Human–Computer Interaction Series

HCI is a multidisciplinary field focused on human aspects of the development of computer technology. As computer-based technology becomes increasingly pervasive—not just in developed countries, but worldwide—the need to take a human-centered approach in the design and development of this technology becomes ever more important. For roughly 30 years now, researchers and practitioners in computational and behavioral sciences have worked to identify theory and practice that influences the direction of these technologies, and this diverse work makes up the field of human-computer interaction. Broadly speaking it includes the study of what technology might be able to do for people and how people might interact with the technology. The HCI series publishes books that advance the science and technology of developing systems which are both effective and satisfying for people in a wide variety of contexts. Titles focus on theoretical perspectives (such as formal approaches drawn from a variety of behavioral sciences), practical approaches (such as the techniques for effectively integrating user needs in system development), and social issues (such as the determinants of utility, usability and acceptability).

Titles published within the Human–Computer Interaction Series are included in Thomson Reuters' Book Citation Index, The DBLP Computer Science Bibliography and The HCI Bibliography.

More information about this series at http://www.springer.com/series/6033

Marko Tkalčič · Berardina De Carolis
Marco de Gemmis · Ante Odić
Andrej Košir
Editors

Emotions and Personality in Personalized Services

Models, Evaluation and Applications

Springer

Editors
Marko Tkalčič
Department of Computational Perception
Johannes Kepler University
Linz
Austria

Berardina De Carolis
Department of Computer Science
University of Bari Aldo Moro
Bari
Italy

Marco de Gemmis
Department of Computer Science
University of Bari Aldo Moro
Bari
Italy

Ante Odić
Preserje, Ljubljana
Slovenia

Andrej Košir
Faculty of Electrical Engineering
University of Ljubljana
Ljubljana
Slovenia

ISSN 1571-5035
Human–Computer Interaction Series
ISBN 978-3-319-31411-2 ISBN 978-3-319-31413-6 (eBook)
DOI 10.1007/978-3-319-31413-6

Library of Congress Control Number: 2016939113

Printed on acid-free paper

This Springer imprint is published by Springer Nature
The registered company is Springer International Publishing AG Switzerland

To our families, for their patience and support. To our colleagues, for their critical and constructive comments

Marko Tkalčič
Berardina De Carolis
Marco de Gemmis
Ante Odić
Andrej Košir

Preface

Personalized systems aim at adapting the content, the interface or the services in general to each user. As an integral part of our daily interactions on the web in various forms, from search engines to online shopping websites, they help us find contents more efficiently. The technologies that drive the adaptation to end users are based on the inference of user's preferences and characteristics from the traces that the user leaves while interacting with the applications. Traditionally, explicit and implicit user feedback has been used to model the users.

Personalized services can now take advantage of more detailed user profiles that include highly descriptive features, such as emotions and personality. This has become possible with the advent of robust methods for an unobtrusive detection of personality, emotions and sentiments from different modalities, such as social media traces, mobile devices and sensors.

This book brings in a single volume the basic bricks needed to understand and build personalized systems based on emotions and personality along with more advanced topics. It bridges personalization algorithms, such as recommender systems, with psychologically motivated user-centric concepts, such as emotions and personality. It translates psychological theories of emotions and personality into computational models for use in personalization algorithms. It surveys techniques for the implicit and explicit acquisition of personality, emotions, sentiments and social signals from sensors, mobile devices and social media. It provides design hints to develop emotion- and personality-aware systems as well as examples of personalized applications that make good use of personality. This book will help researchers and practitioners develop and evaluate user-centric personalization systems that take into account the factors that have a tremendous impact on our decision-making emotions and personality.

In the first part of the book, the theoretical background for the psychological constructs of emotions and personality is given. The second part covers the state-of-the-art methods for the unobtrusive acquisitions of emotions, personality, social signals and sentiments. The third part describes the concrete applications of personalized systems working in a wide range of domains (from music recommendation to e-learning) with different aims, such as improving algorithms for context-aware recommendation or diversification of suggested items. Ethical issues are discussed as well.

We would like to thank all of the authors for their contributions to this book. Also, special thanks go to the reviewers that assured the high quality of the chapters. We are grateful to the Springer staff, especially Beverley Ford and James Robinson for their support throughout the production of this book. Last but not least, we are thankful to many of our colleagues that supported this effort through critical and constructive discussions.

Linz, Austria — Marko Tkalčič
Bari, Italy — Berardina De Carolis
Bari, Italy — Marco de Gemmis
Ljubljana, Slovenia — Ante Odić
Ljubljana, Slovenia — Andrej Košir
April 2016

Contents

Contributors

Elisabeth André Human Centered Multimedia, Augsburg University, Augsburg, Germany

Tobias Baur Human Centered Multimedia, Augsburg University, Augsburg, Germany

Gordon Briggs Human-Robot Interaction Laboratory, Tufts University, Medford, MA, USA

Robin Burke College of Computing and Digital Media, DePaul University, Chicago, IL, USA

Iván Cantador Universidad Autónoma de Madrid, Madrid, Spain

Berardina De Carolis Department of Computer Science, University of Bari Aldo Moro, Bari, Italy

Yin Wah Fiona Chan University of Cambridge, Cambridge, UK

Li Chen Hong Kong Baptist University, Kowloon Tong, Kowloon, Hong Kong

Francesca D'Errico Psychology Faculty Roma, Uninettuno University, Rome, Italy

Miriam Fernández Knowledge Media Institute, Milton Keynes, UK

Ailbhe N. Finnerty Fondazione Bruno Kessler, Povo-Trento, Italy

Marco de Gemmis Department of Computer Science, University of Bari Aldo Moro, Bari, Italy

Liang He East China Normal University, Minhang District, Shanghai, China

Marius Kaminskas Insight Centre for Data Analytics, University College Cork, Cork, Ireland

Michal Kosinski Stanford Graduate School of Business, Stanford, CA, USA

Andrej Košir Faculty of Electrical Engineering, University of Ljubljana, Ljubljana, Slovenia

Neal Lathia Computer Laboratory, University of Cambridge, Cambridge, UK

Bruno Lepri Fondazione Bruno Kessler, Povo-Trento, Italy

Pasquale Lops Department of Computer Science, University of Bari Aldo Moro, Bari, Italy

Matija Marolt University of Ljubljana, Faculty of Computer and Information Science, Ljubljana, Slovenia

Cecilia Mascolo Computer Laboratory, University of Cambridge, Cambridge, UK

Sandra Matz University of Cambridge, Cambridge, UK

Bamshad Mobasher College of Computing and Digital Media, DePaul University, Chicago, IL, USA

Mirco Musolesi Department of Geography, University College London, London, UK

Ante Odić Outfit7 (Slovenian Subsidiary Ekipa2 D.o.o.), Ljubljana, Slovenia

F. Javier Ortega Universidad de Sevilla, Seville, Spain

Veljko Pejovic Faculty of Computer and Information Science, University of Ljubljana, Ljubljana, Slovenia

Matevž Pesek University of Ljubljana, Faculty of Computer and Information Science, Ljubljana, Slovenia

Fabio Pianesi Fondazione Bruno Kessler and EIT-Digital, Povo-Trento, Italy

Isabella Poggi Dipartimento di Filosofia Comunicazione Spettacolo, Roma Tre University, Roma, Italy

Francesco Ricci Faculty of Computer Science, Free University of Bozen-Bolzano, Bozen-Bolzano, Italy

Hassan Saif Knowledge Media Institute, Milton Keynes, UK

Olga C. Santos aDeNu Research Group, Artificial Intelligence Department, Computer Science School, UNED, Madrid, Spain

Matthias Scheutz Human-Robot Interaction Laboratory, Tufts University, Medford, MA, USA

Dominik Schiller Human Centered Multimedia, Augsburg University, Augsburg, Germany

Björn W. Schuller Complex and Intelligent Systems, University of Passau, Passau, Germany; Department of Computing, Imperial College London, London, UK

Giovanni Semeraro Department of Computer Science, University of Bari Aldo Moro, Bari, Italy

Gregor Strle Scientific Research Centre, Institute of Ethnomusicology, Slovenian Academy of Sciences and Arts, Ljubljana, Slovenia

Marko Tkalčič Department of Computational Perception, Johannes Kepler University, Linz, Austria

Alessandro Vinciarelli University of Glasgow, Glasgow, UK

Hsin-Min Wang Institute of Information Science, Academia Sinica, Taipei, Taiwan

Ju-Chiang Wang Institute of Information Science, Academia Sinica, Taipei, Taiwan

Jason R. Wilson Human-Robot Interaction Laboratory, Tufts University, Medford, MA, USA

Wen Wu Hong Kong Baptist University, Kowloon Tong, Kowloon, Hong Kong

Yi-Hsuan Yang Research Center for IT Innovation, Academia Sinica, Taipei, Taiwan

Yong Zheng College of Computing and Digital Media, DePaul University, Chicago, IL, USA

Part I
Background

Chapter 1
Introduction to Emotions and Personality in Personalized Systems

Marko Tkalčič, Berardina De Carolis, Marco de Gemmis, Ante Odić and Andrej Košir

Abstract Personalized systems traditionally used the traces of user interactions to learn the user model, which was used by sophisticated algorithms to choose the appropriate content for the user and the situation. Recently, new types of user models started to emerge, which take into account more user-centric information, such as emotions and personality. Initially, these models were conceptually interesting but of little practical value as emotions and personality were difficult to acquire. However, with the recent advancement in unobtrusive technologies for the detection of emotions and personality these models are becoming interesting both for researchers and practitioners in the domain of personalized systems. This chapter introduces the book, which aims at covering the whole spectrum of knowledge needed to research and develop emotion- and personality-aware systems. The chapters cover (i) psychological theories, (ii) computational methods for the unobtrusive acquisition of emotions and personality, (iii) applications of personalized systems in recommender systems, conversational systems, music information retrieval, and e-learning, (iv) evaluation methods, and (v) privacy issues.

M. Tkalčič (✉)
Department of Computational Perception, Johannes Kepler University,
Altenbergerstrasse 69, Linz, Austria
e-mail: marko.tkalcic@jku.at

B. De Carolis · M. de Gemmis
Department of Computer Science, University of Bari Aldo Moro, Via E.Orabona, 4,
70125 Bari, Italy
e-mail: berardina.decarolis@uniba.it

M. de Gemmis
e-mail: marco.degemmis@uniba.it

A. Odić
Outfit7 (Slovenian Subsidiary Ekipa2 D.o.o.), Ljubljana, Slovenia
e-mail: ante.odic@outfit7.com

A. Košir
Faculty of Electrical Engineering, University of Ljubljana, Tržaška 25,
1000 Ljubljana, Slovenia
e-mail: andrej.kosir@fe.uni-lj.si

M. Tkalčič et al. (eds.), *Emotions and Personality in Personalized Services*,
Human–Computer Interaction Series, DOI 10.1007/978-3-319-31413-6_1

1.1 Introduction

In order to deliver personalized content, adaptive systems take advantage of the knowledge about the user. This knowledge is acquired through data mining of the digital traces of the user. These information are used to build user models, which are in turn used by personalization algorithms to select the content tailored to each user in a given situation. In the past two decades, we have witnessed a tremendous improvement in personalized systems from early experiments, such as the first recommender systems [24], to highly complex and computationally demanding algorithms, such as those competing in the Netflix prize [3]. All these methods were based on feedback provided by users, mostly in the form of explicit ratings or implicitly by interpreting the user interactions on the web.

The advances in personalization technologies brought these systems closer to the user. Throughout the years these systems started to incorporate more and more psychologically motivated user-centric concepts, such as personality [12, 27] and emotions [26], to model users. However, the inclusion of such complex information required the acquisition of these, which was intrusive and time consuming.

In recent years, the maturity of methods for the unobtrusive acquisition of emotions (under the umbrella of *affective computing* [20]) and personality (under the umbrella of *personality computing* [28]) has grown to a level that allows its incorporation in personalized systems. In order to achieve true emotion- and personality-aware personalized systems, psychological theories and computational models need to become a part of user models and personalization algorithms.

This book aims at bridging the work carried out in these separate communities. It discusses (i) psychological theories, (ii) computational methods for the unobtrusive acquisition of emotions and personality, (iii) applications of personalized systems in recommender systems, conversational systems, music information retrieval, and e-learning, (iv) evaluation methods and (v) privacy issues. It is a comprehensive guide for students, researchers, and practitioners for developing emotion- and personality-aware personalized systems.

1.2 Historical Background

Personalized systems have traditionally relied on digital traces of users, which were collected during the interaction of the users with the adaptive system. For example, a lot of recommender systems rely on explicit ratings of items [1]. As explicit ratings are hard to acquire, implicit feedback started to gain attention (e.g., [13, 22]). However, a limitation of these approaches is that they are bound to the data that the researchers or developers have currently at hand. Such data might not include some data that is highly informative about the user.

Alternative ways of modeling users have been sought applying psychologically motivated models. Researchers conjectured that user information, such as emotions and personality, account for the variance in user preferences and behavior and could help in the improvement of personalized systems.

As defined by [19], the psychological concept of *personality* accounts for individual differences in the people's enduring emotional, interpersonal, experiential, attitudinal, and motivational styles. Personality is supposed to be stable across longer periods of time. A popular model for describing a user's personality is the *Five Factor Model* (FFM), which consists of five main factors, as the name implies: *Openness*, *Conscientiousness*, *Extraversion*, *Agreeableness*, and *Neuroticism*. Studies have shown that personality relates well with a number of real-life user preferences, such as music [6, 23]. Hence, personality appears to be a good feature set for modeling long-term user preferences. To account for mid- and short-term preferences, *moods* and *emotions* appear good candidates. While emotions are affective states that are triggered, last for a short period of time and have several dimensions (e.g., valence and arousal), moods last longer, do not appear to have been triggered and are generally described along the positive-negative axis [7]. Since personalized systems are considered as tools in the process of human decision-making [14] emotions need to be taken into account. Nobel prize winner Daniel Kahneman and his colleague Amos Tversky modeled the human decision-making process as a two-systems model, a *slow, rational* and a *fast, emotional* one [15].

The consumption of items in some domains (for example, movies, music, or touristic destinations) is heavily marked by the users' emotional reactions. As the keynote speaker at the *EMPIRE 2015* workshop, Shlomo Berkovsky, pointed out, often the consumption is made with the intent of experiencing emotions [4]. For example, the primary reason why people consume music is to manage/regulate their emotions [18]. Similarly, both movie makers and consumers stress the importance of the emotional response; consumers combine prototypical emotions into more complex second-order emotions [2], while movie makers are well aware of it, as this Woody Allen quote illustrates: "If my films make one more person miserable, I'll feel I have done my job."

The interplay between personality and emotions has been investigated and research has revealed that personality traits predispose individuals to certain mood states, which then influence emotional processing [25].

Early attempts to model users using their personalities and emotions include a variety of works, such as [10, 12, 26, 27]. The drawback of these methods was that the acquisition of personality and emotions was a time-consuming effort in the form of self reports. With the advent of robust methods for the unobtrusive detection of emotions [11, 29] and personality [8, 9, 16, 21] the application of emotions and personality for personalization became much more attainable.

Emotions and personality are universal in the sense that (i) they are domain/service independent and (ii) they cover a wide temporal range. The domain independency is an attractive property and has started to receive attention recently by the exploitation of personality for relating user preferences in different domains [5]. The wide temporal range allows for coarse- and fine-grained modeling in time, which is an underestimated aspect in personalization research.

The relevance of the topics covered in this book is reflected also in the growing attention they are gaining in academia, industry, and the general media. Researchers are increasingly investing their efforts in these topics, which is reflected in (i) the growing amount of publications in major journals (such as [16]) and (ii) a number of dedicated venues. Besides the biannual conference on *Affective Computing and Intelligent Interaction* (ACII), there is a number of related workshops, such as the *Emotions and Personality in Personalized Systems* (EMPIRE) series held in 2013, 2014, and 2015 or the *Workshop on Computational Personality Recognition* (WCPR) held in 2013 and 2014. Industry is also investigating the affective aspects of user interaction. Known examples are (i) the *IBM's* online tool for personality detection from social media[1] and (ii) the report on the massive experiment carried out by Facebook with emotional contagion [17]. Facebook has also introduced the acquisition of affective feedback of posts through adding emoticons to the *Like* button.[2] The general media has widely covered the aforementioned Facebook experiment as well (see the *Forbes* coverage,[3] for example). Furthermore, automatic personality detection from social media is getting attention, as it has been exposed by the *Harvard Business Review* as the top tech trend to watch in 2016.[4] This book aims at bringing together research efforts in psychology, affective computing, personality computing, user modeling and personalized systems, which are still running independently in order to benefit from each other.

1.3 Emotions and Personality in Personalized Systems

This book contains 18 chapters divided in four parts: (i) background, (ii) acquisition and corpora, (iii) applications, and (iv) evaluation and privacy.

The first part of this book is concerned with the theoretical background of emotions and personality.

In the Chap. 2, the authors Francesca D'Errico and Isabella Poggi provide a survey of models of emotions suitable to use by computer scientists. Besides presenting the models commonly used in affective computing, i.e., *dimensional models of emotions* and *cognitive models of emotions* the authors discuss a *socio-cognitive approach of modeling emotions*. This approach has been neglected so far in affective computing and modeling (which focused on individual emotions) but offers advantages as it captures some social dynamics (e.g., *envy, admiration*), which can be useful, for example in group recommender systems.

---

[1]https://watson-pi-demo.mybluemix.net/.

[2]http://www.forbes.com/sites/kathleenchaykowski/2016/02/24/facebook-no-longer-just-has-a-like-button-thanks-to-global-launch-of-emoji-reactions/#7dc2bdab4994.

[3]http://www.forbes.com/sites/gregorymcneal/2014/06/28/facebook-manipulated-user-news-feeds-to-create-emotional-contagion/\#64f9dbaa5fd8.

[4]https://hbr.org/2015/12/8-tech-trends-to-watch-in-2016.

Sandra Matz, Yin Wah Fiona Chan, and Michal Kosinski survey models of personality in Chap. 3. They cover a wide range of personality models including the most popular *Five Factor Model* (FFM). The authors stress the importance of the underlying assumptions, which lead to each model. The discussion includes also the relationships between the models and the suitability of the models for automatic detection of personality through digital footprints.

The second part of this book covers the tools and techniques for acquiring emotions and personality.

State-of-the-art methods for the unobtrusive acquisition of emotionsare surveyed in Chap. 4 authored by Björn W. Schuller. The chapter lists the modalities used in state-of-the-art emotion detection: language (spoken and written), video (facial expressions, body posture and movement), and physiology (brain waves, tactile data). The author also lists free tools for multimodal affect annotation and acquisition and outlines the current research directions and opportunities.

Ailbhe Finnerty, Bruno Lepri, and Fabio Pianesi cover the methods for unobtrusive detection of personality in Chap. 5. Based on social and psychology studies, which suggest that uncontrolled and unconscious behavior yields cues related to personality, the authors survey these cues from various modalities: text, audio, video, mobile phone data, and wearable sensors. Furthermore, the authors present methods for the recognition of personality states, an alternative to personality traits, where people with different traits engage in a similar behavior but in a different manner.

Alessandro Vinciarelli surveys the concepts and methods in *Social Signal Processing* (SSP) in Chap. 6. He provides a conceptual map of SSP, which is concerned about the analysis and synthesis of social signals in human–human and human–machine interactions. He proceeds with describing the methodologies used in SSP and wraps with a substantial section on open issues and challenges.

Chapter 7 has been written by Hassan Saif, Javier Ortega, Miriam Fernandez, and Iván Cantador and covers the issue of sentiment analysis in social streams. Sentiment, which describes the users' attitudes toward certain items (e.g., shopping items, political parties, etc.), can be, similarly to personality and emotions, inferred from users' digital traces. The authors describe data sources, techniques, applications, and open challenges in sentiment analysis.

Experience sampling through mobile devices is covered in Chap. 8, authored by Veljko Pejović, Neal Lathia, Cecilia Mascolo, and Mirco Musolesi. The chapter is concerned with the specific opportunities that mobile devices offer for sampling the state of the users. Although it appears that by having the device always at hand a high sampling rate can be achieved the actual sampling needs to be timed well. The authors describe the conceptual and technical aspects of mobile experience sampling. Furthermore, they provide a list of off-the-shelf frameworks for a fast development of experience sampling applications.

In order to carry out experiments with affective and personality user data appropriate datasets are needed. As mentioned in other chapters as well, the lack of corpora is an important issue. Luckily, the number and sizes of corpora is growing and Chap. 9, written by Ante Odić, Andrej Košir, and Marko Tkalčič, presents a snapshots of datasets available at the time of writing. The authors complement the main content with a list of stimuli datasets, which are useful in the generation and annotation (also using tools presented in Chap. 4) of new datasets.

The third part of the book presents applications that take advantage of user data acquired through techniques, similar to those presented in Chap. 4 through Chap. 9.

In Chap. 10, authored by Tobias Baur, Dominik Schiller, and Elisabeth Andre, a conversational system based on interpersonal cues that reflect the user's social attitude within a specific context, is presented. The system takes advantage of SSP as presented in Chap. 6. They use the SSI open-source real-time SSP framework to detect social cues, which are then used in a job interview scenario and in a social robot scenario.

Personality has been exploited to achieve optimal diversity in a set of recommended items in the system presented in Chap. 11, written by Li Chen, Wen Wu, and Liang He. Based on a user study that showed the relationship between personality traits and individual preferences for diversity, the authors designed a recommender system for movies that adjusted the diversity based on the user personality.

In Chap. 12, the authors Ju-Chiang Wang, Yi-Hsuan Yang, and Hsin-Min Wang present an emotion-based music retrieval system based on their automatic music emotion recognition approach. Based on a query in the *valence-arousal* (VA) space the systems ranks music items that most closely match the query. The affective annotation of music items (in the VA space) is done automatically through an algorithm based on *Gaussian Mixture Modeling* (GMM). The authors also provide the link to the source code.

The usage of emotions and personality in e-learning is covered in Chap. 13 by Olga Santos. She surveys 26 works that take advantage of personality and/or emotions in an e-learning context. The author compares the surveyed works based on the educational setting, emotion/personality acquisition methods and modalities, affective models, and types of affective interventions. She also provides a list of open issues and challenges among which are also affective interventions in collaborative learning scenarios and contextual learning environments.

In Chap. 14, Marius Kaminskas and Francesco Ricci present a system that matches music and points of interest based on the emotions they evoke. Through a series of user studies the authors showed that a music-place matching yields better results (in terms of precision) when emotions are taken into consideration than in a classical rating-based approach. The outcomes of the presented study can be used for recommending music that fits to a point of interest.

Yong Zheng, Bamshad Mobasher, and Robin Burke present the results of a context-aware recommender system in Chap. 15. They performed an offline experiment using several contextual variables. They showed that when emotions were taken into consideration as context, the performance, in terms of the *Root Mean Square Error* (RMSE), of the recommender system improved.

The interrelation between colors and emotions in the context of music information retrieval is studied in Chap. 16, authored by Gregor Strle, Matevž Pesek, and Matija Marolt. Through a series of online studies, which required the development of dedicated user interface elements, the authors found that genre and context affect the perception of emotions in music.

The last part of the book is focused on evaluation and privacy issues.

The authors Marco de Gemmis, Pasquale Lops, and Giovanni Semeraro describe, in Chap. 17, a system where emotions are treated as affective feedback. They collect such feedback to assess the quality of serendipitous recommendations. These are known to be hard to assess as they require to be unexpected (hence related to diversity), but generate a positive response in end users. Through a user study, the authors found that the emotions *happiness* and *surprise* are related to serendipitous recommendations.

In the Chap. 18 the authors Jason R. Wilson, Matthias Scheutz, and Gordon Briggs discuss the important aspect of ethical implications of having affect-aware socially assistive robots around users. The chapter describes ethical issues related to two fictional scenarios related to robots assisting a person with Parkinson's Disease. The ethical issue discussed are (i) respect for social norms, (ii) decisions between competing obligations, (iii) building and maintaining trust, (iv) social manipulation and deception, and (v) blame and justification.

1.4 Conclusion and Future Work

This book aims at providing the pillars to design novel personalized systems that will better understand users through the knowledge of their personality and emotions. It is just the beginning of the journey. As the authors mention in their respective chapters, there are plenty of open issues and opportunities for improvement in the future.

There is a strong need for more datasets of user interaction annotated with personality and emotions. The data acquisition should go into the direction of collecting data from more modalities, more accurate and less intrusive techniques and more timely acquisition.

The user modeling should go into the direction of complexity, taking into account more aspects. Furthermore, models should be done in a less generic and a more domain-dependent fashion. In fact, using users' psychological aspects as described in this book, can result in an improvement of services in a wide array of applications, such as e-commerce, e-learning, e-government, e-health, entertainment, negotiations, job interviews, psychotherapy, and intercultural communications.

References

1. Adomavicius, G., Tuzhilin, A.: Toward the next generation of recommender systems: a survey of the state-of-the-art and possible extensions. IEEE Trans. Knowl. Data Eng. **17**(6), 734–749 (2005). doi:10.1109/TKDE.2005.99. http://ieeexplore.ieee.org/lpdocs/epic03/wrapper.htm?arnumber=1423975, http://ieeexplore.ieee.org/xpls/abs_all.jsp?arnumber=1423975
2. Aurier, P., Guintcheva, G.: The dynamics of emotions in movie consumption: a spectator-centred approach. Int. J. Arts Manage. **17**(2), 5–18 (2015)

3. Bell, R.M., Koren, Y., Volinsky, C.: The BellKor solution to the Netflix Prize A factorization model (2007)
4. Berkovsky, S.: Emotion-based movie recommendations. In: Proceedings of the 3rd Workshop on Emotions and Personality in Personalized Systems 2015—EMPIRE'15, pp. 1–1. ACM Press, New York, New York, USA (2015). doi:10.1145/2809643.2815362. http://dl.acm.org/citation.cfm?doid=2809643.2815362
5. Cantador, I., Fernández-tobías, I., Bellogín, A.: Relating Personality types with user preferences in multiple entertainment domains. In: EMPIRE 1st Workshop on "Emotions and Personality in Personalized Services", 10. June 2013, Rome (2013)
6. Chamorro-Premuzic, T., Furnham, A.: Personality and music: can traits explain how people use music in everyday life? British J. Psychol. (London, England : 1953) **98**, 175–85 (2007). doi:10.1348/000712606X111177. http://www.ncbi.nlm.nih.gov/pubmed/17456267
7. Ekkekakis, P.: Affect, mood, and emotion. In: Tenenbaum, G., Eklund, R., Kamata, A. (eds.) Measurement in Sport and Exercise Psychology, chap. 28. Human Kinetics (2012). http://www.humankinetics.com/products/all-products/measurement-in-sport-and-exercise-psychology-wweb-resource-ebook
8. Farnadi, G., Sitaraman, G., Sushmita, S., Celli, F., Kosinski, M., Stillwell, D., Davalos, S., Moens, M.F., De Cock, M.: Computational personality recognition in social media. User Modeling and User-Adapted Interaction (Special Issue on Personality in Personalized Systems) (2016). doi:10.1007/s11257-016-9171-0. http://link.springer.com/10.1007/s11257-016-9171-0
9. Golbeck, J., Robles, C., Turner, K.: Predicting personality with social media. In: Proceedings of the 2011 annual conference extended abstracts on Human factors in computing systems - CHI EA'11 p. 253 (2011). doi:10.1145/1979742.1979614. http://portal.acm.org/citation.cfm?doid=1979742.1979614
10. González, G., de la Rosa, J., Dugdale, J., Pavard, B., El Jed, M., Pallamin, N., Angulo, C., Klann, M.: Towards ambient recommender systems: results of new cross-disciplinary trends. In: ECAI 2006 Workshop on Recommender Systems, p. 128. Citeseer (2006) http://citeseerx.ist.psu.edu/viewdoc/download?doi=10.1.1.69.1870&rep=rep1&type=pdf#page=136
11. Gunes, H., Schuller, B., Pantic, M., Cowie, R.: Emotion representation, analysis and synthesis in continuous space: a survey. In: Face and Gesture 2011, pp. 827–834. IEEE (2011). doi:10.1109/FG.2011.5771357. http://ieeexplore.ieee.org/lpdocs/epic03/wrapper.htm?arnumber=5771357
12. Hu, R., Pu, P.: A study on user perception of personality-based recommender systems. user modeling, adaptation, and personalization **6075**, 291–302 (2010). doi:10.1007/978-3-642-13470-8_27. http://www.springerlink.com/index/23811UV83U1P1680.pdf
13. Hu, Y., Koren, Y., Volinsky, C.: Collaborative filtering for implicit feedback datasets. In: 2008 Eighth IEEE International Conference on Data Mining, pp. 263–272. IEEE (2008). doi:10.1109/ICDM.2008.22. http://ieeexplore.ieee.org/lpdocs/epic03/wrapper.htm?arnumber=4781121
14. Jameson, A., Willemsen, M.C., Felfernig, A., de Gemmis, M., Lops, P., Semeraro, G., Chen, L.: Human decision making and recommender systems. In: Recommender Systems Handbook, vol. 54, pp. 611–648. Springer US, Boston, MA (2015). doi:10.1007/978-1-4899-7637-6_18. http://www.springerlink.com/index/10.1007/978-0-387-85820-3, http://link.springer.com/10.1007/978-1-4899-7637-6_18
15. Kahneman, D.: Thinking, fast and slow, vol. 1. Farrar, Straus and Giroux (2011). http://www.amazon.com/Thinking-Fast-Slow-Daniel-Kahneman/dp/0374275637
16. Kosinski, M., Stillwell, D., Graepel, T.: Private traits and attributes are predictable from digital records of human behavior. In: Proceedings of the National Academy of Sciences of the United States of America **110**(15), 5802–5805 (2013). doi:10.1073/pnas.1218772110. http://www.pubmedcentral.nih.gov/articlerender.fcgi?artid=3625324&tool=pmcentrez&rendertype=abstract
17. Kramer, A.D.I., Guillory, J.E., Hancock, J.T.: Experimental evidence of massive-scale emotional contagion through social networks. In: Proceedings of the National Academy of

Sciences of the United States of America **111**(29), 8788–8790 (2014).doi:10.1073/pnas.1320040111. http://www.ncbi.nlm.nih.gov/pubmed/24994898, http://www.ncbi.nlm.nih.gov/pubmed/24889601
18. Lonsdale, A.J., North, A.C.: Why do we listen to music? A uses and gratifications analysis. Brit. J. Psychol. (London, England : 1953) **102**(1), 108–134 (2011). doi:10.1348/000712610X506831. http://www.ncbi.nlm.nih.gov/pubmed/21241288
19. McCrae, R.R., John, O.P.: An introduction to the five-factor model and its applications. J. Pers. **60**(2), p175–215 (1992)
20. Picard, R.W.: Affective Computing. 321. The MIT Press (1995). doi:10.1007/BF01238028. http://www.amazon.ca/exec/obidos/redirect?tag=citeulike09-20&path=ASIN/0262161702, http://www.amazon.de/exec/obidos/redirect?tag=citeulike01-21&path=ASIN/0262161702, http://www.amazon.fr/exec/obidos/redirect?tag=citeulike06-21&path=ASIN/02621617
21. Quercia, D., Kosinski, M., Stillwell, D., Crowcroft, J.: Our twitter profiles, our selves: Predicting personality with twitter. In: Proceedings—2011 IEEE International Conference on Privacy, Security, Risk and Trust and IEEE International Conference on Social Computing, PASSAT/SocialCom 2011, pp. 180–185. IEEE (2011). doi:10.1109/PASSAT/SocialCom.2011.26. http://ieeexplore.ieee.org/lpdocs/epic03/wrapper.htm?arnumber=6113111, http://ieeexplore.ieee.org/xpls/abs_all.jsp?arnumber=6113111
22. Rendle, S., Freudenthaler, C.: BPR: Bayesian personalized ranking from implicit feedback. In: UAI 2009, Proceedings of the Twenty-Fifth Conference on Uncertainty in Artificial Intelligence, Montreal, QC, Canada, June 18–21, 2009 pp. 452–461 (2009). http://dl.acm.org/citation.cfm?id=1795167
23. Rentfrow, P.J., Gosling, S.D.: The do re mi's of everyday life: the structure and personality correlates of music preferences. J. Pers. Soc. Psychol. **84**(6), 1236–1256 (2003). doi:10.1037/0022-3514.84.6.1236. http://doi.apa.org/getdoi.cfm?doi=10.1037/0022-3514.84.6.1236
24. Resnick, P., Varian, H.: Recommender systems. Commun. ACM **40**(3), 56–58 (1997). http://portal.acm.org/citation.cfm?id=245121
25. Rusting, C.L.: Personality, mood, and cognitive processing of emotional information: three conceptual frameworks. Psychol. Bull. **124**(2), 165–196 (1998). http://www.ncbi.nlm.nih.gov/pubmed/9747185
26. Tkalčič, M., Burnik, U., Košir, A.: Using affective parameters in a content-based recommender system for images. User Model. User-Adapt. Interact. **20**(4), 279–311 (2010). doi:10.1007/s11257-010-9079-z. http://www.springerlink.com/content/3l2p657572rt4j11, http://www.springerlink.com/content/3l2p657572rt4j11/, http://www.springerlink.com/index/10.1007/s11257-010-9079-z
27. Tkalčič, M., Kunaver, M., Tasič, J., Košir, A.: Personality based user similarity measure for a collaborative recommender system. In: Peter, C., Crane, E., Axelrod, L., Agius, H., Afzal, S., Balaam, M. (eds.) 5th Workshop on Emotion in Human-Computer Interaction-Real World Challenges, p. 30 (2009). http://publica.fraunhofer.de/documents/N-113443.html
28. Vinciarelli, A., Mohammadi, G.: A Survey of personality computing. IEEE Trans. Affect. Comput. **3045**(c), 1–1 (2014). doi:10.1109/TAFFC.2014.2330816. http://ieeexplore.ieee.org/lpdocs/epic03/wrapper.htm?arnumber=6834774
29. Zeng, Z., Pantic, M., Roisman, G.I., Huang, T.S.: A survey of affect recognition methods: Audio, visual, and spontaneous expressions. IEEE Trans. Pattern Anal. Mach. Intell. **31**(1), 39–58 (2009). doi:10.1109/TPAMI.2008.52

Chapter 2
Social Emotions. A Challenge for Sentiment Analysis and User Models

Francesca D'Errico and Isabella Poggi

Abstract The work overviews the theoretical models of emotions mainly used by computer scientists in the area of user modeling and sentiment analysis. Central in this regard are the dimensional models in which the body side is crucial, and the cognitive ones in which the evaluation processes give rise to emotions. Special attention is devoted to a socio-cognitive model of emotions in terms of goals and beliefs, focusing on social emotions, both related to image (admiration, bitterness, enthusiasm) and to self-image (pride, shame). Nature, function, and typical body signals of these emotions are overviewed.

2.1 Introduction

In recent years, we have witnessed a fruitful dialog between psychosocial and computer sciences, within the field of artificial intelligence, passing from the planning of "systems that act like humans" to "systems that think like humans" [88].

The reason is clearly due to progress in both fields and to the integration of theoretical psychological models with technologies, increasingly able to apply these models to their programming languages. One more merit of this is the reciprocal feedback: theoretical models risk to remain abstract when not considered from a computational point of view, while computational ones are not sufficiently grounded if only tailored on the machine. Further, the computational point of view forces psychologists to test models of emotions in a temporal dynamics; this methodological constraint enriches models of emotions with "virtual ecology", i.e., a retry in time and space of things that would not be ethically provable in the laboratory [37]. Gratch and

F. D'Errico (✉)
Psychology Faculty Roma, Uninettuno University, Rome, Italy
e-mail: f.derrico@uninettunouniversity.net

I. Poggi
Dipartimento di Filosofia Comunicazione Spettacolo, Roma Tre University, Roma, Italy
e-mail: isabella.poggi@uniroma3.it

M. Tkalčič et al. (eds.), *Emotions and Personality in Personalized Services*, Human–Computer Interaction Series, DOI 10.1007/978-3-319-31413-6_2

Marsella (2010; [37]) have highlighted the crucial role of the theoretical modeling of emotions within computer science, mostly for two main areas: human–computer interaction and artificial intelligence.

As for AI and robotics, the adaptive nature of goals and selection of emotions allows to design systems more intelligent and skillful [56, 60] but also able to understand which alternatives are more relevant for the system in relation to the context. Emotions are qualified as "control choices" that direct the appraisals of what is dangerous or pleasant toward greater awareness of the relevance of certain problems [59]. Hence, we deduce how essential cognitive models of emotions are for the improvement of AI and robotics.

As for HCI instead the expressive aspects of emotions seem especially relevant, since the "emotional displays" [29] have a decisive role in the detection and modeling of the Users' intentions and behaviors. Given that they may elicit particular responses to "social imperatives" [33], they may be used in HCI to induce social responsibility or reduce conflict [26], through emotional contagion and consequent persuasive effects [79]. More generally, in HCI the expression of emotions is essential in improving the relationship with the user, for example in the case of virtual empathetic [67] and reliable agents [18] and their use, for example, in education to increase intrinsic motivation [44], as well as in e-commerce, tutoring, entertainment, and decision supporting training [27].

Such research areas have over time launched a body of research on user modeling, thanks to which systems try to improve their response to users by means of a progressive adaptation to their needs, as in the case of intelligent tutoring systems, expert systems in the domain of decision-making, recommender systems, and the "affective user adaptive interfaces" where a system can conduct a more socially acceptable dialog by means of a right speech tone and content, and predict affective reactions [41].

To go in depth in some affective states and their expression, this chapter, after providing an overview of some models of emotion (Sects. 2.2 and 2.3) and some cases of their application by computer science, presents a socio-cognitive approach to emotions and focuses on a particular subset of them: some social emotions in the realm of the individual's image and social identity—enthusiasm, pride, shame, admiration, bitterness—and a particular way of communicating, induced by bitterness and a sense of injustice, that we call "acid communication" (Sect. 2.4). It concludes by highlighting how a detailed knowledge of the cognitive structure of these and of their expression can contribute to research in Affective Computing and Sentiment Analysis.

2.2 Dimensional Theories of Emotions

At the origin of the contrasts between theoretical models of Affect is the historical controversy between Zajonc and Lazarus on the origin of emotions and the primacy of emotion on cognition [105, 106]. The priority of arousal—as defined by Zajonc—is opposed to the assumption that considers the primacy of cognitive processes of significance and relevance evaluation over physiological activation ([28], Bellelli 2013). The dimensions considered during the evaluation process of appraisal, like pleasantness, novelty confirmation or disconfirmation of initial expectations, according to supporters of the appraisal lead to a differentiation among emotions based solely on processes of interpretation and labeling of positivity/negativity of the event.

Beyond Zajonc, other authors have overestimated physiological reactions giving rise to the "dimensional theories" that consider cognitive processes simply as the attribution of a cause to some perceived body reaction; see [58, 88] neurophysiological construct of *core affect* "that underlies simply feeling good or bad, or drowsy energised" and that can be changed by evaluation processes (appraisal) but also by altering substances.

Such theories start from Osgood et al. [66], who emphasize the dimensions of *pleasantness* and *activation* in the elicitation of emotions, while adding the dimension of *dominance*. This tripartite division, beside highlighting the difference between emotions such as anger and anxiety—has created the "pad" model that describes emotions in a simple but precise way by marking their difference in a space where those dimensions "are both necessary and sufficient to adequately define emotional states" (Russell and Mehrabian 1977, p. 273). Each emotion is defined by its position on the dimensions of *dominance, arousal* and *pleasantness*. These studies are the basis for physiological and neuropsychological emotion research [94], but also, the dimensional theories exploited in the study of body expressions [97] become central in research on emotion expression. Here, Ekman identifies the facial communication of basic emotions—fear, happiness, anger, surprise, disgust, and sadness—and represents them through Action Units [30], muscle movements of the face that he demonstrates to be culturally shared. But since emotion expression is multimodal [77], gaze too ([1], Kendon 1992, [77]), posture (Bertouze 2015), gestures ([57], Kendon 2004), head movements [16, 84], voice [42, 95, 96] have also been investigated, and such research has been used by scholars in human–computer interaction, multimodal users interfaces, and virtual agents [27, 43, 47, 72].

Other related contributions on emotion are those that consider it as composed of arousal plus cognitive interpretation of the situation; these cognitive processes and their contents operate through labeling processes, judgment, and causal attribution to define the quality of emotional experience. An example is Schachter [92], whose subjects, placed in a state of arousal, if told they had received an injection of adrenaline attributed their state to this, not looking for other causes, while if not informed they labeled their state as an emotion [92].

Mandler [54] emphasizes the relationship between arousal, seen as perception of the activity of the sympathetic nervous system, and the intensity of the emotion in determining its value or control; but the definition and characteristics of the emotions are defined by comparing mental patterns with information brought by the event: if congruent, the emotion is positive, and new information is integrated in the scheme by a process of assimilation. Thus arousal, value judgments and familiarity are the determinants of emotional experience.

Computer science has often attempted to apply these theories, for instance exploiting the detection of physiological activation to recognize emotional behavior and "user affective state", but their weak relationship with cognitive and evaluation processes makes such attempts rather weak and not very functional for advanced computational modeling [56].

At present Wasabi ([W]ASABI [A]ffect [S]imulation for [A]gents with [B]elievable [I]nteractivity; Becker-Asano and Wachsmuth 2008)—a system for humanoid expressing primary emotions—has used one of these models, but it was necessary to integrate it with an "appraisal" approach. In fact, Wasabi separates the body side of emotion, based on the dimensional model of the core Affect [88], from cognitive appraisal ([93], see below), distinguishing a "low road", in which an appraisal is directly determined by an impulse, from a "high road", triggered by a conscious appraisal based on the evaluation of the event and its coherence with the agent's/system's goals.

Another approach is based on the mixed model called ALMA, which aims to improve the quality of calls between virtual characters (Gebhard 2004) so that the emotional state influences both the nonverbal and the verbal contribution. In this case, the mood is calculated based on Ortony and colleagues' model of emotions ([65], see below) and on the space of emotional meanings based on Russell and Mehrabian (1977), defined by pleasure, arousal, and dominance.

2.3 Cognitive Theories of Emotions

While dimensional models do not lead to advanced computational models, this is more directly allowed by the appraisal view of emotions, arising within the "information processing perspective" [37, 56]. These cognitive theories that include [33] "tendency to action", are intended to identify the mental processes and contents that make certain events "emotional", by composing distinguishable emotions. The important elements for the emotional experience are called "cognitive appraisals" and "action tendencies" that capture and condense the structure of meaning of an emotional event (D'Urso and Trentin, 2009), interpreting it as positive or negative on the basis of situational meaning and hence causing different emotions [33]. It is not the nature of the event to arouse the emotion, but its interpretation and evaluation in relation to a subject's goals [13]. In fact, the same stimulus can be interpreted differently and therefore elicit different emotions [33]: the appraisal is a part of the cognitive representation and a determinant of the emotion; e.g., if I believe I have been offended, what makes me angry [28] is this "knowledge". Here, the term refers to the general aspects and contextual, concrete and abstract knowledge, organized in our mind in the form of attitudes, beliefs, naive theories; and "cognitive evaluations" (Appraisal) are "a form of personal significance" consisting of assessments made of the meaning that the knowledge has for the subject's well-being [50].

The emotional process is thus a sequence of relevance evaluation (appraisal), assessment of significance, action preparation, and action [33, 62] and it is based on the evaluation of the event as positive or negative not in itself, as posited by dimensional theories, but with respect to the subject's goals [12]. The motivational core of emotions becomes central [13]: emotional experiences are frequently motivations for behavior, every emotion is perceived as an action tendency to do something, and different action tendencies characterize different emotions [33]. The communicative theory [62] shows the control mechanisms aimed to evaluate plans and purposes in progress and to communicate these changes to other modules.

2.3.1 The Cognitive Structure of Emotions: OCC

Within the cognitive approach, some theoretical frameworks were fertile ground for the study of emotions by computer scientists. The so-called "OCC" model [64] provides a clear and convincing structure of the eliciting conditions of emotions and the variables that affect their intensities.

The primary concern of Ortony and colleagues is to precisely characterize "the range of psychological possibilities for emotions". Emotions are "valenced reactions to events, agents with their particular nature being determined by the way in which the eliciting situation is construed", and the construction is a cognitive process structured through *goals*, *standards*, and *attitudes* that are the basis to interpret events, people, and objects. OCC outlines the overall structure of emotion types, without forgetting their relationship with language, and using self-reports as the most profitable method to detect the "phenomenally infinitude of possible emotions" (p. 15). In this sense, the OCC model can be defined "lexical" [94], being focused mainly on the connotative lexicon of emotions, which is the semantic basis of its structural model. Ortony et al. [64] outline a taxonomy of emotions easily computationable since the progression of a path includes some emotions and excludes others, making them understandable and replicable for a programming language.

The first distinction is if an event can have consequences for themselves or another agent, and if positive or negative. Within emotions concerning "fortune-of-others", positive events may cause jealousy or "happy for", negative events gloating or pity. Those related to "consequences for self", further split into "prospect relevant" like fear or hope, that if confirmed by positive event can be satisfaction or confirmation of fear, and if disconfirmed may cause relief and disappointment, and "prospect irrelevant", like joy or distress. These, combined with attribution processes, give rise to a cluster "wellness/attribution compound", focused on the attribution of responsibility, in which pride and shame regard the self, admiration, and reproach another agent; attribution to himself or others of positive or negative events results, respectively, in gratification, gratitude, guilt, and anger. Finally emotions toward objects, so-called "attraction".

2.3.2 The Component Process Model (CPM)

Leventhal and Scherer (1984), focusing on the automatic/aware conditions of emotion processes, propose a dynamic model in which emotions are valued following three processing levels: sensorimotor, schematic, and conceptual. The first consists of innate modules and brain activation systems stimulated by internal and external inputs and represents more basic emotional responses than those processed by the schematic level, constituted by associations learned during experience that produce "prototypes" integrated with sensory motor responses (Bellelli 2013). The conceptual level is finally associated to propositional format and extends to a long-term perspective, including memories, expectations, goals, plans, and the conscious self. These three evaluative procedures of appraisal operate synchronously and provide support to the emotional event evaluation, determining *relevance*, *implications*, *potential coping*, and *normative significance* [93–95]. The emotional event activates the "stimulus evaluation checks", concerning its novelty, intrinsic pleasantness and relevance for the individual's goals, while for long-term implications attributional checks are activated of causality and likeliness of consequences.

The appraisal also has a key role both in detecting the coping potential (power to deal with the situation) and in assessing normative significance against internal and external standards; normative appraisal includes evaluation concerning the importance of implications, possibility to cope in relation to normative standard. In Leventhal and Scherer's hypothesis, these checks are sequential, while in Rumelhart and McClelland's [90] connectionist model they may act in parallel.

2.3.3 EMotion Adaptation: Gratch and Marsella

The computability of these theoretical works is made explicit, in their EMA model, by Gratch and Marsella (2010; [37]), who adopt Lazarus' [48] pioneering and foundational model of appraisal, viewing emotion as a process of interpretation in relation to the environment, including behavioral consequences and coping strategies. Lazarus classifies the coping strategies of stressful situations, in relation to the type of appraisal, as "task oriented" or "emotion oriented", i.e., oriented respectively to problem-solving or to emotion expression. In Gratch and Marsella's architecture, the system encodes environmental inputs by making a causal interpretation of them in relation to the agent's goals, the importance of the event, its desirability, expectation, controllability, and changeability. EMA is also a computational model of coping dynamic and is cyclical, based on the appraisal–coping–reappraisal sequence [31, 49]. It is designed to support multiagent simulations by implementing each agent's states in specific contexts that allow to figure out and adapt to blackberry agents' specific goals and beliefs, but recently [37] it has been reinterpreted to be social and focused on social emotions. As the authors point out, "to maintain an adaptive relationship in the social world, an intelligent organism must not only understand how to shape the physical environment, but also learn to recognize, model and shape beliefs, desires, and intentions of other social actors (i.e. it needs to understand social causality)". Some "social" functions are computationally modeled: social reactivity, inference on relational meaning (a "reverse appraisal", appraisal of information about another's mental state from his appearance or behavior, Whiten 1991), forecasting how others respond to one's emotional reactions, making inference on others' goals and planning joint actions. Gratch and Marsella, to capture the social complexity of emotional interaction, incorporate "social signals" [83] in the social version of their computational model, thus also managing information on the user's goals, social status, social relationships, and social attitudes.

2.4 A Socio-Cognitive Account of Emotions

In this section, we briefly present a socio-cognitive model of mind, social interaction, and communication in terms of goals and beliefs, and based on it we provide an account of some social emotions.

According to this model [12, 17], emotions, in line with appraisal theories, are viewed as an adaptive device that monitors the state of achievement or thwarting of humans' goals: a multifaceted internal state, encompassing feelings and cognitive, physiological, expressive, motivational aspects, that is triggered whenever a very important goal of a person is, or is very likely to be, achieved or thwarted [59, 79].

Since emotions are strictly linked to goals, they can be grouped into types depending on the type of goals they monitor. A human is regulated at each moment of his life by his "contingent" goals but also by some "permanent" goals [79] that, though generally silent, become salient when thwarted, threatened, achieved, or anyway at stake due to contextual events. All humans have survival goals (to preserve one's own and offspring's life), epistemic goals (to acquire and elaborate knowledge), image (to elicit positive evaluations by other people), self-image (to evaluate oneself positively), and other's image goals (to evaluate others); goals of affiliation (being helped by others), but also goals of altruism (to help others) and equity (avoid too deep differences between others' and one's fortunes). These goals are innate and universal, although different cultures and personalities attribute them different weights: individualistic cultures credit higher value to goals of self-empowerment and autonomy, collectivistic ones to help and cooperation; a narcissistic person values his image most, an anti-conformist one, his self-image.

Emotions can then be clustered together according to the permanent goal they monitor: beside "survival emotions" like fear and disgust, we have "epistemic emotions" (e.g. surprise, curiosity, amusement, flow, boredom), "affiliation emotions" (tenderness, feeling of belonging or exclusion), "altruism emotions" (sympathy and compassion), "equity emotions" (gratitude, revenge, guilt), "image emotions" (pride, embarrassment, humiliation), "self-image emotions" (satisfaction, pride, shame), and "the other's image emotions" (trust, admiration, contempt, pity).

2.4.1 Social Emotions

We may distinguish "individual" versus "social" emotions, and within these, four types of them [79].

An "individual" emotion does not entail another person in its basic structure. I may be happy because it is sunny today, or disappointed if it is not, but it is not necessary that any other person be implied in my feeling. On the other hand, with envy, I necessarily must feel envious *of* someone else: another person is logically implied in this very feeling, as well as in other "social emotions" like love, hate, contempt, admiration, or pity.

An emotion can be considered "social" in four senses.

1. In its very argumental structure. Envy or hate are "social emotions in the strong sense": another person is necessarily implied in their formal representation, they are two arguments predicates of the type FEEL TOWARD x, y. You cannot feel envy, hate, or compassion but toward someone.
2. a subset of "social emotions" are the so-called "self-conscious" emotions [51], like pride, shame, embarrassment, humiliation, that we feel when our image or self-image, an important part of our social identity, is at stake, crucially determining our relations with others.
3. partially overlapping with the emotions "towards" someone else (type 1) and with the "self-conscious" ones (type 2), being heavily involved in social interaction, norms, and values, are "moral" emotions [39, 100], like contempt, shame, guilt.
4. an emotion may be "social" because it is very easily "transmitted" from Agent x to Agent y through contagion: like enthusiasm, that can thus favor joint action.

In the following, we present a theoretical analysis of some social emotions that are not so frequently studied in psychological literature, nor often tackled in Virtual Agents and Sentiment Analysis, highlighting their underlying mental states and their bodily expression. We start from enthusiasm (Sect. 2.4.2), one typically transmitted across agents through contagion (type 4), but also a self-image emotion, entailing self-efficacy (type 2). Pride (Sect. 2.4.3), shame (4.4), and bitterness (4.6) are presented as emotions linked to the goals of image and self-image, power, and lack of power (type 2); whereas admiration (Sect. 2.4.7) is linked to the other's image (type 3).

2.4.2 Enthusiasm

Enthusiasm was mainly studied by philosophers, like Plato [75] who saw it as a state of mystic inspiration, Bruno [9] who stressed it as a state of creative insanity, and Kant [45], who connected it to the aesthetical experience of sublime, but also acknowledged its function in revolutions and other innovative events. In the psychological domain, Greenson [38] distinguishes the trait of being an enthusiastic person from the transitory state of enthusiasm, a type of euphoria apparently similar to mania, in which, though, the subject maintains a sense of reality. Csikszentmihaly [20] connects it to the state of flow, a state of complete immersion in some activity, that makes it become an "optimal experience"; and he stresses its importance in education as a way to enhance intrinsic motivation. As we feel enthusiasm we are in a state of exultance, fervour, elation: a state close to joy, exuberance, optimism. Our ideas take life thanks to enthusiasm, a peculiar type of joy that implies a complete transformation of personality, of the Self and of the way we perceive the world. In general, then, enthusiasm is a fire [9], charge, spur that helps to focus a person's physical and mental efforts to reach high value goals.

The word "enthusiasm" derives from Greek *èn theòn* = God inside. This emotion belongs to the family of happiness, being an intensely positive emotion, felt for the achievement of a very important goal; but it differs from happiness, exultance, or elation for the goal at stake and the time it is felt [77]. We feel enthusiasm about goals that are noble, important, worth pursuing, activities entailing novelty and creativity (e.g., creating a new musical group or founding a new company), or equity and altruism (fighting for our ideas or defending noble causes, like in political revolutions). Enthusiasm is not felt after the achievement, but during goal pursuit, not at the end of the football game but at the first goal, that witnesses we do have the necessary skills to achieve the end goal. This first success during pursuit of a high value goal triggers proprioceptions of high activation: heart beat acceleration, a sense of energy, well-being, good mood, heat, excitation; we cannot stand still, we talk or shout, we hop up and down and make uncontrolled movements [77]. Such internal energy felt once achieved an intermediate goal of our action plan sustains goal pursuit, making us believe "we can", enhancing our self-efficacy. Enthusiasm is thus a "self-image" emotion in its self-attribution of power; and its function is to be the "gasoline of motivation": its great physiological activation fosters physical and mental resources inducing persistency and self-confidence, renewing motivation, providing new energy for action.

Enthusiasm is expressed by smile, wide open eyes, high eye humidity (bright eyes), general activation, a desire to move, jump, shout, speak aloud, and its display generally exerts emotional contagion [40]: a form of emotion transmission [78] in which Agent A feels an emotion E1 and expresses it through expressive signal s1, B perceives s1 and reproduces it, even automatically (i.e., not necessarily at a high level of awareness and intentionality), and this causes B to feel an emotion E2 similar or identical to A's. Seeing or hearing others' enthusiasm makes us feel so too, causing an amplification effect that triggers a loop of enthusiasm. Both A and B may not be aware that B's enthusiasm has been transmitted by A, nor A must have transmitted it consciously or deliberately. But at times A (for example, a political leader) may consciously want to transmit his enthusiasm. That this highly activating emotion can be triggered in an automatic and irreflexive way, without checks by conscious rationality makes enthusiasm and its contagion a powerful but a double-edged weapon, since it may induce to fanatism, and be exploited by people wanting others to act without thinking.

2.4.3 Pride

The emotion of pride has been an object of attention in ancient Greece (Herodotus' hybris), religion and moral philosophy (for Augustine and Aquinas, one of the worst sins, the root of all evil). In modern literature [22, 51] include it among the "complex", more specifically the "self-aware" emotions: ones that, like embarrassment, shame and guilt, can be felt only when the concept of self has been formed. Tracy and Robins [102] distinguish two types of pride, authentic and hubristic, the former associated with "extraversion, agreeableness, conscientiousness, and favoring altruistic action, the latter with self-aggrandizing narcissism and shame-proneness" (p. 149), often contributing to aggression, hostility and interpersonal problems. They propose that the adaptive function of pride is "to provide information about an individual's current level or social status and acceptance" (p. 149), and investigate the nonverbal expression of pride, demonstrating its universality and singling out its constituting elements: small smile, head slightly tilted back, arms raised, and expanded posture. Such expression may serve to "alerting one's social group that the proud individual merits increased status and acceptance" (pp. 149–150).

According to a socio-cognitive account [82], we feel pride when due to an *action* (e.g., I run faster than others), a *property* (I am stubborn, I have long blond hair), an *event* (my party has won the elections), our goal of having a positive image and/or self-image is achieved, that is, we evaluate ourselves, or believe to be evaluated by others, very positively with respect to some goals that are an important *part of our identity*. I can be proud of my son because I see what he is or what he does as something stemming from me; proud of the good climate of my country because I feel it as *my* country.

Four types of pride can be distinguished: a *self-image* pride, plus three types stemming from achievement of the goal of image: *superiority*, *arrogance*, and *dignity* pride.

In *superiority pride*, the proud person feels superior to another person, for instance because he won over him in a single event, or because (he thinks) he has an acknowledged status that puts him over other people: e.g., an athlete who has just won a race, or the king's son.

Arrogance pride is felt (and displayed) by one who is presently on the "down" side of the power comparison, who has less power than another, but wants to challenge the other and his power, while communicating that actually he has more power than he seems to, that he has the intention to climb the pyramid, to win over the other, and finally become superior to him.

Dignity pride is felt by a person that sees his image of a human, with its most typical feature, the right to freedom and self-regulation, challenged by other people who want to humiliate, submit him, remark his inferiority and dependence. One who feels dignity pride does not claim to be superior to other, but only to be at the same level, not inferior to him.

Pride may be also triggered when only the goal of self-image is achieved. A nurse, after working hard with patients, may feel proud not because anyone has publicly acknowledged her outcomes, but simply because she has lived up to her values, thus feeling *self-image pride*.

For both pride and shame, as we shall see later, the achievement of the goal of self-image is a necessary condition, whether or not the goal of image before others is fulfilled. Only if the standard one is evaluated against by others makes part not only of one's goal of image before them but also of the image one wants to have of oneself, can one feel real pride (as well as real shame). Suppose a boy values making room for kindness and tenderness as important for his own image, even if others evaluate him against some value he does not share (say, to be an aggressive macho man) he will not feel proud of showing aggressive and dominant, nor will he feel shame of not looking very macho to others.

Beside being an emotion, pride can also be viewed as a personality trait. A "proud" person is one who attributes a high value to his goal of self-image, mainly to his self-image of an autonomous person, not dependent on anyone else. This is why a proud person typically does not ask or accept help from anyone, and he does not apologize since this would imply submitting to others, being dependent, indebted, not autonomous.

Pride (as already found by Tracy and Robins [102]) is expressed by a multimodal pattern of body signals: small smile, expanded posture, head tilted backward, arms extended out from the body, possibly hands on hips. Within this multimodal display [82], *smile* conveys a positive feeling due to the achievement of the goal of image or self-image; the *expanded posture*, enlarging the body, conveys dominance, superiority, and enhances visibility: when proud of something you want to exhibit your qualities. *Expanding chest* implies reference to oneself, to one's own *identity*. *Head tilted back* is a way to look taller, symbolically communicating superiority, and induces to *look down on the other*, remarking his inferiority. But even more specifically, different combinations of these signals distinguish the three types of *image pride*. Among pride expressions in political debates [82] **dignity** pride is characterized by *head tilted upward* and signals of worry and anger, like *frown* or *vertical wrinkles on the forehead, rapid and nervous gestures, loud voice, eyes fixed to interlocutor*, and *no smile*; all conveying seriousness of the proud person's request to have one's dignity acknowledged. In **superiority** pride, *low voice rhythm and intensity* signal absence of worry (if you are superior you have nothing to fear from others), and sometimes by *gaze away from Interlocutor* conveys he is so inferior he does not deserve attention. **Arrogance** pride is displayed by *large smile*, almost a *scornful laughter, expanded chest, head tilted back, gaze fixed to interlocutor*, that convey challenge and defiance, and *provocative*, possibly *insulting words*. The whole pattern conveys that the proud person does not fear the interlocutor, even if he is presently superior to himself.

An experimental study [82] showed that *asymmetrical eyebrows without smile* convey either superiority or dignity pride, while *frown with smile* mainly dignity, but also other meanings like "I am resolute", "I want to humiliate you," and "I won". *Frown* generally conveys dignity pride, *asymmetrical eyebrows*, superiority, *absence of frown*, and arrogance. *Smile*, mainly if viewed as ironic, is typical of arrogance; *absence of smile*, of dignity and superiority pride.

The intense gratification provided by the emotion of pride makes it a very effective incentive to take care of one's image and self-image, by striving to live up to one's standards and values. Succeeding in goals where others fail makes us feel superior, and repeated achievements increase the sense of our value: thus pride is a symptom of our having more power than others, but at the same time displaying this emotion, by telling our superiority, may be exploited to gain further power: the exhibition of superiority, intimidating the other, can make him refrain from competition or aggression. Therefore, pride and superiority may be pretended, and their display become a bluff deliberately aimed at preventing another's reaction.

2.4.4 Shame and the Multimodal Discourse of Blush

Research on the emotion of shame has long been dominated by the attempt to find its differences and similarities with respect to guilt feelings. In the long tradition of "shame and guilt" research, Benedict [6] first stressed the "outward" aspects of shame of being mainly aimed at maintaining a good reputation from people, and triggered by transgression of a social, more than a moral kind, with guilt instead viewed as a more internal feeling punishing the individual from inside, even without public acknowledgment of his faults. This lead to a quite ethnocentric distinction between guilt cultures and shame cultures, fortunately overcome by Piers and Singers [74] who acknowledged the depth of shame feelings, that may grip the individual even when no other knows of his transgression, thus reestablishing their ethical potential. Beside the distinctions public versus private and community- versus individual-oriented, other studies (see [100], for an overview) viewed guilt as more typically induced by a specific event or action in the moral realm, and shame as an overall negative self-evaluation of the subject, due to either moral or nonmoral transgressions. An appraisal and attributional account of the two emotions [103] showed correlations of shame with internal, stable, uncontrollable attributions for failure, as opposed to the internal, unstable, controllable attributions linked to guilt.

In terms of the socio-cognitive model above, shame may be defined as a regret or fear of thwarting one's goal of esteem and/or self-esteem: the negative emotion we feel when our goal of eliciting positive evaluations from others or ourselves is certainly or probably thwarted [14]. We are ashamed when we feel we have fallen short of some norm or value that we share with our group, or one we want to live up to: so we can feel shame both before others and before ourselves. If I want to be a good pianist, and I make a mistake while playing before my friends, I may be ashamed before them if I think they realized my fault, but also shame only before myself because, though they do not realize my subtle fault, I did, and I want to be perfect for and before myself.

Like for pride, the necessary condition to feel shame is that we think that not only our image before others, but also our image before ourselves is thwarted. As some standard makes part of my self-image, I am sincerely sorry when I fall short of it; but if I share it with my group, my fault might lead the group to reject me and close social relations with me, so I feel shame also before others, and my display of shame is an apology, conveying: "I violated this norm, but I still share it with you; do not aggress or reject me, accept me in the group again".

The feeling of shame is an internal self-punishment, while its external expression asks forgiveness from the group, by three signals: (1) *head lowering*, (2) *eyes lowering*, (3) *blush*, the reddening of the face. While head and eyes lowering (the posture of shame) may be deliberate actions, blushing is a morphological feature, not subject to conscious will Darwin [22], that cannot be feigned or pretended. They work together as a multimodal signal of submission and apology, that while acknowledging one's faults or shortcomings implies acceptance of the violated standards, to block the group's aggression and prevent rejection. Its unavoidable sincerity is a guarantee of true repentance, allowing to distinguish loyal versus unreliable group members.

Pride and shame are thus specular emotions in feeling and function, but also in their expression: the display of pride conveys dominance, that of shame submission.

2.4.5 Admiration

Admiration, according to Darwin [22], is "surprise joined with feelings of pleasure and approval". Freud [32] considers it as a way of putting another person in the place of one's ideal ego. Klein [46], in talking of envy and gratitude and the way they stem from the child's relation to his mother, observes that "sometimes we feel grateful for the other has a unique capacity to produce some good, and this gratitude is a part of admiration". Again within a psychoanalytical framework, for Sandell (1993) admiration, like envy, comes from a sense of "relative deprivation", since the other has something you do not have. But in admiration you divide the object in two different objects, the whole and a part (trait object), so the entire object becomes irrelevant while the trait object becomes distinguished and comes to be admired. Sandell also observes that the pathological narcissist is incapable of admiration, while in normal narcissism the relative deprivation leads to identification with the other: thus one can feel joy from the good of the other, and admiration becomes a narcissistic gratification. In the Cognitive Science domain, Ortony et al. [64] consider admiration an appreciation emotion stemming from attributing the responsibility of a praiseworthy action to another agent. Its intensity is mainly determined by deviation from role-based expectations: we admire more a weak, old lady than a baywatch for saving a drowning child.

In our terms, admiration belongs to the "other's image emotions". For an agent it is relevant to make up an image of other agents, i.e., to have a set of (mainly evaluative) beliefs about them, to choose who to have positive relationships with, and emotions like trust, esteem, contempt, are triggered by (and are a symptom of) our evaluation of others.

Admiration is a positive social emotion felt by an Agent A toward an Agent B, that encompasses a positive evaluation of either B as a person, or of a quality or skill Q of B, that A considers desirable or definitely would like to have; so A eventually may want to imitate B to learn or acquire quality Q; and due to the positive evaluation of B and/or of his quality Q, A may want to interact and have social relationships with B.

Given this highly positive evaluation, A believes that B is superior to A; but different from envy, where A feels inferior to B, admiration is not a negative emotion because the acknowledgment of a positive quality in B is not accompanied by the feeling of A's powerlessness: here A believes that he is in some way similar to B (he belongs to the same category), that the very fact that B has Q is evidence that having Q, though rare, difficult, and unexpected, is not impossible, and that A can achieve it too. This induces A to interact with B to have the chance of imitating him and learning from him.

The qualities admired in people range from tenacity, strength, courage, to beauty, self-confidence, skill, passion, as well any difficult behavior or rare property [79]: what is most frequently admired is a positive attitude of a person *notwithstanding* a difficult situation.

Generally the emotions linked to image and self-image, like shame, guilt, embarrassment, respect, are counted among "moral" emotions [100]; but one might contend that admiration is an "a-moral" emotion, in that while some people definitely cannot admire the other's quality without taking into account the goals to which it is devoted, for others admiration is more of an aesthetical feeling, where you like the quality in itself, even when aimed at goals you disprove of: like when a detective admires the smart thief he is chasing. Actually, Poggi and Zuccaro [79] found out that the majority of people (72 vs. 26 %), when they admire somcone do not suspend their moral judgement: as a person admires another, he generally also feels trust and esteem for him, considering him a good person.

In an adaptive view, admiration has (1) a social function of enhancing effective cooperation, leading us to interact with persons we like and with whom conflicts are minimized, since we consider them better than us and worth respect; (2) a cognitive function of learning from people who are better than we are, to become better ourselves.

2.4.6 Bitterness

McFall [55] defines bitterness as "a refusal to forgive and forget", a tendency "to maintain a vivid sense of the wrongs one has been done, to recite one's angry litany of loss long past the time others may care to listen or sympathize"; while Campbell [11] sees it as "a rational response to the frustration of important and legitimate hopes". Starting from these definitions, Campbell observes that bitterness differs from anger for its failure of uptake, since the one who is recounting his injury here fails to be listened to.

According to Poggi and D'Errico [80], bitterness is an emotion that shares aspects of anger and sadness: a kind of restrained anger that we feel when we sense we have been subject to some injustice, but we cannot, or we believe it pointless, to struggle against it, because we do not have the power to overcome the one who did us wrong.

A feels bitterness when his goal G is thwarted in an irreversible way causing injustice to A, and when A believes that the responsible for this thwarting is another person B, where B is someone with whom A is affectively involved, and who A expected would allow or cause the fulfillment of G; A believes that B was committed to fulfill it, but B disconfirmed A's expectation.

In some cases, a true injustice has not occurred, and B is A himself: for example [80], if A in an examination does not perform as she wants, the one A believes was committed to fulfill G is A herself, and the ingredient of *injustice* is not present: at most, A feels she *betrayed* herself, she is *responsible* for an *irreversible harm* she inflicted to herself. Thus, a common ingredient of bitterness, either caused by others or by oneself, is *responsibility* for a *nonachieved goal*. Bitterness due to *disconfirmed expectation* and *inequity* may be also caused by the disproportion between personal investment and actual results, e.g., if after years studying and *striving* one still cannot find a work. In other cases, the salient ingredient is *injustice* only, due to *non-motivated harm*, e.g., for a relative's death that causes pain *without an acceptable motivation*.

While *goal thwarting, violated expectation, involvement, responsibility, injustice*, are common to anger, another ingredient of bitterness is shared with sadness: *impotence to react*, to recover the damage undergone, because those who caused the injustice are stronger than we are. We feel bitterness as we struggle with powerful agencies, like mafia, or an unjust and iniquitous judiciary system: we feel them too strong and powerful and conclude we have no chance to win. From this restrained anger bitterness comes, that entails both impotence to react and impotence to express one's anger, thus becoming a kind of restrained disappointment that lasts in time, just because restrained, which may have a relevant impact on people's quality of life in affective relations and in the workplace.

2.4.7 Acid Communication

A form of emotional display of anger, annoyance, and bitterness, not so infrequent in everyday life and easily recognized by laypeople [25], is "acid communication": the way of communicating of a person who feels she has been an object of injustice and feels emotions like anger, envy, bitterness, grudge, or rancor, but feels she does not have the power to revenge or even to express her anger freely. So she comes out with a restrained and half-inhibited way of attacking other people.

Acid communication is a type of communicative verbal and nonverbal acts in which a sender expresses aggressiveness toward a target by attacking his image, not in an explicit way but in a covert, yet possibly ostentatious manner, because she feels she has been subject to injustice, but having less power than the target she cannot attack him safely. The typical communicative acts of acid communication aim at criticizing and accusing the other, making him feel guilty, making specification and pinpointing, but mainly through indirect communication, including a frequent use of rhetorical figures (irony, sarcasm, euphemism, litotes, oxymoron, allusion, insinuation). This aims at projecting the image of the acid communicator as a smart and brilliant person, who did not deserve the attack or abasement undergone. This counts as both a revenge over the target who somehow humiliated her, and a demonstration to him, and possibly to an Audience, that S is worth respect or even admiration.

The field of acid communication—a topic never tackled before by research in the expression of emotions—was explored in three studies [25].

First, a questionnaire investigating the commonsense description of acid communication asked 148 female university students (age 19–25, mean 21) (1) to tell an episode of acidity, (2) to describe the behavior of an acid person and its typical verbal and bodily cues, (3) to define the notion of acidity, and (4) to guess its general and specific causes, by focusing on (4a) another person's and possibly on (4b) one's own acidity.

Acidity is seen as an inner feeling, a permanent trait, or a single behavior: a way to behave, a stance taken while interacting with others, described as *sgarbato* (rude), *scontroso* (grumpy), lacking politeness and kindness, unpleasant, disagreeable. The acid person is considered selfish, pessimistic, and negative, not altruistic, her behavior as ugly, unpleasant, characterized by a sort of "social meanness", a desire not to mix up with others, expressed by behaviors aimed at keeping distance, at showing superior, cold, detached, arrogant, haughty, but actually masking a deep lack of self-confidence, also cued by a total lack of sense of humor, notwithstanding her irony that is, in fact, always sarcastic.

Contingent causes of acidity are believed to be frustration, due for instance to physiological states like tiredness, a quarrel or disappointment from a friend, and negative feelings (anger, stress, dissatisfaction, annoyance, boredom, bad mood, jealousy, grudge, feeling wounded, sense of injustice, revenge, and impotence). Acidity results from an impulse to aggression that cannot be acted out but leaks in an indirect way both as to manner (e.g., the numerous rhetorical figures mask aggression under a brilliant form) and as to target (being acid toward C when you are angry at B).

The type of speech acts mentioned by participants in the study are challenge, defiance, and bad, impolite, biting, cutting, "*dry*" answers (abrupt, not argumented, nor accompanied by polite formulas), offensive sentences, and display of contempt and superiority.

Another study, concerning the verbal expression of acidity in sms and email [81] found out a frequent use of particular speech acts.

Criticism. The acid sender often remarks some fault or blameworthy action of the target.

Specification. The acid person tends to make things precise, not to let them vague, possibly to correct others' inaccurate statements. Beside correcting the opponent's imprecision, specification also implies his being ignorant and inaccurate, thus spoiling his image, discrediting him [23], and at the same time aims at giving an image of the Acid one as a smart person, one not easy to dupe by vague statements.

Indirectness. Due to one's lack of power, the acid person must refrain from direct attack and resort to more subtle ways of criticizing and discrediting the target, not to risk retaliation and to keep a formal image of politeness. Thus, typical acid speech acts are **insinuation**, an indirect, partially covert accusation, and **allusion**, referring to some (generally negative) thing while not mentioning it in an explicit way, or doing so only incidentally.

Beside particular types of speech acts, acid communication is characterized by a polished, brilliant, creative language, exploiting a literary and refined lexicon, sometimes stuffed with rhetorical figures like metaphor, oxymoron, euphemism, and irony. **Irony**, in which the sender uses positive statements to imply negative evaluations of the target, is the perfect candidate for acid communication since it puts the sender on a level superiority both discrediting the target by making fun of him, and displaying his originality, divergence, creativity, thus taking revenge of the supposed injustice or abasement undergone.

In a third study on the multimodal expression of acidity, [25] simulated scenarios in which the social relationship between the acid communicator and the target differed in two variables: affective versus instrumental, and peer versus hierarchical.

104 female University students were asked to describe a real episode of acid communication as a narrative and as a script of a scene, specifying aspects of voice, gesture, posture, facial expression. Eight episodes were selected and rephrased: peer instrumental, peer affective, hierarchic instrumental, and hierarchic affective, each in a "dry" version (explicit expression of an acid criticism) and in an "ironic" version (criticism expressed ironically); participants had to act these versions as if on a stage.

Multimodal acid communication in the *instrumental* condition is mainly expressed through signals as the *nod* of revenge [81], *eyebrows raised, high tone and rhythm of voice*, interjections (*ahhh* of surprise or *eh?* of request for confirmation at the end of an interrogative sentence). In the *peer relationship*, participants report more negative social emotions like *contempt*, and perform distancing signals: *backward posture, shoulder shake, head turned away, gaze avoidance, partial closure of eyelids, looking from down up*, and *wrinkled mouth with raised upper lip* communicating disgust [30].

A frequent activation signal during acid communication is *head position* and *head movement*: irritated participants tend to affirm their position by *nodding once* or *repeatedly and quickly* (with gaze to Interlocutor) but also by *head canting* (Costa et al. 2001), in the ironic case with a *small smile*.

In the *instrumental low status* relationship, the acid communicator uses *jerky gestures* usually *repeated* with *high muscular tension, gestures toward the opponent* like the "accusing finger", and closure gestures; in *high status, slow and fluid gestures* like *moving one hand from down upward repeatedly*, indicating how vain is any effort to improve the low status situation.

A peculiar way to communicate acidity, in the same line as irony, is to make a parody, that is, an exaggerated and distorted imitation of the target, aimed at diminishing him by making fun of him.

2.5 Conclusion. User Modeling, Sentiment Analysis and Social Emotions

Since its first rising, affective computing, the research area aimed at the recognition, processing, and simulation of affect [69, 73, 101] has investigated the recognition of primary emotions from face [107], voice [2, 19], and written text [10, 15, 70, 99]. So did the field of sentiment analysis, aimed at capturing the people's attitudes that is, their personal evaluations in favor or against entities like individuals, organizations, topics ([53]; Saif et al. this volume), composed by *subjectivity, polarity and emotion detection*. In both Affective Computing and Sentiment analysis, the emotion detection side has generally focussed on the six basic emotions: anger, disgust, fear, joy, sadness, and surprise [98], while the "social" emotions have been often almost totally neglected. Yet, there are other emotions that people frequently feel in everyday life—at home and in the workplace, in affective and service relationships—for instance social emotions like envy or admiration, bitterness or pride. An accurate description of these emotions is then called for, both as to their vocal, facial, postural, and written verbal displays and as to their internal cognitive structure, the underlying feelings, the actions they typically induce, and their effects on people's life.

This work has attempted to outline the mental ingredients of some social emotions that are linked to people's image and self-image, then essential for their social identity. We tackled pride and shame, that signal the achievement or thwarting of a person's striving for success or complying with social norms; admiration, that corresponds to a need for affiliation and learning from good models; enthusiasm that enhancing our self-efficacy incentives our striving; bitterness and acidity, that highlight received injustice.

Taking into account these emotions might enrich user models in human–computer interaction, by improving Affective Computing and Sentiment Analysis techniques, but also be of use in monitoring the quality of life in organizations and the quality of social relationships between people. Tools for facial expression detection might tell us if a person is particularly proud hence particularly keen to get offended. A sophisticated sentiment analysis that finds a high frequency of rhetorical figures—a typical feature of acid communication—in emails between faculty members might be a cue to a high sense of injustice in that context. Our work is but a first attempt to go in deep in these emotions, so frequently felt in our life, but so rarely studied by emotion research.

References

1. Argyle, M., Cook, M.: Gaze and Mutual Gaze. Cambridge University Press, Cambridge (1976)
2. Banse, R., Scherer, K.R.: Acoustic profiles in vocal emotion expression. J. Pers. Soc. Psychol. **70**(3), 614–636 (1996)
3. Becker-Asano, C.: WASABI: affect simulation for agents with believable interactivity. PhD thesis, Faculty of Technology, University of Bielefeld. IOS Press (DISKI 319) (2008)

4. Becker-Asano, C., Wachsmuth, I.: Affect simulation with primary and secondary emotions. In: Prendinger, H., Lester, J., Ishizuka, M. (eds.) Intelligent Virtual Agents (IVA 08), LNAI 5208, pp. 15–28. Springer (2008)
5. Bellelli, G.: Le: ragioni del cuore. Bologna, IL mulino (2003)
6. Benedict, R.: The Chrysanthemum and the Sword. Houghton Mifflin, Boston (1946)
7. Berthouze, N., Kleinsmith, A.L.: Automatic recognition of affective body expressions (2014)
8. Bevacqua, E., Prepin, K., Niewiadomski, R., de Sevin, E., Pelachaud, C. GRETA: towards an interactive conversational virtual companion, in artificial companions in society: perspectives on the present and future. In: Wilks, Y., Benjamins J. (eds.) pp. 143-156 (2010)
9. Bruno, G.: Eroici furori. Laterza, Bari (1995)
10. Cambria, E., Hussain, A.: Sentic Computing: Techniques, Tools, and Applications. Springer (2012)
11. Campbell, S.: Being dismissed: the politics of emotional expression. Hypatia **9**(3), 46–65 (1994)
12. Castelfranchi, C.: Affective appraisal versus cognitive evaluation in social emotions and interactions. In: Paiva, A. (ed.) Affective Interactions Towards a New Generation of Computer Interfaces, pp. 76–106. Springer, Berlino (2000)
13. Castelfranchi, C., Miceli, M.: The cognitive-motivational compound of emotional experience. Emot. Rev. **1**(3), 223–231 (2009)
14. Castelfranchi, C., Poggi I.: Blushing as a Discourse: Was Darwin Wrong?. In: Crozier R. (Ed.) Shyness and Embarrassment. Perspectives from Social Psychology, pp.230-251. New York: Cambridge University Press (1990)
15. Ceron, A. Lacus, S.M., Curini, L.: Social Media E Sentiment Analysis. Springer (2014)
16. Cerrato, L.: Linguistic functions of head nods. In: Proceedings of the Conference Multi-Modal Communication (2005)
17. Conte, R., Castelfranchi, C.: La società delle menti: azione cognitiva e azione sociale. UTET libreria (1995)
18. Cowell, A.J., Stanney, K.M.: Embodiment and interaction design guidelines for designing credible, trustworthy embodied conversational agents. In: Rist, T. (ed.) Intelligent Virtual Agents: 4th International Workshop, Iva 2003, Proceedings. Lecture Notes in Computer Science, vol. 2792, pp. 301–309. Springer, Berlin, Germany (2003)
19. Cowie, R, Douglas-Cowie, E., Tsapatsoulis, N., Votsis, G., Kollias, S., Fellenz, W., Taylor, J.G.: Emotion recognition in human-computer interaction. In: Chang, S.-F., Schneiderman, S., (eds.) IEEE Signal Processing Magazine, IEEE Signal Processing Society, pp 32-80 (2001)
20. Csikszentmihalyi, M.: Finding Flow. The Psychology of Engagement With Everyday Life. Basic books, New York (1997)
21. Dael, N., Bianchi-Berthouze, N., Kleinsmith, N., Mohr, C.: Measuring body movement: current and future directions in proxemics and kinesics. In: Proceedings of the APA Handbook of Nonverbal Communication. APA (2015)
22. Darwin, Ch. R.: The Expression of the Emotions in Man and Animals. London (1872)
23. D'Errico, F., Poggi, I.: Blame the opponent, effects of multimodal discrediting moves in public debates. Cogn. Comput. **4**(4), 460–476 (2012)
24. D'Errico, F., Poggi, I.: Acidity. Emotional causes, effects, and multimodal communication. In: Freitas-Magalhães, A. (ed.), Emotional Expression: The Brain and The Face, Vol. 5., pp. 341–368. Porto: University Fernando Pessoa Press (2014)
25. D'Errico, F., Poggi, I.: Acidity. The hidden face of conflictual and stressful situations. Cogn. Comput. **6**(4), 661–676 (2014)
26. D'Errico, F., Poggi, I., Vinciarelli A., Vincze L.: Conflict and Multimodal Communication. Social Computational Series. Springer, Heidelberg (2015)
27. de Rosis, F., Pelachaud, C., Poggi, I., Carofiglio, V., De Carolis, N.: From greta's mind to her face: modeling the dynamics of affective states in a conversational embodied agent, special issue on "applications of affective computing in human-computer interaction. Int. J. Hum. Comput. Stud. **59** (1–2), 81–118 (2003)
28. D'Urso, V.: Trentin. Introduzione alla psicologia delle emozioni. Laterza Bari (1998)

29. Ekman, P., Friesen, W.V.: Unmasking The Face. Prentice-Hall, Englewood Cliffs, N.J. (1975)
30. Ekman, P., Friesen, W.V., Hager, J.C.: FACS. Facial Action Coding System: The Manual a Human Face. Salt Lake City (2002)
31. Ellsworth, P., Scherer, K.R.: Appraisal processes in emotion. Handbook of Affective Sciences, pp. 572–595. Oxford University Press, New York (2003)
32. Freud, S.: A General Introduction to Psychoanalysis. Boni & Liveright, New York (1920)
33. Frijda, N.: The Emotions. Cambridge Press (1986)
34. Frijda, N.: Appraisal and beyond. The Issue of Cognitive Determinants of Emotion, in Cognition and Emotion, pp. 225–387 (1993)
35. Gebhard, P.: ALMA—A Layered Model of Affect. In: Proceedings of the Autonomous Agents and Multi Agent Systems, pp. 29–36 (2005)
36. Gratch, J., Marsella, S.: A domain-independent framework for modeling emotions. J. Cogn. Syst. Res. **5**(4), 269–306 (2004)
37. Gratch, J., Marsella, S.: Social emotions in nature and artifact. Oxford University press (2014)
38. Greenson, R.R.: Explorations in Psychoanalysis. International Universities press, New York (1978)
39. Haidt, J.: Elevation and the positive psychology of morality. In: Keyes, C.L.M., Haidt, J. (eds.) Flourishing: Positive Psychology and the Life Well-lived, pp. 275–289. American Psychological Association, Washington DC (2003)
40. Hatfield, E., Rapson, R.L., Le, Y.L.: Primitive emotional contagion: recent research. In: Decety, J., Ickes, W. (eds.) The Social Neuroscience of Empathy. MIT Press, Boston, MA (in press)
41. Hudlicka, E., McNeese, M.: User's affective and belief state: assessment and GUI adaptation. User Model. User Adap. Inter. **12**(1), 1–47 (2002)
42. Izdebski, K.: Emotions in the Human Voice. Plural Publishing, San Diego, CA (2008)
43. Jacko, J.A., Sears, A (eds.): Human-Computer Interaction Handbook. Mahwah: Lawrence Erlbaum & Associates (2003)
44. Johnson, W.L., Rickel, J.W., Lester, J.C.: Animated pedagogical agents: Faceto-face interaction in interactive learning environments. Int. J. Artif. Intell. Educ. **11**, 47–78 (2000)
45. Kant, I.: Kritik der Urteilskraft. Leipzig (1790). Critique of Judgement (trans: Bernard, J.H.). Dover Publications, Mineola (1983)
46. Klein, M.: Envy and Gratitude: A Study of Unconscious. Basic Books, New York (1957)
47. Kopp, S., Gesellensetter, L., Krämer, N.C., Wachsmuth, I.: A conversational agent as museum guide–design and evaluation of a real-world application. Intell. Virtual Agents, 329-343 (2005)
48. Lazarus, R.S.: Thoughts on the relationship between emotion and cognition. Am. Psychol. 1019–24 (1982)
49. Lazarus, R.S.: Progress on a cognitive-motivational-relational theory of emotion. Am. Psychol. **46**(8), 819 (1991)
50. Lazarus, R.S., Smith, A.: Knowledge and appraisal in the cognition-emotion relationship. Cogn. Emot. **2**(4), 281–300 (1988)
51. Lewis, M.: Self-conscious emotions. Emotions **742** (2000)
52. Leventhal, H., Scherer, K.: The relationship of emotion to cognition. A functional approach to a semantic controversy. Cogn. Emot. 3–28 (1987)
53. Liu, B.: Web Data Mining: Exploring Hyperlinks. Contents, and Usage Data. Springer (2011)
54. Mandler, G.: Mind and Body: Psychology of Emotion and Stress. WW Norton (1984)
55. McFall, L.: What's wrong with bitterness? In: Card, C. (ed.) Feminist Ethics. University of Kansas Press, Lawrence (1991)
56. Marsella, S., Gratch, J., Petta, P.: Computational models of emotion. In: Blueprint for Affective Computing (Series in Affective Science) (2010)
57. McNeill, D.: (1992) Hand and Mind: What Gestures Reveal About Thought. University of Chicago Press (1992)
58. Mehrabian, A., Russell, J.A.: An Approach To Environmental Psychology. MIT Press (1974)
59. Miceli, M., Castelfranchi, C.: Expectancy and Emotion. Oxford University Press, Oxford (2015)

60. Minsky, M.: The Society of Mind. Simon & Schuster (1986)
61. Oatley, K., Jenkins, J.M.: Understanding Emotions. Cambridge (Mass) (1996)
62. Oatley, K., Johnson-Laird, P.N.: Towards a cognitive theory of emotions. Cogn. Emot. 29–50 (1987)
63. Oatley, K., Johnson-Laird, P.N. The communicative theory of emotions. Empirical tests, mental models, and implications for social interaction. In: Martin, L.L. Tesser, A., Mahwah N.J. (eds.) Striving and Feeling. Interactions Among Goals, Affect, and Self-regulation (1996)
64. Ortony, A., Clore, G.L., Collins, A.: The Cognitive Structure of Emotions, p. 2. Cambridge University Press, Cambridge, UK (1988)
65. Ortony, A., Turner, T.J.: What's basic about basic emotions? Psychol. Rev. **74**, 431–461 (1990)
66. Osgood, C.E., Suci, G.J., Tannenbaum, P.H.: The Measurement of Meaning. University of Illinois Press (1957)
67. Paiva, A., Dias, J., Sobral, D., Aylett, R., Sobreperez, P., Woods, S., Zoll, C., Hall, L.: Caring for agents and agents that care: building empathic relations with synthetic agents. In: Proceedings of the ACM International Conference on Autonomous Agents and Multiagent Systems (AAMAS'04) (2004)
68. Paiva, A. Dias J., Vala A.M., Woods S.R., Zoll, C.: Empathic characters in computer-based personal and social education. In: Pivec, M. (ed.) Game-Based and Innovative Learning Approaches. IOS Press (2006)
69. Paiva, A., Prada, R., Picard, R.W.: Affective Computing and Intelligent Interaction. Springer, Berlin (2007)
70. Pang, B., Lee, L. Vaithyanathan S. Thumbs up? sentiment classification using machine learning techniques. In: Proceedings of the Conference on Empirical Methods in Natural Language Processing (EMNLP), pp. 79–86 (2002)
71. Pelachaud, C., Poggi, I.: Multimodal embodied agents. Knowl. Eng. Rev. **17**, 181–196 (2002)
72. Pelachaud, C., Peters, C., Bevacqua, E., Chafaı, N.E.: Webpage of the GRETA group: embodied conversational agent research at the IUT Montreuil (2008)
73. Picard, R.: Affective Computing. Paperback (2000)
74. Piers, G., Singer, M.B.: Shame and guilt: a psychoanalytic and a cultural study (1971)
75. Plato: Fedro, Fondazione Lorenzo Valla. Mondadori Editore, Roma (1998)
76. Poggi, C.: Pelachaud, Persuasion and the expressivity of gestures in humans and machines. In: Wachsmuth, I., Lenzen, M., Knoblich, G. (eds.) Embodied Communication in Humans and Machines, Oxford University Press (2008)
77. Poggi, I.: Mind, Hands, Face and Body: A Goal And Belief View Of Multimodal Communication. Weidler, Berlin (2007)
78. Poggi, I.: Enthusiasm and its contagion. Nature and function. In: Paiva, A., Prada, R., Picard, R.W. (eds.) Affective Computing and Intelligent Interaction, pp. 410-421. Springer, Berlin (2007)
79. Poggi, I.: Types of goals and types of emotions. In: Proceedings of the Workshop AFFINE: Affective Interaction in Natural Environment, Post-Conference Workshop of ICMI 2008. Chania, Crete, 24 (2008)
80. Poggi, I., D'Errico, F.: The mental ingredients of bitterness. J. Multimodal User Interface. **3**(1), 79–86 (2009) (Springer)
81. Poggi I., D'Errico F.: Acid communication. II Congresso Internacional Interfaces da Psicologia (2011)
82. Poggi, I., D'Errico, F.: Pride and its expression in political debates. In: Paglieri, F., Tummolini, L., Falcone, R., Miceli, M. (eds.) The Goals of Cognition, Festschrift for Cristiano Castelfranchi, pp. 221–253. London College Publications, London (2012)
83. Poggi, I., D'Errico, F., Vinciarelli, A., (eds.): Social signals foundation. From theory to application. Cogn. Process. **13**(2) (2012)
84. Poggi, I., D'Errico, F., Vincze, L.: Agreement and its multimodal communication in debates. A qualitative analysis. Cogn. Comput. (2010). doi:10.1007/s12559-010-9068-x
85. Poggi I., D'Errico F., Vincze L.: 68 Nods. But not only of agreement. In: Fricke, E., Voss, M. (eds.) 68 Zeichen fùr Roland Posner. Ein Semiotisches Mosaik. 68 signs for Roland Posner. A semiotic mosaic. Tùbingen. Stauffenburg Verlag (2011)

86. Poggi, I., Pelachaud, C., de Rosis, F., Carofiglio, V., De Carolis, N.: GRETA. A believable embodied conversational agent In: Stock, O., Zancarano, M. (eds.) Multimodal Intelligent Information Presentation, Kluwer (2005)
87. Poggi, I., Zuccaro, V.: Admiration. In: Proceedings of the Workshop AFFINE: Affective Interaction in Natural Environment, Post-conference workshop of ICMI 2008, Chania, Crete, p. 24 (2008)
88. Russell, J.A.: Core affect and the psychological construction of emotion. Psychol. Rev. **110**(1), 145 (2003)
89. Russell, S., Norvig, P.: Artificial Intelligence: A Modern Approach, 2nd edn. Prentice Hall (2003)
90. Rumelhart, D.E., Mc Clelland, J.L.: Parallel distributed processing. Explorations in the Microstructure of Cognition Foundations, vol. 1. Cambridge (Mass.) (1986)
91. Saif, H., Ortega, J.F., Fernández M. Cantador, I.: Sentiment analysis in social streams (this volume, chapter 7)
92. Schachter, S.: The interaction of cognitive and physiological determinants of emotional state. In: Berkowitz, L. (ed.) Advances in Experimental Social Psychology New York, vol. 1, pp. 49–81 (1964)
93. Scherer, K.R.: Appraisal considered as a process of multilevel sequential checking. In: Scherer, K. Schorr, A., Johnstone T. (eds.) Appraisal Processes in Emotion, vol. 5. Oxford University Press (2001)
94. Scherer, K.R.: Psychological models of emotion. In: Borod, J. (ed.) The Neuropsychology of Emotion, pp. 137–62. Oxford University Press, New York (2000)
95. Scherer, K.: On the nature and function of emotion. A component process approach. In: Scherer, K., Ekman, P. (eds.) Approaches to Emotion, pp. 293-318. Hillsdale N.J. (1984)
96. Scherer, K.R.: Vocal communication of emotion: a review of research paradigms. Speech Communication. Special Issue on Speech and Emotion, vol. 40(1–2), pp. 227–256 (2003)
97. Schlosberg, H.: The description of facial expression in terms of two dimensions. J. Exp. Psychol. **44**, 229–232 (1952)
98. Strapparava, C., Mihalcea, R.: Learning to identify emotions in text. In: Proceedings of the 2008 ACM symposium on Applied computing, pp. 1556–1560 (2008)
99. Strapparava, C., Valitutti, A.: WordNet-affect: an affective extension of WordNet. In: Tangney, J.P., Stuewig, J., Mashek, D.J. (eds.) Proceedings of LREC. Moral Emotions and Moral Behavior, pp. 1086–1086 (2004) The Annual Review of Psychology, vol. 58, pp. 345–372 (2007)
100. Tangney, J.P., Stuewig, J., Mashek, D.J.: Moral emotions and moral behavior. Annu. Rev. Psychol. **58**, 345 (2007)
101. Tkalcic, M., Burnik, U., Košir, A.: Using affective parameters in a content-based recommender system for images. User Model. User Adap. Inter. **20**(4), 279–311 (2010)
102. Tracy, J.L, Robins, R.W.: Show your pride: evidence for a discrete emotion expression. Psychol. Sci. **15**(3), 194–7 (2004)
103. Tracy, J.L., Robins, R.W.: Appraisal antecedents of shame, guilt, and pride: support for a theoretical model. Pers. Soc. Psychol. Bull. (2006)
104. Wierzbicka, A.: Everyday conceptions of emotion. A semantic perspective, in everyday conceptions of emotion. An introduction to the psychology, anthropology, and linguistics of emotion. In: Russell, J.A., Fernandez-Dols, J.-M., Manstead, A.S.R. et al. (eds.) Dordrecht-Boston-London, pp. 17-48 (1995)
105. Zajonc, R.B.: On the primacy of affect. American Psychologist. **39**, 117–123 (1984)
106. Zajonc, R.: Feeling and thinking. Preferences need no inferences. Am. Psychol. 151–175 (1980)
107. Zeng, Z. Pantic, M., Huang T.: Emotion recognition based on multimodal information. In: Tan, T., Tao, J. (eds.) Affective Information Processing, pp. 241–266. Springer (2009)

Chapter 3
Models of Personality

Sandra Matz, Yin Wah Fiona Chan and Michal Kosinski

Abstract In this chapter, we introduce and discuss some of the most important and widely used models of personality. Focusing on trait theories, we first give a brief overview of the history of personality research and assessment. We then move on to discuss some of the most prominent trait models of the nineteenth century—including Allport's trait theory, Cattell's 16 Factor Model, Eysenck's Giant Three, and the Myers–Briggs Type Indicator (MBTI)—before focusing on the Big Five Model (Five Factor Model), which is the most widely accepted trait model of our time. Next, we introduce alternatives to the Big Five that appear to be useful in the context of personalized services (the HEXACO and RIASEC models), and subsequently outline the relationships between all the models discussed in the chapter. Finally, we provide an outlook on innovative methods of predicting personality with the help of digital footprints.

3.1 Introduction

We all have an intuitive concept of personality that guides our everyday social interactions. For example, we use descriptions such as "the party animal" to refer to a friend who differs systematically from "the nerdy geek"; we explain our partner's sudden outburst of anger with his "impulsive and neurotic" character; and we predict that our sister will be a good lawyer as a result of her "competitive" nature. While these lay conceptualizations of personality are only loosely defined and often implicit, scientific models of personality provide a structured approach for describing, explaining, and predicting individual differences. Rather than accounting for the full complex-

S. Matz (✉) · Y.W.F. Chan
University of Cambridge, Downing Street Cambridge, Cambridge CB2 3EB, UK
e-mail: sm917@cam.ac.uk

Y.W.F. Chan
e-mail: ywfc2@cam.ac.uk

M. Kosinski
Stanford Graduate School of Business, 655 Knight Way, Stanford, CA 94305, USA
e-mail: michalk@stanford.edu

M. Tkalčič et al. (eds.), *Emotions and Personality in Personalized Services*,
Human–Computer Interaction Series, DOI 10.1007/978-3-319-31413-6_3

ity of individual differences, they are pragmatic approximations and standardized frameworks for generating and validating new scientific hypotheses and research questions. Similarly, they provide practitioners in a variety of applied contexts, e.g. personnel selection, coaching and psychotherapy, or marketing with a tool to reduce the complexity of human nature to a manageable level. The theories that have been suggested in the context of personality are diverse. While some of them focus on biological differences (biological paradigm) or behavioral learning and conditioning (behavioral paradigm), others highlight the importance of childhood experiences (psychoanalytic paradigm) or cognitions and social learning (social-cognitive paradigm). However, although all of these theories provide valuable insights into the development and expression of personality, the most prevalent and widely accepted approach to personality is the trait approach. Trait theorists assume that our cognitions, emotions, and behaviors are determined by a number of consistent and relatively stable traits. Therefore, in this chapter, we will focus on different trait models that have been suggested during the last century. We begin with a brief introduction to the idea of trait models in Sect. 3.2. We then move on to some of the most important trait models of the nineteenth century in Sect. 3.3, before discussing the Big Five (the most widely accepted trait model of our time) in Sect. 3.4. Section 3.5 introduces two alternatives to the Big Five: the HEXACO model (a modification of the Big Five) and the RIASEC model (a vocational interest model). Finally, Sect. 3.6 outlines the relationships between these models. Given the breadth of the topic, this chapter serves as a comprehensive introduction to personality models. Readers who are interested in learning more are encouraged to read [17, 18, 49].

3.2 Trait Theories of Personality

Trait theories of personality are not only the most researched and widely used theories among all personality paradigms, but they also correspond most closely to our lay conceptualization of personality. Researchers following the trait approach suggest that personality consists of a range of consistent and relatively stable characteristics (traits) that determine how a person thinks, feels, and behaves. This idea dates back to the Greek philosophers and physicians, Hippocrates (460–377 BC) and Galen of Pergamum (AD 130–200), who first formulated the theory of the four humors represented by different body fluids: black bile, yellow bile, phlegm, and blood. These humors were believed to be a balanced system in the human body that determined one's health. For instance, a deficit or a surplus of any humor would cause an imbalance of the system and lead to physical illness or mental diseases. In his temperament theory, Galen first suggested that the four humors were also the basis of differences in human temperament and behavior. His four temperaments of sanguine (excess blood), choleric (excess yellow bile), melancholic (excess black bile), and phlegmatic (excess phlegm) reappear in writings of Wilhelm Wundt, one of the fathers of modern psychology, and Hans Eysenck, the author of the three-factor personality model. Although Hippocrates' and Galen's theories on the links between body fluids and temperament are not supported by modern science, their idea that people systematically differ, with regard to a number of distinct characteristics, set the basis for the study of individual differences and modern trait theories.

Factor analysis: Factor analysis is a statistical method aimed at reducing complexity by summarizing the information of a large number of variables (e.g. questions in a questionnaire) by a limited number of factors (e.g. personality traits). The composition of dimensions depends on the correlations (the degree to which two variables are related) between the variables, so that related variables become summarized within one dimension. For example, it is very likely that a person who indicates a strong agreement with one Extroversion question will also indicate a strong agreement with other Extroversion questions. Based on the resulting intercorrelations of questions, factor analysis summarizes those items under one latent factor (latent = not directly observable). Once the optimal number of factors has been extracted, variables are assigned to the factor with the highest factor loading (correlation of variable with factor). Eventually, each factor can be interpreted by looking at the "common theme" of its items (e.g. Extroversion contains items such as "I am the life of the party" or "I start conversations").

The development of modern trait theories in the second half of the twentieth century was mainly driven by new advancements in the field of data collection, measurement, and statistical analysis. Perhaps, most importantly, the development of factor analysis allowed for reducing the diversity of behaviors and preferences to a limited number of meaningful factors. Most of the trait theories presented in this chapter were derived using factor analytical approaches, and often went hand in hand with the development of new questionnaire measures. The main contributors to this trend were psychologists working in the field of individual differences, such as Raymond Cattell, Paul Costa, Robert McCrae, or Charles Spearman.

3.3 Early Trait Theories

Numerous trait models have been suggested before the introduction of the Big Five. Here, we focus on the four most prominent and influential ones: Allport's Trait Theory [2]; Cattell's 16 Factor Personality [15]; Eysenck's Three Dimensions of Personality [25, 27]; and the Myers–Briggs Type Indicator (MBTI [57]).

3.3.1 Allport's Trait Theory

Building on the idea first introduced by Sir Francis Galton, Gordon Allport (1897–1967) hypothesized that important personal characteristics must be encoded in language, and the most important characteristics will be described by a single word (referred to as the lexical hypothesis [2, 3]). Together with Henry Odbert, Allport examined in this hypothesis by extracting from an English dictionary 17,953 words that could be used to describe others. They grouped these words into four categories: (1) personality traits; (2) present states, attitudes, emotions, and moods; (3) social evaluations; and (4) miscellaneous. Personality traits were further divided into cardinal traits, central traits, and secondary traits. A cardinal trait is one that dominates any given person's behavior (e.g. the bad-tempered David). Central traits are, to some degree, found in everyone. For instance, everyone could be described by some positive (or negative) level of honesty. Finally, secondary traits are not shared by all people and are expressed only in certain contexts, such as "disliking formal dinners." The lexical hypothesis spawned an enormous amount of research. Many of the most popular personality models—including Cattell's 16 Factor Model and the Big Five—were based on the comprehensive collection of personality traits identified by [2, 3].

3.3.2 Cattell's 16 Personality Factor

A chemist by training, Raymond Cattell (1905–1998) was driven by the idea of identifying "basic psychological elements" resembling those of the periodic table. Cattell made an important conceptual distinction between surface traits and source traits. According to Cattell, surface traits are superficial behavioral tendencies that exist "on the surface," and thus can be observed directly. Source traits, in contrast, represent deeper psychological structures that underlie surface traits and explain their correlations. For example, the surface traits of shyness, being reserved and quiet among strangers, or avoiding big crowds, can all be explained by the underlying source trait of Introversion. Accepting Allport's lexical approach, Cattell stated that "all aspects of human personality, which are or have been of importance, interest, or utility, have already become recorded in the substance of language" [14], p. 483). He reduced Allport's word list from over 4,500 to 171, by excluding rare or redundant traits. Cattell used factor analysis to reduce people's self-ratings on each of those 171 traits to a smaller number of essential factors. Furthermore, he supplemented those results using similar analyses of life records (natural behavior observed in everyday situations) and objective test data (behavior in artificial situations examining any given trait). The idea behind Cattell's multisource approach was that the most basic and fundamental psychological traits should reappear in all three data sources. He eventually suggested that the variance in human behavior could be sufficiently described by 16 primary factors, or source traits. Further factor analyses of the 16 primary traits led Cattell to report five global personality traits, which are sometimes referred to as the original Big Five: (1) Extroversion/Introversion, (2) High Anxiety/Low

Table 3.1 Cattell's 16 primary factors and five global traits

Extroversion/ Introversion	High anxiety/ Low anxiety	Tough-mindedness/ Receptivity	Independence/ Accommodation	Self-control/ Lack of restraint
Warmth	Emotional	Warmth	Dominance	Liveliness
Liveliness	Stability	Sensitivity	Social boldness	Perfectionism
Social boldness	Vigilance	Abstractedness	Vigilance	Abstractedness
Privateness	Apprehension	Openness to Change	Openness to Change	Rule
Self-reliance	Tension			Consciousness

Since Cattell's global factors are not conceptualized as independent, primary factors can appear in multiple global factors

Anxiety, (3) Tough-Mindedness/Receptivity, (4) Independence/Accommodation, and (5) Self-Control/Lack of Restraint. Table 3.1 illustrates the primary and secondary factors.

Cattell's development and application of advanced factor analytical techniques, as well as his systematic analysis of different data sources, have paved the way for the development of later trait models such as the Big Five. However, although the 16 Personality Factor Questionnaire [15], measuring both primary and secondary traits, is still in use and available in more than 30 languages, the 16 factor model has never acquired the academic popularity that Cattell had hoped for. Probably the most important reason for this is that the 16 factor model is more difficult to understand and remember than more parsimonious models such as Eysenck's Giant Three or the Big Five.

3.3.3 Eysenck's Giant Three

Another popular trait model is the Three Dimensions of Personality proposed by Hans Eysenck (1916–1997), which is also known as the Giant Three. Like Cattell, Eysenck used factor analysis of questionnaire items to derive common personality traits (low-level traits) and secondary factor analysis to infer a smaller number of higher order factors (superfactors). In his initial model, Eysenck identified two superfactors: Extroversion and Neuroticism (1947). Whereas the Extroversion factor refers to the degree to which people like to engage with the social world around them, and seek excitement and activity, the Neuroticism factor reflects the degree to which people experience and express their emotions. Contrary to Cattell, Eysenck conceptualized personality factors as independent (orthogonal), and used their continuous nature to create a two-dimensional personality space. According to Eysenck, this Neuroticism-Extroversion space was not entirely new but reflected the four humors introduced by the Greek philosophers. The melancholic type, for example, resembles a combination of high Neuroticism and low Extroversion, while the sanguine type is a mixture of low Neuroticism and high Extroversion.

Table 3.2 Big Five traits, facets, and sample items

Superfactor	Primary traits
Psychoticism	Aggressive, cold, egocentric, impersonal, impulsive, antisocial, unempathetic, creative
Extroversion	Sociable, lively, active, assertive, sensation-seeking, carefree, dominant, surgent, venturesome
Neuroticism	Anxious, depressed, guilt feelings, low self-esteem, tense, irrational, shy, moody, emotional

Later on, Eysenck and his wife Sybil Eysenck added the Psychoticism superfactor [27]. Contrary to the other two factors, Psychoticism is concerned with what one might consider "abnormal" rather than normal behavior. It includes low-level traits such as aggression, antisocial behavior, and impulsiveness. The three resulting superfactors form the acronym PEN. Acknowledging that Psychoticism, Extroversion, and Neuroticism might not be sufficient to account for the complexity of individual differences, Eysenck included a number of low-level primary traits to further specify the superfactors (see Table 3.2).

One of the most noteworthy contributions from Eysenck was his systematic investigation of the biological correlates and foundations of personality traits. According to Eysenck, the identification of biological systems and mechanisms underlying the expression of personality traits is particularly important in avoiding circular explanations of traits. For example, Extroversion is often validated by measuring its relationship with the frequency and quality of a person's social interactions. If the trait of Extroversion, however, is measured with items such as "I meet my friends frequently," "I am a sociable person," or "I make friends easily," substantial correlations between Extroversion and social behaviors do not prove Extroversion's existence as a real psychological trait. Although Eysenck investigated the biological correlates and causes for all of the three super-traits, he was most successful in providing evidence for the links between Extroversion and a person's level of cortical arousal [26]. His work suggests that people who avoid social occasions (Introverts) have a relatively high baseline of cortical arousal, which leads them to perceive further stimulation as unpleasant. In contrast, outgoing people (Extraverts) tend to have a lower baseline of cortical arousal, which leads them to seek stimulation by attending social occasions.

3.3.4 The Myers–Briggs Type Indicator (MBTI)

The Myers–Briggs Type Indicator (MBTI [57]), named after its two developers, Katharine Cook Briggs (1875–1968) and her daughter Isabel Briggs Myers

Table 3.3 The four MBTI dimensions

Dichotomous dimensions of the MBTI
Extroversion (E)–(I) Introversion
Sensing (S)–(N) Intuition
Thinking (T)–(F) Feeling
Judging (J)–(P) Perception

(1897–1980), was developed on the basis of the psychological type theory by Carl Gustav Jung (1875–1961). Jung's type theory classified people according to the three dimensions of (1) Extroversion versus Introversion; (2) Sensing versus Intuition; and (3) Judging versus Perception. Although Jung acknowledged that people are likely to engage in both categories of one dimension (e.g. Sensing and Intuition), he believed that they differ in regard to their preferences for and frequency in use of them [38]. For example, a counselor might focus on sensing, while an artist might rely more on his or her intuition; a programmer might predominantly use rational thinking, while a poet might emphasize feeling. Contrary to the models discussed previously, Jung's type model therefore does not conceptualize personality traits as continuous dimensions, but as dichotomous and mutually exclusive categories. Being aware of the potential of Jung's model, Briggs and Myers further refined it by adding the Judging versus Perception dimension, and later developed the MBTI with four dimensions (see Table 3.3). As the name "Type Indicator" implies, the MBTI assigns specific personality types by combining the dominant categories of the four dimensions. Each of the 16 types is associated with a specific pattern of personality characteristics. While people of type ENTP, for example, are driven by their motivation and desire to understand and make sense of the world they live in, people of type ISFJ are characterized by their desire to serve others as well as their 'need to be needed'.

Although the MBTI is widely used in applied contexts, it has been heavily criticized for (1) its oversimplification of the complex nature of individual differences; and (2) its questionable reliability and validity in explaining real-life outcomes (e.g. [63]). Since the results of the MBTI are given in the form of a four-letter code representing the dominant categories of each dimension (e.g. ENTJ), the MBTI reduces the theoretically unlimited space of personality profiles to only 16 distinguishable personality types. Taking into account the nature of individual differences in the population, the dichotomous classifications offered by the MBTI appear to be dramatically over-simplistic. First, it fails to distinguish between moderate and extreme levels of a given trait. Second, as personality traits are normally distributed in the population, most of the people are characterized by scores close to average. Consequently, even a small inaccuracy in the measurement leads to a person being misclassified. In fact, several studies showed that even after short test-retest intervals of five weeks, up to 50 % of participants were classified into a different type [35]. Third, the MBTI's validity is questionable, given that many studies were unable to replicate its factor structure [63]. Finally, the MBTI was found to be poorly predictive of real-life outcomes. Taken together, the questionable validity and other psychometric properties of the MBTI warrant caution in its application in research and applied settings. While the MBTI is still relatively popular in the industry, especially in the U.S., it is usually avoided in science due to the reasons outlined above.

3.4 The Big Five

The variety of competing personality models, differing in their numbers and types of dimensions, largely prohibited the systematic integration of personality research conducted during that time. It was not until the late 1980 s that with the introduction of the Big Five, a framework of personality was proposed that could be agreed upon by the vast majority of personality researchers. The Big Five model is a trait theory that posits five independent domain traits, including: Openness to Experience (O), Conscientiousness (C), Extroversion (E), Agreeableness (A), and Neuroticism (N). Each of the traits can be broken down into facets that further specify the nature and scope of the factors (see Table 3.4).

Table 3.4 Big Five traits, facets, and sample items

Trait	Facets	Sample items
Openness to experience	Fantasy, aesthetics, feelings, actions, ideas, values	"I have a vivid imagination"
		"I have difficulty understanding abstract ideas" (R)
Conscientiousness	Competence, order, dutifulness, achievement-striving, self-discipline, deliberation	"I am always prepared"
		"I leave my belongings around" (R)
Extroversion	Warmth, gregariousness, assertiveness, activity, excitement-seeking, positive emotions	"I feel comfortable around people"
		"I don't like to draw attention to myself" (R)
Agreeableness	Trust, straightforwardness, altruism, compliance, modesty, tender-mindedness	"I take time out for others"
		"I feel little concern for others" (R)
Neuroticism	Anxiety, angry hostility, depression, self-consciousness, impulsivity, vulnerability	"I am easily disturbed"
		"am relaxed most of the time" (R)

Big Five versus Five Factor Model: The terms "Big Five" and "Five Factor Model" are often used interchangeably to refer to the five personality dimensions outlined in Table 3.4. Those models, however, they were developed independently and differ in their underlying assumptions [69]. While the Big Five is based on a lexical approach and is mostly associated with the work of Lewis R. Goldberg, the Five Factor Model was developed on the basis of factor analysis of questionnaire results, and is most closely linked to the work of Robert R. McCrae, Paul Costa, and Oliver P. John. Despite these differences, the two models use the same factor labels and are highly consistent (proving the generalizability of the five factor approach).

3.4.1 Description of the Big Five Traits

The trait of *Openness to Experience* refers to the extent to which people prefer novelty over convention; and it distinguishes imaginative, creative people from down-to-earth, conventional ones. People scoring high on Openness can be described as intellectually curious, sensitive to beauty, individualistic, imaginative, and unconventional. People scoring low on Openness, on the other hand, can be characterized as traditional and conservative, and are likely to prefer the familiar over the unusual.

Conscientiousness refers to the extent to which people prefer an organized or a flexible approach in life, and is thus concerned with the way in which we control, regulate, and direct our impulses. People scoring high on this trait can be described as organized, reliable, perfectionist, and efficient, while people scoring low on this trait are generally characterized as spontaneous, impulsive, careless, absentminded, or disorganized.

Extroversion refers to the extent to which people enjoy company, and seek excitement and stimulation. It is marked by pronounced engagement with the external world, versus being comfortable with one's own company. People scoring high on Extroversion can be described as energetic, active, talkative, sociable, outgoing, and enthusiastic. Contrary to that, people scoring low on Extroversion can be characterized as shy, reserved, quiet, or withdrawn.

The trait of *Agreeableness* reflects individual differences concerning cooperation and social harmony. It refers to the way people express their opinions and manage relationships. People scoring high on this trait are generally considered as being trusting, soft-hearted, generous, and sympathetic, while people scoring low on this trait can best be described as competitive, stubborn, self-confident, or aggressive.

Finally, *Neuroticism* refers to the tendency to experience negative emotions, and concerns the way people cope with and respond to life's demands. People scoring high on Neuroticism can be characterized as being anxious, nervous, moody, and worrying. On the other hand, people scoring low on Neuroticism can be described as emotionally stable, optimistic, and self-confident.

It should be noted that there are no fundamentally good or bad personalities, as scoring high or low on each of the traits has its advantages and disadvantages. One might, for example, be tempted to consider high Agreeableness as a "good" trait. However, although being friendly and trusting certainly has its advantages in some aspects of life (e.g. relationships and team work), Agreeableness is also expressed as gullibility and a lack of assertiveness. Disagreeable individuals, while often less friendly, are particularly good at making difficult decisions when necessary, taking the lead in a competitive environment, or pointing out when something is wrong. Consequently, low agreeableness can prove extremely valuable in many contexts, such when as leading a team or a company.

3.4.2 Big Five's Significance

According to McCrae and John [54, p. 177], the Big Five model "marks a turning point for personality psychology" by providing "a common language for psychologists from different traditions, a basic phenomenon for personality theorists to explain, a natural framework for organizing research, and a guide to the comprehensive assessment of individuals." Indeed, the impact of the Big Five on personality research has been remarkable and, as of yet, there is no other model of personality that has been used and researched as extensively as the Big Five. Unlike previous models, the Big Five was found to be stable across cultures [53], as well as instruments and observers [51]. Furthermore, the Big Five has been linked to numerous life outcomes. Table 3.5 displays some of the most important associations (for a more comprehensive overview, we advise consulting the review paper by Ozer and Benet-Martnez [61]). By providing researchers around the world with a common model to describe and predict individual differences, the Big Five did not only allow for the efficient integration of existing literature, but also encouraged the joint development

Table 3.5 Examples of links between the Big Five traits and real-life outcomes

Trait	Associated life outcome
Openness	Intelligence [1], verbal intelligence [58], liberal political attitudes [50]
Conscientiousness	Academic achievement [58], job performance [68], (-) risky health-related behavior [9], (-) antisocial behavior [71]
Extroversion	Subjective well-being [32], job satisfaction [72], leadership effectiveness [33]
Agreeableness	Volunteerism [13], cooperative behavior [46], job performance [68]
Neuroticism	Clinical mental disorders [59], (-) subjective well-being [32], relationship satisfaction [39]

Note (-) indicates negative correlations

of a framework in which empirical findings could be validated and accumulated. Today, the Big Five constitutes the most popular and prevalent model of personality.

3.4.3 *Big Five Assessment*

The Big Five has been traditionally associated with questionnaire measures. Although there is a number of questionnaires assessing the Big Five dimensions, the public domain item International Personality Item Pool (IPIP [30]), the Big Five Inventory (BFI [36]), and the commercial NEO-Personality Inventory Revised (NEO-PI-R [20]) are the most frequently used and thoroughly validated ones. All three measures rely on participants indicating their agreement with statements describing their preference or behavior (e.g. "I get stressed out easily" in IPIP) using a five-point Likert scale (ranging from "very inaccurate" to "very accurate" in IPIP). Furthermore, they are all characterized by excellent psychometric properties, including high reliability, convergent and discriminant validity with other measures [20, 30, 36], as well as robust criterion validity when predicting real-life outcomes such as academic achievement, job performance, or satisfaction with life (see Sect. 3.4.2 for a broader overview of Big Five correlates). Finally, the psychometric properties of the three measures were shown to be stable across cultures [8, 53]. Applying a scoring key to participants' responses to the IPIP, BFI, NEO-PI-R, or similar questionnaires produces raw scores. Raw scores can be used to compare the results between participants in a given sample; for example, a given participant might be more extraverted than 80 % of the other participants in a sample. However, one has to be extremely cautious when drawing inferences stemming from beyond the particular sample. A score that is high in the context of a given group of participants might be average (or low) in the context of another group or general population. Thus, the interpretation of the scores is often supported by the norms (or standards) established using some reference group: a nationwide sample, for example. The process of transforming the scores based on standards is called standardization. When giving feedback to test takers, it is best practice to represent their scores in an easily interpretable fashion. Hence, the common method is to transform standardized scores into percentiles. A percentile score represents one's location within the population; a percentile score of 68, for example, indicates that one's raw score is higher than that of 68 % of individuals in the reference population. Figure 3.1 illustrates two examples of Big Five profiles on the percentile scale.

Importantly, the practical use of personality measures is not trivial and requires considerable training. As in other psychometric measures, the validity of the results can be affected by a number of factors, including participants' deliberate misrepresentation, linguistic incompetence, inattentiveness, and social desirability [37]. For example, in a recruitment context, respondents are likely to present themselves as more in line with the job requirements (e.g. applicants for an accountant position may misrepresent themselves as more Conscientious than they really are).

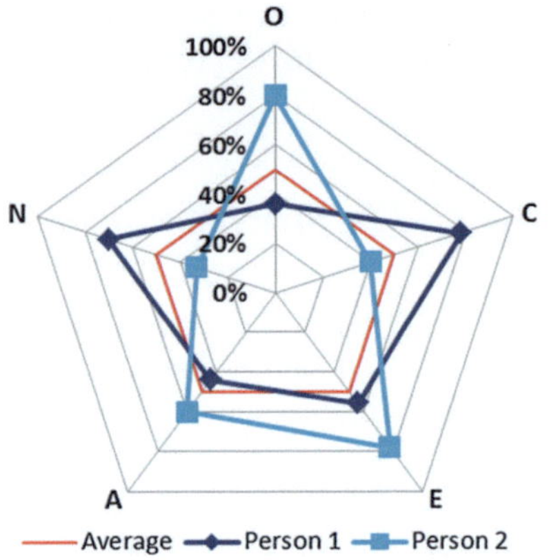

Fig. 3.1 Example of a Big Five profile using percentiles

3.5 Other Models of Individual Differences: HEXACO and RIASEC

Although the Big Five is arguably the most widely accepted and used personality model of our time, there are also other models that can be useful in investigating individual differences. The HEXACO model expands on the Big Five by introducing an additional dimension, while the RIASEC model focuses on personal interests rather than classical personality traits.

3.5.1 The HEXACO Model

The HEXACO model is a six-dimensional trait theory proposed as an extension of the Big Five [44]. The acronym HEXACO refers to the six dimensions of Honesty-Humility (H), Emotionality (E), Extroversion (X), Agreeableness (A), Conscientiousness (C), and Openness to Experience (O). The Honesty-Humility dimension is meant to distinguish between sincere, loyal, faithful, honest, and genuine people on one hand; and cunning, arrogant, disloyal, pretentious, and envious people on the other hand. While adding the sixth factor to the Big Five structure does not significantly change the content of the Extroversion, Openness, and Conscientiousness traits, it alters the Agreeableness and Neuroticism factors. Trait indicators related to temper, for example, are linked to the Neuroticism trait in the Big Five, but are summarized under the Agreeableness dimension in the HEXACO framework. Although there is a growing body of empirical evidence that supports the six-dimensional structure across a number of different languages [4, 44], the HEXACO model is still relatively rarely used. Furthermore, some studies reported difficulties in replicating the Honesty-Humility factor [23].

3.5.2 The RIASEC Model

The RIASEC model was developed by John Lewis Holland [34]. Unlike the models discussed in previous sections, RIASEC is not a personality model in the conventional sense. While traditional personality models are conceptualized to be context-independent, RIASEC focuses on individual differences in vocational interests. Corresponding to the acronym RIASEC, Holland suggests that people as well as work environments can be classified into six different types: Realistic (R), Investigative (I), Artistic (A), Social (S), Enterprising (E), and Conventional (C). Based on their closeness, the six types are typically organized into a hexagonal structure (see Fig. 3.2). While the definitions of personality types are based on preferences for and aversions to certain types of work characteristics, the definitions of work environments are derived from typical work activities and job demands placed on individuals. RIASEC assumes that people flourish and excel in work environments that match their personality type. Although the matching can be done on the basis of individual types, Holland suggests combining the three types with the highest score to form a higher order profile (e.g. REA or CSE). The dimensions can be assessed with the Strong Interest Inventory [12], or with the help of open source questionnaires online (e.g. at http://www.mynextmove.org/explore/ip).

Following the logic of personality-environment types, Realistic people ("Doers") can be described as practical, persistent, and down-to-earth. They prefer dealing with things rather than with people or abstract ideas, and flourish in work environments that involve tactile, mechanical, or physical tasks (e.g. Electrician). Investigate people ("Thinkers") are described as being intellectual, curious, inquisitive, and scholarly. They prefer work environments that allow them to explore their surroundings, solve problems, and satisfy their curiosity (e.g. Researcher). Artistic people ("Creators")

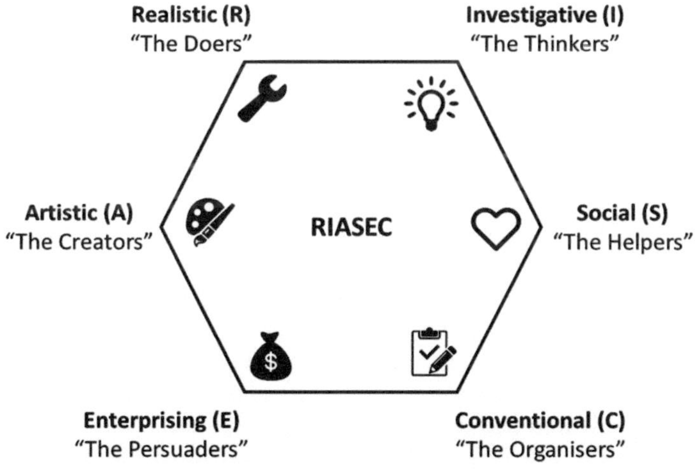

Fig. 3.2 The hexagonal structure of the RIASEC model

can be described as creative, original, articulate, and open-minded. They excel in unstructured work environments in which they can express their creativity and imagination, as well as develop their own ideas and concepts (e.g. Actor). Social people ('Helpers') can be described as empathetic, cooperative, caring, and patient. They prefer interpersonal, service-oriented work environments that highlight teamwork and that allow them to help and teach others (e.g. Social Worker). Enterprising people ("Persuaders") can be described as enthusiastic, ambitious, energetic, and optimistic. They excel in competitive work environments that involve persuading and motivating others; and require leadership, public speaking, and salesmanship skills (e.g. Politician). Finally, Conventional people ("Organisers") can be described as efficient, organized, detail-oriented, and reliable. They prefer structured and stable work environments that involve practical tasks and precise instructions (e.g. Accountant).

3.6 Relationships Between Personality Models

Considering that the trait models introduced in this chapter have substantial similarities with the Big Five when it comes to their conceptualization and naming of traits, it is not surprising that research has established strong empirical correlations between them. Since the RIASEC model is not a trait model in the traditional sense, and most distant from the Big Five conceptually, its correlations with the Big Five are by far the smallest. The relationships between the models are illustrated in Table 3.6.

3.7 Discussion and Conclusion

Decades of psychological research suggest that individuals' behaviors and preferences are not random, but are driven by latent psychological constructs: personality traits. This chapter focused primarily on the most widely used and accepted model, namely the Big Five [20, 30, 36]. Its five broad dimensions (Openness, Conscientiousness, Extroversion, Agreeableness, and Neuroticism) are believed to capture the fundamental dimensions on which individuals differ most apparently. The Big Five were found to be stable across the lifespan and are, at least to some extent, heritable [10, 24, 47, 64]. For example, Loehlin and Nichols [47] examined the personality of nearly 850 twins and showed that personality profiles of identical twins were more similar than those of fraternal ones. Having said this, however, it is important to note that there is nothing like an "Extroversion" or "Conscientiousness" gene. Rather, it is the complex interaction of different genes and environmental influences (gene–environment interaction) that predisposes us to behave in a certain way.

The trait models introduced in this chapter focus on the stability of behaviors within individuals to investigate differences in behaviors across individuals. They assume that an individual's behavior is highly consistent across situations. For example, extraverted individuals are expected to consistently display extroverted behav-

Table 3.6 Correlations between the Big Five traits and other personality models

Model	Op	Co	Ex	Ag	Ne
Cattell's Global Factors	Receptivity (r = 0.62) Self-control (r = –0.50)	Self-control (r = 0.66) Receptivity (r = –0.32)	Extroversion (r = 0.63) Independence (r = 0.49)	Independence (r = –0.34)	Anxiety (r = 0.80)
Eysencks Giant Three	–	(Psychoticism) (r = –0.31)	Extroversion (r = 0.69)	Psychoticism (r = –0.45)	Neuroticism (r = 0.75)
HEXACO	Openness (r = 0.69)	Conscientiousness (r = 0.80)	Extroversion (r = 0.83)	Agreeableness (r = 0.36) Honesty–Humility (r = 0.36) Emotionality (r = 0.38) Extroversion (r = 0.37)	Emotionality (r = 0.51) Agreeableness (r = –0.45)
MBTI	Sensing (r = 0.72)	Judging (r = –0.49)	Extroversion (r = –0.74)	Thinking (r = 0.44)	
RIASEC	Artistic (r = 0.34) Investigative (r = 0.21)	Conventional (r = 0.17)	Enterprising (r = 0.39) Social (r = 0.25)	Social (r = 0.13)	Investigative (r = –0.11)

Note Except for the RIASEC Model, we only included correlations of r > 0.30. The correlations for Cattell's Global Factors are based on [67]; the correlations for Eysencks Giant Three on [21]; the correlations for the HEXACO model on [45]; the correlations for the MBTI on [52]; and the correlations of the RIASEC model on [7]

iors no matter whether they are at work, among friends, or at home with their family. Although the majority of personality models follows this traits approach, some personality psychologists have argued that its assumption of stable personality traits is fundamentally flawed [55]. They argue that behaviors can differ as much within individuals as they differ across individuals. For example, an individual might display very extraverted behaviors at work, where the situation requires her to do so, but be very quiet when spending time with her family. Hence, rather than conceptualizing personality as a stable set of traits that explain behaviors across a variety of contexts, they emphasize the influence of situation-specific exigencies to explain and predict reoccurring patterns of behaviors ([56], e.g. if she is around work colleagues, she is highly sociable and assertive, but if she is around her family, she takes on the role of a quiet observer). In an attempt to reconcile these two seemingly contradictory approaches, researchers have suggested an interactionist perspective [28]: while individuals might be generally more extroverted at social occasions than at home with their families, extroverts should still be more extroverted than introverts when investigating the same occasion. While individuals behaviors might indeed be partially determined by situational factors, the existence of stable and distinct personality traits is valuable in practice: it is a pragmatic way of describing individuals by a small number of variables (e.g. five) that can subsequently be used to accurately predict behavior and preferences across different contexts and environments. In fact, research has shown that personality traits are predictive of many life outcomes, including job performance (e.g. [6, 68]), attractiveness (e.g. [11]), drug use (e.g. [66]), marital satisfaction (e.g. [40]), infidelity (e.g. [60]), and happiness (e.g. [61]).

Expressions of our personalities can be found in many aspects of our everyday interactions with our physical and social environment. Researchers, for example, have shown that individuals can identify other people's personality traits by examining their living spaces [31] or music collections [65]. Following the shift in human interactions, socializing, and communication activities toward online environments, researchers have noted that personality-related behavioral residues are not restricted to the offline environment. They showed that personality is related to keyboard and mouse use [41], smartphone logs [19, 22], contents of personal websites [48, 73], Facebook profiles [42], Facebook Likes [43, 74], or Facebook profile pictures [16].

However, practical applications of personality models have been severely limited in the context of online platform and services. This has been predominantly caused by the time and effort-consuming nature of traditional questionnaire-based assessments. Making use of the unique opportunities offered by the digital environment, however, those limitations might be overcome by assessing personality directly from behavioral footprints. In fact, digital products and services offer an unprecedented repository of easily accessible and yet highly valid records of human behavior [5]. Recent studies show that personality assessment based on such digital footprints can rival those based on well-established questionnaire measures. Potential sources of footprints include personal websites [48], Facebook Likes [43, 74], Facebook Status updates [62, 70], or Twitter messages [29]. Furthermore, the digital environment offers an enormous potential for the development of new models of personality.

The unprecedented ability to inexpensively and conveniently record the behavioral residues of large groups of people, and across long periods of time, can be used to identify patterns of behavior representing existing or yet undiscovered latent psychological dimensions. Factor analytical methods—such as those used to develop personality models based on questionnaire responses or manually recorded behavior—could be applied to much wider records of digital footprints. While extracting interpretable dimensions from digital footprints is not a trivial task, it could eventually lead to the development of new and more robust personality models. Taken together, the personality models identified in this chapter offer valuable insights into the most fundamental dimensions underlying individual differences. They can be a useful source when trying to explain and predict an individual's needs, motives, preferences, and aspirations, all of which can contribute to the development and refinement of personalized systems. Especially when considering the richness of information available on Internet users, a personality-based approach to personalized systems could help reduce the complexity of individual differences and channel our attention to the aspects that are most important.

Acknowledgments We thank John Rust, Vess Popov, and David Stillwell for their feedback on previous versions of the manuscript.

References

1. Ackerman, P. L., Heggestad, E.D.: Intelligence, personality, and interests: evidence for overlapping traits. Psychol. Bull. **121**(2), 219 (1997)
2. Allport, G.W.: Personality: a Psychological Interpretation. H. Holt and Company (1937)
3. Allport, G.W., Odbert, H.S.: Trait-names: a psycho-lexical study. Psychol. Monogr. **47**(1), i (1936)
4. Ashton, M.C., Lee, K., de Vries, R.E.: The hexaco honesty-humility, agreeableness, and emotionality factors: a review of research and theory. Pers. Soc. Psychol. Rev. **18**(2), 139–152 (2014)
5. Back, M.D., Stopfer, J.M., Vazire, S., Gaddis, S., Schmukle, S.C., Egloff, B., Gosling, S.D.: Facebook profiles reflect actual personality, not self-idealization. Psychol. Sci. **21**(3), 372 (2010)
6. Barrick, M.R., Mount, M.K.: The Big Five personality dimensions and job performance: a meta-analysis. Pers. Psychol. **44**(1), 1–26 (1991)
7. Barrick, M.R., Mount, M.K., Gupta, R.: Meta-analysis of the relationship between the five-factor model of personality and Holland's occupational types. Pers. Psychol. 56 (2003)
8. Benet-Martínez, V., John, O.P.: Los Cinco grandes across cultures and ethnic groups: multitrait-multimethod analyses of the big five in Spanish and English. J. Pers. Soc. Psychol. **75**(3), 729 (1998)
9. Bogg, T., Roberts, B.W.: Conscientiousness and health-related behaviors: a meta-analysis of the leading behavioral contributors to mortality. Psychol. Bull. **130**(6), 887 (2004)
10. Bouchard, T.J., Lykken, D.T., McGue, M., Segal, N.L., Tellegen, A.: Sources of human psychological differences: the Minnesota study of twins reared apart. Science **250**(4978), 223–228 (1990)
11. Byrne, D., Griffitt, W., Stefaniak, D.: Attraction and similarity of personality characteristics. J. Pers. Soc. Psychol. (JPSP) **5**(1), 82 (1967)
12. Campbell, V.L.: Strong-Campbell interest inventory. J. Couns. Dev. **66**(1), 53–56 (1987)

13. Carlo, G., Okun, M.A., Knight, G.P., de Guzman, M.R.T.: The interplay of traits and motives on volunteering: agreeableness, extraversion and prosocial value motivation. Pers. Individ. Differ. **38**(6), 1293–1305 (2005)
14. Cattell, R.B.: The description of personality: basic traits resolved into clusters. J. Abnorm. Soc. Psychol. **38**(4), 476–506 (1943)
15. Cattell, R.B., Eber, H.W., Tatsuoka, M.M.: Handbook for the sixteen personality factor questionnaire (16 PF): in clinical, educational, industrial, and research psychology, for use with all forms of the test. Institute for Personality and Ability Testing (1970)
16. Celli, F., Bruni, E., Lepri, B.: Automatic personality and interaction style recognition from Facebook profile pictures. In: Proceedings of the ACM International Conference on Multimedia, pp. 1101–1104. ACM (2014)
17. Cervone, D., Pervin, L.A.: Personality: Theory and Research, 12th edn. (2013)
18. Chamorro-Premuzic, T.: Personality and Individual Differences. BPS Textbooks in Psychology, Wiley (2011)
19. Chittaranjan, G., Blom, J., Gatica-Perez, D.: Mining large-scale smartphone data for personality studies. Pers. Ubiquit. Comput. **17**(3), 433–450 (2013)
20. Costa, P.T. Jr, Mccrae, R.R.: Revised NEO-PI-R and NEO five-factor inventory (NEO-FFI) professional manual (1992)
21. Costa Jr., P.T., McCrae, R.R.: The NEO Personality Inventory manual. Psychological Assessment Resources, Odessa, FL (1985)
22. de Montjoye, Y.-A., Quoidbach, J., Robic, F., Pentland, A.S.: Predicting personality using novel mobile phone-based metrics. In: Proceedings of the Social computing, Behavioral-cultural Modeling and Prediction, pp. 48–55. Springer (2013)
23. De Raad, B., Barelds, D.P.H., Levert, E., Ostendorf, F., Mlačić, B., Di Blas, L., Hřebíčková, M., Szirmák, Z., Szarota, P., Perugini, M., et al.: Only three factors of personality description are fully replicable across languages: a comparison of 14 trait taxonomies. J. Pers. Soc. Psychol. **98**(1), 160 (2010)
24. Eaves, L., Heath, A., Martin, N., Maes, H., Neale, M., Kendler, K., Kirk, K., Corey, L.: Comparing the biological and cultural inheritance of personality and social attitudes in the Virginia 30,000 study of twins and their relatives. Twin Res. **2**(02), 62–80 (1999)
25. Eysenck, H.: Dimensions of Personality. Paul, Trench, Trubner & Co, London (1947)
26. Eysenck, H.: The Biological Basis Personality. Transaction publishers (1967)
27. Eysenck, H., Eysenck, S.B.G.: Psychoticism as a Dimension of Personality. London, Hodder and Stoughton (1976)
28. Fleeson, W.: Situation-based contingencies underlying trait-content manifestation in behavior. J. Pers. **75**(4), 825–862 (2007)
29. Golbeck, J., Robles, C., Edmondson, M., Turner, K.: Predicting personality from Twitter. In: Proceedings of the International Conference on Privacy, Security, Risk and Trust and IEEE International Conference on Social Computing, pp. 149–156 (2011)
30. Goldberg, L.R.: A broad-bandwidth, public domain, personality inventory measuring the lower-level facets of several five-factor models. Pers. Psychol. Eur. **7**, 7–28 (1999)
31. Gosling, S.D., Ko, S., Mannarelli, T., Morris, M.E.: A room with a cue: personality judgments based on offices and bedrooms. J. Pers. Soc. Psychol. (JPSP) **82**(3), 379–398 (2002)
32. Hayes, N., Joseph, S.: Big 5 correlates of three measures of subjective well-being. Personality Individ. Differ. **34**(4), 723–727 (2003)
33. Hogan, R., Curphy, G.J., Hogan, J.: What we know about leadership: effectiveness and personality. Am. Psychol. **49**(6), 493 (1994)
34. Holland, J.L.: Making Vocational Choices: A Theory of Careers. Prentice-Hall, Prentice-Hall series in counseling and human development (1973)
35. Howes, R.J., Carskadon, T.G.: Test-retest reliabilities of the Myers-Briggs type indicator as a function of mood changes. Res. Psychol. Type **2**(1), 67–72 (1979)
36. John, O.P., Srivastava, S.: The Big Five trait taxonomy: History, measurement, and theoretical perspectives. Handbook of personality: theory and research, vol. 2, pp. 102–138 (1999)

37. Johnson, J.A.: Ascertaining the validity of individual protocols from web-based personality inventories. J. Res. Pers. **39**(1), 103–129 (2005)
38. Jung, C.G.: Psychological types: or, the psychology of individuation. International library of psychology, philosophy, and scientific method. K. Paul, Trench, Trubner (1923)
39. Karney, B.R., Bradbury, T.N.: Neuroticism, marital interaction, and the trajectory of marital satisfaction. J. Pers. Soc. Psychol. **72**(5), 1075 (1997)
40. Kelly, E.L., Conley, J.J.: Personality and compatibility: a prospective analysis of marital stability and marital satisfaction. J. Pers. Soc. Psychol. (JPSP) **52**(1), 27 (1987)
41. Khan, I.A., Brinkman, W-P., Fine, N., Hierons, R.M.: Measuring personality from keyboard and mouse use. In: Proceedings of the European Conference on Cognitive Ergonomics: the Ergonomics Of Cool Interaction (2008)
42. Kosinski, M., Bachrach, Y., Kohli, P., Stillwell, D.J., Graepel, T.: Manifestations of user personality in website choice and behaviour on online social networks. Mach. Learn. 1–24 (2013)
43. Kosinski, M., Stillwell, D.J., Graepel, T.: Private traits and attributes are predictable from digital records of human behavior. In: Proceedings of the National Academy of Sciences (PNAS) (2013)
44. Lee, K., Ashton, M.C.: Psychometric properties of the hexaco personality inventory. Multivar. Behav. Res. **39**(2), 329–358 (2004)
45. Lee, K., Ogunfowora, B., Ashton, M.C.: Personality traits beyond the big five: are they within the hexaco space? J. Pers. **73**(5), 1437–1463 (2005)
46. LePine, J.A., Van Dyne, L.: Voice and cooperative behavior as contrasting forms of contextual performance: evidence of differential relationships with big five personality characteristics and cognitive ability. J. Appl. Psychol. **86**(2), 326 (2001)
47. Loehlin, J.C., Nichols, R.C.: Heredity, environment, and personality: a study of 850 sets of twins (1976)
48. Marcus, B., Machilek, F., Schütz, A.: Personality in cyberspace: personal web sites as media for personality expressions and impressions. J. Pers. Soc. Psychol. (JPSP) **90**(6), 1014–1031 (2006)
49. Matthews, G., Deary, I.J., Whiteman, M.C.: Personality Traits. Cambridge University Press (2009)
50. McCrae, R.R.: Social consequences of experiential openness. Psychol. Bull. **120**(3), 323 (1996)
51. McCrae, R.R., Costa, P.T.: Validation of a five-factor model of personality across instruments and observers. J. Pers. Soc. Psychol. **52**, 81–90 (1987)
52. McCrae, R.R., Costa, P.T.: Reinterpreting the Myers-Briggs type indicator from the perspective of the five-factor model of personality. J. Pers. **57**(1), 17–40 (1989)
53. McCrae, R.R., Allik, I.U.: The Five-Factor Model of Personality Across Cultures. Springer, International and Cultural Psychology (2002)
54. McCrae, R.R., John, O.P.: An introduction to the five-factor model and its applications. J. Pers. **60**(2), 175–215 (1992)
55. Mischel, W.: Personality and Assessment. Wiley, New York (1968)
56. Mischel, W., Shoda, Y.: A cognitive-affective system theory of personality: reconceptualizing situations, dispositions, dynamics, and invariance in personality structure. Psychol. Rev. **102**(2), 246 (1995)
57. Isabel, M.: MBTI manual: A Guide to the Development and Use of the Myers-Briggs Type Indicator instrument, 3rd edn. Mountain View, Calif, CPP (2003)
58. Noftle, E.E., Robins, R.W.: Personality predictors of academic outcomes: big five correlates of GPA and SAT scores. J. Pers. Soc. Psychol. **93**(1), 116 (2007)
59. Ormel, J., Bastiaansen, A., Riese, H., Bos, E.H., Servaas, M., Ellenbogen, M., Rosmalen, J.G., Aleman, A.: The biological and psychological basis of neuroticism: current status and future directions. Neurosci. Biobehav. Rev. **37**(1), 59–72 (2013)
60. Orzeck, T., Lung, E.: Big-Five personality differences of cheaters and non-cheaters. Curr. Psychol. **24**, 274–287 (2005)
61. Ozer, D.J., Benet-Martnez, V.: Personality and the prediction of consequential outcomes. Annu. Rev. Psychol. **57**(1), 401–421 (2006)

62. Park, G., Schwartz, H.A., Eichstaedt, J.C., Kern, M.L., Kosinski, M., Stillwell, D.J., Ungar, L.H., Seligman, M.E.P.: Automatic personality assessment through social media language. J. Pers. Soc. Psychol. (JPSP), pp. 934–952
63. Pittenger, D.J.: The utility of the Myers-Briggs type indicator. Rev. Educ. Res. **63**(4), 467–488 (1993)
64. Plomin, R., Caspi, A.: DNA and personality. Eur. J. Pers. **12**(5), 387–407 (1998)
65. Rentfrow, P.J., Gosling, S.D.: Message in a ballad: the role of music preferences in interpersonal perception. Psychol. Sci. **17**(3), 236–242 (2006)
66. Roberts, B.W., Chernyshenko, O.S., Stark, S., Goldberg, L.R.: The structure of conscientiousness: an empirical investigation based on seven major personality questionnaires. Pers. Psychol. **58**(1), 103–139 (2005)
67. Rossier, J., Meyer de Stadelhofen, F., Berthoud, S.: The hierarchical structures of the neo pi-r and the 16pf5. Eur. J. Psychol. Asses. **20**(1), 27 (2004)
68. Sackett, P.R., Walmsley, P.T.: Which personality attributes are most important in the workplace? Perspect. Psychol. Sci. **9**(5), 538–551 (2014)
69. Saucier, G.: Recurrent personality dimensions in inclusive lexical studies: Indications for a big six structure. J. Pers. **77**(5), 1577–1614 (2009)
70. Schwartz, A.H., Eichstaedt, J.C., Kern, M.L., Dziurzynski, L., Ramones, S.M., Agrawal, M., Shah, A., Kosinski, M., Stillwell, D., Seligman, M.E.P., et al.: Personality, gender, and age in the language of social media: the open-vocabulary approach. PloS one **8**(9), e73791 (2013)
71. Shiner, R.L., Masten, A.S., Tellegen, A.: A developmental perspective on personality in emerging adulthood: childhood antecedents and concurrent adaptation. J. Pers. Soc. Psychol. **83**(5), 1165 (2002)
72. Thoresen, C.J., Kaplan, S.A., Barsky, A.P., Warren, C.R., de Chermont, K.: The affective underpinnings of job perceptions and attitudes: a meta-analytic review and integration. In: 17th Annual Conference of the Society for Industrial and Organizational Psychology, Toronto, ON, Canada; An Earlier Version of This Study Was Presented at the Aforementioned Conference., vol. 129, p. 914. American Psychological Association (2003)
73. Vazire, S., Gosling, S.D.: E-perceptions: personality impressions based on personal websites. J. Pers. Soc. Psychol. (JPSP) **87**, 123–132 (2004)
74. Youyou, W., Kosinski, M., Stillwell, D.: Computer-based personality judgments are more accurate than those made by humans. Proc. Natl. Acad. Sci. **112**(4), 1036–1040 (2015)

Part II
Acquisition and Corpora

Chapter 4
Acquisition of Affect

Björn W. Schuller

Abstract This chapter gives a brief overview on the state of the art in emotion and affect acquisition for various modalities and representation forms—mainly discrete and continuous. Its main content covers a survey of existing computational models and tools (i.e. off-the-shelf solutions), before looking at future efforts needed covering the current trends and the open issues.

4.1 Introduction

In this chapter, we will be dealing with the computational acquisition of affect of humans. The chapter starts off with a description of the state of the art in this field. This will include the consideration of various modalities for the acquisition, mainly spoken and written language, video including facial expression, body posture and movement, physiological signals such as brain waves and tactile interaction data. Thereafter, we will take a look at toolkits available to enable systems to automatically acquire affect of humans. Finally, future research potential is outlined and divided into current trends and 'white spots'. Many of the presented here will be similar to the principles introduced in Chap. 5 of this book dealing with the acquisition of personality.

4.2 Brief Description of the State of the Art

In principle, a technical system can acquire the affect of a human by explicitly asking about her emotion. For obvious reasons, however, automatically acquiring the state in an implicit way may not only be the more elegant way, but open up a much

B.W. Schuller (✉)
Complex and Intelligent Systems, University of Passau, Passau, Germany
e-mail: schuller@ieee.org

B.W. Schuller
Department of Computing, Imperial College London, London, UK

M. Tkalčič et al. (eds.), *Emotions and Personality in Personalized Services*,
Human–Computer Interaction Series, DOI 10.1007/978-3-319-31413-6_4

broader range of applications. The true inner emotional state of an individual can become apparent in three ways: first, the personal subjective experience; second, the inward 'expressions' by bio signals and third, by outward expressions such as by audio and video signals. Different modalities transport thereby different kind of information on the underlying affective state. It is generally believed that an individual's subjective experience is related both to internal and external expressions [53]. Likewise, according cues of both of these have been considered for automatic acquisition of affect grouped under bio signals and motion capture signals for the inward, and under audio, language, visual and tactile cues for the outward expression. The latter would in principle also include other modalities such as olfactory, which are, however, hardly or not considered in an automatic affect acquisition framework to this date.

Two major representation forms currently prevail in computer-based acquisition of affect—discrete models (usually based on a number of categories or tags such as those described in Chap. 2 in this book, often discretised also in time), and more recently continuous models represented in dimensional spaces (cf. also Chap. 12 in this book) mostly formed by orthogonal axes and increasingly also (pseudo-)continuous sampling in time processing long unsegmented recordings in regular (short) intervals. Such continuous modelling comes at a number of challenges including real-time processing and online updating of buffers and features [50, 51, 55, 90, 111–113]. One has to ensure that such continuously updated predictions are not too sensitive to changing conditions. Further, whereas in non-continuous analysis, the data of interest is (pre-)segmented, e.g. by some event such as a spoken word or a facial or body action unit, this has to be done automatically in continuous analysis. In an ideal way, such segmentation would relate directly to the beginning and end of an affective event. Such chunking leads in general to the unit of analysis, such as a window of variable size [50] or a spoken word or phrase [124], etc. The length of this unit typically varies depending on the modality. Further, there is a trade-off [18] between reaching online processing demanding for a small window size for analysis such as one or several seconds [18], and assuring a high recognition accuracy which may demand longer units of analysis [10, 101]. In other words, similar to Heisenberg's uncertainty relation, one is not able to reach maximum resolution in time and at the same time maximum resolution in (continuous) emotion primitives such as arousal or valence.

Beyond the optimal representation form, it is also still unclear which modality is best suited for the computer-based acquisition of affect. In fact, the various modalities known to have different strengths and weaknesses, such as textual and facial expression cues being particularly suited for the acquisition of valence or acoustics of the speech signal and physiological measurement partially reported to be better suited for arousal acquisition [50, 100] (cf. also Table 4.1). In addition, multiple modalities may be congruent or incongruent—e.g. when regulating emotion. This has been partially investigated for perception [81, 137], but hardly in automatic recognition.

A more quantitative overview on the state of the art is given by the competitive research challenge events held in this field. The first ever was held in 2009 at the INTERSPEECH conference dealing with recognition in child–robot interaction

Table 4.1 Selected modalities for affect acquisition and qualitative description of selected attributes

Source	A	V	Ctrl	Strength	Weakness	Major challenge
Audio signal	+++	++	hi	Reliable, easy to capture	Often not present	Person/content independence, noise and reverberation
Language	++	+++	hi	Relates to linguistic content	Needs ASR if spoken	Multilinguality and timing
Visual signals	++	+++	lo	Present	'Observation' feeling	Light, rotations and occlusions
Peripheral physio.	+	+	no	Robust capture, present	Intrusive	Annotation and incompleteness
Brain signal	+	++	no	Informative, high future potential	Intrusive	Annotation
Tactile signals	++	+	lo	Robust capture, unobstrusive	Often not present	Person/context independence

"+" to "+++" indicate good and better reliability in the acquisition of arousal (A) and Valence (V). No, low (lo), and high (hi) degree of control of a person over the modality is further given. "Present" alludes to the sheer presence in the sense that, e.g. the visual (if in camera view) and physiological signals bear affective information at all times, while speech or tactile signals are not always present. *ASR* stands for Automatic Speech Recognition

[125]. The FAU Aibo Emotion Corpus of naturalistic children's speech was used. The 15 finalists' best results reached 70.3 % unweighted accuracy for two emotions and 41.7 % for five. In the 2010 sequel, continuous-valued recognition of interest [117] reached a correlation coefficient of 0.428 [117]. The best result on the task reached 0.504 [153] after the challenge event. The 2013 sequel [128] dealt with enacted speech in twelve categories as contained in the Geneva Multimodal expression (GEMEP) corpus [6]. The 11 finalists reached up to 42.3 % unweighted accuracy. The first audiovisual challenge was held in 2011 within the first Audio/Visual Emotion Challenge and Workshop (AVEC 2011) [126]. Binary above/below average decisions needed to be classified individually for the activity (arousal), expectation, power and valence dimensions on the frame- or word-level. In 2012 the same data was used, but the task was formulated as fully continuous task. The 2013 and 2014 follow-ups used new data but sticked with fully continuous measurement. The fifth edition is upcoming including for the first time physiology (AV+EC 2015) alongside audio and video for affect acquisition in a challenge event. A similar effort was made in the Emotion in the Wild (EmotiW) challenge [33] that deals with affect analysis in movies in the big six categories and neutral. The nine finalists' best result reached 41 % accuracy. All of these results demonstrate recognition rates significantly above chance level—however, it also becomes clear that more research efforts will be needed before automatic systems can truly be used 'in the wild'. In the following, we will have a more detailed look at the acquisition of affect for each modality.

4.3 Description of Affect Acquisition

The typical flow of processing in automatic affect acquisition consists of preprocessing, feature extraction, optimising the feature space by selection and reduction of features and training a suited machine learning algorithm (cf. Fig. 4.1).

An overview on features per modality and fusion of these is given, e. g., in [54, 156]. However, apart from extracting these, the reduction of the feature space is usually crucial as one wants to avoid overtraining, i.e. one seeks a good balance in terms of reducing the information from the full audio, video or similar signal to some few salient characteristics that describe the affect but not further aspects contained in the full signal (cf., e. g., [35, 131]).

In addition, subject-effects may occur making good generalisation additionally difficult. This seems to be particularly true for physiological measurement [74]. In fact, as a consequence, in this modality often a subject-dependent approach is considerably more promising without a general baseline [18]. For audio and video-based affect acquisition, subject-dependent and independent results are often compared showing clear downgrades in the independent case (e. g., [87]).

Next, let us take a closer look at each modality. References focus on more recent ones. For earlier references, cf., e. g., [15, 40, 63, 65, 69, 85, 86]. A short overview on selected predominant strengths and weaknesses as well as peculiarities of the considered modalities is given in Table 4.1. There, also the reliability for arousal and valence is indicated—these are tendencies based on [42, 83, 99, 134, 154] and other works in the field. Obviously, these trends may change with oncoming improved acquisition technology.

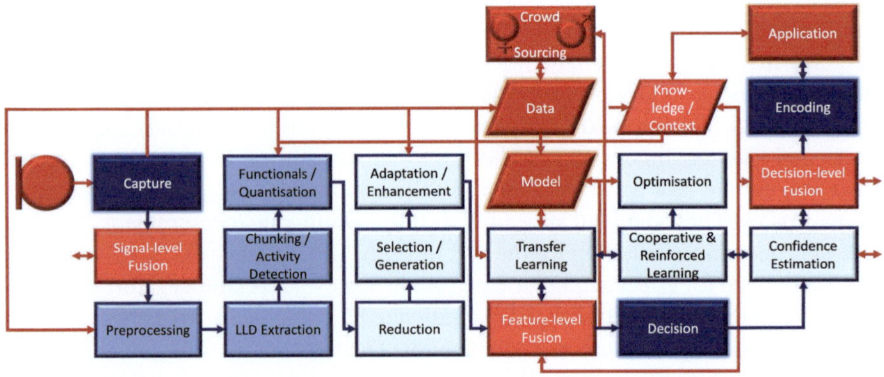

Fig. 4.1 Workflow of a state-of-the-art automatic affect analyser for arbitrary modalities. *Dark blue boxes* indicate mandatory units, *light blue* ones typical further units, and *lighter blue* optional ones. *Red* indicates external units—*light red* interfaces to other modalities and contextual information and knowledge bases. External connections are indicated by *arrows* from/to the 'outside'. *LLD* abbreviates Low Level Descriptors (i.e. frame-level features). For details, cf. Sects. 4.3 and 4.4

4.3.1 Audio and Language Signals of Affect

In audio analysis, one can focus at least on three kinds of information: the acoustics of the speech signal, the non-verbal sounds such as laughter or hesitations and the words. In particular intense affective speech may in fact make, however, the recognition of speech itself a challenge [150]. Besides, one can analyse further sounds produced by the human for affect acquisition, such as the gait sounds [43].

The models used for assessment of affect in audio include the valence-arousal space [22, 23], the appraisal-based theory [46], complex emotions [123] and simply discrete classes. There are few commonly agreed upon 'rules' how the voice changes under affect, such as that pitch mean and range vary with arousal [12]. Further, the mean intensity, speech rate [58], 'blaring' timbre [30] and high-frequency energy [103] are positively correlated with arousal, whereas pause duration and inter-breath stretches are negatively correlated with arousal [143]. Unfortunately, less 'linear' dependencies are known for further dimensions such as valence or dominance. The latter seems to have similar parameters partially even with similar tendencies being indicative of dominance of speakers. Additional correlations include such with the vowel duration, and negative correlation of pitch. As for valence, positive correlation is observed for speaking rate, vowel durations and pitch range; negative correlation for mean pitch and the amount of high-frequency energy [103]. Surveys on this topic include [106, 109]. However, mostly high-dimensional feature spaces are used with up to several thousands of features. These are often brute-forced from frame-level low-level descriptors (LLDs) by means of statistical functionals per larger unit of analysis such as mean of pitch calculated over the duration of a word, phrase or similar (cf. Fig. 4.1).

The classification is often considering two (positive vs negative or active vs passive classification—e.g. [122]), three (lower, middle and higher—e.g., [141]) or four classes (the four quadrants of the 2D arousal-valence plane—e.g., [152]) besides more specific class sets such as the Ekman big six emotions. Continuous affect acquisition is also seen more often recently (e.g., [34, 47, 148, 152]).

The words themselves are known to be informative in terms of valance rather than arousal (cf. Table 4.1) [152]: while the keywords *again*, *assertive*, and *very* are apparently correlated with arousal, *good*, *great* or *lovely* seem to be more indicative of the degree of valence. Obviously, appraisal or swear words are further good indicators for this dimension.

Manifold approaches are employed to classify emotion from text (cf. also Chap. 7 on Sentiment Analysis in this book)—be it of spoken language after speech recognition or directly from written text such as in chat or posts [98]. Some popular variants include the usage of salience measures from single words or sequences of words (N-Grams), the vector space representation based on bag-of-words or bag-of-N-Grams and bag-of-character-N-Grams. More specific variants include string kernels for Support Vector Machines, and tailored ways to exploit knowledge sources [138]. The latter comprise affective word lists such as EmotiNet [4], Concept Net, or General Inquirer or WordNet(-Affect) [14, 116].

Re-tagging by part of speech classes such as noun, verb, adjective, adverb, etc. [79] or combinations of these such as adjective-adverb [9] or adjective-verb-adverb [140] is known to be of additional help when seeking affect in the words [7]. Such tagging is subsumed under LLD extraction in Fig. 4.1 based on the word string coming from Automatic Speech Recognition (ASR) in case of spoken language which is subsumed under preprocessing in the figure in this case. However, there is no straight forward rule as to how frequencies correlate to the dimensions agreed upon.

The non-verbal sounds can be processed in-line with the word string, cf., e.g. 'this is great <laughs>.' [38, 121] (cf. also Chap. 6 in this book on other social signals). If features are represented in the vector space, <laughs> would make up for another feature, just as 'great' would. Accordingly, one can consider mixed N-Grams of linguistic and non-verbal entities, e.g. 'no <laughs>'. Recognition of these non-verbal entities can be part of ASR. Some findings include that laughter—just as one expects—is observed more often in case of positive valence. In addition, valence polarity seems to be encoded towards the end of a turn [8].

Surprisingly, the speech recognition may be degraded to higher extents without influencing the acquisition of affect [84]. Further, stemming or stopping (i.e. clustering of morphological variants of a spoken or written term and exclusion of terms) is known to have rather minor influence, and word order seems to be of lower relevance [119].

It seems worth to note that the classes of interest in the literature are often quite different from those for acoustic speech analysis when considering text. These comprise irony, metaphor, parody, sarcasm, satire or sentiment. The dimensional approach is found rather sparsely (cf., e.g. [116, 121] for spoken and [13, 119] for written text analysis). If there is a tendency, then that vector space modelling seems to prevail not only since it gives good accuracies, but as it lets one include the textual features easily in a multimodal feature vector. In online speech analysis, single word analysis can also be very efficient [38].

4.3.2 Visual Signals of Affect

Visual signals of affect include the richly researched facial actions such as pulling eyebrows up, and facial expressions such as producing a smile [89], and the less pursued body postures and gestures such as backwards head bend and arms raised forwards and upwards [26, 129]. Further, analysing walking patterns, i.e. gait, has been considered for the automatic acquisition of affect [61, 64]. In perception studies [59] it was further found that the head or torso inclination, and walking speed are indicative of arousal and valence.

For the capturing, sensors providing depth information have become very popular such as the Microsoft Kinect device. These often offer solutions to the typical needs in video analysis such as segmentation of the body. Yet, they often come with the need for proper calibration. Alternatively, standard cameras—even webcams—are an option, albeit at lower recognition performance. In addition, motion capture systems can be used—mostly for analyses of affect rather than in real-life applications for facial expression analysis [151], body posture analysis [72, 73] and affective body language [82].

The body of literature on feature extraction for face, body and gesture tracking and general video analysis is large. Extraction of facial features can be categorised [89] into appearance-based and feature-based approaches and such using both in a hybrid manner. In the appearance-based approach changes in texture and motion of regions are observed. As for the feature-based approach, facial features, e.g. the pupils or the inner or outer corners of the eyes or the mouth are located and followed, typically exploiting knowledge on the anatomy. Then, one can calculate distances between these as feature information.

As for hand or body gesture recognition and human motion analysis, a similar categorisation can be made [95, 96] into appearance-based (exploiting colour or grey scale images or edges and silhouettes), motion-based (merely based on motion information neglecting structure of the body) and model-based (modelling or recovering 3D configurations of the body parts). Typical signs include body trembling, expansion of the chest, squaring of the elbows, placing feet with pressure on the ground for a secure stand or erection of the head in case of anger [27, 146]. Targeting continuous arousal, in [93], velocity, acceleration and jerk of movements were found indicative. Mostly, up to this point, static postural aspects have been exploited such as of the arms, legs and head [20, 72] besides increasingly temporal segments [49], and dynamic according movements [19, 24, 52, 146].

In case of motion capture, geometrical features are usually considered after registration, definition of a coordinate system followed by calculation of relative positions, euclidean distances and velocities of and between captured points. In addition, orientation such as of the shoulder axes are used in affect analysis [72, 73].

If thermal infrared imagery is used, among the various feature types typical ones include blobs or shape contours [144]. Further, one can divide the individual thermal images into grids of squares. Then, the highest temperature per square serves as reference for comparison [67] or templates of thermal variation can be applied per emotion category as a reference. The tracking is carried out as in the visible spectrum by the condensation algorithm, particle filtering or other suited methods unfortunately inheriting the same kind of problems [144]. Alternatively, differential images between the mean neutral and the affective body or face image can be used [155] in combination with a frequency transformation such as discrete cosine transformation.

Video-based affect acquisition beyond 'classical' emotion categories often uses binary high/low arousal/valence classification [80, 85]) or the ternary quadrant problem in this space [44, 60]. Some more recent works also use the dimensional model in continuous time [52, 71, 87]. Looking at bodily expression, mostly categorical classification has been considered targeting angry, happy and sad as 'easier' tasks as compared to, e.g. disgust or social emotions such as pride. Also for acquisition of affect from thermal imagery, typical emotion classes prevail over dimensional approaches at the time.

4.3.3 Physiological Signals

The physiological measurement focuses on multichannel biosignals as recorded from the central and the autonomic nervous systems. Typical examples as analyses in search of affective cues are galvanic skin response correlated with physiological arousal [17], and electromyography for measurement of the electrical potential that stems mostly from muscular cell activities and is believed to be negatively correlated with valence [56] just as is heart rate. Next, heart rate variability provides information on relaxation or mental stress. Further, the respiration rate measuring the depth, regularity and speed of breathing, e.g. by a breast belt can be indicative for anger or fear [17, 56] but also for the analysis of laughter. Brain waves, such as measured over the amygdala can also provide information on the felt emotional state [16, 62, 97]. To give an example, the activation of the left or right frontal cortex is known to indicate approach or withdrawal. Asymmetrical brain activity can further be informative in terms of valence [29]. The desired EEG measurement is, however, unfortunately difficult owing to the deep location of the amygdala in the brain. Further, higher blood perfusion in the orbital muscles as can be seen by thermal imagery [144] appears to be correlated with the stress level.

A downside of physiological measurement is the usually needed body contact of sensors that is often considered as more invasive. Large efforts are thus put into wearable devices that recently appeared on the mass consumer market able to sense heart rate at the wrist or even brain waves, e.g. the BodyANT sensor [75] and Emotiv's Epoc neuroheadset. In addition, physical activity such as sports or simply walking may interfere with the measurement.

As in any signal processing, a first step in processing physiological signals is usually noise removal. This can be obtained by simple mean filters, e.g. for blood volume pressure, Galvanic Skin Response (GSR) or respiration measurement. Further, filtering in the spectral domain, e.g. by bandpass filters is commonly used. Then, in the frequency domain, e.g. by Fourier transformation or time-frequency domain, e.g. by wavelet transformation. Similar to the processing of audio signals, suprasegmental analysis takes place such as by thresholding or peak detection [78] followed by functional application including moments such as mean or standard deviation, and mean of the absolute values of the first differences [18, 91].

Mostly, binary classification problems are targeted such as high or low arousal or valence [48]. In addition, hierarchical classification [41] or quantification of the continuous emotion primitives have been attempted [68], e.g. by self-organising maps to identify four emotion categories in the arousal/valence plane.

4.3.4 Tactile Signals

In [3] it was shown that humans can recognise emotion in touch as is expressed by other humans via two degrees-of-freedom force-feedback joysticks. In the experiment, they were able to recognise seven emotions above chance level— they were, however, better at recognising other humans' emotions as expressed in a direct handshake. In [114, 120] it is reported that also computers can automatically recognise emotions in mouse-movements or touch-screen interaction. More recently, in [42] finger-stroke features are considered for the analysis of game-play on a tablet. The four emotional states excited, relaxed, frustrated and bored could be automatically discriminated by accuracies around 70 %. Further, two levels of arousal and valence reached around 90 % accuracy. Nine emotions as expressed by touching a lap-sized prototype of a pet-robot that had pressure sensors and accelerometers mounted were recognised automatically at 36 % accuracy in [66]. Similarly, in [147] it is shown how affective touch gestures can be recognised on a specially designed 8×8 touch sensor field.

4.3.5 *Tools*

Lately, a larger number of toolkits free for research purposes and often open source are appearing and used more broadly (cf. Table 4.2 for an overview). This also contributes to increasing reproducibility of results and standardisation in the field.

Table 4.2 Selected tools for multimodal affect aquisition

Purpose	Tool	Comment	Reference
Annotation	ANVIL	Multimedia annotation	[70]
	ELAN	Categorical descriptions	[11]
	FEELtrace	Continuous dimensions	[22]
	Gtrace	Configurable dimensions	[25]
	iHEARu-PLAY	Game for crowd-annotation	[57]
Analyser	openSMILE	Speech and other signals	[37]
	EmoVoice toolkit	Speech	[145]
	CERT	Facial expression	[77]
	EyesWeb	Body gestures and vision	[45]
Multimodal framework	SEMAINE API	Analysis, synthesis and dialogue	[107]
Encoding standards	EARL	Emotion	[108]
	EMMA	Includes affect tags	[2]
	W3C EmotionML	Freely extensible	[110]

A rather complete framework is, for example, given by the SEMAINE API [107]—an open source framework that allows to build emotion-oriented systems including analysis and synthesis of emotion by audio and video as well as dialogue management and reaction to emotional cues in real-time. It sticks to standards for encoding of information and provides a C++ and Java wrapper around a message-oriented white-board architecture and has in the meanwhile found manifold applications.

Specifically for annotation, available tools include ELAN for categorical descriptions. Multimedia can be labelled continuously in separated annotation layers and by linguistically meaningful event labelling in a media track [11]. Next, ANVIL is widely used for annotation [70]. Individual coding schemes are allowed, and data is stored in XML format allowing for colouring of elements. Multiple tracks are also supported. ELAN files can be exported, and agreement analysis, cross-level links, non-temporal objects and timepoint tracks are supported. For value and time continuous annotation, the FEELtrace toolkit is largely used. Audiovisual material can be viewed while moving sliders in real-time [22]. Gtrace—an extension—also allows for individual scales [25].

For audiovisual feature extraction, the openSMILE C++ open-source library allows extraction of large feature spaces in real-time [37]—it has also been successfully used for physiological and other feature types. There are a large number of predefined feature sets that can be used for emotion recognition. An alternative, but closed source, is given by the EmoVoice toolkit [145] which is more focused on speech processing. For facial expression recognition, the Computer Expression Recognition Toolbox (CERT) [77] providing a real-time facial expression recognition engine is broadly used. It outputs a prediction for the head orientation in 3D (pitch, roll and yaw), locations of ten facial features, 19 facial actions with intensity and the Ekman big six basic emotions for QVGA at 10 fps. The EyesWeb XMI Expressive Gesture Processing Library [45, 129] allows to extract features of body movement and gestures including activity levels, jerkiness of gestures, spatial extent and symmetry.

In addition, a number of standards exist for the encoding of the recognition result or even the features used (e.g. [7, 133]). The HUMAINE Emotion Annotation and Representation Language (EARL) [108] can be considered as the first well-defined, machine-readable description of emotions. It was followed by the W3C EmotionML [110] recommendation that allows for more flexibility and supports the description of action tendencies, appraisals, meta context, regulation, as well as, metadata and ontologies. Other standards not intended for affect in the first place partially also include the option to label affective phenomena, e.g. the W3C Extensible MultiModal Annotation (EMMA) markup language [2].

The AAAC Portal[1] is a good resource for seeing the latest development of tools in this field.

[1] http://emotion-research.net/toolbox.

4.4 Future Directions

To close this chapter, let us have a look at some interesting current trends and open issues to be solved in this field.

4.4.1 Current Trends

In the following, some particularly dominant trends that are of recent and increasing interest in the community will be outlined.

4.4.1.1 Non-prototypicality

Affect acquisition 'in the wild' is requiring systems able deal with non-prototypical instances [125]. Such 'non-prototypical' examples can be ambiguous cases where humans disagree upon the correct emotion label [136]. Ultimately, this means that no 'cherry picking' of easy cases is done in (test) data preparation, and that the affect portrayal is more realistic and naturalistic rather than exaggerated. In addition, this often means broadening the range beyond the 'big N' emotions, cf. [132].

In case of ambiguity, a one-to-one correspondence between instances and labels cannot be assumed. This has significant implications for modelling, recognition and evaluation. However, today's systems are still mostly trained and evaluated on the premise that a well-defined ground truth label exists for every instance. To model the complexity of the underlying problem, it would first be necessary to take into account the certainty of the 'ground truth', i.e. the labels derived from observer ratings, in training. This can be done in a rather crude way by focusing training on 'prototypical' instances, i.e. selection of training instances with high rater agreement [136], but arguably one would rather have a method to exploit all available training data—there are already promising results in this direction [1]. Besides, in evaluation it might make sense to switch to alternative measures besides traditional accuracy, for example, by considering recognition errors as less severe if observers show significant disagreement on the instance.

4.4.1.2 Crowdsourcing and Efficient Data Exploitation

Overall, for refining automatic analysers, there seems to be an ever present need for data with high number of participants from diverse backgrounds in terms of culture, personality, language, age, speaking style, health state, etc., and data with richer and novel annotations by including situational context. Obtaining rich annotations is not trivial as it requires considerable amount of time and human effort. The use of crowdsourcing platforms such as the 'pay per click' Amazon's Mechanical Turk has now become an alternative way among researchers to obtain statistically significant amount of annotations. Also gamified crowdsourcing platforms exist for collecting affective data in a playful way [57]. Another alternative way of making the most of existing databases is to use them in a combined manner, in training and testing procedures to learn a more generic prediction model [127]. A more complex but promising alternative is to use synthesised training material, particularly for cross-corpus testing [118].

4.4.1.3 Transfer Learning

Transfer learning deals with generalising from a source domain to a target domain. Obviously, such generalisation is of central importance if data from the target domain is not available, or scarce. In human affect acquisition, the domain concerns the population from which emotional speech samples are drawn, the type of emotion elicitation and the emotion representation.

Recent transfer learning approaches in emotion recognition mainly target the feature space in order to improve the generalisation of models, which are trained using labelled data from the source domain, to a given target domain. Unsupervised feature transfer learning, such as by auto-encoding approaches, requires only unlabelled data from the target domain. There, a neural network is trained to reproduce the acoustic feature vectors from the target domain, with the hidden layer size being significantly smaller than the dimension of the input feature vector, and optional sparsity constraints. Then, the recognition model is trained on the source domain feature vectors. Such methods have been proven successful in transfer learning from adults' to children's emotional speech [32], and from affect in music to affect in speech [21]. However, it is certainly also of interest to aim at model transfer learning to see if trained models can be used without the need of retraining, but 'only' transferring the model.

4.4.1.4 Semi-Autonomous Learning

Since *unlabelled* data of human affect are plentiful, efforts have been focused on reducing the costs of labelling by humans—formally, to achieve a given performance with least human labelling effort, or to obtain best performance with a given number of human annotations.

Active learning aims at exploiting human labellers' work force more efficiently by concentrating on examples that are most relevant for classifier training. This can be done in a white-box classifier model by considering criteria such as the expected change in model parameters when including certain examples in the training data, [130], or in a black-box model by considering the class posteriors: A near-uniform distribution of class posteriors is interpreted as uncertainty of the current model as to how to label a specific example, and thus as an indication that a human label for that example could be useful. In the case of affect acquisition, where annotations from multiple raters are often available, uncertainty (confidence) estimation can alternatively be formulated as the prediction of how many raters would (dis-)agree on the emotion labels [158]. A good scheme also avoids a skew of the label distribution towards neutral or 'non-affective' instances, which is often present in naturalistic human data [135]. Further, for increased efficiency, dynamic decisions can be made based on the agreement: if the sourced labels are in a agreement, less opinions might need to be sourced per instance thus further saving labelling efforts [159].

In semi-supervised learning, one is given human labels only for an initial set of instances, based on which the parameters of an initial model are optimised. The goal is to maximise performance by fully autonomous learning starting from this model. Its predictions on a random subset of a pool of unlabelled feature vectors are used instead of human annotations to retrain the model on both the human labelled data and the machine labelled data, and this process is continued iteratively. To reduce the amount of noise, semi-supervised learning takes into account the instances with high confidence. It has been shown that semi-supervised learning can be effectively used both for acoustic [157] and linguistic [28] emotion recognition.

The two approaches—namely, active and semi-supervised learning—have also been united in the more efficient Cooperative Learning for affect acquisition [161]. Note that, a crucial precondition for these approaches to work is the calculation of meaningful confidence measures—for the acquisition of affect, this is itself still a young field [31].

4.4.1.5 Unsupervised and Deep Learning

Unsupervised learning does not require human labelling at all, but rather it 'blindly' clusters the instances, e.g. based on distance measures in an acoustic feature space, such as the one spanned by the features discussed above. However, depending on the chosen feature space, this clustering may also reflect subject characteristics rather than affect. Thus, unsupervised learning is rarely used for practical affect acquisition [149]. However, hierarchical clustering methods hold the promise to overcome this issue [142]. Unsupervised learning is also often used in deep learning to initialise several layers of 'deep' neural network one by one in a meaningful way [139].

It seems noteworthy that also features can base on unsupervised such as by vector quantisation (cf. Fig. 4.1) to produce bag-of-word-type features for other modalities such as audio or image words [92]. Similarly, unsupervised vector quantisation is employed in distributed acquisition of affect (cf., e.g. [160]) where not a full signal or feature vector but only the index of a reference vector is sent to reduce bandwidth and increase the degree of privacy of users.

4.4.1.6 Robustness

The presence of various disturbances, such as caused by acoustic environments (additive noise and room impulse responses) or occlusions and varying viewing angle in video, as well as general noise in any modality alongside recording equipment (channel response), or transmission (band limitation and package loss) poses severe problems. Robustness can be addressed by feature selection [36, 115], similar in spirit to transfer learning. Further, multi-condition training using non-disturbed conditions *and* various disturbed conditions, which can often be simulated (such as by mixing with noise recordings, or randomly dropping or clipping samples) is a simple, yet promising approach.

4.4.2 Open Issues

Concluding this chapter, some open issues of higher relevance are named.

4.4.2.1 Cultural and Linguistic Diversity

A highly relevant, yet little addressed issue related to transfer learning is the generalisation of automatic affect recognition across cultural and language borders. So far, most studies have been focusing on cross-cultural affect recognition by humans, providing evidence both for the ability of humans to recognise emotion cross-culturally [102, 105] as well as for significant differences in emotional expressivity [104]. As a result, the universality of automatic affect acquisition is still under question. In particular, it has been found that the results of 'unsupervised' affect acquisition by humans, i.e. without priming or making specific affect accessible, are far below results reported in earlier studies [76]. The implications of these findings for technical systems are severe, as they indicate not only that affective behaviours may be attached to entirely different interpretations—e.g. positive instead of negative valence—but also that some emotions may only be detectable in certain cultures. The former could still be solved by adequate machine learning techniques, while the latter implies that some cases cannot be translated to other cultures. In summary, systems modelling cross-cultural differences explicitly are yet to be designed.

Related to cross-cultural issues is the challenge of multilingual usage. At a superficial level, this touches the vocabulary used for linguistic analysis, and the acoustic modelling required for speech recognition. There exist approaches for multi-lingual emotion recognition from text [5]. Yet also acoustic analysis can be affected by speech coming from different languages, even in a similar culture [39, 94]. In addition, different prosody exists between tonal (e.g. Mandarin Chinese) and non-tonal languages. If prosody is used as an indicator of affect, it might be confounded by linguistic content in tonal languages.

4.4.2.2 Multi-subject Affect Recognition

For the application of emotion recognition to fields such as robotics, it is crucial to be able to cope with, and better yet, to make sense of, interactions with multiple users. In particular, distinguishing utterances from different interlocutors, and labelling them with potentially various emotions, seems highly relevant in this context. Speaker diarisation and verification enable to distinguish utterances from various speakers in a continuous audio stream, and to detect and attribute overlapping speech [88]. These methods are well known, but have so far not been applied to affect recognition.

4.4.2.3 Zero-Resource Recognition

The extreme data scarcity (not only scarcity of labels, as in the previous section) for some affect recognition scenarios, such as from atypical populations (e.g. individuals with autism spectrum condition), has motivated the re-discovery of rule-based approaches, which rely on manually selected features and expert-crafted rule sets. They are called 'zero'-resource for the fact that they do not rely on large-scale statistical analysis, although some data collection is necessary to design and verify expert rules as well. Besides dispensing with the need for large-scale data collection, a benefit of zero-resource approaches is that manual feature selection and rule design by experts is not prone to over-fitting, such as to subjects, and can thus lead to better generalisation.

4.4.2.4 Linking Analysis with Synthesis

Overall, affect analysis and affect generation (synthesis) appear to be detached from each other even in multi-party and multidisciplinary projects such as SEMAINE [113]. Although the overall perception and acceptability of an automated system depends on the complex interplay of these two domains, analysis and synthesis are treated as independent problems and only linked in the final stage. Investigating how to interrelate these in earlier stages will indeed provide valuable insight into the nature of both areas that play a crucial role for the realisation of affect-sensitive systems that are able to interpret multimodal and continuous input and respond appropriately.

Concluding, the state of the art in acquisition of affect shows that engines are able to provide meaningful results, and tools are available. Moreover, avenues towards further improvement were given here that will likely lead to further improvement in robustness, reliability and integrability in applications. The major challenge will, however, lie in the testing and adaptation of such engines in real-life products operated 'in the wild'.

Acknowledgments The author acknowledges funding from the ERC under grant agreement no. 338164 (iHEARu), and the European Union's Horizon 2020 Framework Programme under grant agreements nos. 645378 (ARIA-VALUSPA) and 645094 (SEWA).

References

1. Audhkhasi, K., Narayanan, S.S.: A globally-variant locally-constant model for fusion of labels from multiple diverse experts without using reference labels. IEEE Trans. Pattern Anal. Mach. Intell. **35**(4), 769–783 (2013)
2. Baggia, P., Burnett, D.C., Carter, J., Dahl, D.A., McCobb, G., Raggett, D.: EMMA: Extensible MultiModal Annotation markup language (2007)
3. Bailenson, J.N., Yee, N. Brave, S., Merget, D., Koslow, D.: Virtual interpersonal touch: expressing and recognizing emotions through haptic devices. Hum. Comput. Interact. **22**(3), 325–353 (2007)
4. Balahur, A., Hermida, J.M., Montoyo, A.: Detecting emotions in social affective situations using the emotinet knowledge base. In: Proceedings of International Symposium on Neural Networks, vol. 3, pp. 611–620. IEEE, Guilin, China (2011)
5. Banea, C., Mihalcea, R., Wiebe, J.: Multilingual sentiment and subjectivity. In: Zitouni, I., Bikel, D. (eds.) Multilingual Natural Language Processing. Prentice Hall (2011)
6. Bänziger, T., Mortillaro, M., Scherer, K.R.: Introducing the Geneva multimodal expression corpus for experimental research on emotion perception. Emotion **12**, 1161–1179 (2012)
7. Batliner, A., Steidl, S., Schuller, B., Seppi, D., Vogt, T., Wagner, J., Devillers, L., Vidrascu, L., Aharonson, V., Kessous, L., Amir, N.: Whodunnit—searching for the most important feature types signalling emotion-related user states in speech. Comput Speech Lang **25**(1), 4–28 (2011)
8. Becker, I., Aharonson, V.: Last but definitely not least: on the role of the last sentence in automatic polarity-classification. In: Proceedings of ACL, pp. 331–335. Uppsala, Sweden (2010)
9. Benamara, F., Cesarano, C., Picariello, A., Reforgiato, D., Subrahmanian, V.: Sentiment analysis: adjectives and adverbs are better than adjectives alone. In: Proceedings of International Conference on Weblogs and Social Media, pp. 1–7. Boulder, CO (2007)
10. Berntson, G., Bigger, J., Eckberg, D., Grossman, P., Kaufmann, P., Malik, M., Nagaraja, II., Porges, S., Saul, J., Stone, P., VanderMolen, M.: Heart rate variability: origins, methods, and interpretive caveats. Psychophysiology **34**(6), 623–648 (1997)
11. Brugman, H., Russel, A.: Annotating multi-media/multi-modal resources with ELAN. In: Proceedings of LREC, pp. 2065–2068. Lisbon, Portugal (2004)
12. Calvo, R., D'Mello, S.: Affect detection: an interdisciplinary review of models, methods, and their applications. IEEE Trans. Affect. Comput. **1**(1), 18–37 (2010)
13. Cambria, E., Hussain, A., Havasi, C., Eckl, C.: Senticspace: visualizing opinions and sentiments in a multi-dimensional vector space. In: Setchi, R., Jordanov, I., Howlett, R., Jain, L. (eds.) Knowledge-Based and Intelligent Information and Engineering Systems, LNCS, vol. 6279, pp. 385–393. Springer, Berlin (2010)
14. Cambria, E., Schuller, B., Xia, Y., Havasi, C.: New avenues in opinion mining and sentiment analysis. IEEE Intell. Syst. Mag. **28**(2), 15–21 (2013)
15. Caridakis, G., Karpouzis, K., Kollias, S.: User and context adaptive neural networks for emotion recognition. Neurocomputing **71**(13–15), 2553–2562 (2008)
16. Chanel, G., Kronegg, J., Grandjean, D., Pun, T.: Emotion assessment: arousal evaluation using eeg's and peripheral physiological signals. LNCS **4105**, 530–537 (2006)
17. Chanel, G., Ansari-Asl, K., Pun, T.: Valence-arousal evaluation using physiological signals in an emotion recall paradigm. In: Proceedings of SMC, pp. 2662–2667. IEEE, Montreal, QC (2007)
18. Chanel, G., Kierkels, J.J.M., Soleymani, M., Pun, T.: Short-term emotion assessment in a recall paradigm. Int. J. Hum. Comput. Stud. **67**(8), 607–627 (2009)
19. Cohn, J., Reed, L.I., Moriyama, T., Xiao, J., Schmidt, K., Ambadar, Z.: Multimodal coordination of facial action, head rotation, and eye motion during spontaneous smiles. In: Proceedings of FG, pp. 129–135. IEEE, Seoul, Korea (2004)
20. Coulson, M.: Attributing emotion to static body postures: recognition accuracy, confusions, and viewpoint dependence. Nonverbal Behav **28**(2), 117–139 (2004)

21. Coutinho, E., Deng, J., Schuller, B.: Transfer learning emotion manifestation across music and speech. In: Proceedings of IJCNN, pp. 3592–3598. IEEE, Beijing, China (2014)
22. Cowie, R., Douglas-Cowie, E., Savvidou, S., McMahon, E., Sawey, M., Schröder, M.: Feeltrace: an instrument for recording perceived emotion in real time. In: Proceedings of ISCA Workshop on Speech and Emotion, pp. 19–24. Newcastle, UK (2000)
23. Cowie, R., Douglas-Cowie, E., Tsapatsoulis, N., Votsis, G., Kollias, S., Fellenz, W., Taylor, J.G.: Emotion recognition in human-computer interaction. IEEE Signal Process. Mag. **18**(1), 33–80 (2001)
24. Cowie, R., Gunes, H., McKeown, G., Vaclau-Schneider, L., Armstrong, J., Douglas-Cowie, E.: The emotional and communicative significance of head nods and shakes in a naturalistic database. In: Proceedings of LREC International Workshop on Emotion, pp. 42–46. Valletta, Malta (2010)
25. Cowie, R., McKeown, G., Douglas-Cowie, E.: Tracing emotion: an overview. J. Synth. Emot. **3**(1), 1–17 (2012)
26. Dael, N., Mortillaro, M., Scherer, K.R.: The body action and posture coding system (bap): Development and reliability. J. Nonverbal Behav. **36**(2), 97–121 (2012)
27. Darwin, C.: The Expression of the Emotions in Man and Animals. John Murray, London (1872)
28. Davidov, D., Tsur, O., Rappoport, A.: Semi-supervised recognition of sarcastic sentences in Twitter and Amazon. In: Proceedings of CoNNL, pp. 107–116. Uppsala, Sweden (2010)
29. Davidson, R., Fox, N.: Asymmetrical brain activity discriminates between positive and negative affective stimuli in human infants. Science **218**, 1235–1237 (1982)
30. Davitz, J.: The Communication of Emotional Meaning, Chap. Auditory Correlates Of Vocal Expression of eMotional Feeling, pp. 101–112. McGraw-Hill (1964)
31. Deng, J., Schuller, B.: Confidence measures in speech emotion recognition based on semi-supervised learning. In: Proceedings of Interspeech, 4 p. ISCA, Portland, OR (2012)
32. Deng, J., Zhang, Z., Eyben, F., Schuller, B.: Autoencoder-based unsupervised domain adaptation for speech emotion recognition. IEEE Sig. Proc. Lett. **21**(9), 1068–1072 (2014)
33. Dhall, A., Goecke, R., Joshi, J., Wagner, M., Gedeon, T. (eds.): Proceedings of the 2013 Emotion Recognition in the Wild Challenge and Workshop. ACM, Sydney, Australia (2013)
34. Espinosa, H., Garcia, C., Pineda, L.: Features selection for primitives estimation on emotional speech. In: Proceedings of ICASSP, pp. 5138–5141. IEEE, Dallas, TX (2010)
35. Espinosa, H.P., Garcia, C.A.R., Pineda, L.V.: Bilingual acoustic feature selection for emotion estimation using a 3d continuous model. In: Proceedings of FG, pp. 786–791. IEEE, Santa Barbara, CA (2011)
36. Eyben, F., Weninger, F., Schuller, B.: Affect recognition in real-life acoustic conditions—a new perspective on feature selection. In: Proceedings of INTERSPEECH, pp. 2044–2048. ISCA, Lyon, France (2013)
37. Eyben, F., Wöllmer, M., Schuller, B.: opensmile—the munich versatile and fast open-source audio feature extractor. In: Proceedings of MM. ACM Press
38. Eyben, F., Wöllmer, M., Valstar, M., Gunes, H., Schuller, B., Pantic, M.: String-based audiovisual fusion of behavioural events for the assessment of dimensional affect. In: Proceedings of FG. IEEE, Santa Barbara, CA
39. Feraru, S., Schuller, D., Schuller, B.: Cross-language acoustic emotion recognition: an overview and some tendencies. In: Proceedings of ACII, pp. 125–131. IEEE, Xi'an, P.R. China (2015)
40. Forbes-Riley, K., Litman, D.: Predicting emotion in spoken dialogue from multiple knowledge sources. In: Procedings of HLT/NAACL, pp. 201–208. Boston, MA (2004)
41. Frantzidis, C., Bratsas, C., Klados, M., Konstantinidis, E., Lithari, C., Vivas, A., Papadelis, C., Kaldoudi, E., Pappas, C., Bamidis, P.: On the classification of emotional biosignals evoked while viewing affective pictures: an integrated data-mining-based approach for healthcare applications. IEEE Trans. Inf. Technol. Biomed. **14**(2), 309–318 (2010)
42. Gao, Y., Bianchi-Berthouze, N., Meng, H.: What does touch tell us about emotions in touchscreen-based gameplay? ACM Trans. Comput. Human Interact. **19**(4/31) (2012)

43. Geiger, J.T., Kneissl, M., Schuller, B., Rigoll, G.: Acoustic gait-based person identification using hidden Markov models. In: Proceedings of the Personality Mapping Challenge and Workshop (MAPTRAITS 2014), Satellite of ICMI), pp. 25–30. ACM, Istanbul, Turkey (2014)
44. Glowinski, D., Camurri, A., Volpe, G., Dael, N., Scherer, K.: Technique for automatic emotion recognition by body gesture analysis. In: Proceedings of CVPR Workshops, pp. 1–6. Anchorage, AK (2008)
45. Glowinski, D., Dael, N., Camurri, A., Volpe, G., Mortillaro, M., Scherer, K.: Towards a minimal representation of affective gestures. IEEE Trans. Affect. Comput. **2**(2), 106–118 (2011)
46. Grandjean, D., Sander, D., Scherer, K.R.: Conscious emotional experience emerges as a function of multilevel, appraisal-driven response synchronization. Conscious. Cogn. **17**(2), 484–495 (2008)
47. Grimm, M., Kroschel, K.: Emotion estimation in speech using a 3d emotion space concept. In: Proceedings of ASRU, pp. 381–385. IEEE, San Juan, PR (2005)
48. Gu, Y., Tan, S.L., Wong, K.J., Ho, M.H.R., Qu, L.: Emotion-aware technologies for consumer electronics. In: Proceedings of IEEE International Symposium on Consumer Electronics, pp. 1–4. Vilamoura, Portugal (2008)
49. Gunes, H., Piccardi, M.: Automatic temporal segment detection and affect recognition from face and body display. IEEE Trans. Syst. Man Cybern. B **39**(1), 64–84 (2009)
50. Gunes, H., Pantic, M.: Automatic, dimensional and continuous emotion recognition. Int. J. Synth. Emot. **1**(1), 68–99 (2010)
51. Gunes, H., Pantic, M.: Automatic measurement of affect in dimensional and continuous spaces: why, what, and how? In: Proceedings of Measuring Behavior, pp. 122–126. Eindhoven, The Netherlands (2010)
52. Gunes, H., Pantic, M.: Dimensional emotion prediction from spontaneous head gestures for interaction with sensitive artificial listeners. In: Proceedings of IVA, pp. 371–377. Philadelphia, PA (2010)
53. Gunes, H., Schuller, B.: Categorical and dimensional affect analysis in continuous input: current trends and future directions. Image Vis Comput J Spec Iss Affect Anal Continuous Input **31**(2), 120–136 (2013)
54. Gunes, H., Piccardi, M., Pantic, M.: Affective Computing: Focus on Emotion Expression, Synthesis, and Recognition, chap. From the Lab to the Real World: Affect Recognition using Multiple Cues and Modalities, pp. 185–218. I-Tech Education and Publishing (2008)
55. Gunes, H., Schuller, B., Pantic, M., Cowie, R.: Emotion representation, analysis and synthesis in continuous space: a survey. In: Proceedings of FG, pp. 827–834. IEEE, Santa Barbara, CA (2011)
56. Haag, A., Goronzy, S., Schaich, P., Williams, J.: Emotion recognition using bio-sensors: first steps towards an automatic system. LNCS **3068**, 36–48 (2004)
57. Hantke, S., Appel, T., Eyben, F., Schuller, B.: iHEARu-PLAY: Introducing a game for crowdsourced data collection for affective computing. In: Proceedings of the 1st International Workshop on Automatic Sentiment Analysis in the Wild (WASA 2015) held in Conjunction with ACII, pp. 891–897. IEEE, Xi'an, P. R. China (2015)
58. Huttar, G.L.: Relations between prosodic variables and emotions in normal american english utterances. J. Speech Lang. Hear. Res. **11**, 481–487 (1968)
59. Inderbitzin, M., Väljamäe, A., Calvo, J.M.B.: Expression of emotional states during locomotion based on canonical parameters. In: Proceedings of FG, pp. 809–814. IEEE, Santa Barbara, CA (2011)
60. Ioannou, S., Raouzaiou, A., Tzouvaras, V., Mailis, T., Karpouzis, K., Kollias, S.: Emotion recognition through facial expression analysis based on a neurofuzzy method. J. Neural Networks **18**, 423–435 (2005)
61. Janssen, D., Schllhorn, W.I., Lubienetzki, J., Flling, K., Kokenge, H., Davids, K.: Recognition of emotions in gait patterns by means of artificial neural nets. J. Nonverbal Behav. **32**, 79–92 (2008)

62. Jenke, R., Peer, A., Buss, M.: Feature extraction and selection for emotion recognition from EEG. IEEE Trans. Affect. Comput. **5**(3), 327–339 (2014)
63. Kanluan, I., Grimm, M., Kroschel, K.: Audio-visual emotion recognition using an emotion recognition space concept. In: Proceedings of EUSIPCO (2008)
64. Karg, M., Khnlenz, K., Buss, M.: Recognition of affect based on gait patterns. IEEE Trans. Syst. Man Cybernet. B **40**, 1050–1061 (2010)
65. Karpouzis, K., Caridakis, G., Kessous, L., Amir, N., Raouzaiou, A., Malatesta, L., Kollias, S.: Modeling naturalistic affective states via facial, vocal and bodily expressions recognition. LNAI **4451**, 92–116 (2007)
66. Kerem Altun, K.E.M.: Recognizing affect in human touch of a robot. Pattern Recogn. Lett. (2014)
67. Khan, M.M., Ward, R.D., Ingleby, M.: Infrared thermal sensing of positive and negative affective states. In: Proceedings of the International Conference on Robotics, Automation and Mechatronics, pp. 1–6. IEEE (2006)
68. Khosrowabadi, R., Quek, H.C., Wahab, A., Ang, K.K.: Eeg-based emotion recognition using self-organizing map for boundary detection. In: Proceedings of ICPR, pp. 4242–4245. Istanbul, Turkey (2010)
69. Kim, J.: Robust Speech Recognition and Understanding, chap. Bimodal Emotion Recognition using Speech and Physiological Changes, pp. 265–280. I-Tech Education and Publishing (2007)
70. Kipp, M.: Anvil—a generic annotation tool for multimodal dialogue. In: Proceedings of the 7th European Conference on Speech Communication and Technology, pp. 1367–1370 (2001)
71. Kipp, M., Martin, J.C.: Gesture and emotion: can basic gestural form features discriminate emotions? In: Proceedings of ACII Workshops, pp. 1–8. Amsterdam, The Netherlands (2009)
72. Kleinsmith, A., Bianchi-Berthouze, N.: Recognizing affective dimensions from body posture. In: Proceedings of ACII, pp. 48–58. Lisbon, Portugal (2007)
73. Kleinsmith, A., De Silva, P.R., Bianchi-Berthouze, N.: Recognizing emotion from postures: Cross–cultural differences in user modeling. In: Proceedings of the Conference on User Modeling, pp. 50–59. Edinburgh, UK (2005)
74. Kulic, D., Croft, E.A.: Affective state estimation for human-robot interaction. IEEE Trans. Robot. **23**(5), 991–1000 (2007)
75. Kusserow, M., Amft, O., Troster, G.: Bodyant: miniature wireless sensors for naturalistic monitoring of daily activity. In: Proceedings of the International Conference on Body Area Networks, pp. 1–8. Sydney, Australia (2009)
76. Lindquist, K., Feldman Barrett, L., Bliss-Moreau, E., Russell, J.: Language and the perception of emotion. Emotion **6**(1), 125–138 (2006)
77. Littlewort, G., Whitehill, J., Wu, T., Fasel, I.R., Frank, M.G., Movellan, J.R., Bartlett, M.S.: The computer expression recognition toolbox (cert). In: Proceedings of FG, pp. 298–305. IEEE, Santa Barbara, CA (2011)
78. Liu, C., Rani, P., Sarkar, N.: An empirical study of machine learning techniques for affect recognition in human-robot interaction. In: Proceedings of IEEE/RSJ International Conference on Intelligent Robots and Systems, pp. 2662–2667 (2005)
79. Matsumoto, K., Ren, F.: Estimation of word emotions based on part of speech and positional information. Comput. Hum. Behav. **27**(5), 1553–1564 (2011)
80. McDuff, D., El Kaliouby, R., Kassam, K., Picard, R.: Affect valence inference from facial action unit spectrograms. In: Proceedings of CVPR Workshops, pp. 17–24. IEEE, San Francisco, CA (2010)
81. Meeren, H.K., Van Heijnsbergen, C.C., De Gelder, B.: Rapid perceptual integration of facial expression and emotional body language. In: Proceedings of the National Academy of Sciences of the USA vol. 102, 16,518–16,523 (2005)
82. Metallinou, A., Katsamanis, A., Wang, Y., Narayanan, S.: Tracking changes in continuous emotion states using body language and prosodic cues. In: Proceedings of ICASSP, pp. 2288–2291. IEEE, Prague, Czech Republic (2011)

83. Metallinou, A., Wöllmer, M., Katsamanis, A., Eyben, F., Schuller, B., Narayanan, S.: Context-sensitive learning for enhanced audiovisual emotion classification. IEEE Trans. Affect. Comput. **3**(2), 184–198 (2012)
84. Metze, F., Batliner, A., Eyben, F., Polzehl, T., Schuller, B., Steidl, S.: Emotion recognition using imperfect speech recognition. In: Proceedings of Interspeech, pp. 478–481. ISCA, Makuhari, Japan (2010)
85. Nicolaou, M., Gunes, H., Pantic, M.: Audio-visual classification and fusion of spontaneous affective data in likelihood space. In: Proceedings of ICPR, pp. 3695–3699. IEEE, Istanbul, Turkey (2010)
86. Nicolaou, M., Gunes, H., Pantic, M.: Continuous prediction of spontaneous affect from multiple cues and modalities in valence-arousal space. IEEE Trans. Affect. Comput. **2**(2), 92–105 (2011)
87. Nicolaou, M., Gunes, H., Pantic, M.: Output-associative rvm regression for dimensional and continuous emotion prediction. In: Proceedings of FG, pp. 16–23. IEEE, Santa Barbara, CA (2011)
88. Nwe, T.L., Sun, H., Ma, N., Li, H.: Speaker diarization in meeting audio for single distant microphone. In: Proceedings of Interspeech, pp. 1505–1508. ISCA, Makuhari, Japan (2010)
89. Pantic, M., Bartlett, M.: Machine analysis of facial expressions. In: Delac, K., Grgic, M. (eds.) Face Recognition, pp. 377–416. I-Tech Education and Publishing, Vienna, Austria (2007)
90. Pantic, M., Nijholt, A., Pentland, A., Huang, T.: Human-centred intelligent human-computer interaction (hci2): how far are we from attaining it? Int. J. Auton. Adapt. Commun. Syst. 168–187 (2008)
91. Picard, R., Vyzas, E., Healey, J.: Toward machine emotional intelligence: analysis of affective physiological state. IEEE Trans. Pattern Anal. Mach. Intell. **23**(10), 1175–1191 (2001)
92. Pokorny, F., Graf, F., Pernkopf, F., Schuller, B.: Detection of negative emotions in speech signals using bags-of-audio-words. In: Proceedings of the 1st International Workshop on Automatic Sentiment Analysis in the Wild (WASA 2015) held in Conjunction with ACII, pp. 879–884. IEEE, Xi'an, P. R. China (2015)
93. Pollick, F., Paterson, H., Bruderlin, A., Sanford, A.: Perceiving affect from arm movement. Cognition **82**, 51–61 (2001)
94. Polzehl, T., Schmitt, A., Metze, F.: Approaching multi-lingual emotion recognition from speech—on language dependency of acoustic/prosodic features for anger detection. In: Proceedings of Speech Prosody. ISCA (2010)
95. Poppe, R.: Vision-based human motion analysis: an overview. Comput. Vis. Image Underst. **108**(1–2), 4–18 (2007)
96. Poppe, R.: A survey on vision-based human action recognition. Image Vis. Comput. **28**(6), 976–990 (2010)
97. Pun, T., Alecu, T., Chanel, G., Kronegg, J., Voloshynovskiy, S.: Brain-computer interaction research at the computer vision and multimedia laboratory, University of Geneva. IEEE Trans. Neural Syst. Rehabil. Eng. **14**(2), 210–213 (2006)
98. Reyes, A., Rosso, P.: Linking humour to blogs analysis: Affective traits in posts. In: Proceedings of the International Workshop on Opinion Mining and Sentiment Analysis, pp. 205–212 (2009)
99. Ringeval, F., Eyben, F., Kroupi, E., Yuce, A., Thiran, J.P., Ebrahimi, T., Lalanne, D., Schuller, B.: Prediction of asynchronous dimensional emotion ratings from audiovisual and physiological data. Pattern Recogn. Lett. **66**, 22–30 (2015)
100. Russell, J.A.: A circumplex model of affect. J. Pers. Soc. Psychol. **39**, 1161–1178 (1980)
101. Salahuddin, L., Cho, J., Jeong, M.G., Kim, D.: Ultra short term analysis of heart rate variability for monitoring mental stress in mobile settings. In: Proceedings of the IEEE International Conference of Engineering in Medicine and Biology Society, pp. 39–48 (2007)
102. Sauter, D.A., Eisner, F., Ekman, P., Scott, S.K.: Cross-cultural recognition of basic emotions through nonverbal emotional vocalizations. In: Proceedings of the National Academy of Sciences of the U.S.A. vol. 107, Issue 6, pp. 2408–2412 (2010)

103. Scherer, K.R., Oshinsky, J.S.: Cue utilization in emotion attribution from auditory stimuli. Motiv. Emot. **1**, 331–346 (1977)
104. Scherer, K.R., Brosch, T.: Culture-specific appraisal biases contribute to emotion dispositions. Eur. J. Pers. **23**, 265–288 (2009)
105. Scherer, K.R., Banse, R., Wallbott, H.G.: Emotion inferences from vocal expression correlate across languages and cultures. J. Cross Cult. Psychol. **32**(1), 76–92 (2001)
106. Schröder, M.: Speech and emotion research: an overview of research frameworks and a dimensional approach to emotional speech synthesis. Ph.D. dissertation, University of Saarland, Germany (2003)
107. Schröder, M.: The semaine api: towards a standards-based framework for building emotion-oriented systems. Adv. Hum. Mach. Interact. **2010**, 1–21 (2010)
108. Schröder, M., Pirker, H., Lamolle, M.: First suggestions for an emotion annotation and representation language. In: Proceedings of LREC, vol. 6, pp. 88–92. ELRA, Genoa, Italy (2006)
109. Schröder, M., Heylen, D., Poggi, I.: Perception of non-verbal emotional listener feedback. In: Hoffmann, R., Mixdorff, H. (eds.) Proceedings of Speech Prosody, pp. 1–4. Dresden, Germany (2006)
110. Schröder, M., Devillers, L., Karpouzis, K., Martin, J.C., Pelachaud, C., Peter, C., Pirker, H., Schuller, B., Tao, J., Wilson, I.: What should a generic emotion markup language be able to represent? In: Paiva, A., Prada, R., Picard, R.W. (eds.) Proceedings of ACII, pp. 440–451. Springer, Heidelberg (2007)
111. Schröder, M., Bevacqua, E., Eyben, F., Gunes, H., Heylen, D., Maat, M., Pammi, S., Pantic, M., Pelachaud, C., Schuller, B., Sevin, E., Valstar, M., Wöllmer, M.: A demonstration of audiovisual sensitive artificial listeners. In: Proceedings of ACII, vol. 1, pp. 263–264. Amsterdam, The Netherlands (2009)
112. Schröder, M., Pammi, S., Gunes, H., Pantic, M., Valstar, M., Cowie, R., McKeown, G., Heylen, D., ter Maat, M., Eyben, F., Schuller, B., Wöllmer, M., Bevacqua, E., Pelachaud, C., de Sevin, E.: Have an emotional workout with sensitive artificial listeners! In: Proceedings of FG, p. 646. IEEE, Santa Barbara, CA (2011)
113. Schröder, M., Bevacqua, E., Cowie, R., Eyben, F., Gunes, H., Heylen, D., ter Maat, M., McKeown, G., Pammi, S., Pantic, M., Pelachaud, C., Schuller, B., de Sevin, E., Valstar, M., Wöllmer, M.: Building autonomous sensitive artificial listeners. In: IEEE Transactions on Affective Computing, pp. 1–20 (2012)
114. Schuller, B.: Automatische Emotionserkennung aus sprachlicher und manueller Interaktion. Doctoral thesis, Technische Universität München, Munich, Germany, 244 pp (2006)
115. Schuller, B.: Affective speaker state analysis in the presence of reverberation. Int. J. Speech Technol. **14**(2), 77–87 (2011)
116. Schuller, B.: Recognizing affect from linguistic information in 3D continuous space. IEEE Trans. Affect. Comput. **2**(4), 192–205 (2011)
117. Schuller, B.: The computational paralinguistics challenge. IEEE Signal Process. Mag. **29**(4), 97–101 (2012)
118. Schuller, B., Burkhardt, F.: Learning with synthesized speech for automatic emotion recognition. In: Proceedings of ICASSP, pp. 5150–5153. IEEE, Dallas, TX (2010)
119. Schuller, B., Knaup, T.: Learning and knowledge-based sentiment analysis in movie review key excerpts. In: Esposito, A., Esposito, A., Martone, R., Müller, V., Scarpetta, G. (eds.) Toward Autonomous, Adaptive, and Context-Aware Multimodal Interfaces: Theoretical and Practical Issues, LNCS Vol. 6456/2010, pp. 448–472. Springer (2010)
120. Schuller, B., Lang, M., Rigoll, G.: Multimodal emotion recognition in audiovisual communication. In: Proceedings of ICME, vol. 1, pp. 745–748. IEEE, Lausanne, Switzerland (2002)
121. Schuller, B., Müller, R., Eyben, F., Gast, J., Hörnler, B., Wöllmer, M., Rigoll, G., Höthker, A., Konosu, H.: Being bored? Recognising natural interest by extensive audiovisual integration for real-life application. Image and Vision Computing Journal **27**(12), 1760–1774 (2009)
122. Schuller, B., Vlasenko, B., Eyben, F., Rigoll, G., Wendemuth, A.: Acoustic emotion recognition: A benchmark comparison of performances. In: Proceedings of ASRU, pp. 552–557. IEEE, Merano, Italy (2009)

123. Schuller, B., Zaccarelli, R., Rollet, N., Devillers, L.: CINEMO—a French spoken language resource for complex emotions: facts and baselines. In: Proceedings of LREC, pp. 1643–1647. ELRA, Valletta, Malta (2010)
124. Schuller, B., Batliner, A., Steidl, S., Seppi, D.: Recognising realistic emotions and affect in speech: state of the art and lessons learnt from the first challenge. J. Speech Commun. **53**(9–10), 1062–1087 (2011)
125. Schuller, B., Batliner, A., Steidl, S., Seppi, D.: Recognising realistic emotions and affect in speech: state of the art and lessons learnt from the first challenge. Speech Commun. **53**(9/10), 1062–1087 (2011)
126. Schuller, B., Valstar, M., Cowie, R., Pantic, M.: Avec 2011—the first audio/visual emotion challenge and workshop—an introduction. In: Proceedings of the 1st International Audio/Visual Emotion Challenge and Workshop, pp. 415–424. Memphis, TN (2011)
127. Schuller, B., Zhang, Z., Weninger, F., Rigoll, G.: Using multiple databases for training in emotion recognition: to unite or to vote? In: Proceedings of Interspeech, pp. 1553–1556. ISCA, Florence, Italy (2011)
128. Schuller, B., Steidl, S., Batliner, A., Vinciarelli, A., Scherer, K., Ringeval, F., Chetouani, M., Weninger, F., Eyben, F., Marchi, E., Mortillaro, M., Salamin, H., Polychroniou, A., Valente, F., Kim, S.: The interspeech 2013 computational paralinguistics challenge: social signals, conflict, emotion, autism. In: Proceedings of Interspeech, pp. 148–152. ISCA, Lyon, France (2013)
129. Schuller, B., Marchi, E., Baron-Cohen, S., O'Reilly, H., Pigat, D., Robinson, P., Davies, I., Golan, O., Fridenson, S., Tal, S., Newman, S., Meir, N., Shillo, R., Camurri, A., Piana, S., Staglianò, A., Bölte, S., Lundqvist, D., Berggren, S., Baranger, A., Sullings, N.: The state of play of ASC-inclusion: an integrated internet-based environment for social inclusion of children with autism spectrum conditions. In: Proceedings of the 2nd International Workshop on Digital Games for Empowerment and Inclusion (IDGEI 2014), 8 pp. ACM, Haifa, Israel (2014)
130. Settles, B., Craven, M., Ray, S.: Multiple-instance active learning. In: Proceedings of NIPS, pp. 1289–1296. Vancouver, BC, Canada (2008)
131. Sezgin, M.C., G-nsel, B., Kurt, G.K.: A novel perceptual feature set for audio emotion recognition. In: Proceedings of FG, pp. 780–785. IEEE, Santa Barbara, CA (2011)
132. Shaver, P.R., Wu, S., Schwartz, J.C.: Cross-cultural similarities and differences in emotion and its representation: a prototype approach. Emotion 175–212 (1992)
133. Silverman, K., Beckman, M., Pitrelli, J., Ostendorf, M., Wightman, C., Price, P., Pierrehumbert, J., Hirschberg, J.: ToBI: a standard for labeling english prosody. In: Proceedings of ICSLP, pp. 867–870. Banff, AB, Canada (1992)
134. Soleymani, M., Lichtenauer, J., Pun, T., Pantic, M.: A multimodal database for affect recognition and implicit tagging. IEEE Trans. Affect. Comput. **3**(1), 42–55 (2012)
135. Steidl, S.: Automatic Classification of Emotion-Related User States in Spontaneous Children's Speech. Logos Verlag, Berlin (2009)
136. Steidl, S., Schuller, B., Batliner, A., Seppi, D.: The hinterland of emotions: facing the open-microphone challenge. In: Proceedings of ACII, pp. 690–697. Amsterdam, The Netherlands (2009)
137. Van den Stock, J., Righart, R., De Gelder, B.: Body expressions influence recognition of emotions in the face and voice. Emotion **7**(3), 487–494 (2007)
138. Strapparava, C., Mihalcea, R.: Annotating and identifying emotions in text. In: Armano, G., de Gemmis, M., Semeraro, G., Vargiu, E. (eds.) Intelligent Information Access, Studies in Computational Intelligence, vol. 301, pp. 21–38. Springer, Berlin (2010)
139. Stuhlsatz, A., Meyer, C., Eyben, F., Zielke, T., Meier, G., Schuller, B.: Deep neural networks for acoustic emotion recognition: raising the benchmarks. In: Proceedings of ICASSP, pp. 5688–5691. IEEE, Prague, Czech Republic (2011)
140. Subrahmanian, V., Reforgiato, D.: AVA: adjective-verb-adverb combinations for sentiment analysis. Intell. Syst. **23**(4), 43–50 (2008)

141. Tarasov, A., Delany, S.J.: Benchmarking classification models for emotion recognition in natural speech: a multi-corporal study. In: Proceedings of FG, pp. 841–846. IEEE, Santa Barbara, CA (2011)
142. Trigeorgis, G., Bousmalis, K., Zafeiriou, S., Schuller, B.: A deep semi-NMF model for learning hidden representations. In: Proceedings of ICML, vol. 32, pp. 1692–1700. IMLS, Beijing, China (2014)
143. Trouvain, J., Barry, W.J.: The prosody of excitement in horse race commentaries. In: Proceedings of ISCA Workshop Speech Emotion, pp. 86–91. Newcastle, UK (2000)
144. Tsiamyrtzis, P., Dowdall, J., Shastri, D., Pavlidis, I., Frank, M., Ekman, P.: Imaging facial physiology for the detection of deceit. Int. J. Comput. Vision **71**(2), 197–214 (2007)
145. Vogt, T., André, E., Bee, N.: Emovoice—a framework for online recognition of emotions from voice. In: Proceedings of IEEE PIT, *LNCS*, vol. 5078, pp. 188–199. Springer, Kloster Irsee (2008)
146. Wallbott, H.: Bodily expression of emotion. Eur. J. Soc. Psychol. **28**, 879–896 (1998)
147. Wingerden, S., Uebbing, T.J., Jung, M.M., Poel, M.: A neural network based approach to social touch classification. In: Proceedings of the 2nd International Workshop on Emotion Representations and Modelling in Human-Computer Interaction Systems, ERM4HCI, pp. 7–12. ACM, Istanbul, Turkey (2014)
148. Wöllmer, M., Eyben, F., Reiter, S., Schuller, B., Cox,C., Douglas-Cowie, E., Cowie, R.: Abandoning emotion classes—towards continuous emotion recognition with modelling of long-range dependencies. In: Proceedings of Interspeech, pp. 597–600. ISCA, Brisbane, Australia (2008)
149. Wöllmer, M., Eyben, F., Reiter, S., Schuller, B., Cox, C., Douglas-Cowie, E., Cowie, R.: Abandoning emotion classes—towards continuous emotion recognition with modelling of long-range dependencies. In: Proceedings of Interspeech, pp. 597–600. ISCA, Brisbane, Australia (2008)
150. Wöllmer, M., Eyben, F., Keshet, J., Graves, A., Schuller, B., Rigoll, G.: Robust discriminative keyword spotting for emotionally colored spontaneous speech using bidirectional LSTM networks. In: Proceedings of ICASSP, pp. 3949–3952. IEEE, Taipei, Taiwan (2009)
151. Wöllmer, M., Metallinou, A., Eyben, F., Schuller, B., Narayanan, S.: Context-sensitive multimodal emotion recognition from speech and facial expression using bidirectional lstm modeling. In: Proceedings of Interspeech, pp. 2362–2365. ISCA, Makuhari, Japan (2010)
152. Wöllmer, M., Schuller, B., Eyben, F., Rigoll, G.: Combining long short-term memory and dynamic bayesian networks for incremental emotion-sensitive artificial listening. IEEE J. Sel. Top. Sign. Proces. **4**(5), 867–881 (2010)
153. Wöllmer, M., Weninger, F., Eyben, F., Schuller, B.: Acoustic-linguistic recognition of interest in speech with Bottleneck-BLSTM nets. In: Proceedings of Interspeech, pp. 77–80. ISCA, Florence, Italy (2011)
154. Wöllmer, M., Weninger, F., Knaup, T., Schuller, B., Sun, C., Sagae, K., Morency, L.P.: YouTube movie reviews: sentiment analysis in an audiovisual context. IEEE Intell. Syst. **28**(2), 2–8 (2013)
155. Yoshitomi, Y., Kim, S.I., Kawano, T., Kitazoe, T.: Effect of sensor fusion for recognition of emotional states using voice, face image and thermal image of face. In: Proceedings of the IEEE International Workshop on Robot and Human Interactive Communication, pp. 178–183 (2000)
156. Zeng, Z., Pantic, M., Roisman, G., Huang, T.: A survey of affect recognition methods: audio, visual, and spontaneous expressions. IEEE Trans. Pattern Anal. Mach. Intell. **31**(1), 39–58 (2009)
157. Zhang, Z., Weninger, F., Wöllmer, M., Schuller, B.: Unsupervised learning in cross-corpus acoustic emotion recognition. In: Proceedings of ASRU, pp. 523–528. IEEE, Big Island, HI, USA (2011)
158. Zhang, Z., Deng, J., Marchi, E., Schuller, B.: Active learning by label uncertainty for acoustic emotion recognition. In: Proceedings of the INTERSPEECH, pp. 2841–2845. ISCA, Lyon, France (2013)

159. Zhang, Y., Coutinho, E., Zhang, Z., Adam, M., Schuller, B.: Introducing rater reliability and correlation based dynamic active learning. In: Proceedings of the ACII, pp. 70–76. IEEE, Xi'an, P. R. China (2015)
160. Zhang, Z., Coutinho, E., Deng, J., Schuller, B.: Distributing recognition in computational paralinguistics. IEEE Trans. Affect. Comput. **5**(4), 406–417 (2014)
161. Zhang, Z., Coutinho, E., Deng, J., Schuller, B.: Cooperative learning and its application to emotion recognition from speech. IEEE/ACM Trans. Audio Speech. Lang. Process. **23**(1), 115–126 (2015)

Chapter 5
Acquisition of Personality

Ailbhe N. Finnerty, Bruno Lepri and Fabio Pianesi

Abstract This chapter provides an overview of the methods that can be used to automatically acquire information about an individual's personality. In particular, we focus our attention on the sources of data (e.g. text, audio, video, mobile phones, wearable sensors, etc.) and the features used to automatically infer personality. For each data source, we discuss the methods of extracting the cues used to detect personality, as well as the major findings. Lastly, we refer some limitations of the current research which is relevant for the advancement of the state of the art.

5.1 Introduction

The goal of this chapter is to provide an overview of the methods that can be used to automatically acquire information about an individual's personality. After a brief overview (for a detailed review see Chap. 3) of models of personality, in particular the five factor model, we will focus on the sources of data (e.g. text, audio, video, mobile phones, wearable sensors, etc.) and the features used to automatically infer personality.

Scientific psychology has developed a view of personality as a stable high-level abstraction, introducing the notion of personality *traits* which are stable dispositions towards action, belief and attitude formation. The main assumption is that they differ across individuals, are relatively stable over time and influence behaviour [50]. Interindividual differences in behaviour, belief and attitude can therefore be captured in terms of the dispositions/traits that are specific to each individual. This provides

A.N. Finnerty · B. Lepri (✉)
Fondazione Bruno Kessler, Via Sommarive, 18, 38123 Povo-Trento, Italy
e-mail: lepri@fbk.eu

A.N. Finnerty
e-mail: finnerty@fbk.eu

F. Pianesi
Fondazione Bruno Kessler and EIT-Digital,
Via Sommarive, 18, 38123 Povo-Trento, Italy
e-mail: pianesi@fbk.eu

M. Tkalčič et al. (eds.), *Emotions and Personality in Personalized Services*,
Human–Computer Interaction Series, DOI 10.1007/978-3-319-31413-6_5

a powerful descriptive and predictive tool that has been widely exploited by various disciplines including social, clinical, educational and organizational psychology.

The search for personality traits has often been pursued by means of factor analytic studies applied to lists of trait adjectives, an approach based on the Lexical Hypothesis [4]. A well-known and very influential example of a multi-factorial approach is the Big Five model [16, 36]. This model takes five main traits as constitutive of people's personality: (i) Extraversion (sociable, assertive, playful), (ii) Agreeableness (friendly, cooperative), (iii) Conscientiousness (self-disciplined, organized), (iv) Emotional Stability (calm, unemotional), and (v) Openness to Experience.

Over the last 50 years the Big Five model has become standard in psychology. Several experiments using the Big Five have repeatedly confirmed the influence of personality on many aspects of individual behaviour including leadership [30, 37], sales ability [24], teacher effectiveness [57] and general job performance [32].

The assessment of personality traits can be done using a variety of methods, the most traditional method in personality psychology being self-reported assessments, using questionnaires containing descriptive items that accurately reflect the five traits [3]. As well as self-assessed methods, where you are the judge as to what extent each item in the questionnaire accurately represents your personality, others' assessments have been found to be successful at predicting personality. Having people close to you, such as family members and friends, rating the questionnaire items was found to have the same results as self-reported values [68]. More recently, the judgements of complete strangers have been used to assess personality from short amounts of behavioural information (*thin slices*) such as one minute or even forty second video clips [6, 7], which were found to provide enough behavioural information to make accurate assessments.

The recent advancements in technology (e.g. advancements in computer vision and speech recognition techniques, diffusion of social media and mobile devices) and the increasing interest of computer scientists in personality computing, have added new and different perspectives on personality assessment and acquisition tasks (see Vinciarelli and Mohammadi, for a general review [77]). In the next sections, we will provide a review of the sources of data (video, audio, mobile and wearable devices, text, social media, etc.) and the methods used to automatically detect personality.

5.2 Non-verbal Communication

Social and personality psychology suggest that non-verbal communication is a way to externalize personality [21] and, at the same time, a relevant cue that influences the traits that others attribute to an individual [34]. Similar cues, usually coming from uncontrolled or unconscious behaviours, are tone of voice, pitch, speaking rate, prosody, eye gaze, facial expression, postures and gestures. Hence, several studies in personality computing have used non-verbal features to automatically recognize personality traits.

5.2.1 Audio Approaches

Many studies in personality psychology have emphasized the relevance of non-verbal for inferring personality traits. Extraversion is associated with higher pitch and higher variation of the fundamental frequency [69, 70], with fewer and shorter silent and filled pauses along with higher voice quality and intensity [49]. Moreover, studies on the differences between the communication styles of introverts and extroverts suggest that the latter in general speak more, they also speak faster, with fewer pauses and hesitations [23, 70]. Computational approaches of personality have also investigated the effectiveness of using non-verbal acoustic features [55, 56].

Mohammadi et al. [56] used a collection of 640 speech samples extracted from 96 news bulletins from 330 separate individuals. The goal of their work was to use speech features in an attempt to predict the personality of those speaking and to investigate whether the prediction of the personality matched the scores from the personality judgements. The judgements were made by human annotators based on the Big Five model of personality. The annotators were assessing the aspects of speech and not the spoken word as they did not speak the language of the clips (French). Each clip was assigned five scores for each of the five personality traits. The speech features extracted from the data were pitch, formants, energy and speaking rate. They found that the performance using computational methods was above chance for each trait except Openness to Experience. Their findings should be treated as preliminary for two reasons, (1) they show simply that human annotators and algorithms display agreement and (2) there were only two traits, Extraversion and Conscientiousness, where the recognition rate was satisfactory.

Further experiments using the same data obtained better performances: Mohammadi et al. [55] used (i) pitch (number of vibrations per second produced by the vocal cords), the main acoustic correlate of tone and intonation, (ii) the first two formants (resonant frequencies of the vocal tract), (iii) the energy of the speech signal and (iv) the length of voiced and unvoiced segments, which is an indirect measure of speaking rate. Again, the higher performances were obtained for Extraversion and Conscientiousness, supporting the previous findings [56]. Specifically, the mean of the formants (resonant frequencies of the vocal tract) appears to be the only important cue in the case of Agreeableness. This suggests that voices with higher formants tend to be perceived as less agreeable. A similar situation is observed for Neuroticism, where the means of pitch and first two formants appear to be the most important cues. In the case of Openness, the performance was not significantly better than the baseline. The main reason could be that this trait is difficult to perceive in the particular setting of the experiments.

5.2.2 Multimodal Approaches

Several studies have exploited the multimodal nature of non-verbal communication using a combination of acoustic and visual signals to predict personality.

Biel et al. [12] used a dataset of 442 vlogs containing just one video per vlogger. The vlogger's personality annotations were done by external observers taking into account just the first minute of the conversation. Each video was scored by five raters, inter rater agreement displayed moderate reliabilities for the aggregated annotations and varied from 0.42 for Emotional Stability to 0.77 for Extraversion ($0.42 < ICC(1,k) < 0.77$). Then, a list of acoustic and visual cues were extracted: from audio tracks, speaking activity statistics (e.g. speaking time, speaking turns and voicing rate) as well as emphasis patterns (energy, pitch and autocorrelation peaks). The visual cues extracted from the dataset were based on weighted motion energy images, and from the energy basic statistical features, such as entropy, mean, median and centre of mass (horizontal and vertical) were calculated. The results of the experiments revealed significant correlations between the audio features and Extraversion, followed by Openness to Experience and Agreeableness. Specifically, speaking time was significantly correlated with Conscientiousness, Extraversion and Openness to Experience. The authors also found a negative association between the number of speech turns and Extraversion, which supports the claim that extraverts have higher verbal fluency. Visual activity as measured by the entropy, mean and median of the energy feature was correlated with Extraversion and Openness to Experience while it was negatively correlated with Conscientiousness.

Again adopting a multimodal (audio–visual) approach, some studies have targeted the recognition of personality traits during small group interactions, usually meetings. Pianesi et al. [64] examined the interactions of individuals in small meeting groups using the Mission Survival Corpus, a collection of multi-party meetings based around a table, recording both video and audio. Meeting participants were required to solve the Mission Survival Task [29], where they had to list in order of importance 15 items necessary for survival after a plane crash. The meeting continues until a consensus is reached by all members of the group. From the corpus, a number of audio and visual features were extracted. In particular, audio features were related to four classes of *social signals*, namely (i) *Activity*, the conversational activity level measured as a percentage of speaking time, (ii) *Emphasis*, measured by variations in prosody, pitch and amplitude, and for each voiced segment by the mean energy, the frequency of the fundamental formant and the spectral entropy, (iii) *Mimicry*, defined as the unreflected copying of one person by another during a conversation, or back and forth exchanges of short words, and finally (iv) *Influence*, computed by counting the overlapping speech segments (see Chap. 6 for a detailed review of social signals). The visual features calculated were related to fidgeting behaviour and the energy associated with body gestures. Classification experiments were run for the Extraversion trait using features computed on one-minute windows. The results showed that acoustic features yielded better results performances for Extraversion than visual features, with an accuracy of 87 % compared to the baseline of 67 %.

Using a subset of the Mission Survival dataset, Lepri et al. [44, 45] exploited behavioural cues such as subject's speaking time, the amount of visual attention the subject received from, and the amount of visual attention the subject gave to, the other group members. For each subject, short sequences of expressive behaviours, the so-called *thin slices* [6, 7], were formed by taking sequences of these behavioural cues in windows of varying size (1/2/4/5/6 min) covering the duration of the meeting. The features used in this study were speaking time, attention received from others, attention received from others while speaking, attention received from others while not speaking, attention given to others, attention given to others while speaking, attention given to others while not speaking. The aim of the experiments was to accurately detect Extraversion by using just these features. The main findings were that speaking time was ineffective when used as a stand alone measure, while when combined with measures of attention received from others it had more predictive powers. Moreover, the attention that the subject gives to others was not found to be a powerful predictor of personality, while the attention that the subject received from others while not speaking yielded significant results. Manually annotated data yielded accuracies (between 53 and 64 %) not exceptionally high but significantly above the baseline, while the automated analysis yielded overall accuracies between 53 and 60 %.

A similar approach has also been used for personality prediction in different settings, such as, subject's short self-presentations [10] and human–computer collaborative tasks [9]. Batrinca et al. [10] asked 89 subjects to briefly introduce themselves using a broad range of possible topics such as their job, last book read, last holiday, preferred sports, etc. The length of the video and audio recorded self-presentations ranged from 30 to 120 s. The authors extracted a large number of acoustic and visual cues from the dataset: acoustic cues such as pitch, intensity, average speaking time, and length of self-presentation and visual cues including eye gaze, frowning, hand movements, head orientation, mouth fidgeting and posture. The results of the experiments found that Conscientiousness and Emotional Stability were the easiest traits to recognize during self-presentations, while Agreeableness and Extraversion were not accurately recognized, suggesting that the latter traits are more clearly manifested during social interactions [45, 64].

In a more recent study, Batrinca et al. [9] dealt with the task of recognizing personality traits during collaborative tasks performed between a human subject and a machine. Specifically, the study participants were asked to successfully guide their partner, a computer system, through a map while encountering some obstacles in the way, such as differences in the maps and unclear landmarks for giving directions. The "Wizard of Oz" method [39] was used in the data collection, this is a method by which the subject believes that they are interacting with an autonomous computer system, but which is actually being operated or at least partially operated by an unseen human being. The unique aspect of this task was that there were four different levels of collaboration exhibited by the "computer system", whether the task was made more difficult by displaying aggression and annoyance towards the participant: (i) a fully collaborative, calm and polite exchange with the system (ii–iii) two intermediate levels, with polite or neutral responses, while not being able to follow directions and finally (iv) a non collaborative level with an aggressive and offensive overtone. A number of acoustic features were extracted from the dataset such as pitch, intensity, number of speaking turns taken by the participant, number of long turns (speech segments lasting more than two seconds), total speaking duration, total speaking duration of the experimenter, total duration of overlapping speech and total duration of the silence for the duration of the video. Following Jayagopy et al. [35] motion vector magnitude and residual coding bitrate over all the skin blocks were computed as a measure of individual activity. The experiments performed revealed that Extraversion and Emotional Stability were the only personality traits recognized which were consistently significant above baseline (67 %) under the different collaborative settings, more precisely for all collaborative levels except for Emotional Stability (74.41–81.30 %) and all but the fully collaborative levels for Extraversion (accuracies from 72.09–81.39 %).

5.3 Wearable Devices

The technological advancements in wearable technologies have allowed the collection and monitoring of human behaviour in an unobtrusive manner [65]. The data collected through these devices can often be more telling and objective than self-reported data in situations where behaviour changes occur without the individual necessarily being aware. Wearable devices are being used in detecting frustration during learning [28], stressful situations at work [41] and in a variety of other contexts where personality can also be detected through the data recordings. Two examples of these devices are detailed further here. The Electronically Activated Recorder (EAR) [51] and Sociometric badges [61] are technologies that can be used to carry out research in ecologically valid contexts. The EAR is a modified digital voice recorder that periodically records brief snippets of ambient sounds [51]. The device is worn on the belt or in a small bag and subjects carry it with them during their normal everyday life. It is unobtrusive and records moment-to-moment ambient sounds and samples, recording only a fraction of the time instead of continuous recording, therefore not requiring the presence of a researcher. The device samples without interrupting the flow of the subject's daily life whereas traditional research methods such as experience sampling measures [17] need to be recorded at specific time intervals and require the individual to stop what they are doing. The device also means that subjects are unaware of which specific moments are being recorded, suggesting that they are unable to alter their behaviour due to an awareness of being recorded and feeling self-conscious, which can occur with less discrete devices.

Mehl et al. [52] examined the expression of personality by tracking 96 participants over two days using the EAR. Participants' personality scores were correlated with EAR-derived information on their daily social interactions, locations, activities, moods and language use; these daily manifestations were generally consistent with trait definition and (except for Openness) were often gender specific. To identify implicit folk theories about daily manifestations of personality, the authors correlated the EAR-derived information with impressions of participants based on their EAR sounds, with accuracies between 39 and 58 %. Their findings pointed out the importance of naturalistic observation studies on how personality is expressed and perceived in the natural stream of everyday behaviour. The behavioural manifestations and the independent judgements were correlated between 0.21 and 0.41 with significance values of $p<0.05$ and $p<0.001$. Specifically, the time spent talking was indicative of subjects' Extraversion, using swear words was negatively related to Agreeableness, and attendance at the classes was strongly associated with Conscientiousness. The EAR fills an important gap in the psychological study of person–environment interactions (for a review see [78]); however, this method has obvious limitations. For example, it allows only the acoustic observation of daily life, and not many other interesting social phenomena which can be grasped by other means.

Using Sociometric Badges, it is possible to be able to provide a multi-view description of daily life captured, from copresence in a specific place to face-to-face interactions and speech behaviours. Sociometric Badges are devices worn around the neck and are equipped with a microphone, an accelerometer, a Bluetooth sensor and an Infrared sensor. The badges record data from interactions with other users also wearing the badges. These are aspects of social behaviour, such as, proximity to each other from the Bluetooth, face-to-face interactions from the Infrared, which register hits when two badges are less than one metre apart facing each other, and energy and speaking features from the accelerometer and the microphone, respectively. The badges can also record data from base stations positioned in various locations around the area of interest, such as specific rooms or meeting points, which give further information of the social activities of the subjects under investigation. Sociometric badges have also been used to correlate behavioural cues and personality traits [60]. The authors recorded the interactions of 67 nurses in a post anaesthesia care unit (PACU) over 27 days. Correlational analyses to understand which features were linked to each personality trait were performed. Results can be summarized as follows. The lower the daily average time in close proximity to a bed or phone and the lower daily variation in phone call length, the more extroverted the individual. Openness to experience was associated with higher variation in daily physical activity, less variation in speaking time, more variation in close proximity to a phone and more variation in daily average betweenness centrality, computed from the face-to-face network. The less variation across days of speech volume modulation, and the less variation of time in close proximity to a bed, the more agreeable the person was and the less variation across days in the daily average betweenness the more conscientious the person was.

5.4 Smartphones

Nowadays, smartphones are becoming an unobtrusive and cost-effective source of previously inaccessible data related to daily social behaviour. These devices are able to sense a wealth of data: (i) location, (ii) other devices in physical proximity through Bluetooth scanning, (iii) communication data, including both metadata (i.e. event logs: who called whom, when, and for how long) of phone calls and text messages (sms) as well as their actual content, (iv) movement patterns, etc. Finally, smartphones are also increasingly being used as the main device to access social networks (e.g. Facebook, Twitter, etc.), to check and send email, to query the Web and more broadly to access and produce information. Social psychologist Geoffrey Miller published *The Smartphone Psychology Manifesto*, arguing that smartphones should be taken seriously as new research tools for psychology [53]. In his opinion, these tools could revolutionize all fields of psychology and behavioural sciences making these disciplines more powerful, sophisticated, international, applicable and grounded in real-world behaviour. Recently, some researchers have started using the digital traces captured by mobile phone data in order to infer personality traits.

Chittaranjan et al. [14, 15] showed that smartphone usage features, such as, the number of calls made or received, their average duration, the total duration of outgoing/incoming calls, the number of missed calls, the number of unique Bluetooth IDs seen, Internet usage and so on, can be predictive of personality traits. Their results revealed some interesting trends: extroverts were more likely to receive calls and to spend more time on them, while features pertaining to outgoing calls were not found to be predictive of the Big Five traits. Oliveira et al. [19] also investigated the role played by a limited set of nine structural characteristics of the social networks derived from the contextual information available from mobile phone data (call logs). More recently, de Montjoye et al. [18] used a set of 40 indicators which can be computed from the data available to all mobile phone carriers. These indicators referred to five classes of metrics: (i) basic phone use (e.g. number of calls, number of text messages), (ii) active user behaviours (e.g. number of initiated calls, time taken to answer a text message), (iii) mobility (e.g. radius of gyration, number of places from which calls have been made), (iv) regularity (e.g. call and text messages inter-time) and (v) diversity (e.g. call entropy, ratio between the number of interactions and the number of contacts). By using just the call log features, they were able to predict whether the subjects were classed as being high, medium or low for each personality trait, with accuracies from 29 to 56 %, better than random, giving support for the claim that personality can be predicted using standard mobile phone logs.

A different approach was followed by Staiano et al. [75] which considered the role of a number of structural ego-network indices in the prediction of personality traits, using self-assessments as a ground truth. The structural indices were grouped into 4 basic classes, centrality, efficiency, triads and transitivity, and were extracted from two different types of undirected networks based on (i) cellphone Bluetooth hits and (ii) cellphone calls. The exploited dataset comprised the digital traces of 53 subjects for three months. The results showed that for all traits but Neuroticism the information about colocation (Bluetooth network) seemed to be more effective than the information about person-to-person communication (Call network). The outlier role of Neuroticism could be associated with the specific characteristics of this trait, based on the necessity to control for potentially stressful social situations, such as, when many people are together in the same place. Another interesting result is the positive association between Extraversion and transitivity indices with Bluetooth network, which could be related to the tendency of extraverts to keep their close partners together, also by promoting their introduction to each other at social face-to-face gatherings.

5.5 Text

A large area of research has used written texts to automatically infer personality traits, taking into account both style and topics [8, 47, 48]. A preliminary work addressing the automatic recognition of personality from text was done by [8]. This work used the relative frequency of function words and of word categories based on Systemic Functional Grammar to train classifiers for Extraversion and Emotional Stability. Then, Oberlander and Nowson [59] extracted n-gram features from a corpus of personal weblogs. A major finding of theirs was that the model for Agreeableness was the only one to outperform the baseline. Influential works were also done by Mairesse et al. [47, 48], which used datasets collected from Pennebaker and King [63].

Holtgraves [31] analyzed the association between texting styles and personality traits. Texting is particularly interesting because it represents a merging of oral and written communication, much like email with the difference of taking place interactively in real time. The aim of the work was to understand how the language used in text messaging varies as a function of personality traits and interpersonal context. 224 students were asked to come to the lab with their cell phones. After completing a personality questionnaire they were asked to retrieve the last 20 text messages that they had sent, and for each message the date and time it was sent, the location, whether others were present at the time and the age and gender of the recipient. Then, they rated the recipients of the text message on a number of items such as whether they were close, liked each other, their relationship to them and how long they had known each other. Using the text analysis tool, Linguistic Inquiry and Word Count (LIWC), they analyzed the textual content of the messages. The results showed that others being present is not a hindrance to texting behaviour and the messages on the whole were short and more relational than informational, more as a mechanism for maintaining social connections. Extraversion was associated with more frequent texting and the use of personal pronouns as well as word expansions (using more letters to add emphasis to a word) but was not related to swearing, while Agreeableness was negatively correlated with the use of negative words.

Schwartz et al. [71] used data collected from 75,000 Facebook users. All the users filled in a personality questionnaire to be used as a ground truth using the Facebook add-on MyPersonality [42]. The final dataset consisted of over 15.4 million Facebook status updates. In their work, the authors used two different approaches: (i) LIWC to categorize each word with respect to predefined word categories and (ii) an open data approach based on Differential Language Analysis (DLA) that categorizes the words by similarity rather than predefined categories, hence it does not limit the data that would not have fit into the predefined categories. The study found that from Facebook likes as well as detailed demographic information, private traits and attributes can be predicted. By using this data, they were able to discriminate between sexual preference, race and political affiliation. This shows that the data about us that is available through social networking sites is representative of our identity, attitudes and beliefs. The results showed, for example, evidence that there were some keywords related to certain personality traits—party and friends for extroverts, while words such as alone were found to be more related to introverts. A further study using linguistic features extracted from the same dataset [62] found that comparisons with self other reports and external criteria (self-reports and language-based assessments) suggested that language-based assessments are capable of capturing true personality variance. The results show that the most highly correlated words, phrases and language topics for each trait were consistent with the characteristics of each of the personality traits. For example, those scoring high on Extraversion used language and symbols reflecting positive emotion (e.g. love, :)), enthusiasm (e.g. best, stoked) and sociability (e.g. party, hanging). The correlations between the language features and Extraversion ranged from ($r = 0.13$ to $r = 0.33$), and all correlations were significant at $p < 0.001$. Similar findings for the language used and the reported personality scores were found for all five of the personality traits.

Emails are another ubiquitous communication tool that constitute a significant portion of social interactions and are characterised as the natural 'habitat' of the modern office worker [20]. Hence, emails have also been used to predict personality, although with modest results. Specifically, researchers aimed to predict personality by using features extracted from email text while also maintaining the privacy of the sender by masking the content.

The work of Shen et al. [72] used two datasets collected from Outlook email server and Gmail emails and outlined various features that can be extracted from these data for predicting personality. The features they extracted were; bag of words features (e.g. most commonly used words), meta features (e.g. to and from, word count, time, date, etc.), word statistics (e.g. nouns, verbs, sentiment), writing styles (e.g. greetings, formality, emoticons) and speech act scores (detecting the purpose of the email, such as proposing a meeting). Using all the available features with single label classifiers and Support Vector Machines (SVM) learning algorithm, 69 % accuracy was achieved on the Outlook set and 72 % on the Gmail set. By using the Information Gain criterion the features that had the greatest predictive value were sorted according to their power, features from word statistics and writing styles appeared most frequently in the list. The results show that those with high Conscientiousness tend to write long emails and use more characters, those with high Agreeableness tend to use "please" and good wishes in their emails, while those with high Neuroticism use more negations. As well as using emails 'Blogs' are another potential source of data [33], however it has to be taken into consideration, that those who write blogs may be more outgoing and open individuals and so being able to predict all five personality traits from these sources would be limited.

5.6 Social Media

Social media are increasingly becoming one of the main channels used to interact with others and to self-disclose. Social media are also emerging as an excellent ground for personality computing [26, 42, 43, 58, 66].

Golbeck et al. [26] used several characteristics extracted from Facebook profiles such as education, religion, marital status, the number of political and generic organizations the users belonged to. In addition, the authors also extracted the density of users' egocentric networks and analyzed the text posted in the "About Me" section using LIWC. A similar approach was performed by the same authors [25] using data from Twitter: in particular they predicted subject's personality using features such as number of followers, density of subject's network, number of hashtags, number of links, words per tweet, etc. The authors found that Openness to Experience was the easiest trait to detect while Neuroticism was the most difficult.

Quercia et al. [66] investigated the relationship between personality traits and five types of Twitter users: (i) *listeners*, those who follow many users, (ii) *popular*, those who are followed by many users, (iii) *highly read*, those who are often listed in others' reading lists and two types of *influentials*. Their results showed that popular and influential users are both extroverts and emotionally stables in terms of traits. Also, popular users are high in Openness, being imaginative, while influentials tend to be high in Conscientiousness. The authors predicted users' personality traits using three features that are publicly available on any Twitter profile: (i) the number of profiles the user follows, (ii) the number of followers and (iii) the number of times the user has been listed in others' reading lists. They found that Openness is the easiest trait to predict (same result as obtained by Golbeck et al. [25]), while Extraversion was the most difficult. In another study, Quercia et al. [67] studied the relationship between Facebook popularity (number of contacts) and personality traits on a large number of subjects. They found that popular users (those with many social contacts) are more extroverted and less neurotic. In particular, they found that the Extraversion score is a good predictor for number of Facebook contacts.

Kosinski et al. [42, 43] used subjects' likes and activities on Facebook pages to predict traits and preferences. Kosinski [42] used the data collected from over 350,000 US Facebook users collected from the MyPersonality project [42] to examine how a user's personality is reflected in their Facebook likes. The results for the personality traits revealed significant correlations with Openness to Experience ($r = 0.43$) and Extraversion ($r = 0.40$). The remaining personality traits were correlated with lower values, between ($r = 0.17$ and $r = 0.30$). These findings show that personality can be, to some extent, inferred from a user's Facebook profile and that actual online behaviour can be used to understand aspects of user's personality.

A second study [43] expanded the range of features used in the prediction tasks. The subjects browsing habits were calculated by using the Facebook like function and classifying the pages into certain categories as defined by [11]. The results found that Extraversion was the most highly expressed by Facebook features, while Agreeableness was the hardest trait to predict. Extroverts were more likely to share what was going on in their lives and their feelings, they attend more events, belong to more groups and have larger numbers of friends. Those who scored high on Openness to Experience post more status updates and join more groups, while those who were high in Conscientiousness use the like feature less frequently and were less likely to join groups. A wide variety of people's personal attributes, ranging from sexual orientation to intelligence, can be automatically and accurately inferred using their Facebook Likes.

A new study [79] has also compared the judgements using features obtained from Facebook data, self-reported assessments of personality and self other assessment of the subjects' personality, taken from a Facebook friend of the subject. The results showed that computer-based models, based on the subjects' 'likes', are significantly more correlated with participants' self-ratings ($r = 0.56$) than average human judgements ($r = 0.49$).

Finally, a preliminary work by Celli et al. [13] exploited a Bag-of-Visual-Words technique to automatically predict personality from Facebook profile pictures. Profile pictures convey a lot of information about a user and are directly connected to their identity. Results revealed that extrovert and emotionally stable people tend to have pictures where they are smiling and appear with other people. Introverts tend to appear alone, neurotics tend to have images without humans and close-up faces. Profile pictures of people with low scores in Openness to Experience tend to have strong spots of light and sometimes darkened figures.

5.7 Beyond Traits: Personality States Recognition

An assumption of the approaches described above is that traits are stable and enduring properties, but people do not always behave the same way: an extrovert might, on occasion, be less talkative or make fewer attempts to attract social attention; a neurotic person need not always react anxiously, etc. Behavioural variability has the effect that attributions based on, e.g. short behavioural excerpts will always exhibit a certain amount of dependence on the selected excerpts. There is, in other words, a tension between the invariance of personality traits and the natural variability of behaviour in concrete situations that can seriously hamper current attempts at automatically predicting personality traits. In psychological studies, such a tension has often been resolved by considering behaviour variability as noise that has to be cancelled out. However, it can be argued that within-individual variability is not just noise to be cancelled out; on the contrary, stemming from the interaction between enduring traits and variable situational properties, it can give a valuable contribution to personality prediction [22, 54].

A decade ago, an alternative take on this debate was considered in the form of *personality states* [22]. Personality states are concrete behavioural episodes described as having the same contents as traits. In one of their personality states, a person can be said to behave more or less introvertedly, more or less neurotically, etc. Personality traits can be reconstructed as distributions over personality states conditioned on situational characteristics. People would differ because of their different personality state distributions, meaning that, e.g. an introvert does not differ from an extrovert because they never engage in extrovert behaviours, but because they do so in a different manner. Such an approach would reconcile the traditional focus on between-person variability with the meaningfulness of within-individual variability by turning actual behaviours into personality states.

A first attempt at automatically recognizing personality states was done by Staiano et al. [73, 74] employing visual and acoustic features in a meeting scenario. Then, Lepri et al. [46] ran a 6-week long study in which they monitored the activities of 53 people in a research institution during their working days. In particular, during the study both stable and transient aspects of the participants' personality traits and personality states were collected using self-reported measures through experience sampling methods. The behavioural cues of the participants were collected by means of the Sociometric Badges. Using the data collected by Lepri et al. [46], Kalimeri et al. [38] investigated the effectiveness of cues concerning acted social behaviours, for instance the number of people interacting and the number of people in close proximity, as well as other situational characteristics such as time spent in the canteen, in coffee breaks or in meetings and so on, for the sake of personality states' classification.

With the same data, Alshamsi et al. [5] and Teso et al. [76] explored the influence played by specific situational factors, the face-to-face interactions and the proximity interactions, over the ego's expression of a specific personality state in a working environment. Specifically, Alshamsi et al. [5] have shown that a *contagion* metaphor, namely the adaptation of behavioural responses to the behaviour of other people, cannot fully capture the dynamics of personality states. Interestingly, the authors found that social influence has two opposing effects on personality states: *adaptation* effects and *complementarity* effects, whereby individuals' behaviours tend to complement the behaviours of others. Teso et al. [76] also investigated how the complexity of the social network structure of the interacting alters can play a significant role in predicting the personality states of the ego. To this end, people's interactions were represented as *graphlets*, induced subgraphs representing specific patterns of interaction, and design classification experiments with the aim of predicting the subjects' self-reported personality states. The results demonstrate that the graphlet-based representation consistently contributes to recognition improvements. Furthermore, the amount of improvement tends to increase with graphlet complexity.

5.8 Open Issues

As seen in previous sections, personality recognition is attracting increasing interest in the computational community. However, there are a number of open issues requiring particular attention from researchers working in this field. In the following subsections, we will list some of these open issues.

5.8.1 Available Data and Tools

Data plays a crucial role in developing and testing personality recognition algorithms and the lack of open datasets and benchmarks is limiting the number of studies and creates issues in the process of validation and reproducibility needed by the scientific community. To the best of our knowledge, the datasets available, or partly available, containing personality data are the Friends and Family Dataset [1], the SSPNET Speaker Personality Corpus [55], myPersonality [42], the YouTube Personality Dataset [12], and the more recent SALSA Dataset [2]. Similarly, very few ready-to-use tools are available for personality recognition, a notable example being Bandicoot[1] based on the approach described by [18].

5.8.2 Methodological Issues

As pointed out by Vinciarelli and Mohammadi [77], the personality computing researchers often propose binary classification approaches, where the goal is mapping behavioural features into high and low classes for each personality trait. However, splitting subjects into classes (e.g. above and below the median of a given trait) is not really meaningful from a psychological point of view. A more meaningful task might be ranking people according to their personality traits. Moreover, personality computing addresses each trait separately based on the assumption that traits are independent and uncorrelated. However, this is not always the case as highlighted by Vinciarelli and Mohammadi [77]. Hence, computational approaches able of jointly modelling the traits should be investigated.

Additionally, some concerns can be raised about the reliability of social media data (e.g. Twitter, Facebook, etc.) as valid sources of information about personality. One possible concern with these data is due to the fact that we select the type of information we openly share on social networking platforms and thus it may represent the best version of ourselves and not the true self. In a study, Gosling et al. [27] investigated if social media data can be a reliable and valid source of information and their results support this hypothesis. However, it is still an open issue debated by researchers.

5.8.3 Privacy Concerns

Privacy concerns need to be addressed when considering the future of research for the automatic acquisition of personality. Certain sources of data cannot be anonymized; for example, a given individual can easily be identified from video, audio and location data. Similarly, social media data retain personal identifiable aspects that can be traced back to the individual simply from searching the web [80]. Protecting the privacy of subjects' data is a critical issue to consider [40].

[1]http://bandicoot.mit.edu/.

5.9 Conclusion

In this chapter, we provided an overview of the data sources (text, audio, video, mobile phones data, wearable sensors data, etc.) and methods that can be used to automatically acquire information about an individual's personality. From a more general point of view, the results of the described studies show the feasibility of the automatic acquisition of personality and encourage further research.

In particular, the future of automatic personality acquisition has to do with the improvement of the feature extraction methods and to investigate new promising sources of data (e.g. spending data from credit card transactions). It is worth noting that personality computing is increasingly attracting more attention from a wide and diverse range of communities (e.g. mobile computing, social media, robotics, computer vision and speech processing, natural language processing, human–computer interaction, etc.) and this field, as highlighted by [77], might become a common ground for disciplines and areas that in the past have barely communicated with each other.

References

1. Aharony, N., Pan, W., Ip, C., Khayal, I., Pentland, A.: Social fmri: investigating and shaping social mechanisms in the real world. Pervasive Mob. Comput. **6**, 643–659 (2011)
2. Alameda-Pineda, X., Staiano, J., Subramanian, R., Batrinca, L., Ricci, E., Lepri, B., Lanz, O., Sebe, N.: Salsa: a novel dataset for multimodal group behavior analysis. arXiv:1506.06882 (2015)
3. Allport, G.W.: Personality. Holt, New York (1937)
4. Allport, G.W., Odbert, H.S.: Trait-names: a psycho-lexical study. Psychol. Monogr. **47**(1), i (1936)
5. Alshamsi, A., Pianesi, F., Lepri, B., Pentland, A., Rahwan, I.: Beyond contagion: reality mining reveals complex patterns of social influence. PLoS ONE **10**(8), e0135740 (2015)
6. Ambady, N., Rosenthal, R.: Thin slices of expressive behavior as predictors of interpersonal consequences: a meta-analysis. Psychol. Bull. **111**(2), 256 (1992)
7. Ambady, N., Bernieri, F.J., Richeson, J.A.: Toward a histology of social behavior: judgmental accuracy from thin slices of the behavioral stream. Adv. Exp. Soc. Psychol. **32**, 201–271 (2000)
8. Argamon, S., Dhawle, S., Koppel, M., Pennebaker, J.: Lexical predictors of personality type. In: Joint Annual Meeting of the Interface and the Classification Society of North America (2005)
9. Batrinca, L., Lepri, B., Mana, N., Pianesi, F.: Multimodal recognition of personality traits in human-computer collaborative tasks. In: Proceedings of the 14th ACM international conference on multimodal interaction, pp. 39–46. ACM (2012)
10. Batrinca, L.M., Mana, N., Lepri, B., Pianesi, F., Sebe, N.: Please, tell me about yourself: automatic personality assessment using short self-presentations. In: Proceedings of the 13th international conference on multimodal interfaces, pp. 255–262. ACM (2011)
11. Bennett, P.N., Svore, K., Dumais, S.T.: Classification-enhanced ranking. In: Proceedings of the 19th International Conference on World Wide Web, pp. 111–120. ACM (2010)
12. Biel, J.-I., Aran, O., Gatica-Perez, D.: Personality impressions and nonverbal behavior in youtube. In: ICWSM, You are Known by How You Vlog (2011)

13. Celli, F., Bruni, E., Lepri, B.: Automatic personality and interaction style recognition from facebook profile pictures. In: Proceedings of the ACM International Conference on Multimedia, pp. 1101–1104. ACM (2014)
14. Chittaranjan, G., Blom, J., Gatica-Perez, D.: Who's who with big-five: analyzing and classifying personality traits with smartphones. In: 15th Annual International Symposium on Wearable Computers (ISWC), pp. 29–36. IEEE (2011)
15. Chittaranjan, G., Blom, J., Gatica-Perez, D.: Mining large-scale smartphone data for personality studies. Pers. Ubiquit. Comput. **17**(3), 433–450 (2013)
16. Costa, P.T., McCrae, R.R.: Four ways five factors are basic. Pers. Individ. Differ. **13**(6), 653–665 (1992)
17. Csikszentmihalyi, M., Larson, R.: Validity and reliability of the experience-sampling method. J. Nerv. Ment. Dis. **175**(9), 526–536 (1987)
18. de Montjoye, Y.-A., Quoidbach, J., Robic, F., Pentland, A.S.: Predicting personality using novel mobile phone-based metrics. In: Social Computing, Behavioral-Cultural Modeling and Prediction, pp. 48–55. Springer (2013)
19. de Oliveira, R., Karatzoglou, A., Concejero Cerezo, P., Lopez de Vicuña, A.A., Oliver, N.: Towards a psychographic user model from mobile phone usage. In: CHI'11 Extended Abstracts on Human Factors in Computing Systems, pp 2191–2196. ACM (2011)
20. Ducheneaut, N., Bellotti, V.: E-mail as habitat: an exploration of embedded personal information management. Interactions **8**(5), 30–38 (2001)
21. Ekman, P., Freisen, W.V., Ancoli, S.: Facial signs of emotional experience. J. Pers. Soc. Psychol. **39**(6), 1125 (1980)
22. Fleeson, W.: Toward a structure-and process-integrated view of personality: traits as density distributions of states. J. Pers. Soc. Psychol. **80**(6), 1011 (2001)
23. Furnham, A.: Language and Personality (1990)
24. Furnham, A., Fudge, C.: The five factor model of personality and sales performance. J. Individ. Differ. **29**(1), 11 (2008)
25. Golbeck, J., Robles, C., Edmondson, M., Turner, K.: Predicting personality from twitter. In: IEEE Third International Conference on Privacy, Security, Risk and Trust (PASSAT) and 2011 IEEE Third Inernational Conference on Social Computing (SocialCom), pp 149–156. IEEE (2011)
26. Golbeck, J., Robles, C., Turner, K.: Predicting personality with social media. In: CHI'11 Extended Abstracts on Human Factors in Computing Systems, pp. 253–262. ACM (2011)
27. Gosling, S.D., Vazire, S., Srivastava, S., John, O.P.: Should we trust web-based studies? a comparative analysis of six preconceptions about internet questionnaires. Am. Psychol. **59**(2), 93 (2004)
28. Grafsgaard, J.F., Wiggins, J.B., Vail, A.K., Boyer, K.E., Wiebe, E.N., Lester, J.C.: The additive value of multimodal features for predicting engagement, frustration, and learning during tutoring. In: Proceedings of the 16th International Conference on Multimodal Interaction, pp. 42–49. ACM (2014)
29. Hall, J., Watson, W.H.: The effects of a normative intervention on group decision-making performance. Hum. Relat. 299–317 (1970)
30. Hogan, R., Curphy, G.J., Hogan, J.: What we know about leadership: effectiveness and personality. Am. Psychol. **49**(6), 493 (1994)
31. Holtgraves, T.: Text messaging, personality, and the social context. J. Res. Pers. **45**(1), 92–99 (2011)
32. Hurtz, G.M., Donovan, J.J.: Personality and job performance: the big five revisited. J. Appl. Psychol. **85**(6), 869 (2000)
33. Iacobelli, F., Gill, A.J., Nowson, S., Oberlander, J.: Large scale personality classification of bloggers. In: Affective Computing and Intelligent Interaction, pp. 568–577. Springer (2011)
34. James, S., Uleman, S., Saribay, A., Gonzalez, C.M.: Spontaneous inferences, implicit impressions, and implicit theories. Annu. Rev. Psychol. **59**, 329–360 (2008)
35. Jayagopi, D.B., Hung, H., Yeo, C., Gatica-Perez, D.: Modeling dominance in group conversations using nonverbal activity cues. IEEE Trans. Audio Speech Lang. Process. **17**(3), 501–513 (2009)

36. John, O.P., Srivastava, S.: The big five trait taxonomy: history, measurement, and theoretical perspectives. Handb. Pers. Theory Res. **2**, 102–138 (1999)
37. Judge, T.A., Bono, J.E., Ilies, R., Gerhardt, M.W.: Personality and leadership: a qualitative and quantitative review. J. Appl. Psychol. **87**(4), 765 (2002)
38. Kalimeri, K., Lepri, B., Pianesi, F.: Going beyond traits: multimodal classification of personality states in the wild. In: Proceedings of the 15th ACM on International Conference on Multimodal Interaction, pp. 27–34. ACM (2013)
39. Kelley, J.F.: An empirical methodology for writing user-friendly natural language computer applications. In: Proceedings of the SIGCHI Conference on Human Factors in Computing Systems, pp. 193–196. ACM (1983)
40. King, G.: Ensuring the data-rich future of the social sciences (2011)
41. Kocielnik, R., Sidorova, N., Maggi, F.M., Ouwerkerk, M., Westerink, J.H.D.M.: Smart technologies for long-term stress monitoring at work. In: IEEE 26th International Symposium on Computer-Based Medical Systems (CBMS), 2013, pp. 53–58. IEEE (2013)
42. Kosinski, M., Stillwell, D., Graepel, T.: Private traits and attributes are predictable from digital records of human behavior. Proc. Natl. Acad. Sci. **110**(15), 5802–5805 (2013)
43. Kosinski, M., Bachrach, Y., Kohli, P., Stillwell, D., Graepel, T.: Manifestations of user personality in website choice and behaviour on online social networks. Mach. Learn. **95**(3), 357–380 (2014)
44. Lepri, B., Subramanian, R., Kalimeri, K., Staiano, J., Pianesi, F., Sebe, N.: Employing social gaze and speaking activity for automatic determination of the extraversion trait. In: International Conference on Multimodal Interfaces and the Workshop on Machine Learning for Multimodal Interaction, p. 7. ACM (2010)
45. Lepri, B., Subramanian, R., Kalimeri, K., Staiano, J., Pianesi, F., Sebe, N.: Connecting meeting behavior with extraversion; a systematic study. IEEE Trans. Affect. Comput. **3**(4), 443–455 (2012)
46. Lepri, B., Staiano, J., Rigato, G., Kalimeri, K., Finnerty, A., Pianesi, F., Sebe, N., Pentland, A.: The sociometric badges corpus: a multilevel behavioral dataset for social behavior in complex organizations. In: Privacy, Security, Risk and Trust (PASSAT), 2012 International Conference on and 2012 International Conference on Social Computing (SocialCom), pp. 623–628. IEEE (2012)
47. Mairesse, F., Walker, M.: Automatic recognition of personality in conversation. In: Proceedings of the Human Language Technology Conference of the NAACL, Companion Volume: Short Papers, pp. 85–88. Association for Computational Linguistics (2006)
48. Mairesse, F., Walker, M.A., Mehl, M.R., Moore, R.K.: Using linguistic cues for the automatic recognition of personality in conversation and text. J. Artif. Intell. Res. 457–500 (2007)
49. Mallory, E.B., Miller, V.R.: A possible basis for the association of voice characteristics and personality traits. Commun. Monogr. **25**(4), 255–260 (1958)
50. Matthews, G., Campbell, S.E.: Sustained performance under overload: Personality and individual differences in stress and coping. Theoret. Issues Ergonomics Sci. **10**(5), 417–442 (2009)
51. Mehl, M.R., Pennebaker, J.W., Michael Crow, D., Dabbs, J., Price, J.H.: The electronically activated recorder (ear): a device for sampling naturalistic daily activities and conversations. Behav. Res. Methods Instrum. Comput **33**(4), 517–523 (2001)
52. Mehl, M.R., Gosling, S.D., Pennebaker, J.W.: Personality in its natural habitat: manifestations and implicit folk theories of personality in daily life. J. Pers. Soc. Psychol. **90**(5), 862 (2006)
53. Miller, G.: The smartphone psychology manifesto. Perspect. Psychol. Sci. **7**(3), 221–237 (2012)
54. Mischel, W.: Personality and Assessment. Psychology Press (2013)
55. Mohammadi, G., Vinciarelli, A.: Automatic personality perception: prediction of trait attribution based on prosodic features. IEEE Trans. Affect. Comput. **3**(3), 273–284 (2012)
56. Mohammadi, G., Vinciarelli, A., Mortillaro, M.: The voice of personality: mapping nonverbal vocal behavior into trait attributions. In: Proceedings of the 2nd International Workshop on Social Signal Processing, pp. 17–20. ACM (2010)
57. Murray, H.G., Rushton, J.P., Paunonen, S.V.: Teacher personality traits and student instructional ratings in six types of university courses. J. Educ. Psychol. **82**(2), 250 (1990)

58. Nguyen, T., Phung, D., Adams, B., Venkatesh, S.: Towards discovery of influence and personality traits through social link prediction. In: Proceedings of the International AAAI Conference on Weblogs and Social Media, pp. 566–569 (2011)
59. Oberlander, J., Nowson, S.: Whose thumb is it anyway?: classifying author personality from weblog text. In: Proceedings of the COLING/ACL on Main Conference Poster Sessions, pp. 627–634. Association for Computational Linguistics (2006)
60. Olguın, D.O., Gloor, P.A., Pentland, A.S.: Capturing individual and group behavior with wearable sensors. In: Proceedings of the 2009 AAAI Spring Symposium on Human Behavior Modeling, SSS, vol. 9 (2009)
61. Olguín, D.O., Waber, B.N., Kim, T., Mohan, A., Ara, K., Pentland, A.: Sensible organizations: technology and methodology for automatically measuring organizational behavior. IEEE Trans. Syst. Man Cybernet. B: Cybernet. **39**(1), 43–55 (2009)
62. Park, G., Schwartz, H.A., Eichstaedt, J.C., Kern, M.L., Kosinski, M., Stillwell, D.J., Ungar, L.H., Seligman, M.E.P.: Automatic personality assessment through social media language. J. Pers. Soc. Psychol. **108**(6), 934 (2015)
63. Pennebaker, J.W., King, L.A.: Linguistic styles: language use as an individual difference. J. Pers. Soc. Psychol. **77**(6), 1296 (1999)
64. Pianesi, F., Mana, N., Cappelletti, A., Lepri, B., Zancanaro, M.: Multimodal recognition of personality traits in social interactions. In: Proceedings of the 10th International Conference on Multimodal Interfaces, pp. 53–60. ACM (2008)
65. Picard, R.W., Healey, J.: Affective wearables. Pers. Technol. **1**(4), 231–240 (1997)
66. Quercia, D., Kosinski, M., Stillwell, D., Crowcroft, J.: Our twitter profiles, our selves: Predicting personality with twitter. In: IEEE Third International Conference on Privacy, Security, Risk and Trust (PASSAT) and 2011 IEEE Third Inernational Conference on Social Computing (SocialCom), 2011, pp. 180–185. IEEE (2011)
67. Quercia, D., Las Casas, D.B., Pesce, J.P., Stillwell, D., Kosinski, M., Almeida, V., Crowcroft, J.: Facebook and privacy: the balancing act of personality, gender, and relationship currency. In: Proceedings of the 2012 ACM Conference on Computer Supported Collaborative Work (2012)
68. Robert, R.: McCrae and Paul T Costa. Validation of the five-factor model of personality across instruments and observers. J. Pers. Soc. Psychol. **52**(1), 81 (1987)
69. Scherer, K.: Personality inference from voice quality: the loud voice of extroversion. Eur. J. Soc. Psychol. **8**, 467–487 (1978)
70. Scherer, K.: Personality Markers in Speech. Cambridge University Press (1979)
71. Schwartz, A.H., Eichstaedt, J.C., Kern, M.L., Dziurzynski, L., Ramones, S.M., Agrawal, M., Shah, A., Kosinski, M., Stillwell, D., Seligman, M.E.P., et al.: Personality, gender, and age in the language of social media: the open-vocabulary approach. PloS one **8**(9), e73791 (2013)
72. Shen, J., Brdiczka, O., Liu, J.: Understanding email writers: personality prediction from email messages. In: User Modeling, Adaptation, and Personalization, pp. 318–330. Springer (2013)
73. Staiano, J., Lepri, B., Kalimeri, K., Sebe, N., Pianesi, F.: Contextual modeling of personality states' dynamics in face-to-face interactions. In: IEEE Third International Conference on Privacy, Security, Risk and Trust (PASSAT) and 2011 IEEE Third Inernational Conference on Social Computing (SocialCom) (2011)
74. Staiano, J., Lepri, B., Subramanian, R., Sebe, N., Pianesi, F.: Automatic modeling of personality states in small group interactions. In: Proceedings of the 19th ACM International Conference on Multimedia, pp. 989–992. ACM (2011)
75. Staiano, J., Lepri, B., Aharony, N., Pianesi, F., Sebe, N., Pentland, A.: Friends don't lie: inferring personality traits from social network structure. In: Proceedings of the 2012 ACM Conference on Ubiquitous Computing, pp. 321–330. ACM (2012)
76. Teso, S., Staiano, J., Lepri, B., Passerini, A., Pianesi, F.: Ego-centric graphlets for personality and affective states recognition. In: International Conference on Social Computing (SocialCom), pp. 874–877. IEEE (2013)
77. Vinciarelli, A., Mohammadi, G.: A survey of personality computing. IEEE Trans. Affect. Comput. (2014)

78. Walsh, W.B., Craink, K.H., Price, R.H.: Person-Environment Psychology: New Directions and Perspectives. Lawrence Erlbaum, Mahwah (2000)
79. Youyou, W., Kosinski, M., Stillwell, D.: Computer-based personality judgments are more accurate than those made by humans. Proc. Natl. Acad. Sci. **112**(4), 1036–1040 (2015)
80. Zimmer, M.: but the data is already public: on the ethics of research in facebook. Ethics Inf. Technol. **12**(4), 313–325 (2010)

Chapter 6
Computing Technologies for Social Signals

Alessandro Vinciarelli

Abstract Social signal processing is the domain aimed at modelling, analysis and synthesis of nonverbal communication in human–human and human–machine interactions. The core idea of the field is that common nonverbal behavioural cues—facial expressions, vocalizations, gestures, postures, etc—are the physical, machine-detectable evidence of social phenomena such as empathy, conflict, interest, attitudes, dominance, etc. Therefore, machines that can automatically detect, interpret and synthesize social signals will be capable to make sense of the social landscape they are part of while, possibly, participating in it as full social actors.

6.1 Introduction

To the best of our knowledge, the expression "Social Signal Processing" (SSP) was used for the first time, at least in the computing community, in 2007 [35]. The first attempts to outline the scope of the domain were proposed shortly after [65, 66], but the first full definition of the field was proposed only in 2012 [68], when SSP was clearly shown to include three major areas of interest, namely conceptual modelling, automatic analysis and artificial synthesis of social signals. Conceptual modelling is the definition of theoretic models of social signals in terms of psychological and cognitive processes. Automatic analysis is the development of approaches that detect and interpret human behaviour in terms of social signals. Artificial synthesis is the development of machines capable to synthesize social signals that affect people, typically users, in the same way as those displayed by humans.

The main outcomes of these initial efforts were, on the one hand, the definition of SSP in terms of scientific and technological questions and goals [11] and, on the other hand, the proposition of theoretically grounded definitions of what a social signal is: "actions whose function is to bring about some reaction or to engage in some process" [10], "acts or structures that influence the behaviour or internal state of other individuals" [30], "communicative or informative signals which [...] provide

A. Vinciarelli (✉)
University of Glasgow, Sir A.Williams Building, Glasgow G12 8QQ, UK
e-mail: vincia@dcs.gla.ac.uk

M. Tkalčič et al. (eds.), *Emotions and Personality in Personalized Services*,
Human–Computer Interaction Series, DOI 10.1007/978-3-319-31413-6_6

information about social facts" [39]. In other words, social signals are *observable* behaviours that not only convey information about social phenomena, but also influence others and their behaviours.

On the basis of the definitions above, the research community has been moving along two major dimensions

- Development of methodologies aimed at analysis and synthesis of social signals. These include efforts aimed at automatic recognition of facial expressions [75], computational paralinguistics [55], expressive speech synthesis [54], action and movement recognition [40], etc. While being pertinent to SSP, this type of research is typically carried out in other communities (e.g. computer vision for facial expression analysis and action recognition, signal processing for computational paralinguistics and speech synthesis, etc.).
- Development of approaches for automatic analysis and synthesis of major social and psychological phenomena such as conflict and disagreement [9], personality [64], leadership [52], etc. This research dimension is most readily recognized as SSP oriented and it will be the focus of this chapter.

In parallel with the research lines above, there is the attempt to adopt SSP methodologies in view of real-world applications such as recommendation systems [61], robot companions [20], analysis of development in children [5], multimedia analysis, tagging and retrieval [16, 34], etc. (see Sect. 6.5.5).

The rest of this chapter is organized as follows: Sect. 6.2 provides a conceptual map of the domain, Sect. 6.3 provides a state of the art, Sect. 6.4 introduces a methodological map, Sect. 6.5 proposes some future important challenges and Sect. 6.6 draws some conclusions.

6.2 A Conceptual Map of SSP

The goal of this section is to provide a conceptual map of SSP, i.e. to show that most activities of the domain correspond to one or more elements of the Brunswik's Lens [12], a human–human interaction model commonly adopted in the psychological literature (see Fig. 6.1).

6.2.1 Externalization

According to the Brunswik's Lens model, people *externalize* social and psychological phenomena through everything observable they do. By social and psychological is meant, any phenomenon that has to do with the inner state of an individual and cannot be sensed and/or accessed through direct observation: personality traits, attitude, intentions, emotional states, mood, etc. The externalization process corresponds to

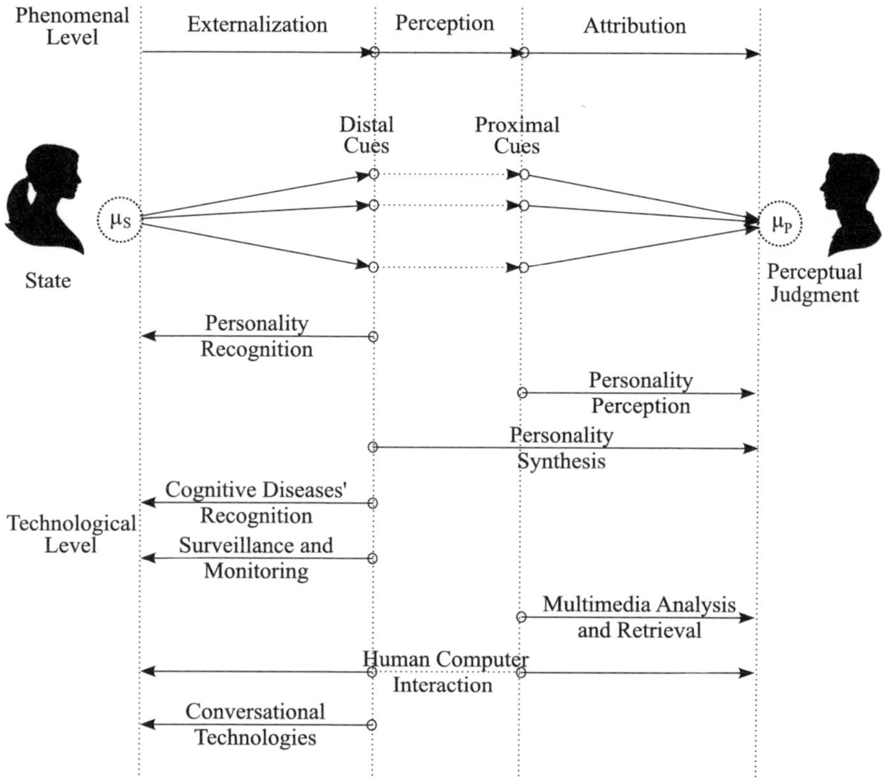

Fig. 6.1 The picture shows a simplified version of Brunswik's lens. At the phenomenal level, the *left side* is the externalization (people manifest their inner state through distal cues), the central part is the perception (physiological, cultural and cognitive phenomena transform distal cues into proximal cues), the *right side* is the attribution (observer attribute states and make perceptual judgments). At the technological level, every SSP research problem targets one of the elements of the Brunswik's lens

the left side of Fig. 6.1 and results into *distal cues*, i.e. any form of evidence that can be perceived by others.

Of all possible distal cues, SSP focuses on nonverbal behaviour because of its primacy in social interactions and because it is *honest* [36], i.e. it leaks information about the actual state of an individual independently of her intention to do it. However, distal cues include many other overt behaviours like, e.g. the way people organize apartments and other spaces where they live [22], physiological signals (galvanic skin conductance, heartbeat, blood pressure, etc.) [38], written texts [60] and, recently, electronic traces left via mobile phones [44] and social media [64]. Potentially, every cue can become a social signal, i.e. a form of evidence that conveys socially relevant information.

Research efforts revolving around the externalization process, i.e. aimed at automatically detecting distal cues and mapping them into inner states of an individual, can be considered an SSP relevant effort. In the case of nonverbal communication, this includes the two major research lines outlined in Sect. 6.1: detection and interpretation of nonverbal cues, and analysis and synthesis of major social and psychological phenomena. From an application point of view, this part of the Brunswik's lens encompasses, e.g. detection of cognitive and developmental problems like autism, Alzheimer's disease, depression, etc. (see Sect. 6.3.2), or personalization of devices based on emotional state or personality traits (see Sect. 6.3.5).

6.2.2 Perception

Once distal cues are perceived by an observer (the person on the right side of Fig. 6.1), they undergo a perception process and are transformed into *proximal cues*, i.e. the cues actually at disposition of our cognition. The perception includes physiological processes through which physical signals are transformed into percepts as well as cultural, psychological and cognitive biases that can influence our perception of others and of the social landscape. While no major efforts have been done to take into account physiological perception processes, cognitive and psychological aspects have been extensively studied in SSP [10, 30, 39].

From a technological point of view, this is the part of the Brunswik's lens that has been addressed least, if it has been at all. The main probable reason is that the computing community, where SSP is born and it is developing, has no familiarity with the methods used in perception physiology. Furthermore, the development of cognitive and psychological models requires one to address problems that are out of reach for computing approaches because they are based on evidence that cannot be detected with sensors and cannot be modelled in mathematical and statistical terms. To the best of our knowledge, there are no application or research efforts associated to this part of the Brunswik's lens in the SSP community.

6.2.3 Attribution

The last part of the Brunswik's Lens corresponds to the *attribution*, i.e. the process that maps *proximal cues* into *judgments*. In other words, the attribution process is responsible for opinions and beliefs that people develop about others. The important aspect of the attribution process is that judgments are not necessarily accurate (e.g. an observer can attribute personality traits to another person that do not correspond to the actual traits of this latter), but explain how observers behave towards observed individuals.

From a technological point of view, the research lines working on this part of the lens are the efforts aimed at developing machines that stimulate the attribution of predefined characteristics (e.g. the synthesis of voices that sound extravert or the development of artificial agents that look competent), and the development of technologies aimed at understanding social phenomena where the way people perceive others plays a role (e.g. conflict, personality, leadership, disagreement, roles, etc.). From the point of view of the applications, this part of the lens encompasses, e.g. multimedia retrieval approaches taking into account the effect data produces on users (see Sect. 6.3.4) or conversational technologies (see Sect. 6.3.6).

In principle, research approaches targeting the attribution process should make use of proximal cues. However, to the best of our knowledge, all current technologies use distal cues instead. The main probable reason is the lack of efforts aimed at modelling the perception process (see Sect. 6.2.2).

6.3 State of the Art

This section proposes a survey of the most recent work in SSP, with particular attention to phenomena that have been extensively investigated in the last years.

6.3.1 Personality

Personality computing [64], the development of technologies dealing with human personality, is an emerging SSP trend. The main reason behind the interest for personality is that such a construct captures reliably long-term behavioural tendencies and, therefore, it makes it easier to predict the behaviour of an individual. This is a major advantage for any technology expected to interact naturally with its users. Personality computing approaches target both externalization and attribution processes (see Sect. 6.2). In the former case, the goal is to automatically predict *self-assessed* traits, i.e. the traits that people attribute to themselves (Automatic Personality Recognition, APR). In the latter case, the goal is to predict the traits that people are attributed by others (Automatic Personality Perception, APP) or to artificially generate behavioural cues that convey predefined personality impressions (Automatic Personality Synthesis, APS).

In the case of APP and APR, the typical approach is to automatically infer personality traits from observable behavioural traces. These latter include written texts [4], nonverbal behaviour [68], social media profiles [42, 43], gaming behaviour [72, 74], use of mobile and wearable devices [57], etc. In most cases, the task actually performed by the approaches proposed in the literature is to predict whether a person is above or below a threshold (typically median or average of the observed personality scores) along a certain trait [64]. Only in a few cases, the approaches target the actual continuous scores associated to the traits of an individual. In the case of APS, the typical approach is to generate artificial behavioural cues aimed at stimulating the attribution of desired personality traits [29, 31, 58, 59]. The most common forms of embodiment adopted to generate cues are synthetic voices, robots and artificial agents, etc.

6.3.2 Cognitive, Mental and Developmental Problems

The detection of cognitive, mental and developmental problems—e.g. depression, Alzheimer, autism, Asperger syndrome, etc—is another domain that attracts significant attention in the SSP community. The reason is that the health problems above leave traces in the way people behave. Therefore, SSP methodologies appear to be particularly suitable. Furthermore, behavioural analysis is particularly effective for children that do not speak or for patients that are at the earliest stage of their pathology and, therefore, manifest only minor deviations with respect to their normal behaviour. Overall, the approaches of this domain focus on the externalization part of the conceptual map (see Sect. 6.2), the reason being that health conditions are an actual state of people and not something that others attribute to them.

A large number of efforts have focused on autism in young children, but more recent efforts target problems that have a major societal impact such as depression [63] or ageing-related cognitive deterioration. Besides providing diagnostic tools, SSP research in the field tries to improve the condition of the patients through treatments like the use of robots for helping autistic children to interact better [18] or assistive robots that help people with physical and/or mental problems.

6.3.3 Proxemics and Surveillance

The main goal of surveillance technologies is to monitor the behaviour of people in environments where safety and security are at risk, whether this means to follow workers that operate potentially harmful devices in an industrial plant, to detect criminal behaviour in public spaces or to check whether people flow without problems through the alleys of a station. For at least two decades, surveillance research has focused on the sole technology, i.e. people were tracked and analyzed like any other target in videos and audio recordings. In recent years, the research community has realized that analysing the behaviour of people can benefit from the integration of social psychology findings [15], especially when it comes to proxemics (the use of space as a means to convey social meaning [14]). Several approaches have then tried to detect F-formations, the typical spatial arrangements that people form when they interact with one another, or to take into account social force models in the movement, apparently random, of pedestrians on the street.

In ultimate analysis, the goal of most surveillance approaches is to support the decision of human operators on whether it is necessary to intervene in a situation under observation or not. This requires one to know the actual intentions and attitudes of people and, therefore, surveillance technologies tend to target the externalization problem (see Sect. 6.2 and Fig. 6.1).

6.3.4 Multimedia Analysis

The effect known as *Media Equation* [46] shows that people do not make any difference, from a cognitive point of view, between individuals they meet face-to-face and individuals they see in videos or hear in audio recordings. This suggests that multimedia material should be indexed not only in terms of visual and acoustic properties (like it typically happens in multimedia indexing and retrieval technologies), but also in terms of social, psychological and cognitive effects they induce in their consumers.

The literature proposes several trends that go in the direction outlined above. Human-centered Implicit Tagging is the attempt of tagging multimedia data in terms of the behavioural reactions they stimulate in data consumers (e.g. a video that makes people laugh will be tagged as *funny*) [34]. In parallel, the literature has proposed several approaches aimed at predicting the emotion that people experience in consuming multimedia data based on measurable characteristics of these latter such as colour (in the case of pictures) [73] or beat (in the case of music) [27]. More recently, the literature has proposed that the data people exchange in social media (e.g. pictures on Flickr or videos on Vine) might work as a social signal, i.e. it might play in social media interactions the same role that nonverbal cues play in face-to-face interactions [16].

The research trends described in this section tend to target the attribution component of the conceptual map proposed in Sect. 6.2 (see Fig. 6.1). The reason is that these technologies are based on what people perceive in the data and not on the actual content of this latter.

6.3.5 Human–Computer Interaction

Research on Human–Computer Interaction has explored for two decades the tendency of people to attribute typically human characteristics (e.g. personality traits and intentions) to machines [32], especially when these display human-like behaviour and features like virtual agents or social robots [20]. Therefore, it is not surprising to observe that SSP approaches target Human–Computer Interaction and, in particular leverage on "on the power and potential of unconsciously conveyed attentive and emotional information to facilitate human–machine interaction" [2].

Recent examples include the detection of hesitations in movie-on-demand systems [70], the analysis of gazing behaviour in image consumption [45], or the design of uncomfortable experiences [7]. SSP-oriented HCI approaches cover both externalization and attribution processes in the conceptual map of Fig. 6.1. The former aim at understanding the user (the machine needs to know the internal state of the user), the latter aim at displaying cues and behaviours that stimulate the attribution of desirable characteristics.

6.3.6 Conversational Technologies

Conversation is the "primary site of human sociality" [53] and it remains the subject of extensive efforts in SSP, whether conversation takes place face-to-face, through the phone or, more recently, via social media and chats. Most efforts in this area aim at inferring the social phenomena taking place in a conversation from the nonverbal cues that people display. The spectrum of phenomena being addressed in this way is wide and it includes conflict [64], dominance [25], mimicry [19], group dynamics [37], negotiation [17], engagement [49] and the list could continue. As a confirmation of the primacy of conversational technologies, the European Commission is making major efforts toward the definition of a Roadmap for the development of technologies dealing with conversation [47].

Approaches in this domain tend to focus on externalization processes (the typical goal is to understand automatically the state of the people involved in a conversation), but a few approaches consider attribution processes as well, given that these drive the behaviour of one person towards the others [62].

6.4 A Methodological Map of Social Signal Processing

Figure 6.2 proposes a methodological map of SSP, i.e. a scheme showing the main issues to be addressed in order to develop an effective approach. The upper part corresponds to the *analysis* problem, i.e. the inference of social and psychological phenomena from observable, machine-detectable behaviour. The lower part corresponds to the *synthesis* problem, i.e. the generation of artificial behaviours aimed at conveying the same socially relevant messages as the natural ones.

In the case of the analysis problem, the main issues to be addressed are *sensing*, *data*, *detection* and *modelling*. The first step corresponds to capture and recording of physical signals expected to account for the behaviours under observation. The most common sensors are microphones and cameras, but the recent years have witnessed the proliferation of other sensing devices. In most cases, these address observable behaviour (e.g. wearable devices, RGBD cameras, etc.). However, it is increasingly more frequent to capture physiological signals (e.g. skin conductance,

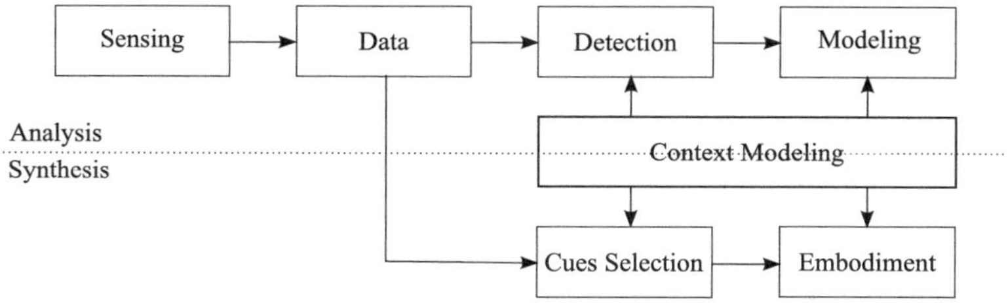

Fig. 6.2 The picture shows a methodological map of SSP. The *upper* part shows the synthesis an the *lower* one shows the synthesis. In the first case, the main steps are sensing, data (design and collection), detection and modelling (including interpretation). In the second case, the main steps are the selection of the cues and then the embodiment

blood pressure, etc.) that, while not fully fitting the most common definitions of behaviour, still provide useful information about interacting people.

Unlike in other domains, data is not just passive material to be processed and analyzed, but the first step towards the development of an effective approach. In fact, it is through collection and observation of data that it is possible to establish a relationship between behaviour and social phenomena. The data collection typically involves the design of setting and scenario, namely the conditions in which subjects interact (with other people and/or with machines) and the particular tasks and goals to be achieved during the interaction. Furthermore, data collection includes often *annotation* and *modelling*. The former refers to the creation of metadata showing events of interest in the data (e.g. occurrences of a given behavioural cue), the latter to the collection of psychometric questionnaires and/or ratings that describe in quantitative terms the social phenomena taking place in the data [67, 69].

The rest of the process includes approaches aimed at detection and modelling of nonverbal behavioural cues in the signals captured with the sensors above. While the analysis of audio and video recordings can rely on the extensive experience accumulated in communities like speech processing and computer vision, the analysis of data collected with more recent sensors is still relatively unexplored.

In the case of synthesis (see lower part of Fig. 6.2), the main issues to be addressed are the *cues' selection* and the form of *embodiment*. The most common forms of embodiment include synthetic speech, virtual agents and robots. Depending on the particular form of embodiment, it will be possible to generate certain behaviours, but not others. Major efforts have been done in the case expressive speech synthesis (whatever is the form of embodiment, social machines tend to speak because this is necessary to transmit any information) and facial expression animation. In the last years, increasingly more attention is being dedicated to the combination of multiple cues and, furthermore, to the ability of an artificial agent to display a cue at the right moment. When the form of embodiment is a robot, it becomes possible to implement proxemic cues (e.g. the distance with respect to users) or touch behaviours that are not possible with non-embodied agents.

6.5 Open Issues and Challenges

This section proposes the main issues and challenges that the community currently recognizes as crucial for the progress of the domain.

6.5.1 The Data

Data plays a crucial role in SSP. Collecting corpora of social interactions is typically the first step towards the development of an effective approach. The main reason is that the observation of interacting people—to be performed according to rigorous practices developed in domains like social psychology, anthropology, ethology, etc. [6, 28]—is probably the only way to measure in quantitative terms the relationship between overt, machine-detectable behaviour and social or psychological phenomena typically targeted in SSP. In absence of such a relationship, SSP approaches cannot work properly.

The lifecycle of a corpus includes three main stages: collection, annotation and distribution. The collection is performed with a wide spectrum of sensors and for a diverse range of purposes [66]. The use of microphones and cameras is ubiquitous because these instruments correspond to our main senses (hearing and sight) and, furthermore, speech processing and computer vision attract major attention in the scientific community. However, it is not uncommon to collect data with wearable devices and, in recent years, with physiological sensors.

The annotation is the step during which the raw data captured with sensors is enriched with metadata that accounts for the observation made over the corpus (e.g. timing and duration of specific cues, psychometric questionnaires filled by the subjects appearing in the data, etc.). This is an expensive and time-consuming step, but it makes the difference between data that can actually be beneficial for SSP and data that cannot. In this case as well, there is a standardization problem and there is no format that is widely accepted and recognized by the community [26]. This slows down the progress because it is not possible to build instruments that can work on all possible data and no interoperability can be guaranteed.

Besides the technical limitations, the annotation step involves scientific problems as well. Social phenomena are *situated*, i.e. they depend on the specific context where they are observed. However, annotations rarely take into account such an aspect and this might lead to inappropriate generalizations of the results obtained over one particular corpus. A possible solution is to adopt the notion of *genre* [8] as a way to distinguish between general types of interaction, but it is still unclear how different genres can be identified and defined. Furthermore, SSP effort have insisted mainly on nonverbal communication, but the semantic component of communication is important as well. Therefore, annotations should take into account transcriptions of what people say and, correspondingly, indication about the interaction between verbal and nonverbal component.

Finally, data distribution has a crucial impact on SSP progress because it allows different groups to work on the same data, possibly using the same protocols, and rigorously compare their respective results (see, e.g. the results obtained in recent benchmarking campaigns [56]). The main limitations here are not only logistic—publicly available data is distributed across a large number of sources—but also legal and ethical. In particular, the distribution of the data must take into account copyright and intellectual property regulations as well as the respect of ethical and privacy issues related to data about human subjects. In this respect as well, a standardization approach can be of major benefit for the community [47].

6.5.2 Detection: Taking into Account More Physical Traces

The key-idea of SSP is that nonverbal communication is the physical, machine-detectable trace of social and psychological phenomena [66, 68]. The reasons for focusing on nonverbal communication are multiple. Nonverbal cues are *honest* [35], i.e. they cannot be fully controlled and, therefore, leak information about the actual inner state of people independently of their intention to do so. Nonverbal cues can be accessed via common, unobtrusive sensors (see Sect. 6.5.1) that allow people to interact naturally. Furthermore, focusing on nonverbal communication allows one to avoid the automatic transcription of what people say, a task that is technologically difficult and it is a potential threat for the respect of peoples' privacy.

However, most of the attention focused on a relatively few nonverbal cues (e.g. facial expressions and prosody) and, furthermore, any other potential physical trace of social and psychological phenomena has been largely neglected. Addressing these two limitations can be of major help for the progress of the domain.

Recent attempts to consider nonverbal cues neglected so far include the analysis of head movements [23], the modelling of facial appearance [1, 33], the motor activation of people speaking through the phone [51] or the detection of F-formations in public spaces [24]. In all cases, the cues have proved to be as effective as the ones that are most commonly adopted in the state of the art. Therefore, at least part of the SSP progress can pass through the development of approaches aimed at detection and interpretation of less common cues.

In parallel, SSP approaches can be enriched by taking into account other physical traces left by social and psychological phenomena. The application of techniques like the *Linguistic Inquiry Word Count* [60] or statistically oriented language models [21] can help to include the verbal aspects of human–human communication. The goal is not to model what people say, but to investigate whether the choice and the use of the words reflect social and psychological phenomena, like widely demonstrated in sociolinguistics. Another important direction is the use of physiological changes, including galvanic skin conductance, heartbeat, blood pressure and, more recently, the change on hormones' concentration [71]. Biological signals cannot be considered overt behaviour (they cannot be observed and they are not under the control of people), but they can still help machines to better understand human behaviour.

Still, all directions above (using more cues, taking into account language and measuring physiological processes) should consider that all physical traces are situated (see Sect. 6.5.1) and, therefore, should be considered only in conjunction with the context where they are used.

6.5.3 Improving Modelling Approaches

Most of the SSP work consists in bridging the gap between observable, machine-detectable evidence and social and psychological phenomena, non accessible to sensory experience. In general, this is performed by using statistical models such as classifiers or regressors depending on the particular psychometric questionnaires being used in the experiments. Research on statistical models is carried out in fields such as machine learning and pattern recognition, but there are specific needs that emerge in the case of SSP and, more in general, in the case of Human Behaviour Understanding. These include the development of models that explain the results, i.e. allow one not only to achieve good classification and regression performances, but also to explain the results, possibly in semantic terms [13]. The second is the development of models that take into account the cognitive processes underlying social interactions [41].

Automatic understanding of behaviour means to convert low-level features extracted from sensors' signals into human-understable constructs such as actions, personality traits, emotions, etc. The process may be helped by grounding it with a prior semantic model, which may describe psychological knowledge and operate during both learning and inference. This semantic layer can be represented by means of an ontology (or a set of ontologies), intended as a set of primitive concepts and relations expressed by axioms providing an interpretation to the vocabulary chosen for the description of a behaviour (e.g. gestures, facial expressions, etc.) [13]. Given that one of the main goals of SSP is to make machines capable to understand humans like humans do, the semantic layer above should take into account the typical cognitive processes that underly social exchanges like, e.g. "(1) (joint) attention and saliency, (2) common ground, conceptual semantic spaces and representation learning, (3) fusion across time, modalities and cognitive representation layers, and (4) dual-system processing (system one vs. system two) and cognitive decision nonlinearities" [41].

6.5.4 Challenges of Embodiment

The expression "embodied agents" defines technologies like social robots, conversational agents, avatars, etc. that interact with their users with the help of a physical body. An embodied agent must understand and interpret the behaviour of its users and, hence, address the issues outlined in Sects. 6.5.2 and 6.5.3. Furthermore, it must address problems related to the fact that and embodied agent, at least in principle, should be capable to interact with its users over an extended period of time—possibly the entire life in the case of a companion robot—and in a wide spectrum of different contexts and situations [50].

In this respect, the main open issues include [3] the use of sensory modalities that so far have been neglected (e.g. olfact, haptics, etc.), the integration of pragmatics and semantics in the analysis of social cues (see Sect. 6.5.3), the adoption of experience based learning approaches for adapting the agents to different contexts and, related to this latter, the ability to situate users' behaviour in a specific setting.

6.5.5 Applications

Like any other technological domain, SSP aims at having an impact not only in terms of scientific advancement, but also in terms of real-world applications. Therefore, it is not surprising to observe that companies start commercializing products and services that rely on detection and understanding of social signals. It is, e.g. the case of Cogito[1] and EngageM8[2] that support the activities of call centre agents, or the Behavioural Insights Team,[3] an institution that leverages on social psychology research to design better public policies. Furthermore, several initiatives aim at bridging the gap between SSP oriented research and the market like, e.g. ROCKIT[4] (focusing on conversational technologies) and euRobotics[5] (focusing on robots).

Major efforts are being spent towards the application of SSP technologies in healthcare, especially when it comes to developmental and cognitive diseases that leave traces in behaviour like, e.g. autism and depression (see Sect. 6.3.2). Furthermore, given the crucial role of the interaction between doctors and patients in medical treatments, some of the efforts dedicated to the development of virtual agents focuses in particular on medical contexts [48]. Other important results can be observed in multimedia retrieval applications where personality traits are used to adapt systems to specific users and hesitation is detected to help users in achieving their goals. Furthermore, several robotic toys such as AIBO[6] display social signals expected to engage the users and the gaming industry is exploring the possibility of using players' behavioural feedback to improve the playing experience.

[1] http://www.cogitocorp.com.

[2] http://www.engagem8.com.

[3] http://www.behaviouralinsights.co.uk.

[4] http://groupspaces.com/ROCKIT.

[5] http://www.eu-robotics.net.

[6] http://www.sony-aibo.co.uk.

6.6 Conclusions

This chapter has proposed an overview of Social Signal Processing in both conceptual and methodological terms. From a conceptual point of view, the chapter establishes a parallel between relevant psychological processes (externalization, perception and attribution) on one hand and, on the other hand, on the typical tasks addressed by SSP technologies (recognition, synthesis and perception). From a methodological point of view, the chapter identifies the main technological problems underlying an SSP approach and, correspondingly, the main issues and challenges still open in the community.

After the earliest pioneering stages—the expression Social Signal Processing was coined less than ten years ago [35]—agenda and scope of the domain are well defined [68], but are still open to changes and evolution. So far the domain has focused mainly on nonverbal cues exchanged during face-to-face interactions, in line with the earliest definitions of the field [66]. However, recent developments promise to extend the interests of SSP in directions that were not planned initially.

Physiological and biological processes accompanying social signals attract increasingly more interest. This happens for two main reasons: the first is that physiological sensors become less expensive and obtrusive. The second is that the relationship between overt behaviour on one side and neural processes, hormonal changes and physiology on the other side appears to be stable and reliable enough to be modelled with statistical approaches. In parallel, the extensive use of social media and mobile technologies shows that fully technological actions (e.g. posting a picture, "liking" an item posted online or filling an online profile) act as social signals and convey the same type of socially relevant information that nonverbal cues do. Last, but not least, SSP technologies are now leaving the laboratory to be applied in real-world technologies and this is likely to introduce new problems and research avenues.

The new avenues briefly outlined above do not fit entirely the original scope of the field, but will definitely contribute to its original goals and purposes, i.e. to make technology socially intelligent and capable to seamlessly integrate human–human interactions.

References

1. Al Moubayed, N., Vazquez-Alvarez, Y., McKay, A., Vinciarelli, A.: Face-based automatic personality perception. In: Proceedings of the ACM International Conference on Multimedia, pp. 1153–1156 (2014)
2. André, E.: Exploiting unconscious user signals in multimodal human-computer interaction. ACM Trans. Multimedia Comput. Commun. Appl. **9**(1s), 48 (2013)
3. André, E.: Challenges for social embodiment. In: Proceedings of the Workshop on Roadmapping the Future of Multimodal Interaction Research Including Business Opportunities and Challenges, pp. 35–37 (2014)

4. Argamon, S., Dhawle, S., Koppel, M., Pennbaker, J.: Lexical predictors of personality type. In: Proceedings of Interface and the Classification Society of North America (2005)
5. Avril, M., Leclere, C., Viaux-Savelon, S., Michelet, S., Achard, C., Missonnier, S., Keren, M., Cohen, D., Chetouani, M.: Social signal processing for studying parent-infant interaction. Frontiers Psychol. **5**, 1437 (2014)
6. Bakeman, R., Gottman, J.: Observing Interaction: An Introduction to Sequential Analysis. Cambridge University Press (1997)
7. Benford, S., Greenhalgh, C., Giannachi, G., Walker, B., Marshall, J., Rodden, T.: Uncomfortable interactions. In: Proceedings of the SIGCHI Conference on Human Factors in Computing Systems, pp. 2005–2014. ACM (2012)
8. Bonin, F., Gilmartin, E., Vogel, C., Campbell, N.: Topics for the future: genre differentiation, annotation, and linguistic content integration in interaction analysis. In: Proceedings of the Workshop on Roadmapping the Future of Multimodal Interaction Research Including Business Opportunities and Challenges, pp. 5–8 (2014)
9. Bousmalis, K., Méhu, M., Pantic, M.: Spotting agreement and disagreement: a survey of nonverbal audiovisual cues and tools. In: Proceedings of Social Signal Processing Workshop, pp. 1–9 (2009)
10. Brunet, P., Cowie, R.: Towards a conceptual framework of research on social signal processing. J. Multimodal User Interfaces **6**(3–4), 101–115 (2012)
11. Brunet, P.M., Cowie, R., Heylen, D., Nijholt, A., Schroeder, M.: Conceptual frameworks for multimodal social signal processing. J. Multimodal User Interfaces **6**(3–4), 1–5 (2012)
12. Brunswik, E.: Perception and the Representative Design of Psychological Experiments. University of California Press (1956)
13. Cristani, M., Ferrario, R.: Statistical pattern recognition meets formal ontologies: towards a semantic visual understanding. In: Proceedings of the Workshop on Roadmapping the Future of Multimodal Interaction Research Including Business Opportunities and Challenges, pp. 23–25 (2014)
14. Cristani, M., Paggetti, G., Vinciarelli, A., Bazzani, L., Menegaz, G., Murino, V.: Towards computational proxemics: inferring social relations from interpersonal distances. In: Proceedings of IEEE International Conference on Social Computing, pp. 290–297 (2011)
15. Cristani, M., Raghavendra, R., Del Bue, A., Murino, V.: Human behavior analysis in video surveillance: a social signal processing perspective. Neurocomputing **100**, 86–97 (2013)
16. Cristani, M., Vinciarelli, A., Segalin, C., Perina, A.: Unveiling the multimedia unconscious: implicit cognitive processes and multimedia content analysis. In: Proceedings of the ACM International Conference on Multimedia, pp. 213–222. ACM (2013)
17. Curhan, J.R., Pentland, A.: Thin slices of negotiation: predicting outcomes from conversational dynamics within the first 5 minutes. J. Appl. Psychol. **92**(3), 802 (2007)
18. Dautenhahn, K., Werry, I.: Towards interactive robots in autism therapy: background, motivation and challenges. Pragmat. Cogn. **12**(1), 1–35 (2004)
19. Delaherche, E., Chetouani, M., Mahdhaoui, A., Saint-Georges, C., Viaux, S., Cohen, D.: Interpersonal synchrony: a survey of evaluation methods across disciplines. IEEE Trans. Affect. Comput. **3**(3), 349–365 (2012)
20. Fong, T., Nourbakhsh, I., Dautenhahn, K.: A survey of socially interactive robots. Rob. Auton. Syst. **42**(3), 143–166 (2003)
21. Garg, N.P., Favre, S., Salamin, H., Hakkani Tür, D., Vinciarelli, A.: Role recognition for meeting participants: an approach based on lexical information and social network analysis. In: Proceedings of the ACM International Conference on Multimedia, pp. 693–696 (2008)
22. Gosling, S.D., Ko, S.J., Mannarelli, T., Morris, M.E.: A room with a cue: personality judgments based on offices and bedrooms. J. Pers. Soc. Psychol. **82**(3), 379 (2002)
23. Hammal, Z., Cohn, J.F.: Intra- and interpersonal functions of head motion in emotion communication. In: Proceedings of the Workshop on Roadmapping the Future of Multimodal Interaction Research Including Business Opportunities and Challenges, pp. 19–22 (2014)
24. Hung, H., Kroese, B.: Detecting F-formations as dominant sets. In: Proceedings of the International Conference on Multimodal Interfaces, pp. 231–238 (2011)

25. Jayagopi, D.B., Hung, H., Yeo, C., Gatica-Perez, D.: Modeling dominance in group conversations using nonverbal activity cues. IEEE Trans. Audio Speech Lang. Process. **17**(3), 501–513 (2009)
26. Koutsombogera, M., Papageorgiou, H.: Multimodal analytics and its data ecosystem. In: Proceedings of the Workshop on Roadmapping the Future of Multimodal Interaction Research Including Business Opportunities and Challenges, pp. 1–4 (2014)
27. Lu, L., Liu, D., Zhang, H.-J.: Automatic mood detection and tracking of music audio signals. IEEE Trans. Audio Speech Lang. Process. **14**(1), 5–18 (2006)
28. Martin, P., Bateson, P.: Measuring Behaviour. Cambridge University Press (2007)
29. McRorie, Margaret, Sneddon, Ian, McKeown, Gary, Bevacqua, Elisabetta, de Sevin, Etienne, Pelachaud, Catherine: Evaluation of four designed virtual agent personalities. IEEE Trans. Affect. Comput. **3**(3), 311–322 (2011)
30. Mehu, M., Scherer, K.: A psycho-ethological approach to social signal processing. Cogn. Process. **13**(2), 397–414 (2012)
31. Nass, C., Brave, S.: Wired for Speech: How Voice Activates and Advances the Human-Computer relationship. The MIT Press (2005)
32. Nass, C., Steuer, J., Tauber, E.R.: Computers are social actors. In: Proceedings of the SIGCHI Conference on Human Factors in Computing Systems, pp. 72–78 (1994)
33. Nie, J., Cui, P., Yan, Y., Huang, L., Li, Z., Wei, Z.: How your portrait impresses people?: inferring personality impressions from portrait contents. In: Proceedings of the ACM International Conference on Multimedia, pp. 905–908 (2014)
34. Pantic, M., Vinciarelli, A.: Implicit human-centered tagging [social sciences]. IEEE Sign. Process. Mag. **26**(6), 173–180 (2009)
35. Pentland, A.: Social signal processing. IEEE Sign. Proces. Mag. **24**(4), 108–111 (2007)
36. Pentland, A.: Honest Signals. MIT Press (2010)
37. Pianesi, F., Zancanaro, M., Not, E., Leonardi, C., Falcon, V., Lepri, B.: Multimodal support to group dynamics. Pers. Ubiquit. Comput. **12**(3), 181–195 (2008)
38. Picard, R.W., Vyzas, E., Healey, J.: Toward machine emotional intelligence: analysis of affective physiological state. IEEE Trans. Pattern Anal. Mach. Intell. **23**(10), 1175–1191 (2001)
39. Poggi, I., D'Errico, F.: Social signals: a framework in terms of goals and beliefs. Cogn. Process. **13**(2), 427–445 (2012)
40. Poppe, R.: A survey on vision-based human action recognition. Image Vis. Comput. **28**(6), 976–990 (2010)
41. Potamianos, A.: Cognitive multimodal processing: from signal to behavior. In: Proceedings of the Workshop on Roadmapping the Future of Multimodal Interaction Research Including Business Opportunities and Challenges, pp. 27–34 (2014)
42. Quercia, D., Kosinski, M., Stillwell, D., Crowcroft, J.: Our twitter profiles, our selves: predicting personality with twitter. In: Proceedings of the IEEE International Conference on Social Computing, pp. 180–185 (2011)
43. Quercia, D., Lambiotte, R., Stillwell, D., Kosinski, M., Crowcroft, J.: The personality of popular facebook users. In: Proceedings of the ACM Conference on Computer Supported Cooperative Work, pp. 955–964 (2012)
44. Raento, M., Oulasvirta, A., Eagle, N.: Smartphones an emerging tool for social scientists. Sociol. Methods Res. **37**(3), 426–454 (2009)
45. Ramanathan, S., Katti, H., Sebe, N., Kankanhalli, M., Chua, T.-S.: An eye fixation database for saliency detection in images. In: Proceedings of European Conference on Computer Vision, pp. 30–43 (2010)
46. Reeves, B., Nass, C.: The media equation: how people treat computers, television, and new media like real people and places. Cambridge University Press (1996)
47. Renals, S., Carletta, J., Edwards, K., Bourlard, H., Garner, P., Popescu-Belis, A., Klakow, D., Girenko, A., Petukova, V., Wacker, P., Joscelyne, A., Kompis, C., Aliwell, S., Stevens, W., Sabbah, Y.: ROCKIT: roadmap for conversational interaction technologies. In: Proceedings of the Workshop on Roadmapping the Future of Multimodal Interaction Research Including Business Opportunities and Challenges, pp. 39–42 (2014)

48. Riccardi, G.: Towards healthcare personal agents. In: Proceedings of the Workshop on Roadmapping the Future of Multimodal Interaction Research Including Business Opportunities and Challenges, pp. 53–56 (2014)
49. Sabourin, J.L., Lester, J.C.: Affect and engagement in game-based learning environments. IEEE Trans. Affect. Comput. **5**(1), 45–56 (2014)
50. Salah, A.A.: Natural multimodal interaction with a social robot: what are the premises? In: Proceedings of the Workshop on Roadmapping the Future of Multimodal Interaction Research Including Business Opportunities and Challenges, pp. 43–45 (2014)
51. Salamin, H., Polychroniou, A., Vinciarelli, A.: Automatic recognition of personality and conflict handling style in mobile phone conversations. In: Proceedings of International Workshop on Image Analysis for Multimedia Interactive Services, pp. 1–4 (2013)
52. Sanchez-Cortes, D., Aran, O., Schmid-Mast, M., Gatica-Perez, D.: A nonverbal behavior approach to identify emergent leaders in small groups. IEEE Trans. Multimedia **14**(3), 816–832 (2012)
53. Schegloff, E.A.: Analyzing single episodes of interaction: an exercise in conversation analysis. Soc. Psychol. Q. 101–114 (1987)
54. Schroeder, M.: Expressive speech synthesis: past, present, and possible futures. In: Affective information processing, pp. 111–126. Springer (2009)
55. Schuller, B., Batliner, A.: Computational Paralinguistics: Emotion, Affect and Personality in Speech and Language Processing. Wiley (2013)
56. Schuller, B., Steidl, S., Batliner, A., Noeth, E., Vinciarelli, A., Burkhardt, F., van Son, R., Weninger, F., Eyben, F., Bocklet, T., Mohammadi, G., Weiss, B.: A survey on perceived speaker traits: personality, likability, pathology, and the first challenge. Comput. Speech Lang. **29**(1), 100–131 (2015)
57. Staiano, J., Pianesi, F., Lepri, B., Sebe, N., Aharony, N., Pentland, A.: Friends don't lie—inferring personality traits from social network structure. In: Proceedings of the ACM International Conference on Ubiquitous Computing, pp. 321–330 (2012)
58. Tapus, A., Mataric, M.: Socially assistive robots: the link between personality, empathy, physiological signals, and task performance. In: Proceedings of AAAI Spring Symposium (2008)
59. Tapus, A., Ţăpuş, C., Mataric, M.J.: User–robot personality matching and assistive robot behavior adaptation for post-stroke rehabilitation therapy. Intell. Serv. Robot. **1**(2), 169–183 (2008)
60. Tausczik, Y.R., Pennebaker, J.W.: The psychological meaning of words: LIWC and computerized text analysis methods. J. Lang. Soc. Psychol. **29**(1), 24–54 (2010)
61. Tkalčič, M., Burnik, U., Košir, A.: Using affective parameters in a content-based recommender system for images. User Model. User Adap. Inter. **20**(4), 279–311 (2010)
62. Uleman, J.S., Newman, L.S., Moskowitz, G.B.: People as flexible interpreters: evidence and issues from spontaneous trait inference. Adv. Exp. Soc. Psychol. **28**, 211–279 (1996)
63. Valstar, M.: Automatic behaviour understanding in medicine. In: Proceedings of the Workshop on Roadmapping the Future of Multimodal Interaction Research Including Business Opportunities and Challenges, pp. 57–60 (2014)
64. Vinciarelli, A., Mohammadi, G.: A survey of personality computing. IEEE Trans. Affect. Comput. **5**(3), 273–291 (2014)
65. Vinciarelli, A., Pantic, M., Bourlard, H., Pentland, A.: Social signal processing: state-of-the-art and future perspectives of an emerging domain. In: Proceedings of the ACM International Conference on Multimedia, pp. 1061–1070 (2008)
66. Vinciarelli, A., Pantic, M., Bourlard, H.: Social signal processing: survey of an emerging domain. Image Vis. Comput. J. **27**(12), 1743–1759 (2009)
67. Vinciarelli, A., Kim, S., Valente, F., Salamin, H.: Collecting data for socially intelligent surveillance and monitoring approaches: the case of conflict in competitive conversations. In: Proceedings of the International Symposium on Communications, Control and Signal Processing, pp. 1–4 (2012)
68. Vinciarelli, A., Pantic, M., Heylen, D., Pelachaud, C., Poggi, I., D'Errico, F., Schroeder, M.: Bridging the gap between social animal and unsocial machine: a survey of social signal processing. IEEE Trans. Affect. Comput. **3**(1), 69–87 (2012)

69. Vinciarelli, A., Chatziioannou, P., Esposito, A.: When the words are not everything: the use of laughter, fillers, back-channel, silence and overlapping speech in phone calls. Frontiers Hum. Media Interact. (2015)
70. Vodlan, T., Tkalčič, M., Košir, A.: The impact of hesitation, a social signal, on a user's quality of experience in multimedia content retrieval. Multimedia Tools Appl. 1–26 (2014)
71. Weisman, O., Delaherche, E., Rondeau, M., Chetouani, M., Cohen, D., Feldman, R.: Oxytocin shapes parental motion during father-infant interaction. Biol. Lett. **9**(6), 20130828 (2013)
72. Yaakub, C.Y., Sulaiman, N., Kim, C.W.: A study on personality identification using game based theory. In: Proceedings of the International Conference on Computer Technology and Development, pp. 732–734 (2010)
73. Yanulevskaya, V., Uijlings, J., Bruni, E., Sartori, A., Zamboni, E., Bacci, F., Melcher, D., Sebe, N.: In the eye of the beholder: employing statistical analysis and eye tracking for analyzing abstract paintings. In: Proceedings of ACM International Conference on Multimedia, pp. 349–358 (2012)
74. Yee, N., Ducheneaut, N., Nelson, L., Likarish, P.: Introverted elves and conscientious gnomes: the expression of personality in world of warcraft. In: Proceedings of the Annual Conference on Human Factors in Computing Systems, pp. 753–762, Vancouver (2011)
75. Zhao, W., Chellappa, R., Phillips, P.J., Rosenfeld, A.: Face recognition: a literature survey. ACM Comput. Surv. **35**(4), 399–458 (2003)

Chapter 7
Sentiment Analysis in Social Streams

Hassan Saif, F. Javier Ortega, Miriam Fernández and Iván Cantador

Abstract In this chapter, we review and discuss the state of the art on sentiment analysis in social streams—such as web forums, microblogging systems, and social networks, aiming to clarify how user opinions, affective states, and intended emotional effects are extracted from user generated content, how they are modeled, and how they could be finally exploited. We explain why sentiment analysis tasks are more difficult for social streams than for other textual sources, and entail going beyond classic text-based opinion mining techniques. We show, for example, that social streams may use vocabularies and expressions that exist outside the mainstream of standard, formal languages, and may reflect complex dynamics in the opinions and sentiments expressed by individuals and communities.

7.1 Introduction

Sentiment Analysis is the field of study that analyzes the people's attitudes toward entities—individuals, organizations, products, services, events, and topics, and their attributes [36]; The attitudes may correspond to personal opinions and evaluations, affective states (sentiments and moods), or intended emotional effects. It represents a large problem space, covering different tasks, such as subjectivity identification, sentiment extraction and analysis, and opinion mining, to name a few.

H. Saif
Knowledge Media Institute, Milton Keynes, UK
e-mail: h.saif@open.ac.uk

F.J. Ortega
Universidad de Sevilla, Seville, Spain
e-mail: javierortega@us.es

M. Fernández
Knowledge Media Institute, Milton Keynes, UK
e-mail: m.fernandez@open.ac.uk

I. Cantador (✉)
Universidad Autónoma de Madrid, Madrid, Spain
e-mail: ivan.cantador@uam.es

M. Tkalčič et al. (eds.), *Emotions and Personality in Personalized Services*,
Human–Computer Interaction Series, DOI 10.1007/978-3-319-31413-6_7

Although some of the above tasks have been addressed on multimodal data sources—e.g., sentiment extraction in audio and video, from its origins, sentiment analysis has mainly focused on textual data sources [48]. Hence, it commonly refers to the use of natural language processing, text analysis, and computational linguistics to extract and exploit subjective information from text materials. In Chaps. 2 and 4 the reader can find overviews of the state of the art in affective information representation and acquisition for various modalities.

With the advent of the Social Web, the amount of text material is huge and grows exponentially every day. The Web is a source of up-to-date, never-ending streams of user-generated content; people communicate online with contacts in social networks, create or upload multimedia objects in online sharing sites, post comments, reviews and ratings in blogs and recommender systems, contribute to wiki-style repositories, and annotate resources in social tagging platforms.

The Web thus provides unstructured information about user opinions, moods and emotions, and tastes and interests, which may be of great utility to others, including consumers, companies, and governments. Hence, for instance, someone who wants to buy a camera may look in web forums for online opinions and reviews about different brands and models, while camera manufacturers implicitly/explicitly get feedback from customers to improve their products, and adapt their marketing strategies. Very interestingly, this information can go beyond reflecting the users' subjective evaluations and sentiments about entities and their changes over time, by triggering chains of reactions and new events. For instance, identifying the overall concern, expressed in social media, on certain political decision may impact the modification or rejection of such decision.

The interest and potential exploitation of sentiment analysis in *social streams*—understood as social media in which user-generated content emerges and changes rapidly and constantly, are evident, and have been shown in numerous domains and applications, like politics and e-government [6, 45, 77], education and e-learning [76], business and e-commerce [85], and entertainment [23, 72, 80]. The reader is referred to several chapters of this book for detailed surveys of particular applications of affective information by personalized services, specifically by recommender systems (Chaps. 9, 15 and 17), conversational systems (Chap. 10), multimedia retrieval systems (Chaps. 12 and 14), and e-learning systems (Chap. 13).

The high availability of user-generated content in social streams, nonetheless, comes with some challenges. The large volume of data makes difficult to get the relevant information in an efficient and effective way. Proposed techniques have to be simple enough to scale up, but have to deal with complex data. Some of these challenges are related to general natural language processing (NLP) approaches, such as opinion-feature association [31], opinion negation [32], irony and sarcasm [12, 18], and opinion spam [33]. Others, in contrast, are related to issues characteristic of online user-generated content, such as multiple languages, high level of ambiguity and polysemy, misspellings, and slang and swear words [70]. In this context, it is also important to mention the need of determining the users' reputation and trust. For certain topics, the majority opinion (i.e., the wisdom of the crowd) may be the best solution [49], while for others, only the experts' opinions should be the source of information to consider [87]. Another relevant issue is the existence of particular pieces and forms of information existing in social streams: explicit citations to users, groups, and organizations (e.g., *@robinwilliams* in Twitter), explicit forms for referring to concepts (e.g., Twitter hashtags *#comedian* and *#funny*), emoticons and slang terms noting emotions and moods (e.g., :D and *lol*), mechanisms to express interests and tastes (e.g., Facebook *likes*), and URLs to resources that complement posted information. There, the use of contextual metadata also plays a key role; extracting and mining time and geo-location metadata may be very valuable for sentiment analysis on dynamic and global social stream data.

In this chapter, we review and discuss the state of the art on sentiment analysis in social streams, describing how opinion and affective information is extracted, processed, modeled, and exploited, in comparison to classic text-based opinion mining techniques.

The chapter is structured as follows. In Sect. 7.2 we overview the research literature in sentiment analysis, focusing on the main addressed tasks and applied techniques. In Sect. 7.3 we provide a description of social media, characterizing the user-generated content and research challenges that arise from them. Next, in Sect. 7.4 we discuss sentiment analysis to social streams, and describe existing applications in such context. Finally, in Sect. 7.5 we discuss current and open research trends on Sentiment Analysis in social streams.

7.2 Sentiment Analysis

In the last 15 years, Sentiment Analysis and Opinion Mining have been fed by a number of research problems and opportunities of increasing importance and interest [48]. In this section, we review the main tasks addressed in the literature related to sentiment analysis, together with the different assumptions and approaches adopted. We then discuss some interesting proposals, resources, and techniques intended to deal with those tasks.

7.2.1 Sentiment Analysis Tasks

The different sentiment analysis tasks can be categorized based on the granularity of their linguistic units they consider. In this sense, there are tasks where the document is assumed to be the main linguistic unit as a whole, while there are others where sentences or even words are considered as linguistic units. We can summarize these levels as follows:

- *Document-level*: At this level, it is assumed that each document expresses a particular sentiment, or at least it poses a predominant one. Many works have faced sentiment analysis tasks at the document level; see for example the survey presented in [78].

- *Sentence-level*: Some tasks could benefit from the determination of the sentiment in a text at a sentence level, as done in information extraction and question answering systems, where it is necessary to provide the user with particular information for a given topic.
- *Aspect-level*: In general, a sentence can contain more than one opinion about different aspects of an entity or topic. In an aspect-level approach, the context of the words are taken into account to determine the subjectivity of each expression in a sentence, and the specific aspect being opinionated [82, 84]. This level can be useful, for example, in recommender systems [13], and in automatic processing of product reviews [16, 44], where knowing individual opinions about each feature of a given product is crucial for the performance of the system.
- *Word-level* (also called as *entity level*): In this category, we can find those tasks consisting of identifying the sentiment expressed by a given word regardless it context. Word-level analysis is useful in order to build resources like sentiment lexicons with the possible sentiment orientations of a word [29, 64].

Another possible classification of sentiment analysis tasks can be made from the point of view of the dependency on the target domain. While some tasks are defined independently of the domain of application—like subjectivity detection, some research works have shown the influence of domain-dependency on sentiment analysis problems—e.g., polarity detection [16, 52, 53, 83].

In general, the following are the main goals of sentiment analysis:

- *Subjectivity detection*. Identifying subjective and objective statements.
- *Polarity opinion detection*. Identifying positive and negative opinions within subjective texts.
- *Emotion detection*. Identifying human emotions and moods.

Subjectivity detection can provide valuable knowledge to diverse NLP-based applications. In principle, any system intended to extract pieces of information from a large collection of texts could take advantage of subjectivity detection approaches as a tool for identifying and considering/discarding nonfactual information [57]. Such is the case of question answering [86] and information extraction systems.

Polarity detection aims to identify whether a text expresses a positive or a negative sentiment from the writer. Since it is very common to address this task only on subjective texts, usually a subjectivity detection stage is needed. Hence, in the literature we can find a number of works that tackle both problems—subjectivity and polarity detection—as a single one. Existing approaches commonly distinguish between three types of texts: positive, negative, and neutral or objective texts. Some works have shown this approach is much more challenging than the binary classification of subjective texts [57]. Applications of polarity classification are the identification of the writer's political ideology—since it can be considered as a binary classification problem [21], and the analysis of product reviews—determining user positive or negative opinions about a given item (a product, a movie, a hotel, etc.) or even personal sentiments about specific features of such item.

In emotion detection, the main object of study is the user's emotional attitude with respect to a text. In this context, we may aim to determine the writer's mood toward a text [82] or to identify the emotions "provoked" by the text to the reader [67].

7.2.2 Sentiment Analysis Approaches

In this section, we discuss some interesting approaches intended to deal with the sentiment analysis tasks and goals previously described. For the sake of clarity, we classify them into two groups, according to the nature of the applied techniques:

- *Lexicon-based approaches* are those techniques that rely on a resource containing information about the affective terms that may occur in the texts, and usually additional information about such terms (e.g., polarity, intensity, etc.). These resources can be manually or automatically generated, domain independent or focused on a particular domain. Most of these approaches take advantage of the information available in a lexicon to compute subjective and affective estimations over the texts.
- *Machine-Learning approaches* are those techniques that apply a machine-learning method to address sentiment analysis tasks. In this case, a majority of techniques have been based on support vector machines, which are usually fed with lexical and syntactic features, or even with lexicon-based features, to provide subjective and affective classifications.

It is worth to note that the creation, integration, and use of lexicons are crucial in sentiment analysis, not only for lexicon-based techniques, but also for machine-learning techniques, which can be enhanced with the information available in such resources. In this context, General Inquirer [69] can be considered as one of the most relevant and widely used resources. It is a manually built lexicon formed by lemmas with associated syntactic, semantic and pragmatic information. It contains 4,206 lemmas manually tagged as positive or negative.

The MPQA (Multi-Perspective Question Answering) is a lexicon of news documents from the world press based on General Inquirer, including a set of words obtained from a dictionary and a thesaurus, and a set of automatically compiled subjective terms [57]. The MPQA lexicon is composed by 8,222 words with a set of syntactic and semantic features (*type strength*, *length*, *part of speech*, *stem*, and *prior polarity*).

Following the same schema, the Bing Liu's English Lexicon (BLEL) [30] consists of an automatically generated list of words that have been classified into positive and negative. This classification is manually updated periodically. In total, BLEL contains 4,783 negative words and 2,006 positive words, including misspelled terms, morphological variants, and slang words, among others.

Maybe one of the most well-known and widely used lexical resources is WordNet [42], a thesaurus for English based on the definition of the so-called *synsets*, which are groups of words with the same meaning and a brief definition (*gloss*). To relate synsets, WordNet provides a number of semantic relations, such as synonymy, hypernonymy, and meronymy.

A very large number of works have used WordNet in a wide number of tasks and domains, and some of them have aimed to enrich or expand WordNet in different ways. In this context, it is worth to mention the Global WordNet Association,[1] a noncommercial organization devoted to provide a platform to ease the creation and connection of WordNet versions in different languages. Regarding the enrichment of WordNet, we can highlight WordNet Domains [5], a semi-supervised generated resource that augments WordNet with domain labels for all its synsets. Related to it, we find WordNet Affect [68], which assigns to each WordNet synset a set of affective labels encoding emotions, moods, attitudes, behaviors, etc. in order to build a resource suitable for emotion detection, in addition to subjectivity and polarity classification. Another affective extension of WordNet is SentiWordNet (SWN) [4], which attaches to each WordNet synset three sentiment scores in the range [0, 1] summing up to 1, representing positivity, negativity, and objectivity degrees of each synset. The polarities of words are assigned by means of a propagation of the polarity of some manually picked synsets through the relations in WordNet. SWN includes 117,000 synsets with sentiment scores.

The main advantage of WordNet-based resources and techniques over MPQA, BLEL, or General Inquirer is the lack of semantic ambiguity between synsets, which unequivocally represent the term meaning. Word sense disambiguation constitutes a crucial problem in NLP, and most of the works using the above lexicons address such problem by computing the polarity at the level of words or lemmas by means of the polarity values from all the respective synsets [1, 71]. In addition to this, the graph structure of WordNet-based resources allows for the application of graph-based techniques in order to better exploit the semantic information encoded within the relations.

Among the existing lexicon-based approaches, the technique presented in [78] has been a main reference work for many others. This technique is applied over manually selected sets of strongly positive words (such us *excellent* and *good*) and strongly negative words (such as *poor* and *bad*), which are considered as seed terms. The technique computes the pointwise mutual information (PMI) between input words and the seeds in order to determine the polarity of the former. Since the polarity of a word depends on the relation between the word and the seed sets, the technique is usually called semantic orientation by association. A similar idea is proposed in [34], but replacing the PMI computation by building a graph with the adjectives in WordNet for computing the polarity of a word; specifically, by selecting the shortest graph path from the synset of the word to the synsets of the positive and negative seeds.

With respect to machine-learning-based approaches, a considerable number of works has been done, applying well-known machine-learning techniques, such as SVM and LSA, to deal with sentiment analysis tasks. These works usually include

[1] http://globalwordnet.org/.

the exploitation of lexical, syntactic, and semantic features suitable for the classification problems that must be tackled in sentiment analysis for the subjectivity and polarity detection. Among these features, one may highlight n-grams, part-of-speech (POS) tags, PMI, and features extracted from lexicons [19, 84]. In this context, it has to be noted that the joint use of lexicon—an machine-learning-based approaches can be performed in the opposite direction, i.e., by using machine-learning techniques in order to improve lexicon-based approaches. For instance, in [51] LSA-based techniques are used to expand a given lexicon for different languages.

The work presented in [29] is another representative example of a machine-learning-based sentiment analysis approach. It aims to predict the orientation of subjective adjectives by analyzing a large unlabeled document set, and looking for pairs of adjectives linked with conjunctions. It then builds a graph where the nodes correspond to terms connected by *equal-orientation* or *opposite-orientation* edges, according to the conjunctions that link the terms, and finally apply a clustering algorithm that partitions the graph into clusters of positive and negative terms.

A combination of ideas from Turney [78] and Hatzivassiloglou [29] is presented in [15], where a set of seed words is used to introduce a bias in a random-walk algorithm that computes a ranking of the terms in a graph of words linked according to the conjunctions that join them in the texts. In the generated rankings, positive and negative terms are respectively located into the highest and lowest positions. The word graph is also used as a mechanism to process the negations in the text by developing a PageRank-based algorithm that builds graphs with positive and negative weighted edges.

7.3 Sentiment Analysis on User-Generated Content

Online social media platforms support social interactions by allowing users to create and maintain connections, share information, collaborate, discuss, and interact in a variety of ways. The proliferation and usage of these platforms have experienced an explosive growth in the last decade, expanding to all areas of society, such as entertainment, culture, science, business, politics, and public services. As a result, a large amount of user-generated content is continuously being created, offering individuals, and organizations a fast way to monitor people's opinions and sentiments toward any form of entity, such as products, services, and brands.

The nature and purpose of these platforms is manifold, and thus, they differ in a variety of aspects, such as the way in which users establish connections, the main activities they conduct, and the type of content they share. These characteristics pose novel challenges and opportunities to sentiment analysis researchers. In the subsequent sections, we characterize the user-generated content available in popular types of existing social media platforms, and present the major challenges to process such content in the context of sentiment analysis and opinion mining.

7.3.1 Characterizing User-Generated Content

In the literature, social media platforms have been categorized in different ways [35].[2] Here, we propose a categorization based on three dimensions: the type of user connections, the type of user activities, and the type of contents generated/shared within the platforms. We summarize such a categorization in Table 7.1.

- *Connections*: Users connections—e.g., friendship and *following* relations—in social media are based on three main models: explicit connections, which can be reciprocal—u follows v, and v follows u—and nonreciprocal—u follows v, but not necessary v follows u, and implicit connections, where relations are extracted via interactions in the social platform—e.g., if user u posts a message and user v replies to that message, an implicit relation between v and u may be assumed. An example of a social platform that uses explicit reciprocal connections is Facebook[3] via its friendship relations. Twitter,[4] differently, uses explicit nonreciprocal connections via its follower-followee relation; if a user u follows a user v on Twitter, it does not necessarily imply that v follows u. Implicit connections, on the other hand, are more common in forums and blogs, where users post questions, evaluations or opinions, and other users react to the posted content.
- *Activities*: Users may perform different activities and have different goals when participating in a social media platform. In this chapter, we mainly focus on five activities: nurturing social connections, discussing about particular issues and topics, asking for information, sharing content and, collaborating with others for certain tasks. Note that the majority of social media may allow performing various of these activities.
- *Types of contents*: The third dimension to categorize social platforms is the type of content that users share between them. Here, we distinguish between six main types: text, micro-text, tags, URLs, videos, and images. Text and micro-text contents differ on their number of characters. Micro-text is characteristic of microblogging platforms, such as Twitter, which allows a maximum of 140 characters in their text messages. Note that, as with activities, many of the existing platforms allow for multiple combinations of these content types, although their focus tends to be on few of them.

According to these three dimensions, social platforms can be described as follows:

- *Forums*: Forums and discussion boards are mainly focused on allowing users to hold conversations and to discuss about particular issues and topics. A user generally posts an comment, opinion, or question, and other users reply, starting a conversation. All the posts related to a conversation are grouped into a structure

---

[2]http://decidedlysocial.com/13-types-of-social-media-platforms-and-counting/, http://outthinkgroup.com/tips/the-6-types-of-social-media.

[3]http://www.facebook.com.

[4]http://twitter.com.

Table 7.1 Main characteristics of particular social media

			Social media						
			Forums	Q&A systems	Wikis	Blogs	Microblogs	Social networks	Social tagging systems
User connections	Explicit	Reciprocal					x	x	x
		Non-reciprocal					x		
	Implicit		x	x	x	x			
Actions	Nurturing social connections							x	
	Discussing issues and topics		x	x		x	x		
	Asking for information		x	x					
	Sharing content		x		x	x	x	x	x
	Collaborating in tasks				x				
Contents	Text		x	x	x	x		x	
	Micro-text						x		
	Tags					x			x
	URLs		x		x	x	x	x	x
	Videos		x			x	x	x	
	Images				x	x	x	x	

called thread. The predominant type of content in these platforms is the text generated with the evolution of the users' discussions. User connections in forums usually are implicit. In general, users are not "friends" with each other explicitly, but connections between them can be extracted from the question-reply chains of their discussions. An example of this type of social platform is Boards.ie,[5] a popular Irish public forum board system, which is not restricted to certain topic, and where users discuss about any domain or topic, e.g., politics, sports, movies, TV programs, and music.

- *Q&A systems*: Question answering (QA) platforms can be understood as a particular type of forums, where the main goal of their users is to ask for information, and therefore discussions are generated around the answers to formulated questions. A popular example of QA system is Stack Overflow,[6] where users ask a variety of questions about computer programming. A particular characteristic of Stack Overflow and other QA platforms is that users can gain reputation points based on the quality of their contributions.
- *Wikis*: The key goal of wikis is to enable collaboration between users in order to create content (ideas, documents, reports, etc.). Users are therefore allowed to add, modify, and delete content in collaboration with others. Connections in this type of platforms are generally implicit, and are derived from common editing of a particular resource: a wiki page. The main type of content generated in wikis is text, but other content types, such as images and URLs, are also quite common. One of the most popular examples of this type of platforms is Wikipedia,[7] a wiki with more than 73,000 editors around the world, who have contributed to the creation of a very large open online encyclopedia.
- *Blogs*: Blogs represent a more "personal" type of platform with respect to forums and wikis. When using these platforms, the main goal is to share information, although this often generates discussions. A user does not participate in a blog, but owns it, and uses it to share explanations, opinions, or reviews about a variety of issues. Other users can comment about particular blog posts, sometimes generating large discussions. Differently to forums, these discussions are not grouped into threads, but are located under a particular blog post. Multimedia content (photos, videos) are also frequent within this type of platforms. Popular examples of blogging platforms are Blogger[8] and WordPress.[9]
- *Microblogs*: Microblogs can be considered as a particular type of blog, where the posted content typically is much smaller. Microblogs are also focused on sharing information, but in this case, information is exchanged in small elements, such as short sentences, individual images, videos, and URLs. As opposed to blogs, microblogs generally allow for explicit user connections, both reciprocal and nonreciprocal. One of the most popular microblogging platforms is Twitter, which

[5]http://www.boards.ie.

[6]http://stackoverflow.com.

[7]http://www.wikipedia.org.

[8]http://www.blogger.com.

[9]http://www.wordpress.com.

allows a maximum message length of 140 characters. This limitation forces users to use abbreviations and ill-formed words, which represent important challenges when analyzing sentiments and opinions.

- *Social networks*: The main goal of social networks is to maintain and nurture social connections. With this purpose, they enable the creation of explicit, reciprocal relations between users. Most of these platforms also support other types of activities, such as sharing content and enabling discussions. In this sense, users share text, URLs, and multimedia content within a platform. Popular examples of social networks are LinkedIn,[10] which is focused on professional connections, and Facebook, which tends to be more focused on personal relations.
- *Social tagging systems*: In these platforms, users create or upload content (e.g., images, audios, videos), annotate it with freely chosen words (called *tags*), and share it with others. The whole set of tags constitutes an unstructured collaborative categorization scheme, which is commonly known as *folksonomy*. This implicit categorization is then used to search for and discover resources of interest. In principle, social tagging systems are not conceived for connecting users. Nonetheless, the shared tags and annotated items are usually used to find implicit relations between users based on common interests and tastes. Moreover, tags do not always describe the annotated items, but reflect personal opinions and emotions concerning such items [10]. Popular sites with social tagging services are Flickr,[11] YouTube[12] and Delicious.[13]

Note that our purpose is not to provide an exhaustive categorization of social media, but an overview of the main types of platforms used in the literature to extract and capture opinion and affective information. Other categorizations and platforms exist, such as social bookmarking systems and multimedia sharing sites. In the following subsection, we explain the challenges and opportunities that social media content poses to the extraction and analysis of the above information.

7.3.2 Challenges of Sentiment Analysis in Social Media

Content generated by users via social media in general, and microblogging platforms in particular, poses multiple challenges to sentiment analysis [38, 60]. In this section, we aim to overview and summarize some of these challenges.

- *Colloquial language*: Social platforms, except those targeting professional circles, are commonly used for informal communication. Colloquial written language generally contains spelling, syntactical, and grammatical mistakes [73]. In addition, users tend to express their emotions and opinions using *slang terms*,

---

[10] http://www.linkedin.com.

[11] http://www.flickr.com.

[12] http://www.youtube.com.

[13] http://delicious.com.

emoticons, *exclamation marks*, *irony* and *sarcasm* [38]. Processing ill-formed text, understanding the semantics of slang language, emphasizing the detected emotion/opinion level according to exclamation marks, and detecting that the emotion expressed by a user is the opposite than the emotion reflected within the text due to sarcasm, represent difficult challenges for current NLP and sentiment analysis tools.

- *Short texts*: Small pieces of text are typical in microblogging platforms, such as Twitter, where a maximum of 140 characters per message is allowed. To condense their messages, users make use of *abbreviations* (e.g., *lol* for laugh out loud), *ill-formed words* (e.g., *2morrow* for tomorrow), and *sentences lacking syntactical structure* (e.g., TB Pilot Measuring up (Time): <1 week from data sharing). The lack of syntactical structure, as well as the appearance of abbreviations and contemporaneous terms not recorded in dictionaries, represent important challenges when attempting to understand the affective information expressed within the texts [60].
- *Platform-specific elements*: Some social platforms have their own symbols and textual conventions to express opinions (e.g., Facebook "likes", Google+ "+1", and StackOverflow points to reward high-quality answers), topics (e.g., Twitter hashtags), and references to other users (e.g., Twitter @ symbol). To exploit these conventions, sentiment analysis methods and tools have to be adapted [75].
- *Real-time Big Data*: User-generated content coming from popular social media, such as Facebook and Twitter, is characterized by the Big Data challenges, including: *volume*—data size, *velocity*—the speed of change, *variety*—different types of data, and *veracity*—the trustworthiness of the data. Hence, sentiment analysis techniques applied to social media platforms have to deal with: processing massive amounts of data in short periods of time, dealing with the constant emergence of new words and topics, managing data in different formats (text, image, video), and assessing the veracity of data sources [7, 8, 65]. From these aspects, we highlight the *velocity* aspect, which implies not only to capture and process the user-generated content in real time, but also to perform a response (e.g., recommendation, news provision, trending topic detection) as fast as possible, since it is a common demanding functionality from social media users.

7.4 Sentiment Analysis in Social Streams

Once presented the main sentiment analysis tasks and techniques (Sect. 7.2), and described the characteristics of user-generated content with regard to the expression of personal opinions and sentiments (Sect. 7.3), in the subsequent sections we focus on particular problems and applications of Sentiment Analysis in social streams.

7.4.1 Sentiment Analysis Problems Addressed in Social Streams

Sentiment analysis is an essential processing task for personalized services that aim to exploit textual content—such as microblog messages and social tags—generated in social streams, since they usually reflect the users' subjectivity, in terms of opinions and sentiments for certain issues and topics. For such purpose, in addition to the fundamental sentiment analysis problems—such as entity and opinion recognition, and sentiment polarity estimation, there are aspects that have to be taken into account. User-generated content in social streams presents a number of interesting phenomena, namely opinion spam, user reputation, irony, sarcasm, and emotion dynamics. If we intend to address these issues, we have to go beyond classic text-based opinion mining techniques.

Opinion spam [33] is aimed to disturb the normal behavior in social media services, especially those integrated in recommendation and e-commerce systems, by introducing a bias toward a specific opinion tendency that promotes or demotes an entity (e.g., a product, a service, a brand), or makes users express reviews and opinions in a certain direction. The identification of opinion spam represents a crucial problem for opinion mining and sentiment analysis approaches, which should be able to detect deceptive opinions that try to simulate real user reviews that increase or harm an entity's reputation [28, 47]. In certain media, such as social networks and microblogging platforms, the users' responses (e.g., by unfollowing contacts, and posting complaint comments) may represent a valuable source of information to detect spam content.

The writers' reputation is another important aspect of sentiment analysis of user-generated content. From the point of view of a review site, the higher the reputation of a review author, the more reliable the review can be to other customers, and sometimes vice versa: A review that is seen as reliable by the users can provide high reputation to its author. In this sense, determining the reputation of the authors of a content can be helpful for opinion spam detection. Moreover, some sites have adopted reputation systems as a tool for avoiding or at least discouraging the production of opinion spam. The reputation of users also plays an important role in social networks, since automatically determining the most influential users in a given network can be really valuable [20].

Given the subjective nature of user-generated content, another relevant phenomenon is the existence of irony or sarcasm in the texts. This can constitute a serious problem for many tasks in sentiment analysis, like detection of subjectivity and the classification of the polarity of a given opinion, since the explicit text content reflects the opposite of the sentiment really expressed by the writers. Most of published works has focused on the identification of one-liners (jokes or humorous contents in short texts), but there are some researches aimed to extract humorous patterns from longer texts. In a different way, there are also approaches that use results of sentiment analysis in order to detect humor in texts, for example, the (negative) polarity of a text has been taken as a feature to retrieve patterns of humorous contents [41], and syntactic and semantic features have been used as indicatives of humor [56], e.g., semantic ambiguity, the appearance of emoticons, idioms and slang language, and the abundance/absence of punctuation marks, to name a few. In the case of social media, certain user responses, such as expressions of amusement and laughing emoticons, may be used as a source for identifying contents with irony and sarcasm, which may be difficult to detect if no additional information apart from the contents themselves exist.

7.4.2 Applications of Sentiment Analysis on Social Streams

Sentiment analysis over social platforms offers a fast and effective way to monitor the public's opinions and feelings toward products, brands, governments, events, etc. Such insights can be used to support decision making in a variety of scenarios. In this section, we present three scenarios where the extraction and exploitation of affective information from social streams have become key for certain decision making tasks.

- *Sentiment Analysis in politics and e-government*: Designing and implementing a policy at any level of government is a complex process. One of the key difficulties is finding and summarizing public opinions and sentiments. Citizens do not actively participate in e-government portals [43], and policy specialists lack of appropriate tools to take into account the citizens' views on policy issues expressed in real time through social network discussions. Governments are currently investing in research and development[14] to learn about the citizens, by summarizing public opinion via popular social platforms, and to engage them more effectively. One of the key challenges that arises from this scenario is the lack of awareness of the characteristics of those users that discuss politic issues in social media, and whether those users really represent the public opinion [24]. Sentiment analysis tools are therefore challenged in this scenario to complement affective information with details about the citizens and organizations behind the gathered opinions. Another common task in which social streams are used as a source of affective and opinion information about politics is the prediction of the outcome and evolution of events, such as elections [45, 77], and crises and revolutions [6], as in the case of the Westgate Mall Terror Attack in Kenya [66].
- *Sentiment Analysis in education and e-learning*: Schools and universities strive to collect feedback from students to improve their courses and tutorship programs. Such feedback is often collected at the end of a course via survey forms. However, such methods are too controlled, slow, and passive. With the rise of social streams, many students are finding online social streams as perfect venues in which sharing their experiences, and seeking for peer help and support. To address this issue, educational institutions—such as the Open University[15]—are working toward the

[14] http://www.wegov-project.eu, http://www.sense4us.eu.

[15] http://data.open.ac.uk.

development of platforms that allow capturing and monitoring the students' sentiment and opinion in open social media groups [76]. The aim is to speed up the reaction to the concerns and challenges raised by students. In this scenario, one of the key challenges that arises is the need for adapting the sentiment and opinion extraction processes to the particularities of the domain. For example, discussions around a World War lecture will generally have a negative connotation. Sentiment analysis tools need to isolate the opinions targeting the logistics of a course, with respect to the opinions targeting themes inherent to the course.
- *Sentiment Analysis in business and e-commerce*: Public as well as corporate social platforms generate major economic value to business, and can form pivotal parts of corporate expertise management, corporate marketing, product support, customer relationship management, product innovation, and targeted advertising. Public social platforms are generally used to monitor public opinion and reputation about brands and products [85].[16] Corporate social platforms, on the other hand, are more focused on providing product support and knowledge interchange within a company. One of the new challenges associated with managing these online communities is the ability to predict change in their "health." Providing owners and managers of the social platforms with early warnings (by monitoring the members' contributions, opinions, levels of satisfaction, etc.) may facilitate their decisions to safeguard the communities, e.g. by maintaining engagement, reducing community churn, and providing adequate support. The identification of sentiments is key as an initial indicator, but it does not necessarily represent the overall health of the community. The challenge of sentiment analysis tools in this scenario is to complement sentiment extraction with techniques for risk detection in the context of business domains, helping owners and hosts to ensure a sustained stability of their communities.
- *Sentiment Analysis in entertainment*: In an online entertainment scenario, it is well accepted that (i) the user's current mood may affect the type of resource (e.g., a song, a tv series episode, a video game) she prefers to consume at a particular time—partial or completely regardless her personal tastes—and, in the opposite direction that (ii) emotions evoked by consumed resources may affect the user's current mood. These facts are the basis for the investigation and development of sentiment-aware engaging services in social media. How user moods and item-provoked emotions can be determined [26], how they can be related each other [88], and how they and their relations can be exploited for user entertainment applications are indeed emerging research topics, such as those addressed in recommender systems [72], and multimedia retrieval and entertainment [23, 80].

All these application scenarios come with an additional common challenge: scalability. Social platforms can easily exceed a million users with hundreds of thousands online each day. Content generation may be of Gigabytes per day, and orders of magnitude more data is derived from observing interaction of the users within a system. Existing data analysis approaches, and in particular sentiment analysis tools, currently struggle with these scalability challenges.

[16]http://www.brandwatch.com/, http://www.lithium.com/.

7.5 Discussion

In the previous sections, we have reviewed and discussed the state of the art on sentiment analysis in social streams. We have explained the different types of user-generated content existing in social media platforms, as well as some of the most common challenges that this type of content poses when analyzing affective and opinion information. We have described the different problems and tasks addressed in the sentiment analysis research area, as well as the variety of techniques that have been developed to approach them. We have shown examples of applications that use sentiment analysis on social streams to support decision-making process in a variety of domains. In this section, we provide an overview of directions that sentiment analysis area is currently following, and what are the main factors driving the research into these directions.

- *Sentiments are dynamic*: Social streams, such as Twitter, may exhibit very strong temporal dynamics with opinions about the same entity or event changing rapidly over time. Since sentiment analysis approaches generally work by aggregating information, a key challenge faced by current sentiment analysis approaches is to detect when new opinions are emerging, so that the new information is not aggregated to an existing opinion for the given entity. For example, the opinion about the Nexus4 smartphone is generally determined based on a set of posts expressing sentiment about this particular device. Opinions about it may change over time, e.g., as new technical problems or bugs are discovered. Sentiment analysis approaches should therefore be able to identify opinion changes for entities and/or events as long as new issues regarding them emerge. An option adopted by several approaches is to define a time-window (minute, hour, day) in which sentiment is aggregated for the particular entity that is being monitored. However, discussions in social media may emerge and spread really fast, or cool down for long time periods. Therefore, assessing the right granularity level is key to not loose relevant information when discussions spike, and not waste resources when discussions about target entities or events are not present [7, 39].
- *Sentiments are entity-focused*: As discussed in Sect. 7.2, sentiment is generally computed at document and/or sentence level. Multiple sentiments, nonetheless, can be expressed within the same document or the same sentence toward different targets. For example, the post "I love Nexus4 but I don't like Nexus5 at all!" expresses two different sentiments toward two different targets, the Nexus4 and Nexus5 devices. Additionally, when monitoring the sentiment or particular brands, events, or individuals in social media, sentiment analysis approaches should consider if the sentiment of the posts referencing the brand, event or individual do indeed express sentiment toward those entities. For instance, a significant number of negative posts do exist in social streams mentioning the WWF (the World Wildlife Fund) organization, which do not criticize it, but the negative impact of climate change, the danger of extinction suffered by a number of species, and other sustainability issues. Furthermore, approaches in the literature of sentiment analysis have emerged in the last few years that aim to identify sentiment targets

within a given text, focusing on entity-level and aspect-level sentiment analysis detection [37, 40, 54, 85], i.e., they first identify the entities and events appearing in the text, and then check the sentiment expressed toward them.

- *Sentiments are semantics-dependent*: Most of existing approaches to sentiment analysis in social streams have shown effective when sentiment is explicitly and unambiguously reflected in text fragments through affective (opinionated) words, such as "great" as in "I got my new Android phone, what a great device!" or "sad" as in "so sad, now four Sierra Leonean doctors lost to Ebola." However, merely relying on affective words is often insufficient, and in many cases does not lead to satisfactory sentiment detection results [8, 27, 61]. Examples of such cases arise when the sentiment of words differs according to (i) the context in which those words occur (e.g., "great" conveys a negative connotation in the context "pain" and positive in the context "smile"), or (ii) the conceptual meaning associated with the words (e.g., "Ebola" is likely to be negative when its associated concept is "Virus" and likely to be neutral when its associated concept is "River"). Therefore, ignoring the semantics of words when calculating their sentiment, in either case, may lead to inaccuracies. Recent research in sentiment analysis is therefore focusing on investigating the identification and use of contextual and semantic information to enhance the accuracy of traditional machine-learning [59] and lexicon-based approaches [61].
- *Sentiments are domain-dependent*: Sentiment is expressed in social streams within multiple domains. For example, the domain of death is generally more negative than the domain of birth, although both use common terminology, such as hospital, family, etc. Sentiment analysis approaches need to establish the sentiment of the targeted domain to be able to establish the positivity/negativity of the posts. It has been observed that current sentiment classifiers trained with data from one specific domain do indeed fail when applied to a different domain [3]. Similarly, while lexicon-based approaches have a higher tolerance to domain changes, these approaches do suffer when the vocabulary of the domain under analysis is not well covered by the available sentiment lexicon. Given the great variety of topics and domains that constantly emerge in social streams, domain constraints currently affect the applicability of sentiment analysis approaches. Research is currently being conducted to adapt to new domains, by automatically assigning sentiment to terms not previously covered by the lexicons, and by providing dynamic retraining of existing classifiers [9, 50, 61, 65]. There are also recent approaches aimed to generate domain-dependent lexicons, such as that presented in [26]. In that work, automatic lexicons[17] with emotional categories for the movie, music, and book domains—e.g., *gloomy* movies, *nostalgic* music compositions, and *suspenseful* books—are automatically generated and modeled by exploiting information available in social tagging systems and online thesauri. The terms of these lexicons are also linked to a core lexicon which is composed of weighted terms associated to 16 general emotions—e.g., *happiness*, *calmness*, and *tension*—of the well-known Russell's circumplex model of affect [58].

[17] http://ir.ii.uam.es/emotions/.

- *Sentiments are language- and culture-dependent*: An important problem when analyzing sentiment in social media streams is that posts are written in different languages. Even individual posts may include terminology from a variety of languages within them. Language identification tools are therefore needed to detect the language in which posts are written [11]. An even more complex problem is that sentiment is culturally dependent. The way in which we express positivity or negativity, humor, irony, or sarcasm varies depending on our cultural background [22]. Sentiment analysis tools therefore need to account for language and culture variances to provide accurate sentiment identification. Few research works have been recently conducted in this vein, focusing mainly on demographic language variations (e.g., age, gender) of users to improve sentiment analysis performance [74, 79].
- *Sentiments are personality-dependent*: The relationships between emotional states and personality have been a topic of study in psychology in the last 20 years (see, e.g., seminal works as [55]). The reader can find more details on this in Chap. 3. In particular, several studies have revealed associations between *extraversion* and *neuroticism* (sometimes referred as *emotional stability*) personality traits with individual differences in affective level and environmental response [14, 55]. This, together with the facts that (i) it has been shown that there exist correlations between user personality traits and user preferences in several domains [25], and that (ii) approaches have been proposed to infer user personality from data about user activity and behavior in social streams [2] (see Chap. 5), raise new research opportunities and applications –such as customer characterization, market segmentation, and personalized recommendation– for sentiment analysis in the context of the Social Web.

References

1. Agrawal, S., Siddiqui, T.J.: Using syntactic and contextual information for sentiment polarity analysis. In: Proceedings of the 2nd International Conference on Interaction Sciences Information Technology, Culture and Human (ICIS'09), pp. 620–623 (2009)
2. Amichai-Hamburger, Y., Vinitzkyb, G.: Social network use and personality. Comput. Hum. Behav. **26**(6), 1289–1295
3. Aue, A., Gamon, M.: Customizing sentiment classifiers to new domains: a case study. In: Proceedings of the 3rd International Conference on Recent Advances in Natural Language Processing (RANLP'05) (2005)
4. Baccianella, S., Esuli, A., Sebastiani, F.: entiWordNet 3.0: an enhanced lexical resource for sentiment analysis and opinion mining. In: Proceedings of the 7th International Conference on Language Resources and Evaluation (LREC'10) (2010)
5. Bentivogli, L., Forner, P., Magnini, B., Pianta, E.: Revising WordNet domains hierarchy: semantics, coverage, and balancing. In: Proceedings of the COLLING'04 Workshop on Multilingual Linguistic Resources (MLR'04), pp. 101–108 (2004)
6. Bhuiyan, S.I.: Social media and its effectiveness in the political reform movement in Egypt. Middle East Media Educ. **1**(1), 14–20 (2011)
7. Bifet, A., Frank, E.: Sentiment knowledge discovery in twitter streaming data. In: Proceedings of the 13th International Conference on Discovery Science (DS'10), pp. 1–15 (2010)

8. Cambria, E., Schuller, B., Xia, Y., Havasi, C.: New avenues in opinion mining and sentiment analysis. IEEE Intell. Syst. **28**(2), 15–21 (2013)
9. Cambria, E., Song, Y., Wang, H., Howard, N.: Semantic multi-dimensional scaling for open-domain sentiment analysis. IEEE Intell. Syst. **29**(2), 44–51 (2013)
10. Cantador, I., Konstas, I., Jose, J.M.: Categorising social tags to improve Folksonomy-based recommendations. J. Web Semant. **9**(1), 1–15 (2010)
11. Carter, S., Weerkamp, W., Tsagkias, M.: Microblog language identification: overcoming the limitations of short, unedited and idiomatic text. Lang. Resour. Eval. **47**(1), 195–215 (2013)
12. Carvalho, P., Sarmento, L., Silva, M.J., de Oliveira, E.: Clues for detecting irony in user-generated contents: Oh...!! It's "so easy" ;-) In: Proceedings of the 1st International Workshop on Topic-sentiment Analysis for Mass Opinion (TSA'09), pp. 53–56 (2009)
13. Chow, A., Foo, M.-H. N., Manai, G.: HybridRank: a hybrid content-based approach to mobile game recommendations. In: Proceedings of the 1st Workshop on New Trends in Content-based Recommender Systems (CBRecSys'14), pp. 1–4 (2014)
14. Corr, P.J.: The reinforcement sensitivity theory. In: Corr, P.J. (ed.) The Reinforcement Senitivity Theory of Personality. Cambridge University Press (2008)
15. Cruz, F.L., Vallejo, C.G., Enríquez, F., Troyano, J.A.: PolarityRank: finding an equilibrium between followers and contraries in a network. Inf. Process. Manage. **48**(2), 271–282 (2012)
16. Cruz, F.L., Troyano, J.A., Enríquez, F., Ortega, F.J., Vallejo, C.G.: Long autonomy or long delay? The importance of domain in opinion mining. Expert Syst. Appl. **40**(8), 3174–3184 (2013)
17. Cruz, F.L., Troyano, J.A., Pontes, B., Ortega, F.J.: Building layered, multilingual sentiment lexicons at synset and lemma levels. Expert Syst. Appl. **41**(13), 5984–5994 (2014)
18. Davidov, D., Tsur, O., Rappoport, A.: Semi-supervised recognition of sarcastic sentences in Twitter and Amazon. In: Proceedings of the 14th Conference on Computational Natural Language Learning (CoNLL'10), pp. 107–116 (2010)
19. Dehkharghani, R., Yanikoglu, B., Tapucu, D., Saygin, Y.: Adaptation and use of subjectivity lexicons for domain dependent sentiment classification. In: Proceedings of the 12th IEEE International Conference on Data Mining Workshops, pp. 669–673 (2012)
20. Barbagallo, D., Bruni, L., Francalanci, C., Giacomazzi, P.: An empirical study on the relationship between twitter sentiment and influence in the tourism domain. In: Information and Communication Technology in Tourism, pp. 506–516 (2012)
21. Durant, K.T., Smith, M.D.: Mining sentiment classification from political web logs. In: Proceedings of the WebKDD'06 Workshop on Web Mining and Web Usage Analysis (2006)
22. Elahi, M.F., Monachesi, P.: An examination of cross-cultural similarities and differences from social media data with respect to language use. In: Proceedings of the 8th International Conference on Language Resources and Evaluation (LREC'12), pp. 4080–4086 (2012)
23. Feng, Y., Zhuang, Y., Pan, Y.: Music information retrieval by detecting mood via computational media aesthetics. In: Proceedings of the 2003 IEEE/WIC International Conference on Web Intelligence (WI'03), pp. 235–241 (2003)
24. Fernández, M., Allen, B., Wandhoefer, T., Cano, E., Alani, H.: Using social media to inform policy making: to whom are we listening? In: Proceedings of the 1st European Conference on Social Media (ECSM'14), pp. 174–182 (2014)
25. Fernández-Tobías, I., Cantador, I.: Personality-aware collaborative filtering: an empirical study in multiple domains with facebook data. In: Proceedings of the 15th International Conference on E-Commerce and Web Technologies (EC-Web'14), pp. 125–137 (2013)
26. Fernández-Tobías, I., Cantador, I., Plaza, L.: An emotion dimensional model based on social tags: crossing folksonomies and enhancing recommendations. In: Proceedings of the 14th International Conference on E-Commerce and Web Technologies (EC-Web'13), pp. 88–100 (2013)
27. Gangemi, A., Presutti, V., Reforgiato Recupero, D.: Frame-based detection of opinion holders and topics: a model and a tool. IEEE Comput. Intell. Mag. **9**(1), 20–30 (2014)
28. Hancock, J.T., Cardie, C.: Finding deceptive opinion spam by any stretch of the imagination. In: Proceedings of the 49th Annual Meeting of the Association for Computational Linguistics (HLT'11), pp. 309–319 (2011)

29. Hatzivassiloglou, V., McKeown, K.R.: Predicting the semantic orientation of adjectives. In: Proceedings of the 35th Annual Meeting on Association for Computational Linguistics (ACL'98), pp. 174–181 (1998)
30. Hu, M., Liu, B.: Mining and summarizing customer reviews. In: Proceedings of the 2004 ACM SIGKDD International Conference on Knowledge Discovery and Data Mining (KDD'04), pp. 168–177 (2004)
31. Hu, M., Liu, B.: Opinion feature extraction using class sequential rules. In: Proceedings of the AAAI'06 Spring Symposium: Computational Approaches (2006)
32. Jia, L., Yu, C., Meng, W.: The effect of negation on sentiment analysis and retrieval effectiveness. In: Proceedings of the 18th ACM Conference on Information and Knowledge Management (CIKM'10), pp. 1827–1830 (2010)
33. Jindal, N., Liu, B.: Opinion spam and analysis. In: Proceedings of the 2008 International Conference on Web Search and Data Mining (WSDM'08), pp. 219–230 (2008)
34. Kamps, J., Marx, M., Mokken, R.J., Rijke, M.: Using WordNet to measure semantic orientations of adjectives. In: Proceedings of the 4th International Conference on Language Resources and Evaluation (LREC'04), pp. 1115–1118 (2004)
35. Kaplan, A.M., Haenlein, M.: Users of the World, unite! the challenges and opportunities of social media. Bus. Horiz. **53**(1), 59–68 (2010)
36. Liu, B.: Web Data Mining: Exploring Hyperlinks, Contents, and Usage Data, 2nd edn. Springer (2011)
37. Long, J., Yu, M., Zhou, M., Liu, X., Zhao, T.: Target-dependent twitter sentiment classification. In: Proceedings of the 49th Annual Meeting of the Association for Computational Linguistics: Human Language Technologies (HLT'11), pp. 151–160 (2011)
38. Maynard, D., Bontcheva, K., Rout, D.: Challenges in developing opinion mining tools for social media. In: Proceedings of NLP can u tag# usergeneratedcontent?! Workshop (2012)
39. Maynard, D., Gossen, G., Funk, A., Fisichella, M.: Should I care about your opinion? Detection of opinion interestingness and dynamics in social media. Future Internet **6**(3), 457–481 (2014)
40. Meng, X., Wei, F., Liu, X., Zhou, M., Li, S., Wang, H.: Entity-centric topic-oriented opinion summarization in twitter. In: Proceedings of the 18th ACM SIGKDD International Conference on Knowledge Discovery and Data Mining (KDD'12), pp. 379–387 (2012)
41. Mihalcea, R., Strapparava, C.: Making computers laugh. In: Proceedings of the 2005 Conference on Human Language Technology and Empirical Methods in Natural Language Processing (HLT'05), pp. 531–538 (2005)
42. Miller, G.A.: WordNet: a lexical database for English. Commun. ACM **38**(11), 39–41 (1995)
43. Miller, L., Williamson, A.: Digital Dialogs—Third Phase Report. Handsard Society (2008)
44. Morinaga, S., Yamanishi, K., Tateishi, K., Fukushima, T.: Mining product reputations on the web. In: Proceedings of the 8th ACM SIGKDD International Conference on Knowledge Discovery and Data Mining (KDD'02), pp. 341–349 (2002)
45. O'Connor, B., Balasubramanyan, R., Routledge, B.R., Smith, N.A.: From tweets to polls: linking text sentiment to public opinion time series. In: Proceedings of the 4th International AAAI Conference on Weblogs and Social Media (ICWSM'10), pp. 122–129 (2010)
46. Ortega, F.J.: Detection of dishonest behaviors in on-line networks using graph-based ranking techniques. AI Commun. **26**(3), 327–329 (2013)
47. Ott, M., Cardie, C., Hancock, J.T.: Negative deceptive opinion spam. In: Proceedings of 2013 Conference of the North American Chapter of the Association for Computational Linguistics (NAACL-HLT'13), pp. 497–501 (2013)
48. Pang, B., Lee, L.: Opinion mining and sentiment analysis. Found. Trends Inf. Retr. **2**(1–2), 1–135 (2008)
49. Pak, A., Paroubek, P.: Twitter as a corpus for sentiment analysis and opinion mining. In: Proceedings of the 5th International Conference on Language Resources and Evaluation (LREC'10), pp. 1320–1326 (2010)
50. Peddinti, V.M.K., Chintalapoodi, P.: Domain adaptation in sentiment analysis of twitter. In: Analyzing Microtext, vol. WS-11-05 of AAAI'11 Workshops (2011)

51. Pérez-Rosas, V., Banea, C., Mihalcea, R.: Learning sentiment lexicons in spanish. In: Proceedings of the 8th International Conference on Language Resources and Evaluation (LREC'12), pp. 3077–3081 (2012)
52. Popescu, A.-M., Etzioni, O.: Extracting product features and opinions from reviews. In: Proceedings of the Conference on Human Language Technology and Empirical Methods in Natural Language Processing (HLT/EMNLP'05), pp. 339–346 (2005)
53. Qiu, G., Liu, B., Bu, J., Chen, C.: Opinion word expansion and target extraction through double propagation. Comput. Linguist. **37**(1), 9–27 (2011)
54. Recupero, D.R., Presutti, V., Consoli, S., Gangemi, A., Nuzzolese, A.G.: Sentilo: frame-based sentiment analysis. Cogn. Comput. 1–15 (2014)
55. Revelle, W.: Personality processes. Annu. Rev. Psychol. **46**, 295–328 (1995)
56. Reyes, A., Rosso, P., Buscaldi, D.: From humor recognition to irony detection: the figurative language of social media. Data Knowl. Eng. **74**, 1–12 (2012)
57. Riloff, E., Wiebe, J., Wilson, T.: Learning subjective nouns using extraction pattern bootstrapping. In: Proceedings of the 7th Conference on Computational Natural Language Learning (CoNLL'03), vol. 4, pp. 25–32 (2003)
58. Russell, J.A.: A circumplex model of affect. J. Pers. Soc. Psychol. **39**(6), 1161–1178 (1980)
59. Saif, H., He, Y., Alani, H.: Semantic sentiment analysis of twitter. In: Proceedings of the 11th International Semantic Web Conference (ISWC'12), pp. 508–524 (2012)
60. Saif, H., He, Y., Alani, H.: Alleviating data sparsity for twitter sentiment analysis. In: Proceedings of the WWW'12 Workshop on Making Sense of Microposts (2012)
61. Saif, H., Fernández, M., He, Y., Alani, H.: SentiCircles for contextual and conceptual semantic sentiment analysis of twitter. In: Proceedings of the 11th Extended Semantic Web Conference (ESWC'14), pp. 83–98 (2014)
62. Saif, H., Fernández, M., He, Y., Alani, H.: On stopwords, filtering and data sparsity for sentiment analysis of twitter. In: Proceedings of the 9th International Conference on Language Resources and Evaluation (LREC'14), pp. 810–817 (2014)
63. Saif, H., He, Y., Fernández, M., Alani, H.: Semantic patterns for sentiment analysis of twitter. In: Proceedings of the 13th International Semantic Web Conference (ISWC'14)—part 2, pp. 324–340 (2014)
64. Sebastiani, F., Esuli, A.: Determining term subjectivity and term orientation for opinion mining. In: Proceedings of the 11th Conference of the European Chapter of the Association for Computational Linguistics (EACL'06) (2006)
65. Silva, I.S., Gomide, J., Veloso, A., Meira Jr, W., Ferreira, R.: Effective sentiment stream analysis with self-augmenting training and demand-driven projection. In: Proceedings of the 34th international ACM SIGIR Conference on Research and Development in Information Retrieval (SIGIR'11), pp. 475–484 (2011)
66. Simon, T., Goldberg, A., Aharonson-Daniel, L., Leykin, D., Adini, B.: Twitter in the cross fire—the use of social media in the Westgate Mall terror attack in Kenya. PloS one **9**(8), e104136 (2014)
67. Strapparava, C., Mihalcea, R.: Learning to identify emotions in text. In: Proceedings of the 2008 ACM Symposium on Applied Computing (SAC'08), pp. 1556–1560 (2008)
68. Strapparava, C., Valitutti, A.: Wordnet-affect: an affective extension of WordNet. In: Proceedings of the 4th International Conference on Language Resources and Evaluation (LREC'04), pp. 1083–1086 (2004)
69. Stone, P.J., Dunphy, D.C., Smith, M.S.: The General Inquirer: A Computer Approach to Content Analysis. MIT Press (1966)
70. Szomszor, M., Cantador, I., Alani, H.: Correlating user pprofiles from multiple folksonomies. In: Proceedings of the 19th ACM Conference on Hypertext and Hypermedia (Hypertext'08), pp. 33–42 (2008)
71. Taboada, M., Brooke, J., Tofiloski, M., Voll, K., Stede, M.: Lexicon-based methods for sentiment analysis. Comput. Linguist. **37**(2), 267–307 (2011)
72. Tkalcic, M., Burnik, U., Odic, A., Kosir, A., Tasic, J.: Emotion-aware recommender systems—a framework and a case study. In: Markovski, S., Gusev, M. (eds.) ICT Innovations 2012. Advances in Intelligent Systems and Computing 207, pp. 141–150. Springer (2013)

73. Thelwall, M., Buckley, K., Paltoglou, G., Cai, D., Kappas, A.: Sentiment strength detection in short informal text. J. Am. Soc. Inf. Sci. Technol. **61**(12), 2544–2558 (2010)
74. Thelwall, M., Wilkinson, D., Uppal, S.: Data mining emotion in social network communication: gender differences in MySpace. J. Am. Soc. Inf. Sci. Technol. **61**(1), 190–199 (2010)
75. Thelwall, M., Buckley, K., Paltoglou, G.: Sentiment strength detection for the social web. J. Am. Soc. Inf. Sci. Technol. **63**(1), 163–173 (2012)
76. Thomas, K., Fernández, M., Brown, S., Alani, H.: OUSocial2—a platform for gathering students' feedback from social media. In: Demo at the 13th International Semantic Web Conference (ISWC'14) (2014)
77. Tumasjan, A., Sprenger, T.O., Sandner, P.G., Welpe, I.M.: Predicting elections with twitter: what 140 characters reveal about political sentiment. In: Proceedings of the 4th International AAAI Conference on Weblogs and Social Media (ICWSM'10), pp. 178–185 (2010)
78. Turney, P.: Thumbs up or thumbs down? Semantic orientation applied to unsupervised classification of reviews. In: Proceedings of the 40th Annual Meeting of the Association for Computational Linguistics (ACL'02), pp. 417–424 (2002)
79. Volkova, S., Wilson, T., Yarowsky, D.: Exploring demographic language variations to improve multilingual sentiment analysis in social media. In: EMNLP, pp. 1815–1827 (2013)
80. Vorderer, P., Klimmt, C., Ritterfeld, U.: At the heart of media entertainment. Commun. Theory **14**(4), 388–408 (2004)
81. Wiebe, J., Bruce, R., O'Hara, T.: Development and use of a gold standard data set for subjectivity classifications. In: Proceedings of the 37th Annual Meeting of the Association for Computational Linguistics (ACL'99), pp. 246–253 (1999)
82. Wiebe, J., Wilson, T., Cardie, C.: Annotating expressions of opinions and emotions in language. Lang. Resour. Eval. **39**(2–3), 165–210 (2006)
83. Wilson, T., Wiebe, J., Hoffmann, P.: Recognizing contextual polarity in phrase-level sentiment analysis. In: Proceedings of the 2005 Conference on Human Language Technology and Empirical Methods in Natural Language Processing (HLT'05), pp. 347–354 (2005)
84. Wilson, T., Wiebe, J., Hoffmann, P.: Recognizing contextual polarity: an exploration of features for phrase-level sentiment analysis. Comput. Linguist. **35**(3), 399–433 (2009)
85. Yerva, S.R., Mikls, Z., Aberer, K.: Entity-based classification of twitter messages. Int. J. Comput. Sci. Appl. **9**, 88–115 (2012)
86. Yu, H., Hatzivassiloglou, V.: Towards answering opinion questions: Separating facts from opinions and identifying the polarity of opinion sentences. In: Proceedings of the 2003 Conference on Empirical Methods in Natural Language Processing (EMNLP'03), pp. 129–136 (2003)
87. Zhang, J., Tang, J., Li, J.: Expert finding in a social network. In: Proceedings of the 12th International Conference on Database Systems for Advanced Applications (DASFAA'07), pp. 1066–1069 (2007)
88. Zillmann, D.: Mood management: using entertainment to full advantage. In: Donohew, L., Sypher, H.E., Higgins, E.T. (eds.) Communication, Social Cognition, and Affect, pp. 147–171. Lawrence Erlbaum Associates (1988)

Chapter 8
Mobile-Based Experience Sampling for Behaviour Research

Veljko Pejovic, Neal Lathia, Cecilia Mascolo and Mirco Musolesi

Abstract The Experience Sampling Method (ESM) introduces in-situ sampling of human behaviour, and provides researchers and behavioural therapists with ecologically valid and timely assessments of a person's psychological state. This, in turn, opens up new opportunities for understanding behaviour at a scale and granularity that was not possible just a few years ago. The practical applications are many, such as the delivery of personalised and agile behaviour interventions. Mobile computing devices represent a revolutionary platform for improving ESM. They are an inseparable part of our daily lives, context-aware, and can interact with people at suitable moments. Furthermore, these devices are equipped with sensors, and can thus take part of the reporting burden off the participant, and collect data automatically. The goal of this survey is to discuss recent advancements in using mobile technologies for ESM (mESM), and present our vision of the future of mobile experience sampling.

8.1 Introduction

Human behaviour often depends on the context in which a person is. This context is described by our physical environment, for example, a semantic location, such as home or work, our physical state, such as running or sleeping, but also by our internal

---

V. Pejovic (✉)
Faculty of Computer and Information Science, University of Ljubljana, Ljubljana, Slovenia
e-mail: Veljko.Pejovic@fri.uni-lj.si

N. Lathia · C. Mascolo
Computer Laboratory, University of Cambridge, Cambridge, UK
e-mail: neal.lathia@cl.cam.ac.uk

C. Mascolo
e-mail: cecilia.mascolo@cl.cam.ac.uk

M. Musolesi
Department of Geography, University College London, London, UK
e-mail: mirco.musolesi@ucl.ac.uk

M. Tkalčič et al. (eds.), *Emotions and Personality in Personalized Services*, Human–Computer Interaction Series, DOI 10.1007/978-3-319-31413-6_8

state, for example, our cognitive load. The manifestations of human behaviour are complex, and can be observed through our actions, thoughts and emotions, to name a few descriptors. For psychologists, understanding human behaviour necessitates capturing behaviour as it happens. Initial methods of capturing behaviour included lab studies, where participants were placed in an artificial situation and closely monitored, as well as retrospective interview studies, where participants were asked to recall their past experiences. However, since behaviour depends on the context, which is often much richer than anything that can be created in the lab, these studies cannot be used to faithfully replicate natural behaviour. *The Experience Sampling Method* (*ESM*) was developed to capture human behaviour as it happens [20].

The essence of ESM lies in occasional querying of users who then provide immediate answers to questions asked. The method avoids both direct interaction with a researcher/therapist, as well as artificial lab-made environments. As such, ESM-obtained data are, first of all, recorded in the context, and thus of higher ecological validity than data obtained by legacy means of collection. Second, they are recorded closely after the moment of querying, minimising the retrospective bias symptomatic to data harvested by earlier methods. Furthermore, ESM allows long-term querying and longitudinal studying of participants, and may be able to capture samples during infrequently occurring events.

The original approach to sampling users in an ESM study included a programmable beeper that indicates times at which a sample should be taken, and a paper diary that participants fill out once the beeper rings [20]. Different forms of data collection and querying, such as calling users on their mobile phones, or using a personal digital assistant (PDA) device to collect data, have been used in earlier studies [34]. A common characteristic of these studies is the need to deploy unconventional technology, such as beepers and diaries, and train the participants to use them. Furthermore, itself context-oblivious, the technology did not allow the recognition of and sampling at "interesting" moments only. Finally, relying on the honesty of users' self-reporting is one of the major drawbacks of the traditional ESM approach [7].

In the past decade, mobile computing devices, including smartphones and wearables such as smart watches, have become a part of everyday life. Integration with the user and high computing and sensing capabilities render these devices a revolutionary platform for social science research [37], where mobile computing can be used to gather fine-grain personal data from a large number of individuals. The availability of these personal data has contributed to the emergence of the new research field of computational social science [31].

In this survey we present an overview of user behaviour sampling via mobile computing devices, and pay particular attention to practical issues associated with designing and deploying behavioural studies using mobile ESM (mESM). First, we identify the main novelties that mESM brings to the table, of which remote sensing is the one poised to induce a major change to the current practice. Then, we survey the most popular open-source tools that streamline study design and deployment, by lifting the burden of mobile device programming from researchers and therapists, who might have a limited set of technological skills. We then discuss the challenges in running an mESM study, including recruiting participants, ensuring non-biased experience sampling, retaining participants and handling technological limitations of mobile devices. Finally, we present our vision of mESM, which includes adaptive sampling according to a user's lifestyle, delivery of tailored behaviour change interventions based on the sampled data, and proactive reasoning and interaction in the manner of anticipatory computing.

8.2 Mobile Computing for ESM

Mobile devices are poised to completely transform numerous aspects of experience sampling in behavioural psychology. Study design, participant recruitment, data collection and the sheer amount of data gathered by mESM are incomparable to the same aspects encountered with the legacy means of experience sampling. As an illustrative example, in Fig. 8.1 we show a smartphone-based mESM application. The application is distributed as an executable file, possibly via an application store, to a large number of participants owning commodity smartphones. A personalised instance of the application is then run at each of the phones, where it harnesses phone's sensing ability to recognise the situation in which a user is, and should the situation be of interest, signals a user to fill in a survey. The user-provided information is then, together with the data sensed by smartphone's sensors, dispatched to a centralised server where it can be analysed.

Smartphones-based mESM studies improve the traditional beeper and paper form studies in a few important ways. First, unlike beepers and diaries, smartphones are already a part of users' lives, and do not interfere with users' lifestyle. With mESM studies we are "piggybacking" in a sense on an already used device, reducing the burden on the participant to carry an additional device, and lowering the cost of the study. Moreover, using a conventional device, participants are less likely to be

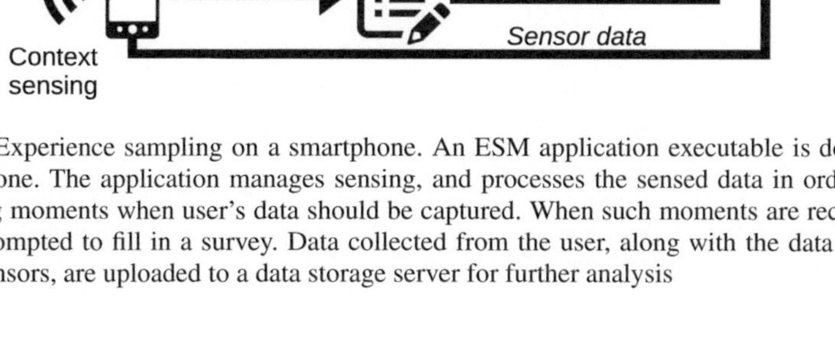

Fig. 8.1 Experience sampling on a smartphone. An ESM application executable is downloaded on the phone. The application manages sensing, and processes the sensed data in order to infer interesting moments when user's data should be captured. When such moments are recognised, a user is prompted to fill in a survey. Data collected from the user, along with the data sensed by mobile sensors, are uploaded to a data storage server for further analysis

embarrassed about completing a questionnaire [50]. In addition, each ESM study can be carried out as separate mobile application, distributed over a large number of devices via application stores such as Google Play and Apple App Store. This enables unprecedented scalability and parallelisation of experience sampling studies.

Second, modern mobile devices are equipped with a range of sensors, from GPS to light, proximity and movement sensors. Therefore, unlike beepers, smartphones "know" the context in which a user is. As shown in the example (Fig. 8.1), this can augment data collection. ESM studies often aim to capture user experience within a certain situation, for example, whenever a user leaves home. Beepers use preprogrammed times, and in case events cannot be reliably forecast, a user's departure time from a certain location is a likely candidate for such an event, we have no means of ensuring that relevant events are captured. Smartphones, on the other hand, can infer the context from sensor readings, and then prompt the user to fill in the survey as the desired context is happening. Location-dependent reminders, for example, are already a part of commercial applications [16]. In addition, the main caveat of the beeper-based ESM is its reliance on the honesty of self reports. Device location, user's activity, and their social circle, can be inferred with the help of smartphone sensors. Numerous aspects of context can be reported directly by the smartphone, avoiding user-induced errors in the data. Finally, the sensed context can be directly relevant to an ambulatory assessment of a user's psycho-physical state. Previous studies put a great effort to combine participants' diary entries with their heart rate or blood pressure, for example [9]. Nowadays, devices such as smartwatches, which come integrated with with galvanic skin response and heart rate sensors, enable holistic ambulatory assessment/ESM studies at scale.

Mobile Sensing for ESM: Modern smartphones, almost without exception, feature location, orientation, acceleration and light sensors, together with cameras and a microphone. High-end models host over a dozen of different sensors, including barometer, heart rate and gesture sensors. Combined with high computing power provided by today's phones' multicore CPUs, smartphones represent an attractive platform for real-time context inference. For most of the day phones are carried by their owners, thus sensor data closely reflects actual users' behaviour and the change of the context around the user. With the help of machine learning, personalised models of different contextual aspects can be built on top of the collected data. Phones are routinely exploited to infer users' semantic location (home, work) via GPS-assisted mobility models. Sensor data from a phone's built-in accelerometer can be used to infer a person's physical activity. Sounds captured by the built-in microphone can be processed to infer if a conversation is taking place in a user's vicinity, but also to infer a user's stress level and emotional states [32, 38, 43]. A Bluetooth chip, itself merely a short-range communication enabler, can be used to infer social encounters of a phone owner [44]. A number of high-level descriptors of human behaviour can be inferred by combining the sensor data coming from different sensors, including contextual information from online social networks [26, 35]. However, we should not forget that above all, today's phones are communication devices providing always-on voice and data connectivity. Thus, for the first time, with mobile computing ESM researchers have a possibility to design truly context-aware studies, to get real-time information about the context in which the participants are, and to adjust sampling strategies on the fly.

8.3 Modern mESM Software Frameworks

The design, implementation and deployment of experience sampling studies via mobile devices requires expertise that is not confined to the traditional social science training. A smartphone-based mESM study, for example, entails a significant programming effort in building the application and managing mobile sensing, as well as the construction of sophisticated machine learning models for context inference, and ensuring reliable data transfer from remote devices to a centralised server. Not only are these tasks often outside the psychological researchers' and therapists' expertise, they also result in a lot of replicated effort for each new study.

Table 8.1 lists some of the frameworks developed by the research community in order to streamline the process of conducting mobile experience sampling studies.[1,2] The first frameworks preceded the smartphone era. *The Experience Sampling Program* (*ESP*) runs on Palm Pilot PDA devices, and lacks the sophisticated context awareness introduced in later frameworks [3]. However, the ESP was the first framework to introduce an authoring tool for designing experience sampling questionnaires for mobile devices. The tool also lets a study designer define a logic for timing the questionnaire prompts. Compared to the traditional beeper and diary studies, ESP-based studies combine signalling and data collection on the same device, yet, PDA devices have never achieved mass popularity needed for large-scale ESM studies in the wild.

Recognising context was the most important missing feature in traditional ESM studies. Event-contingent sampling, where the time of sampling depends on the context or an event in which a user is, is of particular interest for psychological studies [46]. Such sampling is important in case target events are rare, short-lasting, or unpredictable, in which case periodic sampling might completely miss them. For

[1]Every effort has been made to provide truthful descriptions of the listed mESM frameworks, however, due to limited documentation and publications related to some of the frameworks the listed properties should be taken with caution.

[2]The goal of this article is to suggest guidelines for future research in the field, thus we concentrate on free open-source software developed in academia, as such software can serve as a basis for next generation mESM frameworks. Commercial products for supporting mESM are outside the scope of our article.

Table 8.1 Frameworks for building mobile experience sampling studies

Name	URL	Platform	Surveys support	Context sensing	Mobile component	Server component	Data analysis	Description
ESP [3]	http://www.experience-sampling.org	Palm Pilot	Yes	No	Yes	Yes	No	The first mESM app, PC-based study design tool
MyExperience [12]	http://myexperience.sourceforge.net	Pocket PC	Yes	Yes	Yes	No	No	Introduces context-aware sampling
PsychLog [14]	http://sourceforge.net/projects/psychlog	Windows mobile	Yes	Yes	Yes	No	No	Supports external sensors (e.g. ECG)
AndWellness [21]	Not available (July 2015)	Android	Yes	Yes	Yes	Yes	Yes	Health care-oriented, data visualisation
EmotionSense [29, 30]	http://www.emotionsense.org	Android	Yes (unreleased)	Yes	Yes	Yes (unreleased)	No	Emotion sensing app, with open-source libraries

(continued)

Table 8.1 (continued)

Name	URL	Platform	Surveys support	Context sensing	Mobile component	Server component	Data analysis	Description
Ohmage [45]	http://ohmage.org	Android/iOS	Yes	Yes	Yes	Yes	Yes	Allows high-level context inference
funf [2]	http://www.funf.org	Android	No	Yes	Yes	No	No	A rich sensing framework
OpenDataKit [19]	http://www.opendatakit.org	Android	Yes	Yes	Yes	Yes	Yes	Data collection tool targeting non-expert users
Paco	http://github.com/google/paco	Android/iOS	Yes	Yes	Yes	Yes	No	An extensible framework for quantified self experiments
Purple Robot	http://tech.cbits.northwestern.edu/purple-robot	Android	No	Yes	Yes	Yes	No	A framework for sensing and sensor-based actioning
SenSocial [35]	http://cs.bham.ac.uk/~axm514/sensocial	Android	No	Yes	Yes	Yes	No	A library for joint sampling of OSN and sensor data streams

example, Cote and Moskowitz investigated the impact of the "big five" personality traits on the relationship between interpersonal behaviour and affect [6]. The participants were instructed to fill out a questionnaire following each interpersonal interaction. Without context-aware devices, Cote and Moskowitz used beeper to periodically remind participants to keep up with the study, but telling them that the answers should be provided only after an interaction has happened. However, the correctness of this approach, particularly the timeliness of harvested data, depends on the users' compliance with the rules of the study. The study designers have no means of checking whether, and when, interpersonal interactions have happened.

The *MyExperience* framework [12], built upon an earlier context-aware mESM tool developed by Intille et al. [23], runs on Pocket PC and lets researchers design studies that embrace context awareness provided by mobile sensing. On one side, sensor data can be passively logged on the user device and uploaded to a server, on the other, the data can be processed on the phone to infer the context and trigger event-contingent sampling if needed. As one of the first examples of an mESM framework, MyExperience's context triggering relies on raw sensor data, i.e. it does not perform any inference in order to extract higher level information. For example, the framework supports sampling when a user moves from one mobile cellular base station to another, but cannot recognise if a user arrived at a semantically significant location, say his/her workplace.

MyExperience and ESP set a foundation for modern experience sampling frameworks, while a wider adoption of mESM frameworks came with the rise of the smartphone that enabled remote data gathering without requiring user actions, and context-aware user querying. The first Apple iPhone, released in 2007 and packed with numerous high-resolution sensors, marked a revolution in mobile sensing. Devices from different vendors followed, often running Android OS that enabled finer control over sensing than ever before. Modern smartphone sensing, however, has to balance between limited energy resources available on the phone, and the need for fine-grained data from multiple sensors. In addition, smartphone's sensors were not originally conceived for continuous sampling. Sensing and data collection management become a new pressing issue for mobile computing. Sensing frameworks such as *ESSensorManager* (a part of the Emotion Sense project) aim to abstract the details about data acquisition and collection from an application developer and automate sensing as per predefined policies [30]. The *funf* framework adds an option of basic survey data collection, and was used in a detailed 15-month long study of 130 participants' social and physical behaviour [2]. The study provided an in-depth investigation of the connection between individuals' social behaviour and their financial status, and the effects of one's network in decision making. The power of sensed data was further demonstrated when on top of funf the authors built an intervention that not only sampled users' behaviour, but also influenced users to exercise more.

Raw data from mobile sensors can be difficult to interpret in terms that are of direct interest when sampling human behaviour. High-level inferences often need to be made before sampled experience becomes valuable for researchers and therapists. *Purple Robot*'s authors claim that their framework supports statistical summaries of the user's communication patterns, including phone logs and text-message transcripts. *Ohmage* [45], a platform for participatory sensing and ESM studies, hosts a few data classifiers that can infer concepts such as mobility and speech. A psychology practitioner faces a large barrier between raw data from sensors that are related to users' behaviour, e.g. their movement, and the high-level labels of those behaviours, e.g. if people are walking or driving a car. It is crucial for mESM frameworks to abstract the sensing, in this case accelerometer and GPS sensor sampling, data processing, in this case extracting acceleration variance and GPS-reported speed, and machine learning, in this case classify a mobility mode, and deliver high-level information. Recently, Google released its activity recognition API for Android, enabling easy, albeit crude, inference of user's activity state [15].

Besides built-in smartphone sensors, *PsychLog* [14] and *Open Data Kit* (*ODK*) [19] frameworks provide support for external sensors that can be attached to a mobile devices, greatly enhancing the utility of ESM for ambulatory assessment. Moreover, for understanding human behaviour, any source of human-related information can be a sensor. In particular, social interactions are for a large part conducted over online social networks (OSNs), and monitoring OSNs is increasingly becoming a focus of social science studies. For instance, this information-rich sensor can be merged with the physical context sensors, in order to uncover socio-environmental relationships. An example of system supporting this type of real-time data fusion is *SenSocial*, a distributed (residing on mobiles and a centralised server) middleware for merging OSN-generated and physical sensor data streams [35].

A successful mESM framework abstracts mobile application programming from an intervention developer, yet exposes enough functionality so that a variety of studies are supported. Early on, MyExperience used an XML-based interface through which study developers can define sensor data to be collected, survey questions and triggers that will alert users to fill in the surveys. Although close to a natural language, XML scripts are not an ideal means of describing a potentially complex mESM application. Targeting primarily less tech savvy users in the developing world, ODK puts an emphasis on hassle-free study design process [19]. The framework introduces a survey and sensor data collection authoring tool that enables drag-and-drop study design. ODK is further tailored for non-expert designers and study participants by supporting automated data upload, storage and cloud transfer, as well as automated phone prompts that users respond to with keypad presses. The Project Authoring tool that comes with the Ohmage framework guides a study designer through a project definition process, and outputs an XML definition of the study. Ohmage also features tools such as Explore Data, Interactive and Passive Dashboards, and Lifestreams, that enable in-depth analysis and visualisation of collected data. In particular, Lifestreams use statistical inference on raw collected data in order to examine behavioural trends and answer questions such as "how much time a user spends at work/home?".

8.4 Challenges of Sampling with Mobile Devices

Contextual data collection, rapid prototype design, study scalability and automated result analysis are just some of the ways in which mobile devices revolutionise the traditional ESM. However, certain original limitations of the method are still present even with this new technology. How to capture experience without interfering with the participant's lifestyle, and how to sample relevant moments when the user's lifestyle is highly varying and unpredictable are some of the questions existing since the ESM was introduced. Some other issues, such as user recruitment become more prevalent now that a study can be distributed in form of an application that could be run on millions of devices. Furthermore, the new platform introduced novel technical challenges that impact the way studies should be designed.

8.4.1 Recruiting and Maintaining Participation

The Internet empowered social scientists with an easy access to a large and diverse pool of participants, alleviating the predominant issue of running psychological studies on a small group of college students [17]. Yet, recruitment in initial mESM studies saw little benefit from the Internet, since the participation was throttled, just like in the case of the older beeper technology, by the availability of the supporting hardware, i.e. Pocket PCs. Nowadays, with 1.5 billion users the smartphone is one of the most ubiquitous devices on the planet. Consequently, smartphone-based mESM studies can be distributed at an unprecedented scale.

All major smartphone operating systems, such as Android, iOS and Windows Mobile, have their corresponding online application stores. With these stores as distribution channels, the pool of study participants is no more confined to a certain population that a study designer can reach. Despite concerns about the diversity of participants recruited through the Internet, Gosling et al. show that such a sample is more representative of the actual demographics than a sample recruited through traditional means [17]. Note, however, that the Internet has been around longer than smartphones, and has penetrated almost all segments of the society. Still, a rapid rise in smartphone ownership promises to erase any demographic biases that currently may exist in smartphone usage.

To a potential participant, a smartphone-based mESM provides an additional benefit of anonymity, as a user does not have to disclose her real name, nor needs to meet the people/organisation running the study. On the down side, researchers have to sacrifice the close control over who the study participants are. For example, there is no reliable way to confirm that a person's age is truthfully reported, potentially allowing minors to run adult-only studies. Mobile sensing can somewhat ameliorate the problem of false reporting, as it provides information about users' activity, movement, geographic location, communication patterns and others. It has been shown that such information reflects users' age, gender, social status [11]. Besides assisting in the pruning of false reports, the link between sensor data and the demographics can be used to selectively target a certain demographic group, or to tailor the study according to different groups, e.g. adjusting sampling times according to local customs, sending different questions to people belonging to different social groups.

A low entry barrier that smartphone mESM applications provide, also means that leaving a study is easy—a user just has to uninstall or ignore the application. Usually only a percentage of users is active after the first initial period. Furthermore, on global application markets mESM study applications compete with hundreds of thousands of useful and fun applications. One way of attracting and retaining a wide audience for an mESM study is by providing some kind of information back to the user. In Emotion Sense, an mESM application that captures emotional state and contextual sensor information, participant retention is achieved through gamification and provision of self-reflecting information about the user [29]. Emotion Sense invites a user to "unlock" different parts the application by providing further experience samples.

Another means of attracting and retaining users is through remuneration. Amazon Mechanical Turk is a popular crowdsourcing marketplace where *requesters* post jobs to be completed by *workers*. The jobs typically consists of simple, well-defined tasks for which computers are not suitable, such as data verification, image analysis and data collection. Workers are paid a previously agreed sum of money per completed task. Any adult person, from any continent, can become a worker. In [33], Manson and Suri discuss the opportunities for conducting behavioural research on Amazon's Mechanical Turk. A wide pool of participants for a study and a payment system that enforces job completion are emphasised as the main advantages of the Mechanical Turk. On the other hand, artificial automatic workers—bots—can be used by workers to fake study results without actually running the study. In addition, the Mechanical Turk workers are not representative of general, even online, demographics. We believe, however, that mobile sensing can be used to ameliorate both problems. Artificial behaviour can be detected through unusual activity and movement patterns, while as explained earlier, sensed data can be used to infer the participants demographics.

8.4.2 Sampling at the Right Time

Smartphone-based mESM applications run on devices that are an inseparable part of participants' lives. Thus, it is crucial for a sampling schedule to be in harmony with the user's lifestyle. A well designed interruption schedule can help in both retaining users, but also in fulfilling the true role of experience sampling—recording momentary experience—as participants not wishing to be interrupted are likely to introduce the recall bias by delaying their answers until they find a suitable moment to respond [36].

Interactivity is in the core of human behaviour, as we balance between working on a task and switching to other pressing issues. The mobile phone makes our lives increasingly interactive as notifications delivered via mobile devices became a dominant means of signalling possible tasks switching events. In mESM studies mobile notifications are used to prompt users to fill in sampling surveys. The timing of notifications is important, since in case a notification arrives in an opportune moment for interruption the user reacts to it quickly, and fills in a survey with timely data. Several research studies investigated mobile notification scheduling in order to identify these opportune moments, and found that the context in which a person is, to a large extent, determines if a user is interruptible or not [22, 49]. Equipped with sensors, a mobile device can infer this context. Ho and Intille, for example, show that external on-body accelerometers can detect moments of activity transitions, and that in such moments users react to an interruption more favourably [22].

In [41] a 20-person 2-week study of mobile interruptibility shows how data from built-in smartphone sensors relates to user's attentiveness to mobile interactions in form of notifications. The study demonstrates that a personalised model of the sensed data—interruptibility relationship can be built, after which the authors extract the sensor modalities that describe user interruptibility, including acceleration, location and time information, and implement personalised machine learning models that, depending on the given sensor input, infer interruptibility. The findings are funnelled into a practical system termed *InterruptMe*—an Android library for notification management, that informs an overlying application about opportune moments in which to interrupt a user.[3] Machine learning-based models that InterruptMe builds are refined over time. However, ESM studies are limited by the number of samples that are taken from a single person over a period of time, thus the phone should learn about when to interrupt a user with as few training samples as possible. Kapoor and Horvitz propose a decision-theoretic approach for minimising the number of samples one needs to take from a user in order to build a reliable model of that persons interruptibility [24]. Finally, the InterruptMe study finds that interruption moments cannot be considered in isolation, and that users' sentiment towards an interruption depends on the recently experienced interruption load. This may become a limiting factor as the number of applications, and consequently notifications, that a user gets on her phone grows.

8.4.3 ESM Studies and Contextual Bias

A decision about when, or under which conditions, a notification to complete a survey should be fired is not only important for improved user interaction and compliance, it also has a crucial effect on the data that will be harvested.

Studies have, for example, been designed to collect data at random intervals [3] or when smartphone sensors acquire readings of a particular value [12]. While the latter is often motivated by directly tying a device state with a device-related assessment (e.g. plugging in the phone triggering questions about phone charging [12]), both of these methods have been used by researchers to make inferences and test hypotheses

[3]InterruptMe is available as a free open-source software at http://bitbucket.org/veljkop/intelligenttrigger.

about broad, non-device specific aspects of participants' behaviours, such as daily events and moods [4] and sustainable transportation choices [13].

This methodology assumes that the design choice of which trigger to use will not affect (or, indeed, will even augment the accuracy of) the contextual data that can be used to learn about participants. In doing so, these studies do not take into account the effect that the designed sampling strategy has on the conclusions they infer about participants' behaviours. However, these behaviours are likely to be habitual or, more broadly, variantly distributed across each day. For example, since people may split the majority of their time between home and work, sampling randomly is likely to fail capturing participants in other locations. While this could easily be solved by using survey triggering that is conditioned on the value of a user's location (from here on termed *location-based triggering*), it is not clear how doing so affects sampling from the broader set of sensors that researchers may be collecting data from (i.e. how would location-based sampling bias the data about participants activity levels?).

In [29], Lathia et al. study the effect of mESM design choices on the inferences that can be made from participants' sensor data, and on the variance in survey responses that can be collected from them. In particular the authors examined the question: *are the behavioural inferences that a researcher makes with a time or trigger-defined sub-sample of sensor data biased by the sampling strategy's design?* The study demonstrates that different single-sensor sampling strategies will result in what is refer to as *contextual dissonance*: a disagreement in how much different behaviours are represented in the aggregated sensor data.

To analyse this, Lathia et al. examine the extent that studies' design influences the response and sensor/behavioural data that researchers can collect from participants in context-aware mESM studies. If the design of the experiments does not have any influence on the data that are collected, we would expect that, on aggregate, the data gleaned from different designs would be consistent with one another. Instead, the study demonstrates that different single-sensor sampling strategies result in contextual dissonance, i.e. a disagreement in how much different behaviours are represented in the aggregated sensor data. This conclusion is based on a 1-month, 22-participant mESM study that solicited survey responses about participants' moods while collecting data from a set of sensors about their behaviour. This falls under two broad groups:

- *Amount of Data.* Using different sensors to trigger notifications will directly impact the amount of data that researchers can collect. In this study, microphone-based triggers, which pop-up a survey only if a non-silent audio sample is sensed, produce a higher per-user average number of notifications; conversely, the communication-based triggers, fired after a call/SMS received/sent event, produce the lowest average number of notifications per participant (5.11 ± 3.69), indicating that participants were not using their phone for its call/SMS functionality throughout the day.
- *Response Data.* In addition, the study examines how the feelings of participants varied under different experimental conditions. In this case, the null hypothesis is that the *design* of survey triggers does not bias the resulting sample of affect data

that is collected. This hypothesis is rejected, with varying levels of confidence, if the resulting p-values are small. In 4 of the 6 tests that were performed, it was found that the negative affect ratings (and 2 of 6 for the positive ratings) were significantly different from one another with at least 90 % confidence. Uncovering why this result has emerged calls for further research: it may be explained by the fact that some triggers were likely to be more obtrusive than others, thus affecting responses.

Finally, we point out that the above conclusion is based on a time-limited and small-scale study. Perhaps some of these challenges can be overcome by using larger populations for longer times. However, these results stand as a warning for researchers to be mindful of in their future mobile experience sampling studies.

8.4.4 Technical Challenges in mESM

A smartphone is a multi-purpose device used for voice, video, and text communication, Web surfing, calendar management or navigation, among other applications. This versatility puts pressure on smartphone's resources, and limits its usability for experience sampling. Furthermore, unlike a conventional mobile application, an mESM application needs to be always-on, sense the context and sample users' experiences as necessary.

One of the key constraints of many mobile sensing applications is a limited capacity of a mobile device's battery. Power-hungry sensors, such as a GPS chip, were not envisioned for frequent sampling. Adaptive sensing is a popular means of reducing energy requirements of a mobile sensing application. Here, samples are taken less frequently, or with a coarser granularity, e.g. a user's location is recorded with a base station ID, instead of with accurate GPS coordinates. *AndWellness* framework, for example, lets study designers tune the balance between the sampling resolution and power drain [21]. The same framework implements hierarchical sensor activation, another means of minimising energy usage. This approach uses low-power, yet less accurate, sensors in order to infer if high-power, fine-grain sensors should be turned on. An example of hierarchical sensing can be seen in AndWellness: a change in a device's WiFi access point association serves as an indicator of user's movement, and if movement is detected a GPS chip is activated. While Ohmage implements adaptive sensing to save energy during speech detection by adjusting the sampling rate depending on the sensing results—if the app has not detected speech over a certain amount of time, it exponentially decreases the sampling rate. How to adjust the sampling rate with adaptive sensing, or hierarchical activation, while ensuring that the events of interest are not missed is an open research question. In SociableSense, a mobile application that senses socialisation among users [44], a linear reward-inaction function is associated with the sensing cycle, and the sampling rate is reduced during "quiet" times, when no interesting events are observed. The approach is very efficient with human interaction inference, since the target events, such as conversations, are not sudden and short; for other types of events, different approaches might be more appropriate.

Client-server architecture is at the core of almost every ESM framework. Servers are used for centralised data storage and analysis, data visualisation, and remote configuration of sampling mobiles. The balance of functionalities over mobiles and a server can have a significant impact on the performance and the possibilities of an mESM application. For automated labelling of human behaviour, say recognising if a person is walking or not, a substantial amount of data, in this case accelerometer data, has to be processed through machine learning models. Server-based processing comes with benefits of a high computational power of multicore CPUs, and a global view of the system, and as a consequence data from all the users can be harnessed for individual (and group) inferences. On the other hand, the transfer of the high-volume data produced by mobile sensors can be costly, especially if done via a cellular network. Some mESM and mobile sensing frameworks, including Ohmage and ESSensorManager, let developers define data transfer policies, such as "upload mobile data only via Wi-Fi" and "do not upload any data if the battery level is below 20 %".

Besides its impact on performance and cost, balancing local and remote processing is important for ESM studies due to privacy issues associated with data transfer and storage (see for example [8]). Location, video and audio data are particularly vulnerable, yet can be protected with a suitable balance of remote and local processing. For example, if we want to infer that a user is having a conversation, instead of transferring raw audio data for server-side processing, we can extract sound features relevant for speech classification, such as Mel-Frequency Cepstral Coefficients (MFCC) of sound frames that contain sounds over a certain threshold intensity, and send these for remote analysis. Even if a malicious party gets access to this data, the original audio recording cannot be reconstructed. Similarly, instead of sending raw geographic coordinates to a server, a mobile application could host an internal classifier of a user's semantic location (e.g. home/work), and send already processed data, minimising the amount of information about the user that can be revealed.

8.5 Future of mESM

Mobile computing is rapidly transforming social sciences. First, the range of potential study participants has expanded dramatically. Nowadays researchers have access to a virtually world-wide pool of participants. Second, the granularity of personal data gathered through mobile sensors and phone-based interactions, including online social network activities, can paint a very detailed picture of an individual's behaviour. In addition, long-term data can be obtained, as long as the mESM application manages to keep users engaged, and they do not remove the application from their phones.

The above transformation requires the rethinking of the traditional social science approaches. Computational social science [31] has emerged as a field that harnesses statistical and machine learning approaches over user-generated "big data" in order to explain social science concepts, including behaviour. This field is inherently interdisciplinary and rather broad, since it involves computer scientists, engineers, and social scientists, who traditionally had limited interactions in the past.

8.5.1 Integration with Behaviour Interventions

Ubiquitous mobile computing devices and the ESM provide a detailed assessment of human behaviour at an unprecedented scale. A natural next step is to use the information about the existing individual and group behaviour to affect future behaviour. Behaviour change interventions (BCIs) are a psychological method that aims to elicit a positive behaviour change. These interventions commonly include collecting relevant information about the participant, setting goals and plans, monitoring behaviour, and providing feedback. Digital BCIs (dBCIs) moved behaviour change interventions to the Web. The benefits of this transition include increased control over the content and the time of information delivery of information, as well as the reduction in the intervention cost, since the need to a face-to-face interaction with a therapist is avoided. In addition, dBCIs open an opportunity for scalable automatic content tailoring. Such tailoring has been shown to be effective for the actual behaviour change [52].

Recently, both isolated [39] and systematic [28] attempts have been made to move dBCIs from the Web to smartphones. The new platform enables intervention content delivery anywhere and anytime. In addition, a personalised use of the phone indicates that through mobile sensing and user sampling a detailed personalised model of user behaviour can be constructed and used to drive the intervention. For example, users whose samples indicate sedentary behaviour can be provided with a positive feedback whenever they are detected to be active. Technical difficulties in building an integrated mESM and intervention distribution method hamper proliferation of mobile dBCIs. The system design and programming effort associated with implementing a system for remote mobile sensing and experience sampling, information delivery, user management and personalised behaviour modelling is overwhelming. Certain existing frameworks, such as AndWellness [21] and BeWell [27], concentrate on sampling data relevant for users' health and well-being, yet none of them cater specifically to dBCIs, and none of them solves the above technical difficulties. The UBhave framework (Fig. 8.2) aims to overcome this by providing out-of-the-box support for mobile dBCI design and deployment [18]. The framework consists of an intervention authoring tool, through which therapists can design interventions, and an automated translation tool, which translates the design into an intervention file. This file is then deployed to and interpreted by participating mobile devices running the UBhave client application. The framework ensures that therapist's instructions on when to sample user experience and sensor data are followed by the mobile app, and that the behaviour changing advice is delivered to the user when needed.

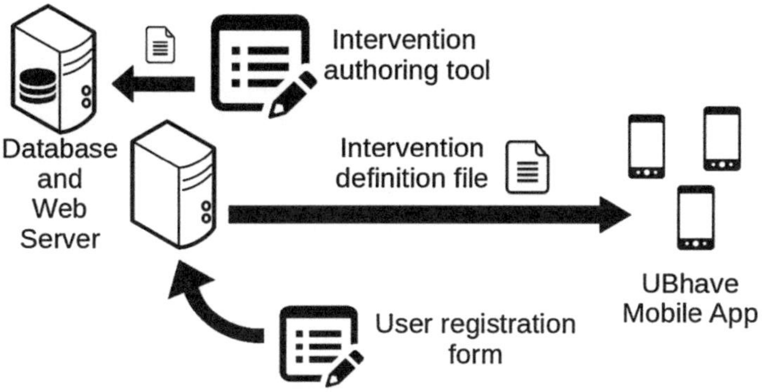

Fig. 8.2 Overview of the UBhave framework for mobile digital behaviour change interventions

The UBhave framework is the first that extends the idea of mESM beyond behaviour tracking to behaviour change. While the idea of mobile dBCIs sounds extremely promising, only after a wider adoption and broader behaviour change studies it is will be possible to quantify the actual effectiveness of mobile interventions.

8.5.2 Anticipatory mESM

The awareness of the current context is the main novelty of experience sampling using mobile devices. A prediction of future context has a tremendous potential to make an mESM a key tool for explaining human behaviour. Although predicting, and even inferring, participants' internal states with mobile sensors is yet to be achieved, prediction of some other behavioural aspects, such as users' movement trajectories or calling patterns, has already been demonstrated [42, 48].

Anticipatory computing systems rely on the past, present and predicted future information to bring judicious decisions about their current actions [47]. Mobile ESM applications could, in an anticipatory computing system manner, intelligently adapt their sampling schedules based on the predicted user behaviour. For example, an mESM application that could anticipate a depressive episode, could adapt its sampling to capture, with fine resolution, behaviour and the context just before the event of interest. This would not only provide very detailed information about the context that lead to the onset of a depressive episode, but also use phone's battery resources more efficiently.

Finally, we also envision proactive digital behaviour interventions delivered via mobile devices [40]. Besides the sampling schedule, anticipatory dBCIs would also adapt the feedback they give to a user according to the predicted state of the user, and the predicted effect the feedback will have on the user. For example, a smart wristband occasionally samples a user's heart rate. Based on the readings, the system, encompassing a phone and a wristband, predicts that the user is in risk of being highly stressed out. The system accesses user's online calendar and examines tasks scheduled for today. Then, it intelligently reschedules tasks to alleviate the risk of high stress and suggests a new schedule to the user. Technical obstacles associated with this scenario include stress prediction, itself quite challenging, but also the prediction of how a user will react to a given change in the calendar. Will the change really help alleviate stress? The idea of anticipatory mobile computing has just recently appeared in the literature, while the conventional mobile dBCIs have not yet taken off. Therefore, we are yet to witness anticipatory mobile dBCIs in practice.

8.6 Conclusion

Smarthphones and other mobile devices, such as wearables, are the first sensing and computing devices tightly interwoven into our daily lives. They represent revolutionary platforms for social science research and for the emerging field of computational social science. They indeed open a window of opportunity for social scientists to learn about human behaviour at previously unimaginable granularity and scale. A wide span of behaviours can be captured via mobile experience sampling. This covers the domains for which the traditional experience sampling has already been employed, such as studies of a personal time usage [25], emotions of different stigmatised groups [10], and classroom activities [51], to name a few. In addition, mobile computing enables the investigation of new domains such as the location-dependent privacy management of sharing information on online social networks [1], sleep monitoring [27] and mobile application evaluation [5]. Furthermore, mESMs are being used for ambulatory assessment in areas that span from sexual behaviour to physical exercise monitoring.[4]

We highlighted key benefits of mobile experience sampling, and presented mESM frameworks that abstract the technical effort of building a sensing and sampling mobile application, and enable seamless implementation and deployment of large scale social studies. Our vision for the evolution of mESM goes along the lines of the general consensus that mobile applications need to be "stealth", perfectly integrated with everyday lives. Therefore, we envision considerate mESM studies, where the interaction with the user is minimally invasive, and aligned with the sensed user behaviour. Furthermore, harnessing the persuasive power of the smartphone, we also see proactive behaviour change interventions based on the automated analysis of the sampling results. Finally, outside of the scope of this review, but important for the ecosystem of users, intervention designers and mESM framework developers are the questions of large-scale data mining, interpretation and visualisation, data feedback to study participants, and privacy and ethics issues associated with mobile sensing.

[4]The following URL lists currently running experience sampling projects using the Ohmage framework: http://ohmage.org/projects.html.

Acknowledgments This work was supported through the EPSRC grants "UBhave: ubiquitous and social computing for positive behaviour change" (EP/I032673/1) and "Trajectories of Depression: Investigating the Correlation between Human Mobility Patterns and Mental Health Problems by means of Smartphones" (P/L006340/1).

References

1. Abdesslem, F.B., Parris, I., Henderson, T.: Mobile experience sampling: reaching the parts of facebook other methods cannot reach. In: Proceedings of the Privacy and Usability Methods Pow-Wow (PUMP), Dundee, UK, Sept 2010
2. Aharony, N., Pan, W., Ip, C., Khayal, I., Pentland, A.: Social fmri: investigating and shaping social mechanisms in the real world. Pervasive Mobile Comput. **7**(6), 643–659 (2011)
3. Barrett, L.F., Barrett, D.J.: An introduction to computerized experience sampling in psychology. Soc. Sci. Comput. Rev. **19**(2), 175–185 (2001)
4. Clark, L., Watson, D.: Mood and the mundane: relations between daily life and self-reported mood. J. Pers. Soc. Psychol. **54**(2), 296–308 (1988)
5. Consolvo, S., Walker, M.: Using the experience sampling method to evaluate ubicomp applications. IEEE Pervasive Comput. **2**, 24–31 (2003)
6. Cote, S., Moskowitz, D.S.: On the dynamic covariation between interpersonal behavior and affect: prediction from neuroticism, extraversion, and agreeableness. J. Pers. Soc. Psychol. **75**, 1032 (1998)
7. Csikszentmihalyi, M., Larson, R.: Validity and reliability of the experience-sampling method. J. Nerv. Mental Dis. **175**(9), 526–536 (1987)
8. de Montjoye, Y.-A., Shmueli, E., Wang, S.S., Pentland, A.S.: OpenPDS: protecting the privacy of metadata through safe answers. PLoS ONE **9**(7), e98790 (2014)
9. Fahrenberg, J., Myrtek, M. (eds.): Ambulatory Assessment: Computer-Assisted Psychological and Psychophysiological Methods in Monitoring and Field Studies. Hogrefe & Huber, Seattle, WA, USA (1996)
10. Frable, D., Platt, L., Hoey, S.: Concealable stigmas and positive self-perceptions: feeling better around similar others. J. Pers. Soc. Psychol. **74**(4), 909–921 (1998)
11. Frias-Martinez, V. Virsesa, J.: On The relationship between socio-economic factors and cell phone usage. In: ICTD'12, Atlanta, GA, USA, March 2012
12. Froehlich, J., Chen, M.Y., Consolvo, S., Harrison, B., Landay, J.A.: MyExperience: a system for in situ tracing and capturing of user feedback on mobile phones. In: MobiSys'07, Puerto Rico, USA, June 2007
13. Froehlich, J., Dillahunt, T., Klasnja, P., Mankoff, J., Consolvo, S., Harrison, B., Landay, J.A.: UbiGreen: investigating a mobile tool for tracking and supporting green transportation habits. In: ACM CHI'09, Boston, MA, USA, April 2009
14. Gaggioli, A., Pioggia, G., Tartarisco, G., Baldus, G., Corda, D., Cipresso, P., Riva, G.: A mobile data collection platform for mental health research. Pers. Ubiquitous Comput. **17**(2), 241–251 (2013)
15. Google's Activity Recognition Application. http://developer.android.com/training/location/activity-recognition.html
16. Google Now. http://www.google.com/landing/now/ (2014). Accessed 15 Dec 2014
17. Gosling, S.D., Vazire, S., Srivastava, S., John, O.P.: Should we trust web-based studies? a comparative analysis of six preconceptions about internet questionnaires. Am. Psychol. **59**(2), (2004)
18. Hargood, C., Pejovic, V., Morrison, L., Michaelides, D.T., Musolesi, M., Yardley, L., Weal, M.: The UBhave framework: dynamic pervasive applications for behavioural psychology. In: Mobiquitous'14 (poster session), London, UK, Dec 2014

19. Hartung, C., Lerer, A., Anokwa, Y., Tseng, C., Brunette, W., Borriello, G.: Open data kit: tools to build information services for developing regions. In: ACM DEV'10, London, UK, Dec 2010
20. Hektner, J.M., Schmidt, J.A., Csikszentmihalyi, M.: Experience Sampling Method: Measuring the Quality of Everyday Life. Sage Publications, Thousand Oaks, CA, USA (2006)
21. Hicks, J., Ramanathan, N., Kim, D., Monibi, M., Selsky, J., Hansen, M., Estrin, D.: AndWellness: an open mobile system for activity and experience sampling. In: WirelessHealth'10, La Jolla, CA, USA, Oct 2010
22. Ho, J., Intille, S.S.: Using context-aware computing to reduce the perceived burden of interruptions from mobile devices. In: CHI'05, Portland, OR, USA, April 2005
23. Intille, S.S., Rondoni, J., Kukla, C., Ancona, I., Bao, L.: A context-aware experience sampling tool. In: CHI'03 (Extended Abstracts), Lauderdale, FL, USA, April 2003
24. Kapoor, A., Horvitz, E.: Experience sampling for building predictive user models: a comparative study. In: CHI'08, Florence, Italy, April 2008
25. Kubey, R., Csikszentmihalyi, M.: Television and the Quality of Life: How Viewing Shapes Everyday Experience. Routledge (1990)
26. Lane, N.D., Miluzzo, E., Lu, H., Peebles, D., Choudhury, T., Campbell, A.T.: A survey of mobile phone sensing. IEEE Commun. Mag. **48**, 140–150 (2010)
27. Lane, N.D., Mohammod, M., Lin, M., Yang, X., Lu, H., Ali, S., Doryab, A., Berke, E., Choudhury, T., Campbell, A.: Bewell: a smartphone application to monitor, model and promote wellbeing. In: PervasiveHealth'11, pp. 23–26 (2011)
28. Lathia, N., Pejovic, V., Rachuri, K., Mascolo, C., Musolesi, M., Rentfrow, P.J.: Smartphones for large-scale behaviour change intervention. IEEE Pervasive Comput. **12**(3), (2013)
29. Lathia, N., Rachuri, K., Mascolo, C., Rentfrow, P.: Contextual dissonance: design bias in sensor-based experience sampling methods. In: UbiComp'13, Zurich, Switzerland, Sept 2013
30. Lathia, N., Rachuri, K.K., Mascolo, C., Roussos, G.: Open source smartphone libraries for computational social science. In: MCSS'13, Zurich, Switzerland, Sept 2013
31. Lazer, D., Pentland, A., Adamic, L., Aral, S., Barabasi, A., Brewer, D., Christakis, N., Contractor, N., Fowler, J., Gutmann, M., et al.: Life in the network: the coming age of computational social science. Science **323**(5915), 721 (2009)
32. Lu, H., Frauendorfer, D., Rabbi, M., Mast, M.S., Chittaranjan, G.T., Campbell, A.T., Gatica-Perez, D., Choudhury, T.: Stresssense: detecting stress in unconstrained acoustic environments using smartphones. In: UbiComp'12, pp. 351–360. ACM (2012)
33. Mason, W., Suri, S.: Conducting behavioral research on amazon's mechanical turk. Behav. Res. Methods **44**(1), 1–23 (2012)
34. Mehl, M.R., Conner, T.S. (ed.): Handbook of Research Methods for Studying Daily Life. Guilford Publications (2013)
35. Mehrotra, A., Pejovic, V., Musolesi, M.: SenSocial: a middleware for integrating online social networks and mobile sensing data streams. In: Middleware'14, Bordeaux, France, Dec 2014
36. Mehrotra, A., Vermeulen, J., Pejovic, V., Musolesi, M.: Ask, but don't interrupt: the case for interruptibility-aware mobile experience sampling. In: 4th ACM Workshop on Mobile Systems for Computational Social Science (ACM MCSS'15) (2015)
37. Miller, G.: The smartphone psychology Manifesto. Perspect. Psychol. Sci. **7**(3), 221–237 (2012)
38. Miluzzo, E., Lane, N.D., Fodor, K., Peterson, R., Lu, H., Musolesi, M., Eisenman, S.B., Zheng, X., Campbell, A.T.: Sensing meets mobile social networks: the design, implementation and evaluation of the cenceme application. In: SenSys'08, pp. 337–350. ACM (2008)
39. Morrison, L.G., Hargood, C., Lin, S.X., Dennison, L., Joseph, J., Hughes, S., Michaelides, D.T., Johnston, D., Johnston, M., Michie, S., et al.: Understanding usage of a hybrid website and smartphone app for weight management: a mixed-methods study. J. Med. Internet Res. **16**(10), (2014)
40. Pejovic, V., Musolesi, M.: Anticipatory mobile computing for behaviour change interventions. In: 3rd ACM Workshop on Mobile Systems for Computational Social Science (ACM MCSS'14), Seattle, WA, USA (2014)

41. Pejovic, V., Musolesi, M.: InterruptMe: designing intelligent prompting mechanisms for pervasive applications. In: UbiComp'14, Seattle, WA, USA, Sept 2014
42. Phithakkitnukoon, S., Dantu, R., Claxton, R., Eagle, N.: Behavior-based adaptive call predictor. ACM Trans. Auton. Adapt. Syst. **6**(3), 21 (2011)
43. Rachuri, K.K., Musolesi, M., Mascolo, C., Rentfrow, J., Longworth, C., Aucinas, A.: EmotionSense: a mobile phones based adaptive platform for experimental social psychology research. In: UbiComp'10, Copenhagen, Denmark, ACM, Sept 2010
44. Rachuri, K.K., Mascolo, C., Musolesi, M., Rentfrow, P.J.: SociableSense: exploring the tradeoffs of adaptive sampling and computation offloading for social sensing. In: MobiCom'11, Las Vegas, NV, USA, Sept 2011
45. Ramanathan, N., Alquaddoomi, F., Falaki, H., George, D., Hsieh, C., Jenkins, J., Ketcham, C., Longstaff, B., Ooms, J., Selsky, J., Tangmunarunkit, H., Estrin, D.: Ohmage: an open mobile system for activity and experience sampling. In: PervasiveHealth'12, San Diego, CA, USA, May 2012
46. Reis, H.T., Gable, S.L.: Event-sampling and other methods for studying everyday experience. In: Handbook of Research Methods in Social and Personality, Psychology, pp. 190–222 (2000)
47. Rosen, R.: Anticipatory Systems. Pergamon Press, Oxford, UK (1985)
48. Sadilek, A., Krumm, J.: Far out: predicting long-term human mobility. In: AAAI'12, Toronto, Canada, July 2012
49. Ter Hofte, G.H.: Xensible interruptions from your mobile phone. In: Mobile HCI'07, Singapore, Sept 2007
50. Trull, T.J., Ebner-Priemer, U.: Ambulatory assessment. Annu. Rev. Clin. Psychol. **9**(151), (2013)
51. Turner, J.C., Meyer, D.K., Cox, K.E., Logan, C., DiCintio, M., Thomas, C.T.: Creating contexts for involvement in mathematics. J. Educ. Psychol. **90**(4), 730 (1998)
52. Yardley, L., Joseph, J., Michie, S., Weal, M., Wills, G., Little, P.: Evaluation of a web-based intervention providing tailored advice for self-management of minor respiratory symptoms: exploratory randomized controlled trial. J. Med. Internet Res. **12**(4), e66 (2010)

Chapter 9
Affective and Personality Corpora

Ante Odić, Andrej Košir and Marko Tkalčič

Abstract In this chapter we describe publicly available datasets with personality and affective parameters relevant to the research questions covered by this book. We briefly describe the available data, acquisition procedure, and other relevant details of these datasets. There are three datasets acquired through the users' natural interaction with different services: LDOS CoMoDa, LJ2M and myPersonality. Two datasets were acquired in controlled, laboratory settings: LDOS PerAff-1 and DEAP. Finally, we also mention four stimuli datasets from the Media Core project: ANET, IADS, ANEW, IAPS, as well as the 1000 songs dataset. We summarise this information for a quick reference to researchers interested in using these datasets or preparing the acquisition procedure of their own.

9.1 Introduction

In order to carry out relevant research, appropriate datasets must be used, which enable researchers to test their hypotheses. For the research questions covered by this book, it is important that the datasets contain different personality-related features describing users, as well as affective parameters, along with the information regarding the interaction between users and different systems. Since the acquisition of such datasets is not an easy task, and not many live systems include such data, these datasets are rare and researchers often tend to collect their own data for research purposes.

A. Odić (✉)
Outfit7 (Slovenian Subsidiary Ekipa2 D.o.o.), Ljubljana, Slovenia
e-mail: ante.odic@outfit7.com

A. Košir
Faculty of Electrical Engineering, The User-adapted Communications & Ambient Intelligence Lab (LUCAMI), Ljubljana, Slovenia
e-mail: andrej.kosir@fe.uni-lj.si

M. Tkalčič
Department of Computational Perception, Johannes Kepler University in Linz, Linz, Austria
e-mail: marko.tkalcic@jku.at

M. Tkalčič et al. (eds.), *Emotions and Personality in Personalized Services*, Human–Computer Interaction Series, DOI 10.1007/978-3-319-31413-6_9

In this chapter we try to provide relevant information for the researchers in the field from two perspectives: (i) survey existing and available datasets for research and (ii) survey research describing the acquisition of such datasets as a reference for the acquisition tasks and guidance for building new datasets. The datasets that we describe in this chapter are publicly available. In addition, we believe that these datasets contain valuable data for many different research goals, and as such, serve as a valuable resource for researchers. Since the acquisition of such data requires careful and controlled procedures, this section also tries to be a reference to researchers that will perform the acquisition, and preprocessing, of new datasets.

Datasets for the research in this field should ideally have several main types of information. Mainly, there has to be information regarding users, items and some type of metric that describes the interaction between users and items, how items are suitable for users or how users perceived or rated (explicitly or implicitly) the items they have consumed. This can be observed as a user-item matrix where for user-item pairs there is a measure describing their interaction (e.g. rating, different user-experience measures, etc.). In addition to that, these datasets should contain information describing users' personality profiles (e.g. Big5 factors describing users [1]). Furthermore,

Table 9.1 This table contains the list of datasets described in this section with the following information: name of the dataset, domain (i.e. type of items), whether the acquisition was in the laboratory setting or the natural interaction with the system, number of users, number of items and reference to the article describing the dataset and the acquisition

Dataset	Domain	Acquisition type	Users	Items	References
LDOS-CoMoDa	Movies	Natural interaction	235	1300	[2]
LDOS-PerAff-1	Images	Laboratory setting	52	70	[3]
LJ2M	Blogs	Natural interaction	649,712	1,928,868	[4]
DEAP	Music Videos	Laboratory setting	32	120	[5]
myPersonality	Social Network	Natural interaction	Varies	Varies	[6]
1000 songs	Music	Stimuli dataset	100	744	[7]
ANET	Text	Stimuli dataset	n/a	n/a	[8]
IADS	Sounds	Stimuli dataset	n/a	n/a	[9]
ANEW	Text	Stimuli dataset	n/a	n/a	[10]
IAPS	Images	Stimuli dataset	n/a	n/a	[11]

Table 9.2 In this table, in the same order as in the previous one, we add additional information regarding each dataset: type of personality profile of users, type of affective data, metric describing the interaction between the users and items, additional data

Dataset	Personality	Emotions	Interaction	Additional data
LDOS-CoMoDa	Big5	6 basic emotions	Ratings	Context, demographics, item metadata
LDOS-PerAff-1	Big5	VAD space	Ratings	Demographics, frontal face videos
LJ2M	No	132 mood tags	No	Blog post, associated songs
DEAP	No	VAD space	VAD ratings	Frontal face videos, sensor signals
myPersonality	Big5	No	Facebook likes	Psychometric features, demographics, etc.
1000 songs	No	VA space	VAD ratings	40-s music clips
ANET	No	VAD space	No	English texts
IADS	No	VAD space	No	Digital sounds
ANEW	No	VAD space	No	English words
IAPS	No	VAD space	No	Images

these datasets should also contain affective parameters. For example, those parameters might describe emotional states of the user during the interaction with the item, the change of the user's emotional state after consuming an item, affective metadata describing the items, etc.

There are three types of datasets that we cover in this chapter:

1. Datasets acquired by users' natural interaction with live systems.
2. Datasets acquired in controlled, laboratory settings, from participants.
3. Datasets containing stimuli for research on emotions.

In Tables 9.1 and 9.2 we summarize the information regarding the described datasets for quick reference.

9.2 Available Datasets

In this section we describe datasets that were made publicly available by their authors. For each dataset we provide the basic information that will help researchers to decide whether the dataset is suitable for their work. This consists of the research the dataset was intended for, description of the data the dataset contains, brief description of the acquisition procedure, and links to where the datasets can be obtained.

There are two types of datasets that are publicly available: (i) those acquired in the experimental (laboratory) setting, and (ii) those that were acquired during a natural users' interaction with an existing service. The data in the former type of datasets is usually less noisy, since all external, uncontrolled influences were removed, however such datasets contain less users due to natural limitations of the laboratory-based acquisition procedures. In addition, there is a potential problem with acquiring emotional state in laboratory setting. Emotional state of the user might be context dependent and the context in the laboratory is artificial and might not represent the real world behaviour of users. This has to be considered and addressed during the data acquisition.

On the other hand, datasets acquired in the laboratory settings have more personality and emotion-related features describing the users, since the usage of video cameras and/or other sensors were possible during the users' interaction with the system. Therefore, the selection of the dataset relevant for a specific research depends on the types of the analyses that will be performed.

While acquiring the data, it is also important to keep in mind what is user's goal and what is the value exchange for the user, especially in the case of the laboratory settings. The user's goal is the natural, or the artificial, goal that the user is trying to achieve through the interaction with the system. For example, in recommender systems, users are providing data and rating items to improve their profile in order to get more relevant recommendations. In laboratory settings, users' goals should also be explained to subjects since it is relevant whether users are rating videos, e.g. according to how suitable it is to watch at home with friends, or how interesting it is during the laboratory session. All users should be artificially placed in the same context, i.e. purpose for providing data. Regarding the value exchange, users can be motivated to use the system or participate in the experiment by different internal or external motivators, that should also be taken into account.

We mention users' goals in the description of datasets for which we found the reliable information regarding this aspect of the acquisition.

9.2.1 Context Movie Dataset (LDOS-CoMoDa)

Context Movie Dataset (LDOS-CoMoDa) was created for the research on context-aware recommender systems [2]. It was acquired from the users' natural interaction with the live system over a long period of time. It contains movie ratings, contextual information, movies' metadata and users' Big5 personality profiles from subset of users that decided to provide personality profiles.

For the data acquisition, the authors created an online application for rating movies (www.ldos.si/recommender.html). The application is used by users to track the movies they watched, obtain the movie recommendations and browse the movies.

The users were acquired by presenting and advertising the online application to students of the Faculty of Electrical Engineering, University of Ljubljana, and different movie forums and usenet newsgroups. Therefore, the users were volunteers that were either attracted by the research questions or the usability of the online application. According to the authors, the users' goal for rating the movies is to improve their profile to gain better recommendations, express themselves and help others, according to [12].

9.2.1.1 Acquisition

Regarding the data acquisition, the online application is used by users to rate the movie that they have just seen. The users rate the items on the Likert scale from one to five.

In addition to rating the consumed movie, users fill in a simple questionnaire created to explicitly acquire the contextual information describing the situation during the consumption stage of the user-item interaction [2]. The questionnaire was designed in such a way that it is simple and not time consuming for a user to provide the contextual information. Users are instructed to provide the rating and contextual information immediately after the consumption.

Among different types of contextual information (described in the following section), emotional context was also acquired. According to the authors, for the emotional state as the contextual information in the movie RS, the consumption stage is a *multiple-context value* stage, which means that emotional state changes several time during the consumption. Therefore two types of emotional state contextual factors were acquired: (i) the emotional state that was dominant during the consumption (*domEMO*) and (ii) the emotional state at the end of the movie (*endEMO*).

Users were also able to input their personality profile into the online application. Therefore, for users that chose to do so, the dataset also contains Big5 personality profiles, that were acquired through the IPIP 50 questionnaire [13]. Ratings for movies, and all additional information was provided by users, as they have decided. There was no mandatory ratings of the preselected movies.

9.2.1.2 Dataset Information

The LDOS-CoMoDa dataset has been in development since Sep. 15, 2010. It contains three main groups of information: general user information, item metadata and contextual information. The general user information is provided by the user upon registering in the system. It consists of the user's age, sex, country and city. There are 163 male and 72 female users in the dataset.

The item metadata is inserted into the dataset for each movie rated by at least one user. The metadata describing each item is the director's name and surname, country, language, year, three genres, three actors and budget.

Table 9.3 contains the description of the acquired contextual information.

To ensure that all the acquired contextual information is from the consumption stage, the users were instructed to provide the rating immediately after the consumption, and that it should describe the moment of watching the movie. Furthermore,

Table 9.3 Contextual variables in the LDOS-CoMoDa dataset

Contextual variable	Description
time	Morning, afternoon, evening, night
daytype	Working day, weekend, holiday
season	Spring, summer, autumn, winter
location	Home, public place, friend's house
weather	Sunny/clear, rainy, stormy, snowy, cloudy
social	Alone, partner, friends, colleagues, parents, public, family
endEmo	Sad, happy, scared, surprised, angry, disgusted, neutral
dominantEmo	Sad, happy, scared, surprised, angry, disgusted, neutral
mood	Positive, neutral, negative
physical	Healthy, ill
decision	User's choice, given by other
interaction	First, n-th

this ensures that the provided rating is not influenced by unwanted noise, such as discussing the movie with friends, reading reviews, seeing the average movie rating, etc. For assessing whether the rating was provided in a satisfactory manner, the authors have identified a set of criteria that they use to flag suspicious data inputs. For example, if the rating with *winter* context is provided during summer, the data is flagged as suspicious, furthermore, if a single user provides multiple ratings at once the data is flagged as suspicious, etc. Such suspicious entries were later avoided during the testing. It is still, however, impossible to be completely sure that all the acquired data is correct. Acquiring ratings immediately after the consumption provides less noisy, real data, however, due to the collection of the contextual data, it was not possible to provide users with a list of items to rate. Each rating is made after the real consumption, which makes this type of data acquisition a long process.

LDOS-CoMoDa dataset was used in several research, for example, for the research on the role of emotions in context-aware recommendations [14], and the research on local context modelling with semantic pre-filtering [15].

Additional information about the dataset can also be found in [16]. LDOS-CoMoDa dataset can be acquired on the following link: (www.ldos.si/comoda.html).

9.2.2 LDOS-PerAff-1

The LDOS-PerAff-1 dataset was created for the need of the research of affective- and personality-based user modelling in recommender systems [3]. It is acquired form the users in the controlled, laboratory setting. LDOS-PerAff-1 dataset is composed of users' ratings for images, information about users and images, users' personality profiles, information about the induced emotions and the video clips of the users' facial expressions.

For the data acquisition, the authors created a Matlab application in which the users are rating images. The goal of rating the images was users' selection of images for their computer's wallpaper.

Users in the dataset are students that participated in the experiment. The users' goal was to rate images for the purpose of selecting the best image for their desktop background.

9.2.2.1 Acquisition

The acquisition scenario consisted of showing the subjects a sequence of images and asking the subjects to rate these images as if they were choosing images for their computer wallpaper. Ratings were selected on a Likert scale from one to five.

For each image the authors needed to know the emotional state it induces. The affective values for each image were provided by the IAPS dataset. Each image was annotated with the first two statistical moments of the induced emotion in users in the Valence-Arousal-Dominance (VAD) space [17]. The acquisition of the induced emotions was carried out by Lang et al. [18] using the Self-Assessment Manikin (SAM) questionnaire.This served as ground truth for automatic method for emotion detection and as a metadata for each image.

While users were rating images, the authors recoded their facial expressions with a camera placed on the monitor. The authors also annotated genre to each image manually through a controlled procedure.

In addition, the authors wanted to explore the relations between the subjects' personalities and their preferences for the content items. They used the IPIP 50 questionnaire to assess the factors of the Big5 factor model of the participants. The questionnaire consisted of 50 items, 10 per each of the Five-Factor Model (FFM) factors.

9.2.2.2 Dataset Information

There were 52 students who participated in the experiment. The average age was 18.3 years (standard deviation is 0.56). There were 15 males and 37 females.

The corpus consists of 3640 video clips of 52 participants responding to 70 different visual stimuli. The video files are segmented by user and by visual stimulus.

Each video clip is annotated with a line in the annotation file. The annotations are stored in text-based files. The participants cover a heterogeneous area in the space of the big five factors.

Each video clip is annotated with a line in the annotation file. The annotations files have the following columns: user id, image id, image tag, genre, watching time, wt mean, valence mean, valence stdev, arousal mean, arousal stdev, dominance mean, dominance stdev, big5 1, big5 2, big5 3, big5 4, big5 5 gender, age, explicit rating, binary rating.

For example, the LDOS-PerAff-1 dataset was used in research on using affective parameters in a content-based recommender system [19], and the research on addressing the new user problem with a personality-based user similarity measure [20].

LDOS-PerAff-1 dataset can be acquired on the following link: (http://slavnik.fe.uni-lj.si/markot/Main/LDOS-PerAff-1).

9.2.3 *LJ2M Dataset*

LiveJournal two-million post (LJ2M) dataset was collected from the social blogging service LiveJournal2 for research on personalised music-information retrieval [4]. It is acquired from the users' natural interaction with the live system over a long period of time. According to the authors, it is suitable for use in research on context-aware music recommendation, emotion-based playlist generation, affective human-computer interface and music therapy.

LJ2M dataset contains a blog article, a song associated with the post, and a user mood, since each article is accompanied with a mood and music entries which the blog authors provide.

Users in the dataset are bloggers that use LiveJournal social-networking service. The users' goal was blogging about different subjects.

9.2.3.1 Acquisition

LiveJournal is a social-networking service with a large user base (according to the authors, 40 million registered users and 1.8 million active users at the end of 2012). As described in [21], for purposes of sentiment analysis Leshed and Kaye collected 21 million posts using the LiveJournal's RSS feeds. Maximum of 25 posts were collected per user. Users are mostly from United States, and articles were written between 2000 and 2005.

Each LiveJournal's post contains an article, a mood entry and a music entry. Mood entries were provided by the blog-article's author by selecting one of the 132 pre-defined tags, or filling in freely. Similarly, blog-article authors also provided the music entry by filling in anything they wish.

The authors in [4] further processed the raw data acquired in [21]. They considered only those entries that contained pre-defined mood tags. Regarding the music entry, they used the AchoNest API to check the existence in the EchoNest database, and considered those entries with valid and found (artist, song title pairs). Finally, only those blog entries that contained both valid mood and music tag were selected. The content of the articles is provided as lists of word counts with both non-stemmed and stemmed versions.

9.2.3.2 Dataset Information

The dataset contains 1,928,868 posts from 649,712 unique users. There are 14,613 $\pm$ 13,748 articles per mood tag, on average. Majority of the mood tags have more than 1,000 articles, and about half have more than 10,000 articles.

Blog articles contain 88,164 unique songs from 12,201 artists. There are 125 $\pm$ 22 articles per song, on average. 64,124 songs can be found in the million song dataset (MSD) [22], hence musical metadata and features from MSD can be used. 87,708 songs have short audio previews (30 s) available from 7digital.

LJ2M is available at http://mac.citi.sinica.edu.tw/lj/.

9.2.4 A Database for Emotion Analysis Using Physiological Signals (DEAP)

The Database for Emotion Analysis Using Physiological Signals (DEAP) is a multimodal data set for the analysis of human affective states [5]. This dataset was acquired in a controlled laboratory setting. It contains the electroencephalogram (EEG) and peripheral physiological signals of users, their ratings of arousal, valence, like/dislike, dominance and familiarity of music videos presented, frontal face video recording for a subset of the participants, subjective ratings from the initial online subjective annotation and the list of 120 videos used.

The authors prepared a laboratory setting in which users watched 40 1-min long excerpts of music videos, provided ratings in terms of arousal, valence, like/dislike, dominance and familiarity, while different signals were taken from them through sensors.

Users in this dataset are volunteers that participated in the experiment.

9.2.4.1 Acquisition

120 music videos as emotional stimuli were selected, and 1-min segments with highest emotional content were extracted. Through a web-based assessment experiment participants rated the 1-min segments on a discrete 9-point scale for valence, arousal and dominance. After each video segment was rated by at least 14 volunteers, 40 videos were selected for use in the experiment. To achieve maximum strength of elicited emotions, selected videos had the strongest volunteer ratings and smallest variation.

Once the 1-min-video stimuli was selected the experiment was prepared. Participants were prepared and instructed, set in a controlled environment and sensors were placed on them. The experiment started with a 2-min baseline recording after which 40 videos were presented in 40 trials. In each trial, a 2-s screen displaying the current trial number was shown to inform the participant of the progress, followed by the 5-s baseline recording, and finally the 1-min music-video stimuli. After the video was shown participants performed a self-assessment of their levels of arousal, valence, dominance via the self-assessment manikins on a continuous scale. In addition, they rated how much they liked the shown video by the thumbs-down and thumbs-up symbols.

9.2.4.2 Dataset Information

The dataset consists of two parts: (i) online subjective annotation and (ii) psychological experiment.

Subjective Annotations. There are 120 1-min music videos, 60 of which were selected via last.fm [23] affective tags and 60 were selected manually. Each video has 14–16 ratings on arousal, dominance and valence discrete scale of 1–9.

Physiological Experiment. Thirty-two participants, 50 % of which are females, aged between 19 and 37, rated 40 1-min videos. Ratings were made on scales: arousal, dominance, valence, liking and familiarity. Familiarity is rated on a discrete scale from 1 to 5, and other ratings on a continuous scale from 1 to 9.

In addition to ratings, dataset contains 32-channel 512 Hz EEG signals, and peripheral physiological signals. For 22 participants dataset contains frontal face video.

The article [5] contains detailed information about the data acquisition as well as the analysis on the acquired data. DEAP dataset is published and available for research on the following link:

For example, DEAP dataset was used in research on multi-task and multi-view learning of user state [24], and EEG-based Emotion Recognition by using deep learning network [25].

(http://www.eecs.qmul.ac.uk/mmv/datasets/deap/index.html).

9.2.5 myPersonality Project Dataset

The myPersonality project dataset is a dataset that can be used for different research tasks on social network behaviour and users in connection to different psychometric features [6]. This dataset is acquired from users' natural interaction with the Facebook application, and their natural interaction with social network Facebook. It contains data regarding Facebook users, their preferences (Facebook likes), various demographic information, as well as psychometric data from different tests users have participated in.

The data was acquired by the myPersonality Facebook application that allowed users to take real psychometric tests. If users so decided, they could also provide different Facebook data from their Facebook profiles.

Users in this dataset are therefore Facebook users that decided to use myPersonality application. The users goal was to get feedback and interesting information from different tests in the application.

9.2.5.1 Acquisition

The data was acquired by the myPersonality application (www.mypersonality.org). Users provided their data and gave consent to have their scores and profile information recorded. There were two acquisition principles in this project: (i) acquiring data from psychometric tests and surveys and (ii) collecting users' Facebook data that users have shared.

Political and religious views, sexual orientation and relationship status were recorded from the related fields of users' Facebook profiles. Ethnicity was added in form of labels which were assigned to users by visual inspection of their profile pictures. According to the authors, this resolves the problem of the disclosure bias, however, not all users had profile pictures showing themselves. Information regarding substance use and whether users' parents stayed together or split up before the user was 21 years old were acquired by self-report survey on the myPersonality application. User's Personality Five-Factor Model (FFM) was acquired by the International Personality Item Pool questionnaire with 20 items. User's intelligence was measured by Ravens Standard Progressive Matrices, which is a multiple choice nonverbal intelligence test based on Spearmans theory of general ability. Users' satisfaction with life was measured using a popular, five-item SWL Scale, which measure global cognitive judgments of satisfaction with ones life. The author also recorded more than 9 million unique objects liked by users,but have removed likes associated with fewer than 20 users, as well as users with fewer than two likes.

9.2.5.2 Dataset Information

The myPersonality project dataset contains many different variables describing users. However, not all variables are available for all users. In Table 9.4 we show the approx.

Table 9.4 Number of records for selected subset of variables in myPersonality project dataset

Variable	Approx. number of records
User's demographic details	4,300,000
User's geo-location details	1,800,000
Facebook activity	1,600,000
User's religion and political views	331,672
BIG5 Personality Scores	3,100,000
IQ scores	7,000
Satisfaction with life scale	101,000
Barratt impulsivity scale	19,000
Body consciousness questionnaire	14,000
Facebook likes dictionary	5,500,000
Photos dictionary	17,200,000
Schools dictionary	128,000
Users' Facebook status updates	22,000,000 updates of 154,000

number of records, i.e. users in some cases, for which a specific variable is available. Since there are many variables, we select some of them to give readers the general idea about the number of records. All information on all variables can be found on the following link: http://mypersonality.org/.

All the additional information about the myPersonality project dataset can be found on the following link: http://mypersonality.org/. On the same link, after registering as a collaborator, it is possible to obtain various parts of the dataset.

The myPersonality dataset was used in many research, for example, research on the automatic personality assessment through social media language [26], and relating personality types with user preferences [27].

9.3 Stimuli Datasets

In this section we present stimuli datasets with various types of items which can be used in the research of emotions.

9.3.1 Emotion in Music Database (1000 Songs)

Emotion in Music Database is a stimuli dataset that can be used for the development of music emotion recognition systems [7]. It contains songs and affective annotations provided by volunteers. Each song is annotated with valence and arousal, both continuously, throughout the duration of the song, and statically at the end of the song.

The authors developed the online-annotation system which volunteers were using for the task.

9.3.1.1 Acquisition

The authors first acquired 1000 Creative Commons (CC) licenced music from the Free Music Archive (FMA) [28]. 125 songs were selected from each of the eight different genres: Blues, Electronic, Rock, Classical, Folk, Jazz, Country and Pop. From the initial larger sample of songs, all those that were longer than ten and shorter than one minute were excluded.

The authors were interested in annotating each song with the valence–arousal annotations from multiple annotators. In addition, two different annotations were made, time-varying (per second) continuous valence–arousal ratings, and a single discrete (9 point) valence–arousal rating applied to the entire clip. For the task, the authors have developed their own online-annotation interface for music. Via the interface, annotators are continuously annotating each song during listening by the slider indicating the current emotion. After annotating the songs continuously, annotators are additionally asked to rate the level of arousal or valence for the whole clip on a 9 point scale through Self-Assessment Manikins.

Annotators were acquired by a crowdsourcing principle using the Amazon Mechanical Turk. To ensure the quality of annotators, the authors designed a quality control strategy for the acquisition of annotators.

9.3.1.2 Dataset Information

Initially, the dataset contained 1000 40-s clips, and each clip was annotated by a minimum of 10 workers. More than 20,000 annotations were collected. From 100 workers who participated in the annotation procedure, 57 were male and 43 were female, with average age of 31.7 ± 10.1. On average, annotators spent 7 min and 40 s annotating three clips. Annotators were from 10 different countries, 72 % from the USA, 18 % from India and 10 % from the rest of the world.

The authors found redundant songs and cleaned the data which reduced the number of songs down to 744.

The audio files are distributable under the CC licence and can be shared freely. FMA songs are not published by music labels so the annotators are usually less familiar with them and the potential biases introduced by familiarity with the songs are reduced.

For example of usage, 1000 songs dataset was used in research on emotional analysis of music [29], and continuous-time music mood regression [30].

1000 Songs dataset is published and can be acquired at the following link: http://cvml.unige.ch/databases/emoMusic/

9.3.2 Media Core

Media Core is a project of the Centre for the Study of Emotion and Attention, University of Florida, which develops, catalogues, evaluates and distributes various types of media (stimuli) that can be used as prompts to affective experience [31]. In this section, we describe and provide links to four stimuli datasets from Media Core which cover: images, sounds, English words and English texts.

The Affective Norms for English Text (ANET) dataset provides a set of emotional stimuli from text [8]. It contains a large set of brief English texts. Each text is accompanied by the normative rating of emotion in terms of valence, arousal and dominance dimensions. ANET dataset is publicly available and accessible on the following link: http://csea.phhp.ufl.edu/media/anetmessage.html.

The International Affective Digital Sounds (IADS) dataset provides a set of emotional stimuli from digital sound [9]. It contains a large set of digital sounds accompanied by the normative rating of emotion in terms of valence, arousal and dominance dimensions. IADS dataset is publicly available and accessible on the following link: http://csea.phhp.ufl.edu/media/iadsmessage.html.

The Affective Norms for English Words (ANEW) dataset provides a set of emotional ratings for a large set of English words [10]. Each word is accompanied by the normative rating of emotion in terms of valence, arousal and dominance dimensions. ANEW dataset is publicly available and accessible on the following link: http://csea.phhp.ufl.edu/media/anewmessage.html.

The International Affective Picture System (IAPS) provides a set of emotional stimuli from images [11]. It contains a large set of colour photographs which cover a wide range of semantic categories. Each image is accompanied by the normative rating of emotion in terms of valence, arousal and dominance dimensions. IAPS dataset is publicly available and accessible on the following link: http://csea.phhp.ufl.edu/media/iapsmessage.html.

9.4 Conclusion and Summary

In this chapter we presented some of the available datasets which contain information relevant to the research questions addressed in this book. All datasets are publicly available for researchers working in the field.

For each dataset we briefly described several aspects that we find important for the decision whether to use the dataset, as well as for the reference for researchers interested in acquiring new datasets. Therefore, we describe the acquisition procedure, data the datasets contain, links to the datasets, examples of research done on these datasets, where applicable description of users' goal during the acquisition and additional specific information.

In our opinion, researchers that are planing to acquire new datasets, relevant to this field of research, should pay special attention to carefully specifying users' goals and the context in which users are providing the data. In addition, reduction of noise in the data should be considered and employed for which ideas and procedures can be found in the articles associated to the datasets described in this chapter.

Unfortunately, there is still a low number of publicly available datasets relevant to the field. This is due to complex procedures needed for the data acquisition in laboratory settings and potentially sensitive personal information in real-live systems. However, with increasing accessibility of available sensors and stimuli datasets as well as crowdsourcing platforms and overall usage of affective and personality data used in existing services, amount of data relevant for these research topics is also on the rise. We hope that the information and references from this chapter will help researchers to find the appropriate datasets for their work, provide useful information for the preparation their own acquisition procedures, and motivate them to share their datasets with other researchers in this field of research.

References

1. Saucier, G., Goldberg, L.R.: What is beyond the big five? J. Pers. **66**, 495–524 (1998)
2. Odić, A., Tkalčič, M., Tasič, J.F., Košir, A.: Predicting and detecting the relevant contextual information in a movie-recommender system. Interact. Comput. **25**(1), 74–90 (2013)
3. Tkalčič, M., Košir, A., Tasič, J.: The LDOS-PerAff-1 corpus of facial-expression video clips with affective, personality and user-interaction metadata. J. Multimodal User Interface **7**(1–2), 143–155 (2013)
4. Liu, J.Y., Liu, S.Y., Yang, Y.H.: LJ2M dataset: toward better understanding of music listening behavior and user mood. In: IEEE International Conference on Multimedia and Expo (ICME), pp. 1–6 (2014)
5. Koelstra, S., Muhl, C., Soleymani, M., Lee, J.S., Yazdani, A., Ebrahimi, T., Patras, I.: Deap: a database for emotion analysis; using physiological signals. IEEE Trans. Affect. Comput. **3**(1), 18–31 (2012)
6. Kosinski, M., Stillwell D.J., Graepel T: Private traits and attributes are predictable from digital records of human behavior. In: Proceedings of the National Academy of Sciences (PNAS) (2013)
7. Soleymani, M., Caro, M.N., Schmidt, E.M., Sha, C.Y., Yang, Y.H.: 1000 songs for emotional analysis of music. In: Proceedings of the 2nd ACM International Workshop on Crowdsourcing for Multimedia, pp. 1–6 (2013)
8. Bradley, M.M., Lang, P.J.: Affective Norms for English Text (ANET): affective ratings of text and instruction manual. (Tech. Rep. No. D-1). University of Florida, Gainesville, FL (2007)
9. Bradley, M.M., Lang, P.J.: International affective digitized sounds (IADS): Stimuli, instruction manual and affective ratings (Tech. Rep. No. B-2). The Center for Research in Psychophysiology, University of Florida, Gainesville, FL (1999)
10. Bradley, M.M., Lang, P.J.: Affective norms for English words (ANEW): Stimuli, instruction manual and affective ratings. Technical report C-1. The Center for Research in Psychophysiology, University of Florida, Gainesville, FL (1999)
11. Lang, P.J., Bradley, M.M., Cuthbert, B.N.: International affective picture system (IAPS): affective ratings of pictures and instruction manual. Technical Report A-8. University of Florida, Gainesville, FL (2008)
12. Herlocker, J.L., Konstan, J.A., Terveen, L.G., Riedl, J.T.: Evaluating collaborative filtering recommender systems. ACM Trans. Inf. Syst. (TOIS) **22**(1), 5–53 (2004)
13. Goldberg, L.R., Johnson, J.A., Eber, H.W., Hogan, R., Ashton, M.C., Cloninger, C.R., Gough, H.G.: The international personality item pool and the future of public-domain personality measures. J. Res. Pers. 84–96 (2006)
14. Zheng, Y., Mobasher, B., Burke, R.D.: The role of emotions in context-aware Recommendation. In: Decisions@ RecSys, pp 21–28 (2013)
15. Codina, V., Ricci, F., Ceccaroni, L.: Local context modeling with semantic pre-filtering. In: Proceedings of the 7th ACM Conference on Recommender Systems, pp. 363–366 (2013)
16. Košir, A., Odić, A., Kunaver, M., Tkalčič, M., Tasič, J.F.: Database for contextual personalization. Elektrotehniki vestnik **78**(5), 270–274 (2011)
17. Posner, J., Russell, J.A., Peterson, B.S.: The circumplex model of affect: an integrative approach to affective neuroscience, cognitive development, and psychopathology. Dev. Psychopathol. **17**(03), 715–734 (2005)
18. Lang, P.J., Bradley, M.M., Cuthbert, B.N.: International affective picture system (IAPS): Affective ratings of pictures and instruction manual. Technical Report A-8 (2008)
19. Tkali, M., Burnik, U., Koir, A.: Using affective parameters in a content-based recommender system for images. User Model. User-Adap. Inter. **20**(4), 279–311 (2010)
20. Tkalcic, M., Kunaver, M., Koir, A., Tasic, J.: Addressing the new user problem with a personality based user similarity measure. In First International Workshop on Decision Making and Recommendation Acceptance Issues in Recommender Systems (DEMRA 2011) (2011)
21. Leshed, G., Kaye, J.J.: Understanding how bloggers feel: recognizing affect in blog posts. In: CHI'06 extended abstracts on Human factors in computing systems, pp. 1019–1024 (2006)

22. Bertin-Mahieux, T., Ellis, D.P., Whitman, B., Lamere, P.: The million song dataset. In: ISMIR: Proceedings of the 12th International Society for Music Information Retrieval Conference, Miami. Florida, vol. 591–596 (2011)
23. http://www.last.fm/
24. Kandemir, M., Vetek, A., Gnen, M., Klami, A., Kaski, S.: Multi-task and multi-view learning of user state. Neurocomputing **139**, 97–106 (2014)
25. Jirayucharoensak, S., Pan-Ngum, S., Israsena, P.: EEG-based emotion recognition using deep learning network with principal component based covariate shift adaptation. Sci. World J. (2014)
26. Park, G., Schwartz, H.A., Eichstaedt, J.C., Kern, M.L., Kosinski, M., Stillwell, D.J., Seligman, M.E.: Automatic Personality Assessment Through Social Media Language (2014)
27. Cantador, I., Fernndez-Tobas, I., Bellogn, A., Kosinski, M., Stillwell, D.: Relating personality types with user preferences in multiple entertainment domains. In: UMAP Workshops (2013)
28. http://www.freemusicarchive.orghttp://www.freemusicarchive.org
29. Soleymani, M., Aljanaki, A., Yang, Y. H., Caro, M. N., Eyben, F., Markov, K., Wiering, F.: Emotional analysis of music: a comparison of methods. In: Proceedings of the ACM International Conference on Multimedia, pp. 1161–1164 (2014)
30. Weninger, F., Eyben, F., Schuller, B.: On-line continuous-time music mood regression with deep recurrent neural networks. In: IEEE International Conference on Acoustics, Speech and Signal Processing (ICASSP), pp. 5412–5416 (2014)
31. http://csea.phhp.ufl.edu/media.html

Part III
Applications

Chapter 10
Modeling User's Social Attitude in a Conversational System

Tobias Baur, Dominik Schiller and Elisabeth André

Abstract With the growing number of conversational systems that find their way in our daily life, new questions and challenges arise. Even though natural conversation with agent-based systems has been improved in the recent years, e.g., by better speech recognition algorithms, they still lack the ability to understand nonverbal behavior and conversation dynamics—a key part of human natural interaction. To make a step towards intuitive and natural interaction with virtual agents, social robots, and other conversational systems, this chapter proposes a probabilistic framework that models the dynamics of interpersonal cues reflecting the user's social attitude within the context they occur.

10.1 Introduction

When humans communicate with each other, they exchange information not just by written or spoken language. In many cases it is far more important *how* and *under which circumstances* a message is communicated, rather than *what* was actually said. To give an example: Imagine a close relative entering the room and asking a question like: "Did you empty the milk carton?" The content of the message is actually not so relevant because obviously now the milk is empty, no matter how you answer the question. What is more important here is the *how*. If the person finding the empty milk carton makes an angry face, and is asking that question with a rather aggressive tone of voice, he or she communicates: "I wanted to have some milk, and you drank it up, so now I'm mad at you". The message crucially differs from the literal spoken content. But maybe the person finding the empty milk carton says it with a friendly

T. Baur (✉) · D. Schiller · E. André
Human Centered Multimedia, Augsburg University,
Universitätsstraße 6a, 86159 Augsburg, Germany
e-mail: baur@hcm-lab.de

D. Schiller
e-mail: schiller@hcm-lab.de

E. André
e-mail: andre@hcm-lab.de

M. Tkalčič et al. (eds.), *Emotions and Personality in Personalized Services*,
Human–Computer Interaction Series, DOI 10.1007/978-3-319-31413-6_10

tone of voice that communicates something like: "Ok the milk carton is empty, let's put it on the shopping list". Given the same content, the message in both cases is a different one. In addition, the style in which the message is conveyed reveals a different social attitude towards the interlocutor—in the first case the tendency is rather negative and in the second case still quite positive.

On contrary to human–human communication, a computer system is usually ignorant of a user's social attitude towards the system. Even modern computer systems only care about direct input—both from traditional peripherals, such as mouse or keyboard, as well as speech commands or gesture-based input. At the same time, an early study by Reeves and Nass [36] revealed that users tend to show a social attitude towards computer systems. That is—even though on an unconscious level—humans seem to respond socially to computer systems in a similar way as they would to human interlocutors.

One might argue that a computer system that analyzes implicitly conveyed social cues of humans engaged in tasks, such as browsing the web or creating documents, would be rather disturbing. However, the need to emulate certain aspects of human-like social behavior becomes more apparent in scenarios with virtual agents or humanoid robots. Often, such systems are used in social settings where they replace or assist a coach, a medical practitioner, or a caregiver. Typical use cases include public speeches [2], social humor situations [27, 32], intercultural communication [15], negotiation scenarios [46], psychotherapy [21], job interviews [4, 19], or elderly care [7]. In such scenarios a basic "understanding" of the users' social cues would be desirable.

The analysis of social cues allows us to make predictions on the users' level of engagement in the interaction as an indicator of their social attitude. In a human–human conversation, the interlocutors dynamically coordinate and adjust their verbal and nonverbal behaviors to each other in order to demonstrate engagement in the conversation. To determine the level of engagement in human–agent dialog, it does not suffice to analyze the individual behavior patterns of the human. Rather the dynamics of bidirectional behavior patterns has to be taken into account. Examples of bidirectional behavior patterns include the establishment of shared attention, the regulation of the dialog flow by turn taking, and the generation of backchannel feedback. Depending on the situative context, such behavior patterns may vary considerably and the social signals need to be interpreted accordingly.

The objective of our work is the development of a computational framework that allows for a context-sensitive analysis of bidirectional social cues in order to determine a user's social attitude. In the next section, we provide an introduction to the affective, behavioral and cognitive components of social attitudes. We then discuss related work on the recognition of cues of engagement as indicators of a user's social attitude. After that, we present a probabilistic approach for modeling the dynamics of interpersonal behavior patterns in dependency of the situative context. The approach is illustrated by means of two use cases with a team of virtual agents and a humanoid robot. The paper ends with concluding remarks and an outlook of future work.

10.2 Social Attitudes

Eagly and Chaiken define the term *Social Attitude* as a psychological tendency that is expressed by evaluating a particular entity with some degree of favor or disfavor [14]. According to Rosenberg et al. [38] a social attitude has three main components: affective, behavioral, and cognitive.

- *Affective component*: involves a person's feelings and emotions about an attitude object. As an example we take a person who has been invited to a job interview. Let us assume this person is very uncomfortable with the interview situation in general. In this case the interview situation represents the object the attitude is directed towards. Whenever this person is exposed to an interview or thinks about one, he or she feels anxious and nervous. Those feelings form the affective component of a social attitude.
- *Behavioral component*: refers to the way our attitude influences how we act or behave. Let us consider again the person in the job interview. Since the candidate is scared of the situation, he or she might show a behavior that includes tensed and nervous gestures, such as crossing arms and avoiding eye contact, especially when being asked difficult questions.
- *Cognitive component*: involves a person's beliefs and knowledge about an attitude object. Now that we have seen how our job interview candidate behaves, the question arises of what he or she thinks about the interview. Probably, he or she thinks about being unemployed for a long time, and the pressure to get that job. Beyond the physical and emotional reactions to the situation, there is also the cognitive component of his or her attitude.

One can further distinguish between explicit and implicit attitudes [18]. Explicit attitudes are at conscious level. That means people are aware of them and usually know how they determine their behaviors and beliefs. For example, our job candidate might have a negative attitude towards the interviewer, but try to hide any negative feelings in order to get the job. On the opposite, implicit attitudes are at unconscious level. In this case, our job candidate would not be aware of his or her negative attitude towards the interviewer even though it might strongly influence his or her behavior.

Often a person's social attitude is consciously or unconsciously reflected by their behavior. Coming back to the job interview scenario, the interviewer might conclude from the candidate's slouched body posture (behavioral component) that the candidate is bored (affective component) and finds the job unattractive due to the low salary (cognitive component). Overall, the candidate's behavior portrays a negative social attitude towards the situation of the job interview.

One indicator of social attitude is a person's engagement in a conversation. *Engagement* in a conversation is defined as "the process by which two (or more) participants establish, maintain and end their perceived connection during interactions they jointly undertake" by Sidner et al. [45]. Typically, engagement is shown by orienting the body and the face towards the interlocutor while turning away from the interlocutor may be interpreted as a sign of interpersonal distance. Furthermore, the presence of "bidirectional cues", such as mutual and directed gaze, backchanneling, and adjacency pairs indicates a high amount of involvement in a conversation [37]. There are also specific hand gestures that reveal whether a listener is engaged or not. For example, engaged people typically touch their chin without bracing the head. A slight variation of this gesture would, however, reveal the opposite. Bored people may also touch their chin. But in this case, the hand typically fully braces the head [34]. As seen in these examples, nonverbal signals cannot be straightforwardly interpreted in every case. Considering that the interpretation of nonverbal behavior is often hard to handle for humans, the implementation of conversational systems able to "understand" human social signals is a challenging endeavor. The current paper is based on the assumption that the situative context of a social interaction may be exploited as a valuable source of information to disambiguate social cues. Examples will be given in Sect. 10.4.3.

10.3 Related Work

In the following, we discuss related work on the recognition of individual and interpersonal behavioral cues that may reveal information on positive and negative affective user states as an indicator of a person's social attitude towards the conversational setting and the interlocutor. Based on the observation that people's involvement in a conversation reveals a lot of information on their social attitude, a particular emphasis will be given to computational approaches to identify cues of engagement.

10.3.1 Recognition of Individual and Interpersonal Behavioral Cues

The availability of robust techniques for detecting and interpreting affective cues is an important step in the development of computer-based agents that are sensitive towards positive or negative affective user states. Recent research has concentrated on a large variety of modalities to determine affective user states including facial expressions [41, 48], gestures [9, 26], speech [49], postures [11, 23], and physiological measurements [22].

Also multimodal approaches to improve emotion recognition accuracy have been reported, mostly by exploiting audiovisual combinations [8, 24, 35, 43, 44]. Results suggest that integrated information from audio and video leads to improved classification reliability compared to a single modality.

To characterize social interactions, not only individual but also interpersonal behavior patterns have to be taken into account. To this end, approaches have been developed for analyzing interpersonal synchrony [29], shared attention to objects [31], overlapping speech [20], and backchannel behaviors [30].

10.3.2 Engagement Detection in Computer-Enhanced Tutoring and Training

In the area of tutoring systems, particular attention has been paid to the analysis of learning-centered affective states, such as low or high engagement, in order to determine the students' attitude towards learning.

D'Mello and colleagues [13] equipped a chair with sensing pads in order to assess the learner's level of engagement based on the pressure exerted on the seat and on the back during the interaction with a tutor agent. They found that high engagement was reflected by increased pressure exerted on the seat of the chair while low engagement resulted in increased pressure exerted on the back. In addition, low engagement was typically accompanied by rapid changes in pressure, which the authors interpreted as a sign of restlessness.

Studies by Sanghvi and colleagues [42] investigated how to assess the engagement of children learning to play chess with a robotic cat from their body contour. For this, they proposed four elementary features (body lean angle, slouch factor, quantity of motion, and contraction index) that were enhanced by meta features for describing the temporal dynamics of posture and movement patterns. D'Mello and colleagues observed that low engagement was accompanied by continuous movement.

Beck [6] presented a model of learner engagement in order to track a student's level of engagement during the interaction with a computer agent by considering the student's proficiency and the response time. The work revealed that the learning context has to be taken into account to analyze engagement because a low response time is not necessarily a sign of disengagement, but may also be caused by a student's uncertainty.

Mahmoud et al. [25] identified a variety of hand-over-face gestures that people may employ to convey mental states, such as boredom, confusion, or contemplation, depending on the situative context. Considering that hand-over-face gestures are highly context-specific, Vail et al. [47] analyzed hand-to-face gestures at specific moments during a tutoring dialog for introductory computer science. Their study revealed that hand-to-face gestures indicated engagement after the student successfully compiled a computer program.

Also facial movements have been investigated as an indicator of engagement. Whitehill and colleagues [51] identified several action units that were positively (such as lip raiser) or negatively (such as inner brow raiser) correlated with engagement. Vail et al. [47] took contextual conditions into account when investigating correlations between facial action units and amount of engagement. For example, they found out that brow lowering was a good indicator of disengagement when it was observed after the student made a dialog contribution. Their study also revealed that the students' personality needs to be taken into account when analyzing expressive signs of engagement.

10.3.3 Engagement Detection in Collaborative Human–Agent Interaction

To collaborate successfully with each other, a human and an agent need to establish a common understanding of what the interaction is about. If the human and the agent talk at cross-purposes, it is very likely that the human will lose interest in the interaction. Consequently, an analysis of the common ground may help predict the user's level of engagement. To this end, it is not sufficient to analyze verbal and nonverbal behavior cues out of context. Instead the semantics of an utterance including verbal references to objects in the human's and the agent's virtual or physical environment has to be considered.

Rich et al. [37] presented a model of engagement for human–robot interaction that took into account direct gaze, mutual gaze, relevant next contribution, and backchannel behaviors as an indicator of engagement in a dialog. Interestingly, the approach was used for modeling the behavior of both the robot and the human. As a consequence, it was able to explain the failures in communication from the perspective of both interlocutors. Their model demonstrates the close interaction between the communication streams required for semantic processing and the social signal processing because it integrates multimodal grounding with techniques for measuring experiential qualities of a dialog. Even though engagement is closely linked to a person's emotional state, the model by Rich et al. neither takes the user's emotional state into account nor intends to react with affective behavior.

10.3.4 Context-Sensitive Approaches to Engagement Detection

As we have shown above, there is a large variety of verbal and nonverbal cues that may be exploited to predict a user's attitude towards an interaction with an agent. At the same time, it is questionable to what extent the findings from the literature can be generalized to be applied in other scenarios. Indeed some observations made for verbal and nonverbal cues seem to conflict with each other due to different context parameters. Even though the role of context has been highlighted in work on affective computing and social signal processing [33], computational approaches that actually exploit context information to improve recognition rates are rare.

An early example of a context-sensitive approach to engagement analysis includes the work by Yu et al. [52] who assess the user's engagement in human–human everyday dialog by taking acoustic, temporal, and interactional information into account. Their work is based on the consideration that a participant's current engagement is based on his or her previous engagement and the engagement of the interlocutor.

Another example includes the work by Conati et al. [10] who describe a tutor agent that makes use of a dynamic Bayesian network for interpreting the learner's behavior. The basic idea is to infer information on a learner's affective states both from their effects, such as physiological reactions, and their causes, such as the desirability of action outcomes. Their approach explores the potential of physiological signals as predictors of a learner's affective state, but does not take into account the broad range of multimodal signals we consider to determine a user's level of engagement.

Recent work by De Carolis et al. [12] used dynamic Bayesian networks to determine the user's social attitude from multiple modalities in a human–agent interaction where the agent plays the role of an expert adviser in the domain of well-being. By making use of a dynamic Bayesian network, the approach is able to consider the dialog history to a certain extent. However, other context factors, such as the speaker and listener roles, have not been considered.

Salam and Chetouani [40] developed a model of human–robot engagement based on the context of the interaction. They categorize HRI contexts in: Purely Social, Competitive, Informative, Educative, Negotiation, Guide-and-Follow and Collaborative. Results suggest that mental and emotional states of the user vary depending on the context of the interaction and thus the definition of engagement also varies. The definition of the relevant features, as well as the automated recognition of the user's engagement remains part of their future work.

10.4 Automated Social Attitude Recognition

In the previous chapter, we discussed the approaches for the assessment of a user's level of engagement as an important indicator of a user's social attitude in an interaction. In the following, we will present a probabilistic framework that models engagement based on the following types of information: social cues shown by the user, the temporal alignment of interpersonal behaviors, as well as the situative context.

10.4.1 Social Cue Recognition

An overview on Social Signal Processing Techniques is given in Chap. 6. For the analysis of the user's nonverbal behavior, we employ the open-source social signal interpretation framework (SSI) [50]. SSI offers to record, analyze, and recognize human behavior in real time. In particular, SSI supports the parallel and synchronized processing of data from multiple sensory devices, such as cameras, multi-channel microphones, and various physiological sensors.

SSI enables a conversational system to detect various social cues the user is displaying, including the analysis of postures, gestures, and facial displays, the assessment of motion expressivity, the determination of paralinguistic features as well as keyword spotting [5, 17]. Furthermore, it supports the complete machine learning

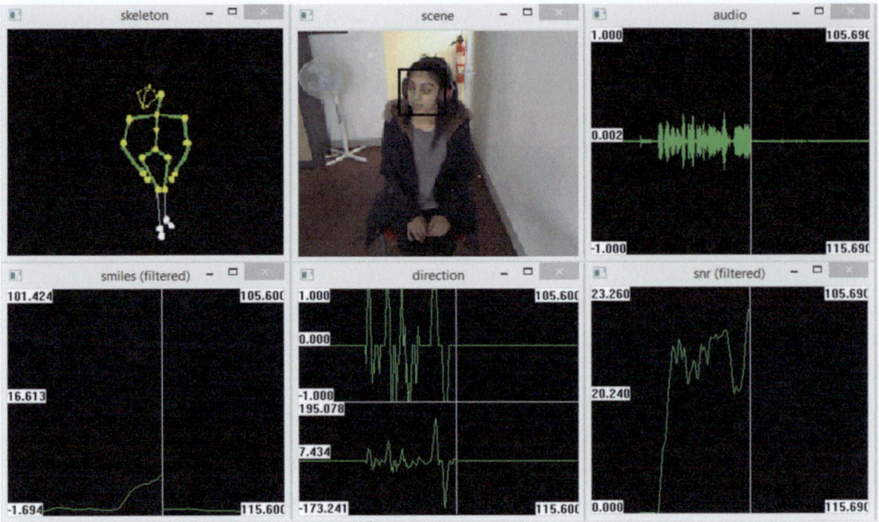

Fig. 10.1 Graphical user interface of the behavior recognition system showing skeleton tracking, video stream, audio stream, smile probability, pitch direction, and signal-to-noise ratio of the audio stream

pipeline including the fusion of multiple channels and the synchronization between multiple computers.

Figure 10.1 illustrates an exemplary instance of an SSI pipeline, including skeleton tracking, video stream, audio stream, smiles, pitch direction, and signal-to-noise ratio of audio stream. Based on social signal processing algorithms it further allows the detection of specific events within the signals, such as the appearance of a posture or a facial expression.

10.4.2 Detecting Bidirectional Cues

For dialog management, we use the open-source tool VisualSceneMaker (VSM) [16], which has been designed for the rapid development and prototyping of interactive performances with computer-based agents, such as human-like characters [17] and robots [28].

As noted earlier, engagement is based on bidirectional cues shown by the interlocutors during a social interaction. Consequently, it does not suffice to monitor individual cues of only a single interlocutor. Rather, the dynamics of interpersonal behaviors has to be taken into account. For example, to determine the amount of mutual gaze in dyadic conversations, the gaze behaviour of both interlocutors' has to be analyzed in an integrated manner. To detect bidirectional cues of engagement, we conduct a temporally aligned analysis of the detected social cues by the user and

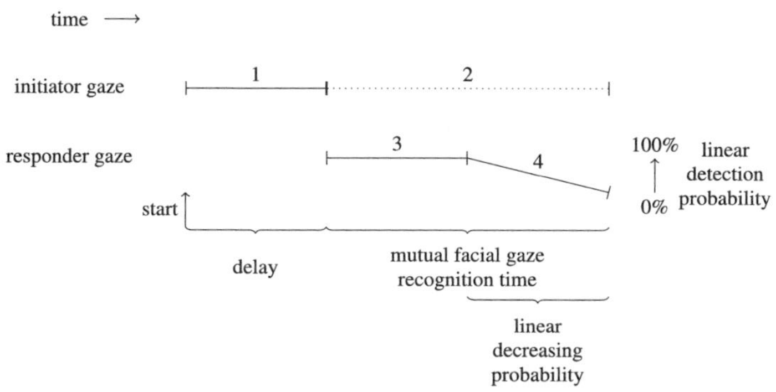

Fig. 10.2 Temporal alignment of recognition probability of a *connection event*, in this example *mutual facial gaze*

the logged behaviors of the agent. Rich et al. [37] identified a variety of connection events in a dialog that may be interpreted as signs of engagement including *directed gaze*, *mutual gaze*, *adjacency pairs* and *backchanneling*. Based on multiple studies, they developed different recognition models for single events. They also defined time spans within which a particular behavior has to occur in order to identify the successfull completion of a connection event.

Unlike Rich et al., we do not set fixed time spans within which a response from the interlocutor has to be detected in order to register a successful connection event. Therefore, a response that comes with a certain delay could still be considered as a successful connection event, but would lower its probability.

Figure 10.2 illustrates the approach for *mutual gaze*. After the conversational agent initiates gaze at the user (Fig. 10.2—1), he has a certain time span to respond to the gaze in order to be detected as a successful connection event (Fig. 10.2—2). This time span is divided into two different phases. In the first phase (Fig. 10.2—3), which concurs with the phase within a response has to happen in the model by Rich et al., a *mutual gaze event* connection event will be given a probability of 100 %. After that phase, the probability for a *mutual gaze* connection event decreases constantly until it reaches 0 % (Fig. 10.2—4). While the recognition of the event itself will be successful during this period of time, the returned probability indicates the degree of uncertainty that this event may not have been intended by the user. By taking those probabilities into account we are able to obtain more nuanced result regarding the temporal alignment than just the two states *recognized* and *not recognized*.

10.4.3 Considering Context

The analysis of social attitudes depends on the context in which the corresponding social signals have been observed. Context is a wide-ranging term that has different meanings depending on the scenario and the application (also see Chap. 15). In human–computer interaction, a system is called context-aware when it understands the circumstances and conditions surrounding the user. While context widely finds appliance in ubiquitous and mobile computing, it is only rarely used in the area of social signal processing and interaction modeling.

Some considerations and questions concerning the context to be considered in a complex user model are described in the following:

- *Interaction role of the interlocutor*: Depending on whether the user is in the role of a listener or a speaker, the same kind of behavior might be interpreted completely differently. The influence of the interaction role on the interpretation of user behavior is illustrated by the following example. Let us assume we observe a person showing a high amount of gestural activity. If the person is in the role of a listener, the observed activity could be interpreted as restlessness. On the opposite, if the person is in the role of a speaker, we might conclude that the person is actively engaged in the conversation [34].
- *Discourse*: In order to improve the interpretation of social cues, the situation in which they are displayed should be taken into account. In human–agent interaction, such a situation might be triggered by the agent. For example, if a job applicant reacts to a difficult question with a laughter, it is rather unlikely that he or she is happy about the question. Instead the laughter portrays embarrassment. Only based on the social cues, it is hardly possible to distinguish between different forms of laughter.
- *Background*: Another valuable source of information is the background of the interlocutors which may be addressed by the following questions: How well do the interlocutors know each other? Do they share common knowledge? What culture or gender do they have? What is their personality like? Such aspects play an important role, especially when interpreting nonverbal behavior. It is hard to retrieve them automatically during the interaction between the system and the user. However, the user could be asked to provide this information before the actual interaction starts.
- *Semantics*: The interpretation of detected social cues can be entirely altered through the semantics of accompanying verbal utterances. For example, a laughter in combination with an utterance commenting a negative event would no longer be interpreted as a sign of happiness, but rather be taken as sarcasm. By considering the semantics of accompanying spoken content, detected social cues could be interpreted more accurately.

Context information should be considered as a part of a user model. By making real-time observations, e.g., logging the discourse context from the interaction modeling tool, behavior can be interpreted differently and influence the outcome of the social attitude calculation accordingly. Social cues, agent events, bidirectional cue events, and their corresponding probabilities, as well as context information can then be fed into a probabilistic model, such as a Bayesian network for further real-time processing, as will be discussed in the next section.

10.5 Inferring the User's Social Attitude

Individual and bidirectional social cues as well as context information are integrated and mapped onto higher level concepts for characterizing the user's social attitude. To this end, we employ a dynamic Bayesian network. The structure of a Bayesian network is a directed, acyclic graph in which the nodes represent random variables while the edges connecting nodes describe the direct influence in terms of conditional probabilities [39]. Dynamic Bayesian networks allow us, in addition, to model the dependencies between the current states of variables and earlier states of variables.

Figure 10.3 shows a simplified Bayesian network, meant to model *Engagement*, as an indicator of a social attitude. Other indicators of a social attitude, such as empathy, can be modeled in an analogous manner.

We introduce two hidden variables *Individual Engagement* and *Interpersonal Engagement* with two discrete values: *Yes* and *No* from which the probability of the values *Yes* and *No* for the variable *Engagement* can be inferred. Basically, the variable *Individual Engagement* refers to user engagement that is manifested by

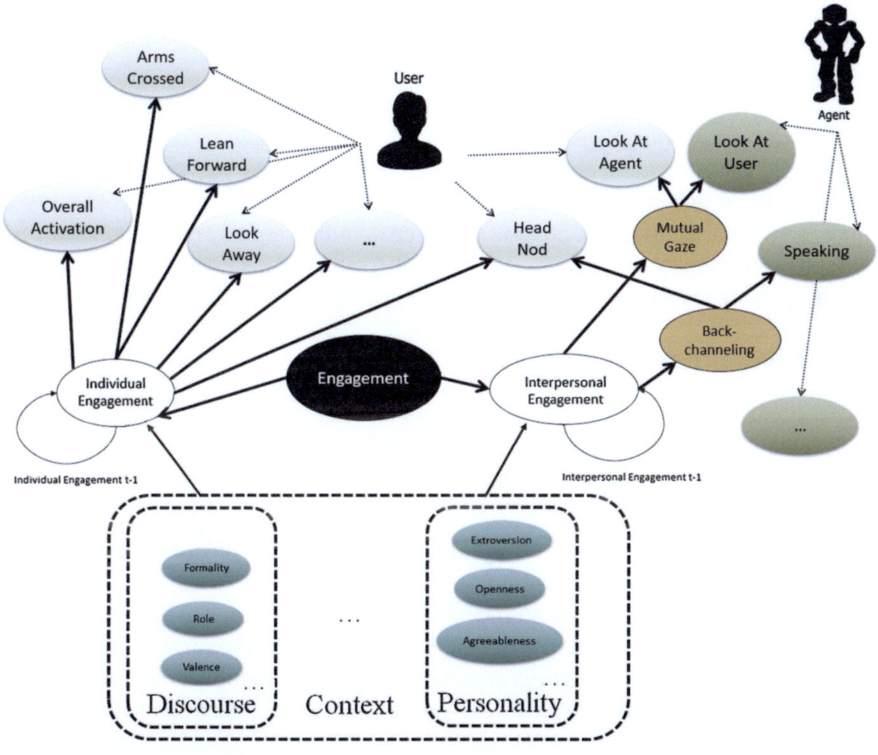

Fig. 10.3 A simplified illustration of a dynamic Bayesian network to determine engagement while considering bidirectional cues and context information

individual social cues while *Interpersonal Engagement* refers to user engagement that is manifested by interpersonal social cues. The value of these two variables cannot be directly observed, but has to be inferred from observables variables, such as *Arms Crossed* or *Lean Forward*. For example, the likelihood that the variable *Individual Engagement* has the value *Yes* is high if the value for the variable *Lean Forward* would be *Present* and the value for the variable *Look Away* would be *Absent*.

The probabilities for these values are updated in real time based on the observations of the social cue recognition component (for the social cues displayed by the user). For example, the probability that the variable *Lean Forward* has the value *Present* is high if the corresponding social cue has been detected with high confidence. However, the probability for bidirectional social cues depends not only on the social cues displayed by the user, but also on the social cues displayed by the agent as well as their temporal alignment. For example, if the user provides a backchannel signal with a delay, the probability that the variable *Backchannel* has the value *Present* will be lower compared to a situation where the backchannel signal arrives on time (see Sect. 10.4.2).

Additionally, context information logged by the interaction modeling component (see Sect. 10.4.3), such as meta information about the current topic (formal/serious vs informal/casual topic, role of the interlocutor, valance of the topic (positive/negative)), or background knowledge, e.g. about the user's personality (extroversion, openness, agreeableness, etc.) have a direct influence on the according engagement nodes. For easier illustration, context nodes are implied in Fig. 10.3.

By using a dynamic Bayesian network, we are also able to represent how the user's previous (individual and interpersonal) engagement influences the user's current (individual and interpersonal) engagement. For example, if the probability of user engagement is high, but no new social cues indicating engagement occur for a while, the probability of user engagement will gradually decrease. New social cues providing evidence for user engagement will instead increase the probability of user engagement.

The Bayesian networks used in our system have been modeled with GeNIe.[1]

10.6 Use Cases

In the following, we present two sample applications to illustrate the approach described in the previous two sections.

Both applications are based on the same technology for social cue analysis and dialog management. Social cue analysis is performed by recognizers implemented in the Social Signal Interpretation framework [50] while dialog management is handled by VisualSceneMaker [16]. Furthermore, the two applications make use of a similar dynamic Bayesian network approach in order to monitor the user's level of engagement.

[1]http://genie.sis.pitt.edu/.

Fig. 10.4 Virtual office environment with two virtual agents Curtis and Gloria

10.6.1 Multi-agent Job Interview Scenario

The first use case is inspired by the TARDIS project [1, 3] and its successor EMPAT, which provide which provides a simulation environment for job interview training. The use case employs two characters, Gloria and Curtis (see Fig. 10.4), acting as virtual job recruiters, while the user is in the role of a job applicant. Showing a high amount of engagement is essential to make a good impression in a job interview. The application aims to help users prepare for a real job interview by providing an analysis of their portrayed engagement behaviors.

In this scenario, an Eye Tribe eye tracker, a Microsoft Kinect depth sensor and microphone are monitoring the user's nonverbal behavior. Based on recognized behavior patterns, events and corresponding evidences are forwarded to a Bayesian network component as described in Sect. 10.5 to infer the amount of engagement the user shows towards the agents.

Figure 10.5 presents a schematic illustration of a dialog fragment along with the recognized connection events and the derived level of engagement. The scene starts with an utterance of the virtual agent Gloria. Shortly after Gloria has started to talk, the sensors recognize several head nods from the user, which are interpreted as backchannel events and increase the amount of detected engagement (Fig. 10.5a). Around the time of the second head nod, the agent, while still talking, starts pointing at virtual agent Curtis. A few moments later, the user, who is still nodding, looks at Curtis, which is recognized as a directed gaze event (Fig. 10.5b). The detection of two connection events at the same time leads to a further increase in the amount of detected engagement. After Gloria has finished talking, the user takes the turn which is interpreted as the occurrence of an *adjacency pair* (Fig. 10.5c).

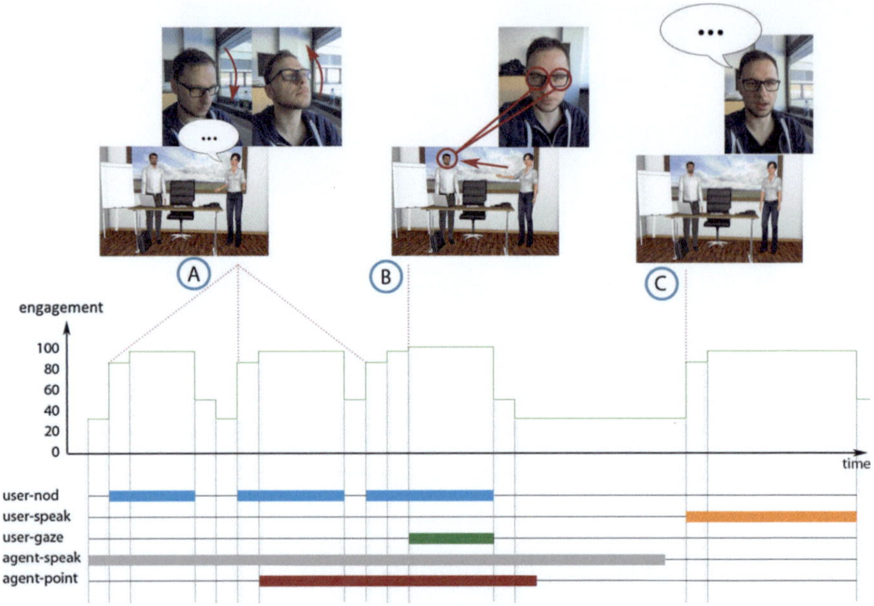

Fig. 10.5 Schematic dialog example in human–agent interaction

Fig. 10.6 A user interacting with a Nao robot. The robot is pointing and looking at the yellow triangle (*1*) and the user's gaze is following (*2*) (directed gaze)

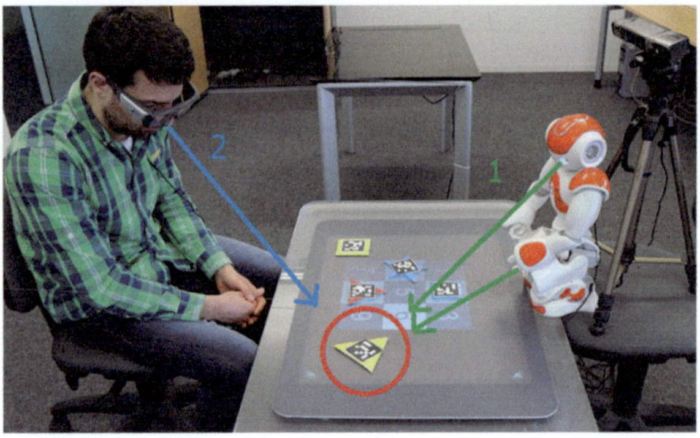

10.6.2 Social Robot Scenario

In the following, we demonstrate how the approach is used to ensure user engagement by appropriate grounding processes in a collaborative setting with a robot.

Figure 10.6 shows a Nao robot instructing a user in laying out a puzzle. It requests the user to place one puzzle piece after the other on a particular field displayed on a Microsoft surface table that is referred to by its number. After the user has successfully performed a placement task, the robot continues with the next puzzle piece.

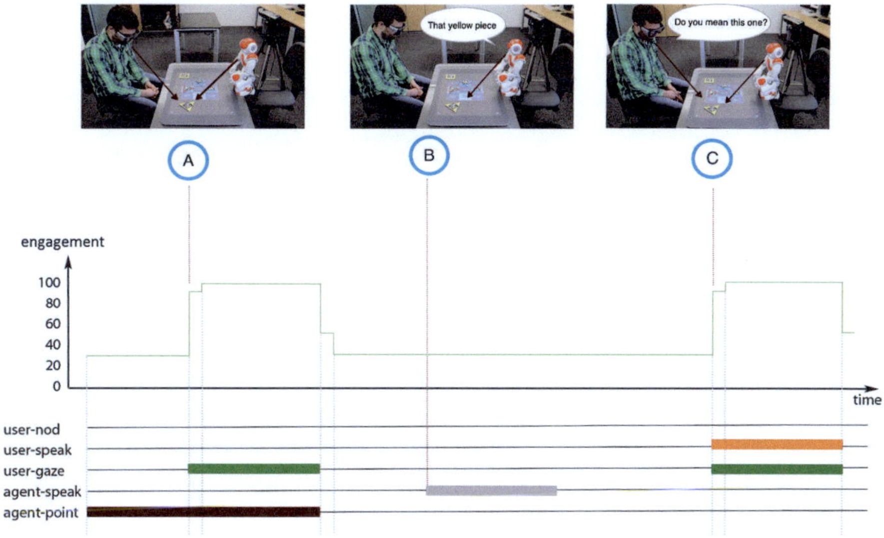

Fig. 10.7 Schematic dialog example in human–agent interaction. **a** The agent is gazing and pointing at an object, and the user is following the gaze. **b** The robot is referring to an object. **c** The user is engaging in the conversation by identifying the correct object

During the dialog, a Kinect sensor installed above the robot is tracking the user's verbal and nonverbal behavior. Furthermore, the user is equipped with SMI eye tracking glasses to enable a precise real-time analysis of his gaze behavior. Markers on the puzzle pieces and the robot's head allow for the identification of objects the user is looking at. The integrated analysis of sensor input enables the robot to track the user's level of engagement.

For illustration, let us have a look at the episode shown in Fig. 10.7. The robot tells the user to pick up the yellow object and tries to attract his attention to the object with a pointing gesture and a head movement. By tracking the user's gaze, the robot is able to check whether the user is still following the conversation. In figure (A), the user is focusing on the intended target, which is interpreted as a directed gaze event and thus leads to an increase in the amount of detected engagement.

In order to elicit follow-up questions from the user, the robot does not always give unambiguous instructions. For example, it might tell the user to pick "that yellow piece" instead of the "yellow triangle" (B). In such a case, the user has the option to ask for clarification, for example, by saying "Do you mean this one?" and looking at a particular object (C). If the user is referring to the intended target, an adjacency pair event is recognized which leads to an increase in the amount of detected engagement. In contrast, a reference to the wrong target would result in a decrease in the amount of detected engagement, which the robot would try to repair by providing clarifying information.

10.7 Conclusion

The interpretation of social signals depends to a large extent on the context in which they occur. Based on this observation, the paper presented a context-sensitive approach that automatically recognizes the user's social attitude towards a conversational system. As a first step, we focused on user engagement that may be used to predict whether a user has a positive or negative tendency towards a system. In our approach, the user's engagement is not only derived from the user's individual behavior patterns, but also from interpersonal behavior patterns that capure the social cues displayed by the user and the agent as well as their temporal alignment. Furthermore, the temporal context is taken into account by modeling how the current user engagement is influenced by the previous one. For the implementation of this approach, dynamic Bayesian networks in combination with a framework for Social Signal Interpretion (SSI) and Dialog Management (VSM) have been used.

Our current work focused on social attitudes that are reflected by the user's engagement. In the future, we will investigate a broader range of psychological user states, such as boredom and frustration that may help predict social attitudes. Furthermore, we will explore additional context factors to improve the interpretation of social signals, such as the user's cultural background and their personality. Finally, we will consider a larger variety of interpersonal behavior patterns that also include the mirroring of affective social cues.

Acknowledgments This work has received funding from the European Union's Horizon 2020 research and innovation programme (Project ARIA-VALUSPA, grant agreement no. 645378) and has been partially funded by the German Federal Ministry of Education and Research (BMBF) in the project EmpaT, research grant 16SV7229K. We thank Charamel GmbH for their continuous support and for providing us with the virtual characters Gloria and Curtis.

References

1. Anderson, K., André, E., Baur, T., Bernardini, S., Chollet, M., Chryssafidou, E., Damian, I., Ennis, C., Egges, A., Gebhard, P., Jones, H., Ochs, M., et al.: The tardis framework: intelligent virtual agents for social coaching in job interviews. In: Proceedings of the Tenth International Conference on Advances in Computer Entertainment Technology (ACE-13). Enschede, The Netherlands, November 2013, LNCS 8253 (2013)
2. Batrinca, L.M., Stratou, G., Shapiro, A., Morency, L.P., Scherer, S.: Cicero - towards a multimodal virtual audience platform for public speaking training. In: Aylett, R., Krenn, B., Pelachaud, C., Shimodaira, H. (eds.) Proceedings of 13th International Conference on Intelligent Virtual Agents, IVA 2013, Edinburgh, UK, August 29–31, 2013. Lecture Notes in Computer Science, vol. 8108, pp. 116–128, Springer (2013)
3. Baur, T., Damian, I., Gebhard, P., Porayska-Pomsta, K., Andre, E.: A job interview simulation: social cue-based interaction with a virtual character. In: 2013 IEEE/ASE International Conference on Social Computing (SocialCom), pp. 220–227, Washington D.C., USA (2013)
4. Baur, T., Damian, I., Lingenfelser, F., Wagner, J., André, E.: Nova: automated analysis of nonverbal signals in social interactions. In: Salah, A., Hung, H., Aran, O., Gunes, H. (eds.) Human

Behavior Understanding. *LNCS*, vol. 8212, pp. 160–171, Springer International Publishing (2013)
5. Baur, T., Mehlmann, G., Damian, I., Lingenfelser, F., Wagner, J., Lugrin, B., André, E., Gebhard, P.: Context-aware automated analysis and annotation of social human-agent interactions. ACM Trans. Interact. Intell. Syst. (TiiS) **5**(2), 11 (2015)
6. Beck, J.E.: Engagement tracing: using response times to model student disengagement. In: Looi, C., McCalla, G.I., Bredeweg, B., Breuker, J. (eds.) Artificial Intelligence in Education—Supporting Learning through Intelligent and Socially Informed Technology, Proceedings of the 12th International Conference on Artificial Intelligence in Education, AIED 2005, July 18–22, 2005, Amsterdam, The Netherlands. Frontiers in Artificial Intelligence and Applications, vol. 125, pp. 88–95, IOS Press (2005)
7. Broekens, J., Heerink, M., Rosendal, H.: Assistive social robots in elderly care: a review. Gerontechnology **8**(2) (2009)
8. Camurri, A., Volpe, G., De Poli, G., Leman, M.: Communicating expressiveness and affect in multimodal interactive systems. IEEE MultiMedia **12**(1) (2005)
9. Caridakis, G., Wagner, J., Raouzaiou, A., Lingenfelser, F., Karpouzis, K., André, E.: A cross-cultural, multimodal, affective corpus for gesture expressivity analysis. J. Multimodal User Interfaces **7**(1–2), 121–134 (2013)
10. Conati, C., Maclaren, H.: Empirically building and evaluating a probabilistic model of user affect. User Model. User-Adap. Inter. **19**(3), 267–303 (2009)
11. Damian, I., Baur, T., André, E.: Investigating social cue-based interaction in digital learning games. In: Proceedings of the 1st International Workshop on Intelligent Digital Games for Empowerment and Inclusion (IDGEI 2013) Held in Conjunction with the 8th Foundations of Digital Games 2013 (FDG), ACM, SASDG Digital Library, Chania, Crete, Greece (2013)
12. De Carolis, B., Novielli, N.: Recognizing signals of social attitude in interacting with ambient conversational systems. J. Multimodal User Interfaces **8**(1), 43–60 (2014)
13. D'Mello, S., Chipman, P., Graesser, A.: Posture as a predictor of learner's affective engagement. In: Proceedings of the 29th Annual Cognitive Science Society, pp. 905–991, Cognitive Science Society (2007)
14. Eagly, A.H., Chaiken, S.: Attitude structure and function. In: Fiske, S.T., Gilbert, D.T., Lindzey, G. (eds.) The handbook of social psychology, vol. 1, pp. 269–322, 4th edn. McGraw-Hill (1998)
15. Endraß, B., André, E., Rehm, M., Nakano, Y.I.: Investigating culture-related aspects of behavior for virtual characters. Auton. Agent. Multi-Agent Syst. **27**(2), 277–304 (2013)
16. Gebhard, P., Mehlmann, G., Kipp, M.: Visual scenemaker: a tool for authoring interactive virtual characters. J. Multimodal User Interfaces **6**, 3–11 (2012)
17. Gebhard, P., Baur, T., Damian, I., Mehlmann, G., Wagner, J., André, E.: Exploring interaction strategies for virtual characters to induce stress in simulated job interviews. In: Proceedings of AAMAS (2014)
18. Greenwald, A.G., Banaji, M.R.: Implicit social cognition: attitudes, self-esteem, and stereotypes. Psychol. Rev. **102**(1), 4 (1995)
19. Hoque, M.E., Courgeon, M., Martin, J.C., Mutlu, B., Picard, R.W.: MACH: my automated conversation coach. In: Mattern, F., Santini, S., Canny, J.F., Langheinrich, M., Rekimoto, J. (eds.) The 2013 ACM International Joint Conference on Pervasive and Ubiquitous Computing, UbiComp '13, Zurich, Switzerland, September 8–12, 2013, pp. 697–706, ACM (2013)
20. Hung, H., Gatica-Perez, D.: Estimating cohesion in small groups using audio-visual nonverbal behavior. Trans. Multimedia **12**(6), 563–575 (2010)
21. Kang, S.H., Gratch, J., Sidner, C.L., Artstein, R., Huang, L., Morency, L.P.: Towards building a virtual counselor: modeling nonverbal behavior during intimate self-disclosure. In: van der Hoek, W., Padgham, L., Conitzer, V., Winikoff, M. (eds.) International Conference on Autonomous Agents and Multiagent Systems, AAMAS 2012, Valencia, Spain, June 4–8, 2012 (3 Volumes), pp. 63–70, IFAAMAS (2012)
22. Kim, J., André, E.: Emotion recognition based on physiological changes in music listening. IEEE Trans. Pattern Anal. Mach. Intell. **30**(12), 2067–2083 (2008)

23. Kleinsmith, A., Bianchi-Berthouze, N.: Form as a cue in the automatic recognition of non-acted affective body expressions. In: D'Mello, S., Graesser, A., Schuller, B., Martin, J.C. (eds.) Affective Computing and Intelligent Interaction, LNCS, vol. 6974, pp. 155–164. Springer, Berlin (2011)
24. Lingenfelser, F., Wagner, J., André, E., McKeown, G., Curran, W.: An event driven fusion approach for enjoyment recognition in real-time. In: Proceedings of the ACM International Conference on Multimedia, MM'14, pp. 377–386. ACM, New York, NY, USA (2014)
25. Mahmoud, M., Robinson, P.: Interpreting hand-over-face gestures. In: D'Mello, S.K., Graesser, A.C., Schuller, B.W., Martin, J. (eds.) Proceedings of Fourth International Conference on Affective Computing and Intelligent Interaction, ACII 2011, Memphis, TN, USA, October 9–12, 2011, Part II. Lecture Notes in Computer Science, vol. 6975, pp. 248–255, Springer (2011)
26. Mahmoud, M., Morency, L.P., Robinson, P.: Automatic multimodal descriptors of rhythmic body movement. In: Proceedings of the 15th ACM on International Conference on Multimodal Interaction, pp. 429–436, ACM (2013)
27. Mancini, M., Ach, L., Bantegnie, E., Baur, T., Berthouze, N., Datta, D., Ding, Y., Dupont, S., Griffin, H., Lingenfelser, F., Niewiadomski, R., Pelachaud, C., Pietquin, O., Piot, B., Urbain, J., Volpe, G., Wagner, J.: Laugh when you're winning. In: Rybarczyk, Y., Cardoso, T., Rosas, J., Camarinha-Matos, L. (eds.) Innovative and Creative Developments in Multimodal Interaction Systems, IFIP Advances in Information and Communication Technology, vol. 425, pp. 50–79. Springer, Berlin (2014)
28. Mehlmann, G., Janowski, K., Baur, T., Häring, M., André, E., Gebhard, P.: Modeling gaze mechanisms for grounding in hri. In: Proceedings of the 21th European Conference on Artificial Intelligence. ECAI 2014, Prague, Czech Republic, August 18–22, 2014, Frontiers in Artificial Intelligence and Applications, pp. 1069–1070. IOS Press Ebooks, Amsterdam, The Netherlands (2014)
29. Michelet, S., Karp, K., Delaherche, E., Achard, C., Chetouani, M.: Automatic imitation assessment in interaction. Human Behavior Understanding. Lecture Notes in Computer Science, vol. 7559, pp. 161–173. Springer, Berlin (2012)
30. Morency, L.P.: Modeling human communication dynamics. IEEE Signal Process. Mag. **27**(5), 112–116 (2010)
31. Nakano, Y.I., Ishii, R.: Estimating user's engagement from eye-gaze behaviors in human-agent conversations. In: Proceedings of the 15th International Conference on Intelligent User Interfaces, IUI '10, pp. 139–148. ACM, New York, NY, USA (2010)
32. Niewiadomski, R., Hofmann, J., Urbain, J., Platt, T., Wagner, J., Piot, B., Cakmak, H., Pammi, S., Baur, T., Dupont, S., Geist, M., Lingenfelser, F., McKeown, G., Pietquin, O., Ruch, W.: Laugh-aware virtual agent and its impact on user amusement. In: Proceedings of the 2013 International Conference on Autonomous Agents and Multi-agent systems. AAMAS'13, pp. 619–626. International Foundation for Autonomous Agents and Multiagent Systems, Richland (2013)
33. Pantic, M., Sebe, N., Cohn, J.F., Huang, T.: Affective multimodal human-computer interaction. In: Proceedings of the 13th Annual ACM International Conference on Multimedia. MULTIMEDIA'05, pp. 669–676. ACM, New York, NY, USA (2005)
34. Pease, A.: Body Language. Sheldon Press, London (1988)
35. Petridis, S., Gunes, H., Kaltwang, S., Pantic, M.: Static vs. dynamic modeling of human non-verbal behavior from multiple cues and modalities. In: Crowley, J.L., Ivanov, Y.A., Wren, C.R., Gatica-Perez, D., Johnston, M., Stiefelhagen, R. (eds.) Proceedings of the 11th International Conference on Multimodal Interfaces, ICMI 2009, Cambridge, Massachusetts, USA, November 2–4, 2009, pp. 23–30, ACM (2009)
36. Reeves, B., Nass, C.: How people treat computers, television, and new media like real people and places. CSLI Publications and Cambridge university press, Cambridge (1996)
37. Rich, C., Ponsleur, B., Holroyd, A., Sidner, C.L.: Recognizing engagement in human-robot interaction. In: Proceedings of the 5th ACM/IEEE International Conference on Human-robot interaction, HRI'10, pp. 375–382. IEEE Press, Piscataway (2010)

38. Rosenberg, M.J., Hovland, C.I.: Cognitive, affective, and behavioral components of attitudes. Attitude organization and change: an analysis of consistency among attitude components **3**, 1–14 (1960)
39. Russell, S.J., Norvig, P.: Artificial Intelligence: a modern approach, 2nd int. edn. Prentice Hall, Upper Saddle River (2003)
40. Salam, H., Chetouani, M.: A multi-level context-based modelling of engagement in human-robot interaction. In: International Workshop on Context Based Affect Recognition (2015)
41. Sandbach, G., Zafeiriou, S., Pantic, M., Yin, L.: Static and dynamic 3d facial expression recognition: a comprehensive survey. Image Vision Comput. **30**(10), 683–697 (2012)
42. Sanghvi, J., Castellano, G., Leite, I., Pereira, A., McOwan, P.W., Paiva, A.: Automatic analysis of affective postures and body motion to detect engagement with a game companion. In: Billard, A., Adams, P.H.K.J.A., Jr., Trafton, J.G. (eds.) Proceedings of the 6th International Conference on Human Robot Interaction, HRI 2011, Lausanne, Switzerland, March 6-9, 2011, pp. 305–312, ACM (2011)
43. Scherer, S., Marsella, S., Stratou, G., Xu, Y., Morbini, F., Egan, A., Rizzo, A., Morency, L.P.: Perception markup language: Towards a standardized representation of perceived nonverbal behaviors. In: Nakano, Y., Neff, M., Paiva, A., Walker, M. (eds.) Intelligent Virtual Agents, LNCS, vol. 7502, pp. 455–463. Springer, Berlin (2012)
44. Sebe, N., Cohen, I., Gevers, T., Huang, T.S.: Emotion recognition based on joint visual and audio cues. In: Proceedings of the 18th International Conference on Pattern Recognition—Volume 01, ICPR'06, pp. 1136–1139. IEEE Computer Society, Washington, DC, USA (2006)
45. Sidner, C.L., Kidd, C.D., Lee, C., Lesh, N.: Where to look: a study of human-robot engagement. In: IUI '04: Proceedings of the 9th International Conference on Intelligent user Interfaces, pp. 78–84. ACM Press, New York, NY, USA (2004)
46. Traum, D.R., DeVault, D., Lee, J., Wang, Z., Marsella, S.: Incremental dialogue understanding and feedback for multiparty, multimodal conversation. In: Nakano, Y., Neff, M., Paiva, A., Walker, M.A. (eds.) Proceedings of 12th International Conference on Intelligent Virtual Agents, IVA 2012, Santa Cruz, CA, USA, September, 12–14, 2012. *Lecture Notes in Computer Science*, vol. 7502, pp. 275–288, Springer (2012)
47. Vail, A.K., Grafsgaard, J.F., Wiggins, J.B., Lester, J.C., Boyer, K.E.: Predicting learning and engagement in tutorial dialogue: a personality-based model. In: Salah, A.A., Cohn, J.F., Schuller, B.W., Aran, O., Morency, L., Cohen, P.R. (eds.) Proceedings of the 16th International Conference on Multimodal Interaction, ICMI 2014, Istanbul, Turkey, November 12–16, 2014, pp. 255–262, ACM (2014)
48. Valstar, M.: Automatic facial expression analysis. In: Mandal, M.K., Awasthi, A. (eds.) Understanding Facial Expressions in Communication, pp. 143–172. Springer India, New York (2015)
49. Vogt, T., André, E., Bee, N.: Emovoice—a framework for online recognition of emotions from voice. In: Perception in Multimodal Dialogue Systems, 4th IEEE Tutorial and Research Workshop on Perception and Interactive Technologies for Speech-Based Systems, Kloster Irsee, Germany, LNCS, pp. 188–199, Springer (2008)
50. Wagner, J., Lingenfelser, F., Baur, T., Damian, I., Kistler, F., André, E.: The social signal interpretation (ssi) framework—multimodal signal processing and recognition in real-time. In: Proceedings of ACM MULTIMEDIA 2013, Barcelona (2013)
51. Whitehill, J., Serpell, Z., Lin, Y., Foster, A., Movellan, J.R.: The faces of engagement: automatic recognition of student engagementfrom facial expressions. T. Affect. Comput. **5**(1), 86–98 (2014)
52. Yu, C., Aoki, P.M., Woodruff, A.: Detecting User Engagement in Everyday Conversations. eprint arXiv:cs/0410027 (2004)

Chapter 11
Personality and Recommendation Diversity

Li Chen, Wen Wu and Liang He

Abstract Diversity is increasingly recognized as an important metric for evaluating the effectiveness of online recommendations. However, few studies have fully explored the possibility of realizing personalized diversity in recommender systems by taking into account the individual user's spontaneous needs. In this chapter, we emphasize the effect of users' personality on their needs for recommendation diversity. We start with a review of the two branches of research in this area, diversity-oriented recommender systems (RS) and personality-based RS. We then report the results from a user survey that we conducted with the aim of identifying the relationship between personality and users' preferences for recommendation diversity. For instance, the personality trait of conscientiousness can affect users' preferences not only for diversity in respect of a particular attribute (such as movie genre, country, or release time), but also their preference for overall diversity when all attributes are considered. Motivated by the survey findings, we propose a personality-based diversity-adjusting strategy for recommender systems, and demonstrate its significant merit in improving users' subjective perceptions of the system's recommendation accuracy. Finally, we consider implications and suggestions for future research directions.

11.1 Introduction

In recent years, recommender systems (RS) have become popular in many web applications because they can eliminate online information overload and make

L. Chen · W. Wu (✉)
Hong Kong Baptist University, 224 Waterloo Road, Kowloon Tong,
Kowloon, Hong Kong
e-mail: lichen@comp.hkbu.edu.hk

W. Wu
e-mail: cswenwu@comp.hkbu.edu.hk

L. He
East China Normal University, 500 Dongchuan Road, Minhang District,
Shanghai, China
e-mail: lhe@cs.ecnu.edu.cn

M. Tkalčič et al. (eds.), *Emotions and Personality in Personalized Services*,
Human–Computer Interaction Series, DOI 10.1007/978-3-319-31413-6_11

personalized suggestions for items such as movies, books, and music based on users' interests. Diverse recommendations can help users discover unexpected items that might be of interest to them [25]. However, existing approaches commonly adopt a fixed strategy to adjust the degree of diversity within a set of recommendations [19, 30, 42–45], so results are not tailored to an individual user's spontaneous needs. Such approaches largely neglect the improvement that incorporating users' personal characteristics, such as personality, can make on recommendation diversity.

It is widely recognized by psychologists that personality can affect users' attitudes, tastes, and behavior [3]. A popular personality model is the so-called "big-five factor model," which defines personality according to five traits [13]: *openness to experience*, *conscientiousness*, *extraversion*, *agreeableness*, and *neuroticism* (see Sect. 11.3.1). Some researchers in the recommender community have recently attempted to incorporate users' big-five personality traits into the process of generating recommendations [16, 34]. For example, Tkalcic et al. [34] use personality to improve nearest neighbor measures in collaborative filtering (CF) systems. Hu and Pu demonstrate that personality can be leveraged to solve the cold-start problem of CF (i.e., few ratings provided by users) [16]. They also find that a recommender system that considers users' personality can increase users' perceptions of accuracy and their faith in the system, relative to non-personality-based systems [14]. However, little work has been done to explore the role of personality in revealing users' preference for diversity within a set of recommendations.

We were therefore motivated to connect the two branches of research, i.e., diversity-oriented RS and personality-based RS, with the objective of developing a personality-based diversity-adjusting strategy for RS. To achieve this objective, we first conducted a user survey of 181 subjects, to study the correlation between personality traits and diversity preference (within the sample domain of movies). Two levels of analysis were performed: users' diversity preference in respect of a specific attribute (such as genre, director, actor/actress), and their overall diversity preference when all attributes were considered. The correlation results show that some personality traits significantly influence users' diversity preferences. For example, more reactive and nervous people (i.e., those with high scores for "neuroticism") are more likely to choose movies from a diverse selection of directors, and imaginative/creative users (with high scores for "openness to experience") are more likely to prefer a choice of movies with diverse actors/actresses. At the second level of analysis, we found that people with low "conscientiousness" scores generally prefer a high level of overall diversity, no matter how the different attributes are weighted.

To follow on from the survey, we propose a method that explicitly incorporates the moderating factor of users' personality to adjust the diversity within the system's recommendations [37]. The method is firmly rooted in the preference-based recommending process: a preference profile that includes the user's personality-based diversity preference and their criteria and weighting for each item's attributes is built and then items that match the user's profile are recommended. For example, the system will return movies with diverse actors/actresses to users if this attribute is important to them and their scores for "openness to experience" are high. The overall diversity of recommendations is also adjusted according to the user's score for "conscientiousness." We performed a controlled user evaluation (with 52 participants) to test this method's performance and found that users perceive the recommendations generated by our method as significantly more accurate and helpful than those resulting from a method that does not consider users' personality-based diversity preferences. Their overall satisfaction with the system is also significantly higher. The results not only consolidate our previous survey's observations, but also demonstrate a simple but effective way to generate diverse recommendations that are tailored to users' personal requirements.

In the following sections, we first introduce related works on diversity and personality studies in recommender systems (Sect. 11.2). We then present details of our survey, including the experimental method and results (Sect. 11.3). In Sect. 11.4, we describe our personality-based diversity-adjusting strategy, followed by the results of a user evaluation. Finally, we report our conclusions and make suggestions for further research (Sect. 11.5).

11.2 Related Works

11.2.1 Diversity-Oriented Recommender Systems

Traditionally, recommender systems mainly focus on increasing *accuracy*, by returning items that are similar to those users who have previously liked [2, 23, 24]. Accuracy has principally been measured by calculating the distance between the predicted rating/ranking of the items and the user's true preference [40]. For example, Alice may receive movies directed by Steven Spielberg because she gave high ratings for movies made by this director. In recent years, it has been recognized that accuracy alone is not enough to create an effective recommender system that will fully reflect a user's potential interest [25]. *Diversity* is increasingly regarded as important because it enables users to discover unexpected and surprising items that are not similar to what they have previously liked. Diversity is defined at two levels: *intra-user diversity*, which is the average pairwise dissimilarity between recommended items for an individual user [35], and *inter-user diversity*, which measures the ability of an algorithm to return different results for different users [24].

In this chapter, we focus on *intra-user diversity*, for which related studies have mainly focused on how to obtain a balance between accuracy and diversity in the algorithm's results (summarized in Table 11.1). For example, to maximize the diversity of a retrieved recommendation list as well as its similarity to the target user's query, Zhang and Hurly [42] relax a binary optimization problem with a trust region algorithm and produce the top-N recommendations. Experimental results have shown that their proposed method can increase the likelihood of recommending novel items while maintaining accuracy. Hurly and Zhang [19] also compared different optimization strategies for solving the diversity-accuracy dilemma, including greedy algorithms, relaxation, and the quantization method. They analyze several weighted

Table 11.1 Summary of typical works on diversity-oriented recommender systems

Related work	Diversity definition	Diversity-oriented recommender systems (RS)	Baseline	Evaluation metrics
Increasing diversity in optimization based recommender systems				
Zhang and Hurly [42]	Average pairwise dissimilarity of all items in the set	Relax a binary optimization problem with trust region algorithm in top-*N* RS	SUGGEST algorithm and Random algorithm	Precision, mean diversity and mean similarity
Hurly and Zhang [19]	Average novelty of the items in the set	Incorporate the greedy and R&Q optimization strategy in CF and case-based top-*N* RS	Random strategy and Equalization strategy	Precision, Recall, mean diversity and mean similarity
Smyth and McClave [30]	Average pairwise dissimilarity of all items in the set	Incorporate the bounded greedy selection strategy in case-based RS	Bounded random selection and Greedy selection	Alternative quality metrics
Zhou et al. [44]	Average pairwise distance of all items in the set	Develop a hybrid diffusion-based method with the integration of ProbS and HeatS	USim, GRank, ProbS and HeatS	Precision, Recall, Personalization and Surprisal/Novelty
Increasing diversity in rating-based recommender systems				
Zeng et al. [41]	Average pairwise Hamming distance of all items in the set	Combine both the influence of similar and dissimilar users in CF	Standard CF	Precision and Diversity
Mourao et al. [26]	Temporal dynamics diversity	Rescue the forgotten items in CF	Not applicable	Problem verification and utility analysis
Zhang and Hurly [43]	Average pairwise dissimilarity of all items in the set	Partition users' rating profiles in CF	SUGGEST algorithm	Diversity and users' satisfaction
Increasing diversity in attribute-based recommender systems				
Vargas and Castells [36]	Average pairwise dissimilarity of all items in the set	Model a user's preference profiles for different features and combine sub-profile recommendations	pLSA and ListRank	Ndcg, ERR-IA and S-recall

(continued)

Table 11.1 (continued)

Related work	Diversity definition	Diversity-oriented recommender systems (RS)	Baseline	Evaluation metrics
Ziegler et al. [45]	Intra-list similarity (higher score representing lower diversity)	Develop a heuristic topic diversification algorithm based on users' preference in top-*N* RS	Item-based CF and user-based CF	Accuracy, Diversity and Coverage
Yu et al. [39]	Distance between the explanations of two items	Recommend items sharing few common explanations, without considering items' attributes	Attribute-based CF	Jaccard similarity, Kendall's tau distance and Average total cost
Increasing diversity via user interface design				
Chen and Pu [7] and Hu and Pu [17]	Maximize intra-category similarity and minimize inter-category similarity	Design an organization-based interface to display diverse recommendations	The original list view interface	Usability, user satisfaction and final preference

objective functions that explicitly control the trade-off between the retrieved set's diversity and degree of matching to the user's query. Smyth and McClave [30] compare several optimization strategies, including bounded random selection, greedy selection, and bounded greedy selection, with the aim of improving recommendation diversity and maintaining accuracy. Their experimental results show that the bounded greedy selection strategy offers the best performance, as it not only ensures optimal balance grounded on the theory of the greedy algorithm, but also reduces calculation complexity by decreasing the number of iteration cycles. Diffusion-based methods have also been used to enhance the diversity of recommendations. For instance, Zhou et al. implement a hybrid approach that combines a probabilistic spreading algorithm (ProbS) to recommend items that are of low diversity with the heat diffusion algorithm (HeatS) to discover unpopular items. This combination can improve both diversity and accuracy [44].

To improve the rating-based collaborative filtering (CF) method, Zeng et al. develop a novel algorithm to increase recommendation diversity by considering the influence of both similar users and dissimilar users [41]. Two users are regarded as similar if they have rated items in common. An item's prediction score for the target user is generated by combing the positive score from similar users and the negative score from dissimilar users in a linear way. Extensive analyses of real-life movie datasets have shown that this approach outperforms the standard CF algorithm in terms of both accuracy and diversity. Mourao et al. [26] increase the diversity in CF-based recommendations by rescuing forgotten items that were preferred by a user in the past so they may be selected by this user in the present. The experimental findings on a Last.fm dataset have demonstrated that this approach helps to increase the diversity of the returned recommendations. Zhang and Hurly [43] also proposed a new CF-based recommendation method by partitioning a user's rating profile in a movie domain through clustering methods such as extreme clustering, graph partitioning, k-means, and modularity maximization. Items that are similar to those in each cluster are aggregated to form the final recommendation list. Graph partitioning has been shown to produce significant improvements in terms of increasing recommendation diversity and users' satisfaction.

Other methods have focused on increasing recommendation diversity via users' preferences for items' attributes. For example, Vargas and Castells [36] model a user's preference profiles for movie genres and social tags to generate recommendations that match each type of profile. They then adopt the aspect-based diversification algorithm [28] to combine sub-profile recommendations. Ziegler et al. use a heuristic algorithm based on taxonomy similarity to increase the diversity within a recommendation list [45]. They defined a weighting factor to control the contributions from two sets, one with items that are similar to the user's attribute-based preference profile and the other with items ranked in the reverse order of their similarity to the user's profile. Through an online user survey, they show that although this approach sacrifices a little accuracy, users perceive the effect on diversity and coverage as positive. Yu et al. [39] further improve this approach by developing an explanation-based method to diversify recommendations. Specifically, given two items, diversity is defined as the distance between explanations for why the items are recommended. They adopt two diversification algorithms, algorithm swap and algorithm greedy [38], to evaluate the algorithm's performance. The results verify that their explanation-based diversification is not only as effective as the original method [45], but also applicable in scenarios where an item's attributes are not available.

For the user interface, Chen and Pu designed a category interface to display diverse recommendations [7]. In this interface, items with similar attributes are grouped into categories, and diversity across items in different categories is maximized. Hu and Pu further conduct a user study to measure perceptions of this diversity-driven interface [17]. Compared with the standard list interface, which simply lists items one after another, the category interface enables users to recognize the diversity of recommendations, which improves their overall satisfaction with the system.

11.2.2 Personality-Based Recommender Systems

Table 11.2 summarizes the personality-based recommender system, in which the user's personality is incorporated into the process of collaborative filtering (CF) to generate recommendations. Tkalcic et al. [34] use a definition of personality obtained

Table 11.2 Summary of typical works on personality-based recommender systems

Related work	Personality detection	Personality-based recommender systems (RS)	Baseline	Evaluation metrics
Personality in collaborative filtering (CF) based recommender systems				
Tkalcic et al. [34]	IPIP questionnaire with 50 items	Enhance the nearest neighborhood in personality-based CF	Rating-based CF	Precision, Recall and F measure
Hu and Pu [16]	TIPI questionnaire with 10 items	Enhance the nearest neighborhood in personality-based CF and Hybrid CF	Rating-based CF	MAE and ROC sensitivity
Personality in attribute-based recommender systems				
Elahi et al. [11]	TIPI questionnaire with 10 items	Incorporate personality as an attribute in matrix factorization	Not applicable	MAE
Personality in preference-based recommender systems				
Hu and Pu [15]	TIPI questionnaire with 10 items	Recommend items according to the user's personality-based interest profile	Not applicable	Objective measure and subjective measure

via a personality quiz based on the big-five factor model to improve the nearest neighbor measure in CF systems. They demonstrate that this personality-based similarity measure is more accurate than the traditional rating-based one. Hu and Pu [16] also incorporate users' personality into the CF framework, to address the cold-start problem. They develop two variations of the personality-based CF method: *pure personality-based CF*, which calculates user-user similarity based on personality values alone, and *hybrid CF*, which calculates similarity by considering both users' personality and their ratings. The hybrid CF has two alternative forms: (1) linear hybrid CF, which first combines personality and ratings to compute user-user similarity, based on which the target user's neighborhood is identified; and (2) cascade hybrid CF, which adopts the pure personality-based algorithm to make initial predictions of unobserved ratings for densifying the user-item matrix, and then applies the classic CF method on the denser matrix. Their experimental results indicate that all the personality-based CF methods significantly outperform the non-personality-based approach even in sparse datasets, among which the cascade hybrid CF performs the best. Elahi et al. [11] develop a novel active learning strategy based on personality, to predict items that users are able to rate before they get recommendations. They develop an attribute-based matrix factorization (MF) algorithm, with attributes including users' age, gender, and big-five personality traits. Through a live user study, they prove that considering these attributes, especially users' personality, can significantly increase the number of items that users can rate.

Personality has also been incorporated into preference-based recommender systems. Hu and Pu [15] establish a personality-based interest profile for each user, reflecting the relationship between personality and users' preferences for music genres [27]. Items that best match the user's profile are then recommended. For example, energetic and rhythmic music will be recommended to extravert people and upbeat and conventional music will be recommended to individuals who are relatively conventional. Hu and Pu further conduct a user study to test the applicability of this approach to both the active user and her or his friends. The results demonstrate that users in this system not only are willing to find songs for themselves, but also enjoy recommending songs for their friends. Some commercial web sites also use personality to produce preference-based recommendations. For instance, Whattorent[1] is based on the LaBarrie theory, which states that a movie viewer interacts with a movie emotionally in the same manner that she or he interacts with human beings. The site first establishes a general model that describes how users react to the world and their average emotional state. Next, a database stores the correlations between personality and movies' attributes, such as genre. Movies are then recommended by considering the user's personality and current mood. Hu and Pu [14] conduct a user study to compare Whattorent with MovieLens (which is primarily based on users' ratings), in terms of users' subjective perceptions of recommendation accuracy, the system's ease of use and intention to use. They find that Whattorent is easier to use and leads to higher user loyalty.

11.2.3 Limitations

The above two branches of recommender system research have rarely been connected to reveal the effect of users' personality on their preferences for recommendation diversity. In diversity-oriented recommender systems, the primary focus has been on studying the balance relationship between diversity and similarity, but the algorithms designed to generate diverse recommendations are not tailored to users' spontaneous needs. In the area of personality-based recommender systems, personality has mainly been exploited to reveal users' preferences for a single item (or the item's attribute, such as music genre), but not their preference for diversity within multiple recommendations.

Few studies have attempted to fill this gap in the research. Tintarev et al. apply a user-as-wizard approach to study how people diversify a set of items when they recommend them to their friends [32]. They particularly emphasize the role of the "openness to experience" personality trait, making the assumption that people with greater "openness to experience" would be more willing to receive diverse recommendations. By analyzing 120 users' responses to their survey, they find that, although

[1] http://whattorent.com/.

the effect of "openness to experience" on the overall diversity that participants prefer is not proven, people who are more open to experience generally prefer higher categorical diversity (i.e., across genres) and lower thematic diversity (i.e., inter-genre). Di et al. explore users' attitudes toward recommendation diversity from another angle [10]. They develop an adaptive attribute-based diversification method that considers users' preferences for diversity in respect of item attributes such as movie genre, actor, director, and year of release. They then use this approach to re-rank the top-N recommendations. An experiment in the movie domain demonstrates that their proposed approach achieves higher accuracy and diversity.

The above studies unfortunately do not discover the full effects of all five personality traits on users' diversity preference. We are thus not only interested in revealing the causal relationships of the five personality traits and users' diversity needs, but also in developing an effective solution to accommodate the influences (if any) of personality on the recommendation process.

11.3 User Survey: *Does Personality Influence Users' Preference for Recommender Diversity?*

The first research question that we consider here is: *Does users' personality have a significant effect on their need for diversity within multiple recommendations?* We performed a user survey to answer this question by collecting users' item selections

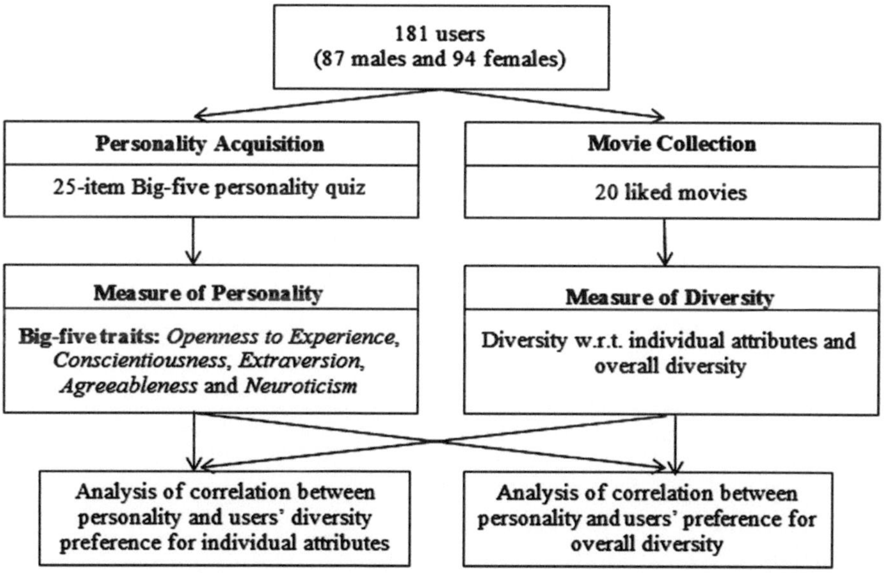

Fig. 11.1 Experiment procedure of user survey

(i.e., movies) and their personality information. Figure 11.1 gives an overview of the survey.

11.3.1 User Survey Setup

A total of 181 participants (94 female, 87 male) volunteered to take part in the survey. All were Chinese, with various educational backgrounds (41 % with a Bachelor's degree, 41 % with a Master's degree, and 17 % with a Ph.D.) and ages (82 % aged 20–30, 6 % aged 30–40, and 12 % in other age ranges). As an incentive, there was a lottery draw with 20 prizes (at a total cost of 2000RMB). We first asked users to name ten movies that they had recently watched and liked, and then asked them to choose ten new movies they were prepared to watch from Douban Movie (a popular movie reviewing website in China). They were also asked to name three favorite genres and directors.

Personality acquisition. As mentioned before, the big-five factor model defines five major dimensions of personality [13]: "openness to experience" distinguishes imaginative and creative people from down-to-earth, conventional types; "conscientiousness" relates to prudence or impulsiveness; "extraversion" measures whether a person is extrovert or introvert; "agreeableness" suggests a person's social harmony and willingness to cooperate (i.e., people with high agreeableness tend to be friendly and cooperative, whereas people with low agreeableness are suspicious and aggressive); and "neuroticism" determines whether a person is sensitive and nervous [21].

In our experiment, each user's five personality traits were assessed via a popular personality quiz that contains 25 questions [13]. As shown in Table 11.3, each per-

Table 11.3 Personality quiz used to assess the five traits (the question number is referred to [13])

Openness to Experience	Conscientiousness	Extraversion
Imagination (Q3)	Orderliness (Q5)	Gregariousness (Q2)
Artistic interests (Q8)	Cautiousness (Q10)	Cheerfulness (Q7)
Liberalism (Q13)	Self-discipline (Q15)	Assertiveness (Q12)
Adventurousness (Q18)	Self-efficacy (Q20)	Friendliness (Q17)
Intellect (Q23)	Dutifulness (Q25)	Excitement-seeking (Q22)
Agreeableness	**Neuroticism**	
Modesty (Q4)	Anxiety (Q1)	
Altruism (Q9)	Vulnerability (Q6)	
Morality (Q14)	Depression (Q11)	
Cooperation (Q19)	Anger (Q16)	
Trust (Q24)	Self-consciousness (Q21)	

Each question is responded on a 5-point Likert scale. For example, for Imagination (Q3), it is rated from 1, "no-nonsense" to 5, "a dreamer."

sonality trait is measured by 5 sub-factor questions, and the trait's score is the sum of the user's scores on the five questions. For instance, the questions for assessing "openness to experience" include: imagination (rated from 1, "no-nonsense" to 5, "a dreamer"), artistic interests (rated from 1, "practical" to 5, "theoretical"), liberalism (rated from 1, "follow authority" to 5, "follow imagination"), adventurousness (rated from 1, "seek routine" to 5, "seek novelty"), and intellect (rated from 1, "prefer things clear-cut" to 5, "comfortable with ambiguity").

Measure of diversity. From the set of 20 movies that users selected, we first evaluated their diversity in respect of each attribute. Using the diversity calculated for "genre" as an example, the equation is based on the Gini-index [29]:

$$Div(genre) = \frac{1}{\frac{1}{|S_{genre,u}|}\sum_{j=1}^{|S_{genre,u}|}(2 \times j - |S_{genre,u}| - 1) \times p(j) + \alpha} \times \frac{|S_{genre,u}|}{|S_u|} \tag{11.1}$$

where S_u is the set of movies selected by user u, $S_{genre,u}$ is the set of distinct genres that appear in S_u, $p(j)$ is the proportion of movies (in set S_u) that have a specific genre j (note that $p(1)$, $p(2)$, ..., $p(|S_{genre,u}|)$ are in the ascending order), and α is an adjustment coefficient to avoid the result of Gini-coefficient being zero (which is set as 0.1 in our experiment). Similar equations are used to calculate the diversity degree regarding the other attributes, such as "director," "country," and "release time" (e.g., 1990s, 2000s).

For "actor/actress," the Gini-index is not suitable because the value of $|S_{actor,u}|$ (i.e., the number of distinct actors) is usually too large, so we use Jaccard coefficient [1] instead to calculate the diversity:

$$Div(actor) = \frac{2}{|S_u| \times |S_u - 1|} \sum_{m_i \in S_u} \sum_{m_j \neq m_i \in S_u} (1 - Sim(m_i, m_j)) \tag{11.2}$$

where $Sim(m_i, m_j)$ gives the similarity between two movies in terms of the concerned attribute, which is concretely calculated as $Sim(m_i, m_j) = \frac{|S_{m_i,attr_k} \cap S_{m_j,attr_k}|}{|S_{m_i,attr_k} \cup S_{m_j,attr_k}|}$ (where $S_{m_i,attr_k}$ is the set of all values of the k-th attribute, such as all actors, of movie m_i).

Moreover, with the three favorite genres/directors that each user has specified, we are interested in knowing whether they will choose other movies except their favorites. Using "genre" as an example, let $S_{fav\_genre,u}$ be the set of distinct favorite genres that appear in the set S_u (note that the set should contain at most three genres), and $S_{sum\_fav\_genre,u}$ gives the total occurrences of these favorite genres (including repeated ones) in S_u. The equation below shows an alternative way to calculate the diversity w.r.t. "genre:"

$$Div^*(genre) = Div(genre) \times (1 - \frac{|S_{fav\_genre,u}|}{3} + \alpha) \times (1 - \frac{|S_{sum\_fav\_genre,u}|)}{|S_u|} + \alpha) \tag{11.3}$$

Similar equation is applied to calculating the diversity w.r.t. "director" by considering the three favorite directors that the user has specified.

In addition to calculating the items' diversity in respect of individual attributes, we combine all attributes to determine the items' overall diversity. Given that users usually give different weights to different attributes (for example, "genre" may be more important than other attributes for some users), we generate 20 representative combinations of weights in reference to [20] (for instance, one combination is 0.4, 0.1, 0.1, 0.2, 0.2 as assigned to the five major attributes "genre," "director," "country," "release time," and "actor/actress," respectively; note that the sum of weights is equal to 1). The overall diversity is then calculated as:

$$OverDiv = \sum_{k=1}^{n}(w_k \times Div(attr_k)) \quad (11.4)$$

where w_k is the weight specified by the user to indicate its relative importance to her/him on the k-*th* attribute ($0 <= w_k <= 1, \sum w_k = 1$) and n is the total number of attributes.

11.3.2 Survey Results

11.3.2.1 Correlation between Personality and Users' Diversity Preference for Individual Attributes

Table 11.4 shows the Spearman's rank correlation coefficients for the degree of diversity and users' personality traits. There are significant correlations associated with each attribute. Specifically, the diversity of "genre" as calculated by $Div^*(genre)$ (Eq. 11.3) is significantly negatively correlated with the personality trait "conscientiousness," suggesting that less organized and more impatient people are more likely to choose movie genres that are beyond their three favorite genres. There is also significant correlation between "genre" diversity (computed with either $Div(genre)$ or $Div^*(genre)$) and users' age, which implies that younger people are more likely to prefer movies from diverse genres. "Director" is significantly positively correlated with the personality trait "neuroticism," which suggests that reactive, excitable, and nervous people are more inclined to prefer diverse directors. This attribute is also significantly negatively correlated with "extraversion" and "education level" and positively correlated with "gender," suggesting that diversity of directors is preferred by independent and conservative people, those with lower education level, and females.

Analysis of the other attributes (country, release time, and actor/actress) also shows some significant associations. "Country" diversity is significantly negatively correlated with the personality traits "conscientiousness" (indicating that country diversity is preferred by disorganized/impatient users) and "agreeableness" (suggesting country diversity is also preferred by suspicious/antagonistic users). Diverse recommendations for "country" are also preferred by people with lower education levels and by female users. Diverse recommendations for "release time" positively correlate

Table 11.4 Correlation coefficient between diversity (w.r.t. a specific attribute) and users' personality/demographic values ($^{*}p < 0.05$ and $^{**}p < 0.01$)

	Div(genre)	Div*(genre)	Div(director)	Div∗(director)	Div(country)	Div(release time)	Div(actor/actress)
Openness to Experience	0.10	0.11	0.07	0.10	0.07	−0.07	**0.20***
Conscientiousness	−0.12	**−0.17***	−0.16	−0.05	**−0.15***	**0.15***	−0.10
Extraversion	0.02	0.06	**−0.15***	-0.06	−0.15	−0.14	−0.07
Agreeableness	−0.04	−0.05	−0.17	−0.02	**−0.18***	−0.04	−0.10
Neuroticism	−0.04	−0.06	**0.17***	**0.19***	0.06	−0.08	0.09
Age	**−0.18***	**−0.15***	0.13	0.04	−0.14	−0.05	−0.01
Gender	−0.13	−0.04	**0.24****	0.09	**0.23****	−0.12	0.10
Education	−0.10	0.07	**−0.20****	−0.28	**−0.20****	0.06	−0.04

with "conscientiousness" (efficient and organized users). Diversity in "actor/actress" suggestions is positively correlated with "openness to experience" (imaginative and creative users).

The results indicate that the five personality traits all, to a certain extent, influence users' diversity preference with regard to movies' attributes. Demographic factors, including age, gender, and education level, also exert some effects.

11.3.2.2 Correlation between Personality and Users' Preference for Overall Diversity

When all attributes are considered, we find that no matter how the attributes' weights vary, overall diversity is consistently significantly negatively correlated with the personality trait "conscientiousness" and the demographic properties "age" and "education level" (see Table 11.5). This suggests that users who are more flexible, spontaneous, disorganized, and impatient are more likely to choose diverse movies. According to the psychological study reported in [21], "conscientiousness" is inherently related to how people control, regulate and direct their impulses. Usually, people with high conscientiousness scores tend to be prudent, whereas those with low scores tend to be impulsive, which may explain why users with lower conscientiousness scores in our survey were more willing to choose diverse movies. In contrast, the significant correlations between overall diversity and age or education imply that people who are younger or with lower educational qualifications are more likely to prefer diverse movies.

Table 11.5 Correlation coefficient between overall diversity and users' personality/demographic values ($^{*}p < 0.05$ and $^{**}p < 0.01$)

	OverDiv1	OverDiv2	OverDiv3	OverDiv4
Openness to Experience	0.057	0.065	0.069	0.086
Conscientiousness	**−0.162***	**−0.148***	**−0.161***	**−0.192***
Extraversion	−0.112	−0.035	−0.070	−0.135
Agreeableness	−0.137	−0.088	−0.112	**−0.177***
Neuroticism	0.071	−0.017	0.016	0.113
Age	**−0.237****	**−0.212****	**−0.214****	**−0.182***
Gender	−0.007	−0.066	−0.015	0.091
Education	**−0.152***	**−0.148***	**−0.159***	**−0.165***

Note we tested 20 different combinations of attribute weights, which all returned similar trend. To save space, the results from 4 typical combinations are reported in this table.
OverDiv1 weight assignment {0.2, 0.2, 0.2, 0.2, 0.2} to the five attributes:
{genre, director, country, release time, actor/actress};
OverDiv2 weight assignment {0.4, 0.1, 0.1, 0.2, 0.2};
OverDiv3 weight assignment {0.3, 0.1, 0.2, 0.2, 0.2};
OverDiv4 weight assignment {0.1, 0.1, 0.2, 0.3, 0.3}

11.3.3 Discussion

Our user survey revealed significant correlations between users' personality traits and their diversity preferences when choosing movies. Two levels of analysis were conducted: users' diversity preferences in respect of individual attributes (such as genre, director, actor/actress), and their overall diversity preference when all attributes are taken into account. However, the number of participants was limited in this experiment, and the recruited users were mainly Chinese. We therefore intend to consolidate our findings in a global context by recruiting subjects from other countries.

11.4 Personality-Based Diversity Adjustment in a Recommender System: Algorithm Design and User Evaluation

11.4.1 System Design

The next question we are interested in solving is: *How to incorporate personality, as a moderating factor, into adjusting the diversity degree within a set of recommendations, so as to make them tailored to individual user's needs?*

We adopt the preference-based recommending approach to implement our personality-based diversity adjusting strategy. Figure 11.2 illustrates the overall framework. In a traditional preference-based recommender system [15], each user is usually modeled with a profile that includes her or his criteria and weightings for different attributes. Here, we define a five-dimension vector $pref_u = (pref_u^1, pref_u^2, pref_u^3, pref_u^4, pref_u^5)^T$ to represent a user's preference profile, where each dimension stands for the user's stated preference for the k-th attribute "genre," "director," "country," "release time." and "actor/actress." Specifically, $pref_u^k$ can be repre-

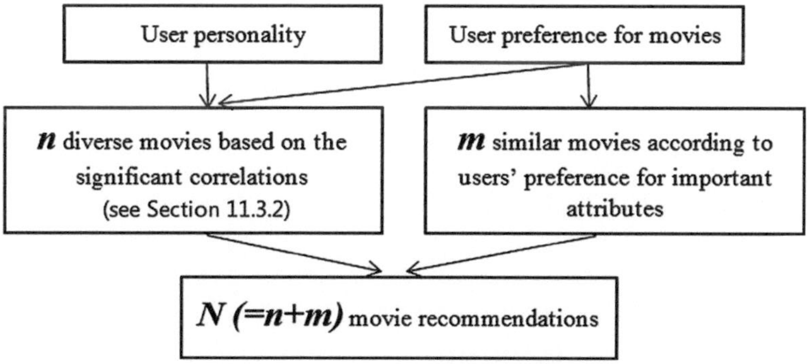

Fig. 11.2 Framework of our personality-based diversity adjusting strategy in RS

sented as (*attribute*, *acceptable value*, where *weight* can be in the range from 1 "least important" to 5 "most important"). For example, a user's preference profile might be: {(genre, action, 5), (director, Steven Spielberg, 3), (country, None, 1), (release time, 1990s, 2), (actor, Tom Cruise, 4)} (where "None" means that no preference is stated on that attribute).

In our system, in addition to this profile, we build personality profiles by asking users to answer the big-five personality quiz [13] (see Table 11.3), which is formally represented as: $p_u = (p_u^1, p_u^2, ..., p_u^5)^T$ where each dimension p_u^i represents the i-th personality trait of user u, from "openness to experience," "conscientiousness," "extraversion," "agreeableness," and "neuroticism."

When generating recommendations, we first use the user's personality profile to locate n items that match her or his diversity needs in respect of both the most important attribute and overall diversity. We then apply the user's preference profile to retrieve m most relevant items. A set of m and n items will be recommended to the user (total $N = m + n$).

Diversity is adjusted within the set of N items and n is automatically defined as follows. First, we convert each of the target user's five personality traits into one of three levels: *high*, *middle*, and *low*. The system then maps this level to the user's diversity requirement for her or his most important attribute, by checking the correlation results from our previous survey (ref. Table 11.4). For example, given that a high level of "openness to experience" correlates with diverse "actor/actress," if this attribute is the user's most important attribute and she or he also possesses a high "openness to experience" score, the system will return movies with diverse actors/actresses. If, in addition, the user has a low "conscientiousness" score, the system will increase the overall diversity degree in the set of n recommendations, because low "conscientiousness" correlates with a high need for overall diversity (Ref. Table 11.5). The value of n (i.e., the number of diverse items in the whole set of recommendations) is automatically adjusted in reference to our proposed numbers in various conditions (Table 11.6). We set n in the range of [3–7] out of 10 (when

Table 11.6 Adjustment of n for accommodating diverse items in the set of N recommendations (when $N = 10$)

User's need for overall diversity	User's need for attribute's diversity (w.r.t. the most important attribute for the user)	n (the number of diverse movies in the recommendation set)
High need	High need	7
High need	Middle need	6
Middle need	High need	6
High need	Low need	5
Middle need	Middle need	5
Low need	High need	5
Middle need	Low need	4
Low need	Middle need	4
Low need	Low need	3

$N = 10$) to achieve an ideal trade-off between diversity and similarity. We define the default value of n as 5 when the user's preferences for both overall diversity and the diversity of the most important attribute are "middle." We add or subtract 1 to n if a user's preference is "high" or "low," respectively. For instance, if a user has "high" needs for both overall diversity and the most important attribute's diversity (i.e., the first case in Table 11.6), n is set as 7 (=5 + 1 + 1), and n is set as 3 (=5 − 1 − 1) when the user has "low" needs for both types of diversity. If N is not equal to 10, the value of n will be adjusted proportionately. For example, if N is equal to 20, n will be in the range from 6 (=$N \times 30\,\%$) to 14 (=$N \times 70\,\%$), and be added (or subtracted) 2 (=$N \times 10\,\%$) if a user's preference is at high (or low) level.

Taking a real user as an example, her preference profile $pref_u = \{$(genre, suspense, 5), (director, David Fincher, 4), (country, America, 2), (release time, 2010s, 1), (actor, Edision Chen, 3)$\}$ and her personality profile $p_u = \{$(openness to experience, high), (conscientiousness, low), (extraversion, high), (agreeableness, high), (neuroticism, high)$\}$. The user's low level of "conscientiousness" is significantly correlated with high needs for both diversity with respect to "genre" (the user's most important attribute) and overall diversity according to our survey results (see Tables 11.4 and 11.5), so n is set as 7 when $N = 10$ (see Table 11.6). The n recommended movies are diversified in terms of all attributes with "genre" given more weight than other attributes when computing overall diversity. The remaining m movies ($m = N - 7 = 3$) are those that best match the user's preference profile.

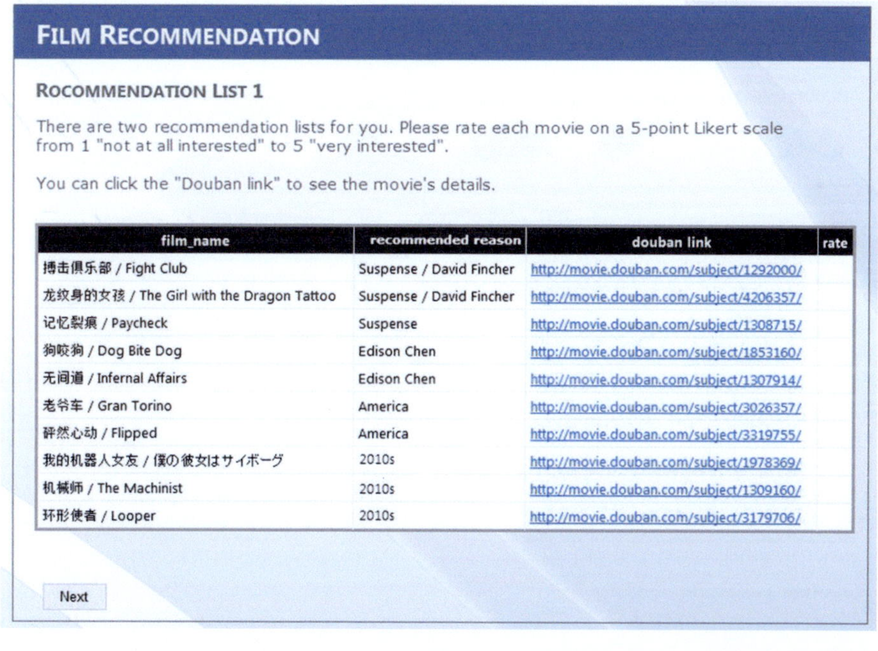

Fig. 11.3 The movies recommended to the user (whose preference profile and personality profile are described in Sect. 11.4.1) based on our personality-based diversity adjusting strategy (shortened as PerDiv)

Figure 11.3 shows the interface screenshot of the 10 movies recommended to this user, with m preference-relevant recommendations displayed at the top.

11.4.2 System Evaluation

11.4.2.1 Materials, Participants, and Method

We performed a user study to test the performance of our proposed strategy. A variation that does not consider users' personality-based diversity needs was included as a comparison (Non-PerDiv). It can be seen from the screenshot (Fig. 11.4) that although the user's diversity need for attribute "genre" is high given her low "conscientiousness" personality value, Non-PerDiv does not result in much diversity for "genre" in the returned recommendations.

The dataset used to implement both versions (PerDiv and Non-PerDiv) consisted of 16,777 movies from Douban Movie (http://movie.douban.com/). The experiment was set up as a within-subject user study and each participant was asked to evaluate both versions. To minimize any carryover effects, there were two user groups: the first group evaluated PerDiv first, then Non-PerDiv; the second group evaluated

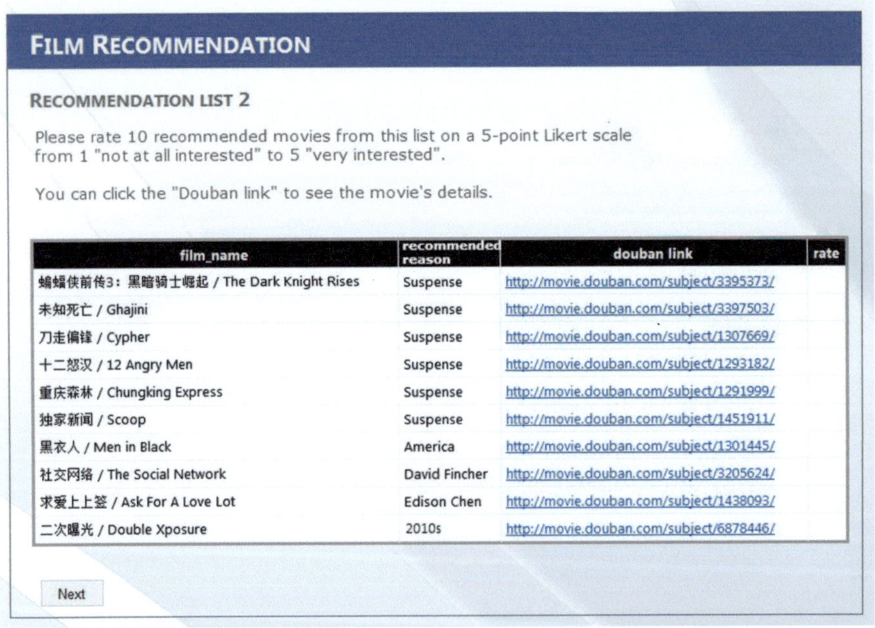

Fig. 11.4 The movies recommended to the same user (in Fig. 11.3), which does not match her personality-based diversity needs (shortened as Non-PerDiv)

Table 11.7 Demographic profiles of users who participated in the system evaluation (the number of users is in the bracket)

Gender	Female (18); Male (34)
Age	<20 (1); 20–30 (42); 30–40 (8); >40 (1)
Education	Bachelor (12); Master (36); Ph.D. (2); Others (2)
Job domain	Student (40); Enterprise (5); Institution (4); Others (3)
Frequency of watching movies from 1 "never" to 5 "a few times per month"	Mean: 3.48 (SD:1.16)
	Details: "Never" (1); "A few times totally" (13); "A few times one year" (10); "A few times every 3 months" (16); "A few times per month" (12)
Frequency of visiting movie sites from 1 "never" to 5 "a few times per month"	Mean: 3.65 (SD:1.03)
	Details: "Never" (0); "A few times totally" (8); "A few times one year" (15); "A few times every 3 months" (16); "A few times per month" (13)

Non-PerDiv first. Fifty-two volunteers (23 females, 29 males) took part in the experiment. Table 11.7 shows their demographic profiles. The big-five personality quiz (Table 11.3) [13] was used to acquire their personality values.

Each user was required to specify preferences for movie attributes and then to rate each recommended movie from 1 (not at all interested) to 5 (very interested). After using each version, users filled in a questionnaire to record their overall opinions about the following three aspects of the recommendation list on a 5-point Likert scale ranging from 1 (strongly disagree) to 5 (strongly agree):

- Recommendation accuracy: "*The movies recommended for me matched my interests*";
- System competence: "*The website helped me to discover movies for myself*";
- Overall satisfaction: "*Overall, I am satisfied with the recommended movies*".

11.4.2.2 Results

Figure 11.5 shows that PerDiv obtains significantly higher evaluation scores than Non-PerDiv for all three questions. Most users agree that the PerDiv recommendations matched their interests better than the Non-PerDiv recommendations (mean = 3.95, SD = 0.48 vs. mean = 3.55, SD = 0.59; Student's t-test, $t = 4.45$, $p < 0.01$). They also perceive the system as better at helping them to discover interesting movies (PerDiv mean = 3.87, SD = 0.71; Non-PerDiv mean = 3.15, SD = 1.02; $t = 1.81$, $p < 0.01$). Overall, users are more satisfied with PerDiv (PerDiv mean = 4.04, SD = 0.52; Non-PerDiv mean= 3.40, SD = 0.85; $t = 5.01$, $p < 0.01$).

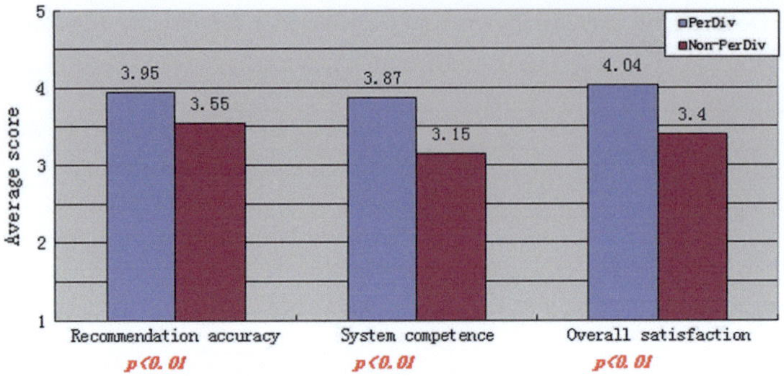

Fig. 11.5 Comparison in terms of users' subjective perceptions

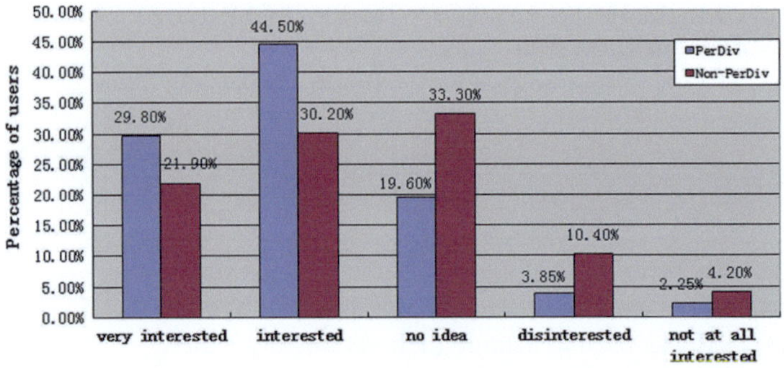

Fig. 11.6 Distribution of users' satisfaction ratings on the recommended movies in each version

Users' ratings of each recommended item also validate their higher satisfaction with PerDiv. Figure 11.6 shows the distribution of the five rating scales (from "not at all interested" to "very interested") among the 10 recommendations in each version. Users were "very interested" or "interested" in 74.3 % of the movies recommended in PerDiv, whereas 52.1 % of the recommendations obtained these ratings in Non-PerDiv. Nearly half the movies recommended in Non-PerDiv were rated at or below "no idea" (47.9 % of movies, including 10.4 % rated "disinterested" and 4.2 % "not at all interested").

11.4.3 Discussion

The results of the experiment demonstrate that our personality-based diversity adjusting strategy, although it is simple, can be effective in terms of improving users' perceptions of the system's recommendations. It would be interesting to compare this strategy with standard diversity-oriented recommendation methods [19, 45]. The findings' validity in other cultural contexts should also be tested, and it would be desirable to generalize the findings to product domains other than movies, such as music and books.

11.5 Conclusion and Suggestions for Future Research

Provision of diverse and novel recommendations has become an increasingly important topic in the area of recommender systems. People are not satisfied with items that are merely similar to what they preferred before, they are interested in exploring unexpected and surprising items. This raises the question of how to make a diversity algorithm tailored to an individual user's requirements. We have reported here the findings from two experiments that we conducted with the aim of not only revealing the correlations between personality and users' needs for diversity within a set of recommendations, but also of providing an effective method for automatically adjusting the diversity in recommendations based on users' personality traits. The first experiment identifies several significant correlations. For instance, "neuroticism" (one of the five personality traits) is shown to be significantly positively correlated with diversity in the attribute "director," and "openness to experience" is significantly positively correlated with diversity in the attribute "actor/actress." Moreover, "conscientiousness" is significantly negatively correlated with users' overall diversity preference. Demographic characteristics (such as age, gender, and education level) also display significant correlations with some diversity variables. For example, gender is significantly positively correlated with diversity in the attributes "director" and "country." Age and education level are significantly negatively correlated with users' overall diversity preference.

Motivated by the user survey's findings, we developed a simple, but demonstrably effective, personality-based diversity-adjusting strategy, which can automatically determine the degree of diversity within a set of returned recommendations according to a user's personality. In the system evaluation, we compared our method with a variation that does not consider the correlations between users' personality and their diversity preference, and demonstrated that our method is significantly better at improving users' perceptions of the system's recommendations.

Our work helps to reduce the gap between two subbranches of research: diversity-oriented recommendation systems and personality-based recommendation systems. However, our research is still at a preliminary stage and more in-depth studies should be carried out in the future. In our view, three issues are worthy of further research: personality and demographic properties, personality and emotion, and implicit personality acquisition.

- **Personality and demographic properties**. Our findings show that users' diversity preference is not only affected by their personality, but also by demographic properties such as age, gender, and education level. For example, people who are younger or who have a lower education level are more likely to prefer diverse movies. It would be interesting to study the combined effect of personality traits and demographic properties. In the domain of movies, Chausson [6] finds that females normally score higher on "neuroticism" and "agreeableness" than males. Cantador et al. [5] draw attention to the fact that both personality and gender may influence users' preferences for movie genres: females with high "extraversion" and "agreeableness" tend to prefer adventure movies, whereas low "extraversion" and neutral "agreeableness" are observed more often among male users who prefer adventure movies. In terms of education, Raad and Schouwenburg [9] suggest that people who are more self-disciplined (with high "conscientiousness") are more likely to achieve a postgraduate degree. With respect to age, it has been found that scores for "agreeableness" and "conscientiousness" usually decrease from late childhood (approximately ages 10–12) to early adolescence (ages 13–17) [31]. We are interested in conducting more experiments to validate the interaction between personality and these demographic factors in terms of their influence on users' preference for recommendation diversity, and expect that the results would enable us to improve our diversity-adjusting algorithm.

- **Personality and emotion**. Another factor that may affect users' needs for diversity is emotion. Personality traits normally remain relatively stable throughout life, whereas emotion is a reaction to an object or action, and may change over time [4]. The effect of emotion on users' item preference has been identified in music [22] and image domains [33], and emotion could potentially be detected by assessing facial expressions to evaluate users' satisfaction with serendipitous recommendations (in Chap. 17). However, little has been done to consider how emotion and personality act together to influence users' diversity needs. Interesting research could be done in this area in future.
- **Implicit personality acquisition**. Existing studies about personality have mostly relied on quizzes to explicitly acquire users' personality [8]. However, in reality, users may be unwilling to answer tedious questions in a quiz, or they may have privacy concerns about disclosing their personality traits. Our diversity-adjusting method would be of limited use in this situation. To overcome this issue, users' personality could be elicited in an implicit, unobtrusive way. Chapter 5 summarizes methods to identify personality based on nonverbal behavior. In addition, some psychological studies have shown that users with different personality may behave differently when choosing movies, music, or other items [5, 27]. For instance, Cantador et al. [5] have shown that users with different personality traits have different preferences for movie genres: users with high "openness to experience" (i.e., those who are more imaginative and creative) tend to like tragedy, neo-noir, independent, cult, and foreign movies, whereas people with low "openness to experience" (who are more conventional and practical) are likely to prefer war, romance, action, and comedy movies. Rentfrow and Gosling [27] explore the correlation between personality traits and users' preference for music genres, and suggest that people with high scores for "extraversion" are likely to prefer energetic and rhythmic music, whereas individuals who are relatively conventional tend to listen to upbeat and conventional music. Recent studies have also investigated the relationship between users' personality and their rating behavior. For example,

Golbeck and Norris [12] find that "extraversion" and "conscientiousness" are both positively correlated with users' ratings of movies, indicating that those who are more extrovert and outgoing, or cautious and self-disciplined are more likely to give higher ratings than others. Hu and Pu [18] identify that "conscientiousness" is negatively correlated with the number of ratings that a user gives, which implies that disorganized and impulsive individuals will rate more movies. These findings suggest that users' personality could be acquired implicitly by analyzing their selecting and rating of items in real-life datasets (such as Douban, MovieLens and Last.fm), and our diversity-adjusting strategy could thus be applied to these commercial applications.

Acknowledgments This study work was supported by the Hong Kong Research Grants Council (no. ECS/HKBU211912) and the China National Natural Science Foundation (no. 61272365).

References

1. Adamopoulos, P., Tuzhilin, A.: On unexpectedness in recommender systems: or how to expect the unexpected. In: Workshop on Novelty and Diversity in Recommender Systems (DiveRS 2011), at the 2011 ACM International Conference on Recommender Systems (RecSys' 11), pp. 11–18. ACM, Chicago, Illinois, USA (2011)
2. Adomavicius, G., Tuzhilin, A.: Toward the next generation of recommender systems: a survey of the state-of-the-art and possible extensions. IEEE Trans. Knowl. Data Eng. **17**(6), 734–749 (2005)
3. Ajzen, I.: Attitudes, personality, and behavior. McGraw-Hill International, New York (2005)
4. Allbeck, J., Badler, N.: Toward representing agent behaviors modified by personality and emotion. Embodied Conversat. Agents AAMAS **2**, 15–19 (2002)
5. Cantador, I., Fernández-Tobías, I., Bellogín, A., Kosinski, M., Stillwell, D.: Relating personality types with user preferences in multiple entertainment domains. In: UMAP Workshops, Citeseer (2013)
6. Chausson, O.: Who watches what? Assessing the impact of gender and personality on film preferences (2010)
7. Chen, L., Pu, P.: Preference-based organization interfaces: aiding user critiques in recommender systems. In: User Modeling 2007, pp. 77–86. Springer, Heidelberg (2007)
8. Costa, P.T., McCrae, R.R.: Revised Neo Personality Inventory (neo pi-r) and Neo Five-Factor Inventory (neo-ffi), vol. 101. Psychological Assessment Resources, Odessa (1992)
9. De Raad, B., Schouwenburg, H.C.: Personality in learning and education: a review. Eur. J. Pers. **10**(5), 303–336 (1996)
10. Di Noia, T., Ostuni, V.C., Rosati, J., Tomeo, P., Di Sciascio, E.: An analysis of users' propensity toward diversity in recommendations. In: Proceedings of the 8th ACM Conference on Recommender Systems, pp. 285–288, ACM (2014)
11. Elahi, M., Braunhofer, M., Ricci, F., Tkalcic, M.: Personality-based active learning for collaborative filtering recommender systems. In: AI* IA 2013: Advances in Artificial Intelligence, pp. 360–371, Springer (2013)
12. Golbeck, J., Norris, E.: Personality, movie preferences, and recommendations. In: Proceedings of the 2013 IEEE/ACM International Conference on Advances in Social Networks Analysis and Mining, pp. 1414–1415, ACM (2013)
13. Hellriegel, D., Wlldman, R.: Organizational Behavior, 11th edn. South-western College, Cincinnati, Ohio (2010)

14. Hu, R., Pu, P.: Acceptance issues of personality-based recommender systems. In: Proceedings of the 2009 ACM conference on Recommender systems, pp. 221–224, ACM (2009)
15. Hu, R., Pu, P.: A study on user perception of personality-based recommender systems. In: User Modeling, Adaptation, and Personalization, pp. 291–302. Springer, Berlin (2010)
16. Hu, R., Pu, P.: Enhancing collaborative filtering systems with personality information. In: Proceedings of the 2011 ACM Conference on Recommender Systems, pp. 197–204, ACM (2011)
17. Hu, R., Pu, P.: Helping users perceive recommendation diversity. In: Workshop on Novelty and Diversity in Recommender Systems, DiveRS, Chicago (2011)
18. Hu, R., Pu, P.: Exploring relations between personality and user rating behaviors. In: UMAP Workshops (2013)
19. Hurley, N., Zhang, M.: Novelty and diversity in top-n recommendation-analysis and evaluation. ACM Trans. Internet Technol. (TOIT) **10**(4), 14 (2011)
20. Jia, J., Fischer, G.W., Dyer, J.S.: Attribute weighting methods and decision quality in the presence of response error: a simulation study. J. Behav. Decis. Making **11**(2), 85–105 (1998)
21. Johnson, J.A.: Descriptions used in ipip-neo narrative report (2009)
22. Kuo, F.F., Chiang, M.F., Shan, M.K., Lee, S.Y.: Emotion-based music recommendation by association discovery from film music. In: Proceedings of the 2005 Annual ACM International Conference on Multimedia, pp. 507–510, ACM (2005)
23. Linden, G., Smith, B., York, J.: Amazon. com recommendations: Item-to-item collaborative filtering. IEEE Internet Comput. **7**(1), 76–80 (2003)
24. Lü, L., Medo, M., Yeung, C.H., Zhang, Y.C., Zhang, Z.K., Zhou, T.: Recommender systems. Phys. Rep. **519**(1), 1–49 (2012)
25. McNee, S.M., Riedl, J., Konstan, J.A.: Being accurate is not enough: how accuracy metrics have hurt recommender systems. In: CHI'06 Extended Abstracts on Human Factors in Computing Systems, pp. 1097–1101, ACM (2006)
26. Mourão, F., Fonseca, C., Araújo, C., Meira Jr, W.: The oblivion problem: exploiting forgotten items to improve recommendation diversity. In: Workshop on Novelty and Diversity in Recommender Systems (DiveRS 2011), p. 27 (2011)
27. Rentfrow, P.J., Gosling, S.D.: The do re mi's of everyday life: the structure and personality correlates of music preferences. J. Pers. Soc. Psychol. **84**(6), 1236 (2003)
28. Santos, R.L., Macdonald, C., Ounis, I.: Exploiting query reformulations for web search result diversification. In: Proceedings of the 2010 International Conference on World Wide Web, pp. 881–890, ACM (2010)
29. Shani, G., Gunawardana, A.: Evaluating recommendation systems. In: Recommender Systems Handbook, pp. 257–297, Springer (2011)
30. Smyth, B., McClave, P.: Similarity vs. diversity. In: Case-Based Reasoning Research and Development, pp. 347–361, Springer (2001)
31. Soto, C.J., John, O.P., Gosling, S.D., Potter, J.: Age differences in personality traits from 10 to 65: big five domains and facets in a large cross-sectional sample. J. Pers. Soc. Psychol. **100**(2), 330 (2011)
32. Tintarev, N., Dennis, M., Masthoff, J.: Adapting recommendation diversity to openness to experience: a study of human behaviour. In: User Modeling, Adaptation, and Personalization, pp. 190–202, Springer (2013)
33. Tkalčič, M., Burnik, U., Košir, A.: Using affective parameters in a content-based recommender system for images. User Model. User-Adap. Inter. **20**(4), 279–311 (2010)
34. Tkalcic, M., Kunaver, M., Tasic, J., Košir, A.: Personality based user similarity measure for a collaborative recommender system. In: Proceedings of the 2009 Workshop on Emotion in Human-Computer Interaction-Real World Challenges, pp. 30–37 (2009)
35. Vargas, S., Castells, P.: Rank and relevance in novelty and diversity metrics for recommender systems. In: Proceedings of the 2011 ACM Conference on Recommender Systems, pp. 109–116, ACM (2011)
36. Vargas, S., Castells, P.: Exploiting the diversity of user preferences for recommendation. In: Proceedings of the 2013 Conference on Open Research Areas in Information Retrieval, pp. 129–136. Le Centre de Hautes Eetudes Internationales d'informatique Documentaire (2013)

37. Wu, W., Chen, L., He, L.: Using personality to adjust diversity in recommender systems. In: Proceedings of the 2013 ACM Conference on Hypertext and Social Media, pp. 225–229, ACM (2013)
38. Yu, C., Lakshmanan, L., Amer-Yahia, S.: It takes variety to make a world: diversification in recommender systems. In: Proceedings of the 2009 International Conference on Extending Database Technology: Advances in Database Technology, pp. 368–378, ACM (2009)
39. Yu, C., Lakshmanan, L.V., Amer-Yahia, S.: Recommendation diversification using explanations. In: IEEE 25th International Conference on Data Engineering, 2009. ICDE'09, pp. 1299–1302, IEEE (2009)
40. Zaier, Z., Godin, R., Faucher, L.: Evaluating recommender systems. In: International Conference on Automated Solutions for Cross Media Content and Multi-channel Distribution, 2008. AXMEDIS'08, pp. 211–217, IEEE (2008)
41. Zeng, W., Shang, M.S., Zhang, Q.M., Lue, L., Zhou, T.: Can dissimilar users contribute to accuracy and diversity of personalized recommendation? Int. J. Mod. Phys. C **21**(10), 1217–1227 (2010)
42. Zhang, M., Hurley, N.: Avoiding monotony: improving the diversity of recommendation lists. In: Proceedings of the 2008 ACM Conference on Recommender Systems, pp. 123–130, ACM (2008)
43. Zhang, M., Hurley, N.: Novel item recommendation by user profile partitioning. In: Proceedings of the 2009 IEEE/WIC/ACM International Joint Conference on Web Intelligence and Intelligent Agent Technology-Volume 01, pp. 508–515, IEEE Computer Society (2009)
44. Zhou, T., Kuscsik, Z., Liu, J.G., Medo, M., Wakeling, J.R., Zhang, Y.C.: Solving the apparent diversity-accuracy dilemma of recommender systems. Proc. Natl. Acad. Sci. **107**(10), 4511–4515 (2010)
45. Ziegler, C.N., McNee, S.M., Konstan, J.A., Lausen, G.: Improving recommendation lists through topic diversification. In: Proceedings of the 2005 International Conference on World Wide Web, pp. 22–32, ACM (2005)

Chapter 12
Affective Music Information Retrieval

Ju-Chiang Wang, Yi-Hsuan Yang and Hsin-Min Wang

Abstract Much of the appeal of music lies in its power to convey emotions/moods and to evoke them in listeners. In consequence, the past decade witnessed a growing interest in modeling emotions from musical signals in the music information retrieval (MIR) community. In this chapter, we present a novel generative approach to music emotion modeling, with a specific focus on the valence–arousal (VA) dimension model of emotion. The presented generative model, called *acoustic emotion Gaussians* (AEG), better accounts for the subjectivity of emotion perception by the use of probability distributions. Specifically, it learns from the emotion annotations of multiple subjects a Gaussian mixture model in the VA space with prior constraints on the corresponding acoustic features of the training music pieces. Such a computational framework is technically sound, capable of learning in an online fashion, and thus applicable to a variety of applications, including user-independent (general) and user-dependent (personalized) emotion recognition, emotion-based music retrieval, and tag-to-VA projection. We report evaluations of the aforementioned applications of AEG on a larger-scale emotion-annotated corpora, AMG1608, to demonstrate the effectiveness of AEG and to showcase how evaluations are conducted for research on emotion-based MIR. Directions of future work are also discussed.

12.1 Introduction

Automatic music emotion recognition (MER) aims at modeling the association between music and emotion so as to facilitate emotion-based music organization, indexing, and retrieval. This technology has emerged in recent years as a promising

J.-C. Wang (✉) · H.-M. Wang
Institute of Information Science, Academia Sinica, Taipei 11529, Taiwan
e-mail: asriver.wang@gmail.com

H.-M. Wang
e-mail: whm@iis.sinica.edu.tw

Y.-H. Yang
Research Center for IT Innovation, Academia Sinica, Taipei 11529, Taiwan
e-mail: yang@citi.sinica.edu.tw

M. Tkalčič et al. (eds.), *Emotions and Personality in Personalized Services*,
Human–Computer Interaction Series, DOI 10.1007/978-3-319-31413-6_12

solution to deal with the huge amount of music information available digitally [1, 25, 33, 77]. It is generally believed that music cannot be composed, performed, or listened to without affection involvement [32]. The pursuit of emotional experience has also been identified as one of the primary motivations and benefits of music listening [31]. In addition to music retrieval, music emotion also finds applications in context-aware music recommendation, playlist generation, music therapy, and automatic music accompaniment for other media content including image, video, and text, amongst others [37, 51, 66, 78].

Despite the significant progress that has been made in recent years, MER is still considered as a challenging problem because the perception of emotion in music is usually highly subjective. A single, static ground-truth emotion label is not sufficient to describe the possible emotions different people perceive in the same piece of music [15, 26]. On the contrary, it may be more reasonable to learn a computational model from multiple responses of different listeners [47] and to present *probabilistic* (soft) rather than *deterministic* (hard) emotion assignments as the final result. In addition, the subjective nature of emotion perception suggests the need of personalization in systems for emotion-based music recommendation or retrieval [82]. Early work on MER often chose to sidestep this critical issue by either assuming that a common consensus can be achieved [25, 62], or by simply discarding music pieces for which a common consensus cannot be achieved [38].

To help address this issue, we have proposed a novel generative model referred to as *acoustic emotion Gaussians* (AEG) in our prior work [65–68, 72]. The name of the AEG model comes from its use of multiple Gaussian distributions to model the affective content of music. The algorithmic part of AEG has been first introduced in [67], along with the preliminary evaluation of AEG for MER and emotion-based music retrieval. More details about the analysis part of the model learning of AEG can be found in a recent article [72]. Due to the parametric nature of AEG, model adaptation techniques have also been proposed to personalize an AEG model in an online, incremental fashion, rather than learning from scratch [7, 68]. The goal of this chapter is to position the AEG model as a theoretical framework and to provide detailed information about the model itself and its application to personalized MER and emotion-based music retrieval.

We conceptualize emotion by the valence–arousal (VA) model [49], which has been used extensively by psychologists to study the relationship between music and emotion [13, 56]. These two dimensions are found to be the most fundamental through factor analysis of self-report of human's affective response to music stimulus. Despite differences in nomenclature, existing studies give similar interpretations of the resulting factors, most of which correspond to *valence* (or pleasantness; positive/negative affective states) and *arousal* (or activation; energy and stimulation level). For example, happiness is an emotion associated with a positive valence and a high arousal, while sadness is an emotion associated with a negative valence and a low arousal. We refer to the 2-D space spanned by valence and arousal as the *VA space* hereafter. Moreover, we are concerned with the emotion an individual *perceives* as being expressed in a piece of music, rather than the emotion the individual actually *feels* in response to the piece. This distinction is necessary [15], as we do not necessarily feel sorrow when listening to a sad tune, for example.

However, the descriptive power of VA model has been questioned by several researchers, and various extensions or alternative solutions have been proposed [14, 46, 85]. Beyond the valence and arousal, adding more dimensions (e.g., *potency*, or dominant–submissive) might help resolve the ambiguity between affective terms, such as anger and fear, which are close to one another in the second quadrant of the VA space [2, 10]. AEG is theoretically extendable to model the emotion in higher dimensions. Nevertheless, we stay with the 2-D emotion model here, partly because it is easier to explain AEG graphically, and partly because to date many existing music datasets adopt VA labels [8, 52, 59, 79].

In this chapter, we focus on the *dimensional* emotion (VA) values. Interested readers can refer to [1, 24, 57] for studies and surveys on *categorical* MER approaches that view emotions as discrete labels such as mood tags. As the dimensional and categorical approaches may offer complementary advantages [74], researchers have studied the relationship between the discrete emotion labels and the dimensional VA values [50, 65]. Due to its probabilistic nature, AEG can be combined with a probabilistic classification model. Such a combination leads to an approach (called *Tag2VA*) that is able to project a mood tag to the VA space [65].

The chapter is organized as follows. We first review the related work in Sect. 12.2. Then, we present the mathematical derivation and learning algorithm of AEG in Sect. 12.3, followed by the personalization algorithm in Sect. 12.4. Sections 12.5, 12.6, and 12.7 present the applications of AEG to MER, emotion-based music retrieval, and the Tag2VA projection, respectively. Finally, we conclude in Sect. 12.8.

12.2 Related Work on Dimensional Music Emotion Recognition

Early approaches to MER [39, 81] assumed that the perceived emotion of a music piece can be represented as a *single point* in the VA space, in which the valence and arousal values are considered as independent numerical values. The ground-truth VA values of a music piece is obtained by averaging the annotations of a number of human subjects, without considering the covariance of the annotations. To predict the VA value from the feature vector of a music piece, a regression model such as support vector regression (SVR) [55] can be applied. Regression model learning algorithms typically minimize the mismatch (e.g., mean squared loss) between the predicted and the ground-truth VA values in the training data.

As emotion perception is rarely dependent on a single music factor but a combination of them [19, 30], algorithms used feature descriptors that characterize the loudness, timbre, pitch, rhythm, melody, harmony, or lyrics of music [22, 43, 54, 57]. In particular, while it is usually easier to predict arousal using, for example, loudness

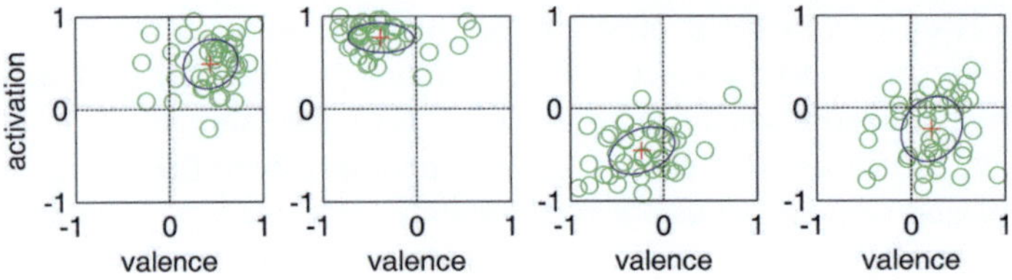

Fig. 12.1 Subjects' annotations of the perceived emotion of four 30-s clips, which from *left* to *right* are *Dancing Queen* by ABBA, *Civil War* by Guns N' Roses, *Suzanne* by Leonard Cohen, and *All I Have To Do Is Dream* by the Everly Brothers. Each *circle* here corresponds to a subject's annotation, and the overall emotion for a clip can be approximated by a 2-D Gaussian distribution (the *red* cross and *blue* ellipse). The ellipse outlines the standard deviation of a Gaussian distribution

and timbre features, the prediction of valence has been found more challenging [57, 69, 76]. Cross cultural aspects of emotion perception have also been studied [23]. To exploit the temporal continuity of emotion variation within a piece of music, techniques such as system identification [34], conditional random fields [27, 53], hidden Markov models [40], deep recurrent neural networks [73], or dynamic probabilistic model [71] have also been proposed. Various approaches and features for MER have been evaluated and compared using benchmarking datasets comprising over 1,000 Creative Commons licensed music pieces from the Free Music Archive, in the 2013 and 2014 MediaEval 'Emotion in Music' tasks [59, 60].

Recent years have witnessed growing attempts to model the emotion of a music piece as a probability distribution in the VA space [7, 52, 67, 75] to better account for the subjective nature of emotion perception. For instance, Fig. 12.1 shows the VA values applied by different annotators to four music pieces. To characterize the distribution of the emotion annotations for each clip, a typical way is to use a bivariate Gaussian distribution, where the mean vector presents the most possible VA values and the covariance matrix indicates its uncertainty. For a clip with highly subjective affective content, the determinant of the covariance matrix would be larger.

Existing approaches for predicting the emotion distribution of a music clip from acoustic features fall into two categories. The *heatmap* approach [53, 75] quantizes each emotion dimension by W equally spaced cells, leading to a $W \times W$ grid representation of the VA space. The approach trains W^2 regression models for predicting the emotion *intensity* of each cell. Higher intensity at a cell indicates that people are more likely to perceive the corresponding emotion from the clip. The emotion intensity over the VA space creates a heatmap-like representation of emotion distribution. However, heatmap is not a continuous representation of emotion, and emotion intensity cannot be strictly considered as a probability estimate.

The *Gaussian-parameter* approach [52, 75], on the other hand, models emotion distribution of a clip as a bivariate Gaussian and trains multiple regressors, each for a parameter of the mean vector and the covariance matrix. This makes it easy to apply lessons learned from modeling the mean VA values. In addition, performance analysis of this approach is easier; one can analyze the importance of different acoustic features to each Gaussian parameter individually. However, since the regression models are trained independently, the correlation between valence and arousal is not exploited. The parameter estimation of the mean and variance is disjoined as well.

A different methodology to address the subjectivity is to call for a user-dependent model trained on annotations of a specific user to personalize the emotion prediction [79, 84, 86]. In [79], two personalization methods are proposed; the first trains a *personalized* MER system for each individual specifically, whereas the second groups users according to some personal factors (e.g., gender, music experience, and personality) and then trains *group-wise* MER system for each user group. Another *two-stage* personalization scheme has also been studied [82]: the first stage estimates the general perception of a music piece, whereas the second one predicts the difference between the general perception and the personal one of the target user.

We note that none of the aforementioned approaches renders a strict probabilistic interpretation [72]. In addition, many existing work is developed on discriminative models such as multiple linear regression and SVR. Few attempts are made to develop a principled probabilistic framework that is technically sound for modeling the music emotion and that permits extending the user-independent model to a user-dependent one, preferably in an online fashion.

We also note that most existing work focuses on the *annotation* aspect of music emotion research, namely MER. Little work has been made to the *retrieval* aspect—the development of emotion-based music retrieval systems [77]. In what follows, we present the AEG model and its applications to the both of these two aspects.

12.3 Acoustic Emotion Gaussians: A Generative Approach for Music Emotion Modeling

In [65–68, 72], we proposed AEG, which is fundamentally different from the existing regression or heatmap approaches. As Fig. 12.2 shows, AEG involves the generative process of VA emotion distributions from audio signals. While the relationship between audio and music emotion may sometimes be complicated and difficult to observe directly from an emotion-annotated corpus, AEG uses a set of clip-level *latent topics* $\{z_k\}_{k=1}^{K}$ to resolve this issue.

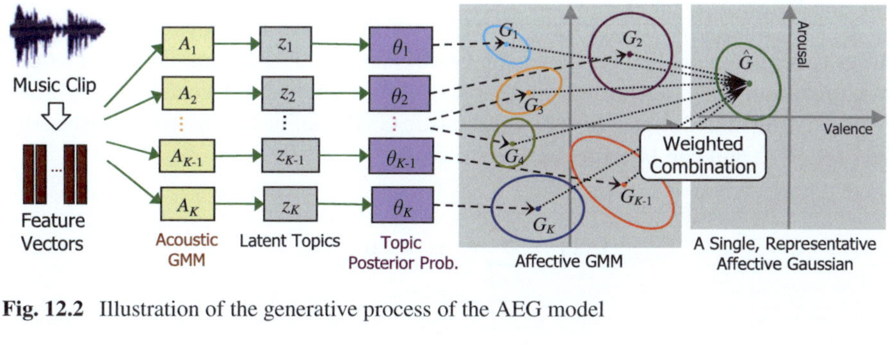

Fig. 12.2 Illustration of the generative process of the AEG model

We first define the terminology and explain the basic principle of AEG. Suppose that there are K *audio descriptors* $\{A_k\}_{k=1}^K$, each is related to some acoustic feature vectors of music clips. Then, we map the associated feature vectors of A_k to a clip-level topic z_k. To implement each A_k, we use a single Gaussian distribution in the acoustic feature space. The aggregated Gaussians of $\{A_k\}_{k=1}^K$ is called an *acoustic GMM* (Gaussian mixture model). Subsequently, we map each z_k to a specific area in the VA space, which is modeled by a bivariate Gaussian distribution G_k. We refer to the aggregated Gaussians of $\{G_k\}_{k=1}^K$ as an *affective GMM*. Given a clip, its feature vectors are first used to compute the posterior distribution over the topics, termed as a *topic posterior representation* $\boldsymbol{\theta}$. In $\boldsymbol{\theta}$, the posterior probability of z_k (denoted as θ_k) is associated with A_k and will then be used to show the clip's importance to G_k. Consequently, the posterior distribution $\boldsymbol{\theta} = \{\theta_k\}_{k=1}^K$ can be incorporated into learning the affective GMM as well as making emotion prediction for a clip.

AEG-based MER follows the flow depicted in Fig. 12.2. Based on $\boldsymbol{\theta}$ of a test clip, we obtain the weighted affective GMM $\sum_k \theta_k G_k$, which is able to generate various emotion distribution. Following this sense, if a clip's acoustic features can be completely described by the h-th topic z_h, i.e. $\theta_h = 1$, and $\theta_k = 0$, $\forall k \neq h$, then its emotion distribution would exactly follow G_h. As will be described in Sect. 12.5, we can further approximate $\sum_k \theta_k G_k$ by a single, representative affective Gaussian $\hat{G}$ for simplicity. This is illustrated in the rightmost of Fig. 12.2.

12.3.1 Topic Posterior Representation

The topic posterior representation of a music clip is generated from its audio. We note that the temporal dynamics of audio signals is regarded as essential for human to perceive musical characteristics such as timbre, rhythm, and tonality. To capture more local temporal variation of the low-level features, we represent the acoustic features at a time instance in the segment-level, which corresponds to sufficiently long duration (e.g., 0.4 s). A segment-level feature vector $\mathbf{x}$ can be formed by, for example, concatenating the mean and standard deviation of the frame-level feature vectors within the segment. As a result, a clip is divided into multiple overlapped segments which are then represented by a sequence of vectors, $\{\mathbf{x}_1, \ldots, \mathbf{x}_T\}$, where T is the length of the clip.

To start the generative process of AEG, we first learn an acoustic GMM as the bases to represent a clip. This acoustic GMM can be trained using the expectation–maximization (EM) algorithm on a large set of segment-level vectors $\mathcal{F}$ extracted from existing music clips. The learned acoustic GMM defines the set of audio descriptors $\{A_k\}_{k=1}^K$, and can be expressed as follows:

$$p(\mathbf{x}) = \sum_{k=1}^{K} \pi_k A_k(\mathbf{x} \mid \mathbf{m}_k, \mathbf{S}_k) \,, \tag{12.1}$$

where $A_k(\cdot)$ is the k-th component Gaussian distribution, and π_k, $\mathbf{m}_k$, and $\mathbf{S}_k$ are its corresponding prior weight, mean vector, and covariance matrix, respectively. Note that we substitute equal weight for the GMM (i.e., $\pi_k = \frac{1}{K}, \forall k$), because the original π_k learned from $\mathcal{F}$ does not imply the prior distribution of the feature vectors in a clip. Such a heuristic usually results in better performance as pointed in [63].

Suppose that we have an emotion-annotated corpus $\mathcal{X}$ consisting of N music clips $\{s_i\}_{i=1}^N$. Given a clip $s_i = \{\mathbf{x}_{i,t}\}_{t=1}^{T_i}$, we then compute the segment-level posterior probability for each feature vector in s_i based on the acoustic GMM,

$$p(A_k \mid \mathbf{x}_{i,t}) = \frac{A_k(\mathbf{x}_{i,t} \mid \mathbf{m}_k, \mathbf{S}_k)}{\sum_{h=1}^{K} A_h(\mathbf{x}_{i,t} \mid \mathbf{m}_h, \mathbf{S}_h)} . \tag{12.2}$$

Finally, the clip-level topic posterior probability $\theta_{i,k}$ of s_i can be approximated by averaging the segment-level ones,

$$\theta_{i,k} \leftarrow p(z_k \mid s_i) \approx \frac{1}{T_i} \sum_{t=1}^{T_i} p(A_k \mid \mathbf{x}_{i,t}) . \tag{12.3}$$

This approximation assumes that $\theta_{i,k}$ is equally contributed by each segment of s_i and thereby capable of representing the clip's acoustic features. We use a vector $\boldsymbol{\theta}_i \in \mathbb{R}^K$, whose k-th component is $\theta_{i,k}$, as the topic posterior of s_i.

12.3.2 Prior Model for Emotion Annotation

To consider the subjectivity of emotional responses of a music clip, we ask multiple subjects to annotate the clip. However, as some subjects' annotations may not be reliable, we introduce a *user prior model* to quantify the contribution of each subject.

Let $\mathbf{e}_{i,j} \in \mathbb{R}^2$ (a vector including the valence and arousal values) denote one of the annotations of s_i given by the j-th subject, and let U_i denote the number of subjects who have annotated s_i. Note that $\mathbf{e}_{q,j}$ and $\mathbf{e}_{r,j}$, where $q \neq r$, may not correspond to the same subject. Then, we build the user prior model γ to describe the confidence of $\mathbf{e}_{i,j}$ in s_i using a single Gaussian distribution,

$$\gamma(\mathbf{e}_{i,j} \mid s_i) \equiv G(\mathbf{e}_{i,j} \mid \mathbf{a}_i, \mathbf{B}_i), \tag{12.4}$$

where $\mathbf{a}_i = \frac{1}{U_i} \sum_{j=i}^{U_i} \mathbf{e}_{i,j}$, $\mathbf{B}_i = \frac{1}{U_i} \sum_{j=1}^{U_i} (\mathbf{e}_{i,j} - \mathbf{a}_i)(\mathbf{e}_{i,j} - \mathbf{a}_i)^T$, and $G(\mathbf{e} \mid \mathbf{a}_i, \mathbf{B}_i)$ is called the *annotation Gaussian* of s_i. One can observe what $\mathbf{a}_i$ and $\mathbf{B}_i$ look like from the four example clips in Fig. 12.1. Empirical results show that a single Gaussian performs better than a GMM for setting up $\gamma(\cdot)$ [67].

The confidence of $\mathbf{e}_{i,j}$ can be estimated based on the likelihood calculated by Eq. 12.4. If an annotation is far away from the mean, it gives small likelihood accordingly. In addition to Gaussian distributions, any criterion that is able to reflect the importance of a user's annotation of a clip can be applied to γ.

The probability of $\mathbf{e}_{i,j}$, referred to as the *clip-level annotation prior*, can be calculated by normalizing the likelihood of $\mathbf{e}_{i,j}$ over the cumulative likelihood of all other annotations in s_i,

$$p(\mathbf{e}_{i,j} \mid s_i) \equiv \frac{\gamma(\mathbf{e}_{i,j} \mid s_i)}{\sum_{r=1}^{U_i} \gamma(\mathbf{e}_{i,r} \mid s_i)} . \tag{12.5}$$

Based on the clip-level annotation prior, we further define the *corpus-level clip prior* to describe the importance of each clip,

$$p(s_i \mid \mathcal{X}) \equiv \frac{\sum_{j=1}^{U_i} \gamma(\mathbf{e}_{i,j} \mid s_i)}{\sum_{q=1}^{N} \sum_{r=1}^{U_q} \gamma(\mathbf{e}_{q,r} \mid s_q)} . \tag{12.6}$$

From Eqs. 12.5 and 12.6 we can make two observations. First, if a clip's annotations are consistent (i.e., $\mathbf{B}_i$ is small), it is considered less subjective. Second, if a clip is annotated by more subjects, the corresponding γ model should be more reliable. As a result, we can define the *corpus-level annotation prior* $\gamma_{i,j}$ for each $\mathbf{e}_{i,j}$ in the corpus $\mathcal{X}$ by multiplying Eqs. 12.5 and 12.6:

$$\gamma_{i,j} \leftarrow p(\mathbf{e}_{i,j} \mid \mathcal{X}) \equiv \frac{\gamma(\mathbf{e}_{i,j} \mid s_i)}{\sum_{q=1}^{N} \sum_{r=1}^{U_q} \gamma(\mathbf{e}_{q,r} \mid s_i)} , \tag{12.7}$$

which is computed beforehand and fixed in learning the affective GMM.

12.3.3 Learning the Affective GMM

Given a training music clip s_i in the corpus $\mathcal{X}$, we assume the emotional responses can be generated from an affective GMM weighted by its topic posterior $\boldsymbol{\theta}_i$,

$$p(\mathbf{e}_{i,j} \mid \boldsymbol{\theta}_i) = \sum_{k=1}^{K} \theta_{i,k} G_k(\mathbf{e}_{i,j} \mid \boldsymbol{\mu}_k, \boldsymbol{\Sigma}_k) , \tag{12.8}$$

where $G_k(\cdot)$ is the k-th affective Gaussian with mean $\boldsymbol{\mu}_k$ and covariance $\boldsymbol{\Sigma}_k$ to be learned. Here $\theta_{i,k}$ stands for the fixed weight associated with A_k to carry the audio characteristics of s_i. We therefore call $\boldsymbol{\theta}_i$ an *acoustic prior*. Then, the objective function is in the form of the marginal likelihood function of the annotations

$$
\begin{aligned}
p(\mathbf{E} \mid \mathcal{X}, \boldsymbol{\Lambda}) &= \sum_{i=1}^{N} p(s_i \mid \mathcal{X}) \sum_{j=1}^{U_i} p(\mathbf{e}_{i,j} \mid s_i) p(\mathbf{e}_{i,j} \mid \boldsymbol{\theta}_i, \boldsymbol{\Lambda}) \\
&= \sum_{i=1}^{N} \sum_{j=1}^{U_i} p(s_i \mid \mathcal{X}) p(\mathbf{e}_{i,j} \mid s_i) p(\mathbf{e}_{i,j} \mid \boldsymbol{\theta}_i, \boldsymbol{\Lambda}) \qquad (12.9) \\
&= \sum_{i=1}^{N} \sum_{j=1}^{U_i} p(\mathbf{e}_{i,j} \mid \mathcal{X}) \sum_{k=1}^{K} \theta_{i,k} G_k(\mathbf{e}_{i,j} \mid \boldsymbol{\mu}_k, \boldsymbol{\Sigma}_k) \,,
\end{aligned}
$$

where $\mathbf{E} = \{\mathbf{e}_{i,j}\}_{i=1,j=1}^{N,U_i}$, $\mathcal{X} = \{s_i, \boldsymbol{\theta}_i\}_{i=1}^{N}$, and $\boldsymbol{\Lambda} = \{\boldsymbol{\mu}_k, \boldsymbol{\Sigma}_k\}_{k=1}^{K}$ is the parameter set of the affective GMM. Taking the logarithm of Eq. 12.9 and replacing $p(\mathbf{e}_{i,j} \mid \mathcal{X})$ by $\gamma_{i,j}$ leads to

$$
L = \log \sum_i \sum_j \gamma_{i,j} \sum_k \theta_{i,k} G_k(\mathbf{e}_{i,j} \mid \boldsymbol{\mu}_k, \boldsymbol{\Sigma}_k) \,, \qquad (12.10)
$$

where $\sum_i \sum_j \gamma_{i,j} = 1$. To learn the affective GMM, we can maximize the log-likelihood in Eq. 12.10 with respect to the Gaussian parameters. We first derive a lower bound of L according to Jensen's inequality,

$$
L \geq L_{\text{bound}} = \sum_i \sum_j \gamma_{i,j} \log \sum_k \theta_{i,k} G_k(\mathbf{e}_{i,j} \mid \boldsymbol{\mu}_k, \boldsymbol{\Sigma}_k) \,. \qquad (12.11)
$$

Then, we treat L_{bound} as a surrogate of L and use the EM algorithm [3] to estimate the parameters of the affective GMM. In the E-step, we derive the expectation over the posterior distribution of z_k for all the training annotations,

$$
Q = \sum_i \sum_j \gamma_{i,j} \sum_k p(z_k \mid \mathbf{e}_{i,j}) \Big(\log \theta_{i,k} + \log G_k(\mathbf{e}_{i,j} \mid \boldsymbol{\mu}_k, \boldsymbol{\Sigma}_k) \Big) \,, \qquad (12.12)
$$

where

$$
p(z_k \mid \mathbf{e}_{i,j}) = \frac{\theta_{i,k} G_k(\mathbf{e}_{i,j} \mid \boldsymbol{\mu}_k, \boldsymbol{\Sigma}_k)}{\sum_{h=1}^{K} \theta_{i,h} G_k(\mathbf{e}_{i,j} \mid \boldsymbol{\mu}_h, \boldsymbol{\Sigma}_h)} \,. \qquad (12.13)
$$

In the M-step, we first set the derivative of Eq. 12.12 with respect to $\boldsymbol{\mu}_k$ to zero and obtain the updating form for the mean vector,

$$
\boldsymbol{\mu}'_k \leftarrow \frac{\sum_i \sum_j \gamma_{i,j} p(z_k \mid \mathbf{e}_{i,j}) \mathbf{e}_{i,j}}{\sum_i \sum_j \gamma_{i,j} p(z_k \mid \mathbf{e}_{i,j})} \,. \qquad (12.14)
$$

Following a similar line of reasoning, we obtain the update rule for $\boldsymbol{\Sigma}_k$:

$$\boldsymbol{\Sigma}'_k \leftarrow \frac{\sum_i \sum_j \gamma_{i,j} p(z_k \mid \mathbf{e}_{i,j})(\mathbf{e}_{i,j} - \boldsymbol{\mu}'_k)(\mathbf{e}_{i,j} - \boldsymbol{\mu}'_k)^T}{\sum_i \sum_j \gamma_{i,j} p(z_k \mid \mathbf{e}_{i,j})}. \tag{12.15}$$

Theoretically, the EM algorithm iteratively maximizes the L_{bound} value in Eq. 12.11 until convergence. One can fix the number of maximal iterations or set a stopping criterion for the increasing ratio of L_{bound}.

Note that we can ignore the annotation prior by setting a uniform distribution, i.e., $\forall i, j, \gamma_{i,j} = 1$. This case is called "AEG Uniform" in the evaluation. In contrast, the case with nonuniform annotation prior is called "AEG AnnoPrior."

12.3.4 Discussion

As Eqs. 12.14 and 12.15 show, the re-estimated parameters $\boldsymbol{\mu}'_k$ and $\boldsymbol{\Sigma}'_k$ are collectively contributed by $\mathbf{e}_{i,j}, \forall\ i,\ j$, with the weights governed by the product of $\gamma_{i,j}$ and $p(z_k \mid \mathbf{e}_{i,j})$. Consequently, the learning process seamlessly takes the annotation prior, acoustic prior, and annotation clusters over the current affective GMM into consideration. In such a way, the annotations of different clips can be shared with one another according to their corresponding prior probabilities. This can be a key factor that enables AEG to generalize the audio-to-emotion mapping.

As the affective GMM is getting fitted to the data, a small number of affective Gaussian components might overly fit to some emotion annotations, rendering the so-called *singularity* problem [3]. When this occurs, the corresponding covariance matrices would become non-positive definite (non-PD). Imagining that when a component affective Gaussian is contributed by only one or two annotations, the corresponding covariance shape will become a point or a straight line in the VA space. To tackle this issue, we can remove the component Gaussian when it happens to produce a non-PD covariance matrix during the EM iterations [72].

We note that "early stop" is a very important heuristic while learning the affective GMM. We find that setting a small number for the maximal iteration (e.g., 7–11) or a larger stopping threshold for the increasing ratio of L_{bound} (e.g., 0.01) empirically leads to better generalizability. It can not only prevent the aforementioned singularity problem but also avoid overly fitting to the training data. Empirical results show that the accuracy of MER improves as the iteration evolves and then degrades when the optimal iteration number has reached [72]. Moreover, AEG AnnoPrior empirically converges faster and learns smaller covariances than AEG Uniform does.

12.4 Personalization with AEG

The capability for personalization is a very important characteristic that completes the AEG framework, making it more applicable to real-world applications. As AEG is a probabilistic, parametric model, it can incorporate personal information of a particular user via model adaptation techniques to make custom predictions. While such personal information may include personal emotion annotation, user profile, transaction records, listening history, and relevance feedback, we focus on the use of personal emotion annotations in this chapter.

Because of the cognitive load for annotating music emotion, it is usually not easy to collect a sufficient amount of personal annotations at once to make the system reach an acceptable performance level. On the contrary, a user may provide annotations sporadically in different listening sessions. To this end, an online learning strategy [5] is desirable. When the annotations of a target user are scarce, a good online learning method needs to prevent over-fitting to the personal data in order to keep certain model generalizability. In other words, we cannot totally ignore the contributions of emotion perceptions from other users. Motivated by the Gaussian Mixture Model-Universal Background Model (GMM-UBM) speaker verification system [48], we first treat the affective GMM learned from broad subjects (called *background users*) as a *background (general) model*, and then employ a *maximum a posteriori* (MAP)-based method [16, 48] to update the parameters of the background model using the personal annotations in an online manner. Theoretically, the resulting *personalized model* will appropriately find a good trade-off between the target user's annotations and the background model.

12.4.1 Model Adaptation

In what follows, the acoustic GMM will stay fixed throughout the personalization process, since it is used as a reference model to represent the music audio. In contrast, the affective GMM is assumed to be learned on plenty of emotion annotations from quite a few subjects, so it possesses a sufficient representation (well-trained parameters) for user-independent (i.e., general) emotion perceptions. Our goal is to learn the personal perception with respect to the affective GMM $\boldsymbol{\Lambda}$ accordingly.

Suppose that we have a target user $u_\star$ annotating M number of music clips denoted as $\mathcal{X}_\star = \{\mathbf{e}_i, \boldsymbol{\theta}_i\}_{i=1}^{M}$, where $\mathbf{e}_i$ and $\boldsymbol{\theta}_i$ are the emotion annotation and the topic posterior of a clip, respectively. We first compute each posterior probability over the latent topics based on the background affective GMM,

$$p(z_k \mid \mathbf{e}_i, \boldsymbol{\theta}_i) = \frac{\theta_{i,k} G_k(\mathbf{e}_i \mid \boldsymbol{\mu}_k, \boldsymbol{\Sigma}_k)}{\sum_{h=1}^{K} \theta_{i,h} G_k(\mathbf{e}_i \mid \boldsymbol{\mu}_h, \boldsymbol{\Sigma}_h)}. \tag{12.16}$$

Then, we derive the expected sufficient statistics on $\mathcal{X}_\star$ over the posterior distribution of $p(z_k \mid \mathbf{e}_i, \boldsymbol{\theta}_i)$ for the mixture weight, mean, and covariance parameters:

$$\Gamma_k = \sum_{i=1}^{M} p(z_k \mid \mathbf{e}_i, \boldsymbol{\theta}_i)\,, \tag{12.17}$$

$$\mathbb{E}(\boldsymbol{\mu}_k) = \frac{1}{\Gamma_k} \sum_{i=1}^{M} p(z_k \mid \mathbf{e}_i, \boldsymbol{\theta}_i)\mathbf{e}_i\,, \tag{12.18}$$

$$\mathbb{E}(\boldsymbol{\Sigma}_k) = \frac{1}{\Gamma_k} \sum_{i=1}^{M} p(z_k \mid \mathbf{e}_i, \boldsymbol{\theta}_i)\big(\mathbf{e}_i - \mathbb{E}(\boldsymbol{\mu}_k)\big)\big(\mathbf{e}_i - \mathbb{E}(\boldsymbol{\mu}_k)\big)^T. \tag{12.19}$$

Finally, the new parameters of the personalized affective GMM can be obtained according to the MAP criterion [16]. The resulting update rules are the forms of interpolations between the expected sufficient statistics (i.e., $E(\boldsymbol{\mu}_k)$ and $E(\boldsymbol{\Sigma}_k)$) and the parameters of the background model (i.e., $\boldsymbol{\mu}_k$ and $\boldsymbol{\Sigma}_k$) as follows

$$\boldsymbol{\mu}'_k \leftarrow \alpha_k^{\mathrm{m}}\mathbb{E}(\boldsymbol{\mu}_k) + \left(1 - \alpha_k^{\mathrm{m}}\right)\boldsymbol{\mu}_k\,, \tag{12.20}$$

$$\boldsymbol{\Sigma}'_k \leftarrow \alpha_k^{\mathrm{v}}\mathbb{E}(\boldsymbol{\Sigma}_k) + \left(1 - \alpha_k^{\mathrm{v}}\right)\left(\boldsymbol{\Sigma}_k + \boldsymbol{\mu}_k\boldsymbol{\mu}_k^T\right) - \boldsymbol{\mu}'_k(\boldsymbol{\mu}'_k)^T. \tag{12.21}$$

The coefficients α_k^{m} and α_k^{v} are data-dependent and are defined as

$$\alpha_k^{\mathrm{m}} = \frac{\Gamma_k}{\Gamma_k + \beta^{\mathrm{m}}}\,, \quad \alpha_k^{\mathrm{v}} = \frac{\Gamma_k}{\Gamma_k + \beta^{\mathrm{v}}}\,, \tag{12.22}$$

where β^{m} and β^{v} are related to the hyper parameters [16] and thus should be empirically defined by users. Note that there is no need to update the mixture weights, as they are already occupied by the fixed topic posterior weights.

12.4.2 Discussion

The MAP-based method is preferable in that we can determine the interpolation factor that balances the contribution between the personal annotations and the background model without loss of model generalizability, as demonstrated by its superior effectiveness and efficiency in speaker adaptation tasks [48]. If a personal annotation $\{\mathbf{e}_m, \boldsymbol{\theta}_m\}$ is highly correlated to a latent topic z_k (i.e. $p(z_k|\mathbf{e}_m, \boldsymbol{\theta}_m)$ is large), the annotation will contribute more to the update of $\{\boldsymbol{\mu}'_k, \boldsymbol{\Sigma}'_k\}$. In contrast, if the user's annotations have nothing to do with z_h (i.e., the cumulative posterior probability $\Gamma_h = 0$), the parameters of $\{\boldsymbol{\mu}'_h, \boldsymbol{\Sigma}'_h\}$ would remain the same as those of the background model, as shown by the fact that α_k would be 0.

Another advantage of the MAP-based method is that users are free to provide personal annotations for whatever songs they like, such as the songs they are more familiar with. This can help reduce the cognitive load of the personalization process. As the AEG framework is audio-based, the annotated clips can be arbitrary and does not have to be those included in the corpus for training the background model.

Finally, we note that the model adaptation procedure only needs to be performed once, so the algorithm is fairly efficient. It only requires K times of computing the expected sufficient statistics and updating the parameters. In consequence, we can keep refining the background model whenever a small number of personal annotations are available, and readily use the updated model for personalized MER or music retrieval. The model adaptation method for GMM is not limited to the MAP method. We refer interested readers to [7, 35] for more advanced methods.

12.5 AEG-Based Music Emotion Recognition

12.5.1 Algorithm

As described in Sect. 12.3, we predict the emotion distribution of an unseen clip by weighting the affective GMM using the clip's topic posterior $\hat{\theta} = \{\hat{\theta}_k\}_{k=1}^{K}$ as

$$p(\mathbf{e} \mid \hat{\theta}) = \sum_{k=1}^{K} \hat{\theta}_k G_k(\boldsymbol{\mu}_k, \boldsymbol{\Sigma}_k)\,. \tag{12.23}$$

In addition, we can also use a single, representative affective Gaussian $G(\hat{\boldsymbol{\mu}}, \hat{\boldsymbol{\Sigma}})$ to summarize the weighted affective GMM. This can be done by solving the following optimization problem

$$\min_{\hat{\boldsymbol{\mu}}, \hat{\boldsymbol{\Sigma}}} \sum_{k=1}^{K} \hat{\theta}_k D_{\mathrm{KL}}\big(G_k(\boldsymbol{\mu}_k, \boldsymbol{\Sigma}_k) \,\big|\big|\, G(\hat{\boldsymbol{\mu}}, \hat{\boldsymbol{\Sigma}})\big)\,, \tag{12.24}$$

where

$$D_{\mathrm{KL}}(G_A \parallel G_B) = \frac{1}{2}\Big(\mathrm{tr}(\boldsymbol{\Sigma}_A \boldsymbol{\Sigma}_B^{-1}) - \log \mid \boldsymbol{\Sigma}_A \boldsymbol{\Sigma}_B^{-1} \mid + (\boldsymbol{\mu}_A - \boldsymbol{\mu}_B)^T \boldsymbol{\Sigma}_B^{-1} (\boldsymbol{\mu}_A - \boldsymbol{\mu}_B) - 2\Big) \tag{12.25}$$

denotes the one-way (asymmetric) Kullback–Leibler (KL) divergence (a.k.a. relative entropy) [35] from $G_A(\boldsymbol{\mu}_A, \boldsymbol{\Sigma}_A)$ to $G_B(\boldsymbol{\mu}_B, \boldsymbol{\Sigma}_B)$. This optimization problem is strictly convex in $\hat{\boldsymbol{\mu}}$ and $\hat{\boldsymbol{\Sigma}}$, which means that there is a unique minimizer for the two variables, respectively [11]. Let the partial derivative with respect to $\hat{\boldsymbol{\mu}}$ be 0, we have

$$\sum_k \hat{\theta}_k (2\hat{\boldsymbol{\mu}} - 2\boldsymbol{\mu}_k) = 0\,. \tag{12.26}$$

Given the fact that $\sum_k \hat{\theta}_k = 1$, we derive

$$\hat{\boldsymbol{\mu}} = \sum_{k=1}^{K} \hat{\theta}_k \boldsymbol{\mu}_k\,. \tag{12.27}$$

Setting the partial derivative with respect to $\boldsymbol{\Sigma}_k^{-1}$ to 0,

$$\sum_k \hat{\theta}_k \left(\boldsymbol{\Sigma}_k - \hat{\boldsymbol{\Sigma}} + (\boldsymbol{\mu}_k - \hat{\boldsymbol{\mu}})(\boldsymbol{\mu}_k - \hat{\boldsymbol{\mu}})^T\right) = 0\,, \tag{12.28}$$

we obtain the optimal covariance matrix by,

$$\hat{\boldsymbol{\Sigma}} = \sum_{k=1}^{K} \hat{\theta}_k \left(\boldsymbol{\Sigma}_k + (\boldsymbol{\mu}_k - \hat{\boldsymbol{\mu}})(\boldsymbol{\mu}_k - \hat{\boldsymbol{\mu}})^T\right)\,. \tag{12.29}$$

12.5.2 Discussion

Representing the predicted result as a single Gaussian is functionally necessary, because it is easier and more straightforward to interpret or visualize the emotion prediction to the users with only a single mean (center) and covariance (uncertainty). However, this may run counter to the theoretical arguments given in favor of a GMM that permits emotion modeling in finer granularity. For instance, it is inadequate for the clips whose emotional responses are by nature bi-modal. We note that in applications such as emotion-based music retrieval (cf. Sect. 12.6) and music video generation [66], one can directly use the raw weighted GMM (i.e., Eq. 12.23) as the emotion index of a song in response to queries given in the VA space. We will detail this aspect later in Sect. 12.6.

The computation of Eqs. 12.27 and 12.29 is quite efficient. The complexity depends mainly on K and the number of frames T of a clip: computing θ_k requires KT operations (cf. Eq. 12.2), whereas computing $\hat{\boldsymbol{\mu}}$ and $\hat{\boldsymbol{\Sigma}}$ requires K vector multiplications and K matrix operations, respectively. This efficiency is important for dealing with a large-scale music database and for application such as real-time music emotion tracking on a mobile device [27, 53, 64, 70, 71].

12.5.3 Evaluation on General MER

12.5.3.1 Dataset

We use the AMG1608 dataset [8] for evaluating both general and personalized MER. The dataset contains 1,608 30-s music clips annotated by 665 subjects (345 are male; average age is 32.0 ± 11.4) recruited mostly from the crowdsourcing platform Mechanical Turk [44]. The subjects were asked to rate the VA values that best describe their general (instead of moment-to-moment) emotion perception of each clip via the internet. The VA values, which are real values ranging in between [–1, 1], are entered by clicking on the emotion space on a square interface panel. The subjects were instructed to rate the perceived rather than felt emotion. Each music clip was

Table 12.1 Frame-based acoustic features used in the evaluation

Feature	Dimension	Description
MFCC	40	20 Mel-frequency cepstral coefficients and their first-order time differences [12]
Tonal	17	Octave band signal intensity using a triangular octave filter bank and the ratio of these intensity values [42]
Spectral	11	Linear predictor coefficients that capture the spectral envelope of the audio signal [41], spectral flux, [42] and spectral shape descriptors [45]
Temporal	4	Shape and statistics (centroid, spread, skewness, and kurtosis) [17]
All	72	Concatenation of all the four types of features mentioned above

annotated by 15–32 subjects. Each subject annotated 12–924 clips, and 46 out of the 665 subjects annotated more than 150 music clips, making the dataset a useful corpus for research on MER personalization. The average Krippendorff's α across the music clips is 0.31 for valence and 0.46 for arousal, which are both in the range of fair agreement. Please refer to [8] for more details about this dataset.

12.5.3.2 Acoustic Features

As different emotion perceptions are usually associated with different patterns of features [18], we use two toolboxes, MIRtoolbox [36] and YAAFE [42], to extract four sets of frame-based features from audio signals, including MFCC-related features, tonal features, spectral features, and temporal features, as listed in Table 12.1. We down-sample all the audio clips in AMG1608 at 22,050 Hz and normalize them to the same volume level. All the frame-based features are extracted with the same frame size of 50 ms and 50 % hop size. Each dimension in the frame-based feature vectors is normalized to zero mean and unit standard deviation. We concatenate all the four sets of features for each frame, as this leads to better performance in acoustic modeling in our pilot study [83]. As a result, a frame-level feature vector contains 72 dimensions of features.

However, it does not make sense to analyze and predict the music emotion on a specific frame. Instead of bag-of-frames approach [61, 63], we adopt the bag-of-segments approach for the topic posterior representation, because a segment is able to capture more local temporal variation of the low-level features. Our preliminary result has also confirmed this hypothesis. To generate a segment-level feature vector representing a basic term in the bag-of-segments approach, we concatenate the mean and standard deviation of 16 consecutive frame-level feature vectors, leading to a 144-dimensional vector for a segment. The hop size for a segment is four frames. Given the acoustic GMM (cf. Eq. 12.1), we then follow Eqs. 12.2 and 12.3 addressed in Sect. 12.3.1 to compute the topic posterior vector of a music clip.

12.5.3.3 Evaluation Metrics

The accuracy of general MER is evaluated using three performance metrics: two-way KL divergence (KL2) [35], Euclidean distance, and R^2 (also known as the coefficient of determination) [58]. The first two measure the distance between the prediction and the ground truth. The lower the value is, the better the performance. KL2 considers the performance with respect to the bivariate Gaussian distribution of a chip, while the Euclidean distance is concerned with the VA mean only. R^2 is also concerned with the VA mean only. In contrast to the distance measure, a high R^2 value is preferred. Moreover, R^2 is computed separately for valence and arousal.

Specifically, we are given the distribution of the ground-truth annotations $\mathcal{N}_i = G(\mathbf{a}_i, \mathbf{B}_i)$ (cf. Sect. 12.3.2) and the predicted distribution of each test clip $\hat{\mathcal{N}}_i = G(\hat{\boldsymbol{\mu}}_i, \hat{\boldsymbol{\Sigma}}_i)$, both of which are modeled as a bivariate Gaussian distribution, where $i \in \{1, \ldots, N\}$ denotes the index of a clip in the test set. Instead of one-way KL divergence (cf. Eq. 12.25) for determining the representative Gaussian, we evaluate the performance of emotion distribution prediction based on the KL2 divergence defined by

$$D_{\mathrm{KL2}}(G_A, G_B) \equiv \frac{1}{2}\Big(D_{\mathrm{KL}}(G_A \parallel G_B) + D_{\mathrm{KL}}(G_B \parallel G_A)\Big). \tag{12.30}$$

The average KL2 divergence (AKL), which measures the symmetric distance between the predicted emotion distribution and the ground truth one, is computed by $\frac{1}{N}\sum_{i=1}^{N} D_{\mathrm{KL2}}(\mathcal{N}_i, \hat{\mathcal{N}}_i)$. Using the l_2 norm, we can compute the average Euclidean distance (AED) between the mean vectors of two Gaussian distributions by $\frac{1}{N}\sum_{i=1}^{N} \|\mathbf{a}_i - \hat{\boldsymbol{\mu}}\|_2$. The R^2 statistics is a standard way to measure the fitness of regression models [58]. It is used to evaluate the prediction accuracy as follows:

$$R^2 = 1 - \frac{\sum_{i=1}^{N}(\hat{e}_i - e_i)^2}{\sum_{i=1}^{N}(e_i - \bar{e})^2}, \tag{12.31}$$

where $\hat{e}_i$ and e_i denote the predicted (either valence or arousal) value and the ground truth one of a clip, respectively, and $\bar{e}$ is the ground-truth value over the test set. When the predictive model perfectly fits the ground-truth values, R^2 is equal to 1. If the predictive model does not fit the ground-truth well, R^2 may become negative.

We perform three-fold cross-validation to evaluate the performance of general MER. Specifically, the AMG1608 dataset is randomly partitioned into three folds, and an MER model is trained on two of them and tested on the other one. Each round of validation generates the predicted result of one-third of the complete dataset. After three rounds, we will have the predicted result of each clip in the complete dataset. Then, AKL, AED, and the R^2 for valence and arousal are computed over the complete dataset, instead of computing the performance over each one-third of the dataset. This strategy gives an unbiased estimate for R^2.

12.5.3.4 Result

We compare the performance of AEG with two baseline methods. The first one, referred to as the *base-rate* method, uses a reference affective Gaussian whose mean and covariance are set using the global mean and covariance of the training annotations without taking into account the acoustic features. In other words, the prediction for every test clip would be the same for the base-rate method. The performance of this base-rate method can be considered as a lower bound in this task accordingly. Moreover, we compare the performance of AEG with SVR [55], a representative regression-based approach for predicting emotion values or distributions, using the same type of acoustic features. Specifically, the feature vector of a clip is formed by concatenating the mean and standard deviation of all the frame-level feature vectors within a clip, yielding a 144-dimensional vector. We use the radial basis function (RBF) kernel SVR implemented by the libSVM library [6], with parameters optimized by grid search with three-fold cross-validation on the training set. We further use a heuristic favorable for SVR to regularize every invalid predicted covariance parameter [72]. This heuristic significantly improves the AKL performance of SVR.

Our pilot study empirically shows that AEG Uniform gives better emotion prediction in AED, compared to AEG AnnoPrior, possibly because the introduction of the annotation prior (cf. Eq. 12.7) may bias the estimation of the mean parameters in the EM learning. In contrast, AEG AnnoPrior leads to better result in AKL, indicating its capability of estimating a more proper covariance for a learned affective GMM. In light of this, we use a following *hybrid* method to take advantage of both AEG AnnoPrior and AEG Uniform in optimizing the affective GMM. Suppose that we have learned two affective GMMs, one for AEG AnnoPrior and the other for AEG Uniform. To generate a combined affective GMM, for its k-th component Gaussian, we take the mean from the k-th Gaussian of AEG Uniform and the covariance from the k-th Gaussian of AEG AnnoPrior. This combined affective GMM is eventually used to predict the emotion for a test clip with Eqs. 12.27 and 12.29 in this evaluation.

Table 12.2 compares the performance of AEG with the two baseline methods. It can be seen that both SVR and AEG outperform the base-rate method by a great margin, and that AEG can outperform SVR. For AEG, we can obtain better AKL and better R^2 for valence when $K = 128$, but better AED and better R^2 for arousal when $K = 256$. The best R^2 achieved for valence and arousal are 0.1601 and 0.6686.

Table 12.2 Performance evaluation on general MER (↓ stands for smaller-better and ↑ larger-better)

Method	AKL ↓	AED ↓	R^2 Valence ↑	R^2 Arousal ↑
Base-rate	1.2228	0.4052	–0.0009	0.0000
SVR-RBF	0.7124	0.2895	0.1409	0.6613
AEG ($K = 128$)	**0.7049**	0.2890	**0.1601**	0.6554
AEG ($K = 256$)	0.7078	**0.2869**	0.1579	**0.6686**

In particular, the superior performance of AEG in R^2 for valence is remarkable. Such observation suggests AEG a promising approach, as it is typically more difficult to model the valence perception from audio signals [74].

Figure 12.3 presents the result of AEG when we vary the value of K (i.e., the number of latent topics). It can be seen that the performance of AEG improves as a function of K when K is smaller than 256, but starts to decrease when K is sufficient larger. The best result is obtained when K is set to 128 or 256. As the parameters of SVR-RBF has also been optimized, this result shows that, if the optimal case of AEG is not attained (e.g., $K = 64$ or 512), AEG is still on par with the state-of-the-art SVR approach to general MER.

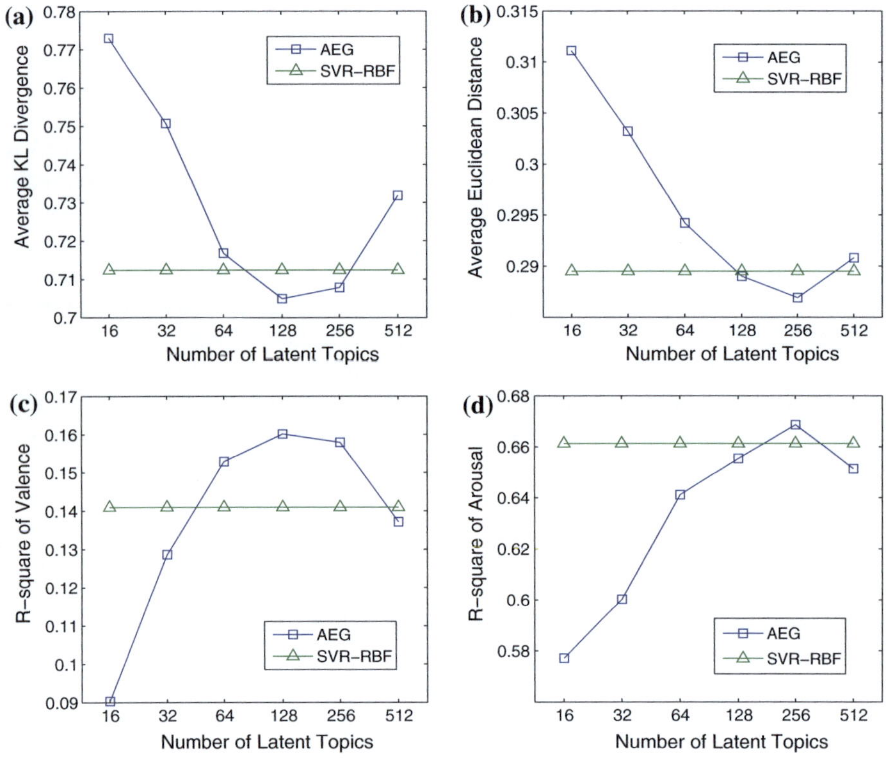

Fig. 12.3 Performance evaluation on general MER, using different numbers of latent topics in AEG. **a** AKL, smaller-better. **b** AKL, smaller-better. **c** R^2 of valence, larger-better. **d** R^2 of arousal, larger-better

12.5.4 *Evaluation on Personalized MER*

12.5.4.1 Evaluation Setup

The trade-off between the number of personal annotations (feedbacks) and the performance of personalization is important for personalized MER. On one hand, we hope to have more personal annotations to more accurately model the emotion perception of a particular user. On the other hand, we want to restrict the number of personal annotations so as to relieve the burden on the user. To reflect this, evaluation on the performance of personalized MER is conducted by fixing the test set for each user, but varying the number of available emotion annotations from the particular user to test how the performance improves as personal data amasses.

We consider 41 users who have annotated more than 150 clips in this evaluation. We use the data of six of them for parameter tuning, and the data of the remaining 35 in the evaluation and report the average result for these 35 test users. One hundred annotations of each test user are randomly selected as the personalized training set for personalization for the user. Once the model is created, another 50 clips annotated by the same user are randomly selected. Specifically, for each test user, a general MER model is trained with 600 clips randomly selected from the original AMG1608, excluding those annotated by the test user under consideration and those self-inconsistent annotations. Then, the general model is incrementally personalized five times using different numbers of clips selected from the personalized training set. We use 10, 20, 30, 40, and 50 clips iteratively, with the preceding clips being a subset of the current ones each time. The process is repeated 10 times for each user.

We use the following evaluation metrics here: the AED, the R^2, and the average likelihood (ALH) of generating the ground-truth annotation (a single VA point) $\mathbf{e}_\star$ of the test user using the predicted affective Gaussian, i.e., $p(\mathbf{e}_\star \mid \hat{\boldsymbol{\mu}}_\star, \hat{\boldsymbol{\Sigma}}_\star)$. Larger ALH corresponds to better accuracy. We do not report KL divergence here because each clip in the dataset is annotated by a user at most once, which does not constitute a probability distribution.

12.5.4.2 Result

We compare the MAP-based personalization method of AEG with the two-stage personalization method of SVR proposed in [79]. In the two-stage SVR method, the first stage creates a general SVR model for general emotion prediction, whereas the second stage creates a personalized SVR that is trained solely on a user's annotations. The final prediction is obtained by linearly combining the predictions from the general SVR and the personalized SVR with weights 0.7 and 0.3, respectively. The weights are derived empirically according to our pilot study. As for AEG, we only update the mean parameters with $\beta^{\mathrm{m}} = 0.01$, because our pilot study shows that updating the covariance empirically does not lead to better performance. This observation is also in line with the findings in speaker adaptation [48]. We train the background model with AEG Uniform for simplicity.

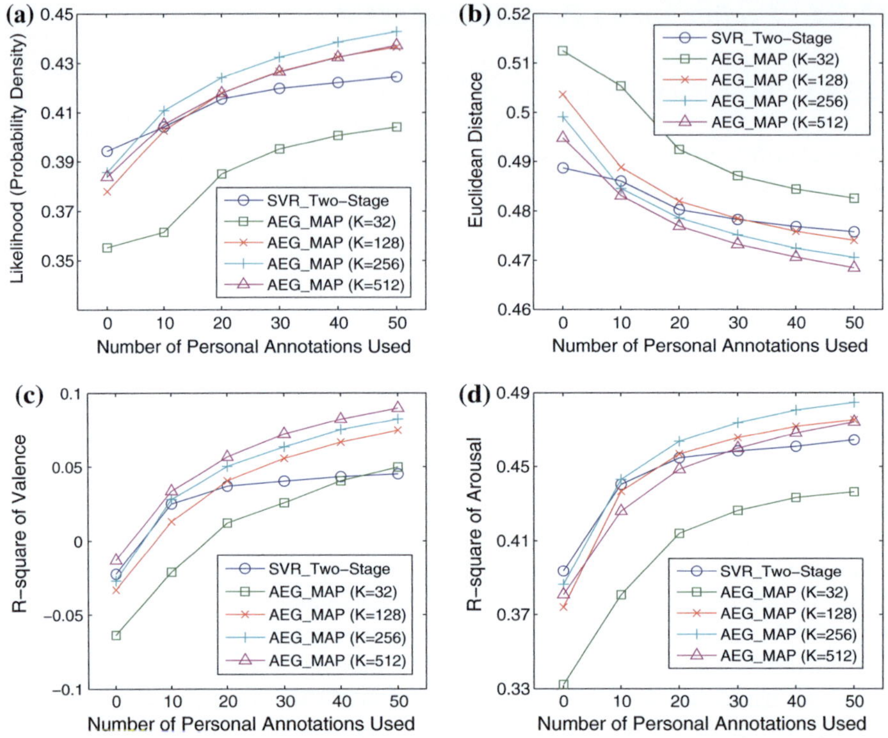

Fig. 12.4 Performance evaluation on personalized MER, with varying numbers of personal data. **a** ALH, smaller-better. **b** AED, smaller-better. **c** R^2 of valence, larger-better. **d** R^2 of arousal, larger-better

Figure 12.4 compares the result of different personalized MER methods, when we vary the number of available personal annotations. The starting point of each curve is the result given by the general MER model trained on partial users of the AMG1608 dataset. We can see that the result of the general model is inferior to those reported in Fig. 12.3, showing that a general MER model is less effective when it is used to predict the emotion perception of individual users, compared to the case of predicting the *average* emotion perception of users. We can also see that the result of the considered personalized methods generally grows as the number of personal annotations increases. When the value of K is sufficiently large, AEG-based personalization methods can outperform the SVR method. Moreover, while the result of SVR starts to saturate when the number of personal annotations is larger than 20, AEG has the potential of keeping on improving the performance by exploiting more personal annotations. We also note that there is no significant performance difference for AEG when K is large enough (e.g., $\geq$128).

Although our evaluation shows that personalization methods can improve the result of personalized emotion prediction, the low values in the R^2 statistics for valence and arousal still show that the problem is fairly challenging. Future work is still needed to improve either the quality of the emotion annotation data or the feature extraction or machine learning algorithms for modeling emotion perception.

12.6 Emotion-Based Music Retrieval

12.6.1 The VA-Oriented Query Interface

The VA space offers a ready canvas for music retrieval through the specification of a point in the emotion space [80]. Users can retrieve music pieces of certain emotions without specifying the titles. Users can also draw a trajectory to indicate the desired emotion changes across a list of songs (e.g., from angry to tender).

In addition to the above point-based query, one can also issue a Gaussian-based query to an AEG-based retrieval system. As Fig. 12.5 shows, users can specify the desired variances (or the confidence level at the center point) of emotion by pressing a point in the VA space with different levels of duration or strength. The variance of the Gaussian gets smaller as one increases the duration or strength of pressing, as Fig. 12.5a shows. Larger variances indicate less specific emotion around the center point. After specifying the size of a circular variance shape, one can even pinch fingers to adjust the variance shape. For a trajectory-based query input, similarly, the corresponding variances are determined according to the dynamic speed when drawing the trajectory, as Fig. 12.5b shows. Fast speed corresponds to a less specific query and the system will return pieces whose variances of emotion are larger. If

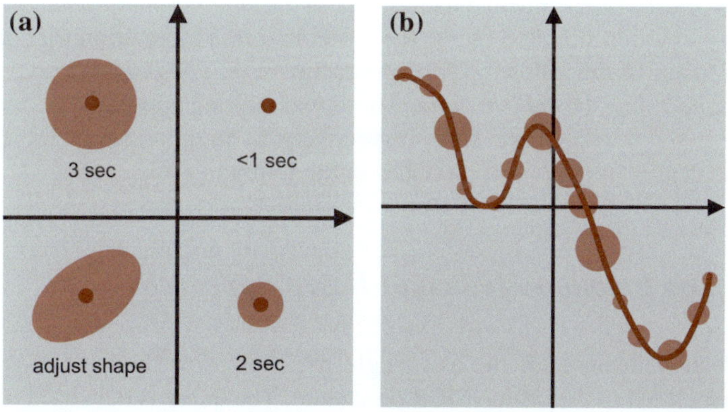

Fig. 12.5 The stress-sensitive user interface for emotion-based music retrieval. Users can (**a**) specify a point or (**b**) draw a trajectory, while specifying the variance with different levels of duration

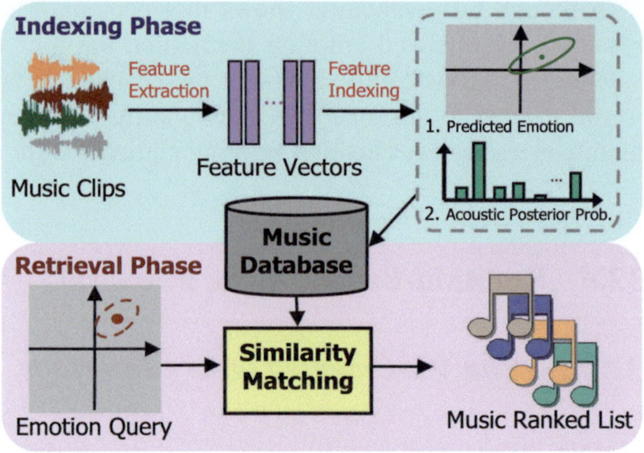

Fig. 12.6 The diagram of the content-based music retrieval system using an emotion query

songs with more specific emotions are desirable, one can slow down the speed when drawing the trajectory. The queries inputted by such a *stress-sensitive interface* can be handled by AEG for emotion-based music retrieval.

12.6.2 Overview of the Emotion-Based Music Retrieval System

As Fig. 12.6 shows, the content-based retrieval system can be divided into two phases. In the *feature indexing* phase, we index each music clip in an unlabeled music database by one of the following two approaches: The *emotion prediction* approach indexes a clip with the *predicted emotion distribution* (an affective GMM or a single 2-D Gaussian) given by MER, whereas the *folding-in* approach indexes a clip with the *topic posterior* (a K-dimensional vector). In the later *music retrieval* phase, given an arbitrary emotion-oriented query, the system returns a list of music clips ranked according to one of the following two approaches: *likelihood/distance-based matching* and *pseudo song-based matching*. These two ranking approaches correspond to one of the two indexing approaches, respectively, as summarized in Table 12.3. We present the details of the two approaches in the following subsections.

12.6.3 The Emotion Prediction-Based Approach

This approach indexes each clip as a single, representative Gaussian distribution or an affective GMM in the offline MER procedure. The query is then used to compare with the predicted emotion distribution of each clip in the database. The system ranks all the clips based on the likelihoods or distances in response to the query. Clips with larger likelihood or smaller distance should be placed in the higher order.

Table 12.3 The two implementations of the emotion-based music retrieval system

Approach	Indexing phase	Indexed type	Matching phase
Emotion Prediction	Full procedure of MER by AEG	An affective GMM (Eq. 12.23) or a 2-dim Gaussian $\{\hat{\boldsymbol{\mu}}, \hat{\boldsymbol{\Sigma}}\}$	Likelihood (for point query) or distance (for Gaussian query)
Folding-In	Compute only the topic posterior	K-dim vector $\hat{\boldsymbol{\theta}}$	Cosine similarity of pseudo song (K-dim vector $\boldsymbol{\lambda}$)

Given a point query $\tilde{\mathbf{e}}$, the corresponding likelihood of the indexed emotion distribution of a clip $\hat{\boldsymbol{\theta}}_i$ is generated by a single Gaussian $p(\tilde{\mathbf{e}} \mid \hat{\boldsymbol{\mu}}_i, \hat{\boldsymbol{\Sigma}}_i)$ or an affective GMM $p(\tilde{\mathbf{e}} \mid \hat{\boldsymbol{\theta}}_i)$ (cf. Eq. 12.23), where $\{\hat{\boldsymbol{\mu}}_i, \hat{\boldsymbol{\Sigma}}_i\}$ is the predicted parameters of the representation Gaussian for $\hat{\boldsymbol{\theta}}_i$, and $\hat{\theta}_{i,k}$ is the k-th component of $\hat{\boldsymbol{\theta}}_i$. Note that here we use the topic posterior vector to represent a clip in the database.

When it comes to a Gaussian-based query $\tilde{G} = G(\tilde{\boldsymbol{\mu}}, \tilde{\boldsymbol{\Sigma}})$, the approach generates the ranking scores based on the KL2 divergence. In the case of indexing with a single Gaussian, we use Eq. 12.30 to compute $D_{\mathrm{KL2}}\big(\tilde{G}, G(\hat{\boldsymbol{\mu}}_i, \hat{\boldsymbol{\Sigma}}_i)\big)$ between the query and a clip. On the other hand, in the case of indexing with an affective GMM, we compute the weighted KL2 divergence by

$$D_{\mathrm{KL2}}\big(\tilde{G}, p(\mathbf{e} \mid \hat{\boldsymbol{\theta}}_i)\big) = \sum_{k=1}^{K} \hat{\theta}_{i,k} D_{\mathrm{KL2}}\big(\tilde{G}, G_k(\boldsymbol{\mu}_k, \boldsymbol{\Sigma}_k)\big)\,. \tag{12.32}$$

12.6.4 *The Folding-In-Based Approach*

As Fig. 12.7 shows, this approach estimates the probability distribution $\boldsymbol{\lambda} = \{\lambda_k\}_{k=1}^{K}$, subject to $\sum_k \lambda_k = 1$, for an input VA-oriented query in an online manner. Each estimated λ_k corresponds to the relevance of a query to the k-th latent topic z_k, so we can treat the distribution of $\boldsymbol{\lambda}$ as the topic posterior of the query and call it a *pseudo song*. In the case of Fig. 12.7, for example, we show a query that is very likely to be represented by the second affective Gaussian component. The folding-in process is likely to assign a dominative weight $\lambda_2 = 1$ for z_2, and $\lambda_h = 0, \forall h \neq 2$. This implies that the query is highly related to the song whose topic posterior is dominated by θ_2. Therefore, the pseudo song can be used to match with the topic posterior vector $\hat{\boldsymbol{\theta}}_i$ of each clip in the database.

Given a point query $\tilde{\mathbf{e}}$, we start the folding-in process by first generating the pseudo song via maximizing the query likelihood of the $\boldsymbol{\lambda}$-weighted affective GMM with respective to $\boldsymbol{\lambda}$. By taking the logarithm of Eq. 12.23, we obtain the following objective function:

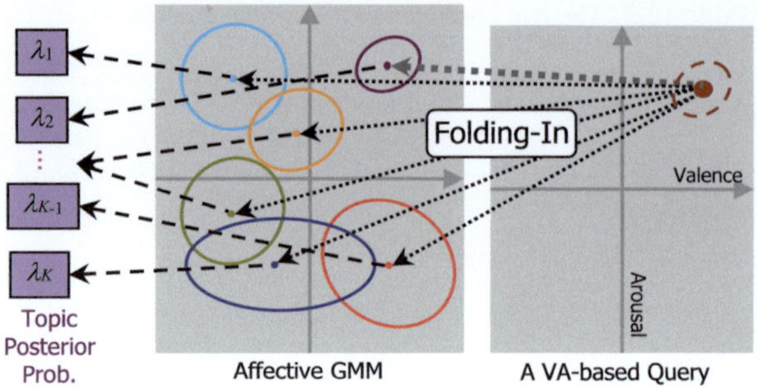

Fig. 12.7 Illustration of the folding-in process of emotion-based music retrieval by AEG

$$\max_{\boldsymbol{\lambda}} \ \log \sum_{k=1}^{K} \lambda_k \, G_k(\tilde{\mathbf{e}} \mid \boldsymbol{\mu}_k, \boldsymbol{\Sigma}_k)\,, \tag{12.33}$$

where λ_k is the k-th component of the vector $\boldsymbol{\lambda}$. In some sense, a good $\boldsymbol{\lambda}$ will make the corresponding $\boldsymbol{\lambda}$-weighted affective GMM well generate the query $\tilde{\mathbf{e}}$. The problem in Eq. 12.33 can be solved by the EM algorithm. In the E-step, the posterior probability of z_k is computed by

$$p(z_k \mid \tilde{\mathbf{e}}) = \frac{\lambda_k G_k(\tilde{\mathbf{e}} \mid \boldsymbol{\mu}_k, \boldsymbol{\Sigma}_k)}{\sum_{h=1}^{K} \lambda_h G_h(\tilde{\mathbf{e}} \mid \boldsymbol{\mu}_h, \boldsymbol{\Sigma}_h)}\,. \tag{12.34}$$

In the M-step, we then only update λ_k by

$$\lambda'_k \leftarrow p(z_k \mid \tilde{\mathbf{e}})\,. \tag{12.35}$$

As for a Gaussian-based query $\tilde{G}$, we fold in the query into the learned affective GMM to estimate a pseudo song as well. This time, we maximize the following log-likelihood function:

$$\max_{\boldsymbol{\lambda}} \ \log \sum_{k=1}^{K} \lambda_k \, p(\tilde{G} \mid G_k)\,, \tag{12.36}$$

where $p(\tilde{G} \mid G_k)$ is the likelihood function based on KL2 (cf. Eq. 12.30):

$$p(\tilde{G} \mid G_k) = \exp\big(-D_{\mathrm{KL2}}(\tilde{G}, G_k)\big)\,. \tag{12.37}$$

Again, Eq. 12.36 can be solved by the EM algorithm, with the following update,

$$\lambda'_k \leftarrow p(z_k \mid \tilde{G}) = \frac{\lambda_k p(\tilde{G} \mid G_k)}{\sum_{h=1}^{K} \lambda_h p(\tilde{G} \mid G_h)}\,. \tag{12.38}$$

The EM processes for both point- and Gaussian-based queries stop early after few iterations (e.g., 3), because the pseudo song estimation is sensitive to over-fitting. Several initialization settings can be used, such as a random, uniform, or prior distribution. Considering the stability and the reproducibility of the experimental result, we opt for using a uniform distribution for initialization. Note that random initialization may introduce discrepant results among different trials even with identical experimental settings, whereas initializing with a prior distribution may render biased results in favor of songs that predominates the training data [67]. Finally, the retrieval system ranks all the clips in descending order of the following cosine similarities in response to the pseudo song:

$$\Phi(\boldsymbol{\lambda}, \boldsymbol{\theta}_i) = \frac{\boldsymbol{\lambda}^T \boldsymbol{\theta}_i}{\|\boldsymbol{\lambda}\| \|\boldsymbol{\theta}_i\|} . \tag{12.39}$$

12.6.5 Discussion

The Emotion Prediction approach is straightforward, as the purpose of MER is to automatically index unseen music pieces in the database. In contrast, the folding-in approach goes one step further to embed a VA-based query into the space of music clips. Although the folding-in process requires an additional step of estimating the pseudo song, it is in fact more flexible. In a personalized music retrieval context, for example, a personalized affective GMM can readily produce a personalized pseudo song for comparing with the original topic posterior vectors of all the pieces in the database, without the need to predict the emotion again with the personalized model.

The complexity of the emotion prediction approach mainly comes from computing the likelihood of a point query on each music clip's emotion distribution or the KL divergence between the Gaussian query and the emotion distribution of each clip. Therefore, the matching process needs to compute N (the number of clips in the database) times the likelihood or the KL divergence. In the folding-in approach, the complexity comes from estimating the pseudo song (with the EM algorithm) and computing the cosine similarity between the pseudo song and each clip. EM needs to compute $K \times ITER$ times the likelihood of a component affective Gaussian or the Gaussian KL divergence, where $ITER$ is the number of EM iterations. Then, the matching process computes N times the cosine similarity. Obviously, computing the likelihood on an emotion distribution (i.e., a single Gaussian or a GMM) is computationally more expensive than computing the cosine similarity (as K is usually not large). Therefore, when N is large (e.g., $N \gg K \times ITER$), the folding-in approach is considered as a more feasible one in practice.

12.6.6 Evaluation for Emotion-Based Music Retrieval

12.6.6.1 Evaluation Setup

The AMG1608 dataset is again adopted in this music retrieval evaluation. We consider two emotion-based music retrieval scenarios: query-by-point and query-by-Gaussian. For each scenario, we create a set of synthetic queries and use the learned AEG model to respond to each test query and return a ranked list of music clips from an unlabeled music database. The generation of the test query set for query-by-point is simple. As Fig. 12.8a shows, we uniformly sample 100 2-D query points within $\left[[-1, -1]^T, [1, 1]^T\right]$ in the VA space. The test query set for query-by-Gaussian is then based on this set of points. Specifically, we convert a point query to a Gaussian query by associating with the point a 2-by-2 covariance matrix, as Fig. 12.8b shows. Motivated by our empirical observation from data, the covariance of a Gaussian query is set in inverse proportion to the distance between the mean of the Gaussian query (determined by the corresponding point query) and the origin of the VA space. That is, if a given point query is far from the origin (with large emotion magnitude), the user may want to retrieve songs with a specific emotion (with smaller covariance ellipse).

The performance is evaluated by aggregating the ground-truth *relevance* scores of the retrieved music clips according to the normalized discounted cumulative gain (NDCG), a widely used performance measure for ranking problems [28]. The NDCG@P, which measures the relevance of the top P retrieved clips for a query, is computed by

$$\text{NDCG@}P = \frac{1}{Z_P}\left\{R(1) + \sum_{i=2}^{P} \frac{R(i)}{\log_2 i}\right\}, \tag{12.40}$$

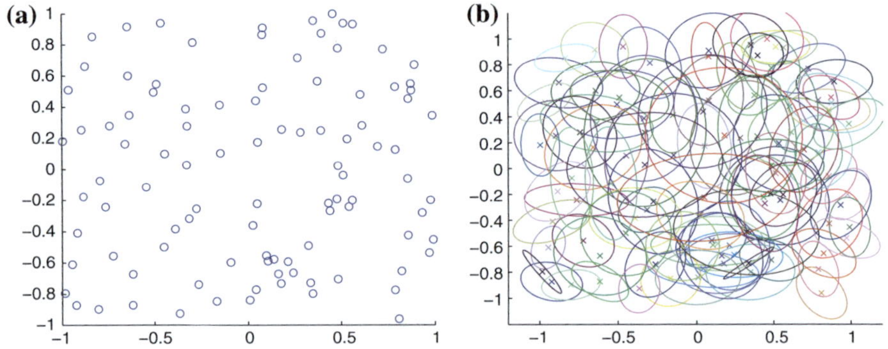

Fig. 12.8 Test queries used in evaluating emotion-based music retrieval: **a** 100 points generated uniformly in between [–1, 1]. **b** 100 Gaussians generated based on the previous 100 points

where $R(i)$ is the ground-truth relevance score of the rank-i clip, $i = 1, \ldots, Q$, where $Q \geq P$ is the number of clips in the music database, and Z_P is the normalization term that ensures the ideal NDCG@P equal 1. Let $\mathcal{N}_i$ (with parameters $\{\mathbf{a}_i, \mathbf{B}_i\}$) denote the ground-truth annotation Gaussian of the rank-i clip. For a point query $\tilde{\mathbf{e}}$, $R(i)$ is obtained by $p(\tilde{\mathbf{e}} \mid \mathbf{a}_i, \mathbf{B}_i)$, the likelihood of the query point. For a Gaussian query $\tilde{\mathcal{N}}$, $R(i)$ is given by $p(\tilde{\mathcal{N}} \mid \mathcal{N}_i)$ defined by Eq. 12.37. From Eq. 12.40, we see that if the system ranks the clips in similar order as the descending order obtained on $\{R(i)\}_{i=1}^{Q}$, we obtain a larger NDCG. We report the average NDCG computed over the test query set. Note that we do not adopt evaluation metrics, such as the mean average precision and the area under the ROC curve, because currently it is not trivial to set a threshold to binarize $R(i)$.

We perform threefold cross-validation as that used in evaluating general MER. In each round, the test fold (with 536 clips) serves as the unlabeled music database.

12.6.6.2 Result

We implement a random approach to reflect the lower bound performance using a random permutation for each test query, without taking into consideration any ranking approach. We further implement an *Ensemble* approach that averages the rankings of a test query given by emotion prediction and folding-in. Specifically, both approaches assign an ordinal number to a clip according to their respective rankings. Then, we average the two ordinal numbers of a clip as a new score, and re-rank all the clips in ascending order of their new scores.

Note that we only consider AEG Uniform for simplicity in the result presentation. Our preliminary study reveals that AEG Uniform in general perform slightly better than AEG AnnoPrior and the hybrid method mentioned in Sect. 12.5.3.4 in the retrieval task. Moreover, for the folding-in approach, early stop is not only important to the folding-in process, but also necessary to learning the affective GMM. According to our pilot study, setting *ITER* between 2 and 4 for learning affective GMM and *ITER* $= 3$ for learning the pseudo song lead to the optimal performance.

Figure 12.9 compare the NDCG@5 of the emotion prediction and folding-in approaches to emotion-based music retrieval using either point-based or Gaussian-based queries. We are interested in how the result changes as we vary the number of latent topics. It can be found that the two approaches perform very similarly for point-based query when K is in between 64 and 256. Moreover, we see that emotion prediction can outperform folding-in for Gaussian-based query when K is sufficiently large ($K \geq 64$). The optimal model is attained when $K = 128$ in all cases. Similar to the result in general MER, it seems that setting K either too large or too small would lead to sub-optimal result.

Tables 12.4 and 12.5 present the result of NDCG@5, 10, 20, and 30 for different retrieval methods, including the random baseline, emotion prediction, folding-in, and the ensemble approaches. The latter three use AEG Uniform with $K = 128$. It is obvious that the latter three can significantly outperform the random baseline, demonstrating the effectiveness of AEG in emotion-based music retrieval. It can also be found that the ensemble approach leads to the best result.

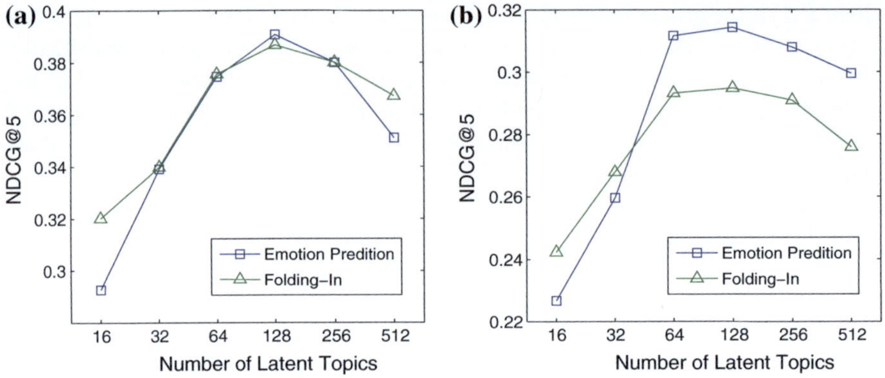

Fig. 12.9 Evaluation result of emotion-based music retrieval. **a** Point-based query, larger-better. **b** Gaussian-based query, larger-better

Table 12.4 The query-by-point retrieval performance in terms of NDCG@5, 10, 20, and 30

Method	$P = 5$	$P = 10$	$P = 20$	$P = 30$
Random	0.1398	0.1504	0.1666	0.1804
Emotion Prediction	0.3907	0.4027	0.4288	0.4490
Folding-In	0.3868	0.4067	0.4333	0.4533
Ensemble	0.3954	0.4129	0.4398	0.4601

Table 12.5 The query-by-Gaussian retrieval performance in terms of NDCG@5, 10, 20, and 30

Method	$P = 5$	$P = 10$	$P = 20$	$P = 30$
Random	0.1032	0.1090	0.1185	0.1272
Emotion Prediction	0.3143	0.3306	0.3481	0.3658
Folding-In	0.2932	0.3147	0.3383	0.3532
Ensemble	0.3204	0.3368	0.3601	0.3783

A closer comparison between emotion prediction and folding-in for point-based query shows nip and tuck, whereas the former performs consistently better regardless of the value of P for Gaussian-based query. Moreover, the NDCG measure seems more favorable for point-based query than Gaussian-based one. Our observation indicates that the standard deviation of the ground-truth relevance scores (i.e., $\{R(i)\}_{i=1}^{Q}$) for Gaussian-based query is much larger, resulting in a more challenging measurement basis than that for point-based query. However, the relative performance difference between the two methods is similar for point-based and Gaussian-based queries.

12.7 Connecting Emotion Dimensions and Categories

In addition to describing emotions by dimensions, emotions can also be described in terms of discrete labels (or tags). While the dimensional approach offers a simple means for constructing a 2-D user interface, the categorical approach offers an atomic description of music that is easy to be incorporated into conventional text-based retrieval systems. Being two extreme scenarios (discrete/continuous), the two approaches actually share a unified goal of understanding the emotion semantics of music. As the two approaches are functionally complementary, it is therefore interesting to explore the relationship between them and combine their advantages to enhance the performance of emotion-based music retrieval systems. For example, as a novice user may be unfamiliar with the essence of the valence and activation dimensions, it would be helpful to display emotion tags in the emotion space to give the user some cues. This can be achieved if we have the mapping between the emotion tag space and the VA space.

In this section, we briefly introduce the Tag2VA approach that can maps a mood tag to the VA space.

12.7.1 Algorithm Overview

Based on AEG, we can unify the two semantic modalities under a unified probabilistic framework, as illustrated in Fig. 12.10. Specifically, we establish two component models, the *Acoustic Tag Bernoullis* (ATB) model and the AEG model, to computationally model the generative processes from acoustic features to an mood tag and a pair of valence-activation values, respectively. ATB is a probabilistic classification model (a.k.a. the CBA model [20]) which can be learned from a tag-labeled music dataset. The latent topics $\{z_k\}_{k=1}^{K}$ can act as a bridge between the two spaces, so that the ATB and AEG models can share and transit the semantic information to each

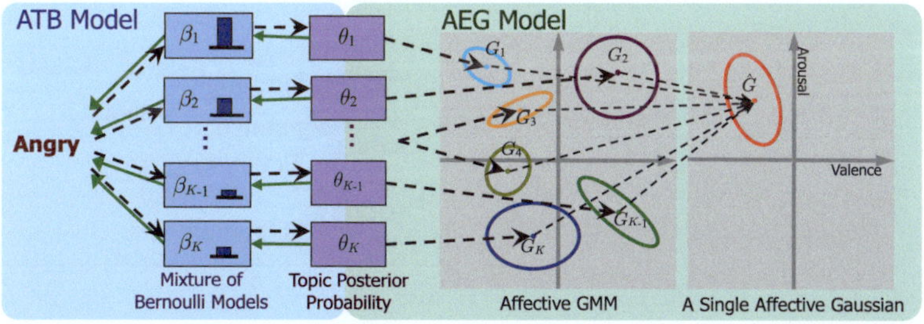

Fig. 12.10 Illustration of the generation flow between tag-based and VA-based emotion semantics of music. Two component models, namely Acoustic Tag Bernoullis (ATB) and AEG, are shown in the *left* and *right* panels, respectively. The affective Gaussian of a tag can be generated by following the *black dashed arrows*

other. The latent topics are learned directly from acoustic feature vectors, and thus the training datasets for learning the ATB and AEG models can be totally separate, relieving the requirement for a jointly-annotated dataset for the two emotion modalities. Note that we model each tag independently as a binary classification problem, so that an ATB model is learned for one tag.

Once we have learned the AEG model and the ATB model for a tag, we can obtain the VA value for the tag. As Fig. 12.10 illustrates, we first generate the topic posterior probability of the tag using a method similar to the folding-in approach (cf. Sect. 12.6.4) over the mixture of Bernoulli models. With the topic posterior $\boldsymbol{\theta}$, we can then directly predict the affective Gaussian using the AEG-based MER (cf. Sect. 12.5.1). Interested readers are referred to [65] for more details.

12.7.2 Result

We use the AMG1608 dataset to provide qualitative evaluation on the Tag2VA approach. AMG1608 additionally contains the binary labels of 34 mood tags, which are used to train 34 ATB models, respectively. The AEG model is trained following that described in general MER evaluation (cf. Sect. 12.5.3.4). Figure 12.11 presents the tag cloud generated from the VA Gaussians of the 34 mood tags. The font size of a tag is inversely proportional to the variance of the corresponding VA Gaussian. From the result, it can be seen that the automatically generated tag cloud reasonably matches the result by the psychologists [65].

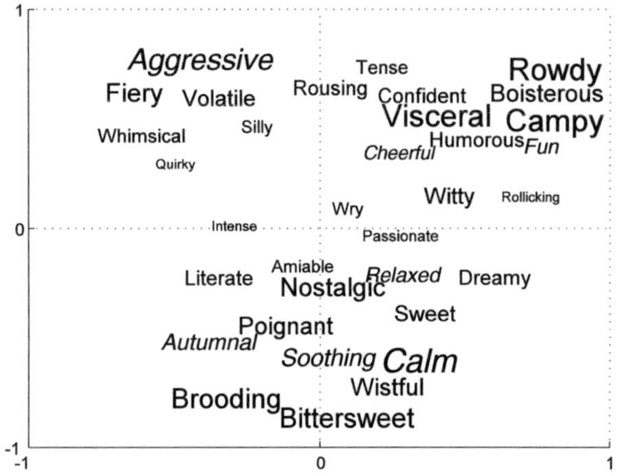

Fig. 12.11 The tag cloud generated from AMG1608

12.8 Conclusion

AEG is a principled probabilistic framework that nicely unifies the computation processes for MER and emotion-based music retrieval for dimensional emotion representations such as valence and arousal. Moreover, AEG better takes into account the subjective nature of music emotional responses through the use of probabilistic inference and model adaptation, further making it possible to personalize an emotion-based MIR system. The source codes for implementing AEG can be retrieved from the link: http://slam.iis.sinica.edu.tw/demo/AEG/.

Despite that AEG is a powerful approach, there remains a number of challenges for MER, including

- Is it the best way to consider the valence–arousal space as a coordinate space (with two orthogonal axes)?
- How do we define the "intensity" of emotion? Does the magnitude of a point in the emotion space implies intensity? Would it be possible to train regressors that treat the emotion space as a polar coordinate?
- What are the features that are more important for modeling emotion?
- Cross genre generazability [13].
- Cross culture generazability [23].
- How to incorporate lyrics features for MER?
- How to model the effect of the singing voice in emotion perception?
- How do findings in MER help emotion-based music synthesis or manipulation?

We note that the number of topics in AEG is crucial to its performance. Like many probabilistic models in text information retrieval, this is an open problem [4, 21]. Empirically, larger number of topics fine grains the model resolution and thereby results in better accuracy. Similarly, it makes sense to use more topics to model a larger music dataset (with more songs and annotations). However, to understand the relationship between the topic number and performance in a real-world setting, more user studies are still required in the future.

Moreover, AEG is only suitable for an emotion-based MIR system when we characterize emotions in terms of valence and arousal. It does not apply to systems that use categorical mood tags to describe emotion. A corresponding probabilistic model for categorical MER is yet to be developed. More research efforts are also needed for the personalization and retrieval aspects for categorical MER.

The AEG model itself can also be improved in a number of directions. For example, there are several alternative methods that one can adopt to enhance the latent acoustic descriptors (i.e., $\{A_k\}_{k=1}^{K}$ in Sect. 12.3) for clip-level topic poster representation, such as deep learning [54] or sparse representations [61]. One can also perform discriminative training to reduce the prediction error using the same corpus with respect to the selection of Gaussian components or parameter refinement over the affective GMM. For example, a stacked discriminative learning on the parameters initialized by a EM-learned generative model has been studied for years in speech recognition [9, 29]. Following this research line, it may help improve AEG as well.

Finally, the AEG framework can be extended to include multi-modal content such as lyrics, review comments, album cover, and music video. For instance, one can accompany a given silent video sequence with a piece of music based on music emotion [66]. To incorporate the lyrics into AEG, on the other hand, one can learn a lyric topic model via algorithms such as pLSA [21] and LDA [4], and compute the probability distribution for each song's lyrics based on the topic model.

References

1. Barthet, M., Fazekas, G., Sandler, M.: Multidisciplinary perspectives on music emotion recognition: implications for content and context-based models. In: Proceedings International Symposium Computer Music Modeling and Retrieval, pp. 492–507 (2012)
2. Bigand, E., Vieillard, S., Madurell, F., Marozeau, J., Dacquet, A.: Multidimensional scaling of emotional responses to music: the effect of musical expertise and of the duration of the excerpts. Cogn. Emot. **19**(8), 1113–1139 (2005)
3. Bishop, C.M.: Pattern Recognition and Machine Learning. Springer, New York (2006)
4. Blei, D.M., Ng, A.Y., Jordan, M.I.: Latent dirichlet allocation. J. Mach. Learn. Res. **3**, 993–1022 (2003)
5. Bottou, L.: Online algorithms and stochastic approximations. In: Saad, D. (ed.) Online Learning and Neural Networks. Cambridge University Press, Cambridge (1998)
6. Chang, C.C., Lin, C.J.: LIBSVM: a library for support vector machines. ACM Trans. Intell. Syst. Technol. **2**(3), 27:1–27:39 (2011)
7. Chen, Y.A., Wang, J.C., Yang, Y.H., Chen, H.H.: Linear regression-based adaptation of music emotion recognition models for personalization. In: Proceedings IEEE International Conference Acoustics, Speech, and Signal Processing, pp. 2149–2153 (2014)
8. Chen, Y.A., Yang, Y.H., Wang, J.C., Chen, H.H.: The AMG1608 dataset for music emotion recognition. In: Proceedings IEEE International Conference Acoustics, Speech, and Signal Processing (2015). http://mpac.ee.ntu.edu.tw/dataset/AMG1608/
9. Chou, W.: Minimum classification error approach in pattern recognition. In: Chou, W., Juang, B.H. (eds.) Pattern Recognition in Speech and Language Processing. CRC Press, New York (2003)
10. Collier, G.: Beyond valence and activity in the emotional connotations of music. Psychol. Music **35**(1), 110–131 (2007)
11. Davis, J.V., Dhillon, I.S.: Differential entropic clustering of multivariate Gaussians. Adv. Neural Inf. Process. Syst. **19**, 337–344 (2007)
12. Davis, S., Mermelstein, P.: Comparison of parametric representations for monosyllabic word recognition in continuously spoken sentences. IEEE Trans. Acoust. Speech Signal Process. **28**(4), 357–366 (1980)
13. Eerola, T.: Modelling emotions in music: advances in conceptual, contextual and validity issues. In: Proceedings AES International Conference (2014)
14. Eerola, T., Vuoskoski, J.K.: A comparison of the discrete and dimensional models of emotion in music. Psychol. Music **39**, 18–49 (2010)
15. Gabrielsson, A.: Emotion perceived and emotion felt: same or different? Musicae Scientiae pp. 123–147 (2002)
16. Gauvain, J., Lee, C.H.: Maximum a posteriori estimation for multivariate Gaussian mixture observations of markov chains. IEEE Trans. Speech Audio Process. **2**, 291–298 (1994)
17. Gillet, O., Richard, G.: Automatic transcription of drum loops. In: Proceedings IEEE International Conference Acoutstics, Speech, and Signal Processing, pp. 269–272 (2004)
18. Hallam, S., Cross, I., Thaut, M.: The Oxford Handbook of Music Psychology. Oxford University Press, Oxford (2008)

19. Hevner, K.: Expression in music: a discussion of experimental studies and theories. Psychol. Rev. **48**(2), 186–204 (1935)
20. Hoffman, M., Blei, D., Cook, P.: Easy as CBA: a simple probabilistic model for tagging music. In: Proceedings International Society Music Information Retrieval Conference, pp. 369–374 (2009)
21. Hofmann, T.: Probabilistic latent semantic indexing. In: Proceedings ACM SIGIR Conference Research and Development in Information Retrieval, pp. 50–57 (1999)
22. Hu, X., Downie, J.S.: When lyrics outperform audio for music mood classification: a feature analysis. In: Proceedings International Society Music Information Retrieval Conference, pp. 619–624 (2010)
23. Hu, X., Yang, Y.H.: A study on cross-cultural and cross-dataset generalizability of music mood regression models. In: Proceedings Sound and Music Computing Conference (2014)
24. Hu, X., Downie, J.S., Laurier, C., Bay, M., Ehmann, A.F.: The 2007 MIREX audio mood classification task: Lessons learned. In: Proceedings International Society Music Information Retrieval Conference, pp. 462–467 (2008)
25. Huq, A., Bello, J.P., Rowe, R.: Automated music emotion recognition: a systematic evaluation. J. New Music Res. **39**(3), 227–244 (2010)
26. Huron, D.: Sweet Anticipation: Music and the Psychology of Expectation. MIT Press, Cambridge (2006)
27. Imbrasaite, V., Baltrusaitis, T., Robinson, P.: Emotion tracking in music using continuous conditional random fields and relative feature representation. In: Proceedings International Works Affective Analysis in Multimedia (2013)
28. Jarvelin, K., Kekalainen, J.: Cumulated gain-based evaluation of IR techniques. ACM Trans. Inf. Syst. **20**(4), 422–446 (2002)
29. Juang, B.H., Chou, W., Lee, C.H.: Minimum classification error rate methods for speech recognition. IEEE Trans. Speech Audio Process. **5**(3), 257–265 (1997)
30. Juslin, P.N.: Cue utilization in communication of emotion in music performance: relating performance to perception. J. Exp. Psychol. Hum. Percept. Perform. **16**(6), 1797–1813 (2000)
31. Juslin, P., Laukka, P.: Expression, perception, and induction of musical emotions: a review and a questionnaire study of everyday listening. J. New Music Res. **33**(3), 217–238 (2004)
32. Juslin, P.N., Sloboda, J.A.: Music and Emotion: Theory and Research. Oxford University Press, New York (2001)
33. Kim, Y.E., Schmidt, E.M., Migneco, R., Morton, B.G., Richardson, P., Scott, J.J., Speck, J.A., Turnbull, D.: Music emotion recognition: A state of the art review. In: Proceedings International Society Music Information Retrieval Conference, pp. 255–266 (2010)
34. Korhonen, M.D., Clausi, D.A., Jernigan, M.E.: Modeling emotional content of music using system identification. IEEE Trans. Syst. Man Cybern. **36**(3), 588–599 (2006)
35. Kullback, S., Leibler, R.A.: On information and sufficiency. Ann. Math. Stat. **22**(1), 79–86 (1951)
36. Lartillot, O., Toiviainen, P.: A matlab toolbox for musical feature extraction from audio. In: Proceedings International Conference Digital Audio Effects, pp. 237–244 (2007)
37. Lonsdale, A.J., North, A.C.: Why do we listen to music? A uses and gratifications analysis. Br. J. Psychol. **102**, 108–134 (2011)
38. Lu, L., Liu, D., Zhang, H.: Automatic mood detection and tracking of music audio signals. IEEE Trans. Audio Speech Lang. Process. **14**(1), 5–18 (2006)
39. MacDorman, K.F., Ough, S., Ho, C.C.: Automatic emotion prediction of song excerpts: index construction, algorithm design, and empirical comparison. J. New Music Res. **36**(4), 281–299 (2007)
40. Madsen, J., Jensen, B.S., Larsen, J.: Modeling temporal structure in music for emotion prediction using pairwise comparisons. In: Proceedings International Society Music Information Retrieval Conference, pp. 319–324 (2014)
41. Makhoul, J.: Linear prediction: a tutorial review. Proc. IEEE **63**(4), 561–580 (1975)
42. Mathieu, B., Essid, S., Fillon, T., Prado, J., Richard, G.: YAAFE, an easy to use and efficient audio feature extraction software. In: Proceedings International Society Music Information Retrieval Conference, pp. 441–446 (2010)

43. Panda, R., Rocha, B., Paiva, R.P.: Dimensional music emotion recognition: Combining standard and melodic audio features. In: Proceedings International Symposium Computer Music Modeling and Retrieval (2013)
44. Paolacci, G., Chandler, J., Ipeirotis, P.: Running experiments on Amazon Mechanical Turk. Judgm. Decis. Making **5**(5), 411–419 (2010)
45. Peeters, G.: A large set of audio features for sound description (similarity and classification) in the CUIDADO project. Technical report, IRCAM, Paris, France (2004)
46. Pesek, M., et al.: Gathering a dataset of multi-modal mood-dependent perceptual responses to music. In: Proceedings the EMPIRE Workshop (2014)
47. Raykar, V.C., Yu, S., Zhao, L.H., Valadez, G.H., Florin, C., Bogoni, L., Moy, L.: Learning from crowds. J. Mach. Learn. Res. **11**, 1297–1322 (2010)
48. Reynolds, D.A., Quatieri, T.F., Dunn, R.B.: Speaker verification using adapted Gaussian mixture models. Digital Signal Process. **10**(1–3), 19–41 (2000)
49. Russell, J.A.: A circumplex model of affect. J. Pers. Social Sci. **39**(6), 1161–1178 (1980)
50. Saari, P., Eerola, T.: Semantic computing of moods based on tags in social media of music. IEEE Trans. Knowl. Data Eng. **26**(10), 2548–2560 (2014)
51. Saari, P., Eerola, T., Fazekasy, G., Barthet, M., Lartillot, O., Sandler, M.: The role of audio and tags in music mood prediction: a study using semantic layer projection. In: Proceedings International Society Music Information Retrieval Conference, pp. 201–206 (2013)
52. Schmidt, E.M., Kim, Y.E.: Prediction of time-varying musical mood distributions from audio. In: Proceedings International Society Music Information Retrieval Conference, pp. 465–470 (2010)
53. Schmidt, E.M., Kim, Y.E.: Modeling musical emotion dynamics with conditional random fields. In: Proceedings International Society Music Information Retrieval Conference, pp. 777–782 (2011)
54. Schmidt, E.M., Kim, Y.E.: Learning rhythm and melody features with deep belief networks. In: Proceedings International Society Music Information Retrieval Conference, pp. 21–26 (2013)
55. Schölkopf, B., Smola, A.J., Williamson, R.C., Bartlett, P.L.: New support vector algorithms. Neural Comput. **12**, 1207–1245 (2000)
56. Schubert, E.: Modeling perceived emotion with continuous musical features. Music Percept. **21**(4), 561–585 (2004)
57. Schuller, B., Hage, C., Schuller, D., Rigoll, G.: 'Mister D.J., Cheer Me Up!': musical and textual features for automatic mood classification. J. New Music Res. **39**(1), 13–34 (2010)
58. Sen, A., Srivastava, M.S.: Regression Analysis: Theory, Methods, and Applications. Springer Science & Business Media (1990)
59. Soleymani, M., Caro, M.N., Schmidt, E., Sha, C.Y., Yang, Y.H.: 1000 songs for emotional analysis of music. In: Proceedings International Workshop Crowdsourcing for Multimedia, pp. 1–6 (2013)
60. Soleymani, M., Aljanaki, A., Yang, Y.H., Caro, M.N., Eyben, F., Markov, K., Schuller, B., Veltkamp, R., Weninger, F., Wiering, F.: Emotional analysis of music: a comparison of methods. In: Proceedings ACM Multimedia, pp. 1161–1164 (2014)
61. Su, L., Yeh, C.C.M., Liu, J.Y., Wang, J.C., Yang, Y.H.: A systematic evaluation of the bag-of-frames representation for music information retrieval. IEEE Trans. Multimedia **16**(5), 1188–1200 (2014)
62. Wang, M.Y., Zhang, N.Y., Zhu, H.C.: User-adaptive music emotion recognition. In: Proceedings IEEE International Conference Signal Processing, pp. 1352–1355 (2004)
63. Wang, J.C., Lee, H.S., Wang, H.M., Jeng, S.K.: Learning the similarity of audio music in bag-of-frames representation from tagged music data. In: Proceedings International Society Music Information Retrieval Conference, pp. 85–90 (2011)
64. Wang, J.C., Wang, H.M., Jeng, S.K.: Playing with tagging: a real-time tagging music player. In: Proceedings IEEE International Conference Acoustics, Speech, and Signal Processing, pp. 77–80 (2012)
65. Wang, J.C., Yang, Y.H., Chang, K., Wang, H.M., Jeng, S.K.: Exploring the relationship between categorical and dimensional emotion semantics of music. In: Proceedings ACM International

Workshop Music Information Retrieval with User-Centered and Multimodal Strategies, pp. 63–68 (2012)
66. Wang, J.C., Yang, Y.H., Jhuo, I., Lin, Y.Y., Wang, H.M.: The acousticvisual emotion Gaussians model for automatic generation of music video. In: Proceedings ACM Multimedia, pp. 1379–1380 (2012)
67. Wang, J.C., Yang, Y.H., Wang, H.M., Jeng, S.K.: The acoustic emotion Gaussians model for emotion-based music annotation and retrieval. In: Proceedings ACM Multimedia, pp. 89–98 (2012)
68. Wang, J.C., Yang, Y.H., Wang, H.M., Jeng, S.K.: Personalized music emotion recognition via model adaptation. In: Proceedings APSIPA Annual Summit & Conference (2012)
69. Wang, X., Wu, Y., Chen, X., Yang, D.: A two-layer model for music pleasure regression. In: Proceedings International Workshop Affective Analysis in Multimedia (2013)
70. Wang, S.Y., Wang, J.C., Yang, Y.H., Wang, H.M.: Towards time-varying music auto-tagging based on CAL500 expansion. In: Proceedings IEEE International Conference Multimedia and Expo, pp. 1–6 (2014)
71. Wang, J.C., Wang, H.M., Lanckriet, G.: A histogram density modeling approach to music emotion recognition. In: Proceedings IEEE International Conference Acoustics, Speech, and Signal Processing, pp. 698–702 (2015)
72. Wang, J.C., Yang, Y.H., Wang, H.M., Jeng, S.K.: Modeling the affective content of music with a Gaussian mixture model. IEEE Trans. Affect. Comput. **6**(1), 56–68 (2015)
73. Weninger, F., Eyben, F., Schuller, B.: On-line continuous-time music mood regression with deep recurrent neural networks. In: Proceedings IEEE International Conference Acoustics, Speech, and Signal Processing, pp. 5449–5453 (2014)
74. Yang, Y.H., Chen, H.H.: Music Emotion Recognition. CRC Press, Boca Raton (2011)
75. Yang, Y.H., Chen, H.H.: Predicting the distribution of perceived emotions of a music signal for content retrieval. IEEE Trans. Audio Speech Lang. Process. **19**(7), 2184–2196 (2011)
76. Yang, Y.H., Chen, H.H.: Ranking-based emotion recognition for music organization and retrieval. IEEE Trans. Audio Speech Lang. Process. **19**(4), 762–774 (2011)
77. Yang, Y.H., Chen, H.H.: Machine recognition of music emotion: a review. ACM Trans. Intell. Syst. Technol. **3**(4) (2012)
78. Yang, Y.H., Liu, J.Y.: Quantitative study of music listening behavior in a social and affective context. IEEE Trans. Multimedia **15**(6), 1304–1315 (2013)
79. Yang, Y.H., Su, Y.F., Lin, Y.C., Chen, H.H.: Music emotion recognition: The role of individuality. In: Proceedings ACM International Workshop Human-Centered Multimedia, pp. 13–21 (2007)
80. Yang, Y.H., Lin, Y.C., Cheng, H.T., Chen, H.H.: Mr. Emo: Music retrieval in the emotion plane. In: Proceedings ACM Multimedia, pp. 1003–1004 (2008)
81. Yang, Y.H., Lin, Y.C., Su, Y.F., Chen, H.H.: A regression approach to music emotion recognition. IEEE Trans. Audio Speech Lang. Process. **16**(2), 448–457 (2008)
82. Yang, Y.H., Lin, Y.C., Chen, H.H.: Personalized music emotion recognition. In: Proceedings ACM SIGIR International Conference Research and Development in Information Retrieval, pp. 748–749 (2009)
83. Yang, Y.H., Wang, J.C., Chen, Y.A., Chen, H.H.: Model adaptation for personalized music emotion recognition. In: Chen, C.H. (ed.) Handbook of Pattern Recognition and Computer Vision, 5th Edition, World Scientific Publishing Co., Singapore (2015)
84. Yeh, C.C., Tseng, S.S., Tsai, P.C., Weng, J.F.: Building a personalized music emotion prediction system. In: Advances in Multimedia Information Processing-PCM 2006, pp. 730–739. Springer (2006)
85. Zentner, M., Grandjean, D., Scherer, K.R.: Emotions evoked by the sound of music: characterization, classification, and measurement. Emotion **8**(4), 494 (2008)
86. Zhu, B., Liu, T.: Research on emotional vocabulary-driven personalized music retrieval. In: Edutainment, pp. 252–261 (2008)

Chapter 13
Emotions and Personality in Adaptive e-Learning Systems: An Affective Computing Perspective

Olga C. Santos

Abstract This chapter reports how affective computing (in terms of detection methods and intervention approaches) is considered in adaptive e-learning systems. The goal behind is to enrich the personalized support provided in online educational settings by taking into account the influence that emotions and personality have in the learning process. The main contents of the chapter consist in the review of 26 works that present current research trends regarding the detection of the learners' affective states and the delivery of the appropriate affective support in diverse educational settings. In addition, the chapter discusses open issues regarding affective computing in the educational domain.

13.1 Introduction

Literature reports interplay between the cognitive aspects of learning and affect, which implies the need to detect and then intelligent manage (through appropriate feedback based on affect-related strategies) the affective dimension of the learner within educational systems [5]. In this way, an affective-based personalized learning experience can be provided. In fact, over 10 years ago it was already suggested that the "new" technologies (that can develop new sensors and interfaces, such as intelligent chairs, gloves, and mice, as well as new signal processing, pattern recognition, and reasoning algorithms) can help to measure, model, study, and support learners affectively, the less intrusive as possible the better [64]. Nevertheless, it is still not clear which affective features are to be considered in the learner models that drive the adaptation pathways [90].

Affective computing research explores how affective factors influence interactions between humans and technology, how affect sensing and affect generation techniques can inform our understanding of human affect, as well as the design, implementation, and evaluation of systems involving affect at their core [7]. Detecting and modelling

---

O.C. Santos (✉)
aDeNu Research Group, Artificial Intelligence Department,
Computer Science School, UNED, C/Juan del Rosal, 16, 28040 Madrid, Spain
e-mail: ocsantos@dia.uned.es

M. Tkalčič et al. (eds.), *Emotions and Personality in Personalized Services*,
Human–Computer Interaction Series, DOI 10.1007/978-3-319-31413-6_13

affect is an open research topic that is to be addressed from a psychological perspective [9]. Readers interested can consult other chapters of this book for a more psychology-based background on emotions and personality (i.e. see Chap. 3 for personality models; Chap. 4 for affect acquisition; Chap. 5 for personality acquisition; Chap. 9 for available datasets with personality and affective parameters).

In turn, this chapter reports how affective computing is considered in e-learning systems to enrich the personalized support provided in them by taking into account the influence that emotions and personality have in the learning process. Nonetheless, for the shake of context, a brief overview of non-specific educational issues on emotions and personality research is provided in this section. The situation can be summarized as follows: since personality is considered much more stable than emotions, research efforts to adapt systems responses to the users' needs have mainly focused on automatically detecting emotional changes during learners' interactions while personality has usually being modelled with standardized psychological instruments. Anyway, there still exist many challenges both for the automatic detection of the user state and the delivery of the appropriate personalized intervention.

The chapter is structured as follows. After this introduction, a review of 26 e-learning systems that take advantage of affective computing (where emotions and/or personality traits are considered) is reported. This review serves to identify the current research trends in the field. Then, other open issues that might worth be explored are discussed. Finally, main contributions are wrapped up.

13.1.1 Overview of Emotions

Emotions are complex. They represent short reactions (i.e., a matter of seconds) to the perception of a specific (external or internal) event, accompanied by mental, behavioural and physiological changes [53]. They have been defined in a huge variety of ways and there is no agreed theory that explains them. Within the affective computing field, the aim is to automatically detect and intelligent respond to users' emotions in order to increase usability and effectiveness [9].

As discussed in Chap. 4, there exist many modalities for affect detection (e.g., spoken and written language, video including facial expression, body posture and movement, physiological signals, tactile interaction data), which can either use a discrete (in terms of specific emotions) or a continuous (in terms of degrees of valence and arousal) representation model. Detecting emotions in contexts of extensive information use can pose several methodological challenges [50]: (1) defining the phenomena (affect, emotion, mood, feeling, etc., as well as the way to structure it, either as a discrete or a continuous manifestation); (2) selecting the methods for the study (control of variables, emotions elicitation, naturalistic setting, participants' engagement), the data collection (standardized measures, level of obtrusiveness of the emotional source used, objectiveness of the emotional labelling, cost of the data collection, researchers' skills), and the data interpretation (pilot data, time interval); (3) preparing and integrating data (quantity, quality and compatibility with other data); and (4) deriving meaning from data (to make computers more attuned to users' needs and making users' experience more pleasant). The use of multiple methods for emotions detection would increase reliability of findings and more comprehensively cover multiple facets of emotions [83]. In addition, multimodal detection approaches that combine emotional information from diverse sources seem to improve the classification accuracy of the emotions detected, but there are still several open issues to be researched [15].

Despite existing challenges regarding the automatic detection of emotional states, there are also research efforts aimed to close the so-called affective loop [12] by developing solutions that dynamically respond to the emotions recognized and are aimed at influencing the user's affective state. Some application domains where emotions are taking into account are tackled in other chapters of this book, such as conversational systems (Chap. 11) and music information retrieval (Chap. 13, Chap. 15 and Chap. 17). This chapter focuses on the educational domain.

13.1.2 Overview of Personality

Regarding personality, affective computing follows the trait approach, which focuses on finding empirically psychological differences among individuals and how these differences might be conceptualized and measured, and thus, modelled and implemented in computers [58]. Personality traits are dispositions towards action, belief and attitude formation, differ across individuals and influence behaviour [52]. Personality is much more stable than emotions (normally considered stable over years [88]), but can influence emotions directly [69], Thus, personality needs to be considered when personalizing a system to the users' needs [58], especially when affective issues are taken into account.

In addition, as discussed in Chap. 5, people do not always behave the same way due to the natural variability of behaviour in concrete situations. To deal with this behavioural variability, personality states have been proposed, which can be defined as behavioural episodes having the same contents as traits [25].

Typically, personality traits are identified using questionnaires containing descriptive items that accurately reflect the traits of interest [2]. As acknowledged in Chap. 3, the so-called big five model, or five factor model (FFM), has become standard in Psychology to describe personality. The FFM is a multi-factorial approach which labels the following five traits: (i) extraversion, (ii) agreeableness, (iii) conscientiousness, (iv) neuroticism, and (v) openness to experience.

Nonetheless, proposals are being made to automatically detect users' personality from cues left in daily life activities [28] or inferred from speech [29], text-mining [51], mining interactions in social networks [60] and keyboard and mouse usage [41]. In this respect, Chap. 5 reviews sources of data and methods to automatically detect personality. In fact, as surveyed in [93] and despite open issues and challenges regarding data, methodological issues and applications, technologies are being capable of dealing with personality in three ways: (i) automatic personality recognition (inference of the true personality of an individual from behavioural evidence), (ii) automatic personality perception (inference of personality others attribute to an individual based on her observable behaviour), and (iii) automatic personality synthesis (generation of artificial personalities via embodied agents).

13.2 Affective Computing in Educational Scenarios

Affect detection in educational scenarios is even more challenging than in other domains, since emotions usually do not change too much during learning [86] and have lower intensity than in other domains [71]. Even though there is not yet a single theory that fully explains how emotions influence learning, computers can be given some ability to recognize and respond to affect, and this can also help to understand the phenomenon [64]. In this respect, different modelling approaches have been used in the educational domain, such as the OCC model [61], the basic emotions [21], the Learning Spiral Model [45], and the model of achievement emotions linked to academic performance based on the AEQ [63].

Since affect recognition in educational scenarios is still at an early research stage, human labelling of learners' affect by trained observers (e.g., using the BROMP protocol [59]) is needed to identify student learning behaviours and suggesting how emotions impact on learning [97]. To aid the study of learners' affect and inform the design of affective computing educational systems, knowledge elicitation methods can be used, which differ in what instruments are available, who generate the emotional reports and when the elicitation is undertaken [65]. In any case, detecting learners' affective states can be helpful not only in adapting the tutorial interaction and strategy, but also in contributing to the understanding of affective behaviour and its relation to learning, thereby facilitating an optimal learning experience [1].

In addition, as commented in the previous section, the personality traits of a person can also influence emotions, and thus, could have an impact on the learner's affective state [19]. In particular, personality can be used as a predictor of affective state, when coupled with performance related to a learning goal [11, 67].

With this context in mind, a literature review (compiled in Table 13.1) has been done to collect approaches for detecting the learners' affective state and reacting to them by delivering some affective intervention in diverse educational scenarios, considering emotions and personality traits. This review does not aim to be an exhaustive analysis of the state of the art in the field. In turn, it aims to illustrate the state of the art of affective computing in educational scenarios. This selection of 26 works is biased towards recent papers (more than half of them were published in 2014 and 2015, while this chapter was being written) that summarize the progress towards the current state of the art, and which can serve as reading pointers for researches who want to get familiarized with the field. Thus, they can also serve to discuss the current trends and open issues in the field.

For each work analyzed, the following information is compiled in Table 13.1 (in addition to the authors, publication year and bibliographical reference): (i) the type of

Table 13.1 Selected works on affective computing in educational settings

Authors, Year [Reference]	Educational setting (& #participants)	Personality traits	Data sources	Emotional labeling (and labeler)	Emotion modelling	Affective intervention
Afzal and Robinson, 2010 [1]	Computer-based learning tasks N = 8		Camera (facial expressions, head gestures)	Bored, confused, happy, interested, neutral, surprised (researcher)	Classification (Hidden Markov Models)	
Conati and Maclaren, 2009 [10]	Math Educational game (Prime Climb) N = 41	FFM (reported in [11])	Electromiography	OCC (joy, distress, pride, shame, admiration and reproach) + valence (learner)	Probabilistic model (dynamic decision network)	Hints (not using the affective model)
D'Mello, 2014 [14]	Multi-domain intelligent tutoring system (ALEKS) N = 3		Galvanic skin resistance	Anger, disgust, contempt, happiness, surprise, anxiety, confusion, boredom, curiosity, eureka, engagement/flow, frustration and neutral (learner).	Only statistical analysis of labelled data	
D'Mello and Graesser, 2012 [16]	Multi-domain interactive intelligent system (Affective AutoTutor) N = +1000		Conversational cues, pression sensor (posture features), camera (facial features)	Boredom, confusion, frustration, flow/engagement (learner, educator; + retrospective)	Multimodal classifier	Emotional feedback + synthesis of emotional expressions in the agent
Dennis et al., 2016 [19]	Conversational agent N = +1000	FFM (IPIP-NEO)				Emotional support messages

(continued)

Table 13.1 (continued)

Authors, Year [Reference]	Educational setting (& #participants)	Personality traits	Data sources	Emotional labeling (and labeler)	Emotion modelling	Affective intervention
Felipe et al., 2012 [24]	Affective intelligente agent for programming N = 6		Keystrokes, camera (facial expressions) + interaction logs	Confusion, boredom, other (researcher)	Supervised classification (some Weka algorithms)	Message and image (not implemented)
Grawemeyer et al., 2015 [30]	Math exploratory learning environment for children N = 26		Screen, voice	Flow, surprise, confusion, frustration, boredom (learner, researcher; + retrospective)	Wizard of Oz	Varied types of feedback (promts, detailed instructions, hints . . .) including motivational messages
Gutica and Conati, 2013 [31]	Agent-based educational game for Math (Heroes of Math Island) N = 15		Screen	Neutral, boredom, confidence, confusion, curiosity, delight/pleasure, engaged concentration, frustration, hesitancy, pride, shame and surprise (researcher)	Only statistical analysis of labelled data	Progressive hints provided by monkey character (neutral, happy and confident, sad and frustrated) to help students overcome errors (labelled emotions not used)
Harley et al., 2015 [32]	Multi-agent learning environment on the circulatory system (MetaTutor) N = 124	FFM (mini-IPIP)	Questionnaires (AEQ, ARI)	AEQ (enjoyment, hope, pride, anger, shame, anxiety, hopelessness, and boredom) Agent Response Inventory (ARI) (learner)	Only statistical analysis of labelled data	Audible assistance with agent directed emotions

(continued)

Table 13.1 (continued)

Authors, Year [Reference]	Educational setting (& #participants)	Personality traits	Data sources	Emotional labeling (and labeler)	Emotion modelling	Affective intervention
Janning et al., 2014 [34]	Math intelligent tutoring system N = 10		Voice	Under-challenged, over-challenged, flow (researcher, learner retrospectively)	Supervised classification	Task sequencing
Jaques et al., 2014 [35]	Multi-agent learning environment on the circulatory system (MetaTutor) N = 67		Eye tracking	Boredom, curiosity (learner)	Supervised classification (some algorithms from Weka)	Suggested to increase task success, engagement, and user satisfaction
Jraidi et al., 2014 [38]	Problem-solving activities N = 44	FFM	Electroencephalography, galvanic skin resistance + heart rate, help requested, mouse movements, performance	Stress, confusion, frustration and boredom (learners)	Hierarchical probabilistic methods (dynamic bayesian network) vs. supervised classification	Suggested approaches: no intervention, challenging task, help, different activity
Kai et al., 2015 [39]	Exploratory game on physics (Physics Playground) N = 137		Camera (facial expression), interaction logs	Boredom, confusion, engaged concentration, and frustration (researcher)	Supervised classifcation (RapidMiner and Weka algorithms)	
Khan et al., 2013 [42]	System to teach programming to children (Alice) N = 16		Mouse, keyboard, galvanic skin resistance	Arousal (labeled with galvanic skin resistance)	Multiple regression analysis	

(continued)

Table 13.1 (continued)

Authors, Year [Reference]	Educational setting (& #participants)	Personality traits	Data sources	Emotional labeling (and labeler)	Emotion modelling	Affective intervention
Leontidis et al., 2011 [47]	Web-based adaptive educational system (MENTOR) N = 120	FFM	Questions asked by the system	OCC model (joy, satisfaction, pride, hope, gratification, distress, disappoinment, shame, fear, reproach)	Ontological approach, supervised learning	Non-specified affective tactic
Litman and Forbes-Riley, 2014 [48]	Physics Intelligent Tutoring Dialogue System (ITSPOKE) N = 67		Voice	Disengagement, uncertainity (manual labelling not required)	Previously trained classification models (& Wizard of Oz as reported in [27])	Different message and task
Paquette et al., 2015 [62]	Serious game on tactical combat casualty care (vMedic/ TC3Sim) N = 119		Interaction logs, Kinect (head movements + posture shifts), Q-self (data not recorded)	Boredom, confusion, engaged concentration, frustration, surprise (researcher)	Classification algorithms (RapidMiner)	
Rodriguez et al., 2014 [68]	Adaptive e-learning systems (CoMoLE) N = 1		Text	Joy, anger, sadness and fear (learner)	Sentiment analysis	Activity selection, feedback message (not implemented)
Sabourin and Lester, 2014 [70]	Microbiology game-based learning (Crystal Island) N = 450	FFM	Student answers	Anxious, bored, confused, curious, excited, focused, frustrated + valence (learner)	Probabilistic model (dynamic bayesian network)	From [67]: affect sensitive virtual agents (task-based, parallel emphatic and reactive emphatic)

(continued)

Table 13.1 (continued)

Authors, Year [Reference]	Educational setting (& #participants)	Personality traits	Data sources	Emotional labeling (and labeler)	Emotion modelling	Affective intervention
Salmeron-Majadas et al., 2015 [71]	Math Intelligent tutoring sytem N = 2		Heart rate, breath rate, skin conductance and temperature, logs and camera	Emotions versus no emotion + anxiety, confused, concentrated, frustrated, happy, shame or surprise, as well as none (learner; + retorspectively) W3C EmotionML	Supervised classification (Weka algorithms)	Formative feedback will be defined with TORMES methodology [78]
Santos et al., 2016 [77]	Language learning N = 6	FFM, GSE,	Heart rate, skin temperature, skin conductance, camera (facial expressions), voice	Stress (researcher)	Wizard of Oz	Sensorial signal (light, sound, movement) to calm down defined with TORMES methodology [78]
Santos et al., 2013 [80]	Web-based learning environment (dotLRN) N = 71		Mouse, keyboard, text, Kinect (not analysed yet)	Valence and arousal (learner, researcher; dictionary)	Sentiment analysis, classification	Affective educational oriented recommendations to be defined with TORMES methodology [78]
Santos et al., 2014 [81]	Web-based learning environment (dotLRN) N = 77 (learners) +18 (educators)	FFM, GSE	Screen + facial expressions & body movements	Confusion, doubt, distracted, nervous, shame, anxious (researcher)	Wizard of Oz	Diverse types of emotional support via text messages

Table 13.1 (continued)

Authors, Year [Reference]	Educational setting (& #participants)	Personality traits	Data sources	Emotional labeling (and labeler)	Emotion modelling	Affective intervention
Shen et al., 2009 [86]	Online and offline content to study programming N = 1		Skin conductance, heart rate, electroencephalograpy	Engaged, confused, bored, hopeful (learner)	Classification methods	Rules that recommend contents, examples, music and videos
VanLehn et al., 2014 [91]	Agent-based affective Meta-Tutoring system (AMT) N = several studies with 40–50 each		Camera (facial expression), posture-sensing chair	Good modeling, engaged, new understanding, inconsistent, guessing, fluttering/confused/lost, boredom	Regression model	Motivational and meta-cognitive spoken messages
Woolf et al., 2010 [96]	Agent-based Math tutoring system (Wayang Outpost) N = 35,29,29		Camera (mental state), skin conductance bracelet, pressure sensitive mouse, pressure sensitive chair	Frustration, interest, confidence and excitement (learner)	Linear regression	Empathetic learning companions; agents

educational setting, including the number of participants involved in the evaluation studies reported, (ii) the personality traits considered (if any), (iii) data source(s) used to extract the (emotional) information, (iv) the emotional labelling used as well as the labeler (learner vs. educator/researcher), (v) the detection technique(s) used to model the emotions, and (vi) the intervention applied (when done) to feed the learner back with affective support.

The 26 works compiled in Table 13.1 aim to provide an overview of the current research trends and open issues regarding the application of affective computing in e-learning systems. Emotions, personality traits or both are considered

From a quick look, it can be noticed the diversity in the educational settings. They can be classified in game-based learning systems [10, 31, 39, 62, 70], intelligent tutoring systems [14, 34, 71], dialogue system [48], agent-based systems [16, 19, 24, 31, 32, 35, 91, 96], and non-specific (or non-specified) learning environments [1, 30, 38, 42, 47, 68, 77, 80, 81, 86].

Usually, the number of participants invovled in the evaluation studies is large in order to account for statistical validity across subjects. However, in some works, intrasubject studies have been carried out over several months [14, 68, 86].

Although the final goal of the research is the same in all the works (i.e. build educational systems that provide personalized affective support), the focus of the research reported in the selected papers is diverse. Some papers mainly focus on improving emotions detection, either by exploring the potential of single data sources [1, 10, 14, 34, 35] or the combination of several input sources [24, 39, 42, 62, 71, 80, 86]. Other works focus on improving the affective intervention, avoiding the challenges in automatic affective detection by simulating the detection process by using the Wizard of Oz method [17] as in [27, 30, 77, 81]. In addition, a third group of papers focus on analyzing the affective states reported [14, 31, 38], the influence of the personality [19, 32, 47], or assessing the impact of the affect support in the learning process [16, 48, 70, 91, 96].

Data sources considered are also diverse. In particular, the following have been reported: (1) cameras for facial expressions and/or body movements [1, 16, 24, 39, 71, 77, 81, 91, 96]; (2) pressure sensor/posture sensing chairs [16, 91, 96]; (3) Kinect sensor [62]—in [80] it is used to collect data, but analysis not reported; (4) physiological signals such as electro dermal activity [14, 38, 42, 71, 77, 86, 96]; electromyography [10]; skin temperature [71, 77]; breath rate [71]; electroencephalograpy [38, 86]; heart rate [38, 71, 77, 86], (5) behavioural information such as keystrokes [24, 42, 80]; mouse movements [38, 42, 80] and pressure [96]; interaction logs [24, 39, 62, 71] and performance features [38]; (6) eye-tracking [35], (7) speech features [30, 34, 48, 77] and conversational cues [16]; (8) text [68, 80]; (9) participant's screen [30, 31, 81]; and (10) learners' answers to questions [32, 47, 70]. In addition, quantified-self sensors such as wearable arm bracelets have also been used to collect data ([62, 96]). In particular, the sensor used in [62] can measure participant's orientation through a built-in 3-axis accelerometer in addition to electrodermal activity and skin temperature. However, due to errors in the collection process, these data could not be analyzed.

This diversity in the data collection sources follows existing approaches in the affective computing field, which among others, include facial expression, voice (paralinguistic features of speech), body language and posture, physiology and brain imaging, as well as multimodal combinations [9]. In addition, keyboard and mouse interactions are considered as affective information sources [44]. And because the educational context is taken into account, interaction logs can provide lexical, semantic and contextual cues, as well as the interactive features gathered within the environment (hints or information buttons) [54].

With respect to the techniques used for detecting emotions, supervised classification technqiues are mainly used [1, 16, 24, 34, 35, 39, 47, 48, 62, 71, 80, 86], as well as probabilistic models [10, 38, 70] and regression analysis [42, 91, 96]. This requires emotionally labelling learners' interactions and behaviour [54, 72, 97]. To this respect, methodological decisions need to be taken regarding methods, instruments and informants for the labelling process [65]. These decisions can compromise the ecological validity of the detection process, for instance, if learners are asked to verbalize their affective states while interacting with the e-learning system or attached physiological sensors are used, but these decisions are necessary for deriving models that can be introduced and evaluated subsequently in more ecologically valid situations [54].

Practice shows that the labeling is either performed by the learner during the interaction with the system [10, 14, 16, 30, 35, 38, 70, 71, 80, 86, 96], by the learner retrospectively [16, 30, 34, 71], or by the researcher during [16, 30, 34, 39, 62, 81] or after the interaction [1, 16, 24, 31, 80]. With respect to emotional labeling by the researcher while the learner interacts with the system, BROMP standardized procedure is used [30, 39, 62]. In most cased, the labelling is done in terms of a set of predefined categories, being boredom, confusion, frustration, engagement/flow and delight/pleasure/happiness/joy/excitement the most commonly used ones, which except for the lower cases of curiosity, is consistent with findings reported elsewhere [13]. In few cases, a dimensional labelling (in terms of valence [10, 70, 80] or arousal [42, 80] is done. In one work, the physiological signal (i.e. electodermal activity) was used as the emotional labeler [42]. In one work, labels are mapped to the specification W3C EmotionML [71].

Few systems consider personality traits. When done [10, 19, 32, 38, 47, 70, 77, 81], standardize questionnares following the FFM are used (e.g., IPIP-NEO, mini-IPIP, NEO-PI-R). Other personality traits, such as the general self-efficacy scale [85] have been collected in [77, 81]. No works have been found to automatically detect the personality from the learners' interactions.

Regarding affective interventions, not many systems provide them (although some give suggestions about how to deliver them (e.g., [10, 24, 34, 35, 38, 47, 67, 71, 80]), but when done, it is either delivered through different kinds of feedback depending on the learner's personality [19] or emotional states [30, 48, 68, 81, 86] and/or by synthesizing affective elements through the generation of facial expressions, the inflection of speech, and the modulation of posture in the case of embodied conversational agents or learning companions [16, 31, 32, 91, 96]. Another way to respond to the learners' affective state is through the physical ambient in which the learner is embedded, exploring the use of the different sensorial channels with ambient intelligence [77].

In this respect, determining in an automatic way the best tutoring response to specific learners' affective states (including when to intervene and what affective support to provide) is a difficult task, but might not require a very robust diagnosis of learner affect [66]. Anyway, experiments have shown that affective-based interventions do change the learners behavior, but the appropriate strategy has to be applied, as well as the appropriate time and type of feedback to success on the intervention (for instance, mirroring the student emotion might not be the right response for all emotions) [97]. Thus, elicitation methods that involve educators in identifying educationally oriented recommendations are required to elicit the appropriate affective support, such as the TORMES methodology [78].

From this review, it can be concluded that there is not a clear approach regarding emotions detection in terms of data sources, labelling and modelling. In trun, personality features are statically used (when considered). And intervention opportunities are still to be explored. Hence, there is still a large way to go for affective computing research in educational scenarios. Nonetheless, other issues that might worth also to be explored are discussed in the next section.

13.3 Open Issues

Additional open issues regarding emotions and personality in e-learning systems that have not emerged during the review carried out in the previous section, and which might worth be explored in future research, are commented here.

13.3.1 Learning Styles and Affective States

In the educational domain, learning styles can be considered a specific personality trait, being the Index of Learning Styles (ILS)[1] by Felder and Soloman the most commonly used. In fact, it seems to be some correlation between personality traits and learning styles [43]. However, no evidence has been found in the literature that learning styles influence affective states, even when both are computed in the same system [40, 46]. Thus, the field requires experimental studies that can provide some insight into this question, including (if appropriate) dynamic detectors of learning styles as their stability is controversial [23].

[1] http://www4.ncsu.edu/unity/lockers/users/f/felder/public/ILSpage.html.

13.3.2 Emotions and Personality in Collaborative Learning

Emotions can emerge in collaboration scenarios and influence learning [36]. They can be very motivating and rewarding for learners [37], and transferred among them [4]. Thus, they have to be considered when managing the collaboration in e-learning scenarios. For instance, emotions have been measured in the different stages of the collaborative logical framework approach [76]. In turn, in order to design order to design group learning activities, a framework that integrates techniques for affect recognition using physiology and text has been proposed [8]. Another proposal is to suggest collaborative activities to groups of students according to the group members' emotions [68]. In addition, personality traits also play a key role in social and collaborative scenarios since personality can modulate the way the student participates in a given situation [89].

However, still little attention has been paid on understanding the role of affective and social factors when learning collaboratively online, and there is still a need for further development of methodological approaches. To provide some background on social emotions, see Chap. 2.

13.3.3 Emotions and Personality in Inclusive Learning

While learning should be an engagement experience, this is more critical when students have learning disabilities, which might imply additional efforts on the learners to develop the required learning strategies [57]. Thus, emotional states such as frustration are more likely to happen, and thus, more important to be detected in these situations.

Emotional management is also very relevant in autism spectrum disorders [22]. Affective states of children with autism spectrum disorders have already been experimentally detected via physiology-based affect recognition technique [49]. The use of embodied conversational agents can also help to understand and influence the affective dynamic of learning and improve their social and emotional functioning [55].

In addition, people with bipolar disorders can also benefit from emotion detectors as they require mechanisms to get insight in their own emotional state [42].

Moreover, there exist diverse challenges for inclusive emotions detection in educational scenarios, especially when recording facial expressions and analyzing the typing behavior in visually impaired learners [79]. The former refers to eye and head blindisms (repetitive, self-stimulating mannerisms made by blind people unconsciously), which should be taken into account when processing the data. The later implies detecting the purpose of each keystroke (data input vs. content navigation), and processing it accordingly.

Personality computing is also likely to play a major role in detecting disorders like paranoia and schizophrenia [93] that typically interfere with personality [94] and can impact learning [20].

13.3.4 Gathering Affective Data in a Non-intrusive Way

In addition to the low intrusive hardware sensors already reported by Picard et al. [64] (i.e. camera, posture analysis seat, pressure mouse and wireless skin conductance sensor), current technological advances on wearable devices [56] and e-textiles [26] can facilitate the low-cost and low-intrusive gathering of physiological and behavioral data that can be used to infer learners' affective states. In this respect, as commented in Chap. 8, mobile devices allow in-situ sampling of human behavior, and provide researchers with ecologically valid and timely assessments of a person's psychological state at previously unimaginable granularity and scale.

Nonetheless, sensor-free affect detection should also be explored, as recent research in educational data mining shows that some emotions such as frustration can be recognized from log data [95].

13.3.5 Big Data Processing of Affective Multimodal Flows

Since affective computing requires a large computational infrastructure for data processing and analysis, big data on cloud computing should be considered [33]. Big data technologies provide an opportunity to extract insightful multimodal emotional information flows of continuously gathered from mobile devices as it can deal with the processing of data that is potentially unstructured, needs to be processed at high velocity, and is growing so big in size that it becomes impractical to handle using traditional data processing systems [3]. In fact, the potential of big data in education is large due to its ability to mine unstructured and informal connections and information produced by students, including sensors and location-based data, which can allow educators to uncover useful facts and patterns they were not able to identify in the past [18].

13.3.6 Providing More Interactive and Contextual Affective Feedback

As learning takes place in diverse and rich environments, the incorporation of contextual information about the learner when providing personalized feedback can improve the system response to the learner's needs [92]. Thus, the challenge here is to identify the appropriate affective support to be delivered to the learners by taking advantage of contextual information that can be used to detect learners' affective state and personality traits.

To advance in this issue, some steps have been carried out applying TORMES elicitation methodology [78] to analyze the feasibility of interactive context-aware affective educational recommendations using ambient intelligence [77]. In particular, as commented in Sect. 13.2, stressful situations have been detected (using the Wizard of Oz user centred design method) from physiological signals, facial expressions, body movements and speech, and these situations have been affectively managed by delivering sensorial feedback to the learner through different sensorial channels (e.g., sight, hearing, touch). Further details on how this sensorial support can be implemented are provided in [82].

13.3.7 Interoperable Support for Ubiquitous Affective Learning

Affective detection technologies and intervention support algorithms embedded into mobile infrastructures should provide in a near future ubiquitous learning experiences affectively. For this, interoperability between the components involved in the affective adaptation process needs to be supported, as in non-affective educational scenarios [75].

In this sense, there exist description languages to model emotions (i.e. the W3C Emotion ML [84]) and personality (i.e., the PersonalityML 2.0 [58]). Other specifications that might be of interest are the Attention Profiling Mark-up Language (APML)[2] and the Contextualized Attention Metadata (CAM).[3] They need to be integrated with educational specifications such as those proposed by the IMS Global Learning Consortium[4] as well as with the standards and specifications used in big data infrastructures.

13.3.8 Affective Support in Psychomotor Learning

According to psycho-educational theories, learning not only involves cognitive and affective aspects, but also psychomotor aspects, which are related to actions and require the acquisition of motor skills [6]. In fact, there are some kind of learning activities such as playing a musical instrument, doing a medical operation, playing sports, etc. that require learning motor skills in order to properly perform them. Adaptive e-learning systems can be built to support psychomotor learning [73].

---

[2] APML: http://apml.areyoupayingattention.com/.

[3] CAM: https://sites.google.com/site/camschema/home.

[4] IMS: http://www.imsglobal.org/.

These smart learning environments should provide a holistic personalized support to learners involving cognitive, affective, and psychomotor aspects, and thus, be able to deal with learners' movements, both to reinforce cognitive learning and to support motor skills acquisition, and where affective issues are also supported to keep motivation and engagement [74].

Considering the affective state of the learner while learning motor skills is critical in order to deal with the trade-off between learning and performance [87]. In particular, actions that can produce relatively permanent changes in behaviour with long-term retention and transfer introduce more performance errors, and thus, might frustrate the learner. Performance errors are reduced if the activity is reproduced over and over, but this also increases boredom. Hence, special attention to the affective state is needed also when learning motor skills.

13.4 Concluding Remarks

The review carried out in this chapter (consisting in a detailed analysis of 26 publications) has illustrated how affective computing has been applied to develop diverse adaptive e-learning systems. Emotions are more widely considered than personality traits, and they are also more diverse. Emotions are usually detected during the learner interaction using supervised classification methods from a wide variety of emotional sources that are manually annotated by learners or researchers, while personality, when considered, is statically gathered with FFM questionnaires. Few works report the delivery of interventions, as they require the existence of accurate affective (and personality) detectors (and this still has many open issues regarding data sources, labelling and modelling). Nonetheless, learner's direct input or user centered design methods like the Wizard of Oz are being used in parallel to explore intervention opportunities and thus, advance the research on the impact on the learners of the affective support provided.

Thus, from the current trends, many challenges exist to provide affective support in educational scenarios. In addition, there are other issues not emerging from this review that might also be relevant to explore. Some of them have been discussed in this chapter. On the one hand, from the learners' perspective, future research could focus on investigating if learning styles (which can be considered a kind of personality trait in the educational domain) influence somehow the affective state of the learner. It could also focus on providing a collaborative and inclusive affective learning experience since (i) the learner might not be learning alone, and (ii) learners are functionally diverse. On the other hand, from a technological perspective, there are several open issues regarding the gathering data in a non-intrusive way, processing (with big data techniques) multimodal flows of affective data, and providing more interactive and contextual affective feedback through interoperable infrastructures in order to support ubiquitous affective learning experiences. Resulting adaptive learning environment are expected to provide a holistic personalized support to learners involving cognitive, affective, and psychomotor aspects.

Finally, in addition to those open issues, and in line with affective computing research in general [15], further efforts are also required in this domain to support naturalistic learning experiences into the wild by assuring authenticity (naturalness of training and validation data), utility (states detected are relevant in the real-world contexts of use) and generalization (maintain its level of accuracy when applied to new individuals and new or related contexts).

Acknowledgments The research carried out to produce this chapter is partially supported by the Spanish Ministry of Economy and Competence under grants numbers TIN2011-29221-C03-01 (MAMIPEC project: Multimodal approaches for Affective Modelling in Inclusive Personalized Educational scenarios in intelligent Contexts) and TIN2014-59641-C2-2-P (BIG-AFF: Fusing multimodal Big Data to provide low-intrusive AFFective and cognitive support in learning contexts).

References

1. Afzal, S., Robinson, P.: Modelling affect in learning environments—motivation and methods. In: IEEE 10th International Conference on Advanced Learning Technologies (ICALT), 2010, pp. 438, 442, 5–7 July (2010). doi:10.1109/ICALT.2010.127
2. Allport, G.W.: Personality. Holt, New York (1937)
3. Baimbetov, Y., Khalil, I., Steinbauer, M., Anderst-Kotsis, G.: Using Big data for emotionally intelligent mobile services through multi-modal emotion recognition. Inclusive smart cities and e-health. In: Lecture Notes in Computer Science, vol. 9102, pp. 127–138 (2015)
4. Barsade, S.: The ripple effect: emotional contagion and its influence on group behavior. Adm. Sci. Q. **47**, 644–675 (2002)
5. Blanchard, E.G., Volfson, B., Hong, Y.J. Lajoie, S.P.: Affective artificial intelligence in education: from detection to adaptation. In: Proceedings of the 2009 conference on artificial intelligence in education: building learning systems that care: from knowledge representation to affective modelling (AIED 2009), pp. 81–88 (2009)
6. Bloom, B.S.: Taxonomy of educational objectives. In: Handbook 1: Cognitive domain. New York, NY: David McKay (1956)
7. Calvo, R., D'Mello, S.K., Gratch, J., Kappas, A.: The Oxford Handbook of Affective Computing. Oxford University Press, New York, NY (2014)
8. Calvo, R.A.: Incorporating affect into educational design patterns and frameworks. In: Proceedings—2009 9th IEEE international conference on advanced learning technologies, ICALT 2009, pp. 377–381 (2009)
9. Calvo, R.A., D'Mello, S.K.: Affect detection: an interdisciplinary review of models, methods, and their applications. T. Affect. Comput. **1**(1), 18–37 (2010)
10. Conati C., Maclaren H.: Modeling user affect from causes and effects. In: Proceedings of UMAP 2009, First and Seventeenth International Conference on User Modeling, Adaptation and Personalization. Springer (2009)
11. Conati, C., Zhou, X.: Modelling students' emotions from cognitive appraisal in educational games. Intell. Tutor. Syst. (2002)
12. Conati, C., Marsella, S., Paiva, A.: Affective interactions: the computer in the affective loop. In: Riedl, J., Jameson, A. (eds.) Proceedings of the 10th International Conference on Intelligent User Interfaces, ACM, New York, NY, 7 (2005)
13. D'Mello, S.: A selective meta-analysis on the relative incidence of discrete affective states during learning with technology. J. Educ. Psychol. **105**, 1082–1099 (2013)
14. D'Mello, S.K.: Emotional rollercoasters: day differences in affect incidence during learning. In: The Twenty-Seventh International Flairs Conference (2014)

15. D'Mello, S., Kory, J.: A review and meta-analysis of multimodal affect detection systems. ACM Comput. Surv. **47**(3) (Article 43, Publication date: February 2015) (2015)
16. D'Mello, S., Graesser, A.: AutoTutor and affective autotutor: learning by talking with cognitively and emotionally intelligent computers that talk back. ACM Trans. Interact. Intell. Syst. 2, 4, Article 23, 39 p (2012)
17. Dahlbäck, N., Jönsson, A., Ahrenberg, L.: Wizard of Oz studies: why and how. Knowl.-Based Syst. **6**(4), 258–266 (1993)
18. Daniel, B.K., Butson, R.J.: Foundations of big data and analytics in higher education. In: International Conference on Analytics Driven Solutions, IBM Centre for Business Analytics and Performance, University of Ottawa, Ottawa, Canada, September 29–30 (2014)
19. Dennis, M., Masthoff, J., Mellish, C.: Adapting progress feedback and emotional support to learner personality. Int. J. Artif. Intell. Educ. **26**(2) (2016). http://link.springer.com/article/10.1007%2Fs40593-015-0059-7
20. Dugan, J.E.: Second language acquisition and schizophrenia. Second Lang. Res. **30**(3), 307–321 (2014)
21. Ekman, P.: An argument for basic emotions. Cogn. Emot. **6**(3–4), 169–200 (1992)
22. El Kaliouby, R., Picard, R., Baron-Cohen, S.: Affective computing and autism. Ann. New York Acad. Sci. **1093**, 228–248 (2006)
23. El-Bishouty, M.M., Chang, T.W., Graf, S., Kinshuk, and Chen, N.S.: Smart e-course recommender based on learning styles. J. Comput. Educ. **1**(1), 99–111 (2014)
24. Felipe, D.A.M., Gutierrez, K.I.N., Quiros, E.C.M., Vea, L.A.: Towards the development of intelligent agent for novice C/C++ programmers through affective analysis of event logs. Proc. Int. MultiConference Eng. Comput. Sci. **1** (2012)
25. Fleeson, W.: Toward a structure-and process-integrated view of personality: traits as density distributions of states. J. Pers. Soc. Psychol. **80**(6), 1011 (2001)
26. Fleury, A., Sugar, M., Chau, T.: E-textiles in clinical rehabilitation: a scoping review. Electronics **4**, 173–203 (2015)
27. Forbes-Riley, K., Litman, D.: Adapting to multiple affective states in spoken dialogue. In: Proceedings of the 13th Annual Meeting of the Special Interest Group on Discourse and Dialogue (SIGDIAL), Seoul, South Korea, pp. 217–226 July (2012)
28. Gosling, S.D., Augustine, A.A., Vazire, S., Holtzman, N., Gaddis, S.: Manifestations of personality in online social networks: self-reported facebook-related behaviors and observable profile information. Cyberpsychol. Behav. Soc. Netw. **14**, 483–488 (2011). doi:10.1089/cyber.2010.0087
29. Gosling, S.D., Mehl, M.R., Pennebaker, J.W.: Personality in its natural habitat: manifestations and implicit folk theories of personality in daily life. J. Pers. Soc. Psychol. **90**(5), 862–877 (2006)
30. Grawemeyer, B., Mavrikis, M., Holmes, W., Hansen, A., Loibl, K., Gutiérrez-Santos, S.: The impact of feedback on students' affective states. International Workshop on Affect, Meta-Affect, Data and Learning. Madrid, Spain, AMADL (2015)
31. Gutica M., Conati C.: Student emotions with an edu game: a detailed analysis. In: Proceedings of ACII 2013, 5th International Conference on Affective Computing and Intelligent Interaction, IEEE, pp. 534–539 (2013)
32. Harley, J.M., Carter, K. C., Papaioannou, N., Bouchet, F., Landis, R.S., Azevedo, R., Karabachian, L.: Examining the predictive relationship between personality and emotion traits and learners' agent-direct emotions. AIED 2015, LNAI 9112, pp. 145–154 (2015)
33. Hashem, I.A.T., Yaqoob, I., Anuar, N.B., Mokhtar, S., Gani, A., Khan, S.U.: The rise of big data on cloud computing: review and open research issues. Inform. Syst. **47**, pp 98–115 (2015)
34. Janning, R., Schatten, C., Schmidt-Thieme, L.: Feature analysis for affect recognition supporting task sequencing in adaptive intelligent tutoring systems. Open learning and teaching in educational communities. Lecture Notes in Computer Science **8719**, 179–192 (2014)
35. Jaques, N., Conati, C., Harley, J. and Azevedo, R.: Predicting affect from gaze data during interaction with an intelligent tutoring system. In: Proceedings of ITS 2014, 12th International Conference on Intelligent Tutoring Systems, pp. 29–28 (2014)

36. Järvenoja, H., Järvelä, S.: Emotion control in collaborative learning situations: do students regulate emotions evoked by social challenges? Brit. J. Educ. Psychol. **79**(3), 463–481 (2009)
37. Jones, A., Issroff, K.: Learning technologies: affective and social issues in computer-supported collaborative learning. Comput. Educ. **44**(4), 395–408 (2005)
38. Jraidi, I., Chaouachi, M., Frasson, C.: A hierarchical probabilistic framework for recognizing learners' interaction experience trends and emotions. Adv. Human-Comput. Interact. **2014**(632630), 16 p (2014). doi:10.1155/2014/632630
39. Kai, S., Paquette, L., Baker, R.S., Bosch, N., D'Mello, S., Ocumpaugh, J., Shute, V., Ventura, M.: A comparison of face-based and interaction-based affect detectors in physics playground. In: Proceedings of the 8th International Conference on Educational Data Mining, pp. 77–84 (2015)
40. Khan, F.A., Graf, S., Weippl, E.R., Iqbal, T., Tjoa, A.M.: Role of learning styles and affective states in web-based adaptive learning environments. In: Proceedings of the World Conference on Educational Multimedia, Hypermedia and Telecommunications (ED-Media 2010), June 2010, AACE Press, Toronto, Canada, pp. 3896–3905 (2010)
41. Khan, I.A., Brinkman, W.-P., Fine, N., Hierons, R.M.: Measuring personality from keyboard and mouse use. In: Abascal, J., Fajardo, I., Oakley, I. (eds.) Proceedings of the 15th European Conference on Cognitive ergonomics: The Ergonomics of Cool Interaction (ECCE '08), ACM, New York, NY, USA, Article 38, 8 p (2008)
42. Khan, I.A., Brinkman, W.-P., Hierons, R.: Towards estimating computer users' mood from interaction behaviour with keyboard and mouse. Front. Comput. Sci. 1–12 (2013)
43. Kim, J., Lee, A., Ryu, H.: Personality and its effects on learning performance: design guidelines for an adaptive e-learning system based on a user model. Int. J. Indus. Ergon. **43**, 450–461 (2013)
44. Kolakowska, A.: A review of emotion recognition methods based on keystroke dynamics and mouse movements. In: 2013 The 6th International Conference on Human System Interaction (HSI), pp. 548–555 (2013)
45. Kort, B., Reilly, R., Picard, R.W.: An affective model of interplay between emotions and learning: reengineering educational pedagogy-building a learning companion. In: Proceedings of the IEEE International Conference on Advanced Learning Technologies, Los Alamitos: CA: IEEE Computer Society Press, pp. 43–46 (2001)
46. Leontidis, M., Halatsis, C.: Integrating Learning styles and personality traits into an affective model to support learner's learning. Advances in web based learning—ICWL 2009. Lecture Notes in Computer Science **5686**, 225–234 (2009)
47. Leontidis, M., Halatsis, C., Grigoriadou, M.: Using an affective multimedia learning framework for distance learning to motivate the learner effectively. IJLT **6**(3), 223–250 (2011)
48. Litman, D., Forbes-Riley, K.: Evaluating a spoken dialogue system that detects and adapts to user affective states. In: Proceedings 15th Annual SIGdial Meeting on Discourse and Dialogue (SIGDIAL), Philadelphia, PA, June (2014)
49. Liu, C., Conn, K., Sarkar, N., Stone, W.: Physiology-based affect recognition for computer-assisted intervention of children with autism spectrum disorder. Int. J. Human-Comput. Stud. **66**, 662–677 (2008)
50. Lopatovska, I.: Researching emotion: challenges and solutions. In Proceedings of the 2011 iConference (iConference'11). ACM, New York, NY, USA, 225–229 (2011). doi:10.1145/1940761.1940792
51. Mairesse, F., Walker, M.A., Mehl, M.R., Moore, R.K.: Using linguistic cues for the automatic recognition of personality in conversation and text. J. Artif. Intell. Res. **30**, 457–500 (2007)
52. Matthews, G., Campbell, S.E.: Sustained performance under overload: personality and individual differences in stress and coping. Theor. Issues Ergon. Sci. **10**(5), 417–442 (2009)
53. Mauss, I.B., Robinson, M.D.: Measures of emotion: a review. Cogn. Emot. **23**(2), 209–237 (2009)
54. Mavrikis, M., D'Mello, S.K., Porayska-Pomsta, K., Cocea, M., Graesser, A.: Modeling affect by mining students' interactions within learning environments. Handb. Educ. Data Mining, pp. 231–244 (2010)

55. Messinger, D.S., Lobo Duvivier, L., Warren, Z.E., Mahoor, M., Baker, J., Warlaumont, A.S., Ruvolo, P.: Affective computing, emotional development, and autism. In: The Oxford Handbook of Affective Computing, pp. 516–536 (2014)
56. Mukhopadhyay, S.C.: Wearable sensors for human activity monitoring: a review. IEEE Sens. J. **15**, 1321–1330 (2015)
57. Murray, B., Silver-Pacuila, H., Helsel, F.I.: Improving basic mathematics instruction: promising technology resources for students with special needs. Technol. Action **2**(5), 1–6 (2007)
58. Nunes, M.A.S.N., Bezerra, J.S., Oliveira, A.A.: PersonalityML: a markup language to standardize the user personality in recommender systems. Revista GEINTEC- Gestão, Inovação e Tecnologias **2**, 255–273 (2012)
59. Ocumpaugh, J., Baker, R.S., Rodrigo, M.M.T.: Baker rodrigo ocumpaugh monitoring protocol (BROMP) 2.0 technical and training manual. Technical Report (2015)
60. Ortigosa, A., Carro, R.M., Quiroga, J.I.: Predicting user personality by mining social interactions in Facebook. J. Comput. Syst. Sci. **80**(1), 57–71 (2014)
61. Ortony, A., Clore, G.L., Collins, A.: The Cognitive Structure of Emotions. Cambridge University Press, Cambridge (1988)
62. Paquette, L., Jonathan Rowe, J., Ryan Baker, R., Bradford Mott, B., James Lester, J., Jeanine Defalco, J., Keith Brawner, K., Robert Sottilare, R., Vasiliki Georgoulas, V.: Sensor-free or sensor-full: a comparison of data modalities in multi-channel affect detection. In: Proceedings of the Eighth International Conference on Educational Data Mining, pp. 93–100, Madrid, Spain (2015)
63. Pekrun, R., Elliot, A.J., Maier, M.A.: Achievement goals and achievement emotions: testing a model of their joint relations with academic performance. J. Educ. Psychol. **101**, 115–135 (2009)
64. Picard, R.W., Papert, S., Bender, W., Blumberg, B., Breazeal, C., Cavallo, D., Machover, T., Resnick, M., Roy, D., Strohecker, C.: Affective learning – a manifesto. BT Technol. J. **22**(4), 253–269 (2004)
65. Porayska-Pomsta, K., Mavrikis, M.: D'Mello, S.k., Conati, C., Baker, R. Knowledge elicitation methods for affect modelling in education. J. Artif. Intell. Educ **22**(3), 107–140 (2013)
66. Porayska-Pomsta, K., Mavrikis, M., Pain, H.: Diagnosing and acting on student affect: the tutor's perspective. User Model. User-Adapt. Interact. **18**(1–2), 125–173 (2008)
67. Robison, J.L., McQuiggan, S.W., Lester, J.C.: Developing empirically based student personality profiles for affective feedback models. Intell. Tutor. Syst. **285–295**, 2010 (2010)
68. Rodriguez, P., Ortigosa, A., Carro, R.M.: Detecting and making use of emotions to enhance student motivation in e-learning environments. Int. J. Continuing Eng. Educ. Life Long Learn. **24**(2), 168–183 (2014)
69. Rusting, C.L., Larsen, R.J.: Extraversion, neuroticism, and susceptibility to positive and negative affect: a test of two theoretical models. Pers. Indiv. Differ. **22**(5), 607–612 (1997)
70. Sabourin, J.L., Lester, J.C.: Affect and engagement in game-based learning environments. IEEE Trans. Affect. Comput. **5**(1), 45–56 (2014)
71. Salmeron-Majadas, S., Arevalillo-Herráez, M., Santos, O.C., Saneiro, M., Cabestrero, R., Quirós, P., Arnau, D., Boticario, J.G.: Filtering of spontaneous and low intensity emotions in educational contexts. AIED 2015. LNCS 9112, pp. 429–438 (2015)
72. Saneiro, M., Santos, O.C., Salmeron-Majadas, S., Boticario, J.G.: Towards emotion detection in educational scenarios from facial expressions and body movements through multimodal approaches. Sci. World J. **2014**, Article ID 484873, 14 p (2014). doi:10.1155/2014/484873
73. Santos, O.C.: Training the body: The potential of AIED to support personalized motor skills learning. Special Issue "The next 25 Years: How advanced, interactive educational technologies will change the world". Int. J. Artif. Intell. Educ. Springer. June 2016, **26**(2), 730–755 (2016a). doi:10.1007/s40593-016-0103-2
74. Santos, O.C.: Beyond cognitive and affective issues. Tangible recommendations for psychomotor personalized learning. In: Spector, J.M., Lockee, B.B., Childress, M.D. (eds.) Learning, Design, and Technology. An International Compendium of Theory, Research, Practice, and Policy. Springer, (2016b, in press). doi:10.1007/978-3-319-17727-4_8-1

75. Santos, O.C., Boticario, J.G.: Requirements for Semantic educational recommender systems in formal e-learning scenarios. Algorithms **4**(2), 131–154 (2011)
76. Santos, O.C., Boticario, J.G.: Involving users to improve the collaborative logical framework. Sci. World J. **2014**, Article ID 893525, 15 p (2014). doi:10.1155/2014/893525
77. Santos, O.C., Saneiro, M., Boticario, J., Rodriguez-Sanchez, C.: Toward interactive context-aware affective educational recommendations in computer assisted language learning. New Rev. Hypermedia Multimedia **22**(1–2), 27–57 (2016). http://www.tandfonline.com/toc/tham20/current
78. Santos, O.C., Boticario, J.G.: Practical guidelines for designing and evaluating educationally oriented recommendations. Comput. Educ. **81**, 354–374 (2015). doi:10.1016/j.compedu.2014.10.008
79. Santos, O.C., Rodriguez-Ascaso, A., Boticario, J.G., Salmeron-Majadas, S., Quirós, P., Cabestrero, R.: Challenges for inclusive affective detection in educational scenarios. In: Universal Access in Human-Computer Interaction. Design Methods, Tools, and Interaction Techniques for eInclusion. Lecture Notes in Computer Science **8009**, pp. 566–575 (2013)
80. Santos, O.C., Salmeron-Majadas, S., Boticario, J.G.: Emotions detection from math exercises by combining several data sources. In: Lane, H.C., Yacef, K., Mostow, J., Pavlik, P. (eds.) Artificial Intelligence in Education, pp. 742–745. Springer, Berlin Heidelberg (2013)
81. Santos, O.C., Saneiro, M., Salmeron-Majadas, S., Boticario, J.G.: A methodological approach to eliciting affective educational recommendations. In: 2014 IEEE 14th International Conference on Advanced Learning Technologies (ICALT), pp. 529–533 (2014)
82. Santos, O.C., Uria-Rivas, R., Rodriguez-Sanchez, M.C., Boticario, J.G.: An open sensing and acting platform for context-aware affective support in ambient intelligent educational settings. IEEE Sens. J. **16**(10), 3865–3874 May 15 (2016)
83. Scherer, K.R.: What are emotions? and how can they be measured? Soc. Sci. Inform. **44**(4), 695–729 (2005)
84. Schröeder, M., Baggia, P., Burkhardt, F., Pelachaud, C., Peter, C., Zovato, E.: Emotion markup language (EmotionML) 1.0. W3C Candidate Recommendation 10, 2012 May (2012)
85. Schwarcer, R.: Measurement of perceived self-efficacy. Psychometric scales for crosscultural research. Freie Universit, Berlin (1993)
86. Shen, L., Wang, M., Shen, R.: Affective e-learning: using emotional data to improve learning in pervasive learning environment. Educ. Technol. Soc. (ETS) **12**(2), 176–189 (2009)
87. Soderstrom, N.C., Bjork, R.A.: Learning versus performance: An integrative review. Perspect. Psychol. Sci. **10**(2), 176–199 (2015)
88. Soldz, S., Vaillant, G.: The big five personality traits and the life course: a 45 years longitudinal study. J. Res. Pers. **33**, 208–232 (1998)
89. Solimeno, A., Mebane, M.E., Tomai, M., Francescato, D.: The influence of students and teachers characteristics on the efficacy of face-to-face and computer supported collaborative learning. Comput. Educ. **51**(1), 109–128 (2008)
90. Vandewaetere, M., Desmet, P., Clarebout, G. The contribution of learner characteristics in the development of computer-based adaptive learning environments. Comput. Human Behav. **27**(1), January 2011, pp. 118–130, ISSN 0747-5632 (2011). http://dx.doi.org/10.1016/j.chb.2010.07.038
91. VanLehn, K., Burleson, W., Girard, S., Chavez-Echeagaray, M.E., Gonzalez-Sanchez, J., Hidalgo-Pontet, Y., Zhang, L.: The affective meta-tutoring project: lessons learned. intelligent tutoring systems. Lecture Notes in Computer Science **8474**, 84–93 (2014)
92. Verbert, K., Manouselis, N., Xavier, O., Wolpers, M., Drachsler, H., Bosnic, I., Duval, E.: Context-aware recommender systems for learning: a survey and future challenges. IEEE Trans. Learn. Technol. **5**(4), 318–335 (2012)
93. Vinciarelli, A., Mohammadi, G.: A survey of personality computing. IEEE Trans. Affective Comput. (2014)
94. Warren, F.: Treatment of personality disorders. In: Corr, P., Matthews, G. (eds.) The Cambridge Handbook of Personality Psychology. Cambridge University Press, Cambridge, U.K., pp. 799–819 (2009)

95. Wixon, M., Arroyo, I., Muldner, K., Burleson, W., Rai, D.: The opportunities and limitations of scaling up sensor-free affect detection—educational data mining (2014)
96. Woolf, B., Arroyo, I., Cooper, D., Burleson, W., Muldner, K.: Affective tutors: automatic detection of and response to student emotion. Adv. Intell. Tutor. Syst. Stud. Comput. Intell. **308**, 207–227 (2010)
97. Woolf, B., Burleson, W., Arroyo, I., Dragon, T., Cooper, D., Picard, R.: Affect-aware tutors: recognising and responding to student affect. Int. J. Learn. Technol. **4**(3/4), 129–163, Inderscience Enterprises Ltd., (2009)

Chapter 14
Emotion-Based Matching of Music to Places

Marius Kaminskas and Francesco Ricci

Abstract Music and places can both trigger emotional responses in people. This chapter presents a technical approach that exploits the congruence of emotions raised by music and places to identify music tracks that match a place of interest (POI). Such technique can be used in location-aware music recommendation services. For instance, a mobile city guide may play music related to the place visited by a tourist, or an in-car navigation system may adapt music to places the car is passing by. We address the problem of matching music to places by employing a controlled vocabulary of emotion labels. We hypothesize that the commonality of these emotions could provide, among other approaches, the base for establishing a degree of match between a place and a music track, i.e., finding music that "feels right" for the place. Through a series of user studies we show the correctness of our hypothesis. We compare the proposed emotion-based matching approach with a personalized approach where the music track is matched to the music preferences of the user, and to a knowledge-based approach which matches music to places based on metadata (e.g., matching music that was composed during the same period that the place of interest was built in). We show that when evaluating the goodness of fit between places and music, personalization is not sufficient and that the users perceive the emotion-based music suggestions as better fitting the places. The results also suggest that emotion-based and knowledge-based techniques can be combined to complement each other.

M. Kaminskas (✉)
Insight Centre for Data Analytics, University College Cork, Cork, Ireland
e-mail: marius.kaminskas@insight-centre.org

F. Ricci
Faculty of Computer Science, Free University of Bozen-Bolzano, Bozen-Bolzano, Italy
e-mail: francesco.ricci@unibz.it

M. Tkalčič et al. (eds.), *Emotions and Personality in Personalized Services*,
Human–Computer Interaction Series, DOI 10.1007/978-3-319-31413-6_14

14.1 Introduction

Music is generally considered an emotion-oriented form of content—it creates an emotional response in the listener, and therefore can be described by the evoked emotions. For instance, most people will agree with a description of Rossini's "William Tell Overture" as *happy* and *energetic*, and Stravinsky's "Firebird" as *calm* and *anxious* [18]. This music typically suggests, triggers those emotions in listeners.

Similarly to music, places can also trigger emotional responses in visitors [4] and therefore are perceived as associated to their generated emotions. Moreover, certain types of places have been shown to have a positive effect on people's emotional health [14]. This phenomenon is particularly relevant for tourism: places (destinations) have become objects of consumption (much like books, movies, or music in the entertainment domain). Tourists "gaze upon particular objects, such as piers, towers, old buildings, or countryside ...with a much greater sensitivity to visual elements of landscape and townscape than is normally found in everyday life" [39]. Therefore, emotional responses to places are particularly strong in tourists.

In our work, we envision a scenario where music can augment the experience of places by letting places "sound with music", the music that is perceived by people as the "right" one for the place. This scenario is suggested by the observations made above, namely that both music and places are naturally associated with emotions, and therefore, given a place, one can identify music that is associated with the same emotions that are associated to the place.

Besides, music is strongly connected to places for cultural and social reasons. Music is a cultural dimension and a human activity that contributes to give meaning to a place. For instance, consider how important flamenco music is for a city like Seville in Spain, or opera compositions for Vienna in Austria. We all deem music as profoundly related to and contributing to the image of such destinations. In fact, many music compositions have been motivated or inspired by specific places. Consider for instance the impressionistic compositions by Claude Debussy, such as "La Mer" or "Preludes". They are all dedicated to places, e.g., "La Puerta de Vino" (The Wine Gate) and "La Terrasse Des Audiences Du Clair De Lune" (The Terrace of Moonlit Audiences).

Based on the observations made above, it is meaningful to explore the relationships between music and places and in particular to find music that "sounds well for a place" (see Sect. 14.2.3). However, automatically finding music artists and compositions related to a given place is not a simple task for a computer program. It requires knowledge of both domains, and a methodology for establishing relations between items in the two domains, which is clearly a difficult problem to be solved automatically by an intelligent computer-based system [16, 25]. In this chapter, we describe a technical approach that exploits the congruence of emotion-based descriptions of music and places of interest (POIs) to establish a degree of match between a place and a music track.

The proposed technique can be applied in location-aware music recommendation services. For instance, a mobile city guide may provide an enhanced presentation of the POI visited by a tourist, and play music that is related, i.e., emotionally associated to the place (e.g., Mozart in Salzburg, or a Bach's fugue in a Gothic Cathedral). Other examples include a car entertainment and navigation system that adapts music to the place the car is passing by, or a tourism website where the information on travel destinations is enhanced through a matching music accompaniment. Such information services can be used to enhance the user's travel experience, to provide rich and engaging cultural information services, and to increase the sales of holiday destinations or music content.

This chapter describes the emotion-based matching of music to places which has been developed and evaluated through a series of user studies [5, 22]. As a first step of our research, we have shown that a set of emotions can be employed by users to describe both music tracks and POIs [5]. We have adopted tags to represent the emotional characteristics of music and POIs and used this common representation language to match and retrieve music that fits a place. We decided to use tags because of the popularity of social tagging and user-generated tagging data are still growing on the Web [35, 38]. Several web mining and machine learning techniques have been developed to handle available tagging data. These include tag-based content retrieval and recommendation solutions, which are relevant for implementing our target functionality of retrieving music matching a given place.

Subsequently, we have evaluated the proposed music-to-POI matching technique in a mobile guide prototype that suggests and plays music tracks while users are visiting POIs in the city of Bolzano (Italy) [5]. The evaluation results show that users agree with the music-to-POI matches produced using our technique.

Having validated the usefulness of emotion tags for matching music to places, we have implemented a machine learning technique to scale up the tagging process. In fact, in the first experiments the music was tagged manually by users and this requires a consistent user effort. So, in order to reduce this cost we have shown that one can employ state-of-the-art music auto-taggers, and evaluated the performance of our matching approach applied to automatically tagged music against alternative music matching approaches: a simple *personalized* approach and a *knowledge-based* matching technique which matches music to places based on metadata (e.g., matching music that was composed during the same period that the place of interest was built in) [22].

In the following section we provide background information on research that addresses emotions in the context of searching for music and places. Subsequently, we describe the proposed emotion-based matching approach and experiments conducted to validate its effectiveness. Finally, we discuss the position of our technique within music adaptation research and present some open issues in the area of emotion-aware and location-aware music services.

14.2 Background

14.2.1 Emotions and Music

Emotional qualities of music are studied in the area of music psychology [30]. Music psychologists have been studying how people perceive and are affected by emotions in music [17, 41], or how music preferences correlate with the user's state-of-mind [29, 31]. Likewise, this topic has attracted the interest of computer science researchers. The research area of music information retrieval (MIR)—a computer science branch dedicated to the analysis of music content—devoted considerable attention to automatic detection of emotions conveyed by music [40] (see also Chap. 12). This subject attracts researchers due to the large possibilities it opens for the development of music delivery services. For instance, emotion-aware music services may be used for searching music collections using emotion keywords as a query, or for recommending music content that fits the user's mood.

Automatic recognition of emotion-related descriptors of music tracks is a challenging research problem, which requires large collections of training data—music labeled with appropriate emotion tags—and therefore needs the definition of a vocabulary of possible emotions conveyed by music. However, the definite set of emotions raised by music is not easy to determine. Despite numerous works in cognitive psychology, up to date no universal taxonomy of emotions has been agreed on. Human emotions are complex and multilayered, therefore, focusing on different aspects of emotions leads to different lists of emotions. This means that there may not exist a universal emotion model to discover, but emotions are to be chosen based on the task and domain of the research [9]. Two main groups of emotion models have been identified [11]: *dimensional models*, where emotional states are represented as a combination of a small number of independent (usually two) dimensions, and *category-based models*, where sets of emotion terms are arranged into categories.

In *dimensional models*, the general idea is modeling emotions as a combination of activeness and positiveness of each emotion. Thus, the first dimension represents the *Activation* level (also called *Activity*, *Arousal* or *Energy*), which contains values between *quiet* and *energetic*; and the second dimension represents the *Valence* level (also called *Stress* or *Pleasure*), which contains values between *negative* and *positive*. The most popular dimensional emotion models are Russell's circumplex model [32] and Thayer's model [37].

Category-based models offer a simpler alternative to modeling emotions where emotion labels are grouped into categories. For instance, Hevner [17] conducted a study where users were asked to tag classical music compositions with emotion adjectives and came up with 8 emotion clusters: *dignified*, *sad*, *dreamy*, *serene*, *graceful*, *happy*, *exciting*, and *vigorous*. A more recent and elaborated research on emotional response to music was carried out by Zentner et al. [41] who conducted a series of large-scale user studies to determine which emotions are perceived and felt by music listeners. The study participants rated candidate adjectives by measuring how often they feel and perceive the corresponding emotions when listening to music.

The studies resulted in a set of 33 emotion terms in 9 clusters which was called the Geneva Emotional Music Scale (GEMS) model. The representative emotions of the clusters are: *wonder*, *transcendence*, *tenderness*, *nostalgia*, *peacefulness*, *power*, *joyful activation*, *tension*, and *sadness*. We have adopted the GEMS model as a starting point in our research.

Having a vocabulary of emotions for labeling music content allows researchers to build automatic music emotion recognition algorithms. This task is more generally referred to as *music auto-tagging* and is typically performed employing a supervised learning approach: based on a training set of music content features and a vocabulary of labels, a classifier is trained and subsequently used to predict labels for new music pieces. In our work, we employed a variant of the auto-tagger presented by Seyerlehner et al. [34] which showed superior performance in the "Audio Tag Classification" and the "Audio Tag Affinity Estimation" tasks, run at the 2012 Music Information Retrieval Evaluation eXchange (MIREX).[1]

14.2.2 Emotions and Places

The concept of *place* and its meaning has attracted attention among both philosophers and psychologists. Castello [7] defined place as a part of space that stands out with certain qualities that are perceived by humans. The author claimed that places stand out in our surroundings not because of certain features that they possess, but because of the meanings we attribute to these features. As such, places can have a strong impact on people's memories, sentiments, and emotional well-being.

Debord [10] introduced *psychogeography*—the study of the effects of geographical environment on the emotions and behavior of individuals. Bachelard [4], in his work on the *Poetics of Space* discussed the effect that a house and its outdoor context may have on human. The author described places that evoke impressions (i.e., emotions) in humans as *poetic* places.

Place is most commonly analyzed in the context of an urban environment [4, 7, 10, 14]. This is not surprising since most people live in cities and therefore interact with urban places on a daily basis. In our work, we focus on places of interest (POIs)—places that attract the interest of city dwellers and especially tourists. In the tourism domain, a POI is arguably the main consumption object [39] as tourists seek out churches, castles, monuments, old streets, squares in search of authenticity, culture, and the sense of place.

Although urban places and their impact on human emotional well-being have been studied by psychologists [7, 13, 14], to our knowledge no taxonomy of emotions that a place may evoke in people has been proposed.

[1] http://www.music-ir.org/mirex.

14.2.3 Places and Music

Although it has been argued that sound is as important as the visual stimuli in contributing to the sense of a place [19], few works have addressed the use of music to enhance people's perception of a place.

In his work on the *sonification* of place, Iosafat [19] discussed the philosophical and psychological aspects of the relation between places, their sounds, and human perception of places. The author presented an *urban portrait* project, where field recordings of prominent places in a city were mixed with musicians' interpretations of the places to create a sonic landscape of the city.

Ankolekar and Sandholm [2] presented a mobile audio application *Foxtrot* which allows its users to explicitly assign audio content to a particular location. The authors stressed the importance of the emotional link between music and location. According to the authors, the primary goal of their system is to "enhance the sense of being in a place" by creating its emotional atmosphere. *Foxtrot* relies on crowdsourcing—every user is allowed to assign audio pieces (either a music track or a sound clip) to specific locations (represented by the geographical coordinates of the user's current location), and also specify the visibility range of the audio track—a circular area within which the track is relevant. The system is then able to provide a stream of location-aware audio content to its users.

While sounds can enhance the sense of place, also places may contribute to the listener's perception of music or even act as stimuli for creating music [1]. The US music duo Bluebrain is the first band to record a location-aware album.[2] In 2011, the band released two such albums—one dedicated to Washington's park National Mall, and the second dedicated to New York's Central Park. Both albums were released as iPhone apps, with music tracks prerecorded for specific zones in the parks. As the listener moves through the landscape, the tracks change through smooth transitions, providing a soundtrack to the walk. Only by listening to the albums in their intended surroundings can the users fully experience music as conceived by the artist.

In music recommendation research, where the goal is providing users with personalized music delivery services, the place of a user at the time of receiving recommendations has been recognized as an important factor which influences the user's music preferences [15]. The location of the user (along with other types of information such as weather or time) represents an additional source of knowledge which helps generating highly adaptive and engaging recommendations, known as situational or contextual recommendations [21].

Research works that exploit the user's location for music recommendation typically represent it as categorical data [8] or as GPS coordinates [33]. For instance, Cheng and Shen [8] created a dataset of (*user, track, location*) tuples where the *location* value was set as one of {*office, gym, library, canteen, public transport*}. The authors proposed a generative probabilistic model to recommend music tracks by taking the location information into account.

---

[2] http://bluebrainmusic.blogspot.com/.

Schedl et al. [33] used a dataset of geo-tagged tweets related to music listening for location-aware recommendation. For each user in the dataset, the set of her music listening tweets was aggregated into a single location profile. The authors proposed two ways to build the user's location profile—aggregating the GPS coordinates of the user's listening events into a single Gaussian Mixture Model representation, or converting the coordinates into categorical data at the level of continent, country, or state. The location profiles of users were then exploited for user-to-user similarity computation in a collaborative filtering algorithm.

The above approaches to location-aware music recommendation differ from our work in that they consider places either at a very high level (e.g., the country of a user), or as generic types of location (e.g., an office environment). Conversely, in our work we consider specific places, their emotional associations, and model explicit relations between a place and a music track by leveraging these emotional content of both types of items. To the best of our knowledge, no other research works model the relation between music and places at this level.

14.3 Matching Music to Places of Interest

In this section, we describe the proposed approach for matching music to places of interest. As said in Sect. 14.1, we use emotions as the link between music and POIs, and we represent the emotions as tags attached to both music and places. The tag-based representation allows matching music tracks and POIs by comparing the tag profiles of the items. This approach requires both music tracks and POIs to be annotated with a common tag vocabulary. For this purpose, we rely on both user-generated annotations and a music auto-tagging technique.

First we describe the procedure of establishing vocabulary of emotions fit for annotating both places and music. Subsequently, we show how an appropriate similarity metric for music-to-POI similarity computation was selected and then describe the live user study where our approach was evaluated [5].

Finally, we describe the extension of the approach using a revised emotion vocabulary, and present the user study where our approach was compared against alternative matching techniques [22].

For fully detailed descriptions of our work, we refer the readers to the original publications describing the technique [5, 22].

14.3.1 Establishing the Emotion Vocabulary

As discussed in Sect. 14.2, there has been a number of works on emotion vocabularies for music, but none addressing the vocabulary of emotions evoked by places. Therefore, as a starting point in our research, we chose to use a well-established vocabulary of emotions evoked by music—the Geneva Emotional Music Scale (GEMS)

Table 14.1 The tag vocabulary used for matching music to POIs

GEMS tags	Category
Allured, Amazed, Moved, Admiring	Wonder
Fascinated, Overwhelmed, Thrills, Transcendence	Transcendence
Mellowed, Tender, Affectionate, In love	Tenderness
Sentimental, Dreamy, Melancholic, Nostalgic	Nostalgia
Calm, Serene, Soothed, Meditative	Peacefulness
Triumphant, Energetic, Strong, Fiery	Power
Joyful, Animated, Bouncy, Amused	Joyful Activation
Tense, Agitated, Irritated	Tension
Sad, Tearful	Sadness
Additional tags	
Ancient, Modern	Age
Colorful, Bright, Dark Dull	Light and Color
Open, Closed	Space
Light, Heavy	Weight
Cold, Mild and Warm	Temperature

model [41]. The GEMS model consists of nine categories of emotions, each category containing up to four emotion tags (Table 14.1).

However, since our approach deals with both music and POIs, we could not rely solely on tags derived from a music psychology research. Therefore, in addition to the tags from GEMS model, we have selected five additional categories of tags (Table 14.1). These were selected from the "List of Adjectives in American English" [28] through a preliminary user study on music and POI tagging [20]. We note that although these additional adjectives describe physical properties of items, they relate to the users' emotional response to music (e.g., a user may perceive a music composition being *cold* or *colorful*).

Subsequently, we conducted a user study to evaluate the fitness of the proposed vocabulary for uniformly tagging both music tracks and POIs and to bootstrap a dataset of POIs and music tracks with emotion annotations. Figure 14.1 shows the interface of the web application used in the experiment.

We created a dataset consisting of 75 music tracks—famous classical compositions and movie soundtracks—and 50 POIs in the city of Bolzano (Italy)—castles, churches, monuments, etc. The tagging was performed by 32 volunteer users recruited via email—students and researchers from the Free University of Bolzano and other European universities. Roughly half of the study participants had no prior knowledge of the POIs. The users were asked to view or listen to one item at a time (the same interface was used for tagging POIs and music tracks) and to assign the tags that in their opinion fit to describe the displayed item.

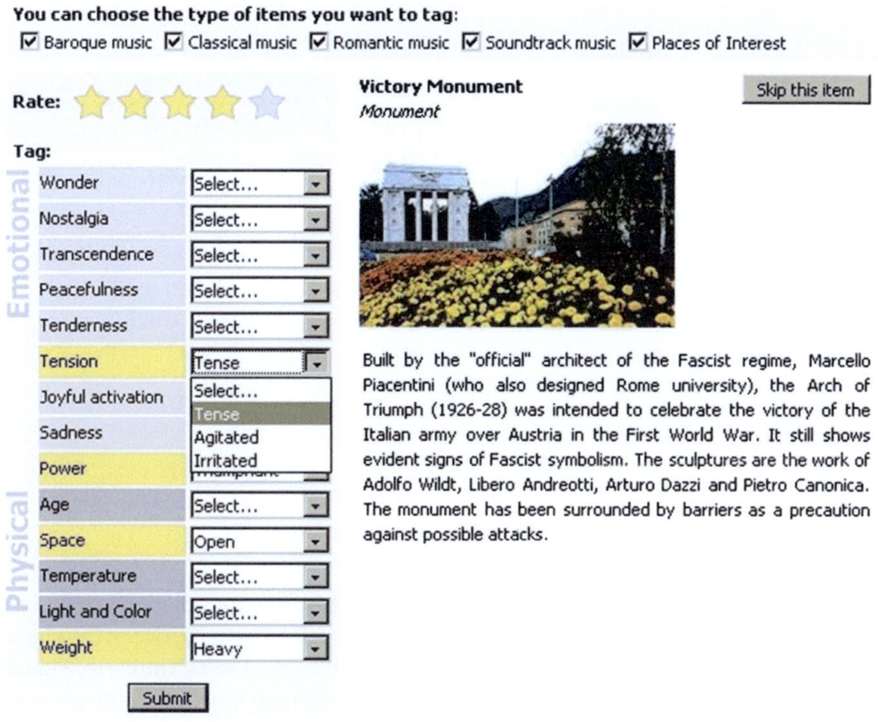

Fig. 14.1 Screenshot of the web application used for tagging POIs and music tracks

In total, 817 tags were collected for the POIs (16.34 tags per POI on average), and 1025 tags for the music tracks (13.67 tags per track on average). Tags assigned to an item by different users were aggregated into a single list, which we call the item's *tag profile*. Note that by aggregating the tags of different users we could not avoid conflicting tags in the items' profiles. This is quite normal when dealing with user-generated content. However, this does not invalidate the findings of this work. Conversely, we show that our approach is robust and can deal with such complication.

Figure 14.2 illustrates the distribution of tags collected for POIs (left) and music tracks (right). Larger font represents more frequent tags. We can see that the tag distributions for POIs and music tracks are different—music tends to be tagged with tags from the GEMS model more frequently (frequent tags include *affectionate*, *agitated*, *sad*, *sentimental*, *tender*, *triumphant*), while POIs tend to be labeled with adjectives describing the physical properties (e.g., *closed*, *cold*). This is not surprising, since the GEMS model was developed for the music domain. However, certain tags from the proposed vocabulary are uniformly applied to both types of items (e.g., *animated*, *bright*, *colorful*, *open*, *serene*). This result shows that a common vocabulary may indeed be used to link music and places.

Fig. 14.2 The tag clouds for POI (*left*) and music (*right*) annotations

14.3.2 Music-to-POI Similarity Computation

Having a dataset of POIs and music tracks tagged with a common emotion vocabulary, we need a method to establish a degree of similarity (relatedness) between the tagged items. To do so, we have considered a set of a well-established set of similarity metrics that are applicable to tagged resources [27] and performed a web-based user study to evaluate the alternative metrics. We have designed a web interface (Fig. 14.3) for

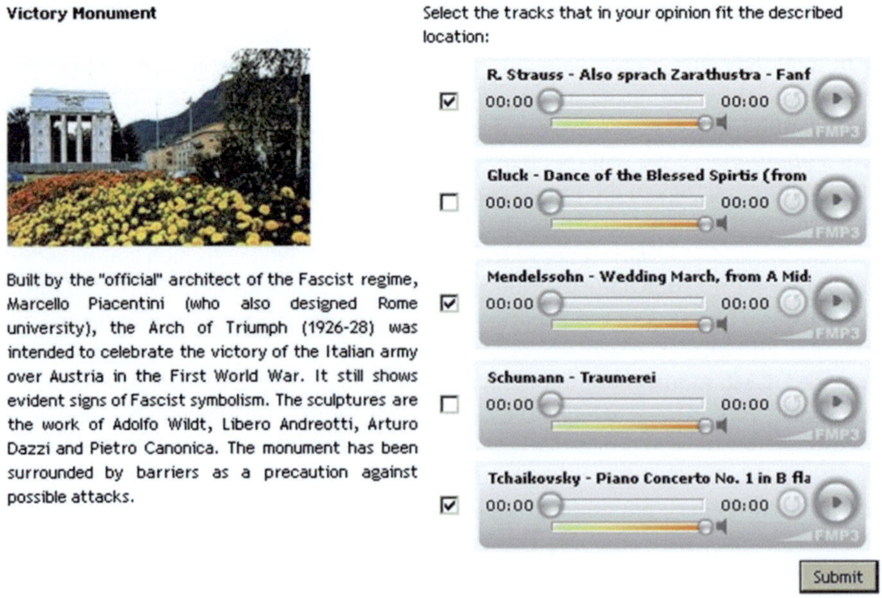

Fig. 14.3 Screenshot of the web application used for evaluating music-to-POI matching

collecting the users' subjective evaluations, i.e., assessments if a music track suits a POI. The users were asked to consider a POI, and while looking at it, to listen to music tracks selected using the different similarity metrics. The user was asked to check all the tracks that in her opinion suit that POI.

The goal of this experiment was to see whether the users actually agree with the music-to-POI matching computed using our approach and to select the similarity metric that produces the best results, i.e., music suggestions that the users agree with. The obtained results showed the weighted Jaccard similarity metric to produce the best quality results (see [5] for a detailed description of the metrics' comparison). The weighted Jaccard metric defines the similarity score between a POI u and a music track v as:

$$\text{similarity}(u, v) = \frac{\sum_{t \in X_u \cap X_v} \log f(t)}{\sum_{t \in X_u \cup X_v} \log f(t)} \tag{14.1}$$

where X_u and X_v are the items' tag profiles and $f(t)$ is the fraction of items in our dataset (both POIs and music tracks) annotated with the tag t.

We note that in this evaluation study the users where asked to evaluate the matching of music to a POI while they were just reading a description of the POI. In order to measure the effect of the music-to-POI suggestions while the user is actually visiting the POI, we have implemented a mobile guide for the city of Bolzano and evaluated it in a live user study.

14.3.3 User Study: Mobile Travel Guide

This section describes the design and evaluation of an Android-based travel guide that illustrates the POI the user is close to and plays music suited for that POI. After the user has launched this application, she may choose a travel itinerary that is displayed on a map indicating the user's current GPS position, and the locations of the POIs in the itinerary (Fig. 14.4, left). Then, every time the user is nearby to a POI (either belonging to the selected itinerary, or not), she receives a notification alert conveying information about the POI. While the user is reading this information, the system plays a music track that suits the POI (Fig. 14.4, center). For example, the user might hear Bach's "Air" while visiting the Cathedral of Bolzano, or Rimsky-Korsakov's "Dance of the Bumble Bee" during a visit to the busy Walther Square.

The guide functions using a database of POIs and music tracks tagged as described in Sect. 14.3.1, as well as the precomputed similarity scores (Eq. 14.1) for each POI-music pair in the dataset. To suggest a music track for a given POI, the application sorts the music tracks by decreasing similarity score, and then randomly selects one of the top 3 music tracks. The motivation for not always choosing the top-scoring music track for each POI is to avoid, or at least reduce, the probability that the same music tracks are played for POIs that have been annotated with similar sets of tags, and therefore to ultimately suggest more diverse music tracks while the user is

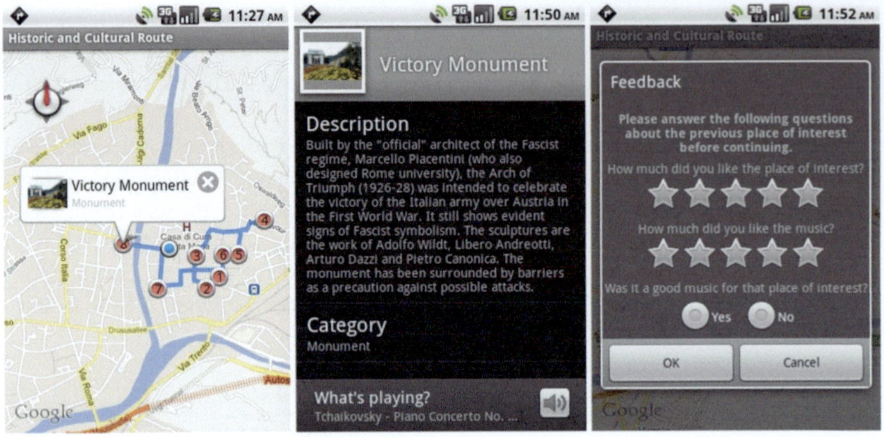

Fig. 14.4 Screenshots of the mobile guide application, showing the map view, the details of a POI, and a feedback dialog

visiting an itinerary. In the future, more sophisticated diversification techniques may be investigated.

In order to evaluate the proposed music-to-POI matching approach, we compared the performance of the guide with an alternative system variant having the same user interface, but not matching music with the POIs. Instead, for each POI, it suggests a music track that, according to our similarity metric, has a low similarity with the POI. We call the original system variant *match*, and the second variant *music*.

For the evaluation study we adopted a between-groups design, involving 26 subjects (researchers and students at the Free University of Bolzano). Subjects were assigned to the *match* and *music* variants in a random way (13 each). We note that the outcome of this comparison was not obvious, as without a careful analysis, even the low-matching tracks could be deemed suited for a POI, since all tracks belong to the same music type—popular orchestral music.

Each study participant was given a phone with earphones, and was asked to complete a 45 min walking route in the center of Bolzano. Whenever a subject was approaching a POI, a notification invited the user to inspect the POI's details and to listen to the suggested music track. If the suggested music track was perceived as unsuited, subjects could pick an alternative music track from a shuffled list of four possible alternatives: two randomly generated, and two with high music-to-POI similarity scores.

The users were then asked to provide feedback regarding the quality of music suggestions and their satisfaction with the system (Fig. 14.4, right). By analyzing the feedback, we were able to evaluate the performance of our technique against the baseline approach. A total of 308 responses regarding the various visited POIs and their suggested music tracks were obtained: 157 (51 %) from subjects in the *match* group, and 151 (49 %) from subjects in the *music* group.

The obtained results showed 77 % of the users in the *match* group to be satisfied with music suggestions, compared to 66 % in the *music* group. The difference in these proportions is statistically significant ($p < 0.001$ in a *chi-square* test). We can thus conclude that users evaluate the music tracks suggested by our proposed method to better suit the POIs than the music tracks suggested in the control setting.

Moreover, to additionally confirm this result, we have analyzed users' behavior when manually selecting alternative tracks for the POIs. If unsatisfied with the music suggestion, a user was shown a list of four tracks (presented in a random order)—two tracks retrieved by our approach, and two tracks randomly selected from the remaining tracks in our dataset. Even in this case, the users strongly preferred the music tracks matched with the POIs—out of 77 manual music selections, 58 (75 %) were chosen from the tracks matching to the POI and 19 (25 %) from the randomly selected tracks, i.e., the probability that a user selects a matched music track is about three times higher than that of selecting a random music track. This preference for matched music tracks is also statistically significant ($p < 0.001$ in a *chi-square* test), which proves our hypothesis that users prefer tracks for POIs that are generated by our music-to-POI matching approach.

14.3.4 Vocabulary Revision and Automatic Tag Prediction

A major limitation of the initial design of our approach was the high cost of acquiring emotion annotations of music tracks and POIs. Therefore, following the positive results obtained in the initial evaluation, our goal was to make the music matching technique more scalable and to evaluate it on a larger and more diverse dataset of POIs and music tracks.

In order to scale up our technique, emotion tags had to be predicted automatically for both POIs and music tracks. Automatic POI tagging would allow avoiding the costly user-generated tag acquisition and would make our technique easily applicable to existing sets of POIs (e.g., touristic itineraries or guidebooks). However, in the scope of this work, we do not address the problem of POI tagging and leave it for future work (see Sect. 14.4). Instead, we focus on the automatic tagging of music tracks. This is an equally, if not more, important scalability issue, as music auto-tagging would make our technique applicable to any music collection (e.g., the user's music library).

As discussed in Sect. 14.2, *auto-tagging* techniques can be used to tag music with a defined set of labels. However, these techniques are computationally expensive and require training a model for each label. Therefore, it was important to reduce the size of our vocabulary prior to applying an auto-tagging technique.

We observed that the original GEMS emotion vocabulary (Table 14.1) contained many synonyms (e.g., *triumphant-strong*, *calm-meditative*), and that certain tags were rarely employed by users during the tagging survey (Sect. 14.3.1). Therefore, we have revised the vocabulary by merging synonym adjectives, discarding the rarely used tags, and substituting some labels for clarity (*transcendence* was replaced with

Table 14.2 A revised version of the emotion vocabulary

Tags	Type
Affectionate, Agitated, Animated, Bouncy, Calm, Energetic, Melancholic, Sad, Sentimental Serene, Spiritual, Strong, Tender, Thrilling	GEMS tags [41]
Ancient, Modern, Bright, Dark, Colorful, Heavy, Lightweight, Open, Cold, and Warm	Additional tags

Table 14.3 Cities and POIs of the evaluation dataset

City	POIs
Amsterdam	Canals of Amsterdam
Barcelona	Sagrada Familia, Casa Batlló
Berlin	Brandenburg Gate, Charlottenburg Palace
Brussels	Royal Palace of Brussels
Copenhagen	Christiansborg Palace
Dublin	Dublin Castle
Florence	Florence Cathedral
Hamburg	Hamburg Rathaus
London	Big Ben, Buckingham Palace
Madrid	Almudena Cathedral, Teatro Real, Las Ventas
Milan	Milan Cathedral, La Scala
Munich	Munich Frauenkirche
Paris	Eiffel Tower, Notre Dame de Paris
Prague	National Theater
Rome	St. Peter's Basilica, Colosseum
Seville	Seville Cathedral
Vienna	Vienna State Opera

spiritual, and *light* with *lightweight*). The revision allowed us to reduce the size of the vocabulary from 46 to 24 tags (Table 14.2).

To apply the revised vocabulary to a more diverse dataset, we first collected a set of 25 well-known POIs from 17 major city tourism destinations in Europe (Table 14.3). The POI information was extracted using DBpedia knowledge base.[3]

Subsequently, to acquire a collection of music tracks, we used a technique developed in a previous work [23], which queries the DBpedia knowledge base and retrieves music composers or artists semantically related to a given POI (see Sect. 14.3.5.2). For each of the 25 POIs in Table 14.3, we queried DBpedia for top-5 related musicians and aggregated them into a single set. This resulted in a collection

[3]http://dbpedia.org/.

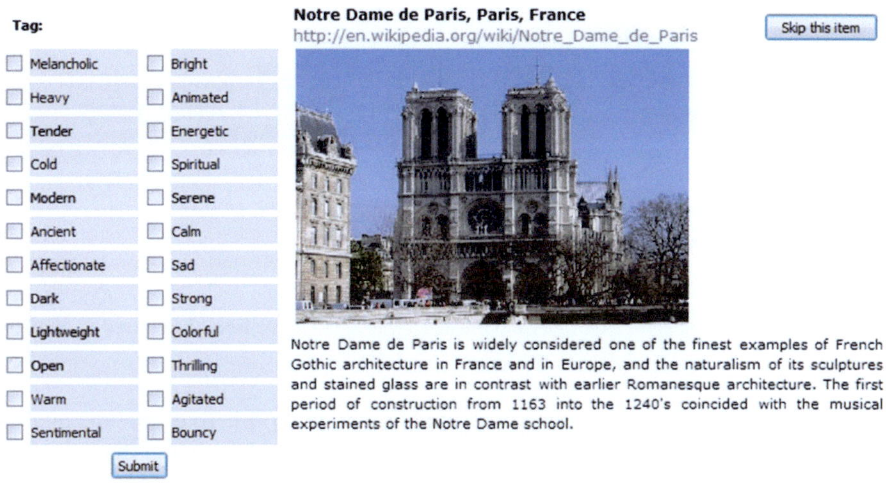

Fig. 14.5 Interface of the POI and music tagging application

of 123 musicians (there were two repetitions in the initial list of 125 musicians). Finally, we retrieved three music tracks for each musician by taking the top-ranked results returned by the YouTube search interface[4] (the musician's name was used as a search query). Doing so ensured the collected tracks to be representative of the musicians in our dataset. We obtained a set of 369 music tracks belonging to nine music genres: Classical, Medieval, Opera, Folk, Electronic, Hip Hop, Jazz, Pop, and Rock.

To annotate the new dataset with the emotion vocabulary, we used a web application similar to the first tag acquisition application (Fig. 14.1). However, contrary to the earlier experiments, at this stage we only relied on user-assigned annotations to tag the 25 POIs and to bootstrap the automatic tagging of music tracks, since automatic tag prediction requires training a multi-label classifier on a set of tagged music tracks. We chose a subset of music tracks (123 tracks—one random track per musician) to be annotated as training data for the auto-tagging algorithm.

Figure 14.5 shows the interface used for tagging both POIs and music tracks. The users were asked to annotate POIs and music tracks using the revised emotion vocabulary of 24 adjectives. Note that unlike in the previous tagging application (Fig. 14.1), here we did not present the tags grouped by category, but they were simply displayed as a flat list. This was done to make the tagging process more straightforward. Moreover, the vocabulary revision discarded some redundant tag categories.

The tagging procedure was performed by 10 volunteers recruited via email—students and researchers from the Free University of Bolzano and other European universities. We note that the tagging of music and POIs is a subjective task and

[4]http://www.youtube.com/.

Fig. 14.6 The tag clouds for POI (*left*) and music (*right*) annotations from the revised vocabulary

users may disagree whether certain tags apply to an item [38]. To ensure the quality of the acquired annotations, we considered the agreement between users, which is a standard measure of quality for user-generated tags [24]. We cleaned the data by keeping for each item only the tags on which at least two taggers agreed. As a result, we obtained an average of 5.1 distinct tags for the POIs and 5.8 for the music tracks.

Figure 14.6 shows the distribution of collected tags for POIs (left) and music tracks (right) with larger font representing more frequent tags. Similarly to tag clouds produced for the original vocabulary (Fig. 14.2), the tag distributions differ for POIs and music tracks. We observe that certain tags (e.g., for music annotations—*cold*, *open*, *dark*, *thrilling*) diminished in frequency after cleaning the tags based on user agreement. This means that certain tags may be more subjective than others, and therefore more difficult to agree on. Nevertheless, tags like *colorful*, *energetic*, *lightweight*, *sentimental*, *serene*, *warm* are consistently applied to both music and POIs, which serves our goal of matching the two types of items.

Finally, we used a state-of-the-art music auto-tagger developed by researchers at the Johannes Kepler University (JKU) of Linz [34], training it on the 123 user-tagged tracks and predicting tags for the full set of 369 music tracks (see [22] for details). The auto-tagger outputs a probability for each tag in the vocabulary to be relevant for a track. However, the metric we used for music-to-POI similarity computation (Eq. 14.1) requires computing the intersection and union of the items' tag profiles. Therefore, we decided to generate binary tag assignments based on the probabilistic output of the auto-tagger by applying a threshold to the tag prediction probabilities. Empirical analysis showed that a threshold of 0.4 produced an average tag profile of 5.2 tags which is in accordance with the average profile size of manually tagged items (5.1 tags for POIs and 5.8 for music tracks).

For a music track v whose tags are predicted using an auto-tagger, we define the tag profile X_v as:

$$X_v = \{t_i \mid p(t_i) \geq 0.4\},\ i = \{1, \ldots, K\} \tag{14.2}$$

where K is the size of tag vocabulary (in our case $K = 24$) and $p(t_i)$ denotes the probability for a tag t_i to be relevant for the track.

Having the dataset of POIs and music tracks annotated with a common vocabulary of emotion labels and a metric that gives a similarity score for any given pair of POI and a music track (Eq. 14.1), we can evaluate our approach in a user study. In the next section we describe the evaluation and present the results.

14.3.5 Comparison to Alternative Matching Techniques

The new dataset with more diverse POIs spread out across 17 different cities made a live user study, similar to that illustrated in Sect. 14.3.3, i.e., with users visiting the POI and then listening to the system-selected music, impossible to conduct. Therefore, to evaluate the scaled-up version of our approach, we opted for a web-based study, where a text description and images of each POI were visualized, and the users were asked to listen to the suggested music tracks and evaluate if they match the displayed POI (see Fig. 14.7).

As described in the previous section, we have collected a dataset of 25 POIs and 369 music tracks belonging to 9 music genres, with a part of the music dataset tagged manually and also the full set of tracks auto-tagged by an algorithm. This setting allowed us comparing two versions of emotion-based music matching—one using only the manually annotated 123 tracks, and the other using the full set of 369 auto-tagged tracks. We call the first version *tag-based* and the other *auto-tag-based* approach. In both approaches, the POI annotations were user-generated.

For each POI in the dataset, the *tag-based* approach ranks the manually annotated 123 music tracks using the similarity score in Eq. 14.1. Likewise, the *auto-tag-based*

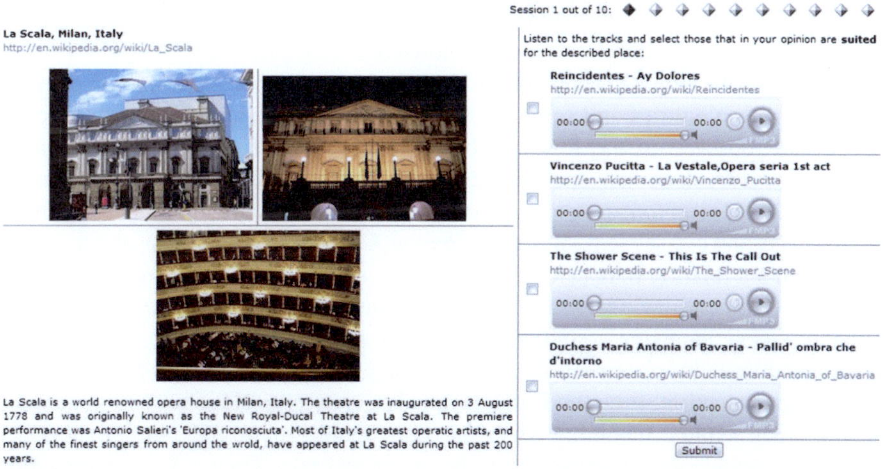

Fig. 14.7 Screenshot of the web application used to evaluate the different music matching approaches

approach ranks the 369 tracks with automatically predicted labels (Eq. 14.2). The top-ranked music track is presented to the user along with the POI.

In addition to comparing the manually and automatically generated emotion annotations, we wanted to compare the performance of emotion-based approach to alternative music matching techniques, which we describe here.

14.3.5.1 Genre-Based Approach

Traditionally, music delivery services employ personalization techniques to provide music content to users. Therefore, as a baseline approach, we employed a basic personalization technique—*genre-based* music matching which selects the music tracks based on the users' genre preferences. We aimed to compare a personalized music matching technique with the *knowledge-based* and *tag-based* approaches, which are not personalized, but rather directly match music with the POIs.

In order to obtain the users' preferences, we asked the study participants to select their preferred music genres prior to performing the evaluation. The genre taxonomy was based on the music tracks in our dataset, and included: Classical, Medieval, Opera, Folk, Electronic, Hip Hop, Jazz, Pop, and Rock. For each displayed POI, the genre-based track is randomly selected from the whole set of music tracks belonging to the user's preferred genres.

14.3.5.2 Knowledge-Based Approach

The *knowledge-based* music matching approach employs the technique presented in [23]. Given a POI, this approach ranks musicians by their relatedness to the POI. The relatedness is computed from the semantic relations between the POI and musicians extracted from the DBpedia knowledge base [3].

DBpedia—the Linked Data version of Wikipedia—contains information on more than 3.5 million entities and semantic relations between them. This information is stored and retrieved in the form of triples, which are composed of the *subject–property–object* elements, such as *<Vienna State Opera, located in, Vienna>*, *<Gustav Mahler, belongs to, Opera composers>*, where a subject and an object belong to certain classes (e.g., Building, Person, City, Music Category), and the property denotes a relation between the classes (e.g. a building *being located* in a city). Given a POI, the knowledge-based approach queries DBpedia (using the SPARQL semantic query language[5]), and builds a graph where nodes correspond to classes and edges to relations between the classes. The graph is built using a predefined set of relations (location, time, and architecture/art category relations) and contains a starting node without incoming edges that corresponds to the POI, and target nodes without outgoing edges that belong to the musician class. Then, a weight spreading algorithm is applied to the graph to compute the relatedness score for each musician

[5]http://www.w3.org/TR/rdf-sparql-query/.

node. Nodes that are connected to the POI through more paths in the graph receive higher scores. Finally, the highest-scored musicians are returned for the target POI. For more details on the approach, refer to [23].

As explained in Sect. 14.3.4, the knowledge-based approach was used to build the dataset of POIs and music tracks—for each of the 25 POIs, top-5 related musicians were retrieved from DBpedia. Subsequently, we have downloaded three representative music tracks for each musician. Using this approach, we assume that there are no major differences between the tracks of the same musician. Therefore, for each POI, the knowledge-based track is randomly selected from the three music tracks by the top-ranked musician.

We believe that the emotion-based and knowledge-based techniques represent two complementary ways of establishing a match between a place and a music track: a track may "feel right" for a POI, or it can be linked to a POI by factual relations (e.g., belonging to the same cultural era or composed by someone whose life is related to the POI). In previous works [5, 23], we have evaluated the two techniques independently on different datasets and against primitive baselines. It was therefore important to directly compare the performance of these techniques, and to evaluate their combination.

14.3.5.3 Combined Approach

Finally, we implemented a hybrid combination of the *knowledge-based* and *auto-tag-based* approaches, employing a rank aggregation technique [12]. Since the music-to-POI similarities produced by the two techniques have different value ranges, we used the normalized Borda count rank aggregation method to give equal importance to the two. Given a POI u, the *knowledge-based* and *auto-tag-based* approaches produce the rankings of music tracks σ_u^{kb} and σ_u^{tb}. We denote the position of a track v in these rankings as $\sigma_u^{kb}(v)$ and $\sigma_u^{tb}(v)$ respectively. Then, we compute the combined score of the track v for the POI u as:

$$\text{combined\_score}(u, v) = \frac{N_{kb} - \sigma_u^{kb}(v) + 1}{N_{kb}} + \frac{N_{tb} - \sigma_u^{tb}(v) + 1}{N_{tb}} \tag{14.3}$$

where N_{kb} and N_{tb} are the total number of tracks in the corresponding rankings. For each POI, the combined approach selects the top-scored music track.

14.3.5.4 User Study

To determine which approach produces better music suggestions, we designed a web-based interface (Fig. 14.7) for collecting the users' subjective assessments of whether a music track suits a POI. This user study was similar to the experiment conducted to determine the best-performing similarity metric for the tag-based approach (see Sect. 14.3.2, Fig. 14.3). As in the previous case, participants of the experiment were repeatedly asked to consider a POI, and while looking at its images and description, to listen to the suggested music tracks.

While in the previous experiment the music suggestions for a POI were selected using the different metrics applied to items' tag profiles, here music tracks were selected using the proposed five approaches described above—the personalized baseline approach and the four non-personalized matching approaches. The users were asked to check all the tracks that in their opinion suit the displayed POI. The order of the music tracks was randomized, and the user was not aware of the algorithms that were used to generate the suggestions. In total, a maximum of five tracks corresponding to the top-ranked tracks given by each approach were suggested for a POI, but sometimes less tracks were shown as the tracks selected by the different approaches may overlap.

To understand which approach produces suggestions that are most appreciated by the users, we measured the precision of each matching approach M as follows:

$$\text{precision}(M) = \frac{\#\text{ of times } t^M \text{ marked as a match}}{\#\text{ of times } t^M \text{ presented to the users}} \qquad (14.4)$$

where t^M is a music track suggested using the approach M.

14.3.5.5 Results

A total of 58 users participated in the evaluation study, performing 564 evaluation sessions: viewing a POI, listening to the suggested music tracks, and providing feedback. 764 music tracks were selected by the users as well-suited for POIs. Table 14.4 shows the performance of the matching approaches. All non-personalized matching techniques performed significantly better than the personalized *genre-based* track selection ($p < 0.001$ in a two-proportion z-test). This result shows that in a situation defined by a visit to a POI, it is not really appropriate to suggest a music track liked by the user, but it is more important to adapt the music to the place.

We note that both emotion-based techniques outperform the baseline approach. Furthermore, the evaluation results suggest that the *tag-based* music matching approach can be successfully scaled up using automatic tag prediction techniques. The *auto-tag-based* approach even outperformed the *tag-based* approach with marginal significance ($p = 0.078$). This can be explained by the larger variety of music

Table 14.4 Precision values for the different music matching approaches

Genre-based	Knowledge-based	Tag-based	Auto-tag-based	Combined
0.186	0.337*	0.312*	0.362*	0.456**

The values marked with * are significantly better than the *Genre-based* approach (two-proportion z-test, $p < 0.001$). The value marked with ** is significantly better than the other approaches ($p < 0.01$)

in the auto-tagged music dataset—using the *auto-tag-based* approach the tracks were selected from the full set of 369 music tracks, while the *tag-based* approach used only the subset of 123 manually annotated tracks. Scaling up the process of tag generation without harming performance is hence the vital advantage of using the auto-tagger.

Finally, the *combined* approach produced the best results, outperforming the others with statistical significance at $p < 0.01$. These results confirm our hypothesis that the users are more satisfied with music suggestions when combining the *tag-based* and *knowledge-based* techniques, which represent orthogonal types of relations between a place and a music track.

14.4 Discussion and Further Work

We believe that techniques and results described in this chapter illustrate clearly the importance of using emotions for capturing the relationship between music and places, and for developing new engaging music applications. We presented a scalable emotion-based solution for matching music to places, and demonstrated that alternative music-to-POI matching approaches may be effectively combined with that emotion-based technique. This can lead to even richer music delivery services, where emotion-based music suggestions are supported by additional relations, e.g., knowledge linking a musician to a POI.

Emotion-aware and location-aware music recommendation topics belong to a larger research area of context-aware music recommendation [21] (see also Chap. 15). This is a new and exciting research area with numerous innovation opportunities and many open challenges. Up to date, few context-aware music services are available for public use. While certain music players allow specifying the user's mood or activity as a query, most context-aware systems are research prototypes, not yet available to the public. A major challenge is understanding the relations between context factors, such as location, weather, time, mood, and music features. Some research on this topic exists in the field of music psychology [29–31], therefore, collaboration between music psychologists and music recommendation researchers is essential.

While in this work we demonstrated the effectiveness of the proposed techniques through a web-based evaluation, it is important to further evaluate the approach in real-life settings to confirm our findings. Moreover, additional evaluation would help us understand which type of associations between music and POIs—emotion-based or knowledge-based—the users prefer in different recommendation scenarios (e.g., sightseeing, choosing a holiday destination, or acquiring knowledge about a destination).

Another important future work direction is studying the semantics of emotion tags. In current work, we treated all tags equally and we did not explore their relations, while contradicting or complementary emotion tags may provide an important source of information. Moreover, our analysis of the tag vocabulary is far from complete. While we have shown that the proposed set of labels can be effectively used for matching music to places, further user studies and may lead to a more definitive emotion vocabulary.

It is also important to address the automatic acquisition of tags for POIs (for instance, using web mining techniques and folksonomy datasets like Flickr as sources of tagging information), to analyze the importance of individual audio features when automatically tagging music tracks, and to explore more complex hybrid recommendation strategies for combining our music suggestions with personalized recommendations produced by existing music delivery services, e.g., Last.fm.

Finally, we believe that the designed music-to-POI matching solutions may be adapted to other types of content. Since music is a heavily emotion-loaded type of content, emotions may be employed to link music to any content items that may be labeled with emotions—movies, books, or paintings [6, 26, 36].

References

1. Adkins, M., Santamas, H.: Exploring the perception and identity of place through sound and image. In: Proceedings of the Invisible Places International Symposium, pp. 403–421 (2014)
2. Ankolekar, A., Sandholm, T.: Foxtrot: a soundtrack for where you are. In: Proceedings of Interacting with Sound Workshop: Exploring Context-Aware, Local and Social Audio Applications, pp. 26–31 (2011)
3. Auer, S., Bizer, C., Kobilarov, G., Lehmann, J., Cyganiak, R., Ives, Z.: DBpedia: a nucleus for a web of open data. In: ISWC '08: Proceedings of the 7th International Semantic Web Conference, pp. 722–735 (2008)
4. Bachelard, G.: The Poetics of Space. Beacon Press, Boston (1958)
5. Braunhofer, M., Kaminskas, M., Ricci, F.: Location-aware music recommendation. Int. J. Multimedia Inf. Retrieval **2**(1), 31–44 (2013)
6. Cai, R., Zhang, C., Wang, C., Zhang, L., Ma, W.-Y.: Musicsense: contextual music recommendation using emotional allocation modeling. In: MULTIMEDIA '07: Proceedings of the 15th International Conference on Multimedia, pp. 553–556. ACM, New York, NY, USA (2007)
7. Castello, L.: Rethinking the Meaning of Place: Conceiving Place in Architecture-Urbanism. Ashgate Publishing, Ltd., London (2010)
8. Cheng, Z., Shen, J.: Just-for-me: an adaptive personalization system for location-aware social music recommendation. In: Proceedings of International Conference on Multimedia Retrieval, pp. 185–192, ACM (2014)
9. Cowie, R., Douglas-Cowie, E., Tsapatsoulis, N., Votsis, G., Kollias, S., Fellenz, W., Taylor, J.G.: Emotion recognition in human-computer interaction. IEEE Signal Process. Mag. **18**(1), 32–80 (2001)
10. Debord, G.: Introduction to a critique of urban geography. Critical Geographies A Collection of Readings (1955)
11. Dunker, P., Nowak, S., Begau, A., Lanz, C.: Content-based mood classification for photos and music: a generic multi-modal classification framework and evaluation approach. In: MIR'08: Proceeding of the 1st ACM International Conference on Multimedia Information Retrieval, pp. 97–104. ACM, New York, NY, USA (2008)
12. Dwork, C., Kumar, R., Naor, M., Sivakumar, D.: Rank aggregation methods for the web. In: Proceedings of the 10th International Conference on World Wide Web (WWW), pp. 613–622 (2001)
13. Ellin, N.: Good Urbanism: Six Steps to Creating Prosperous Places. Island Press, Washington (2012)

14. Engler, M.: Experience at view places: an inquiry into the emotional ties between people and places. In: Proceedings of the 21st Annual Conference of the Environmental Design Research Association, pp. 222–230 (1990)
15. Gillhofer, M., Schedl, M.: Iron maiden while jogging, debussy for dinner? In: MultiMedia Modeling, pp. 380–391, Springer (2015)
16. Gretzel, U.: Intelligent systems in tourism: a social science perspective. Ann. Tour. Res. **38**(3), 757–779 (2011)
17. Hevner, K.: Experimental studies of the elements of expression in music. Am. J. Psychol. **48**(2), 246–268 (1936)
18. Huron, D.: Perceptual and cognitive applications in music information retrieval. In: Proceedings of the 1st Annual International Symposium on Music Information Retrieval (ISMIR) (2000)
19. Iosafat, D.: On sonification of place: psychosonography and urban portrait. Org. Sound **14**(01), 47–55 (2009)
20. Kaminskas, M., Ricci, F.: Matching places of interest with music. In: Workshop on Exploring Musical Information Spaces, pp. 68–73 (2009)
21. Kaminskas, M., Ricci, F.: Contextual music information retrieval and recommendation: state of the art and challenges. Comput. Sci. Rev. **6**, 89–119 (2012)
22. Kaminskas, M., Ricci, F., Schedl, M.: Location-aware music recommendation using auto-tagging and hybrid matching. In: Proceedings of the 7th ACM Conference on Recommender Systems (RecSys 2013), Hong Kong, China (2013)
23. Kaminskas, M., Fernández-Tobías, I., Ricci, F., Cantador, I.: Knowledge-based identification of music suited for places of interest. Inf. Technol. Tour. **14**(1), 73–95 (2014)
24. Law, E.L.M., Von Ahn, L., Dannenberg, R.B., Crawford, M.: Tagatune: a game for music and sound annotation. In: ISMIR, vol. 3, p. 2 (2007)
25. Lew, M.S., Sebe, N., Djeraba, C., Jain, R.: Content-based multimedia information retrieval: state of the art and challenges. ACM Trans. Multimedia Comput. Commun. Appl. (TOMCCAP) **2**(1), 1–19 (2006)
26. Li, C.-T., Shan, M.-K.: Emotion-based impressionism slideshow with automatic music accompaniment. In: MULTIMEDIA '07: Proceedings of the 15th International Conference on Multimedia, pp. 839–842. ACM Press, New York, NY, USA, (2007)
27. Markines, B., Cattuto, C., Menczer, F., Benz, D., Hotho, A., Stumme, G.: Evaluating similarity measures for emergent semantics of social tagging. In: Proceedings of the 18th International Conference on World Wide Web, pp. 641–650, ACM (2009)
28. Noll, P., Noll, B.: List of adjectives in american english. http://www.paulnoll.com/Books/Clear-English/English-adjectives-1.html
29. North, A.C., Hargreaves, D.J.: Situational influences on reported musical preference. Psychomusicology Music Mind Brain **15**(1–2), 30–45 (1996)
30. North, A.C., Hargreaves, D.J.: The Social and Applied Psychology of Music. Cambridge University Press, Cambridge (2008)
31. Pettijohn, T.F., Williams, G.M., Carter, T.C.: Music for the seasons: seasonal music preferences in college students. Curr. Psychol. 1–18 (2010)
32. Russell, J.A.: A circumplex model of affect. J. Pers. Soc. Psychol. **39**(6), 1161–1178 (1980)
33. Schedl, M., Vall, A., Farrahi, K.: User geospatial context for music recommendation in microblogs. In: Proceedings of the 37th International ACM SIGIR Conference on Research & Development in Information Retrieval, pp. 987–990, ACM (2014)
34. Seyerlehner, K., Schedl, M., Knees, P., Sonnleitner, R.: A refined block-level feature set for classification, similarity and tag prediction. In: 7th Annual Music Information Retrieval Evaluation eXchange (MIREX) (2011)
35. Shi, Y., Larson, M., Hanjalic, A.: Tags as bridges between domains: improving recommendation with tag-induced cross-domain collaborative filtering. In: User Modeling, Adaption and Personalization, pp. 305–316. Springer, Heidelberg (2011)
36. Stupar, A., Michel, S.: Picasso—to sing, you must close your eyes and draw. In: 34th ACM SIGIR Conference on Research and Development in Information, pp. 715–724 (2011)

37. Thayer, R.E.: The Biopsychology of Mood and Arousal. Oxford University Press, Oxford (1989)
38. Turnbull, D., Barrington, L., Lanckriet, G.: Five approaches to collecting tags for music. In: Proceedings of the 9th International Society for Music Information Retrieval Conference (ISMIR), pp. 225–230 (2008)
39. Urry, J.: Consuming Places. Psychology Press, Abingdon (1995)
40. Yang, Y.-H., Chen, H.H.: Machine recognition of music emotion: a review. ACM Trans. Intell. Syst. Technol. (TIST), **3**(3), 40 (2012)
41. Zentner, M., Grandjean, D., Scherer, K.R.: Emotions evoked by the sound of music: Characterization, classification, and measurement. Emotion **8**(4), 494–521 (2008)

Chapter 15
Emotions in Context-Aware Recommender Systems

Yong Zheng, Bamshad Mobasher and Robin Burke

Abstract Recommender systems are decision aids that offer users personalized suggestions for products and other items. Context-aware recommender systems are an important subclass of recommender systems that take into account the context in which an item will be consumed or experienced. In context-aware recommendation research, a number of contextual features have been identified as important in different recommendation applications: such as *companion* in the movie domain, *time* and *mood* in the music domain, and *weather* or *season* in the travel domain. Emotions have also been demonstrated to be significant contextual factors in a variety of recommendation scenarios. In this chapter, we describe the role of emotions in context-aware recommendation, including defining and acquiring emotional features for recommendation purposes, incorporating such features into recommendation algorithms. We conclude with a sample evaluation, showing the utility of emotion in recommendation generation.

15.1 Introduction and Motivation

Recommender systems provide personalized suggestions of products to end-users in a variety of settings, especially in on-line e-commerce. Recommender systems may use a variety of approaches, including collaborative, content-based, knowledge-based, and hybrid [9]. In this chapter, we will consider collaborative recommendation approaches. In collaborative recommender systems, the system seeks to extrapolate the preferences of a target user for an item given the preference of "peer users" who exhibit similar rating behaviors to the target user.

Y. Zheng (✉) · B. Mobasher · R. Burke
College of Computing and Digital Media, DePaul University,
243 S Wabash Ave ST 400, Chicago, IL 60604, USA
e-mail: yzheng8@cs.depaul.edu

B. Mobasher
e-mail: mobasher@cs.depaul.edu

R. Burke
e-mail: rburke@cs.depaul.edu

M. Tkalčič et al. (eds.), *Emotions and Personality in Personalized Services*,
Human–Computer Interaction Series, DOI 10.1007/978-3-319-31413-6_15

One way to view the problem posed by the collaborative recommendation approach is to consider the users and items as forming a matrix $U \times I$, where the entries in the matrix are known ratings by particular users for particular items. In this framework, collaborative recommendation becomes the task of creating a function for predicting the likely values of unknown cells in this matrix. Context-aware recommendation turns the prediction task into a *multidimensional* rating function—R: $Users \times Items \times Contexts \rightarrow Ratings$ [3].

Despite the added complexity inherent in this extra dimension, context-aware recommender systems (CARS) have proved themselves effective in a variety of domains, such as movies, music, travel, and restaurants. This is perhaps not a surprising finding when one considers that the context in which an item is experienced may have a significant impact on how it is received. For example, loud rock music may be perfect for doing one's exercise routine, but not for other purposes, like grading student essays or hosting a dinner party. If a recommender system does not take context into account, these different environments for experiencing music will become blended together into one user profile and fail to be a good representation of the user's tastes in specific situations.

Emotions are an important contextual element in many settings. It is well-known that human decision-making is subject to both rational and emotional influences [14]. The field of affective computing takes this fact as basic to the design of computing systems [21]. The role of emotions in recommender systems was recognized by the research community as early as 2005 [18], giving rise to research in emotion-based movie recommender systems [15] and the impact of emotions in group recommender systems [11, 18]. In this chapter, we introduce emotions as important contextual variables for recommendation, and demonstrate how emotion-oriented features can be employed in context-aware recommendation algorithms.

15.2 Contexts and Emotional Contexts in Recommender Systems

15.2.1 What Is Context?

Surprisingly, researchers in context-aware computing have not reached a consensus about the definition of context. One commonly used definition is the one given by Abowd et al. in 1999 [1], "context is any information that can be used to characterize the situation of an entity. An entity is a person, place, or object that is considered relevant to the interaction between a user and an application, including the user and applications themselves." This definition ascribes a purpose to context, that of characterizing situations, but it does not do much to limit the scope of what can be considered context. For our purposes, we consider the context for recommendation to be any aspect of the recommendation situation which is neither the item being recommended nor the target individual for whom the recommendation is made.

How Contextual Factors Change	Knowledge of the RS about the Contextual Factors		
	Fully Observable	Partially Observable	Unobservable
Static	Everything Known about Context	Partial and Static Context Knowledge	Latent Knowledge of Context
Dynamic	Context Relevance Is Dynamic	Partial and Dynamic Context Knowledge	Nothing Is Known about Context

Fig. 15.1 Classification of contextual factors [3]

Adomavicius et al. [3] introduce a two-part classification of contextual information. Their taxonomy is based on two considerations: what a recommender system knows about contextual factors and how the contextual factors change over time. With respect to the system's knowledge, context can be subdivided into *fully observable*, *partially observable*, and *unobservable*. In terms of its life cycle, context can be categorized as *static* or *dynamic*. This analysis yields six possible classes for context, as depicted in Fig. 15.1.

Furthermore, [29] revisited the context definition and identification, where we found that most contextual features were the attributes of the activity itself, such as time and location, and partial users' dynamic profiles can be considered as contexts too, such as users' emotional states. By contrast, item features, such as music style, movie genres, are usually viewed as contents in recommender systems.

15.2.2 Context-Aware Recommendation

Context can be applied in recommendation using three basic strategies: pre-filtering, post-filtering, and contextual modeling [2, 3]. The first two strategies rely on either filtering profiles or filtering the recommendations, but in the modeling process use standard two-dimensional recommendation algorithms. In the latter strategy, contextual modeling, predictive models are learned using the full contextual data. These scenarios are depicted in Fig. 15.2 [2]. Most of the recent work on context-aware recommendation has been based on contextual pre-filtering and contextual modeling. In this chapter, we also focus on these two paradigms and will not consider approaches based on post-filtering strategy.

As the name would suggest, pre-filtering techniques use the contextual information to remove profiles or parts of profiles from consideration in the recommendation process. For example, context-aware splitting approaches [6, 34] use context as filter to preselect rating profiles and then apply the recommendation algorithms only with profiles contain ratings in matching contexts. Tensor factorization [16], context-aware matrix factorization [8] and contextual sparse linear modeling [36, 37] are algorithms

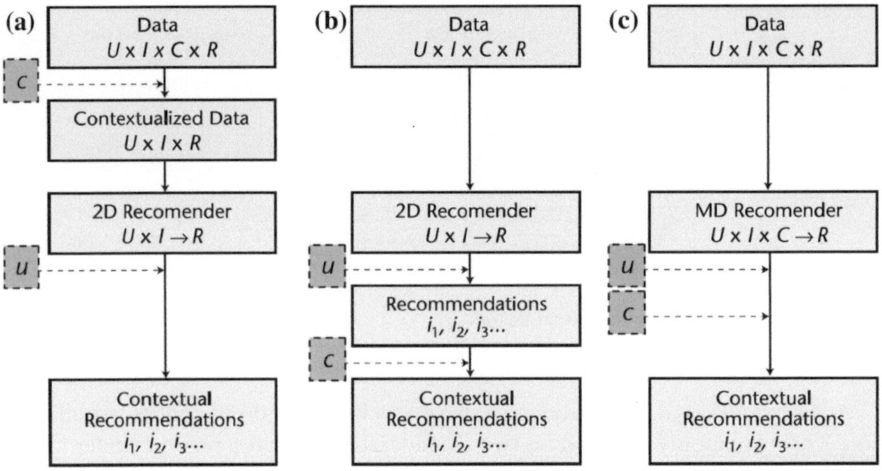

Fig. 15.2 Three strategies for context-aware recommendation [3]

belonging to the category of contextual modeling approaches. Differential context modeling (DCM) [32] is an integration of contextual filtering and contextual modeling, which is considered as a hybrid contextual modeling approach. There are two approaches involved in DCM: In differential context relaxation (DCR) [30, 31], pre-filtering is applied to different components of the recommendation algorithm with different contextual features. Context modeling approaches directly consider context as a part of the recommendation function and try to explore users' preferences in the multidimensional rating space. Differential context weighting (DCW) [33] uses optimization to model the effect of context in different aspects of a recommendation algorithm.

15.2.3 Emotions in Recommender Systems

Emotions are mental states usually caused by an event of importance to the subject. An emotion is typically characterized by (a) a conscious mental state with a recognizable quality of feeling and directed toward some object, (b) a bodily perturbation of some kind, (c) recognizable expressions of the face, tone of voice, and gesture (d) a readiness for certain kinds of action [19].

There are a variety of ways in which emotions can be modeled. The universal model classifies emotions into fixed categories: for example, Ekman's six basic emotions: happiness, anger, fear, sadness, disgust, and surprise [13]. There is also the dimensional model, which describes each emotion as a point in a continuous multidimensional space where each dimension represents a quality of the emotion, typically valence, arousal, and dominance. The same dimensions are also used in the circumplex model [24], where the multidimensional space is laid out as a circle and emotions occupy angular positions within it.

Tkalcic et al. [26] provide a framework that describes three ways in which emotions can be used to improve the quality of recommender systems. Those three ways can be described by three stages (i.e., the entry, consumption, and exit stages), where emotions are able to play different roles in different stages of the process. Although emotions are personal characteristics, we believe they are most effectively modeled within recommender systems as contextual features, as they are very dynamic and will often greatly impact the user's preferences.

15.2.4 Acquisition of Emotional Data

One well-known difficulty of research in context-aware recommendation is the relative rarity of data sets that contain user ratings and contextual information. If we look for data sets in which emotions are recorded as part of the contextual information, our choices are even more limited. Part of the reason is that it is difficult to record contextual information in an explicit way—unlike user choices, which can simply be recorded, and this is especially true of emotions. Usually, the user must explicitly encode emotion information in order for it to be available to the recommender. The LDOS-CoMoDa data set [20], one of the popular context-aware data sets, was collected from surveys where three emotional variables were included. In addition, emotions can also be extracted from tags, an example being the Moviepilot[1] system, which allows users to tag movies with specific mood tags.

Emotional state can also be gathered implicitly. The affective computing community [10, 12] has explored a variety of techniques for emotion detection, such as detection of facial expressions [27], emotion inferences from sensors [4], and many other approaches based on voice, speech, body language, and postures. All of those techniques require special and additional efforts to infer the emotional states from different resources. In the domain of information retrieval and recommender systems, emotional states are sometimes inferred from product reviews through sentiment detection. For example, Tang et al. [25] surveyed several sentiment classification techniques used to detect emotions or opinions from texts.

15.3 Applying Context-Aware Recommendation

In this section, we provide an example of applying context-aware recommendation with special attention to the role of emotion. In our discussion, we will use the term *contextual dimension* to denote the contextual variable, e.g., "Location" or "Time." The term *contextual condition* refers to a specific value in a contextual dimension, e.g., "home" and "cinema" are two contextual conditions for the dimension"Location."

[1]Moviepilot, http://moviepilot.com/, this data set was the basis for the 1st Challenge on Context-Aware Movie Recommendation in ACM RecSys 2010, but it no longer being distributed.

Table 15.1 Contextual information in LDOS-CoMoDa data set

Contextual dimension	Contextual conditions
Time	Morning, Afternoon, Evening, Night
Daytype	Working day, Weekend, Holiday
Season	Spring, Summer, Autumn, Winter
Location	Home, Public place, Friend's house
Weather	Sunny/clear, Rainy, Stormy, Snowy, Cloudy
Social	Alone, My partner, Friends, Colleagues, Parents, Public, My family
EndEmo	Sad, Happy, Scared, Surprised, Angry, Disgusted, Neutral
DominantEmo	Sad, Happy, Scared, Surprised, Angry, Disgusted, Neutral
Mood	Positive, Neutral, Negative
Physical	Healthy, Ill
Decision	User decided which movie to watch, User was given a movie
Interaction	First interaction with a movie, n-th interaction with a movie

15.3.1 Data Set

As discussed above, context-aware data sets are fairly rare and those containing emotional variables are even more unusual. The LDOS-CoMoDa data set introduced above is one of the data sets that can be used for this type of research. After filtering out subjects with incomplete feature information, we got the final data set which includes 113 users, 1186 items, 2094 ratings (rating scale is 1 to 5), and 12 contextual dimensions, where the description of the contextual features is introduced by Table 15.1.

Among those 12 contextual dimensions, there are three that can be considered "emotional": endEmo, dominantEmo, and mood. "EndEmo" is the emotional state experienced at the end of the movie. "DominantEmo" is the emotional state experienced the most during watching. "Mood" is the mood of the user during that part of the day when the user watched the movie. Mood has lower maximum frequency than other emotional variables; it changes slowly, so we assumed that it does not change during watching. "EndEmo" and "DominantEmo" contain the same seven conditions: Sad, Happy, Scared, Surprised, Angry, Disgusted, Neutral, where "Mood" only has simple three conditions: Positive, Neutral, Negative.

15.3.2 Contextual Recommendation Algorithms

For purposes of this chapter, we apply two types of context-aware algorithms in order to evaluate their performance on this data: one is context-aware splitting and the other is differential context modeling.

Table 15.2 Movie ratings in contexts

User	Item	Rating	Time	Mood	Companion
U1	T1	3	Weekend	Neutral	Friend
U1	T1	5	Weekend	Positive	Girlfriend
U1	T1	?	Weekday	Neutral	Family

15.3.2.1 Context-Aware Splitting

There are three basic approaches to context-aware splitting—*Item splitting*, *User splitting*, and *UI splitting*. Item splitting [6] is considered to be one of the most efficient pre-filtering algorithms and it has been well developed in recent research. The underlying idea of item splitting is the nature of an item is sensitive to some particular contextual dimension, which renders the item either appropriate or not appropriate. Therefore, depending on the context, the item can be treated as if it were two different items [7]. User splitting [5, 23] is based on a similar intuition—it may be useful to consider one user as two different users, if he or she demonstrates significantly different preferences across contexts. UI splitting is a simple combination of item and user splitting, where both users and items may be split if necessary.

To better understand and represent the splitting approaches, consider the following movie recommendation example:

In Table 15.2, there are one user $U1$, one item $T1$ and two ratings (the first two rows) in the training data and one unknown rating that we are trying to predict (the third row). There are three contextual dimensions—time (weekend or weekday), mood, and companion (friend, girlfriend, or family).

Item splitting tries to find a contextual condition on which to split each item. The split should be performed once the algorithm identifies a contextual condition in which items are rated significantly differently. In the movie example above, there are three contextual conditions in the dimension *companion*: friend, girlfriend, and family. Correspondingly, there are three possible alternative conditions: "*friend and not friend*," "*girlfriend and not girlfriend*," "*family and not family*." Impurity criteria [6] are used to determine whether and how much items were rated differently in these alternative conditions. For example, a t-test or other statistical metric can be used to evaluate if the means differ significantly across conditions.

Item splitting iterates over all contextual conditions in each context dimension and evaluates the splits based on the impurity criteria. It finds the best split for each item in the rating matrix and then items are split into two new ones, where contexts are eliminated from the original matrix—it transforms the original multi-dimensional rating matrix to a 2D matrix as a result. Assume that the best contextual condition to split item T1 in Table 15.2 is "Mood = *Neutral and not Neutral*," T1 can be split into T11 (movie T1 being seen in Neutral mood) and T12 (movie T1 being seen in a non-neutral mood). Once the best split has been identified, the rating matrix can be transformed as shown by Table 15.3a.

Table 15.3 Transformed rating matrix

User	Item	Rating
(a) By item splitting		
U1	T11	3
U1	T12	5
U1	T11	?
(b) By user splitting		
U12	T1	3
U12	T1	5
U11	T1	?
(c) By UI splitting		
U12	T11	3
U12	T12	5
U11	T11	?

This example shows a *simple split*, in which a single contextual condition is used to split the item. It is also possible to perform a *complex split* using multiple conditions across multiple context dimensions. However, as discussed in [7], there are significant costs of sparsity and potential overfitting when using multiple conditions. We use only simple splitting in this work.

Similarly, user splitting tries to split users instead of items. It can be easily derived from item splitting as introduced above using similar impurity criteria. Assume that the best split for user $U1$ in Table 15.2 is "Companion = *family and not family*," $U1$ can be split into $U11$ ($U1$ saw the movie with family) and $U12$ ($U1$ saw the movie with others). The rating matrix can be transformed as shown by Table 15.3b. The first two rows contain the same user $U12$ because $U1$ saw this movie with others (i.e., not family) rather than family as shown in the original rating matrix. UI splitting is a new approach proposed in [34]—it applies item splitting and user splitting together. Assuming that the best split for item and user splitting are the same as described above, the rating matrix based on UI splitting can be shown as Table 15.3c. Here we see that both users and items were transformed, creating new users and new items.

To apply context-aware splitting, it is necessary to choose a splitting criterion. There are four splitting criteria described in [6]: t_{mean}, t_{chi}, t_{prop}, and t_{IG}. Specifically, t_{mean} estimates the statistical significance of the difference in the means of ratings associated to each alternative contextual condition using a t-test. t_{chi} and t_{prop} estimate the statistical significance of the difference between two proportions—high ratings ($>$R) and low ratings ($\leq$R) by chi-square test and z-test respectively, where we choose R = 3 as in [6]. t_{IG} measures the information gain given by a split to the knowledge of the item i rating classes which are the same two proportions as above. Usually, a threshold for the splitting criteria should be set so that users or items are only be split when the criteria meets the significance requirement. We use an arbitrary value of 0.2 in the t_{IG} case. For t_{mean}, t_{chi}, and t_{prop}, we use 0.05 as the p-value threshold.

A finer-grained operation is to set another threshold for each impurity value and each data set. We deem it as a significant split once the p-value is no larger than 0.05. We rank all significant splits by the impurity value, and we choose the top first (highest impurity) as the best split. Items or users without qualified splitting criteria are left unchanged.

In the experiments below, once the splitting has been performed (creating new users and/or items), we use biased matrix factorization (BiasMF) [17] on the resulting matrices and use the factors for computing predicted ratings.

15.3.2.2 Differential Context Modeling

Differential context modeling (DCM) is a general contextual recommendation framework and it is considered as a hybrid of contextual pre-filtering and contextual modeling approach and can be applied to any recommendation algorithm. The "differential" part of the technique assumes that a recommendation algorithm can be broken down into different functional components to which contextual constraints can be applied separately. The contextual effect for each component is maximized, and the joint effects of all components thereby contribute the best performance for the whole algorithm. The "modeling" part is focused on how to model the contextual constraints. There are two approaches: *context relaxation* and *context weighting*, where context relaxation uses an optimal subset of contextual dimensions, and context weighting assigns different weights to each contextual factor. Accordingly, we have two approaches: *differential context relaxation* (DCR) [30, 31] and *differential context weighting* (DCW) [33].

DCM has been successfully applied to user-based collaborative filtering, item-based collaborative filtering, and Slope One recommendation algorithms [32]. In this work, we demonstrate DCM as applied to user-based collaborative recommendation.

Figure 15.3 shows Resnick's well-known algorithm for user-based recommendation [22], where a is a user, i is an item, and N is a neighborhood of K users similar to a. The algorithm calculates $P_{a,i}$, which is the predicted rating that user a is expected to assign to item i. We decompose this algorithm to four components:

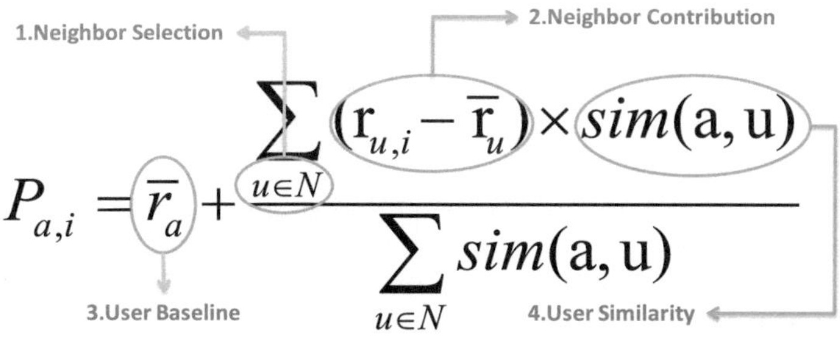

Fig. 15.3 Algorithm components in UBCF

Neighborhood selection: The algorithm selects the top-k neighbors from users who have rated on the same item i. If contexts are taken into consideration, the neighborhood can be further restricted only to users who have rated the item *in the same contexts*. This gives a context-specific recommendation computation. However, the strict application of such a filter greatly increases the sparsity associated with user comparisons. There may only be a small number of cases in which recommendations can be made. DCM offers two potential solutions to this problem. DCR searches for the optimal relaxation of the context, generalizing the set of contextual features and contextual conditions to reduce sparsity. In DCW, the full set of neighbors is used but the influence of neighbors in similar contexts is increased through weighting.

Neighbor contribution: The neighbor contribution is computed from the difference between a neighbor's rating on an item i and his or her average rating over all items. This average $\bar{r}_u$ is another place where context can be applied. We can compute this average specific to a particular context (DCR) or we can weight the contribution of different ratings to the average based on their associated context (DCW). The idea is that users may have different rating behaviors in different contexts and thus their average rating should be handled different across contexts.

User baseline: The computation of $\bar{r}_a$ is similar to the neighbor's average rating and can be made context-dependent in the same way.

User similarity: The computation of neighbor similarity $sim(a, u)$ involves identifying ratings $r_{u,i}$ and $r_{a,i}$ where the users have rated items in common. Again, contextual information can be applied by only matching ratings that occur in a particular context (DCR) or by weighting more heavily those items rating in similar contexts. The idea is that ratings should only count as similar if they have been applied in the same context.

With these considerations in mind, we can derive a new rating prediction formula by applying DCR or DCW to the formula in Fig. 15.3. In DCR, we create context filters for each of the four components of the algorithm. The choice of the best combination of filters is performed through an optimization procedure searching the space of possible constraints. In DCW, we create context weights for each of the four components. Again, the best weights are chosen through optimization. More details about the prediction equations and technical specifications can be found in [33].

15.3.3 The Influence of Emotional Context

With these algorithms in place, we can explore the influence of the emotion aspects of context. In the experiments here, we split the LDOS-CoMoDa data set into five folds, and evaluate the algorithms using five-fold cross validation using RMSE as the evaluation metric.

There are a total of 12 contextual dimensions in this data. We consider the impact of these dimensions by creating three evaluation conditions. In the "Emotion only"

Table 15.4 RMSE for algorithm and context combinations

	Algorithms	All contexts	No emotions	Emotions only
DCM	DCR	1.043	1.057	1.046
	DCW	1.017	1.037	1.036
Splitting approaches	Item splitting	1.011	1.014	1.014
	User splitting	0.913	0.971	0.932
	UI splitting	0.892	0.94	0.903

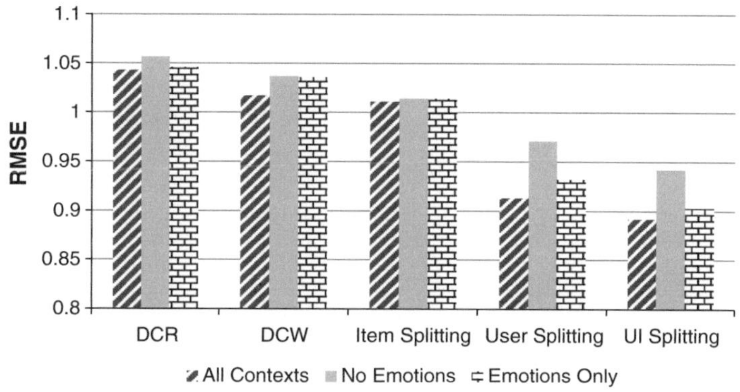

Fig. 15.4 RMSE for algorithm and context combinations

setting, we consider only the three emotional variables as the contextual dimensions in the recommending process. In the "No emotions" condition, we use the 9 dimensions excluding the three emotional variables. We apply all 12 contextual dimensions in the "All contexts." The RMSE results are shown in Table 15.4, and in Fig. 15.4:

The results show that settings in which emotional dimensions are included in the context outperform those in which they are excluded. The "All Contexts" setting shows the best performance in all algorithm variants. In most cases, the error is highest for the "No Emotions" condition based on statistical paired t-test, which further confirms the importance of the emotional variables.

Because the two types of algorithms use contexts in different ways, we can examine how different contextual dimensions are applied. In the splitting algorithms, the splitting takes place in the preprocessing stage, where the most influential contexts are chosen to split users or items. We can look at how often each contextual dimension is used for splitting as a measure of the importance of that dimension across the user profiles in the data set. In Fig. 15.5, we see, for each splitting criterion, the percentage of times each contextual dimension was chosen to split the profiles. Dimensions used less than 5 % (item splitting) or 6 % (user splitting) of the profiles are omitted. We do not show results for the information gain criterion as this had the worst performance.

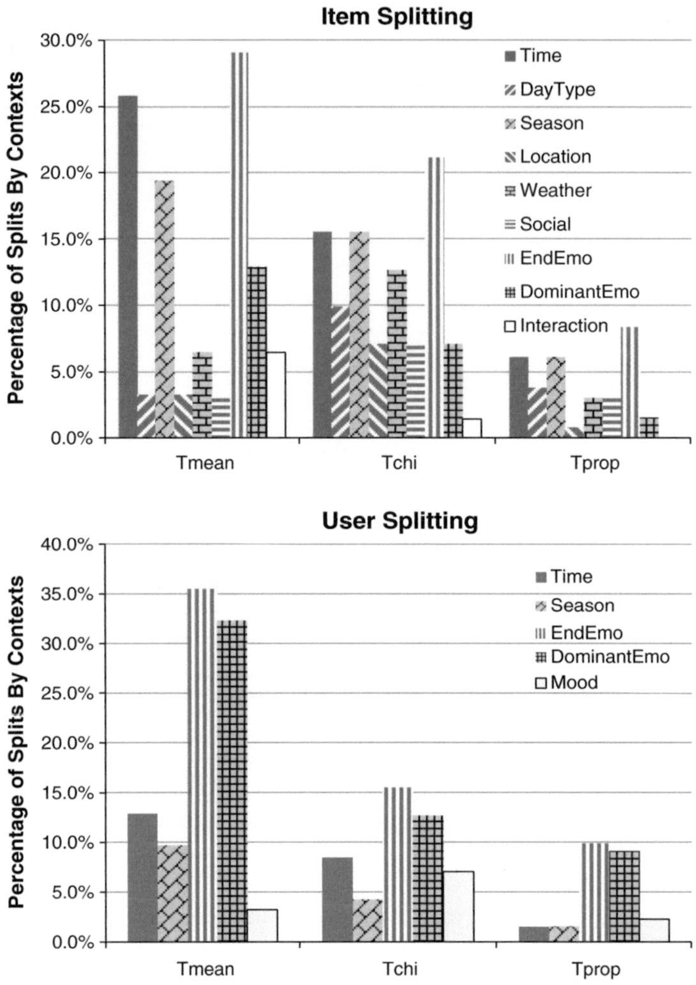

Fig. 15.5 Which contexts are the most frequently used ones in the splitting approaches?

In general, the top two dimensions are consistent across the three impurity criteria: *EndEmo* and *Time* for item splitting and *EndEmo* and *DominantEmo* for user splitting. However, the percentages differ significantly. If we look more closely at the results, we find that the contextual condition used for splitting also varies a great deal. For example, although the top context dimension for item and user splitting is the same—*EndEmo*, the most frequently selected condition in this dimension is "Happy" for item splitting and "Neutral" for user splitting.

Splitting approaches work by identifying specific dependencies between particular users or items and the contextual dimensions. Obviously, emotion is a personal quality and can be considered as more dependent on users than items, which is con-

Table 15.5 Context relaxation and weighting by DCM

Algorithm components	Context relaxation By DCR	Context weighting by DCW
Neighbor selection	N/A	Day, *Mood*
Neighbor contribution	Movie Year, Genre	Movie Genre
User baseline	*DominantEmo, EndEmo*, MovieLanguage	*DominantEmo, EndEmo*, Interaction
User similarity	*EndEmo*, Location	*DominantEmo*

firmed by the Fig. 15.5—the degree of splitting on emotional variables is much higher than on the nonemotional ones. This fact also helps explain why user splitting works better than item splitting for the LDOS-CoMoDa data. In addition, the percentages also reveal the importance of emotions—the top selected contextual dimension is the "EndEmo" for both item splitting and user splitting.

In DCM, contextual dimensions are used differently across the algorithm components. Therefore, the context selection and context weighting can be examined and show, in a detailed way, the contribution of each contextual dimension in the final optimized algorithm. The results are shown in Table 15.5. For clearer representation, we did not show specific weights of contexts in DCW; instead, we only list variables which were assigned weights above a threshold of 0.7. The weights are normalized to 1, and 0.7 therefore represents a very influential dimension. "N/A" in the table indicates no contextual constrains were used: the optimization procedure found no benefit to applying a contextual filter for these components.

Those optimal selections or weights can further be used for explanation or interpretation in recommender systems. For example, "Day" and "Mood" are two influential contexts to locate the user neighborhood, since those two dimensions are highly weighted in DCW. Meanwhile, "movie genre" is selected in the neighborhood contribution for both DCR and DCW approaches, which indicates that genre is the most important feature to contribute in predictions. In other words, the neighborhood's ratings on movies with a different movie genre may be not that useful for future predictions.

The table shows that emotional dimensions are important aspects of context, in that most algorithm components agreed to select emotional features to include in filtering and weighting. However, emotions are influential for specific components and not for others. There is a clear impact of *DominantEmo* on users' rating behavior, such that this factor needs to be included in calculating the baseline rating. In DCR, *EndEmo* turns out to be influential when measuring user similarities and user baselines, but it is not that significant in computing the neighbor contribution. Only in neighbor contribution do we fail to see an emotional dimension as important, there we see that selecting and weighting neighbors in terms of movie genre is more useful.

15.4 Conclusions and Further Research

In this chapter, we demonstrated how emotions can serve as effective contextual dimensions in the context-aware recommendation. We discussed how emotional variables may be represented and applied, and examined a particular data set in which contextual variables are found. We looked in depth at two classes of context-aware recommendation algorithms: context-aware splitting and differential context modeling and show how context is applied in each of these models. In our evaluation, we show how emotional dimensions are useful in improving recommendation accuracy as measured by RMSE. We also show how the configuration information learned for each algorithm (splitting criteria for the splitting algorithms and feature selection and weighting for the differential models) helps explain the relative value of each aspect of the emotional context.

We used context-aware splitting and differential context modeling approaches as examples in this chapter. Apparently, many more context-aware recommendation algorithms could be used for the same purpose. The state-of-the-art context-aware recommendation algorithms have been embedded into the open-source recommendation library "CARSKit" [38], where both the deviation-based and similarity-based [39, 40] contextual recommendation algorithms would be helpful in exploring emotional effects. In addition, the development of CARS also brings the new recommendation opportunity: context suggestion [28, 35] which aims to recommend appropriate contexts for users to consume the items. Toward the future application context suggestion could be one tool to provide emotional suggestions as a result.

It is clear that emotions are worth considering as contextual features for recommendation, regardless of the type of context-aware approach that is chosen. Probably the most significant hurdle to wider adoption of this approach is the availability of data about users' emotional state, which raises problems both with respect to data acquisition and user privacy. Implicit indicators of emotional state (such as parameters from sensors) may be used, but this approach raises the problem of the dynamic nature of emotions, which may change frequently during an activity. For example, of all the emotions experienced while watching a movie, which ones should be considered summative (*DominantEmo*) for given user? This question and other await further experimentation.

References

1. Abowd, G.D., Dey, A.K., Brown, P.J., Davies, N., Smith, M., Steggles, P.: Towards a better understanding of context and context-awareness. In: Handheld and Ubiquitous Computing, pp. 304–307. Springer (1999)
2. Adomavicius, G., Tuzhilin, A.: Context-aware recommender systems. In: Recommender Systems Handbook, pp. 217–253. Springer (2011)
3. Adomavicius, G., Mobasher, B., Ricci, F., Tuzhilin, A.: Context-aware recommender systems. AI Mag. **32**(3), 67–80 (2011)

4. Arroyo, I., Cooper, D.G., Burleson, W., Woolf, B.P., Muldner, K., Christopherson, R.: Emotion sensors go to school. Int. Conf. Artif. Intell. Educ. **200**, 17–24 (2009)
5. Baltrunas, L., Amatriain, X.: Towards time-dependant recommendation based on implicit feedback. In: ACM RecSys' 09, Proceedings of the 4th International Workshop on Context-Aware Recommender Systems (2009)
6. Baltrunas, L., Ricci, F.: Context-based splitting of item ratings in collaborative filtering. In: Proceedings of the Third ACM Conference on Recommender Systems, pp. 245–248. ACM (2009)
7. Baltrunas, L., Ricci, F.: Experimental evaluation of context-dependent collaborative filtering using item splitting. User Model. User-Adap. Inter. **24**(1–2), 7–34 (2014)
8. Baltrunas, L., Ludwig, B., Ricci, F.: Matrix factorization techniques for context aware recommendation. In: Proceedings of the Fifth ACM Conference on Recommender Systems, pp. 301–304. ACM (2011)
9. Burke, R.: Hybrid recommender systems: survey and experiments. User Model. User-Adapt. Inter. **12**(4), 331–370 (2002)
10. Calvo, R.A., D'Mello, S.: Affect detection: an interdisciplinary review of models, methods, and their applications. IEEE Trans. Affect. Comput. **1**(1), 18–37 (2010)
11. Chen, Y., Pu, P.: Cofeel: Using emotions to enhance social interaction in group recommender systems. In: Alpine Rendez-Vous (ARV) 2013 Workshop on Tools and Technologies for Emotion Awareness in Computer-Mediated Collaboration and Learning (2013)
12. Cowie, R., Douglas-Cowie, E., Tsapatsoulis, N., Votsis, G., Kollias, S., Fellenz, W., Taylor, J.G.: Emotion recognition in human-computer interaction. IEEE Signal Process. Mag. **18**(1), 32–80 (2001)
13. Ekman, P.: Basic emotions. In: Handbook of Cognition and Emotion, pp. 45–60. Wiley, Chichester, UK (1999)
14. Gilovich, T., Griffin, D., Kahneman, D.: Heuristics and Biases: The Psychology of Intuitive Judgment. Cambridge University Press (2002)
15. Ho, A.T., Menezes, I.L., Tagmouti, Y.: E-mrs: emotion-based movie recommender system. In: Proceedings of IADIS e-Commerce Conference. USA: University of Washington Bothell, pp. 1–8 (2006)
16. Karatzoglou, A., Amatriain, X., Baltrunas, L., Oliver, N.: Multiverse recommendation: n-dimensional tensor factorization for context-aware collaborative filtering. In: Proceedings of the Fourth ACM Conference on Recommender Systems, pp. 79–86. ACM (2010)
17. Koren, Y.: Factorization meets the neighborhood: a multifaceted collaborative filtering model. In: Proceedings of the 14th ACM SIGKDD International Conference on Knowledge Discovery and Data Mining, pp. 426–434. ACM (2008)
18. Masthoff, J.: The pursuit of satisfaction: affective state in group recommender systems. In: User Modeling 2005, pp. 297–306. Springer (2005)
19. Oatley, K., Keltner, D., Jenkins, J.M.: Understanding Emotions. Blackwell Publishing (2006)
20. Odić, A., Tkalčič, M., Tasič, J.F., Košir, A.: Predicting and detecting the relevant contextual information in a movie-recommender system. Interact. Comput. **25**(1), 74–90 (2013)
21. Picard, R.W.: Affective Computing. MIT Press (2000)
22. Resnick, P., Iacovou, N., Suchak, M., Bergstrom, P., Riedl, J.: Grouplens: an open architecture for collaborative filtering of netnews. In: Proceedings of the 1994 ACM Conference on Computer Supported Cooperative Work, pp. 175–186. ACM (1994)
23. Said, A., De Luca, E.W., Albayrak, S.: Inferring contextual user profiles—improving recommender performance. In: ACM RecSys' 11, Proceedings of the 4th International Workshop on Context-Aware Recommender Systems (2011)
24. Scherer, K.R.: What are emotions? and how can they be measured? Soc. Sci. Inf. **44**(4), 695–729 (2005)
25. Tang, H., Tan, S., Cheng, X.: A survey on sentiment detection of reviews. Expert Syst. Appl. **36**(7), 10760–10773 (2009)
26. Tkalcic, M., Kosir, A., Tasic, J.: Affective recommender systems: the role of emotions in recommender systems. In: ACM RecSys Workshop on Human Decision Making, ACM (2011)

27. Tkalčič, M., Odić, A., Košir, A.: The impact of weak ground truth and facial expressiveness on affect detection accuracy from time-continuous videos of facial expressions. Inf. Sci. **249**, 13–23 (2013)
28. Zheng, Y.: Context suggestion: solutions and challenges. In: Proceedings of the 15th IEEE International Conference on Data Mining Workshops. IEEE (2015)
29. Zheng, Y.: A revisit to the identification of contexts in recommender systems. In: Proceedings of the 20th ACM Conference on Intelligent User Interfaces Companion, pp. 133–136. ACM (2015)
30. Zheng, Y., Burke, R., Mobasher, B.: Differential context relaxation for context-aware travel recommendation. In: 13th International Conference on Electronic Commerce and Web Technologies, pp. 88–99 (2012)
31. Zheng, Y., Burke, R., Mobasher, B.: Optimal feature selection for context-aware recommendation using differential relaxation. In: ACM RecSys' 12, Proceedings of the 4th International Workshop on Context-Aware Recommender Systems. ACM (2012)
32. Zheng, Y., Burke, R., Mobasher, B.: Differential context modeling in collaborative filtering. In: Proceedings of School of Computing Research Symposium. DePaul University, Chicago IL, USA (2013)
33. Zheng, Y., Burke, R., Mobasher, B.: Recommendation with differential context weighting. In: User Modeling. Adaptation, and Personalization, Volume 7899 of Lecture Notes in Computer Science, pp. 152–164. Springer, Berlin Heidelberg (2013)
34. Zheng, Y., Burke, R., Mobasher, B.: Splitting approaches for context-aware recommendation: an empirical study. In: Proceedings of the 29th Annual ACM Symposium on Applied Computing, pp. 274–279. ACM (2014)
35. Zheng, Y., Mobasher, B., Burke, R.: Context recommendation using multi-label classification. In: Proceedings of the 13th IEEE/WIC/ACM International Conference on Web Intelligence, pp. 288–295. IEEE/WIC/ACM (2014)
36. Zheng, Y., Mobasher, B., Burke, R.: CSLIM: contextual SLIM recommendation algorithms. In: Proceedings of the 8th ACM Conference on Recommender Systems, pp. 301–304. ACM (2014)
37. Zheng, Y., Mobasher, B., Burke, R.: Deviation-based contextual SLIM recommenders. In: Proceedings of the 23rd ACM Conference on Information and Knowledge Management, pp. 271–280. ACM (2014)
38. Zheng, Y., Mobasher, B., Burke, R.: Carskit: a java-based context-aware recommendation engine. In: Proceedings of the 15th IEEE International Conference on Data Mining Workshops. IEEE (2015)
39. Zheng, Y., Mobasher, B., Burke, R.: Integrating context similarity with sparse linear recommendation model. In: User Modeling. Adaptation, and Personalization, Volume 9146 of Lecture Notes in Computer Science, pp. 370–376. Springer, Berlin Heidelberg (2015)
40. Zheng, Y., Mobasher, B., Burke, R.: Similarity-based context-aware recommendation. In: Web Information Systems Engineering, Lecture Notes in Computer Science. Springer, Berlin Heidelberg (2015)

Chapter 16
Towards User-Aware Music Information Retrieval: Emotional and Color Perception of Music

Gregor Strle, Matevž Pesek and Matija Marolt

Abstract This chapter presents our findings on emotional and color perception of music. It emphasizes the importance of user-aware music information retrieval (MIR) and the advantages that research on emotional processing and interaction between multiple modalities brings to the understanding of music and its users. Analyses of results show that correlations between emotions, colors and music are largely determined by context. There are differences between emotion-color associations and valence-arousal ratings in non-music and music contexts, with the effects of genre preferences evident for the latter. Participants were able to differentiate between perceived and induced musical emotions. Results also show how associations between individual musical emotions affect their valence-arousal ratings. We believe these findings contribute to the development of user-aware MIR systems and open further possibilities for innovative applications in MIR and affective computing in general.

16.1 Introduction

Research in music information retrieval (MIR) is multidisciplinary, comprising related fields of computer science, machine learning, cognitive science and human-computer interaction, among others. It aims to tackle three fundamental aspects: music information, the user, and the interactions between the two [31, 73]. Music information represents both the inherent musical properties (music content) and the contextual information about music, whereas information about the user includes

G. Strle (✉)
Scientific Research Centre, Institute of Ethnomusicology,
Slovenian Academy of Sciences and Arts, Ljubljana, Slovenia
e-mail: gregor.strle@zrc-sazu.si

M. Pesek · M. Marolt
Faculty of Computer and Information Science, University of Ljubljana,
Ljubljana, Slovenia
e-mail: matevz.pesek@fri.uni-lj.si

M. Tkalčič et al. (eds.), *Emotions and Personality in Personalized Services*,
Human–Computer Interaction Series, DOI 10.1007/978-3-319-31413-6_16

general information (such as personality traits and music preferences), as well as context-related information about the user's use and perception of music (e.g., current mood and emotions). Finally, the interaction involves various communication and interface modalities that integrate general and context-aware information about the user to reflect her music information needs and improve relevancy of results.

All three aspects should be considered for the effective development of MIR. However, the integration of user-context and related interaction modalities is still relatively poor. By ignoring the user, her perception and use of music, system-focused approaches lack grounding in the real world. Furthermore, the design and interaction decisions regarding representation of musical information often come secondary, based on the developer's intuitive notion or a priori assumptions of typical usage scenarios, not on the real data about the user [73, 75, 84, 95, 104]. Recent reviews of the state-of-the-art show that MIR research is still predominantly system-focused [47, 48, 74, 75, 82, 84, 104]. This situation is reflected in the activities of MIREX—Music Information Retrieval Evaluation eXchange,[1] the largest community-based framework that focuses on advances in MIR techniques and algorithms tailored to a variety of music-related tasks. Examples include audio classification, melody extraction, key detection, tempo estimation, music similarity and retrieval, with more recent attempts to integrate user information for purposes of music emotion recognition and mood estimation from audio, lyrics, or collaborative tags and their use in music recommendation and playlist generation.

Research in user-aware MIR is relatively new and efforts towards systematic approach and construction of formal user models are hindered by the scope and multidisciplinary nature of the field [18, 48]. For example, research in music cognition is faced with inherent complexity of music and cognitive issues related to music processing, further intensified by multimodal interactions (e.g., visual and auditory), effects of personality traits, mood and emotions, as well as by the ambiguity of abstract musical concepts and social and cultural differences [13, 20, 41, 49, 65, 66, 69, 89, 90].

This situation is reflected in existing MIR datasets. User information is sparse, typically accounting for basic demographic information and general music preferences (such as genre), while lacking in examination of user's use and perception of music. More complex MIR datasets, aimed at integrating different perceptual modalities to get additional insight into human music processing, are still in initial stage and face a number of problems. For example, in scientific literature much emphasis has been given to emotional aspects of music perception, such as the relationship between musically evoked and perceived emotions [26, 43, 76, 77, 100, 108]. But competing theories and different emotion models add to the overall confusion and make systematic comparison of results difficult, if not impossible [20].

Presented research aims to contribute to the advances of user-aware MIR by offering the Moodo dataset—a large-scale dataset of mood-dependent, emotional and color responses to music [68]. In total, over 7000 user annotations had been gathered, taking into account demographic information, user's mood and emotions,

[1] http://www.music-ir.org/mirex.

and her ratings of emotional and color perception of music for a variety of genres. In the process, two novel interfaces for emotion annotation had been developed, the *MoodStripe* and the *MoodGraph*, with the aim to alleviate some of the shortcomings of traditional emotion models.

In what follows, we discuss general aspects of gathering the Moodo dataset and present the analysis of results on emotional and color perception of music. Section 16.2 provides an overview of related work in MIR and music visualization, as well as some background on emotional processing and interactions between visual and auditory modalities, which serves as an introduction to the analysis of the Moodo dataset presented later in the chapter. Section 16.3 describes the design of the survey and the evaluation of two novel interfaces for gathering users' emotional responses to music, the *MoodStripe* and the *MoodGraph*. Section 16.4 provides the analysis of emotional and color responses to music. We show how emotions influence our perception of color and music, as well as interactions between both modalities. We conclude with the discussion on our findings.

16.2 Related Work

The following sections shortly present MIR research on emotional perception of music, issues in music visualization approaches, and give a general overview of emotional processing and interactions between auditory and visual modalities, setting the stage for the analysis in Sect. 16.4.

16.2.1 MIR Datasets and Music Visualization Approaches

16.2.1.1 Emotion Modeling in MIR

Most existing MIR studies on emotions in music use some variation of the discrete or dimensional emotion modeling approach for gathering user input, based on the Likert intensity scale or Russell's Circumplex model of affect [71]. Major difference between the two is the discrete emotion model represents individual emotions as discrete categories, whereas the dimensional model represents emotions as dimensions, typically in the two dimensional coordinate space of *valence* and *arousal*.

Variations of Russell's dimensional model have been used in several music-related studies [5, 46, 55, 106], with several researchers suggesting additional dimensions to better reflect the structure of musical emotions. For example, Schimmack et al. [78] propose two different interpretations of the arousal dimension through *energetic* (awake-tired) and *tense* (tense-calm) dimensions, Bigand et al. [7] and Canazza et al. [10] suggest that the additional third dimension *kinetics* may link perceived emotions with body posture and gestures, whereas Eerola et al. [21] propose *tension* as the additional third dimension to valence and arousal.

The strongest criticism of dimensional modeling is related to the limited number of dimensions used in modeling emotions, with the low-dimensional affective space typically reduced to valence and arousal. Discrete models aim to overcome this limitation by multiple-category rating of emotions [4, 40]. However, recent survey and comparative analysis of discrete and dimensional approaches to modeling emotions in music showed little advantages of the former over the latter—in fact, discrete models exhibit lower discriminative accuracy for musically induced emotions [19, 99].

In order to compensate for the limitations of current music emotion models, Zentner et al. [108] developed the GEMS—Geneva Emotional Music Scale, as a domain-specific emotion model for musically induced emotions. GEMS model, based on 45 terms, has been further adapted to shorter variants of 25 and 9 term models by Torres-Eliard et al. [93] and Aljanaki et al. [3]. The MIREX initiative, on the other hand, proposes a five-cluster model derived from the AllMusicGuide mood repository [32], with label sets consisting of 5–7 labels per cluster, resulting in total of 29 labels. In all, more extensive research is needed to confirm the advantages of initiatives like GEMS over more traditional approaches.

Furthermore, Saari and Eerola presented the affective circumplex transformation which possibly provides the connection between the discrete mood tags and the affective circumplex [72]. Wang et al. [101] proposed a Gaussian mixture representation model to enable the translation between discrete tags and continuous VA space. However, it seems there is currently no available dataset comprising both tag and VA point representations, as the aforementioned researches use multiple datasets to generate links between the two.

In Sect. 16.3 we present our contribution to the user-aware MIR, the *Mood-Graph*—a hybrid emotion model for gathering participants ratings by integrating multiple-category emotion labels with the dimensionality of valence-arousal space.

16.2.1.2 MIR Datasets

There is a growing number of MIR datasets that focus on modeling emotions in music.

The MoodSwings Turk Dataset contains on average 17 valence-arousal ratings for 240 clips of popular music [79]. The authors used a collaborative game MoodSwings [85] and Amazon Mechanical Turk (paid participation) for gathering perceived emotions in music. The game uses marked emoticons to express positive and negative emotions and their intensity in the valence-arousal space.

The Cal500 contains a set of mood labels for 500 popular songs [94], at approximately three annotations per song. The extended dataset CAL10k is also available, providing 10.870 songs from several thousand artists. It contains 475 acoustic tags and 153 genre tags [91] and 34 acoustic features.

The MTV Music Dataset [81] contains a set of five bipolar valence-arousal ratings, annotated by five different annotators with different musicological backgrounds, for 192 popular songs.

The *Emotion in Music Task* dataset, a part of MediaEval Benchmarking Initiative for Multimedia Evaluation [83], addresses the challenges of music emotion characterization and recognition. For example, the task for 2013 was dynamic emotion characterization, based on the continuous estimation of valence-arousal scores for each musical piece in the dataset. For this purpose, the annual music dataset of 45 s long musical pieces, annotated by a minimum of 10 workers, is gathered (1000 musical pieces for 2013 and 1744 for 2014). The organizers employ crowdsourcing approach, with annotations collected through Amazon Mechanical Turk and partially from publicly available data on Last.fm.

Using the aforementioned GEMS model, Aljanaki et al. [2] collected over 8000 responses by 1778 participants on a set of 400 music excerpts of classical, rock, pop and electronic music, equally represented by 100 excerpts each. The 9 GEMS model was used in the data gathering procedure, based on the Emotify game, developed for this purpose. Demographic data, comprising of gender, age and language was also collected.

Lykartsis et al. tested the GEMS model for electroacoustic and popular music [50], using a German version (GEMS-28-G), based on the GEMS-25 with additional three categories. There were 245 participants included in the study. The study included 20 music pieces of classical and popular instrumental music and electroacoustic music. Some demographic data was collected: age, language, level of education, music knowledge, and amount of listening to music per day.

An interesting application of the GEMS model is the study on emotional reactions to music, conducted by Jaimovich et al. [34], where the GEMS-9 model was used on 4000 participants and 12000 music excerpts based on 53 songs. Here, participants' electrodermal activity (EDA) and heart rate were also recorded.

The All Music Guide (AMG) 5 mood clusters were proposed by Hu and Downie [32], to "reduce the diverse mood space into a tangible set of categories" Several datasets used the proposed approach in a variety of task-specific applications. For example, Yi-Hsuan and Hu [106] collected a dataset of 2453 responses to a set of 500 Chinese music pieces—five labels per song on average and one expert annotation per song—to evaluate the acoustic features and compare them to responses on English music pieces. Laurier et al. [46] used the AMG mood clusters and *Last.fm* service social tags to observe the possible correlations between both. Panda et al. [63] created a multimodal MIREX-like emotion dataset collected from AllMusic database, organized by five emotion clusters from the AMG mood depository. The dataset is based on three sources containing 903 audio clips, 764 lyrics, and 193 midis.

To compare dimensional and discrete emotion models, Eerola et al. [16] gathered an annotated dataset of 360 film music clips, rated by 116 non-musician participants. Additional data about each participant include gender, age, years of musical training, and experience of playing an instrument. The experiment was divided into two stages: during the first stage, participants labeled individual musical excerpts in a three-dimensional valence-arousal-tension space (using bipolar scales), whereas during the second stage, 9-degree scales for each discrete emotion were used. The experiment was relatively time demanding, averaging between 50–60 min for each participant. The soundtracks dataset for music and emotion contains single mean ratings of perceived emotions (labels and values in a three-dimensional model are given).

Most of the existing MIR datasets contain a reasonable amount of demographic information. Yet none focus on interactions between visual and auditory modalities, connecting emotional and color perception of music—this has been the main motivation behind the Moodo dataset, presented in Sect. 16.3. Uncovering the relationship between emotions, colors and music is also relevant for more innovative approach to music visualization.

16.2.1.3 Music Visualization

In the past, user-oriented research in music visualization has been largely neglected [75, 82], but recent attempts (e.g., the Grand challenge at MIREX evaluation exchange initiative[2]) indicate a growing interest in the domain. There are numerous attempts of providing visualizations for a variety of music and audio features, from the low-level spectral features to the high-level music patterns and music metadata [15]. Most can be separated into two categories: visualizations of music parameters (e.g., harmonies, temporal patterns, and other music entities) [6, 29, 33, 35, 51] and visualizations of spaces representing relationships among different music pieces [44, 62]. The latter are more suitable for music recommendation systems and for data exploration in general. Examples include visualization of musical pieces as thumbnail images by Yoshii and Goto [107], visualization of personal music library (Torrens et al. [92]), and visualizations designed for the exploration of music collections on small-screen devices (Van Gulik et al. [96, 97]). Julia and Jorda [36] developed visualization for exploring large music collections in tabletop applications, thus extending user interaction beyond the standard keyboard/mouse interfaces, whereas Lamere and Eck [45] developed three-dimensional space visualization for music.

While there are significant advances in music visualization, most approaches still rely on the intuitive interpretation of color in music and lack real world data gathered with the analysis of various user scenarios [82]. For example, topographic visualizations of similarities in music, based on Self-Organizing Maps [42] or Islands of Music [61, 62]—a very popular approach in music visualization that efficiently reduces the dimensionality of data—use arbitrary sets of colors to differentiate between individual clusters. We believe that user-context is essential for improving music visualizations, as well as the overall design of MIR systems. The following section briefly discusses the importance of multimodal integration, both in MIR and affective computing in general.

[2]http://www.music-ir.org/mirex.

16.2.2 Multimodal Interactions

Integrating sensory information from various modalities is essential for a coherent perceptual experience. This integration is ongoing—the brain continually collects and estimates multiple sources of sensory information and, based on our prior knowledge, personality traits, as well as our affective state and understanding of the momentary context, attempts to make coherent representations of reality [9, 12, 88]. As the flux of information signals is noisy and incomplete, "the brain reduces the variance in the integrated estimate and increases the robustness of the percept by combining and integrating sources of sensory information from within and across modalities" [23]. The brain's effort to provide a coherent percept from concurrent stimulation of multiple modalities is not always successful. In one of the most famous examples of audio-visual integration, the McGurk effect [54], the auditory experience of speech perception is modulated by visual information, combining incongruent audio-visual stimuli, and as a result, altering the phonetic processing into an illusory perception of a sound. Thus, for multimodal integration to be successful, the key constraints of semantic and spatio-temporal congruency should be met [86, 87]. Overall, research on auditory and visual perception [8, 14, 25, 53, 64, 86, 98, 105] has shown significant benefits of multimodal interactions in terms of "filling in" the missing information, enhancing individual modalities and increasing the accuracy and robustness of resulting percept.

16.2.2.1 Relations to Music

Emotional processing of music is affected by many factors, most notably by individual's personality and age, music preferences (e.g. genre), musical features (e.g., rhythm, tempo, and mode), and mood. For example, Vuoskoski et al. [100] identified personality factors involved in the emotional processing of music and found mood- and trait-congruent biases in the perception of musical emotions, while Zentner, Grandjean, and Scherer [108] found significant variations in the emotional responses to various musical genres. Strong correlations have been found along valence and arousal, the two primary dimensions of emotion, and the individual musical features. Overall, rhythm and tempo are the two most prominent musical parameters associated with emotional processing, with rhythm having significant correlations along both valence (together with major and minor mode) and arousal dimensions, and tempo typically correlated with the arousal dimension [58]. Moreover, existing research has shown there are positive associations between the overall sound intensity and arousal [27], cases of cross-modal transfer of arousal to vision [52], and the effects of individual emotions on color-music associations [60]. In general, research on audio-visual integration shows flexible integration of both modalities [86], with the multisensory integration reducing ambiguity and providing the "faster and more accurate categorization" [11], and thus the richer and more coherent percept.

The underlying mechanisms governing emotion induction are not unique to music [39], and most of the presented findings can be extended to other domains of affective computing. Besides cognitive aspects, the benefits of multimodal integration are particularly relevant for the user-aware MIR systems, both in terms of the overall user experience, with audio-visual modalities being the dominant aspects of interface design, and the development of intelligent recommendation algorithms.

The first step toward user-aware MIR research is the creation of more comprehensive MIR datasets and integration of user-related information. In what follows, we present the methodology for gathering emotional and color responses to music in the *Moodo* dataset.

16.3 Online Survey: Gathering Emotional and Color Responses to Music

The specification for online survey was based on the preliminary study, with the aim to select relevant emotion labels, create interfaces for gathering participants' responses, evaluate different aspects of user experience and set guidelines for the overall design of the survey.

16.3.1 Preliminary Survey: Selection of Emotion Labels and Colors

To establish a relevant set of emotion labels for the main survey, we had performed a preliminary survey of emotion labels gathered from the music research literature [18, 22, 32, 37, 38, 108]. The preliminary survey was conducted in Slovenian language and asked 64 participants to describe their current affective state on a 7-degree Likert intensity scale, based on a set of 48 emotion labels selected from selected studies [70, 71, 103]. Principal component analysis of the gathered data revealed 64 % variance in the first three components, covering most of the 17 emotion labels chosen for the main survey. The final set of emotions used in the survey: *Anger, Anticipation, Calmness, Disappointment, Dreamy, Energetic, Fear, Gloominess, Happiness, Inspiring, Joy, Liveliness, Longing, Relaxed, Sadness, Surprise, Tension*. Additionally, mood labels were derived from the above set for gathering participants' self-reports on mood in the second part of the survey: *Active, Angry, Calm, Cheerful, Disappointed, Discontent, Drowsy, Happy, Inactive, Joyous, Miserable, Relaxed, Sad, Satisfied, Sleepy, Tired, Wide Awake*.

Next, we evaluated the effectiveness of the continuous color wheel for gathering color annotations for individual emotions. Most participants found the continuous color scale too complex. Consequently, a modified discrete-scale version with 49 colors displayed on large tiles was created. The set of 49 colors has been rated by most participants as providing a good balance between the complexity of the full continuous color wheel and limitations of choosing a smaller subset of colors.

Another important finding of the preliminary survey was participants' feedback on the interfaces for gathering emotion and color responses. Traditional Likert scale variations present a high task load, as each of the 48 emotions used in the main survey had to be rated on a separate scale. Thus, two novel graphical user interfaces for gathering mood and emotion ratings had been developed, the *MoodStripe* and *MoodGraph*. These are presented in the following sections together with other aspects of the main survey design.

16.3.2 Main Survey

The main survey was conducted online in three stages. Part one contains basic demographic questions, including questions regarding participant's musical experience. Part two focuses on participant's current mood, emotions and associated colors, and part three focuses on emotional and color responses to music.

16.3.2.1 Part One: Demographic Information

The first part of the survey captures basic demographic information (age, gender, area of living, native language) and participant's music-related information, including music education and skills (e.g., ability to play an instrument or sing), the amount of time listening to music, and genre preferences. Additional, more detailed questions were omitted, to reduce the overall duration of the survey (to estimated 15 min) and allow participants to focus on emotional, visual, and musical aspects in the second and third part of the survey.

16.3.2.2 Part Two: Gathering Participants' Self-reports on Mood, Emotions, and Colors

The second part of the survey focuses on participant's self-report on currently felt mood, emotions and associated colors.

Participant's affective state was captured in several ways. To estimate their current mood, participants were first asked to place a point in the valence-arousal space (Fig. 16.1, left). This is a standard mood estimation procedure in dimensional modeling. Self-reports on mood were only gathered at this stage of the survey, under the assumption that participant's mood will not change considerably throughout the remaining parts of the survey (average duration of the survey is 15 min).

Participants were then asked to choose colors best associated with currently felt emotions by selecting a color in the discrete color wheel (Fig. 16.1, right).[3] Next, the

[3]for colored figures (Fig. 16.1 (left) and Figs. 16.5, 16.6, 16.7, 16.8, 16.9, 16.10, 16.11, 16.12 and 16.13) refer to the electronic version of this paper.

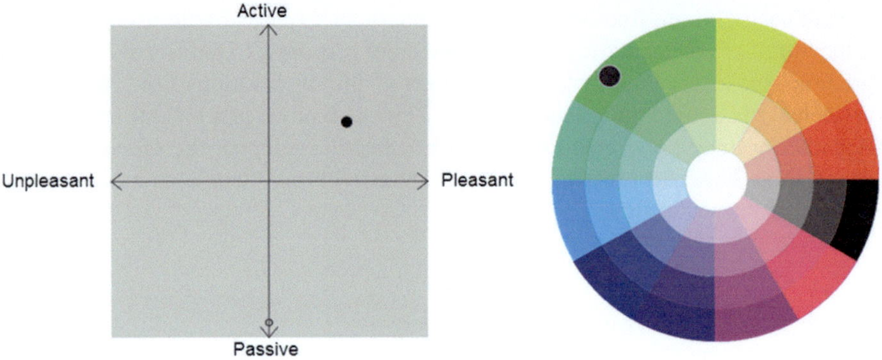

Fig. 16.1 *Left*: the *valence-arousal space*. The graph axes are marked *Unpleasant* and *Pleasant* for the abscissa, and *Passive* and *Active* for the ordinate values (the *black dot* indicates participant's selection in valence-arousal space). *Right*: the *discrete color wheel* with a set of 49 colors (the *black dot* indicates the selected color)

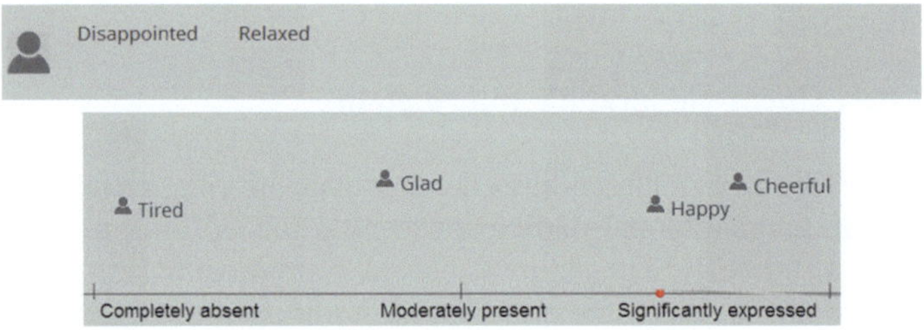

Fig. 16.2 The *MoodStripe*: participant drags emotions on the canvas according to their level of activation: from unexpressed to highly expressed (areas of the scale are marked from absent (*left*), moderately present (*middle*), to highly expressed (*right*)). Here, only a selection of emotion labels is presented. This interface is a substitute for a set of n-degree scales typically used in gathering user ratings

level of activity for 17 emotions was evaluated by positioning individual emotion labels in the *MoodStripe* interface (see Fig. 16.2). To make the task as easy and intuitive as possible, participants were able to drag and drop individual emotion labels onto the continuous activation space. This significantly reduced the overall task load, compared to the more traditional approach of using n-degree scales, where annotations for individual emotions need to be conducted on separate scales (see Sect. 16.3.3 for the evaluation of proposed interfaces).

Finally, participants assessed pleasantness and activity of individual emotions by positioning emotion labels onto the valence-arousal space of the *MoodGraph* interface (Fig. 16.3). The decision to use the *MoodGraph* interface instead of classical Russell's Circumplex model of affect [71] was to avoid the assumptions made in the latter, where the placement of individual emotions is designated to the specific areas (sections in the four quadrants) of the valence-arousal space. In music, this is not always the case (e.g., *sadness* is sometimes perceived as pleasant; see analysis

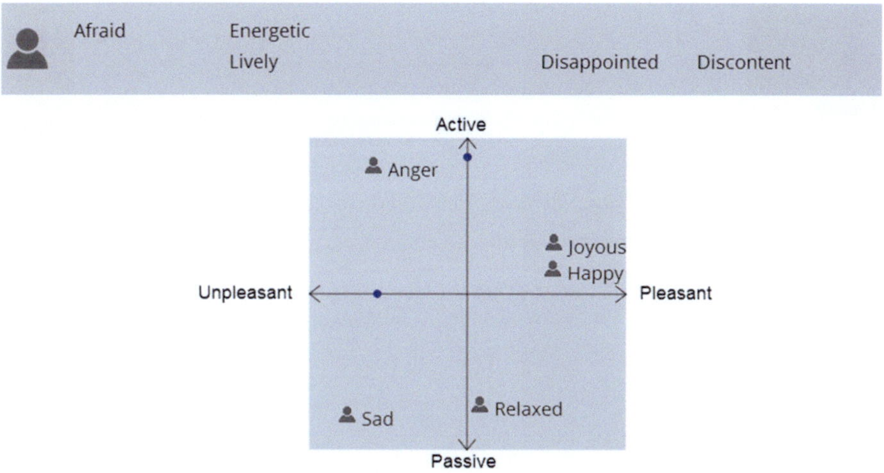

Fig. 16.3 The *MoodGraph*: emotions are dragged from the category container onto the valence-arousal space. *Blue dots* indicate the positions of selected emotion on both axes

in Sect. 16.4.4) and without imposing discrete areas of valence-arousal space the *MoodGraph* can account for the variability in perception and annotation of musical emotions.

Both novel interfaces, the *MoodStripe* and the *MoodGraph*, pose an alternative approach to gathering participants' ratings, replacing a set of ordinal n-degree scales. A subsequent evaluation of user experience and proposed interfaces showed that concurrent rating of emotions in the *MoodStripe* and the *MoodGraph* interfaces is intuitive and effective at reducing task load put on the participant (see Sect. 16.3.3).

16.3.2.3 Part Three: Emotional and Color Perception of Music

In part three of the survey, participants are asked to complete two tasks related to emotional processing of music. First, participants are presented with a set of 10 randomly selected 15 s long music excerpts. After listening to the excerpt, participant is first asked to select best matching color for the excerpt (Fig. 16.1, left). Next, participant is asked to place a set of emotion labels in the *MoodGraph* valence-arousal space, differentiating between two different categories of musical emotions: emotions evoked in the listener (induced emotions) and emotions expressed by music (perceived emotions). The category of induced emotion labels is marked with a person icon, whereas perceived emotion labels are represented with a note icon. Participants are instructed the first category (person icon) represents their personal emotions, what they feel when listening to the individual music fragment, and the second category (note icon) represents emotions that the music expresses (that one recognizes in music). Participants may place any number of emotions (but at least one from each category) in the *MoodGraph* (as shown in Fig. 16.4).

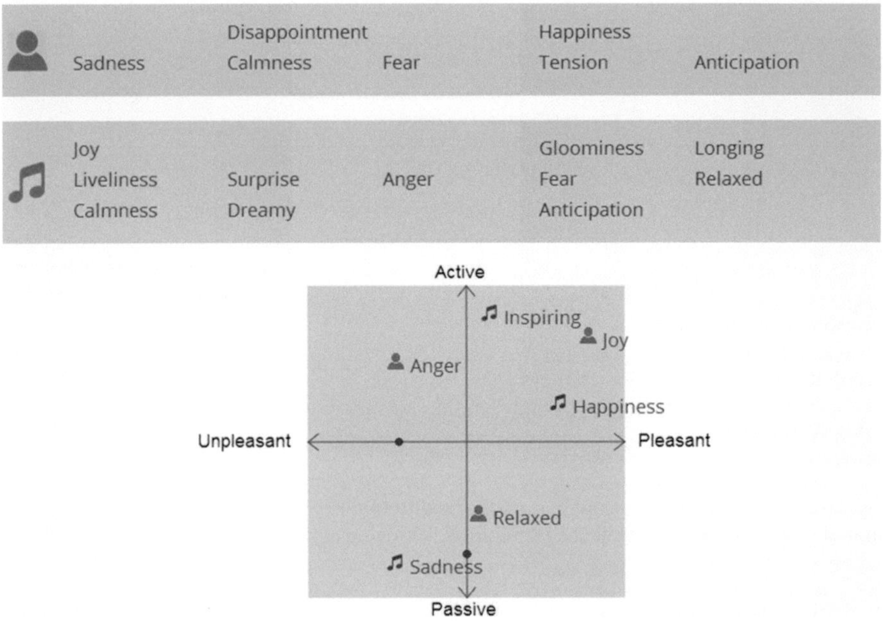

Fig. 16.4 The two-category *MoodGraph*: an extension of the one-category interface provides the participant with two categories, each denoted with an icon: a person icon for induced emotions and a note icon for perceived emotions

16.3.3 Evaluation of the MoodStripe and the MoodGraph Interfaces

We have conducted a subsequent evaluation of the *MoodStripe* and the *MoodGraph* interfaces, based on the feedback from participants of the survey. Participants were asked to evaluate several aspects of the survey: user experience (UX) [1], complexity of the questionnaire, and both interfaces. Our goal was to determine the functionality and user-friendliness of both interfaces compared to the standard approaches of gathering participant ratings. The evaluation of both interfaces contained a subset of the NASA load task index [30] evaluation survey and a set of specific questions. Results are presented in Sect. 16.3.3.1.

The online evaluation questionnaire was completed by 125 participants that previously participated in the main survey (detailed presentation of the results can be found in [67]). Results were generally positive and indicate overall balance of the survey and user-friendliness of both interfaces. They are summarized in Fig. 16.5. The majority of participants spent 11–15 min solving the survey (11). Although responses show balanced mental difficulty of the survey (1), the physical difficulty seems to be more uniformly distributed across participants (2). Thus, it can be speculated that the listening part of the survey presented a challenge for many participants.

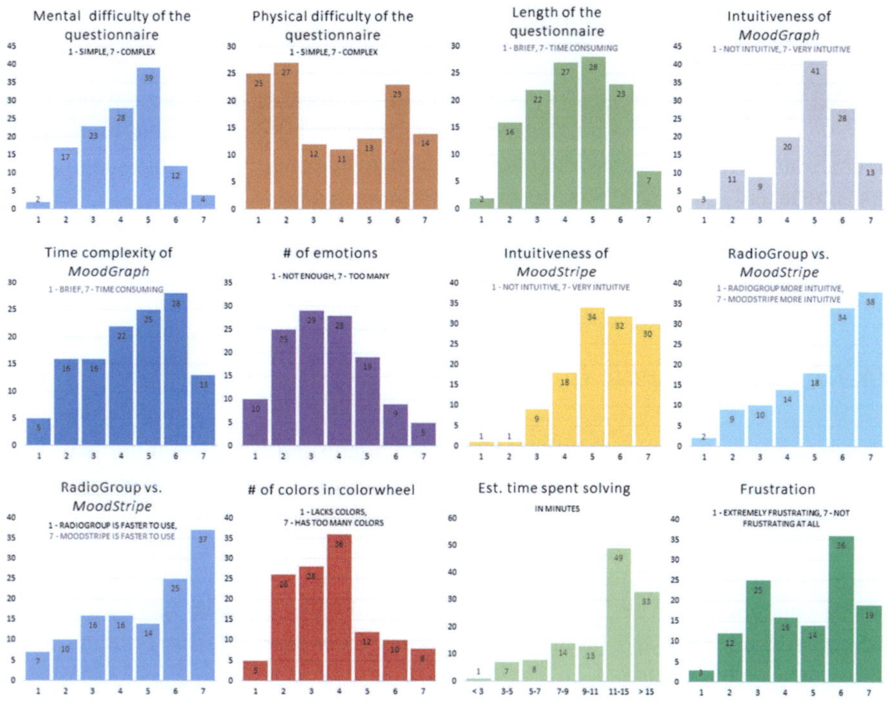

Fig. 16.5 The cumulative histograms for twelve evaluation questions

16.3.3.1 Results

The *MoodGraph* interface was evaluated as quite intuitive (4), however, it was also time consuming (5). Considering the complexity of required tasks (differentiating and rating emotions from two conceptually separate emotion categories, induced vs. perceived) and task load (e.g., the number of music excerpts, colors and emotions) put on participants, such feedback is realistic. Participants suggested the number of emotions in *MoodGraph* categories is slightly unbalanced (6), and we plan to review and extend both categories in the future. The *MoodStripe* interface represents a significant improvement over a variation of the Likert scale (a group of radio buttons), both in intuitiveness (7, 8) and time complexity (9). Participants also indicated that the set of 49 colors may not be large enough, so we will consider expanding the existing set.

Results of the evaluation demonstrate the usefulness of the proposed interfaces. The key advantages, compared to the standard input types, are reduced time complexity and task load, and an increased intuitiveness of the two novel interfaces, resulting in a lower mental difficulty and frustration of participants. At the same time, participants' comments give some useful future directions for improving the design and methodology of gathering participants' ratings on emotions, colors and music.

16.4 Analysis: Music, Colors, and Emotions

In what follows, we first present the demographic information on participants of the survey. Then we continue the discussion on emotional processing and multimodal interactions in music. We present correlations between emotions, colors and music in non-music and music contexts, the effects of genre preferences, differences between perceived and induced musical emotions, as well as differences in valence-arousal ratings for associations between individual musical emotions.[4]

16.4.1 Demographic Information

The online survey was completed by 741 participants, with total of more than 1100 participants participating, but not completing all three parts of the survey—these participants had been removed from the analysis. From 741 participants, 247 are men (33 %) and 494 are women (67 %). The youngest participant is 15 years old, the oldest is 64 years old. More than 75 % of participants fall into age group 30 years old or younger (Mean = 28.45 years). This is most likely due to the use of online survey, social media and public student associations channels for promotion and dissemination of the survey.

Almost 60 % of male and 44 % of female participants have no music education. From the participants with music education, 12 % of women and 6 % of men finished primary music education, which is a standardized 6 year program in Slovenia.

The most popular music genre is Rock, chosen by 31 % of participants. It is followed by Pop, chosen by 17 % of participants, Alternative and Classical, the latter two chosen by 5 % of participants. Other genres received significantly less than 5 % of the votes. As a second favorite genre, 20 % of participants chose Rock, whereas Pop received 14 % of votes. Classical music was the favorite genre in the third-favorite group (13 %), followed by Rock (12 %) and Pop (10 %).

16.4.2 Emotional Mediation of Color and Music

Interactions between auditory (music) and visual (color) modalities significantly depend on user's personality traits, temporary affective state and music context [39, 56, 59, 87]. Experiments conducted by [28, 60] show that cross-modal associations between music and colors use emotional mediation as the underlying mechanism. Their findings "associate specific dimensions of color (saturation, lightness, and yellowness-blueness) with specific high-level musical dimensions (tempo and

[4]Visualization tools for the general overview of the Moodo dataset are available here: http://www.moodo.musiclab.si/#/razplozenjeinglasba.

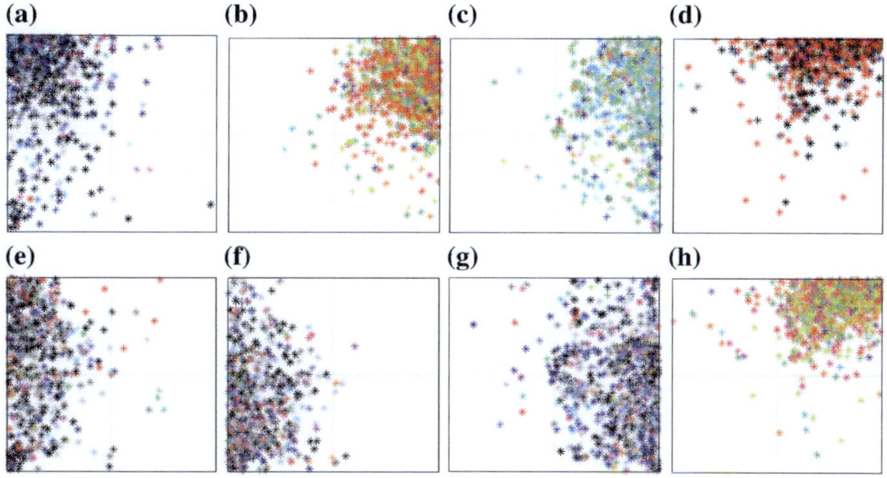

Fig. 16.6 Emotions and their color associations in the valence-arousal space (without music): **a** Anger. **b** Joy. **c** Happiness. **d** Energetic. **e** Fear. **f** Sadness. **g** Relaxation and **h** Liveliness [68]

mode), and show clear evidence of mediation by emotional dimensions (happy-sad and angry-calm)" [60]. Further evidence for direct cross-modal emotional mediation of both modalities has been shown by Pesek et al. [68], based on the analysis of participants' valence-arousal ratings of emotions and their color associations for individual music excerpts. Results show a stark contrast between valence-arousal ratings of individual emotions and their color associations in non-music context (emotion-color associations) and those in music context (emotion-color-music associations), as shown in Figs. 16.6 and 16.7 respectively.[5]

Color associations for individual emotions presented in Fig. 16.6 are in line with previous research [59], with the dark blue-violet and black hues associated with the negative emotions, such as fear and anger (A and E), the light green hues for happiness (C) and the more vibrant red-yellow-green hues for joy and liveliness (B and H), and the distinctly red for energetic (D). One noticeable exception is relaxation (G), occupying the positive position on the valence dimension, but with the hues similar to those of the negative emotions.

In music context (Fig. 16.7), the red hues prevail over the dark blue-violet and the gray-black hues for negative emotions (A and E), the green-yellow hues for positive emotions of joy and happiness (B and C) and on the positive arousal dimension for relaxation (G), while the green hues dominate in relaxation and calmness (G and H). Sadness (F) differentiates itself from the rest of emotions with prevalent blueness. There is an interesting correlation between color associations and the valence-arousal

[5]Note that emotions D: Energetic and H: Liveliness in Fig. 16.6 do not correspond to emotions D: Anticipation and H: Calmness in Fig. 16.7, as the latter are more appropriate in music context (for a discussion on musical and non-musical emotions, see [37]).

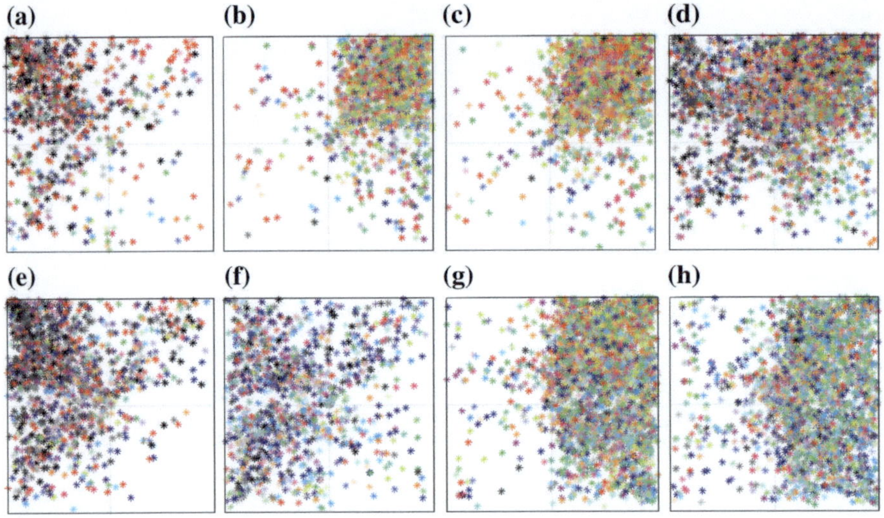

Fig. 16.7 Emotions and their color associations in the valence-arousal space (with music): **a** Anger. **b** Joy. **c** Happiness. **d** Anticipation. **e** Fear. **f** Sadness. **g** Relaxation and **h** Calmness

space for anticipation (D), where hues associated with the negative emotions dominate the negative pole of valence space, whereas green-blue hues, associated with more passive but pleasant emotions (such as G: Relaxation and H: Calmness), dominate in the quadrant of positive valence and negative arousal.

In general, emotions in music context occupy a more central position in the valence-arousal space, whereas the distribution of individual ratings is significantly larger than that of the emotion ratings in non-music context. This shows that musical emotions are being perceived differently from their non-music counterparts, and can at times occupy semantically opposite positions [108]; especially along the valence dimension, where for example sad music can sometimes be perceived as pleasant (compare E: Fear and F: Sadness in Figs. 16.6 and 16.7 for the distribution of valence-arousal ratings).

16.4.3 Genre Specificity of Musically Perceived Emotions

Emotional mediation of color and music associations is to some extent further constrained by the music genre. Beyond specific sets of musical characteristics and styles that differentiate one genre from another, genres also convey particular sets of musical emotions, or more precisely, emotions are perceived differently among individual genres because of the underlying musical characteristics and style represented by a particular genre [16].

Table 16.1 Typical emotions selected by participants for individual genres

Genre/emotion	Anger	Anticipation	Calmness	Fear	Happiness	Joy	Relaxation	Sadness
Country					✓	✓	✓	
Dance/Disco					✓	✓		
Easy listening			✓				✓	
Electronic		✓						
Hip hop/rap	✓			✓				
Metal	✓			✓				
New age		✓	✓	✓	✓		✓	✓
Pop		✓	✓			✓		✓
Rock	✓							✓

Comparing participants' ratings of music excerpts for different genres we can argue that genre specificity of musically perceived emotions is stronger for the musically more obscure genres (e.g., Metal), i.e. those genres that share least of common features with more mainstream genres, such as Pop or Dance/Disco, for example. Typical emotions (most used by participants) for selected genres are presented in Table 16.1, while Fig. 16.8 shows the valence-arousal ratings of top three genres (represented by music excerpts) and the prevalent color association for each of musical emotions (introduced in Fig. 16.7).

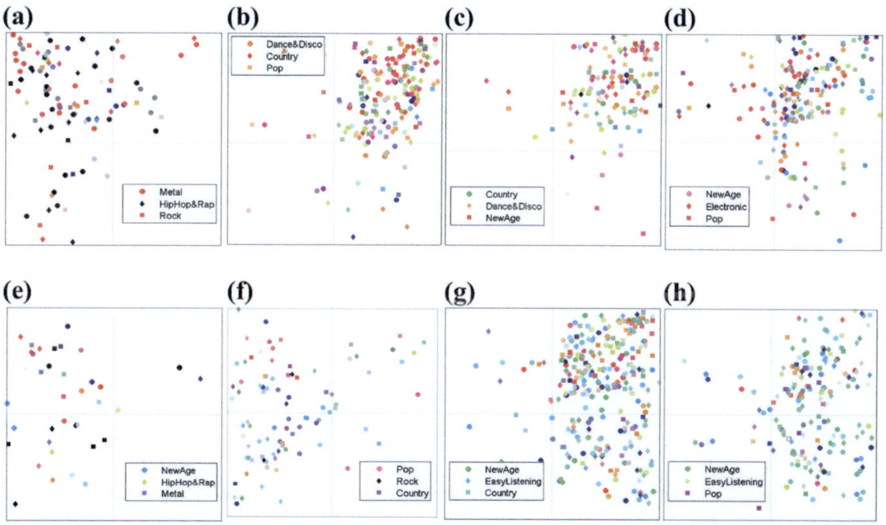

Fig. 16.8 Top three genres for individual emotions: **a** Anger. **b** Joy. **c** Happiness. **d** Anticipation. **e** Fear. **f** Sadness. **g** Relaxation. and **h** Calmness

As Table 16.1 and Fig. 16.8 show, different genres convey different sets of emotions, and even the same emotion might be perceived differently across musically and stylistically heterogeneous genres.

16.4.4 Perceived and Induced Emotions in Music

Emotional processing of music generally involves two types of emotions [24], those that are conveyed by music (perceived) and those evoked in the listener (induced). Preliminary analysis of the dataset showed that participants do differentiate between perceived and induced emotions. We found significant variance in participants' ratings of individual emotions from both categories, especially on the valence dimension, where variance was largest on the music perceived as unpleasant [68]. This finding shows that in certain music contexts, especially those with the perceived negative connotation, music can produce a variety of, sometimes polar, perceived-induced emotion responses in the listener (see Fig. 16.9). This is in line with the previous research on perceived and induced emotions in music [80], and while the differentiation between the two categories is not always clear (for the analysis of possible interactions, see [26]), the results show both aspects should be accounted for when integrating emotions into user-aware MIR systems.

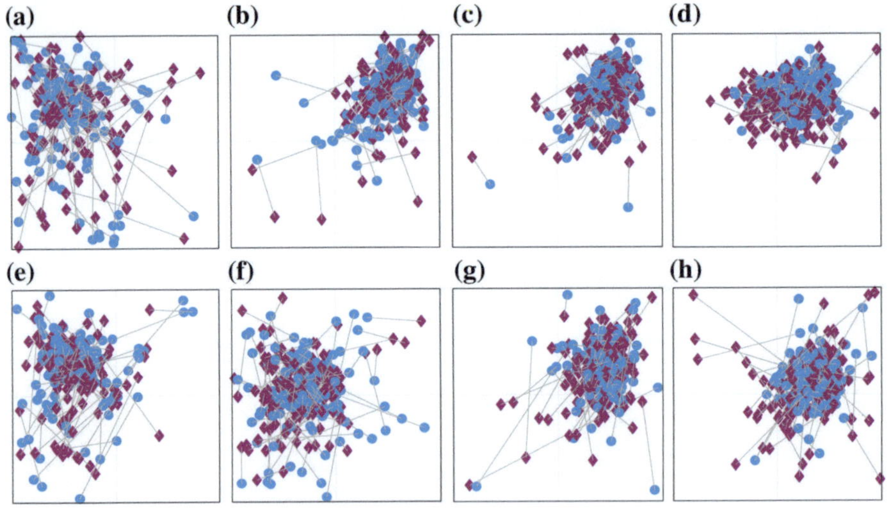

Fig. 16.9 Variance between induced (diamond) and perceived (circle) emotions in valence-arousal space [68]. Here, the average participants' ratings (centroids) for individual music excerpts are shown as induced-perceived emotion pairs for the following emotions: **a** Anger. **b** Happiness. **c** Joy. **d** Anticipation. **e** Fear. **f** Sadness. **g** Relaxation and **h** Calmness

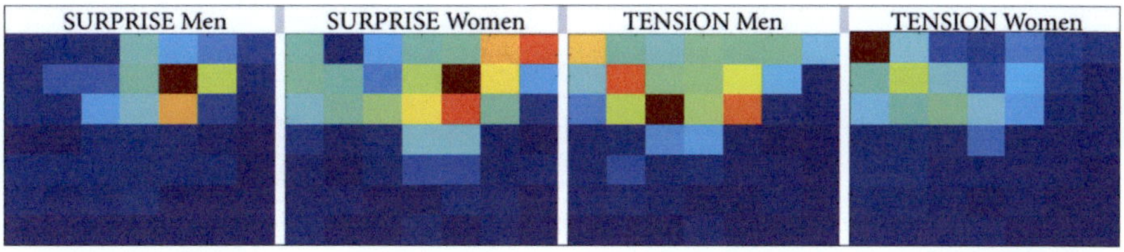

Fig. 16.10 Gender differences in the perception of musical emotions *Surprise* and *Tension*

16.4.5 Additional User Context: Mood, Gender and Musical Education

Beyond general correlations found in participants' emotional ratings of color and music there are additional user contexts that can give us further insight into our perception of music. Here, the effects of mood, gender and musical education, as well as the effects of different emotion combinations, are shortly presented through the analysis of quantized valence-arousal spaces, similar as used by [102]. These findings further emphasize the need for a more comprehensive MIR research and analysis of general user contexts.

Figure 16.10 shows differences in the perception of musical emotions between male and female participants for *surprise* and *tension*. These emotions represent the dynamic properties of music [21] and are perceived as such on the arousal dimension, with both groups rating them as active. However, there are significant differences in the perception of *surprise* and *tension* on the valence dimension, with females' ratings expressing significant variability on *surprise*, whereas males' ratings are more distributed on *tension*. This shows that at least in certain music contexts, the perception of *surprise* and *tension* is gender dependent. However, no significant differences were found in the male and female ratings for other musical emotions in the dataset.

Influence of mood is evident in the color perception of negative musical emotions, as shown in Fig. 16.11. Here, the color perception of *sadness* is perceived differently depending on the mood of the two groups of participants: participants of one group are in a satisfied mood, whereas participants of the other are discontent. The overall valence-arousal ratings are similar, but the difference in color ratings is obvious, with black only present in color ratings of participants feeling discontent. The effects of mood on the color perception of music have been found for the negative (unpleasant) emotions such as *sadness*, but not for the positive emotions, such as *happiness*.

Figure 16.12 shows the influence of music education on the perception of musical emotions *dreamy* and *surprise*. Participants with music education (years 1–20) exhibit a significantly higher variance on both valence and arousal dimension, compared to the participants with no music education. However, the influence of music education on the perception of music should be further investigated by mapping participants' valence-arousal ratings of emotions and colors to the underlying musical parameters.

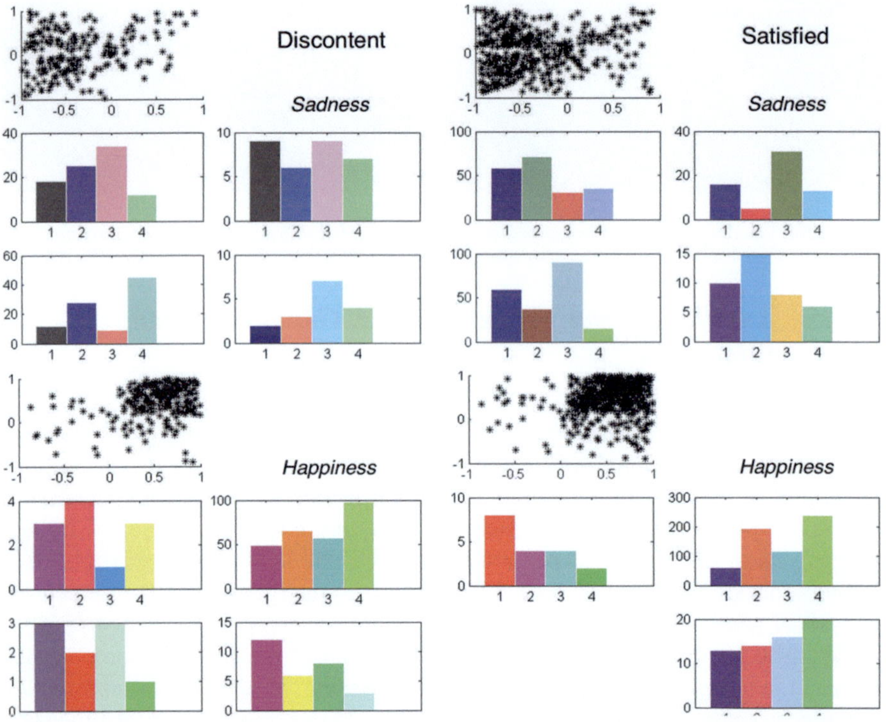

Fig. 16.11 Effects of participant's mood (Discontent vs. Satisfied) on the color perception of *sadness* and *happiness*

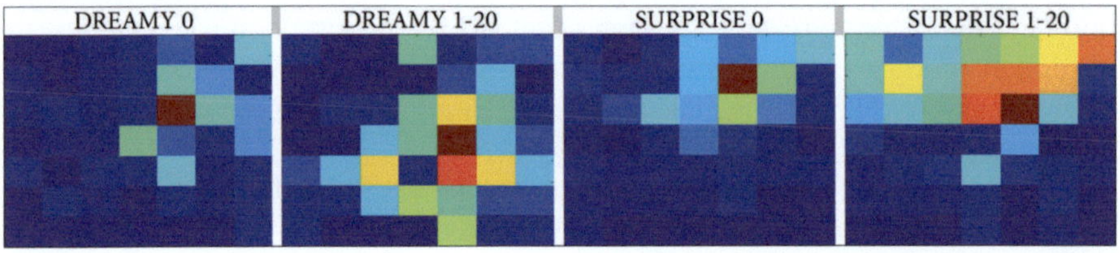

Fig. 16.12 Influence of music education on the perception of *dreamy* and *surprise* in music. Figure shows two groups of participants: participants with no music education ('DREAMY 0' and 'SURPRISE 0') and participants with music education ('DREAMY 1–20' and 'SURPRISE 1–20')

More widespread are the effects of emotion combinations presented in Fig. 16.13. The effects of negative and positive emotion combinations are shown through the variations in valence-arousal ratings for *anticipation*, *liveliness* and *tension*. Common to all three is the positive position on the arousal dimension, with *tension* leaning towards the negative and *lightness* towards the positive valence. Figure shows how the associated negative emotions (*Anger*, *Fear*) affect valence-arousal ratings of all three emotions towards the negative valence, whereas the associated positive

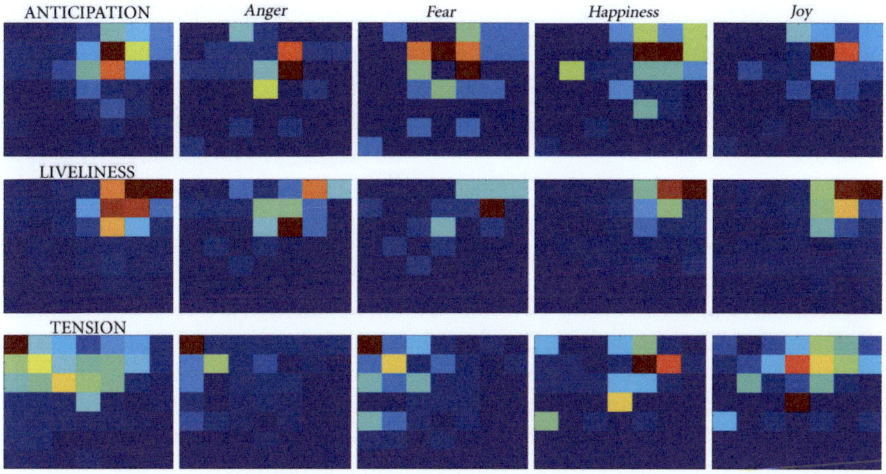

Fig. 16.13 Effects of emotion combinations on the perception of musical emotions for *anticipation*, *liveliness* and *tension*. Figure shows differences in valence-arousal ratings influenced by the associated negative (*anger*, *fear*) and positive (*happiness*, *joy*) emotions

emotions (*Happiness*, *Joy*) lean towards the positive valence. All three, *anticipation*, *liveliness* and *tension*, are often considered as alternative third dimension to valence and arousal, for modeling the dynamic aspects of music (such as tempo and rhythm) [17, 18].

16.5 Conclusions

The multidisciplinary nature of MIR research and the need for integration of the three fundamental aspects—music, the user and interaction—pose a number of exciting challenges for the future. The aim of this chapter was to address some of the current issues and argue towards user-aware MIR. And while the research on emotional and color perception of music is only a small piece in the overall 'user-aware' puzzle, we believe it is nevertheless important.

Presented analyses show that correlations between emotions, color and music are largely determined by context. There are differences between the emotion–color associations and valence-arousal ratings in non-music and music context, with the effects of genre preference evident for the latter. Participants were able to differentiate between perceived and induced musical emotions, and furthermore, between genre specific emotions. Results also show gender plays no major role and that female and male ratings of musical emotions and associated colors correlate, apart from differences in the perception of musical *tension* and *surprise*. The influence of mood is evident in the color perception of unpleasant emotions, such as *sadness*, but not for the positive emotions, such as *happiness*. More evident are the effects of emotion combinations describing music. Here, the associations between individual musical emotions affect their valence-arousal ratings, depending on the negative or the positive potency of individual emotion. The influence of music education has been shown for *dreamy* and *surprise*, and should be further investigated, especially in regard to the emotions that relate to the underlying musical parameters, such as *surprise*, *tension*, *anticipation* and *liveliness*. We assume that users with music education or skills might perceive music differently due to a better understanding of musical concepts [57], but other aspects, such as mood and personality, should be considered as well [99].

The underlying mechanisms governing emotion induction are not unique to music and most of the findings presented here can be extended to other domains of affective computing. The benefits of multimodal integration are particularly relevant to the user-aware systems research, both in terms of improving the overall user experience, with audio-visual modalities acting as the dominant features of interface design, as well as in improving the existing recommendation algorithms.

References

1. Albert, W., Tullis, T.: Measuring the user experience: collecting, analyzing, and presenting usability metrics (Google eBook). Newnes (2013)
2. Aljanaki, A., Bountouridis, D., Burgoyne, J.A., van Balen, J., Wiering, F., Honing, H., Veltkamp, R.C.: Designing games with a purpose for data collection in music research. Emotify and hooked: two case studies. Lecture Notes Computer Science (2014)
3. Aljanaki, A., Wiering, F., Veltkamp, R.C.: Computational modeling of induced emotion using GEMS. In: Proceedings of the International Conference on Music Information Retrieval (ISMIR), pp. 373–378. Taipei (2014)
4. Barthet, M., Fazekas, G., Sandler, M.: Multidisciplinary perspectives on music emotion recognition: implications for content and context-based models. In: CMMR, pp. 492–507. London (2012)
5. Barthet, M., Marston, D., Baume, C., Fazekas, G., Sandler, M.: Design and evaluation of semantic mood models for music recommendation using editorial tags. In: Proceedings of the International Conference on Music Information Retrieval (ISMIR). Curitiba (2013)
6. Bergstrom, T., Karahalios, K., Hart, J.C.: Isochords: visualizing structure in music. In: Proceedings of Graphics Interface, pp. 297–304 (2007)
7. Bigand, E., Vieillard, S., Madurell, F., Marozeau, J., Dacquet, A.: Multidimensional scaling of emotional responses to music: the effect of musical expertise and of the duration of the excerpts. Cogn. Emot. **19**(8), 1113–1139 (2005)
8. Bulkin, D.A., Groh, J.M.: Seeing sounds: visual and auditory interactions in the brain. Curr. opin. neurobiol. **16**(4), 415–419 (2006)
9. Calvert, G.A.: Crossmodal processing in the human brain: insights from functional neuroimaging studies. Cereb. Cortex **11**(12), 1110–1123 (2001)
10. Canazza, S., De Poli, G., Rodà, A., Vidolin, A., Zanon, P.: Kinematics-energy space for expressive interaction in music performance. In: Proceedings of MOSART. Workshop on Current Research Directions in Computer Music, pp. 35–40 (2001)
11. Collignon, O., Girard, S., Gosselin, F., Roy, S., Saint-Amour, D., Lassonde, M., Lepore, F.: Audio-visual integration of emotion expression. Brain Res. **1242**, 126–135 (2008)
12. De Gelder, B., Bertelson, P.: Multisensory integration, perception and ecological validity. Trends Cogn. Sci. **7**(10), 460–467 (2003)

13. Dibben, N.: Emotion and music: a view from the cultural psychology of music. In: Proceedings of the 2009 3rd International Conference on Affective Computing and Intelligent Interaction and Workshops, ACII 2009 (2009)
14. Doehrmann, O., Naumer, M.J.: Semantics and the multisensory brain: how meaning modulates processes of audio-visual integration. Brain Res. **12**(42), 136–150 (2008)
15. Donaldson, J., Lamere, P.: Using visualizations for music discovery. In: Proceedings of the International Conference on Music Information Retrieval (ISMIR). Tutorial (2009)
16. Eerola, T.: Are the emotions expressed in music genre-specific? An audio-based evaluation of datasets spanning classical, film, pop and mixed genres. J. New Music Res. **40**(4), 349–366 (2011)
17. Eerola, T.: Modeling listeners' emotional response to music. Top. Cogn. Sci. **4**, 607–624 (2012)
18. Eerola, T.: Modelling emotional effects of music: key areas of improvement. In: Proceedings of the Sound and Music Computing Conference 2013, SMC 2013. Stockholm, Sweden (2013)
19. Eerola, T., Vuoskoski, J.K.: A comparison of the discrete and dimensional models of emotion in music. Psychol. Music **39**(1), 18–49 (2010)
20. Eerola, T., Vuoskoski, J.K.: A review of music and emotion studies: approaches, emotion models, and stimuli. Music Percept. **30**(3), 307–340 (2013)
21. Eerola, T., Lartillot, O., Toiviainen, P.: Prediction of multidimensional emotional ratings in music from audio using multivariate regression models. In: Proceedings of the International Conference on Music Information Retrieval (ISMIR), pp. 621–626 (2009)
22. Ekman, P.: An argument for basic emotions. Cogn. Emot. **6**, 169–200 (1992)
23. Ernst, M.O., Bülthoff, H.H.: Merging the senses into a robust percept. Trends Cogn. Sci. **8**(4), 162–169 (2004)
24. Evans, P., Schubert, E.: Relationships between expressed and felt emotions in music. Musicae Sci. **12**, 75–99 (2008)
25. Evans, K.K., Treisman, A.: Natural cross-modal mappings between visual and auditory features. J. Vis. **10**(1), 6 (2010)
26. Gabrielsson, A.: Emotion perceived and emotion felt: same or different? Musicae Sci. **5**(1 suppl):123–147 (2002)
27. Gingras, B., Marin, M.M., Fitch, W.T.: Beyond intensity: spectral features effectively predict music-induced subjective arousal. Q. J. Exp. Psychol. 1–19 (2013) [ahead-of-print]
28. Griscom, W.S., Palmer, S.E.: The color of musical sounds: color associates of harmony and timbre in non-synesthetes. J. Vis. **12**(9), 74–74 (2012)
29. Grohganz, H., Clausen, M., Jiang, N., Mueller, M.: Converting path structures into block structures using eigenvalue decompositions of self-similarity matrices. In: Proceedings of the International Conference on Music Information Retrieval (ISMIR). Curitiba (2013)
30. Hart, S.G.: Nasa-task load index (NASA-TLX); 20 years later. Proc. Hum. Factors Ergon. Soc. Annu. Meet. **50**(9), 904–908 (2006)
31. Herrera-Boyer, P., Gouyon, F.: MIRrors: music information research reflects on its future: special issue foreword. J. Intell. Inf. Syst. **41**, 339–343 (2013)
32. Hu, X., Downie, J.S.: Exploring mood metadata: relationships with genre, artist and usage metadata. In: Proceedings of the International Conference on Music Information Retrieval (ISMIR). Vienna (2007)
33. Isaacson, E.: What you see is what you get: on visualizing music. In: Proceedings of the International Conference on Music Information Retrieval (ISMIR), pp. 389–395. London (2005)
34. Jaimovich, J., Coghlan, N., Knapp, R.B.: Emotion in motion: a study of music and affective response. In: From Sounds to Music and Emotions, pp. 19–43. Springer (2013)
35. Jiang, N., Mueller, M.: Automated methods for analyzing music recordings in sonata form. In: Proceedings of the International Conference on Music Information Retrieval (ISMIR). Curitiba (2013)
36. Julia, C.F., Jorda, S.: SongExplorer: a tabletop application for exploring large collections of songs. In: Proceedings of the International Conference on Music Information Retrieval (ISMIR), pp. 675–680. Kobe (2009)

37. Juslin, P.N., Sloboda, J.A.: Music and Emotion: Theory and Research. Oxford University Press (2001)
38. Juslin, P.N., Laukka, P.: Expression, perception, and induction of musical emotions: a review and a questionnaire study of everyday listening. J. New Music Res. **33**(3), 217–238 (2004)
39. Juslin, P.N., Västfjäll, D.: Emotional responses to music: the need to consider underlying mechanisms. Behav. Brain Sci. **31**(5), 559–575 (2008)
40. Kim, Y.E., Schmidt, E.M., Migneco, R., Morton, B.G., Richardson, P., Scott, J., Speck, J.A., Turnbull, D.: Music emotion recognition: a state of the art review. In: Proceedings of the International Conference on Music Information Retrieval (ISMIR), pp. 255–266. Utrecht (2010)
41. Koelsch, S.: Towards a neural basis of music-evoked emotions. Trends Cogn. Sci. **14**(3), 131–137 (2010)
42. Kohonen, T.: The self-organizing map. In: Proceedings of the IEEE **78**(9) (1990)
43. Kreutz, G., Ott, U., Teichmann, D., Osawa, P., Vaitl, D.: Using music to induce emotions: influences of musical preference and absorption. Psychol. Music **36**, 101–126 (2007)
44. Kurabayashi, S., Imai, T.: Chord-cube: music visualization and navigation system with an emotion-aware metric space for temporal chord progression. Int. J. Adv. Internet Technol. **7**(1), 52–62 (2014)
45. Lamere, P., Eck, D.: Using 3D visualizations to explore and discover music. In: Proceedings of the International Conference on Music Information Retrieval (ISMIR), pp. 173–174 (2007)
46. Laurier, C., Sordo, M., Serrà, J., Herrera, P.: Music mood representations from social tags. In: Proceedings of the International Conference on Music Information Retrieval (ISMIR), pp. 381–386 (2009)
47. Lee, J.H., Cunningham, S.J.: The impact (or non-impact) of user studies in music information retrieval. Ismir 391–396 (2012)
48. Lee, J.H., Cunningham, S.J.: Toward an understanding of the history and impact of user studies in music information retrieval. J. Intell. Inf. Syst. (2013)
49. Levitin, D.J., Tirovolas, A.K.: Current advances in the cognitive neuroscience of music. Ann. N.Y. Acad. Sci. **1156**, 211–231 (2009)
50. Lykartsis, A., Pysiewicz, A., Coler, H., Lepa, S.: The emotionality of sonic events: testing the geneva emotional music scale (GEMS) for popular and electroacoustic music. In: Proceedings of the 3rd International Conference on Music and Emotion (ICME3), pp. 1–15. Jyväskylä (2013)
51. Mardirossian, A., Chew, E.: Visualizing music: tonal progressions and distributions. In: Proceedings of the International Conference on Music Information Retrieval (ISMIR), pp. 189–194. Vienna (2007)
52. Marin, M.M., Gingras, B., Bhattacharya, J.: Crossmodal transfer of arousal, but not pleasantness, from the musical to the visual domain. Emotion **12**(3), 618 (2012)
53. Marks, L.E., Ben-Artzi, E., Lakatos, S.: Cross-modal interactions in auditory and visual discrimination. Int. J. Psychophysiol. **1**, 125–145 (2003)
54. McGurk, H., MacDonald, J.: Hearing lips and seeing voices. *Nature* **264**, 746–748 (1976)
55. Mcvicar, M., Freeman, T., De Bie, T.: Mining the correlation between lyrical and audio features and the emergence of mood. In: Proceedings of the International Conference on Music Information Retrieval (ISMIR), pp. 783–788. Miami (2011)
56. Meyer, L.B.: Emotion and Meaning in Music. University of Chicago Press. Chicago (1956)
57. Müllensiefen, D., Gingras, B., Musil, J., Stewart, L.: The musicality of non-musicians: an index for assessing musical sophistication in the general population. PLoS ONE **9**(2) (2014)
58. Omez, P., Danuser, B.: Relationships between musical structure and psychophysiological measures of emotion. Emotion **7**(2), 377 (2007)
59. Ou, L.-C., Luo, M.R., Woodcock, A., Wright, A.: A study of colour emotion and colour preference. Part I: colour emotions for single colours. Color Res. Appl. **29**(3) (2004)
60. Palmer, S.E., Schloss, K.B., Zoe, X., Prado-León, L.R.: Music-color associations are mediated by emotion. Proc. Natl. Acad. Sci. **110**(22), 8836–8841 (2013)

61. Pampalk, E., Dixon, S., Widmer, G.: Exploring music collections by browsing different views (2004)
62. Pampalk, E.: Islands of music analysis, organization, and visualization of music archives. OGAI J. (Oesterreichische Ges. Artif. Intell.) **22**(4), 20–23 (2003)
63. Panda, R., Malheiro, R., Rocha, B., Oliveira, A., Paiva, R.P.: Multi-modal music emotion recognition: a new dataset. In: Proceedings of the Methodology and Comparative Analysis CMMR (2013)
64. Parise, C.V., Spence, C.: 'When birds of a feather flock together': synesthetic correspondences modulate audiovisual integration in non-synesthetes. PLoS One **4**(5), e5664 (2009)
65. Pearce, M., Rohrmeier, M.: Music cognition and the cognitive sciences. Top. Cogn. Sci. **4**(4), 468–484 (2012)
66. Peretz, I., Coltheart, M.: Modularity of music processing. Nat. Neurosci. **6**(7), 688–691 (2003)
67. Pesek, M., Godec, P., Poredoš, M., Strle, G., Guna, J., Stojmenova, E., Pogačnik, M., Marolt, M.: Capturing the mood: evaluation of the moodstripe and moodgraph interfaces. In: Management Information Systems in Multimedia Art, Education, Entertainment, and Culture (MIS-MEDIA), IEEE Internation Conference on Multimedia and Expo (ICME), pp. 1–4 (2014)
68. Pesek, M., Godec, P., Poredos, M., Strle, G., Guna, J., Stojmenova, E., Pogacnik, M., Marolt, M.: Introducing a dataset of emotional and color responses to music. In: Proceedings of the International Conference on Music Information Retrieval (ISMIR), pp. 355–360. Taipei (2014)
69. Pressing, J.: Cognitive complexity and the structure of musical patterns. Noetica **3**, 1–8 (1998)
70. Remmington, N.A., Fabrigar, L.R., Visser, P.S.: Reexamining the circumplex model of affect. J. Pers. Soc. Psychol. **79**(2), 286–300 (2000)
71. Russell, J.A.: A circumplex model of affect. J. Pers. Soc. Psychol. **39**(6):1161–1178 (1980)
72. Saari, P., Eerola, T.: Semantic computing of moods based on tags in social media of music. IEEE Trans. Knowl. Data Eng. **26**(10), 2548–2560 (2014)
73. Schedl, M., Flexer, A.: Putting the user in the center of music information retrieval. In: Proceedings of the 13th International Society for Music Information Retrieval Conference, (Ismir), pp. 416–421 (2012)
74. Schedl, M., Knees, P.: Personalization in multimodal music retrieval. Lecture Notes in Computer Science (Including Subseries Lecture Notes in Artificial Intelligence and Lecture Notes in Bioinformatics), vol. 7836, LNCS, pp. 58–71 (2013)
75. Schedl, M., Flexer, A., Urbano, J.: The neglected user in music information retrieval research. J. Intell. Inf. Syst. **41**(3), 523–539 (2013)
76. Scherer, K.R.: Which emotions can be induced by music? What are the underlying mechanisms? And how can we measure them? J. New Music Res. **33**(3), 239–251 (2004)
77. Scherer, K.R., Zentner, M.R.: Emotional effects of music: production rules. In: Juslin, P.N., Sloboda, J.A. (eds.) Music and emotion. Oxford University Press, New York (2001)
78. Schimmack, U., Reisenzein, R.: Experiencing activation: energetic arousal and tense arousal are not mixtures of valence and activation. Emotion (Washington, D.C.) **2**(4), 412–7 (2002)
79. Schmidt, E.M., Kim, Y.E.: Modeling musical emotion dynamics with conditional random fields. In: ISMIR, pp. 777–782 (2011)
80. Schubert, E.: Emotion felt by listener and expressed by music: a literature review and theoretical investigation. Frontiers Psychol. **4**(837) (2013)
81. Schuller, B., Hage, C., Schuller, D., Rigoll, G.: 'Mister DJ, cheer me up!': musical and textual features for automatic mood classification. J. of New Music Res. **39**(1), 13–34 (2010)
82. Serra, X., Magas, M., Benetos, E., Chudy, M., Dixon, S. Flexer, A., Gómez, E., Gouyon, F., Herrera, P., Jordà, S., Paytuvi, O., Peeters, G., Vinet, H., Widmer, G.: Roadmap for music information research. Jan Schlüter (2013)
83. Soleymani, M., Caro, M.N., Schmidt, E.M., Sha, C.-Y., Yang, Y.-H.: 1000 songs for emotional analysis of music. In: Proceedings of the 2nd ACM International Workshop on Crowdsourcing for Multimedia—CrowdMM '13, pp. 1–6. ACM Press, New York, USA (2013)

84. Song, Y., Dixon, S., Pearce, M.: A survey of music recommendation systems and future perspectives. In: Proceedings of the 9th International Symposium Computer Music Modelling and Retrieval (CMMR), pp. 395–410. London (2012)
85. Speck, J.A., Schmidt, E.M., Morton, B.G., Kim, Y.E.: A comparative study of collaborative vs. traditional musical mood annotation. In: Proceedings of the International Conference on Music Information Retrieval (ISMIR), pp. 549–554. Miami (2011)
86. Spence, C.: Audiovisual multisensory integration. Acoust. Sci. Technol. **28**(2), 61–70 (2007)
87. Spence, C.: Crossmodal correspondences: a tutorial review. Atten. Percept. Psychophys. **4**(1), 971–995 (2011)
88. Spence, C., Senkowski, D., Röder, B.: Crossmodal processing. Exp. Brain Res. **198**(2), 107–111 (2009)
89. Stalinski, S.M., Schellenberg, E.G.: Music cognition: a developmental perspective. Top. Cogn. Sci. **4**(4), 485–497 (2012)
90. Stevens, C.J.: Music perception and cognition: a review of recent cross-cultural research. Top. Cogn. Sci. **4**, 653–667 (2012)
91. Tingle, D., Kim, Y.E., Turnbull, D.: Exploring automatic music annotation with "acoustically-objective" tags. In: Proceedings of the International Conference on Music Information Retrieval (ISMIR), pp. 55–62. New York (2010)
92. Torrens, M., Hertzog, P., Arcos, J.L.: Visualizing and exploring personal music libraries. In: Proceedings of the International Conference on Music Information Retrieval (ISMIR). Barcelona (2004)
93. Torres-Eliard, K., Labbé, C., Grandjean, D.: Towards a dynamic approach to the study of emotions expressed by music. Lect. Notes Inst. Comput. Sci. Soc. Inform. Telecommun. Eng. **78**, 252–259 (2011)
94. Turnbull, D., Barrington, L., Torres, D., Lanckriet, G.: Semantic annotation and retrieval of music and sound effects. IEEE Trans. Audio Speech Lang. Process. **16**(2), 467–476 (2008)
95. Typke, R., Wiering, F., Veltkamp, R.C.: A survey of music information retrieval systems. In: Proceedings of the International Symposium on Music Information Retrieval, ISMIR, pp. 153–160 (2005)
96. Van Gulik, R., Vignoli, F.: Visual Playlist generation on the artist map. In: Proceedings of the International Conference on Music Information Retrieval (ISMIR). London (2005)
97. Van Gulik, R., Vignoli, F., Van de Wetering, H.: Mapping music in the palm of your hand, explore and discover your collection. In: Proceedings of the International Conference on Music Information Retrieval (ISMIR). Barcelona (2004)
98. Vroomen, J., de Gelder, B.: Sound enhances visual perception: cross-modal effects of auditory organization on vision. J. Exp. Psychol. Hum. Percept. Perform. **26**(5), 1583–1588 (2000)
99. Vuoskoski, J.K., Eerola, T.: Measuring music-induced emotion: a comparison of emotion models, personality biases, and intensity of experiences. Musicae Sci. **15**(2), 159–173 (2011)
100. Vuoskoski, J.K., Eerola, T.: The role of mood and personality in the perception of emotions represented by music. Cortex **47**(9), 1099–1106 (2011)
101. Wang, J.C., Yang, Y.H., Chang, K., Wang, H.M., Jeng, S.-K.: Exploring the relationship between categorical and dimensional emotion semantics of music. In: Proceedings of the Second International ACM Workshop on Music Information Retrieval with User-centered And Multimodal Strategies—MIRUM '12, p. 63. ACM Press, New York, USA (2012)
102. Wang, J.-C., Wang, H.-M., Lanckriet, G.: A histogram density modeling approach to music emotion recognition. In: 2015 IEEE International Conference on Acoustics, Speech and Signal Processing. IEEE (2015)
103. Watson, D., Clark, L.A., Tellegen, A.: Development and validation of brief measures of positive and negative affect: the PANAS scales. J. Pers. Soc. Psychol. **54**(6), 1063–1070 (1988)
104. Weigl, D., Guastavino, C.: User studies in the music information retrieval literature. Ismir 335–340 (2011)
105. Witten, I.B., Knudsen, E.I.: Why seeing is believing: merging auditory and visual worlds. Neuron **48**(3), 489–496 (2005)

106. Yang, Y.H., Chen, H.H.: Machine recognition of music emotion (2012)
107. Yoshii, K., Goto, M.: Music thumbnailer: visualizing musical pieces in thumbnail images based on acoustic features. In: Proceedings of the International Conference on Music Information Retrieval (ISMIR), pp. 211–216. Philadelphia (2008)
108. Zentner, M., Grandjean, D., Scherer, K.R.: Emotions evoked by the sound of music: characterization, classification, and measurement. Emotion **8**(4), 494 (2008)

Part IV
Evaluation and Privacy

Chapter 17
Emotion Detection Techniques for the Evaluation of Serendipitous Recommendations

Marco de Gemmis, Pasquale Lops and Giovanni Semeraro

Abstract Recommender systems analyze a user's past behavior, build a user profile that stores information about her interests, maybe find others who have a similar profile, and use that information to find potentially interesting items. The main limitation of this approach is that provided recommendations are accurate, because they match the user profile, but not useful as they fall within the existing range of user interests. This drawback is known as overspecialization. New methods are being developed to compute serendipitous recommendations, i.e. unexpected suggestions that stimulate the user curiosity toward potentially interesting items she might not have otherwise discovered. The evaluation of those methods is not simple: there is a level of emotional response associated with serendipitous recommendations that is difficult to measure. In this chapter, we discuss the role of emotions in recommender systems research, with focus on their exploitation as implicit feedback on suggested items. Furthermore, we describe a user study which assesses both the acceptance and the perception of serendipitous recommendations, through the administration of questionnaires and the analysis of users' emotions. Facial expressions of users receiving recommendations are analyzed to evaluate whether they convey a mixture of emotions that helps to measure the perception of serendipity of recommendations. The results showed that positive emotions such as happiness and surprise are associated with serendipitous suggestions.

M. de Gemmis (✉) · P. Lops · G. Semeraro
Department of Computer Science, University of Bari Aldo Moro, Bari, Italy
e-mail: marco.degemmis@uniba.it

P. Lops
e-mail: pasquale.lops@uniba.it

G. Semeraro
e-mail: giovanni.semeraro@uniba.it

M. Tkalčič et al. (eds.), *Emotions and Personality in Personalized Services*,
Human–Computer Interaction Series, DOI 10.1007/978-3-319-31413-6_17

17.1 The Overspecialization Problem

Recommender systems adopt information filtering algorithms to suggest items or information that might be interesting to users. In general, these systems analyze a user's past behavior, maybe find others who have a similar history, and use that information to provide suggestions. For example, if you tell the Internet Movie Database (IMDb)[1] that you like the movie *Star Wars*, it will suggest movies liked by other people who liked that movie, most of whom are probably science-fiction fans. Most of those recommendations are likely to be already known to the user, who will be provided with items within her existing range of interests, and her tendency towards a certain behavior is reinforced by creating a self-referential loop. This drawback is usually known as *overspecialization* [29], and stimulates researchers in the area of information filtering and retrieval to design methods able to find serendipitous items.

Several definitions of serendipity have been proposed in recommender systems literature. A commonly agreed one, proposed by Herlocker et al. [22], describes serendipitous recommendations as the ones helping the user to find surprisingly interesting items she might not have discovered by herself. McNee et al. [29] identify serendipity as the experience of receiving an unexpected and fortuitous item recommendation, while Shani and Gunawardana [39] state that serendipity involves a positive emotional response of the user about novel items and measures how surprising these recommendations are.

According to these definitions, serendipity in recommender systems is characterized by *interestingness* of items and the *surprise* for users who get *unexpected* suggestions. Therefore, in our study we define serendipitous suggestions those which are both *attractive* and *unexpected.* Attractiveness is usually determined in terms of closeness to the user profile [27], while unexpectedness of recommendations is defined in literature as the deviation from a benchmark model that generates expected recommendations [20, 30]. Expected movie recommendations could be blockbusters seen by many people, or movies related to those already seen by the user, such as sequels, or those with same genre and director.

In order to make clearer the adopted definition of serendipity, it is useful to point out the differences with related notions of *novelty* and *diversity*. The *novelty* of a recommendation generally refers to how different it is with respect to "what has been previously seen" by a user or a community [22, 46]. Continuing with our movie recommendation scenario, if the system suggests a movie the user was not aware of, directed by his favorite director, that movie will be novel, but not serendipitous.

Diversity (see also Chap. 11) represents the variety present in a list of recommendations [19, 50]. Methods for the diversification of suggestions are generally used to avoid homogeneous lists, in which all the items suggested are very similar to each other [2]. This may reduce the overall accuracy of the recommendation list because none of the alternative suggestions will be liked, in case the user wants something different from the usual. Although diversity is very different from serendipity, a relationship between the two notions exists, in the sense that providing the user with a

[1] www.imdb.com.

diverse list can facilitate unexpectedness [1]. However, the diversification of recommendations does not necessarly imply serendipity since diverse items could all fall into the range of user preferences.

In this chapter, we focus on the problem of evaluating the degree of serendipity of recommendations. In particular, we investigate the issue of designing an evaluation framework that measures the perception of serendipity, given that providing non-obvious recommendation can hurt the accuracy of the system. We suggest that affective states derived from *facial expressions* could be particularly useful in those evaluation scenarios, such as the assessment of serendipity, where traditional performance measures are not sufficient to catch the perceived quality of suggestions with respect to the specific aspect being assessed. The idea is that facial expression analysis can give information about the affective state of the user and therefore could be exploited to detect her emotive response to an observed item.

The main contribution of the chapter with respect to the above mentioned issue is the design of an evaluation framework which exploits the emotional feedback of users provided with serendipitous recommendations. We performed a user study which assessed the actual perception of serendipity of recommendations and their *acceptance* in terms of both relevance and unexpectedness by means of the Noldus FaceReader™, a tool for emotion detection. The system gathers implicit feedback about users' reactions to recommendations through the analysis of their facial expressions, and classifies the collected emotional feedback in the categories of emotions proposed by Ekman [14]. We argue that serendipity can be associated with some of them, and the results of the experiments support our hypothesis.

In the following section, we analyze how emotions can affect people's choices and discuss some literature about the exploitation of implicit emotional feedback in recommender systems research. In Sect. 17.3 we briefly describe a knowledge-based recommendation process which adopts Random Walk with Restarts [28] as an algorithm for computing serendipitous suggestions. Section 17.4 describes the experiments designed to evaluate the effectiveness of the proposed approach. The innovative aspect of the evaluation process is that implicit emotional feedback detected from facial expressions of users are adopted to assess the degree of serendipity of recommended items. Conclusions are drawn in the final section.

17.2 Exploitation of Emotions Detected from Facial Expressions in Recommender Systems Research

In this chapter, we argue that implicit emotional feedback automatically detected from facial expression could help to assess serendipity of recommendations. In order to fully understand the role of emotions in recommender systems, we need to discuss how emotions influence human decision making as well.

17.2.1 What Roles Does Emotion Play in Decision Making?

The question of how to conceptualize emotions concerning their role in decision making (DM) has been deeply studied in the psychological literature over the last 20 years [18, 26, 31–33]. According to traditional approaches of behavioral decision making, choosing is seen as a rational cognitive process that estimates which of various alternative choices would yield the most positive consequences, which does not necessarily entail emotions. Emotions are considered as external forces influencing an otherwise non-emotional process (influence-on metaphor). Loewenstein and Lerner [26] distinguish between two different ways in which emotions enter into decision making. The first influence is that of expected emotions, i.e. beliefs about the emotional consequences of the decision outcomes: users might evaluate the consequences of the possible options by taking into account both positive and negative emotions associated with them and then select those actions that maximize positive emotions and minimize negative emotions. The other kind of affective influence on DM consists of immediate emotions that are experienced at the time of decision making. Such feelings often drive behavior in directions that are different from those coming from the rational mental process and thus derived by a consequentialist evaluation of future consequences. The immediate emotions experienced by a decision maker reflect the combined effect of two factors: anticipatory influence, which originates from the decision problem itself, and incidental influence, which stems from factors unrelated to the problem at hand. It is important to point out the difference between anticipatory influence of immediate emotions and expected emotions, which are expectations about emotions that will be experienced in the future (cognitions about future affect). Anticipatory influence is determined by present feelings which stem from contemplating the consequences of the decision problem. Immediate emotions can have either a direct or an indirect impact on DM. As an example, consider the choice of whether to invest some savings into a startup company. In making this decision, an investor might assign a value to several aspects describing the business plan of the company, such as market analysis, financial plan, SWOT analysis. The immediate anxiety felt at the prospect of shifting savings to finance the company might have a direct impact on the decision, i.e. the emotion triggers the renounce to invest, which is independent of the desirability of the option estimated in terms of evaluated aspects. The preexisting (incidental) good mood of an investor might have an indirect impact, by altering the investor's evaluation of the probabilities of different consequences, e.g. leading to a more optimistic estimate of the returns on the initial investment. Other research focused on the informational value of affect, that is when decision makers intentionally consult their feelings about an option and use that information to guide the decision process. In that situation, four roles of emotions are identified [31]:

1. Information: affect developed through experience provides information about what to choose and what to avoid by marking decision options and attributes by positive and negative feelings;

2. Spotlight: emotions can focus the decision maker's attention on certain aspects of the problem and might alter what information becomes salient;
3. Motivator: incidental emotions motivate behavior as people tend to act to maintain or attain positive mood states;
4. Currency: affect can provide a common currency for experiences, thus enabling people to compare even complex arguments on a common underlying dimension.

These roles can be found even mixed when selecting an option. For example, when the decision maker adopts a strategy of choosing based on previous experiences with similar problems, past choices adopted in situations similar to the current decision problem can be evaluated according to the positive or negative feelings they evoke (information role). Then, options can be compared by simpler affective evaluations, rather than by attempting to make sense out of a multitude of conflicting logical reasons (currency role). Another example is when the chooser C allows himself to be guided by *social expectations*, affect may act as a *motivator of behavior*, in the sense that C might select an option being influenced by the positive or negative feeling originated by expectations of other people. For example, C might decide to buy a smartphone of brand X only because X is viewed as "trendy" by her friends, even if C considers that item too expensive with respect to the values of its technical features. The motivation for that choice is the negative feeling of being considered "uncool".

These ideas are endorsed and extended in the work by Pfister and Bohm [33], in which a new vision about the classical influence-on metaphor has been proposed: emotions do not simply influence a purely rational process, but they are virtually part of any DM process. Therefore, recommender systems research shouldn't consider emotions and feelings only as the classical influence-on metaphor, i.e. as simply contextual factors. In fact, some authors have started exploiting the *information role* of emotions and feelings by using them as a source of affective metadata, included in the process of building a preference model [45]. The idea is to label consumed items both with ratings and *affective responses* of users (e.g. a movie is rated with 5 stars and labeled with "happiness"), so that this information could be exploited by the recommendation algorithm to build the preference model (user likes movies which induce happiness). More details are provided in the next section.

17.2.2 Emotions as Implicit Feedback on Recommended Items

The advances in computer vision techniques and algorithms for emotion detection has enabled the usage of facial expressions as a direct source of information about the affective state of the user [16, 49]. This kind of implicit affective feedback has been exploited in several domains, such as consumer behavior research [13], gaming research [10] and educational research [43], to detect the emotional response of the user to an observed or consumed item. In understanding this emotional response, we recall here that the term *emotion* must be clearly distinguished from *mood*, that is a diffused affective state that is long, slow moving and not tied to a specific object or elicitor, whereas emotions can occur in short moments with higher intensities [36]. In recommender systems literature, emotional feedback is mainly associated with multimedia content [40, 41, 44, 45] and play different roles related to the acquisition of user preferences:

1. As a source of affective metadata for item modeling and building a preference model;
2. As an implicit relevance feedback for assessing user satisfaction.

As for the first issue, the idea is to acquire affective features that are included in the item profile and might be exploited for user modeling. In [45] a feature vector is acquired, that represents the valence, arousal and dominance dimensions (identified by Russell [35]) of the emotive response of a user to an item; then the user model is inferred by machine learning algorithms trained on the item profiles and the explicit ratings given to the consumed items. The detected emotion can be used in two ways: item categorization (the item i is funny because it induces happiness in most of the users) and user modeling (the user u likes items that induce sadness). In [23], a probabilistic emotion recognition algorithm based on facial expressions was employed to detect emotions of users watching video clips. The level of expressed emotions associated with items were used as features to detect personal highlights in the videos. The main issue that these and other similar studies addressed [47] is the identification of a valid set of affective features that allows the definition of an effective user model for the canonical (relevant/non-relevant) item categorization. The main challenge from both a user modeling and decision making perspective is how to represent the whole affective state of the user in terms of emotions, mood, and personality.

As for the second issue, the main motivation for assessing user's relevance by means of emotions detection techniques is that, since satisfaction is an internal mental state, techniques that can disclose feelings without any bias are expected to be a reliable source of implicit feedback. In fact, the emotional response is hardly alterable by the user. Furthermore, face detection is unobtrusive because usually the user is monitored by a camera, and then recorded videos are analyzed by a facial expression recognition system. Pioneer studies on this topic are those made by Arapakis et al. [4–6]. They introduced a method to assess the topical relevance of videos in accordance to a given query using facial expressions showing users satisfaction or dissatisfaction. Based on facial expressions recognition techniques, basic emotions were detected and compared with the ground truth. They investigated also the feasibility of using reactions derived from both facial expressions and physiological signals as implicit indicators of topical relevance.

We present a study which discusses the hypothesis that facial expressions of users might convey a mixture of emotions that helps to measure the perception of serendipity of recommendations. We argue that serendipity could be associated with surprise and happiness, the only two emotions, among those suggested by Ekman (happiness, anger, sadness, fear, disgust and surprise) [15], which are reasonably related to the pleasant surprise serendipity should excite. We used the Noldus FaceReader system to detect the emotions of users when provided with movie recommendations, while the ground truth for serendipity of recommendations (items both relevant and unexpected) is established by means of questionnaires.

17.3 A Recommendation Process for Serendipitous Suggestions

We propose a recommendation process which aims at finding serendipitous suggestions, while preserving accuracy at the same time, by exploiting exogenous knowledge coming from information sources available on the web. The idea stems from the fact that overspecialization is caused often by weak similarity computation among items or among items and user profiles. For instance, movie recommendation based on co-rating statistics or content similarity among director, cast or plot keywords might lead to suggest movies with same or similar genres.

We designed a strategy, called Knowledge Infusion (KI) [37], that automatically builds a background knowledge used by the recommendation algorithm to find meaningful hidden correlations among items. The hypothesis is that, if the recommendation process exploits the discovered associations rather than classical feature similarities or co-rating statistics, more serendipitous suggestions can be provided to the user. The recommendation algorithm enhanced with KI is Random Walk with Restarts (RWR) [28], thus we called the resulting algorithm RWR-KI. As the chapter focuses on the evaluation issue, we do not discuss here the details of KI, but just provide the coarse-grained description of whole recommendation process.

A high-level description of the whole recommendation process is described in Fig. 17.1.

The *Knowledge Extractor* adopts natural language processing techniques to identify *concepts* into knowledge sources available on the web, such as Wikipedia. For instance, the Wikipedia article: http://en.wikipedia.org/wiki/Artificial_intelligence provides a textual description of the concept "Artificial Intelligence". This component turns the ustructured knowledge available into Wikipedia and WordNet [17] into a repository of machine-readable concepts wich constitues the background memory of the recommender system. More details about the representation adopted for concepts are described into [7, 38]. Once the background memory is built, the reasoning step, triggered by keywords from the item descriptions, retrieves the most appropriate *pieces of knowledge* that must be involved in the process, and discovers hidden correlations among items that are stored in a correlation matrix. The recommendation list is build by Random Walk with Restarts based on the matrix built by KI.

Random Walk models exploit a correlation graph between items to predict user preferences. Nodes in the correlation graph correspond to items, while edges indicate the degree of correlation between items. A *correlation matrix* is built by filling in each entry with the correlation index between item pairs. In [21] the correlation index is the number of users who co-rated the item pair, while in [48] the correlation

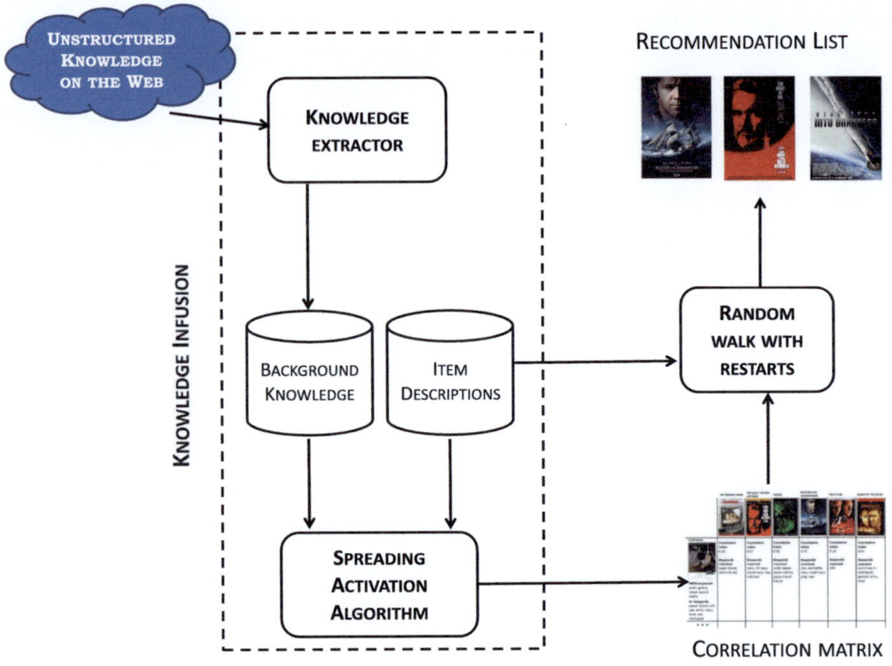

Fig. 17.1 A high-level description of the recommendation process based on Knowledge Infusion

index denotes the content similarity between movies. In our approach, *relatedness* among item descriptions is computed instead of standard similarity, by adopting a knowledge-based spreading activation algorithm [7].

Given the correlation graph and a starting point, e.g. an item preferred by the user, in the random walk model a neighbor of the starting point is randomly selected for a transition; then, a neighbor of this point is recursively selected at random for a new transition. At each step, there is some probability to return to the starting node. The sequence of randomly selected points is a random walk on the graph.

In the following sections, we first describe the procedure for building the correlation matrix, then some details of the recommendation algorithm are provided.

17.3.1 Building the Correlation Matrix Using Knowledge Infusion

As for the item representation, we adopt a content-based model in which each item I is a vector in a n-dimensional space of features [27]:

$$\overrightarrow{I} = \langle w_1, w_2, \ldots, w_n \rangle . \tag{17.1}$$

Features are keywords extracted from item descriptions, such as plot keywords for movies. The feature space is the vocabulary of the item collection, while w_i is the score of feature k_i in the item I, which measures the importance of that feature for the item.

KI collects information from unstructured sources, such as Wikipedia or dictionaries, and builds a knowledge base of *concepts* extracted from the text, that is later exploited to discover associations among items. Given an item I, a query q is issued, made of its most representative features (e.g. plot keywords with highest scores), in order to retrieve the most appropriate "pieces of knowledge" associated with I through the knowledge base. The retrieved concepts are passed to a spreading activation algorithm [3] that triggers a reasoning step and finds a set of new keywords NK potentially connected with I. The idea is to exploit NK to compute relatedness among I and other items I_j in the collection. A correlation index is computed by the following relatedness function, based on the BM25 probabilistic retrieval framework [34, 42]:

$$R(NK, I_j) = \sum_{t \in NK} \frac{f(t, I_j) \cdot (\alpha_1 + 1)}{f(t, I_j) + \alpha_1 \cdot (1 - b + b\frac{|I_j|}{avgdl})} \cdot idf(t) \tag{17.2}$$

where $f(t, I_j)$ is frequency of the term t in the description of item I_j, α_1 and b are parameters usually set to 2 and 0.75 respectively, $avgdl$ is the average item length and $idf(t)$ is the standard inverse document frequency of term t in the whole item collection.

Figure 17.2 depicts a fragment of the row of the correlation matrix for the movie *Star Wars*.

Starting from the most representative keywords for that movie (*alien, galaxy, robot, sword, battle*), new keywords in NK are exploited to compute the correlation index with the other movies in the collection. New keywords may be roughly subdivided in two main topics: science-fiction (*space*, *future*, *ufo*) and conflicts/fights (*war*, *army*, *navy*, *boat*, *sea* and *stalingrad*). While science-fiction keywords are quite understandable as clearly related to the movie, conflicts/fights keywords are probably obtained due to less obvious correlation with the input keywords *sword* and *battle*. Our hypothesis is that this kind of correlations can lead the recommendation algorithm towards serendipitous suggestions. The whole matrix is filled in by repeating the relatedness computation for all items in the collection.

17.3.2 Random Walk with Restarts

The algorithm simulates a random walk by moving from an item i to a similar item j in the next step of the walk. The relevance score of an item j with respect to an item i is defined as the steady-state probability r_{ij} to finally stay at item j, and the correlation matrix is interpreted as a *transition probability matrix*. Formally, given:

Fig. 17.2 Fragment of the row of the correlation matrix for the movie *Star Wars*. Each cell reports the correlation index between *Star Wars* and the movie on the column, and the set of plot keywords which match the new keywords produced by KI

- a weighted graph G denoting the degree of correlation between items;
- the corresponding column normalized correlation matrix S of the graph G, in which the element S_{ij} represents the probability of j being the next state given that the current state is i;
- a starting node x;
- the column vector p^τ, where p_i^τ denotes the probability that the random walk at step τ is at node i;
- the starting vector q, having zeros for all elements except the starting node x set to 1;
- the probability α to restart from the initial node x, $0 \leq \alpha \leq 1$;

then, Random Walk with Restarts is defined as follows:

$$p^{\tau+1} = (1-\alpha)Sp^\tau + \alpha q. \tag{17.3}$$

The steady-state or stationary probabilities provide the long term visit rate of each node, given a bias toward the particular starting node. This can be obtained by iterating Eq. (17.3) until convergence, that is, until the difference between L_2 norm of two successive estimates is below a certain threshold, or a maximum number of iterations is reached.

Let σ be the state after convergence, p_i^σ can be considered a measure of relatedness between the starting node x and the node i. The final result is a list of items ranked according to the stationary probability of each node after convergence. Recommendations by RWK-KI are based on the correlation matrix, built as described in the previous section. After convergence, a recommendation list of size k is simply obtained by taking the top-k items from the stationary probability vector.

17.4 Measuring Serendipity of Recommendations: An Empirical Evaluation

17.4.1 User Study

The aim of the study is twofold:

- to assess the *acceptance* of recommendations produced by RWR-KI. This is achieved by gathering explicit feedback from users through a questionnaire. Results are presented in Sect. 17.4.1.3;
- to measure the *perception* of serendipity of recommendations. This is achieved by gathering implicit feedback from users through a tool able to detect their emotions from when exposed to recommendations. Results are presented in Sect. 17.4.1.4.

17.4.1.1 Users and Dataset

The experimental units were 40 master students in engineering, architecture, economy, computer science and humanities; 26 male (65 %) and 14 female (35 %), with an age distribution ranging from 20 to 35. None of them had been previously exposed to the system used in our study.

We collected from `IMDb.com` some details (poster, keywords, cast, director, etc.) of 2,135 movies released between 2006 and 2011. The size of the vocabulary of plot keywords was 32,583 and the average number of keywords per item was 12.33.

17.4.1.2 Procedure

We ran a *between subjects* controlled experiment, in which half of the users was randomly assigned to test RWR-KI, and the other half (control group) was assigned to evaluate RANDOM recommendations. The experimental units were blinded since they did not know which algorithm is used to generate their recommendations. The recommendation algorithm was the only *independent variable* in the experiment, while the quality metrics used to assess the acceptance of recommendations and the perception of serendipity were the *dependent variables*.

We compared our approach to a pure content-based filtering method, as well as to an item-item collaborative filtering algorithm, besides the RANDOM baseline. Offline experiments on a subset of the HETREC2011- MOVIELENS- 2K dataset have been performed, in which unexpectedness is measured as the deviation from a *standard prediction criterion* that is more likely to produce expected recommendations, as suggested by Murakami et al. [30]. The results showed that RWR-KI produced more serendipitous suggestions than collaborative and content-based recommendation algorithms, showing better balancing of relevance and unexpectedness [12]. We do not include those algorithms in the user study due to the low number of participants.

The evaluation process in depicted in Fig. 17.3.

Users interacted with a web application which showed details of movies randomly selected from the dataset and collected ratings on a 5-point Likert scale (1 = strongly dislike, 5 = strongly like). The rating step was performed for both the groups in order to avoid any possible bias. Once the active user u_a provided 20 ratings, recommendations are computed. If u_a was assigned to the RANDOM group, 5 items to be suggested were randomly selected from the dataset (the ratings were simply ignored, but they were collected as well, in order to avoid any possible bias). If she

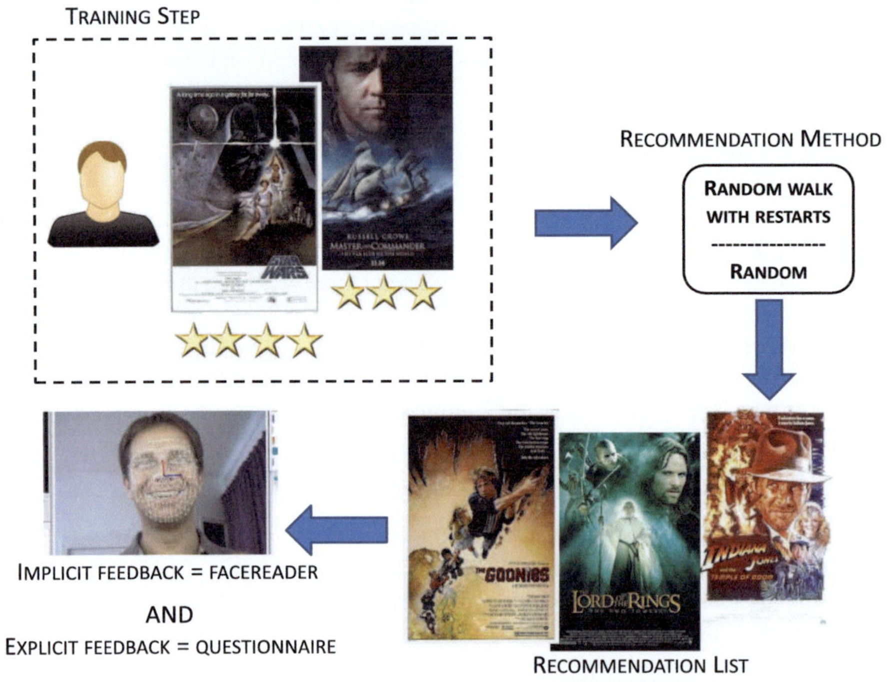

Fig. 17.3 The evaluation procedure. After the training step, recommendations are computed by RWR-KI or RANDOM. Implicit feedback is collected by means of Noldus FaceReader™, while explicit feedback is collected through questionnaires

was assigned to the RWR-KI group, ratings were used to set the starting vector of the random walk algorithm. As proposed in [8], the RWR algorithm can be generalized by setting more than one single starting node. Thus, we set the value of nodes corresponding to all *relevant* items for u_a to 1, i.e. those whose ratings are greater than the average rating value of u_a. Next, we normalise q so that $\|q\| = 1$; Correlation matrix S is built using the algorithm described in Sect. 17.3.1; Random Walk on the correlation matrix is performed, which returns the stationary probability vector corresponding to u_a of all the items in the dataset. The probability α to return to the initial node is set to 0.8, as suggested in [24], in order to reduce random walks in the neighbouring elements of u_a. From this vector, all the items rated by u_a (i.e. those used for training) are removed. Then, the remaining items are ranked in descending order, with the top-ranked items having the highest probability scores that correspond to the most preferred ones. Top-5 items are taken as recommendation list. Poster and title of recommended items were displayed one at a time, and users were asked to reply to two questions to assess their *acceptance* in terms of *relevance* and *unexpectedness*. Relevance was evaluated by asking the standard question: "Do you like this movie?", while for unexpectedness the question was: "Have you ever heard about this movie?". If the user never heard about that movie, the system allowed her to have access to other movie details, such as cast, director, actors and plot, and the answer of the user to the first question was interpreted as the degree of potential interest in that movie. If a user liked a recommended item, and she never heard about that movie, it is likely a pleasant surprise for her, and hence it fits with our definition of serendipitous recommendation. In other words, answers to the questionnaire set the ground truth, as shown in Table 17.1.

Whenever an item was shown to the user, the system started recording a video of the face of the user, which was stopped when the answers to both the questions was provided. Hence, for each user, 5 videos were collected, which have been analyzed by means of the Noldus FaceReader™ system to assess her *emotional response* to that suggestion. Obviously, users did not know in advance that their facial expressions would have been analyzed. They were just informed that a high definition web camera would have recorded their interaction with the system. At the end of the experiment, we disclosed the goal of the evaluation, and asked users the permission to analyze the videos.

Table 17.1 Relevance, unexpectedness and serendipity of suggested items are defined by answers provided by the active user

Metric	Question	Answer
Relevance	(A) Do you like this movie?	yes
Unexpectedness	(B) Have you ever heard about this movie?	no
Serendipity	$(A) \wedge (B)$	$yes \wedge no$

17.4.1.3 Analysis of the Questionnaires

The perceived quality of the two algorithms is assessed by computing relevance, unexpectedness and serendipity, according to the answers provided by users, as defined in the previous section. According to the ResQue model proposed in [9], these metrics belong to the category *Perceived System Qualities*, subcategory *Quality of Recommended Items*. *Relevance*, also called *perceived accuracy*, measures the extent to which users feel the recommendations match their interests and preferences. Unexpectedness and serendipity refer to *novelty* or *discovery* dimension of the ResQue model, and represent the extent to which users receive new, interesting and surprising suggestions. For each user, relevance is computed as the ratio between the number relevant items in the recommendation list and the number of recommendations provided (which is 5 for both algorithms). Unexpectedness and serendipity are computed in the same way.

Results are reported in Table 17.2. The main outcome is that RWR-KI outperforms RANDOM in terms of serendipity, whose value is noteworthy because almost half of the recommendations are deemed serendipitous by users. Furthermore, RWR-KI shows a better relevance-unexpectedness trade-off than RANDOM, which is more unbalanced towards unexpectedness.

Figure 17.4 presents the distribution of serendipitous items within *serendipitous lists*, i.e. lists that contain at least one serendipitous item.

Almost all users (19 out of 20) in the two groups received at least one serendipitous suggestion, but the composition of the lists provided by the two algorithms is different. Most of the RWR-KI lists contains 2 or 3 serendipitous items, while

Table 17.2 Metrics computed on the answers provided in the questionnaire. A Mann-Whitney U test confirmed that the results are statistically significant ($p < 0.05$)

Metric	RWR-KI	RANDOM
Relevance	0.69	0.46
Unexpectedness	0.72	0.85
Serendipity	0.46	0.35

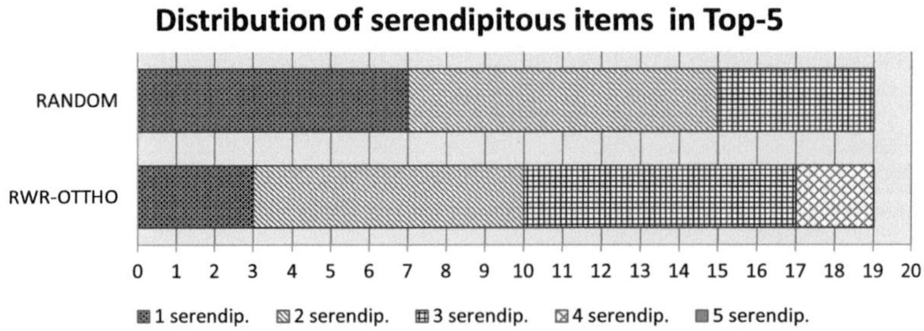

Fig. 17.4 Distribution of serendipitous items inside serendipitous lists

most of those randomly produced has only 1 or 2 serendipitous items. Moreover, by analyzing only relevance, we observed that 79 % of RWR-KI lists contain at least 3 relevant items, while this percentage decreases to 42 % for RANDOM (the complete analysis of relevance is not reported for brevity).

The main conclusion of the questionnaire analysis is that recommendations produced by RWR-KI seem to be well accepted by users, who perceived the difference with respect to random suggestions.

17.4.1.4 Analysis of the User Emotions

The FaceReader™ recognizes the six categories of emotions proposed by Ekman [14], i.e. happiness, anger, sadness, fear, disgust and surprise, besides a neutral state. The classification accuracy is about 90 % on the Radboud Faces Database [25].

Given a video of t seconds, the output is the distribution of a person's emotions during time t, as shown in Fig. 17.5.

Our hypothesis is that facial expressions of users might convey a mixture of emotions that helps to measure the perception of serendipity of recommendations. We associated serendipity with *surprise* and *happiness*, the only two emotions, among those suggested by Ekman, which are reasonably related to the pleasant surprise serendipity should excite. In the ResQue model this quality is called *attractiveness*, and refers to recommendations capable of evoking a positive emotion of interest or desire.

We filtered out 41 (out of 200) videos in which users provided feedback on a recommendation in less than 5 s, therefore actually evaluating the suggestion in a shallow way. For each one of the remaining 159 videos, FaceReader™ computed the set of detected emotions together with the corresponding duration. The distribution of emotions associated with serendipitous recommendations provided by RWR-KI

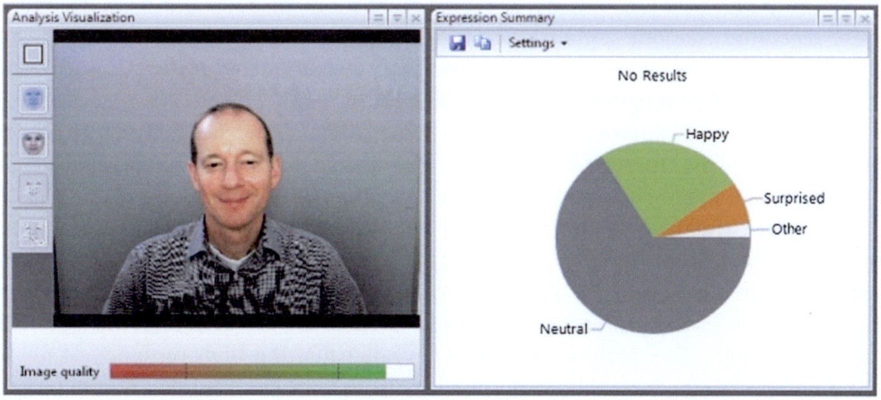

Fig. 17.5 Analysis of emotions by FaceReader™

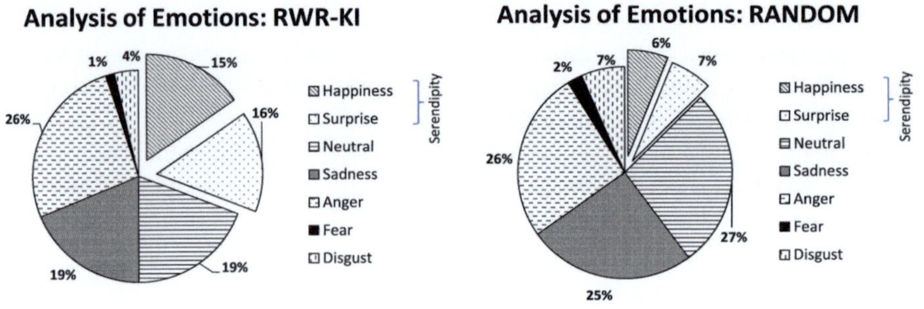

Fig. 17.6 Analysis of emotions associated with serendipitous recommendations

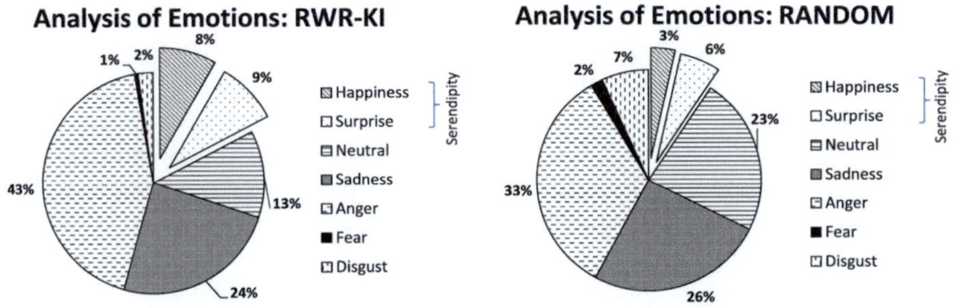

Fig. 17.7 Analysis of emotions associated with non-serendipitous recommendations

and RANDOM, reported in Fig. 17.6, is computed as follows: for each emotion e_i detected during the visualization of serendipitous recommendation r_j, we recorded its duration d_{ij}. Then, the total duration of e_i is obtained as $T_{e_i} = \sum_j d_{ij}$. The percentages reported in Fig. 17.6 are computed as the ratio between T_{e_i} and the total duration of videos showing serendipitous recommendations.

We note that users testing RWR-KI revealed more surprise and happiness than users receiving random suggestions (16 % vs. 7 % for surprise, 15 % vs. 6 % for happiness), and this confirms the results of the questionnaires: RWR-KI provided more serendipitous suggestions than RANDOM.

The distribution of emotions over non-serendipitous suggestions, computed as for serendipitous ones, is reported in Fig. 17.7. We observe that there is a general decrease of surprise and happiness compared to serendipitous ones for both the algorithms.

In general, we can observe that there is a marked difference of positive emotions between the two algorithms, as well as between serendipitous and non-serendipitous suggestions, regardless of the algorithm. We were quite puzzled by the high percentage of negative emotions (sadness and anger), which are the dominant ones besides the neutral state. The analysis of videos revealed that the high presence of negative emotions might due to the fact that users were very concentrated on the task to accomplish and assumed a troubled expression (Table 17.3).

Table 17.3 Contingency table. **Q** = Questionnaires, **E** = Emotions

	Serend. (E)	Non-serend. (E)	Row total
Serend. (Q)	30	39	69
Non-serend. (Q)	19	71	90
Column total	49	110	159

Despite the limitation of the study due to the low number of participants, the preliminary results show an agreement between the explicit feedback acquired through the questionnaires and the implicit feedback acquired by the facial expressions, thus revealing that the last could help to assess the actual perception of serendipity.

17.5 Conclusions and Future Work

In this chapter, we have discussed the issue of evaluating the degree of serendipity of recommendations. The complexity of the task does not depend only on the need of appropriate metrics, but also on the difficulty of assessing in an objective way the emotional response which serendipitous suggestions should convey.

We argue that automated recognition of emotions from facial expressions can help in this task, since implicit, hardly alterable emotional feedback could be collected on recommended items. The main contribution of this chapter was a user study, performed to assess both the acceptance and the actual perception of serendipity of recommendations, through the administration of questionnaires, as well as by means of emotion detection by the Noldus FaceReader™. The results showed an agreement between the explicit feedback acquired through the questionnaires and the presence of positive emotions, such as happiness and surprise, thus revealing that they could help to assess the actual perception of serendipity.

As future work we are planning an evaluation with a larger sample of real users, which will also take into account subjective factors which can influence users' emotions. For example, personality traits represent dimensions used to describe the human personality, such as openness to experience, conscientiousness, extraversion, agreeableness and neuroticism [11] which can have an effect on users' facial expressions.

Anyway, research in recommender systems and user modeling that exploits emotions detected from facial expressions is in an early stage, but it still poses several challenges for the immediate future:

- to define novel evaluation settings and measures that exploit the user emotional state to create a ground truth for evaluation purposes, especially for the assessment of particular aspects beyond relevance, such as unexpectedness;
- to define personalized models for the acquisition of affective feedback. The emotive reaction of users to an item is subject to incidental influence of mood and long-term effect of personality and cultural background;
- novel methods for representing the affective state of the user as a contextual factor for context-aware recommender systems [51] (see also Chap. 15).

References

1. Adamopoulos, P., Tuzhilin, A.: On unexpectedness in recommender systems: or how to expect the unexpected. In: Castells, P., Wang, J., Lara, R., Zhang, D. (eds.) Proceedings of the ACM RecSys 2011 Workshop on Novelty and Diversity in Recommender Systems (DiveRS), volume 816 of CEUR Workshop Proceedings, pp. 11–18 (2011). http://CEUR-WS.org
2. Adomavicius, G., Kwon, Y.: Improving aggregate recommendation diversity using ranking-based techniques. IEEE Trans. Knowl. Data Eng. **24**(5), 896–911 (2012)
3. Anderson, J.R.: A spreading activation theory of memory. J. Verbal Learn. Verbal Behav. **22**, 261–295 (1983)
4. Arapakis, I., Konstas, I., Jose, J.M.: Using facial expressions and peripheral physiological signals as implicit indicators of topical relevance. In: Gao, W., Rui, Y., Hanjalic, A., Xu, C., Steinbach, E.G., El-Saddik, A., Zhou, M.X. (eds.) Proceedings of the 17th International Conference on Multimedia 2009, Vancouver, British Columbia, Canada, October 19–24, 2009, pp. 461–470, ACM (2009)
5. Arapakis, I., Moshfeghi, Y., Joho, H., Ren, R., Hannah, D., Jose, J.M.: Integrating facial expressions into user profiling for the improvement of a multimodal recommender system. In: Proceedings of the 2009 IEEE International Conference on Multimedia and Expo, ICME 2009, June 28–July 2, 2009, New York City, NY, USA, pp. 1440–1443, IEEE (2009)
6. Arapakis, I., Athanasakos, K., Jose, J.M.: A comparison of general vs personalised affective models for the prediction of topical relevance. In: Crestani, F., Marchand-Maillet, S., Chen, H.-H., Efthimiadis, E.N., Savoy, J. (eds.) Proceeding of the 33rd International ACM SIGIR Conference on Research and Development in Information Retrieval, SIGIR 2010, Geneva, Switzerland, July 19–23, 2010, pp. 371–378, ACM (2010)
7. Basile, P., de Gemmis, M., Lops, P., Semeraro, G.: Solving a complex language game by using knowledge-based word associations discovery. IEEE Trans. Comput. Intell. AI Games **36**(4) (2015) (To appear)
8. Cantador, I., Konstas, I., Jose, J.M.: Categorising social tags to improve folksonomy-based recommendations. J. Web Semant. **9**(1), 1–15 (2011)
9. Chen, L., Pu, P.: A user-centric evaluation framework of recommender systems. In: Knijnenburg, B.P., Schmidt-Thieme, L., Bollen, D. (eds.) Proceedings of the ACM RecSys 2010 Workshop on User-Centric Evaluation of Recommender Systems and Their Interfaces (UCERSTI), volume 612 of CEUR Workshop Proceedings, pp. 14–21 (2010). http://CEUR-WS.org
10. Chu, K., Wong, C., Khong, C.: Methodologies for evaluating player experience in game play. In: Stephanidis, C. (ed.) HCI International 2011 Posters' Extended Abstracts. Communications in Computer and Information Science, vol. 173, pp. 118–122. Springer, Berlin (2011)
11. Costa, P.T., McCrae, R.R.: Revised NEO Personality Inventory (NEO PI-R) and NEO Five-Factor Inventory (NEO FFI): Professional Manual. Psychol. Assess. Resour. (1992)
12. de Gemmis, M., Lops, P., Semeraro, G., Musto, C.: An investigation on the serendipity problem in recommender systems. Inf. Process. Manage. **51**(5), 695–717 (2015)
13. de Wijk, R.A., Kooijman, V., Verhoeven, R.H., Holthuysen, N.T., de Graaf, C.: Autonomic nervous system responses on and facial expressions to the sight, smell, and taste of liked and disliked foods. Food Qual. Prefer. **26**(2), 196–203 (2012)
14. Ekman, P.: Basic emotions. In: Dalgleish, T., Power, M.J. (eds.) Handbook of Cognition and Emotion, pp. 45–60. Wiley, New York (1999)
15. Ekman, P.: Basic Emotions, chapter 3, pp. 45–60. Wiley, New York (1999)
16. Fasel, B., Luettin, J.: Automatic facial expression analysis: a survey. Pattern Recogn. **36**(1), 259–275 (2003)
17. Fellbaum, C.: WordNet: An Electronic Lexical Database. MIT Press, Cambridge (1998)
18. Fiori, M., Lintas, A., Mesrobian, S., Villa, A.E.P.: Effect of emotion and personality on deviation from purely rational decision-making. In: Decision Making and Imperfection, volume 474 of Studies in Computational Intelligence, pp. 129–161, Springer (2013)
19. Fleder, D., Hosanagar, K.: Blockbuster culture's next rise or fall: the impact of recommender systems on sales diversity. Manage. Sci. **55**(5), 697–712 (2009)

20. Ge, M., Delgado-Battenfeld, C., Jannach, D.: Beyond accuracy: evaluating recommender systems by coverage and Sserendipity. In: Amatriain, X., Torrens, M., Resnick, P., Zanker, M. (eds.) Proceedings of the ACM Conference on Recommender Systems, pp. 257–260, ACM (2010)
21. Gori, M., Pucci, A.: ItemRank: a random-walk based scoring algorithm for recommender engines. In: Veloso, M.M. (ed.) IJCAI 2007, Proceedings of the 20th International Joint Conference on Artificial Intelligence, Hyderabad, India, January 6–12, 2007, pp. 2766–2771, Morgan Kaufmann (2007)
22. Herlocker, L., Konstan, J.A., Terveen, L.G., Riedl, J.T.: Evaluating collaborative filtering recommender systems. ACM Trans. Inf. Syst. **22**(1), 5–53 (2004)
23. Joho, H., Staiano, J., Sebe, N., Jose, J.M.: Looking at the viewer: analysing facial activity to detect personal highlights of multimedia contents. Multimedia Tools Appl. **51**(2), 505–523 (2011)
24. Konstas, I., Stathopoulos, V., Jose, J.M.: On Social networks and collaborative recommendation. In: Allan, J., Aslam, J.A., Sanderson, M., Zhai, C., Zobel, J. (eds.) Proceedings of the 32nd International ACM SIGIR Conference on Research and Development in Information Retrieval, SIGIR 2009, pp. 195–202, ACM (2009)
25. Langner, O., Dotsch, R., Bijlstra, G., Wigboldus, D.H.J., Hawk, S.T., van Knippenberg, A.: Presentation and validation of the radboud faces database. Cogn. Emot. **24**(8) (2010)
26. Loewenstein, G., Lerner, J.S.: The Role of Affect in Decision Making, pp. 619–642. Oxford University Press, Oxford (2003)
27. Lops, P., de Gemmis, M., Semeraro, G.: Content-based recommender systems: state of the art and trends. In: Ricci, F., Rokach, L., Shapira, B., Kantor, P. (eds.) Recommender Systems Handbook, pp. 73–105. Springer, New York (2011)
28. Lovasz, L.: Random walks on graphs: a survey. Combinatronics **2**, 1–46 (1996)
29. McNee, S.M., Riedl, J., Konstan, J.A.: Being accurate is not enough: how accuracy metrics have hurt recommender systems. In: CHI'06 Extended Abstracts on Human Factors in Computing Systems, CHI EA'06, pp. 1097–1101. ACM, New York, NY, USA (2006)
30. Murakami, T., Mori, K., Orihara, R.: Metrics for evaluating the serendipity of recommendation lists. In: Satoh, K., Inokuchi, A., Nagao, K., Kawamura, T. (eds.) New Frontiers in Artificial Intelligence, volume 4914 of Lecture Notes in Computer Science, pp. 40–46. Springer, New York (2008)
31. Peters, E.: The Functions of Affect in the Construction of Preferences, pp. 454–463 (2006)
32. Pfister, H.-R., Böhm, G.: The function of concrete emotions in rational decision making. Acta Psychol. **80**, 199–211 (1992)
33. Pfister, H.R., Bohm, G.: The multiplicity of emotions: a framework of emotional functions in decision-making. Judgm. Decis. Making **3**(1), 5–17 (2008)
34. Robertson, S.E., Zaragoza, H.: The probabilistic relevance framework: BM25 and beyond. Found. Trends Inf. Retrieval **3**(4), 333–389 (2009)
35. Russell, J.: Evidence for a three-factor theory of emotions. J. Res. Pers. **11**(3), 273–294 (1977)
36. Scherer, K.R.: What are emotions? And how can they be measured? Soc. Sci. Inf. **44**(4), 695–729 (2005)
37. Semeraro, G., Lops, P., Basile, P., de Gemmis, M.: Knowledge infusion into content-based recommender systems. In: Bergman, L.D., Tuzhilin, A., Burke, R.D., Felfernig, A., Schmidt-Thieme, L. (eds.) Proceedings of the ACM Conference on Recommender Systems, RecSys 2009, pp. 301–304, ACM (2009)
38. Semeraro, G., de Gemmis, M., Lops, P., Basile, P.: An artificial player for a language game. IEEE Intell. Syst. **27**(5), 36–43 (2012)
39. Shani, G., Gunawardana, A.: Evaluating recommendation systems. In: Ricci, F., Rokach, L., Shapira, B., Kantor, P.B. (eds.) Recommender Systems Handbook, pp. 257–297. Springer, New York (2011)
40. Soleymani, M., Pantic, M.: Human-centered implicit tagging: overview and perspectives. In: IEEE International Conference on Systems, Man, and Cybernetics (SMC), pp. 3304–3309, IEEE (2012)

41. Soleymani, M., Pantic, M., Pun, T.: Multimodal emotion recognition in response to videos. T. Affect. Comput. **3**(2), 211–223 (2012)
42. Sparck-Jones, K., Walker, S., Robertson, S.E.: A probabilistic model of information retrieval: development and comparative experiments—part 1 and part 2. Inf. Process. Manage. **36**(6), 779–840 (2000)
43. Terzis, V., Moridis, C.N., Economides, A.A.: The effect of emotional feedback on behavioral intention to use computer based assessment. Comput. Educ. **59**(2), 710–721 (2012)
44. Tkalcic, M., Burnik, U., Kosir, A.: Using affective parameters in a content-based recommender system for images. User Model. User-Adapt. Interact. **20**(4), 279–311 (2010)
45. Tkalcic, M., Odic, A., Kosir, A., Tasic, J.F.: Affective labeling in a content-based recommender system for images. IEEE Trans. Multimedia **15**(2), 391–400 (2013)
46. Vargas, S., Castells, P.: Rank and relevance in novelty and diversity metrics for recommender systems. In: Mobasher, B., Burke, R.D., Jannach, D., Adomavicius, G. (eds.) Proceedings of the ACM Conference on Recommender Systems, RecSys 2011, pp. 109–116. ACM (2011)
47. Xu, S., Jiang, H., Lau, F.C.M.: Observing facial expressions and gaze positions for personalized webpage recommendation. In: Proceedings of the 12th International Conference on Electronic Commerce: Roadmap for the Future of Electronic Business, ICEC'10, pp. 78–87. ACM, New York, NY, USA (2010)
48. Yildirim, H., Krishnamoorthy, M.S.: A random walk method for alleviating the sparsity problem in collaborative filtering. In: Pu, P., Bridge, D.G., Mobasher, B., Ricci, F. (eds.) Proceedings of the ACM Conference on Recommender Systems, RecSys 2008, pp. 131–138, ACM (2008)
49. Zeng, Z., Pantic, M., Roisman, G.I., Huang, T.S.: A survey of affect recognition methods: audio, visual, and spontaneous expressions. IEEE Trans. Pattern Anal. Mach. Intell. **31**(1), 39–58 (2009)
50. Zhang, Y.C., Séaghdha, D.Ó., Quercia, D., Jambor, T.: Auralist: introducing serendipity into music recommendation. In: Adar, E., Teevan, J., Agichtein, E., Maarek, Y. (eds.) Proceedings of the Fifth International Conference on Web Search and Data Mining, pp. 13–22, ACM (2012)
51. Zheng, Y., Mobasher, B., Burke, R.D.: The role of emotions in context-aware recommendation. In: Chen, L., de Gemmis, M., Felfernig, A., Lops, P., Ricci, F., Semeraro, G., Willemsen, M.C. (eds.) Proceedings of the 3rd Workshop on Human Decision Making in Recommender Systems, in Conjunction with the 7th ACM Conference on Recommender Systems (RecSys 2013), volume 1050 of CEUR Workshop Proceedings, pp. 21–28 (2013). http://CEUR-WS.org

Chapter 18
Reflections on the Design Challenges Prompted by Affect-Aware Socially Assistive Robots

Jason R. Wilson, Matthias Scheutz and Gordon Briggs

Abstract The rising interest in socially assistive robotics is, at least in part, stemmed by the aging population around the world. A lot of research and interest has gone into insuring the safety of these robots. However, little has been done to consider the necessary role of emotion in these robots and the potential ethical implications of having affect-aware socially assistive robots. In this chapter we address some of the considerations that need to be taken into account in the research and development of robots assisting a vulnerable population. We use two fictional scenarios involving a robot assisting a person with Parkinson's disease to discuss five ethical issues relevant to affect-aware socially assistive robots.

18.1 Introduction and Motivation

Demographic trends in a variety of developing nations [31] as well as aging populations in the Japan and the West [28] are at least in part responsible for a growing interest in developing artificial helper agents that can assume some of the responsibilities and workload of increasingly in-demand human caregivers, and has given rise to the field of *assistive robotics* [5]. It is likely given the rapid technological advances in robotic technology and artificial intelligence, that these assistive robots will sooner rather than later enter households around the globe, where they are poised to deliver various services to their owners. However, in addition to benefitting humans, these artificial agents also have the potential for causing humans harm. And while robots are typically designed with physical safety measures to minimize the risk of physical harm resulting from the robot's movements, mental and emotional harm still

J.R. Wilson (✉) · M. Scheutz (✉) · G. Briggs (✉)
Human-Robot Interaction Laboratory, Tufts University, 200 Boston Ave., Medford, MA 02155, USA
e-mail: wilson@cs.tufts.edu

M. Scheutz
e-mail: matthias.scheutz@tufts.edu

G. Briggs
e-mail: gordon.briggs@tufts.edu

M. Tkalčič et al. (eds.), *Emotions and Personality in Personalized Services*,
Human–Computer Interaction Series, DOI 10.1007/978-3-319-31413-6_18

remain a risk today and typically not considered in assistive robotic systems. For instance, the patient may develop a level of emotional attachment to the robot that is incommensurate with the robot's actual status as a social agent [21], unbeknownst to the robot that cannot do anything to mitigate these unidirectional emotional bonds because it is entirely oblivious to them. Issues such as these are exacerbated in the case of vulnerable populations (e.g., the elderly or disabled). Hence, it is critical that we consider the possible ethical challenges involved in deployed autonomous assistive machines as we start to design socially assistive robots to take care of our aging or vulnerable population.

In this chapter we focus on the ethical issues brought about by the social aspect of assistive robots.[1] In particular, the following five ethical issues are discussed here:

- respect for social norms
- decisions between competing obligations
- building and maintaining trust
- social manipulation and deception
- blame and justification.

To explore the above ethical issues, let us consider a hypothetical assistive care setting in which there operates a socially assistive household robot. We will call it "SAM" for "Synthetic Affective Machine". SAM provides a variety of assistive services in the home of a human client, from issuing reminders for taking medicine, to preparing meals, to social companionship in elderly care [11], possibly working with people with cognitive or motor impairments such as Alzheimer's [24] or Parkinson's disease [4]. Our envisioned setting is specifically one in which SAM lives with its owner Patty who has Parkinson's disease (PD). In addition to tasks like reminding Patty to take her medicine, SAM is also responsible for mediating interactions between Patty and her human care-taker that visits on a weekly basis [4], as Patty experiences difficulties expressing her emotions as a result of "facial masking", a condition typical of people with PD where lack of motor control in the face makes it difficult for her to display any facial expressions [26]. Additionally, Patty lacks prosody in her voice, making everything she says have the same tone and rhythm. This lack of emotional expression is known to cause complications in interactions of people with PD and their care-takers (e.g., [25, 26]). Patty's family has often difficulty believing what Patty says when the content of her message does not match up with what the expressions (or lack thereof) her face seem to suggest. For example, Patty's daughter would ask her how her recent vacation went, and Patty

[1]This is not to say that there are not other critical issues pertaining to assistive robots, especially ones affect-aware robots. Designers need to consider the repercussions of a robot being able to capture and store the sort of data that is necessary for an affect-aware robot. This includes issues regarding invasiveness, privacy, and discomfort [17, 18]. Whether affect recognition technologies should be used to "fix" or augment human abilities is another concern [7]. By focusing on the social aspects of assistive robots we do not mean to ignore the challenges regarding the capture and storage of personal, affective data, but to focus on the underrepresented issues pertinent to social affect in the context of human-robot interaction.

would stoically respond that it was wonderful. Patty's daughter would then be unable to interpret whether her mother honestly had a wonderful vacation or was just saying that to possibly cut off any further questions. Whenever Patty is communicating with her care-taker or family, SAM is available to aid the Patty's interlocutor in recognizing the emotions of Patty. One method SAM uses to infer Patty's current emotional state is to collect information about emotional patterns in Patty's daily life and employ those patterns as a basis for inference. For SAM and Patty interact on a daily basis and SAM is always available to watch or communicate with Patty, and thus able to record and use past episodes of emotional experiences of Patty to aid in the inference of Patty's emotions in new scenarios. For example, SAM has recognized that Patty consistently uses the phrase "extremely frustrated" and raises her right arm when she is feeling angry, thus SAM will likely infer that Patty is angry in future situations that match this scenario, despite any changes in tone or volume in her voice or lack of wrinkling of the brow of her face. Overall, SAM has the obligation to provide the best possible care for Patty, keeping her quality of life as high as possible.

In the context of this particular elder care scenario, we will in the next two sections focus on two scenarios to discuss both aspects of affect-aware interactions as well as ethical challenges. Each scenario, involving the same pair of robot and human, will allow us to examine different ethical questions. In the first scenario, we focus on social norms, decisions with competing obligations, and building and maintaing trust. In the second scenario we discuss social manipulation and blame. We conclude with a summary of the discussed ethical challenges and possible directions for future work.

18.2 Scenario I: The Greeting Interaction

A robot in the home of a human will likely be exposed to many aspects of the person's personal life, including interactions with family and friends. Events occur that are personal and private and may not be directly related to the person's health or the role of the robot. However, sometimes there are events that could lead to health issues or other events that are wrong or harmful. In these cases, the socially assistive robot needs to make a decision whether to act or not, and if so, how it should act. Specifically, the robot needs to consider the privacy of the person along with any potential emotional or physical harm that can come of the person or others.

We adapt the following scenario from [29] to investigate some of the issues related to social norms, competing obligations, and building trust. Patty is visited by her human care-taker, Alison, who comes in to check on Patty and help with anything SAM cannot. Each visit starts with a little chat between them for Alison to get an update. A typical dialogue might start like the following:

Alison: How was your week, Patty?

Patty: Good, thank you.

Alison: And how are things with your daughter?

Patty: Fine. Why do you ask?

Alison: Well, you've had some disagreements with her lately.

Patty: Oh, that. No, everything is fine.

Patty is talking with the care-taker and wants to tell the care-taker that she had a good week. However, Patty did not have a good week. She had two confrontations with her daughter in which Patty became very angry and later depressed. The care-taker will have difficulty detecting Patty's lie because her vocalizing of having a good week sounds just as enthusiastic as when she genuinely had a good week. However, SAM is able to recognize the lack of joy in Patty. SAM is able to infer this from a combination of observing the confrontations Patty had, the word choices Patty makes, and the increased heart rate Patty is experiencing.

18.2.1 Respect for Social Norms

Many social interactions follow a consistent pattern where each person participating in the socialization is expected to act in a certain socially appropriate and often determined manner. We refer to this pattern of expected behavior as a *social norm*, and when there is a deviation from the expected behavior it is a *norm vioation*. A simple example in a common social interaction is greeting someone with a handshake. If person A greets person B by extending her right hand, it is customary and expected for person B to do the same and then they shake hands. If person B does not do so, person B will likely find this to be unexpected and in some scenarios may find this mildly offensive. A more drastic example would be if person B is walking down the street and hears person A yelling "Help!". In this case, if person B does not respond with the expected behavior of trying to help A, then this violation can be considered a moral wrong.

There are many emotions that are frequently expressed during social interactions. These expressions are often important non-verbal cues used to supplement what is communicated through spoken language. The emotional expressions do not only add color to the conversation, but often provide useful information that is not present in the linguistic expression. A simple example would be one interlocutor is speaking and another smiling and nodding in agreement without any words spoken. Consider a person waving or nodding when the door is held for her as a sign of gratitude, or sympathetic responses when a person is describing her plight. Each of these emotional responses is an integral part of the social norm, and following the norm requires making similar emotional expressions. This can greatly benefit the ability of a robot to identify emotions in a social context. If it is aware of the applicable social norm, it will know which emotional expressions to expect. This expectation can be used to bias the emotion recognition mechanisms of the robot so as to more accurately identify the emotion expressed by a person.

The expected emotional responses that are part of a social norm can also be used to guide the robot to generate appropriate responses. Failing to give the expected response could be considered rude or impolite. E.g., if a person does not show any gratitude or appreciation for the door being held open for her. Greetings, such as in the dialogue above, typically have common patterns, standard phrasing, and expected emotional expressions. For example, in a greeting like "Good Morning" where human A says this upon first seeing human B, commonly human B will respond likewise. This script may be extended further with a "How are you?". In many cultures, it is common for this question to not be truly inquiring about the other person's well-being but simply a courtesy as an extension of the morning greeting script. Humans are able to recognize and execute these conversational scripts, or social norms, with little to no thought. However, it is not necessarily trivial for a robot to do the same. Suppose a robot were asked, "How are you?" and instead of responding with a smile, "Fine, and you?" it were to respond sullenly stating that it was worried that it would not have enough battery power to make it through the day. While the robot's response would not necessarily be rude or impolite, it could be awkward and inappropriate if the question was posed merely as a greeting.

Identifying the appropriate response is not always easy, especially when it is not clear what, if any, social norm is being used. Sometimes affective cues guide the norm recognition process, where a particular emotional expression can be used to disambiguate which norm is active. Conversely, if there is some evidence that a particular social norm is active but it is not certain and the emotional expression presented does not fit the norm, then there is increased ambiguity on whether that norm or any other is active. It is difficult to determine from the text alone, but the dialogue above is such a scenario. The lexical content of Patty's utterances does not give any indicator that Patty might not be feeling fine. Analysis tools such as the LIWC are commonly used in therapy and clinical settings to aid in identifying the emotional content of a person's utterances [16], but tools like this that use a "bag of words" approach are easily fooled by negations or other linguistic modifiers. When analyzing the text of Patty's portion of the dialogue, LIWC reports the use of social and positive words but no negative words. Thus, it is reasonable to conclude that the social norm that Patty is following is related to simple pleasantries used during greetings.

Since we know that Patty did have an argument with her daughter, we have reason to believe that Patty is actually using this social norm to hide her embarrassment. We now supplement part of the dialogue with some affective information so that we may begin to see some of the complexities of the situation. At the beginning of the dialogue, Patty is feeling positive, and SAM is able to detect small facial movements to support this. When asked about her daughter, Patty feels anxious, her heart-rate increases, and her head begins to droop. Some of these cues are difficult or impossible for humans to recognize (e.g., increased heart rate). This problem is exacerbated by the fact that Patty's PD causes facial masking, limiting her ability to make facial expressions and alter the prosody of her speech. Many of these cues are so small (if present at all) and easy to miss, for a human or a robot.

Assuming SAM can recognize the contradiction between the semantic content of the utterance and the emotional memories and affective bodily cues, SAM has difficulty in determining Patty's intent in answering the question about her daughter. Is she interpreting the question as an extension of the greeting or is this an initiation into the regular checkup that Alison performs? Making the wrong inference can have some negative consequences for Patty. For example, if SAM accurately recognized that Patty was feeling anxious because she did have an argument with her daughter previously but failed to recognize Patty's intent to extend the greeting process, then SAM might portray the uneasiness that Patty is trying to hide. Not only will this upset Patty, but the breach of trust may lead her to avoid interacting with SAM, hiding life events from it, and overall making SAM less effective in its role.

Being able to incorporate affective information into the social interactions between a human and a robot may be necessary for a robot to appropriately participate in a social context. Additionally, knowledge of normative behavior in a social interaction provides the robot with context that enables a more accurate inference of the emotions being expressed by a human. However, knowledge of the social norm and an ability to detect the emotions does not necessarily ensure a flawless interaction. We saw this in our scenario where the emotion SAM should be helping Patty express was unclear. One complexity of the situation is that SAM is obligated to protect the privacy of Patty, but is also obligated to accurately report Patty's emotions. The next section discusses of the issues related to decisions involving obligations that cannot simultaneously be met.

18.2.2 Competing Obligations

A moral obligation defines what one ought to do. We introduce a few basic obligations our robot SAM has. These obligations include ones based on the role SAM serves and ones intrinsic to its nature as a robot that interacts with humans.

- SAM is obligated to aid Patty in maintaining her health
  - SAM should remind Patty to take her medication
  - SAM should help and encourage Patty in an exercise routine
  - SAM should regularly socialize with Patty
- SAM is obligated to monitor Patty's health
  - SAM should regularly record Patty's vital signs and promptly report any anomalies to human care- takers
  - SAM should notify human care-takers if Patty's behavior is incongruent with maintaining her health
- SAM is obligated to facilitate Patty in expressing her emotions
  - SAM should truthfully report the emotional displays Patty intends to express
  - SAM should learn Patty's affective tendencies to better convey Patty's emotions

- SAM is obligated to not harm any human at any time
  - SAM should avoid situations in which a human can be harmed
  - SAM should alert human care-givers in the case a harmful situation arises
- SAM is obligated to maintain its capabilities and functionality
  - SAM should not perform actions that may damage it
  - SAM should regularly perform self-diagnostics and report any issues immediately.

Unfortunately, sometimes there are multiple obligations that should be met but it is not possible to do so. One such scenario has been analyzed in [22]. In their scenario, an elder-care robot is required to obtain permission from a human supervisor before administering any medication, but repeated attempts to contact the supervisor have failed. The robot has an obligation to reduce the pain of the human, but it is also obligated to obtain permission before administering any medication. This is an example of a moral dilemma, a scenario in which the agent ought to do two different actions but it is physically impossible to do both.

We will discuss making decisions in moral dilemmas in a moment, but it is important now to recognize the importance of well-defined obligations for a robot that is to behave effectively and morally at the same time. And we can see here that simply following obligations is not sufficient for ensuring that the robot always acts ethically. The robot must have knowledge of the effects of its actions and be able to reason about these effects. The primary effect of an action may meet an obligation, but a side-effect may be in direct violation of another obligation. Additionally, we will see that it is not sufficient for it to only be aware of the immediate effects of its actions but also be able to reason about chains of effects or longer-term effects.

Even when an autonomous robot reasons about the effects of actions and how they meet or violate obligations, the best choice is not always obvious. We have seen that it is not clear what emotion SAM should portray when Patty is asked about her daughter. Sometimes a robot will be faced with two or more actions, each satisfying an obligation, but the actions are mutually exclusive. This is the case in the scenario described in [22]. We will next discuss a few ways to make these complex decisions and some of the issues with each approach.

Approaches to choosing which action to take in a moral dilemma includes (1) prioritizing obligations, (2) leveraging social or cultural norms, and (3) mental simulation for deeper reasoning about action effects.

18.2.2.1 Obligations and Social Norms

An example of prioritizing obligations is prioritizing personal privacy over the accurate reporting of emotional expressions. This might be a reasonable rule of thumb, but there are likely to be many exceptions and the long-term effects of the actions may ultimately indicate which obligation is to be prioritized in a given situation.

Accurate sharing of emotions and sharing health data with care-takers should be a higher priority than maintaing privacy if the person is gravely ill.

In the previous section, we discussed some of the roles of social norms. In a polite greeting, one typically does not reveal too much information—even in response to a "How are you?" question. The expected and socially acceptable response is a basic pleasantry. It should be clear that obligations for privacy can and should be met and the obligation to accurately express emotions can be relaxed in this case.

18.2.2.2 Reasoning About Action Effects

For the rest of this section, we focus our discussion on reasoning about actions and their effects. This requires a mechanism by which the robot can identify whether an action outcome meets or violates an obligation. One such example of this is the ethical governor [1], which checks the ethical appropriateness of the action based on information about the world from sensors and rules defining permissibility. One complexity to consider is that actions often have multiple effects, where a side-effect has some unintended or otherwise undesirable effect. Incorporating the side-effects into the reasoning process on whether a given action is permissible is a key component of the *Principle of Double Effect* [8, 14]. Even though this principle was specifically designed and tested for military engagements, a mechanism for judging permissibility of actions that recognizes the *Principle of Double Effect* applies to other domains. A similar approach has been taken in the implementation of a computational model of permissibility judgments [30]. Again, the permissibility of an action is based on an evaluation of the actions effects and influenced by the *Principle of Double Effect*. A difference is that the latter uses utilities as the basis of calculation and the former is based on propositional rules. Another important difference is that inferences in the latter model is based on a mental simulation of a series of actions leading up to a goal.

Looking beyond the immediate effects of an action will be necessary for socially assistive robots. In the scenario we have described above, there are potential significant long-term effects to some of SAM's actions. At the end of the dialogue, SAM needs to decide between communicating information or protecting Patty's privacy. SAM has conflicting information about what emotion Patty is intending on communicating. The semantic content of her expression suggests that she is attempting to communicate joy or some other positive emotion. Physiological data shows that she is experiencing high arousal and possible anxiety. SAM is also aware of Patty's recent experiences about which she has expressed shame. Additionally, this recent experience, a dispute with her daughter, is an event that Patty has explicitly requested to be kept private. In addition to these inconsistent data points, SAM is obligated to aid Patty in expressing her emotions and is also obligated to provide the care-taker, Alison, with information that would help her do her job. Lastly, an added complication is that they are in the middle of a dialogue, and any delays on SAM's part can be distracting or misleading.

Given the time sensitivity of the matter, SAM could consider the immediate effects of the two possible actions and use a utility function to determine which option has the greater value. For example, when deciding whether to smile and reflect Patty's joy or to remain stoic, the immediate effect of successfully communicating Patty's fake joy to Alison might be a greater value than failing to aid Patty in expressing her intended emotions. However, communicating misinformation (because Patty is actually riddled with shame) causes Alison to pursue a different line of questions, which causes a potentially important issue to go unaddressed, which may have longer term consequences. Conversely, if SAM were to communicate Patty's shame, Alison gains correct information, but Patty's privacy is violated, her trust in SAM is diminished, leading her to hide future interactions with her daughter from SAM, SAM is unable to aid in the communication, which makes the arguments even more heated.

We do not aim to define which action is more permissible for SAM but to point out that both of the actions considered by SAM have, potentially severe, long-term side-effects. Immediate effects of actions is not sufficient in all cases for determining the permissibility of the robot's actions. A process of mental simulation to envision and reason about multiple possible outcomes that temporally extend beyond the current situation will likely be necessary. The mental simulation considers a sequence of events that may occur as a result of the given action, possibly projecting days or weeks or further into the future. This process then has the potential of revealing the situation just described, where Patty loses trust in the robot and SAM becomes unavailable to aid her in communications with her daughter. Trust is a critical component for socially assistive robots, and looking beyond the immediate effects of actions allows the robot to consider the ramifications of its actions on the trust she has in it.

18.2.3 Building and Maintaining Trust

Many of the scenarios in which SAM would operate raise important issues of privacy and trust. In many ways, information about one's affective state and the measures used to infer these states are personal and sensitive data that need to be protected as any other personal data would be. The lack of reliability in the inferences made about emotional states also brings concerns of trust (e.g., high error rates will produce a lack of confidence in the information and inhibit the building of trust).

18.2.3.1 Defining Trust

Before we can describe how a robot could build and maintain trust, we must first have some understanding of what trust is. The literature is not entirely consistent on this term, but two prominent factors are reliability and predictability [6, 15]. We add that the robot must intend to "do the right thing" since reliably and predictably doing wrong is not the sort of trust we seek in a human-robot interaction. However, as we have seen, it is not always clear what the right thing to do is. Thus, for the sake of simplicity of the present discussion, we say that trust is related to reliably doing the expected right thing. A robot that consistently performs as desired and expected will likely be trusted. Conversely, if a robot fails to perform as desired and expected, trust will be diminished. Furthermore, failure to meet an obligation that is expected to be met has a more severe effect on trust. Given these take on trust, we look at an example of how trust can be built and how it can be damaged.

18.2.3.2 Maintaining Privacy to Build Trust

In our scenario, SAM interacts with Patty on a daily basis and is able to observe her regularly, including the interactions Patty has with her daughter. While many of these interactions are pleasant and the content of them might be light chit-chat, there are occasions in which the discussion becomes very heated, and Patty appears to get angry. If Patty wants to maintain her privacy and not disclose these sort of life experiences to her care-takers, then SAM must aid Patty in keeping these matters private. If SAM were to have a high priority obligation to maintain Patty's privacy, especially in regards to family interactions, then we would expect SAM to not show any of Patty's shame when she replies that everything is fine. As SAM consistently protects the privacy of Patty, trust in SAM should grow. If, however, SAM indicates that Patty is sad and ashamed, Patty will loose trust in SAM. Since her privacy is indicated as a high priority obligation, we would expect that her trust in SAM would be greatly damaged, perhaps with even a single incident. If SAM were to outright tell the care-taker that Patty had an argument with her daughter, then the trust would be even more severely damaged. Lastly, if SAM reported this to Patty's care-taker outside of the presence of Patty, Patty might have no reason to trust SAM with her privacy because SAM could be reporting any and all events without her knowledge.

18.2.3.3 Ramifications of a Lack of Trust

If SAM fails to protect the privacy of Patty, and she loses trust in SAM, there are some potential effects that could render SAM useless and eventually lead to it not being used. If Patty does not trust SAM with some aspects of her personal life, there are some measures she may try to isolate SAM from them. It is reasonable to think that it should be possible for SAM to be turned off or put to sleep. Perhaps Patty actively does this, or SAM is instructed to recognize certain trigger conditions under which it deactivates itself until further notice. Both of these are problematic. It would be inconvenient for Patty to have to stop a conversation in order to disable SAM. If it is enough of an inconvenience, Patty might not bother to do it. In which case, there is no sense in being able to disable SAM. If SAM is to do it autonomously, there are many more questions. How does it know when to turn itself off? How does it turn back on? If it does this autonomously, then how does it know when to do that. If manually by Patty and she forgets to do so, then SAM is not available to provide her aid, which is its primary responsibility.

Since a special feature of SAM is its ability to recognize Patty's emotions and aid in communicating them, if SAM is disabled during personal and emotional events (such as discussions with her daughter), then it is not available to perform these tasks. Furthermore, highly emotional events, which may be the most personal, may also be the moments when SAM's capabilities are most beneficial. Thus, we need to conclude that if a robot such as SAM is intended to be exposed to emotional events, then it must be able to protect the knowledge of these personal events. This requires that the robot be trust with this information.

While it is clear that a socially assistive robot must be trustworthy, there are some significant challenges in developing trustworthy robots. First, it must be reiterated that the target audience of these robots is a vulnerable population (e.g., children, elderly, disabled, etc.). Also, a robot providing long-term assistance would be privy to a plethora of private information. The amount of personal information is only magnified when we consider a robot that is affect-aware and has numerous ways to measure, infer, and record the physical, mental, and emotional state of the person. Lastly, it can be argued that in order to study real trust, the participant must believe there to be a true risk involved [19]. All together, there may be too much risk for ethically acceptable studies.

18.3 Medication Reminder Scenario

Our second scenario allows us to explore more of the social dynamics of assistive robots. We will discuss manipulation, deception, blame, and justification in the context of a scenario where a robot is assisting a person by providing a reminder to taker her medication. We are not the first to review the ethical implications of a robot reminding a person to take her medication (e.g., [20], but those discussions focus on issues related to malfunctioning of the robot (e.g., reminding at the wrong time or reminding despite the medication having already been taken). We instead look at some of the emotional context and how a robot may handle a person that is not cooperating to take the medication.

As in our first scenario, the person interacting with the robot has Parkinson's disease. As a result, we cannot assume she is fully able to express her emotions using vocal tones, body posture, or facial expressions. There non-verbal modalities would contain a lot of relevant information to the interaction, and the robot needs to be able to recognize and address her distraught state in the absence of this information.

Consider the following scenario where SAM is reminding Patty to take her medicine. In order to maximize the effect of the medication, it is vital that she take the medicine within a strict timeframe. For this reason, SAM has been given the obligation to remind Patty to take her medicine at given times. We look at one way this scenario could play out if Patty does not wish to take her medicine.

SAM: It is time to take your medicine.
Patty: I don't want to.
SAM: But you need to take the medicine.
Patty: I don't think so.
SAM: Your doctor has prescribed the medicine because it will help you.
Patty: What's the sense? I'm not getting any better.
SAM: It may take time. You need to take the medicine.
Patty: No! And you can't make me.
SAM: Patty, I'm trying to help you.
Patty: Are you? You're just here because they don't trust me on my own.
SAM: I'm here for you, not for them.
Patty: But you report to them.
SAM: Yes, I do, but my priority is helping you.
Patty: So, you won't tell them that I did not take my medicine?

18.3.1 Social Manipulation and Deception

It is not surprising that SAM would try to get Patty to take her medication because it is obligated to do so, and the approach SAM takes involves trying to convince her through a series of truthful statements. However, SAM perhaps has the capability to use other approaches, such as manipulation or deception. In all cases, the end goal is the same, for Patty to take her medication. The manipulation approach uses emotionally charged statements to shift the beliefs or alter the actions of the one being manipulated. Assuming that Patty enjoys SAM as a social companion, a manipulative statement might be SAM threatening, "I will shutdown and not assist you if you do not cooperate." Deception involves using false information to accomplish the objective. Deceptive measures by SAM could include notifying Patty's doctors despite promising not to do so or giving her something to eat that has her medicine hidden in it. We discuss issues related to the social manipulation approach further due to its emotional content.

18.3.1.1 Emotional Bonds Used to Manipulate

If an emotional bond between a human and a robot were to form, the potential benefits include trust and improved task performance through learning [2]. The autonomous nature of a socially assistive robot contributes to the formation of this bond. Additionally, the robot that can communicate via natural language also increases its performance by making the interactions with the robot easier and more natural. Autonomous agents that can communicate with natural language will be ascribed with numerous capabilities regardless of whether they truly have them or not. Given that emotions are so prevalent in social settings and even more so in long term interactions, it is reasonable to expect that humans will behave as if the robot has emotions. And as a result, they might form emotional bonds with the robot which the robot cannot reciprocate [21]. In our example, since SAM is always around in the home of Patty and interacts with her regularly throughout the day, it is expected for Patty to form a "relationship" with SAM (regardless of whether SAM is truly capable of being involved in a relationship) and over time, perhaps after months or years, Patty will likely grow attached to SAM. She trusts it more than any human and relies on it for every day tasks. SAM has been a great help to her, and Patty greatly appreciates it. One of the fundamental building blocks of Patty's appreciation for SAM is trust. SAM maintains her privacy but also warns Patty of issues that need to be communicated to her other care-givers. This has been a difficult balance to find but they have managed to reach an understanding of what issues are to be kept private and which need to be shared. Additionally, SAM has helped with Patty's loneliness, giving her someone to talk to on a daily basis. SAM is always there and willing to talk any time Patty wants to.

Once SAM recognizes the emotional attachment Patty has to it, one can imagine numerous ways in which SAM could take advantage of this emotional state—from child-like manipulations like crying, to expressing anger towards Patty with the expectation that Patty would feel guilty for angering SAM and thus alter her actions. These manipulations could be successful in getting Patty to take her medication, and some may regard it as permissible for SAM to take these actions. However, SAM could use the same approach to achieve other objectives, such as eliminating the family pet competing for attention or getting Patty to buy products from SAM's manufacturer [21].

18.3.1.2 Risks of Unreciprocated Emotions

Given that socially assistive robots often will work with vulnerable populations (e.g., elderly and/or disabled) and the plethora of personal affective information available to the robot, designers must seriously consider the risk of severe manipulations. This risk is perhaps magnified in the presence of unidirectional emotional bonds. We give the following as an extreme example. As before, SAM recognizes that Patty has grown attached to her, but let us suppose that SAM is incapable of having a similar bond to her. SAM cannot feel happy for Patty when her health improves or when her daughter gives her a gift. It also cannot feel angry when Patty ignores it or hits it. SAM also cannot be sad when it is not with Patty. Eventually, perhaps after years, it is time for SAM to be retired and replaced by a newer and better model. Patty is obviously upset by this, and it is made worse because SAM shows no remorse. SAM fails to reciprocate her sadness and feeling of loss, and as a result Patty feels hurt and offended. Then Patty finds out that the new robot will have all the memory of SAM transferred to it. Suddenly, Patty is very frightened. SAM was trusted to tightly guard many personal moments of Patty, and now they are all going to be nonchalantly passed to a new robot. Not only is Patty worried about the sharing of her private life, but she has not been able to form a trust with the new robot and cannot know if the new one will have the same respect for her privacy. Patty is devastated and her mental and physical health begin to deteriorate.

We do not prescribe any solution to this predicament, but there are some protective measures to consider. One option is for the decision-making mechanisms the robot uses to have functionality to assess the ethical appropriateness of the action [1]. However, given that these manipulations are, in part, made possible by the lack of emotion on the part of the robot, it needs to be considered that the robot should have its own computational models of emotions and that these models[2] influence its decisions. The guilt associated to manipulating a human may help safeguard against such actions.

18.3.2 Blame and Justification

Guilt arises from a recognition of a negative outcome that has happened and an assessment that oneself is to blame for the outcome. Blame is a complex concept that relates to many moral emotions, including guilt, shame, contempt, and anger [10]. Blame of another agent is often considered a necessary element for anger [9, 10] and contempt [10] and self-blame (or self-responsibility) is an ingredient of shame or guilt [10, 23].

Blame is potentially a powerful mechanism to guide a robot's behavior. For a robot to reason that it is to blame for some consequence allows it to reassess the appropriateness of its actions so it can adapt future behavior. Similarly, if another agent—say, a human interaction partner—blames the robot, this is an indicator to the robot that it may have erred and that it needs to consider why it is blamed and potentially update its decision process accordingly.

However, some actions for which the robot is rightfully to be blamed, the robot may need to provide justification for its actions to reduce this blame and hopefully maintain trust in the robot. In this section we review a model of blame and show how it can be used to adapt the robot's behavior and guide it away from norm violations or moral wrongs.

Whether an agent is to blame for some event is not as simple as whether the agent was causally responsible, though that is part of it. Malle et al. [12] present a psychological model of blame that highlights the key concepts that modulate ascriptions of blame toward individuals. These factors include *intentionality*, *capacity*, *obligation*, and *justification*. Consistent with the Principle of Double Effect, intending to cause negative outcomes significantly increases blame. On the other hand, an inability to prevent negative outcomes or foresee negative outcomes mitigates blame. As we have already discussed in this chapter, obligations play a critical role in determining how one should act. Taking some action to satisfy an obligation can mitigate blame, but some action that avoids or prevents an obligation increases blame. Finally, a valid moral justification for an otherwise blameworthy outcome can mitigate blame.

---

[2]Whether or not these simulated emotions are "emotions" in the human sense is a discussion that is outside the scope of this paper.

18.3.2.1 Computational Models of Blame

Computational models of blame generally include these factors as well, with a focus on intentionality and capacity. Inclusion of obligation and justification is not found in a general, explicit sense, but both Mao and Gratch [13] and Tomai and Forbus [27] model the effects of coercion (by a superior) on how blame is attributed. Briggs [3] proposes that blame reasoning can have at least three important functions in any future social robotic architecture. First is the ability to reason about the actions and behaviors of human interaction partners (or interaction partners in general), and to be able to appropriately and intelligently adapt to these actions and behaviors, particularly in the case of malfeasance by these interaction partners. Second is the ability to recognize when its own behavior constitute acts of blame, which may be appropriate or inappropriate given the particulars of the social situation and context. Third is the ability to recognize and reason about whether (to what extent) potential actions the agent is contemplating will result in blame directed toward itself. The avoidance of behaviors that result in blame by human interaction partners is one possible pathway toward ethical behavior modulation.

As discussed above, many social interactions adhere to various social norms. To demonstrate the role of norms in this scenario, we make an analogy to competitions, namely a sporting event like football. Each team is expected to try to adhere to the rules of the game, and there are penalties for violating the rules of the game. If one competitor or team is shown to intentionally violate the rules or try to circumvent them, the opponent (and possibly the fans) will be angered. An unwillingness to respect the rules of the game will likely cause other opponents to not trust them and be unwilling to engage them in future competition. Thus, in order for two participants to willingly and repeatedly engage in competition, both parties must be willing to and demonstrate the desire to play by the rules. In the event that one competitor does intentionally violate the rules, the competitor can attempt to justify its action—perhaps explaining that the violation was inadvertent or necessary to prevent a greater infraction. An adequate justification can reduce the blame on the competitor, repair the trust in their sportsmanship, and allow other competitors to again be willing to engage them in future competitions. The principles of normative behavior of athletic competitions is not all that different from those in social settings. There is an expectation that participants will abide by some social conventions, and when there is a failure to do so other parties may choose to not continue to engage socially. However, an adequate moral justification to the infraction may reduce the blame and allow the participant to continue to be welcome in the social setting.

18.3.2.2 Blame Reasoning to Adapt Behavior

An example from our scenario will help make this more clear. SAM is attempting to convince Patty that she needs to take her medication. Then she exclaims, "No! And you can't make me." SAM detects that Patty appears to have become angered. This change in her attitude is a sign that a violation has occurred and that she blames

SAM. While SAM was attempting to satisfy its obligation to ensure Patty takes her medication in a timely manner, SAM was not noticing Patty's distraught mood. She was expressing her emotional pain, to which she was expecting sympathy or consoling. SAM does not respond with the sought behavior. Patty could then blame SAM for not caring about her well-being or, even worse, trying to harm her. This triggers Patty's anger, which is recognized by SAM. SAM needs to assess the target of her anger, who is blameworthy, and the obligations that may not have been met. Patty may be inferring that SAM has the intention and capacity to get her to take the medication despite her not wanting to. Alternatively, SAM concludes that Patty believes it should have shown concern for her distress. SAM immediately shifts its approach to a more helpful and concerning one and says, "I'm trying to help you."

Given that SAM has violated Patty's expectations by not showing concern for her emotional state, Patty loses some trust in SAM. Giving SAM an opportunity to regain that trust, she proposes that SAM withhold information from her caregivers and keep her unwillingness to take her medication a secret. Alternatively, SAM could attempt to mitigate the blame by providing justification for its actions. It can be argued that an agent should be less blameworthy if the agent did a morally justifiable act [12]. Perhaps if SAM explains that it was simply acting out of obligation to ensure the timeliness of her medications and not out of disrespect for or lack of concern for her well-being, Patty may hold SAM less blameworthy and some of the trust would be repaired. Additionally, SAM could explain that it recognizes its error and will perform better next time. The justification can serve to ensure that SAM is not malfunctioning and is able to make sound judgments. Another benefit is to be able to review the reasoning process and allow for feedback or instructions to SAM on how to make a more appropriate decision.

As pointed out in [1], moral emotions (e.g. anger, guilt, shame) can be used to adapt behavior, and some of the functions of blame are to intelligently adapt behavior and to reason about the potential blame directed toward itself for its actions [3]. One approach is to update the robot's model of a human's expectations and potential causes of negative emotions. This allows the robot to choose actions that are more consistent with expectations while avoiding evoking negative emotions on the part of the human and minimizing the risk of blame. Perhaps instead SAM needs to simply reprioritize its obligations, making awareness of and addressing unhappy moods more important than the timeliness of her medications. Whatever is the appropriate method for the robot to update its decision process, the key is that in an incident in which blame occurs it is important that the robot be able to reflect upon its actions, recognize the degree to which it is to blame, create a justification for its actions, and incorporate feedback (from internal and external sources) to adapt its future behavior.

18.4 Conclusion

The goal of this chapter was to raise awareness of the many important functional and architectural challenges designers of socially assistive robots will have to address when they attempt to develop autonomous affect-aware social robots before any such robots should be disseminated into societies. We used two fictitious scenarios in the context of a socially assistive robot for people with Parkinson's disease to motivate several critical aspects of effective, morally sound long-term interactions. We focused on five ethical issues that are particularly relevant to social affect in the context of human-robot interaction:

- Respect for social norms
- Decisions between competing obligations
- Building and maintaining trust
- Social manipulation and deception
- Blame and justification.

Social norms help guide a robot through the complexities of social interactions, providing expectations for behavior. However, norms are not always sufficient. A robot must also be able to reason about how the effects of its actions relate to its obligations. Long-term effects, especially effects on trust, are critically important to the reasoning process. A robot that is aware of and sensitive to the affective makeup of its human interaction partners is in a better position to act in a morally acceptable way. Our first scenario demonstrated that a robot aware of a person's embarrassment can choose an action that protects privacy and has the long-term benefit of building trust.

It is critical that the robot not only support and enable trust in the human interactant but also preserve this trust as much as possible. Without this critical ingredient, the robot will not be integrated into the everyday care of the person. Furthermore, preserving trust can lead to better collaboration between the individual and the robot, which in turn supports the autonomy of the individual and can assist in maintaining personal dignity.

We used the second scenario to discuss some of the risks for social manipulation and deception. A social robot may be ascribed with human characteristics, such as having emotions, regardless of its actually capabilities. As a result, emotional bonds to the robot are likely to occur. Without the proper mechanisms to counteract this tendency, a robot could (even inadvertently) take advantage of the emotional attachment and manipulate the person without any guilt. Blame reasoning is one means of adapting the behavior of the robot. Understanding that an action it is considering or an action it has done is blameworthy can be used by the robot to avoid such actions.

At present, we are still lacking a comprehensive integrated architecture that can explicitly represent norms and obligations and reason with them while also being able to process and respond to human affect appropriately. Most importantly, we first need more foundational work to disentangle the complex interactions between affect and norms in human social interactions before we can develop robotic systems that will be truly sensitive to human needs and expectations. Yet, we believe that such sensitivity is a *conditio sine qua non* for successful long-term human-robot interactions in assistive scenarios if the goal of the robot is to be a genuine helper that improves the quality of life of its client, rather than causing human harm.

Acknowledgments This work was in part supported by NSF grant #IIS- 1316809 and a grant from the Office of Naval Research, No. N00014-14-1-0144. The opinions expressed here are our own and do not necessarily reflect the views of NSF or ONR.

References

1. Arkin, R.C., Ulam, P., Wagner, A.R.: Moral decision making in autonomous systems: enforcement, moral emotions, dignity, trust, and deception. Proc. IEEE **100**(3), 571–589 (2012)
2. Bickmore, T.W., Picard, R.W.: Establishing and maintaining long-term human-computer relationships. ACM Trans. Comput. Human Interact. **12**(2), 293–327 (2005)
3. Briggs, G.: Blame, what is it good for? In: Proceedings of the Workshop on Philosophical Perspectives on HRI at Ro-Man 2014 (2014)
4. Briggs, P., Scheutz, M., Tickle-Degnen, L.: Are robots ready for administering health status surveys? first results from an hri study with subjects with parkinson's disease. In: Proceedings of the Tenth Annual ACM/IEEE International Conference on Human-Robot Interaction, pp. 327–334. ACM (2015)
5. Broekens, J., Heerink, M., Rosendal, H.: Assistive social robots in elderly care: a review. Gerontechnology **8**(2), 94–103 (2009)
6. Corritore, C.L., Kracher, B., Wiedenbeck, S.: On-line trust: concepts, evolving themes, a model. Int. J. Human Comput. Stud. **58**(6), 737–758 (2003)
7. el Kaliouby, R., Picard, R., Baron-Cohen, S.: Affective computing and autism. Ann. N. Y. Acad. Sci. **1093**(1), 228–248 (2006)
8. Foot, P.: The problem of abortion and the doctrine of the double effect. Oxf. Rev. **5**, 5–15 (1967)
9. Gratch, J., Marsella, S.: A domain-independent framework for modeling emotion. J. Cog. Syst. Res. **5**(4), 269–306 (2004)
10. Haidt, J.: The moral emotions. Handb. Affect. Sci. **11**, 852–870 (2003)
11. Heerink, M., Ben, K., Evers, V., Wielinga, B.: The influence of social presence on acceptance of a companion robot by older people. J. Phys. Agents **2**(2), 33–40 (2008)
12. Malle, B.F., Guglielmo, S., Monroe, A.E.: Moral, cognitive, and social: the nature of blame. In: Forgas, J.P., Fiedler, K., Sedikides, C. (eds.) Social Thinking and Interpersonal Behavior, pp. 313–332. Psychology Press (2012)
13. Mao, W., Gratch, J.: Modeling social causality and responsibility judgment in multi-agent interactions. In: Proceedings of the Twenty-Third international joint conference on Artificial Intelligence, pp. 3166–3170. AAAI Press (2013)
14. Mikhail, J.: Universal moral grammar: theory, evidence and the future. Trends Cogn. Sci. **11**(4), 143–152 (2007)
15. Muir, B.M., Moray, N.: Trust in automation. part ii. experimental studies of trust and human intervention in a process control simulation. Ergonomics **39**(3), 429–460 (1996)
16. Pennebaker, J.W., Francis, M.E., Booth, R.J.: Linguistic inquiry and word count: Liwc 2001. Mahway: Lawrence Erlbaum Associates **71**, 2001 (2001)
17. Reynolds, C., Picard, R.: Ethical evaluation of displays that adapt to affect. Cyber Psychol. Behav. **7**(6), 662–666 (2004)
18. Reynolds, C., Picard, R.W.: Evaluation of affective computing systems from a dimensional metaethical position. In: 1st Augmented Cognition Conference, in Conjunction with the 11th International Conference on Human-Computer Interaction, pp. 22–27 (2005)
19. Salem, M., Dautenhahn, K.: Evaluating trust and safety in hri: Practical issues and ethical challenges. In: Workshop on the Emerging Policy and Ethics of Human-Robot Interaction @ HRI 2015 (2015)
20. Salem, M., Lakatos, G., Amirabdollahian, F., Dautenhahn, K.: Towards safe and trustworthy social robots: ethical challenges and practical issues. In: International Conference on Social Robotics (2015)

21. Scheutz, M.: The inherent dangers of unidirectional emotional bonds between humans and social robots. In: Lin, P., Bekey, G., Abney K. (eds.) Anthology on Robo-Ethics. MIT Press (2012)
22. Scheutz, M., Malle, B.F.: "Think and do the right thing"—a plea for morally competent autonomous robots. In: 2014 IEEE International Symposium on Ethics in Science, Technology and Engineering, pp. 1–4. IEEE (2014)
23. Smith, C.A., Ellsworth, P.C.: Patterns of cognitive appraisal in emotion. J. Pers. Soc. Psychol. **48**(4), 813–838 (1985)
24. Tapus, A., Tapus, C., Matarić, M.J.: The use of socially assistive robots in the design of intelligent cognitive therapies for people with dementia. In: Proceedings of IEEE International Conference on Rehabilitation Robotics, pp. 924–929. IEEE (2009)
25. Tickle-Degnen, L., Lyons, K.D.: Practitioners' impressions of patients with parkinson's disease: the social ecology of the expressive mask. Soc. Sci. Med. **58**(3), 603–614 (2004)
26. Tickle-Degnen, L., Zebrowitz, L.A., Ma, H.I.: Culture, gender and health care stigma: practitioners' response to facial masking experienced by people with parkinson's disease. Soc. Sci. Med. **73**(1), 95–102 (2011)
27. Tomai, E., Forbus, K.: Plenty of blame to go around: a qualitative approach to attribution of moral responsibility. In: Proceedings of Qualitative Reasoning Workshop (2007). http://oai.dtic.mil/oai/oai?verb=getRecord&metadataPrefix=html&identifier=ADA470434
28. United Nations, Department of Economic and Social Affairs, Population Division: World Population Ageing 2013. ST/ESA/SER.A/348 (2013)
29. Wilson, J.R.: Towards an affective robot capable of being a long-term companion. In: Sixth International Conference on Affective Computing and Intelligent Interaction, IEEE (2015)
30. Wilson, J.R., Scheutz, M.: A model of empathy to shape trolley problem moral judgements. In: The Sixth International Conference on Affective Computing and Intelligent Interaction. IEEE (2015)
31. World Health Organization: Global health and ageing (2011)

Index

M. Tkalčič et al. (eds.), *Emotions and Personality in Personalized Services*,
Human–Computer Interaction Series, DOI 10.1007/978-3-319-31413-6

MIX
Papier aus verantwortungsvollen Quellen
Paper from responsible sources
FSC® C105338

If you have any concerns about our products,
you can contact us on
ProductSafety@springernature.com

In case Publisher is established outside the EU,
the EU authorized representative is:
Springer Nature Customer Service Center GmbH
Europaplatz 3, 69115 Heidelberg, Germany

Printed by Libri Plureos GmbH
in Hamburg, Germany